Writer's Choice

COMPOSITION AND GRAMMAR

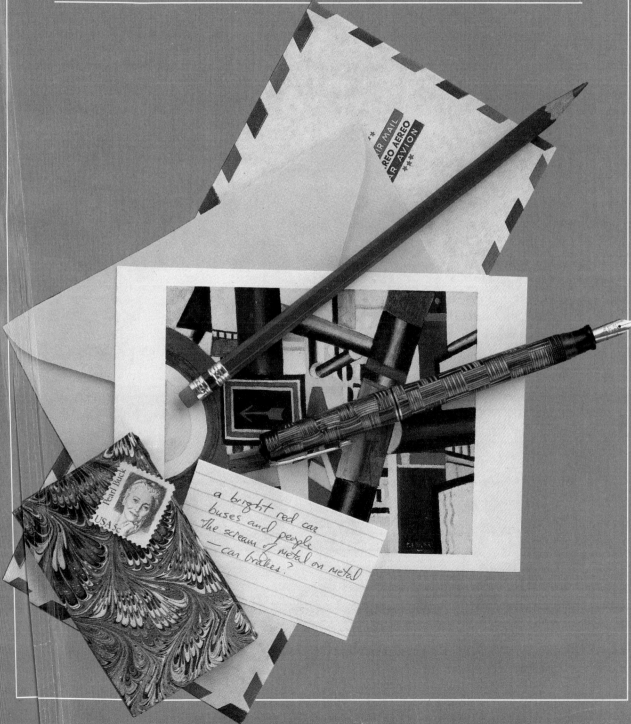

a bright red car
buses and people
The scream of metal on metal
— car brakes?

Case Studies: Writers at Work

Shelley Lauzon
Director of Public Information

Walter Echo-Hawk
Attorney

Cléo Boudreau
Captain of the Melibea

Barbara Brandon
Cartoonist

Samuel Regalado
Historian

Richard MacNeish and Jane Libby
Archaeologists

Student Advisory Board

Arthur Housinger

David Alonzo

Susannah Levine

Michelle Kalski

Becky Byer

Marsha Novak

Peer Ivaska

Mathew Isaac

ii

Writer's Choice

COMPOSITION AND GRAMMAR

Pieter Brueghel, *The Fall of Icarus*, 1564

Consulting Author for Composition
William Strong

Grammar Specialist
Mark Lester

Visual-Verbal Learning Specialists
Ligature, Inc.

GLENCOE
Macmillan/McGraw-Hill

Lake Forest, Illinois   Columbus, Ohio   Mission Hills, California   Peoria, Illinois

Front cover includes
Fernand Léger,
Follow the Arrow.

Back cover includes
Herman Zapf,
*The Sequoya Alphabet of
the Cherokee Indians.*

Send all inquiries to:
GLENCOE DIVISION
Macmillan/McGraw-Hill
15319 Chatsworth Street
P.O. Box 9609
Mission Hills, CA 91346-
9609

ISBN 0-02-635241-9
(Student's Edition)
ISBN 0-02-635242-7
(Teacher's Wraparound
Edition)

Printed in the United States
of America

2 3 4 5 6 7 8 9 10 VHJ 96 95 94 93 92

Consulting Author for Composition

William Strong is Professor of Secondary Education at Utah State University, Director of the Utah Writing Project, and a member of the National Writing Project Advisory Board. A nationally known authority in the teaching of composition, he is the author of many volumes, including, most recently, *Writing Incisively: Do-It-Yourself Prose Surgery* (McGraw-Hill, 1991).

As Consulting Author, Dr. Strong helped to develop the structure and content of Part 1: Composition. He reviewed and edited all Composition units. Dr. Strong also conceived and wrote Unit 8: Style Through Sentence Combining. He collaborated on *Sentence Combining Blackline Masters*, which accompanies *Writer's Choice*.

Grammar Specialist

Mark Lester is Professor of English at Eastern Washington University. He formerly served as Chair of the Department of English as a Second Language, University of Hawaii. He is the author of *Grammar in the Classroom* (Macmillan, 1990) and of numerous professional books and articles.

As Grammar Specialist, Dr. Lester reviewed student's edition material from Part 2: Grammar, Usage, and Mechanics. He collaborated on *Grammar Reteaching Blackline Masters*, which accompanies *Writer's Choice*.

Associate Consultant in Writing

Bonnie S. Sunstein is Associate Professor of English and Director of the Master of Arts in Teaching Program at Rivier College in Nashua, New Hampshire. Dr. Sunstein has taught extensively in New England in colleges and secondary schools, as well as in the New Hampshire Reading and Writing Program. She has published in the area of writing and teaching and is the coeditor of *Portfolio Portraits* (Heinemann, 1992) and the author of a forthcoming book about teachers and writing (Boynton/Cook).

As Associate Consultant in Writing, Dr. Sunstein established the theoretical framework for integrating writing portfolios into *Writer's Choice*.

Contributing Writers

Larry Beason is Assistant Professor of English at Eastern Washington University. Dr. Beason is the writer of *Grammar Reteaching Blackline Masters*, which accompanies *Writer's Choice*.

Willis L. Pitkin Jr. is Professor of English at Utah State University. Dr. Pitkin is the writer of *Sentence Combining Blackline Masters*, which accompanies *Writer's Choice*.

Visual-Verbal Learning Specialists

Ligature, Inc., is an educational research and development company with offices in Chicago and Boston. Ligature is committed to developing educational materials that bring visual-verbal learning to the tradition of the written word.

As visual-verbal and curriculum specialists, Ligature collaborated on conceiving and implementing the pedagogy of *Writer's Choice*.

Acknowledgments

Grateful acknowledgment is given authors, publishers, photographers, museums, and agents for permission to reprint the following copyrighted material. Every effort has been made to determine copyright owners. In the case of any omissions, the Publisher will be pleased to make suitable acknowledgments in future editions.

Elements of Style (Third Edition), by William Strunk Jr. and E. B. White, copyright © 1979, Macmillan Publishing Co., Inc. Earlier editions © 1959 and © copyright 1972 by Macmillan Publishing Co., Inc. Reprinted by permission of Macmillan Publishing Co.

Continued on page 839

Composition Advisers

The advisers reviewed Composition lesson prototypes. Their contributions were instrumental in the development of the Writing Process in Action lessons.

Michael Angelotti
Head of Division of Teacher
   Education
College of Education
University of Oklahoma

Charles R. Duke
Dean of the College of Education and
   Human Services
Clarion University

Carol Booth Olson
Director
University of California, Irvine,
   Writing Project

Judith Summerfield
Associate Professor of English
Queens College, City University of
   New York

Denny Wolfe
Professor and Associate Dean
Darden College of Education
Old Dominion University
formerly Director, Tidewater Writing
   Project

Educational Reviewers

The reviewers read and commented upon manuscripts during the writing process. They also critiqued early drafts of graphic organizers and page layouts.

Lenore Croudy
Flint Community School
Flint, Michigan

John A. Grant
St. Louis Public Schools
St. Louis, Missouri

Vicki Haker
Mead Junior High
Mead, Washington

Frederick G. Johnson
Georgia Department of Education
Atlanta, Georgia

Sterling C. Jones Jr.
Detroit Public Schools
Detroit, Michigan

Barry Kincaid
Raytown School District
Kansas City, Missouri

Evelyn G. Lewis
Newark Public Schools
Newark, New Jersey

M. DeAnn Morris
Crescenta Valley High School
La Crescenta, California

Anita Moss
University of North Carolina
Charlotte, North Carolina

Ann S. O'Toole
Chesterfield County Schools
Richmond, Virginia

Suzanne Owens
Glendale High School
Glendale, California

Sally P. Pfeifer
Lewis and Clark High School
Spokane, Washington

Marie Rogers
Independence High School
Charlotte, North Carolina

Barbara Schubert
Santa Clara County Office of
Education, San Jose, California

Ronnie Spilton
Chattahoochee High School
Alpharetta, Georgia

Robert Stolte
Huntington Beach High School
Huntington Beach, California

Student Advisory Board

The Student Advisory Board was formed in an effort to ensure student involvement in the development of *Writer's Choice*. The editors wish to thank members of the board for their enthusiasm and dedication to the project.

The editors also wish to thank the many student writers whose models appear in this book.

Thanks are also due to Miami University of Ohio for help in the selection of models from student portfolios.

Writer's Choice

COMPOSITION AND GRAMMAR

Writer's Choice was written for you, the student writer. You're the writer in the title, and real students like you contributed to the materials you'll study. The book is organized into three main parts: (1) Composition; (2) Grammar, Usage, and Mechanics; and (3) Resources and Skills.

Part 1 Composition

The lessons in Composition are designed to give you help with specific writing tasks. You can use the units and lessons in order from beginning to end or select just the ones that help with your own writing needs.

Part 2   Grammar, Usage, and Mechanics

In the unique Troubleshooter, you'll learn to identify and correct the most common student writing problems. Throughout the rest of Part 2, you'll find plenty of practice to reinforce what you learn.

Part 3   Resources and Skills

You can use these resources and skills not just in English class but wherever you need to communicate effectively. The tone and approach are user-friendly, with many opportunities to practice and apply the skills you learn.

William
Strunk Jr.
and
E.B. **White**

The
Elements
of
Style

Part 4

Contents

CONTENTS

CONTENTS

Unit 5 Expository Writing: *Here and Now*   201

Unit 6 Persuasive Writing: *At the Podium*   257

CONTENTS

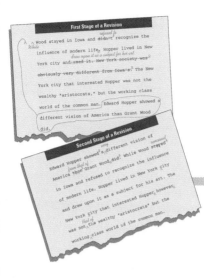

Literature Models by *Benjamin Franklin, Frederick Douglass, President Andrew Jackson, John Ridge, Irving B. Harris, Eleanor Roosevelt, Susan B. Anthony, Dorothy Thompson, President John F. Kennedy, Langston Hughes, Barbara Jordan, Donald Morris*

Part 2 Grammar, Usage, and Mechanics

CONTENTS

Part 3 Resources and Skills

Literature

Each literature selection is an extended example of the mode of writing taught in the unit.

Literature Models

Excerpts from outstanding works of fiction and nonfiction exemplify specific writing skills.

Workshop Literature

Each workshop uses an excerpt from a novel or long work of nonfiction to link grammar, usage, or mechanics to literature.

Case Studies

Each case study focuses on a real writer working on a real-life writing project. Come on backstage!

Fine Art

Fine art—paintings, drawings, photos, and sculpture—is used to teach as well as to inspire.

Writer's Choice

COMPOSITION AND GRAMMAR

Welcome *to Writer's Choice! Your writing and your choices are what this book is all about. The modular format of the book allows you to choose quickly the lesson or handbook section that will help you with a writing problem or task. With this big picture in mind, take a few minutes to get to know each of the main parts of the book, which are illustrated on the upcoming pages.*

Part 1 Composition

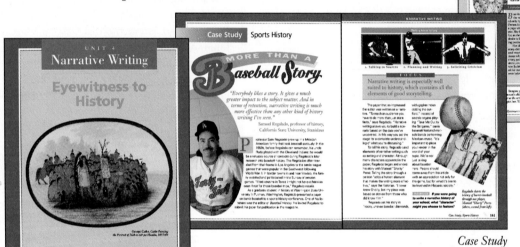

Unit Opener

Case Study

Part 2 Grammar, Usage, and Mechanics

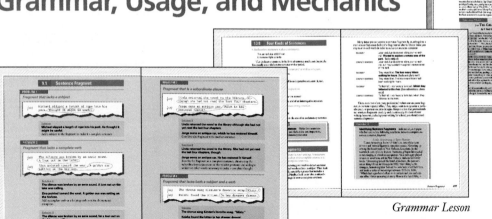

Troubleshooter

Grammar Lesson

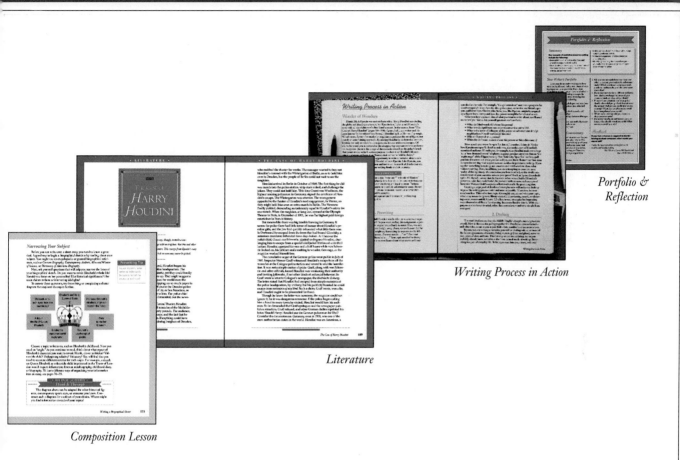

Portfolio & Reflection

Writing Process in Action

Literature

Composition Lesson

Part 3 Resources and Skills

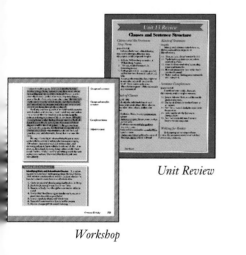

Unit Review

Workshop

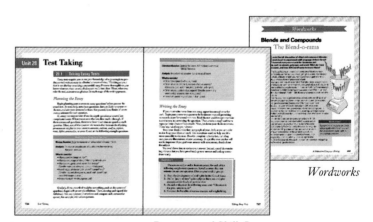

Wordworks

Resources and Skills Lesson

Inside Composition

T*he basic building block of the Composition units is the four-page lesson. Each lesson clearly focuses on a specific writing problem or task. You will always find clear and specific instruction, models of effective writing, and a variety of writing activities.*

Student Models present writing by students like you to help you achieve your own writing goals.

Testing Your Description

It's easy to garble an account of an event. Time gets confused; the vantage point jumps around; information is left out. You've probably heard people recounting events in such a confusing manner that you had to keep interrupting to ask questions. However, your readers can't interrupt you with questions. Look at this model to see what to avoid.

Disarming the burglar alarm should have come at the beginning.

Model

T*he thief rummaged in the drawers for valuables. Before that, he disarmed the burglar alarm. When he found nothing in the dining room, he went into the back bedroom. When he saw the police car pull up in front of the house, he grabbed the earrings and slithered out the back window, leaving a thin trail of blood on the white carpet.*

Which part of the model is inconsistent with the vantage point of the rest of the model?

3.5   Describing an Event

Literature Models help you learn from the pros by showing you how published authors have met the writing challenges you face.

No Time to Think

Have you ever fallen or had an accident and found it difficult to explain what happened? Sometimes you can only say, "It all happened so fast!" Notice how Sue Grafton packs the continuous action of such an event into the following descriptive passage.

Literature Model

B*ehind me, the Dodge had made a U-turn and was now accelerating as it headed straight at me again. I ground at the starter, nearly singing with fear, a terrified eye glued to my rearview mirror where I could see the pickup accumulating speed. The Dodge plowed into me, this time with an impact that propelled the VW forward ten yards with an ear-splitting BAM. My forehead hit the windshield with a force that nearly knocked me out. The safety glass was splintered into a pattern of fine cracks like a coating of frost. The seat snapped in two and the sudden liberation from my seat belt slung me forward into the steering wheel. The only thing that saved me from a half-rack of cracked ribs was the purse in my lap, which acted like an air bag, cushioning the blow.*

Sue Grafton, G is for Gumshoe

How do words like "behind," "straight," "rearview," "forward," and "back" help the reader understand the event?

Grafton uses strong, active verbs in this passage. Identify some of them.

Grafton's account of the collision describes each step in the action. Readers can follow the sequence of events as the Dodge hurtles toward the VW because every incident is portrayed as it is witnessed by the narrator sitting in the front seat of the stalled VW.

Choosing a Vantage Point

Because events involve time and motion, they are sometimes harder to describe than static scenes. Writers need to dissect an event into a logical sequence of clearly linked actions and reactions. The vantage point from which those actions are witnessed must be clear and consistent in order for the reader to follow what's happening.

138   *Descriptive Writing: Mysteries and Clues*

Writer's Choice Activities give you a full page of writing options to help you apply what you have learned in the lesson. You'll also find fine art or a special feature on using computers in writing.

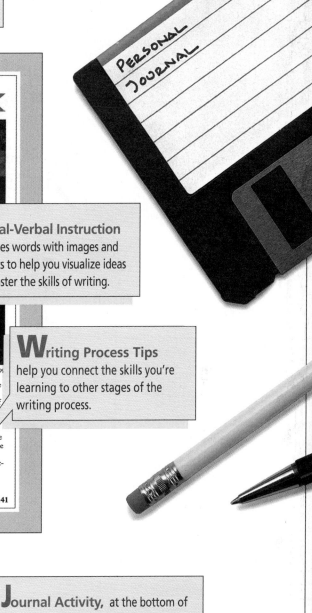

PERSONAL JOURNAL

• ACTIVITIES •
Writer's Choice

The following are some writing options to help you try out what you have learned.

1. Guided Assignment Imagine that you were driving a car over a bridge during an earthquake. *Life* magazine has asked you to write about your experience. Develop a list of details that are consistent with your vantage point to describe the

Visual-Verbal Instruction combines words with images and graphics to help you visualize ideas and master the skills of writing.

Thoughts and Impressions from Different Vantage Points

Neighbor in street:
Is person at window OK? Will he jump? Others in house? Pets out? Will it spread to other houses? What is coming over the firefighters' radio? The firefighter looks hot. The street is closed off. Should I do anything?

Firefighter:
How best to get man down? Others in house? Wind direction could be a problem. Origin of fire? Will it spread? Send for more units? How's the water pressure? Paramedics here? Are there combustibles?

Person at the window:
Choking fumes. Smoke burns my eyes. Too high to jump? Get out on sill? Do I have time to save anything?

Imagine spotting a roaring fire over the rooftops in your neighborhood. You run toward the scene. You hear fire engines. You see your neighbor's house ablaze. How close can you get? How close do you want to get?

It all depends on why you're there. If you intend to rescue a friend, you may need to pound on the door. If you want to interview the firefighters for a story, you'll want to stand near the truck. If you just want to watch the fire being put out, standing across the street may offer the best perspective.

Choosing a vantage point in writing is like finding a place to stand at the scene of a fire; it selects and limits the details available to you. You should, therefore, determine your purpose in writing before choosing your vantage point. Do you simply want the reader to know what has happened? Or do you want the reader to feel involved in the action as it is happening? Are you trying to create a particular reaction to the events described? Fear? Anger? Delight? You have many options.

Writing Process Tips help you connect the skills you're learning to other stages of the writing process.

n Round, 1898

...ing in the ...n your ...iptions of ...l be from ...present ...hou ...ne ...or one ...om the ...f the spec ...nt van-

141

Drafting Tip

As you draft a piece, be sure to alert the reader when you shift vantage points. Begin a new paragraph, or say something like "Meanwhile, at Sue's house . . ."

• JOURNAL ACTIVITY •
Think It Through

Think of an event you described in a way that was different from the way someone else described it. It might have been an accident, a party, an athletic event, even a scene from a movie. List in your journal some reasons why you think your impressions might have differed.

Journal Activity, at the bottom of the second page of every lesson, gives you a chance to reflect and respond to the lesson material.

Describing an Event **139**

Inside Grammar

This grammar handbook works for you, not the other way around. You'll learn how to find and fix errors in your writing. Two special sections—the Troubleshooter and the Workshops—help you expand your grammar skills.

The **Troubleshooter** presents in one place the solutions to the twelve errors most frequently made by student writers. Your teacher may refer you to the Troubleshooter by marking errors in your papers with the abbreviations shown down the far left side of the page.

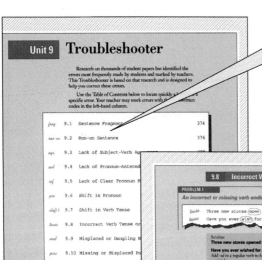

Each of the twelve errors is explained in detail in the Troubleshooter Unit.

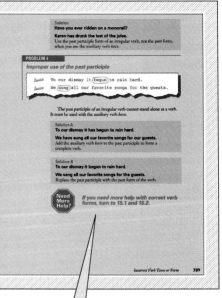

For each common error, the Troubleshooter shows you the solution. If you need more help, the Troubleshooter also refers you to the appropriate lesson.

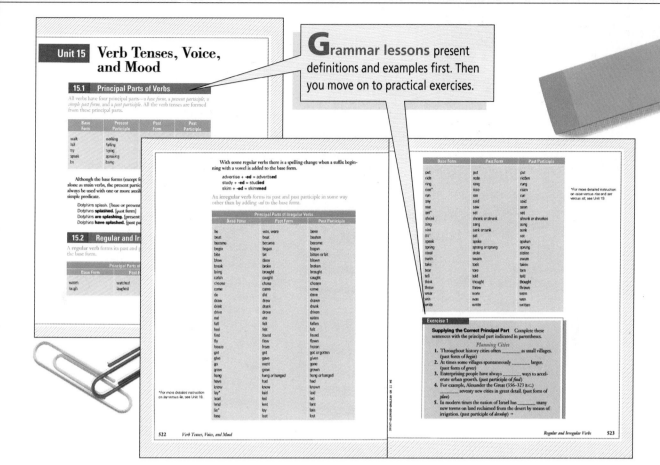

Grammar lessons present definitions and examples first. Then you move on to practical exercises.

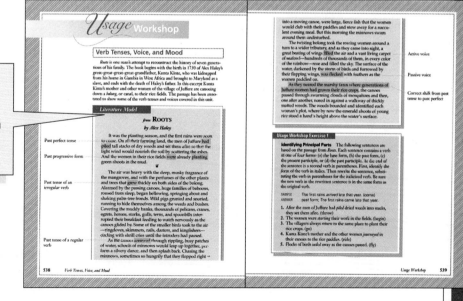

The Workshop at the end of each unit presents exercises based on a selection from a novel or other work of literature.

Inside Resources

T he lessons in this unit give you the skills necessary to prepare and deliver a speech, take a test, use a dictionary, and find books in the library. Each lesson is complete, concise, and easy to use.

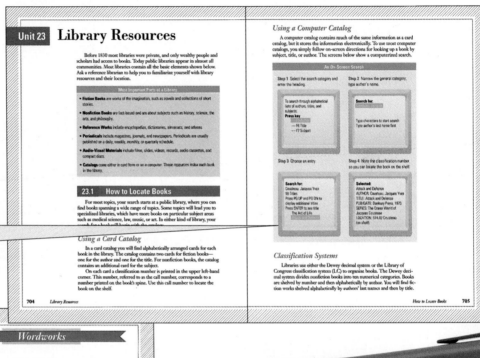

Graphics help you comprehend complex information at a glance.

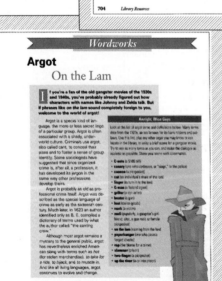

Wordworks pages like this one provide a humorous look at how we use and misuse our language. These features appear in the first unit in Resources, which puts you in command of basic facts about the English language.

Part 1

Composition

Part 1 Composition

Personal Writing

Making Connections

Emil Hansen Nolde, *Portrait of the Artist and His Wife*, 1932

EYEWITNESS TO A

Hurricane

"It came to mind that a great gift had been given to me . . . that of being chosen to witness this awesome natural event, not hiding in some sunken shelter on land, but rather here, on the water, exposed and vulnerable, and, in a very real sense, part of the terrifying drama itself."

Cléo Boudreau, captain of
the *Melibea*

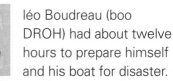

C léo Boudreau (boo DROH) had about twelve hours to prepare himself and his boat for disaster. He had long before made a mental note of a certain mangrove creek on a small island near Puerto Rico, and now he set sail to take shelter in this "hurricane hole." A killer storm, Hurricane Hugo, was bearing down on the northeast Caribbean. Listening to the stream of radio reports from area weather stations, Boudreau knew that he and his forty-foot, single-masted sailboat, the *Melibea*, were in great danger.

By late afternoon on September 17, 1989, the *Melibea* was braced for the storm. Sixteen heavy ropes cinched the small craft to the thick trunks

Writing a Newsletter

1. Reeling in Ideas

2. Drafting at Dawn

3. Revising Until It's Right

FOCUS

Personal writing, whether read by others or written only for yourself, can be spellbinding and colorful.

of the mangrove trees; sails and gear were fastened down. Boudreau put a pot of stew on the stove and waited.

Strong gusts became screeching winds of 135 miles per hour by 2 A.M. Boudreau felt his chances for survival were slim. But, he recalls, "It was such a magnificent occurrence, it seemed to make everything else insignificant."

Saved by two ropes that held tight, the *Melibea* made it through the night. Boudreau participated in relief efforts in the devastated region for the better part of a week. Then, he says, "I began thinking that maybe I should write about it." The impulse to write resulted in a captivating eyewitness account of the storm.

Rich storytelling flows naturally from this sailor, who has been chronicling his personal adventures for nearly a decade. A former professor of humanities and foreign

languages from Massachusetts, Boudreau decided to retire at age fifty-seven, in 1984. Since then he has been enjoying the "complete freedom" and adventure of the sailing life—spending two months each year at St. Thomas and the rest of the time cruising between Jamaica and Venezuela. Despite the dangers of living at sea, Boudreau calls the nautical life "paradise."

But life in paradise presented Boudreau with a problem: staying in touch with people back home. At first his main correspondent was his son Will in Massachusetts, to whom he wrote long, lively accounts of his activities. These letters grew into a twice-yearly newsletter, *The Melibea News,* which is circulated to friends throughout the United States.

Boudreau's adventures aboard the Melibea, *above, include a narrow escape from mysterious pursuers and two days and nights of relentless bailing to get his sinking vessel to Venezuela.*

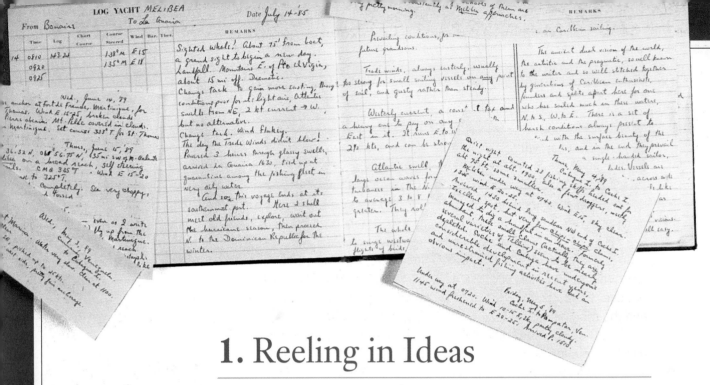

Notes and entries in the ship's log, above, help to jog Boudreau's memory when he writes his newsletters. Ashore at St. Thomas, below, the captain finds a quiet place to think and write.

1. Reeling in Ideas

Before retiring, Boudreau had never attempted any personal writing. Now he says, "To sit down and try to match up a style with an actual event that you have had a part in—I never realized it was such a challenge. To use words as one would use paints—to let them shed their color on each other in a way that highlights an adventure—is rewarding."

His ship's log is "perhaps the chief sourcebook for the newsletters," the captain says. "Of course, some things in the newsletter aren't in the log and vice versa, but I do go back over the logs and try to make little vignettes or anecdotes out of the entries."

The newsletter doesn't always feature life-and-death adventures; in fact, one issue humorously described the process of baking bread. But in the middle of the churning ocean, even baking bread can be an adventure.

INTERFACE *Recall a commonplace activity—such as baking, painting, or going to the store—that became an adventure. Write a brief personal account of your experience.*

2. Drafting at Dawn

A habitual early riser, Boudreau does most of his writing before 10:30 A.M., in an idyllic setting: "From when the sun comes up until the trade winds fill in, it's delightfully cool. I have a cockpit in the sailboat with a canvas top on it. I can just sit there at my writing table with my typewriter, looking out over the harbor, the palm trees, and the mountains."

Usually Boudreau has a definite idea in mind before he begins writing. "I think about it ahead of time and get it down in rough form." He first composes his newsletter in pencil. After writing a couple of drafts, he chooses the best one and revises it again as he types it on his old typewriter.

"I let it sit for a couple of weeks or so. Then I go back and do a final draft," he explains. "About four or five run-throughs is my average."

As he composes, Boudreau doesn't usually imagine any particular reader. But he did write one piece for a special friend. "My best correspondent has been a little girl I met in the Bahamas in 1985. She's blind, and she asked in a letter a year and half ago to tell her something about flying fish. I found it very charming to sit down and, thinking about her, to write something about flying fish."

Boudreau strengthens his writing with vivid description, interesting facts, personal and sensory observations, and a strong sense of narrative. All of those elements came together as he wrote his account of Hugo:

"Air and sea and mangrove branches had become a single tortured element pleading for release from the awesome forces that relentlessly ground them together into a unique, exploding mass," Boudreau later wrote. "The wind screamed in upward spirals of velocity—where was the limit? 180, 190, 200 knots of wind [170 to 230 miles per hour]. The end was near for sure. Nothing could remain standing against these forces. Suddenly, four lines [ropes] parted on *Melibea's* port quarter, one after the other, like pistol shots, pow! pow! pow! pow! She swung instantly broadside to the violence, and to the brink of disaster. . . ."

Do they really fly? Boudreau ponders the question of flying fish (above) in one of his newsletters. Photo below shows Boudreau's recipe for flying fish as well as letters to his son and newsletters reprinted in a St. Thomas newspaper.

3. "Revising Until It's Right"

The *Melibea* was designed by a single shipbuilder to be sailed by a lone sailor. For Boudreau, writing is a solitary endeavor as well. "If there's anybody I write for, it must be myself," says the captain.

He is also his own editor, so he must rely on his own instincts to decide when his work is complete. "Because of my life style," he notes, "I can take time to make sure that I find the pleasure that I'm looking for in it, simply by revising until it's right."

The writer times his editions of *The Melibea News* to coincide with the visits of his son Will, who takes the copy back to the United States for duplication and mailing. A handful of readers has grown to a circulation of more than 150 friends and relatives. Boudreau's "hurricane edition" garnered an even wider audience when it was reprinted as a three-part newspaper series in the *St. Thomas Courier*.

Readers of the newsletter frequently urge Boudreau to reprint some of his other issues, but he laughs, "I don't know why everyone wants to put me to work. I'm having so much fun!"

The Melibea News

St. Thomas
Sept. 25, 1989

#10
Hurricane edition

The mangrove slough at Ensenada Honda is a very wonderful piece of real estate. It's located on the S side of Vieques, a small island off the E coast of Puerto Rico, about 25 miles from St. Thomas. The slough is completely uninhabited, except by mosquitos, of which there are probably more per cubic inch than at any other known spot on God's green earth. There is some transient wildlife. Brown boobies nest there in season, and frigate birds hover, now that the big guns of U.S. Navy warships no longer use the area for gunnery practice.

Unexploded ordinance lies strewn about the hillsides, and it's inadvisable - nay, prohibited - to set foot on dry land there. The slough is rimmed around on three sides by high hills covered with scrub growth, and the open, seaward side to the S is all but closed off by coral reefs so dense that even the resident fish populations can't navigate it without a chart. The bay enclosed here - that's the mean-ing of its Spanish name, Deep Bay - is nowhere deeper than 25 feet, and this depth is found only in a narrow and tortuous passage. Elsewhere the bay averages 8 feet, over a muddy bottom, like brown Jello.

At the head of the bay is a narrow creek that wanders about among acres of red mangroves, and on a high hill to the E the Navy, for reasons best known to itself, maintains an observation post and a small weather station. It's required to radio ahead for permission to enter the area. Usually there's no answer.

The dank, rich smell of rotting vegetation lies heavily over the slough, and at nighttime when the mosquitos swarm and the no-see-'ems fly up in clouds it must appear to the casual observer to be a very un-likely place in which to raise a family, or build a retirement home or a country club. Nonetheless, and all minor inconveniences accepted, this swampy wasteland is the best and finest garden spot created west of Eden, for it has one unique virtue that far outweighs all its blemi-shes; it's a fine hurricane hole.

Melibea, an incorrigible gunkholer, first went to Ensenada Honda in October of 1986 looking for lobster, which are abundant in the off-shore reefs there. She stayed three days knocking about among the coral heads and reefs, exploring the slough by dinghy, spearfishing for mangrove snapper, enjoying the solitude. It struck me at the time

Boudreau considers his current life ideal and regrets only that he didn't start his full-time sailing earlier. If you were to write a personal newsletter from your vision of an "ideal" life, what would it be called and why?

ON ASSIGNMENT

1. People often write personal newsletters such as *The Melibea News* when they have too many correspondents to write to individually. Imagine that you are about to write such a newsletter to a group of friends or relatives to summarize your activities of the past year. List all the events you would want to include. Put an asterisk next to anything you would like to develop more fully into an anecdote. Now set down at least one anecdote that you could put into a newsletter.

2. **Literature Connection** Cléo Boudreau's writing combines humor, dialogue, narrative, description, and reflection. Find a personal account of an incident in an autobiography, nonfiction book, or magazine feature. Write a brief analysis of what makes the account interesting.

3. **Cooperative Learning** Divide into groups of three or four students to prepare a newsletter about life in your school. As a group, decide on possible topics, such as "Lunchroom Life" or "Mr. Mack's Math Class" and agree on the length of each piece. Topics might include social events, homework, clubs, and sports. Assign one member to write each article. Choose members to contribute photos or illustrations. Brainstorm together to contribute ideas and anecdotes to each other's writing.

   Each article should be written from a personal perspective, using colorful first-person narrative. Focus on memorable events, eyewitness accounts, or topics that have a personal or emotional impact on you. Exchange articles and edit one another's work. Together, lay out your pages, and assign members to copy or type all the articles in an interesting style resembling a letter or leaflet. Distribute copies to your class and to the school newspaper for possible republication.

Writing to Discover More About Yourself

Deep in New Territory

"How do I know what I think until I see what I say?" novelist E. M. Forster once asked. Perhaps you know the feeling. You say something you never thought of before, yet the minute you hear it, you know that's what you think.

Taking a paintbrush or a pen in hand reveals thoughts you never knew you had. If you express yourself to see what you feel or think, you'll soon find yourself "deep in new territory." In the excerpt that follows, writer Annie Dillard explains how writing can lead to new discoveries.

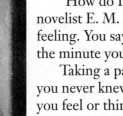

Malvin Gray Johnson, *Self-Portrait (detail), 1934*

What does Dillard mean when she says, "You make the path boldly and follow it fearfully"?

Literature Model

When you write, you lay out a line of words. The line of words is a miner's pick, a woodcarver's gouge, a surgeon's probe. You wield it, and it digs a path you follow. Soon you find yourself deep in new territory. Is it a dead end, or have you located the real subject? You will know tomorrow, or this time next year.

You make the path boldly and follow it fearfully. You go where the path leads. . . . The writing has changed, in your hands, and in a twinkling. . . . The new place interests you because it is not clear. You attend. In your humility, you lay down the words carefully, watching all the angles.

Annie Dillard, *The Writing Life*

Just as painter Malvin Gray Johnson used paint to explore images of himself in his self-portrait, Dillard uses words as tools for digging out ideas that are new, unknown, and interesting.

Writing about your own thoughts, feelings, and experiences is called personal writing. Personal writing can take many forms. It can be a poem, a journal entry, an essay, or a song. It can be written for your eyes only or for the entire world if you choose to share it.

Planning the Journey

Setting off on a voyage of discovery, whether in travel or writing, usually requires planning. Just as a road map can help a traveler plan a trip, a life map may help you identify events in your life that offer intriguing possibilities for you to explore.

Charting the people, places, and events that have been significant to you can give you an overview of the high points, low points, and turning points of your life. If you make a map of challenges you have met and disappointments you've overcome, you'll notice patterns that will help you answer questions such as When do I feel happy? What are my interests? What type of work do I like? Who are my friends? The life map below shows the kinds of events one student might note.

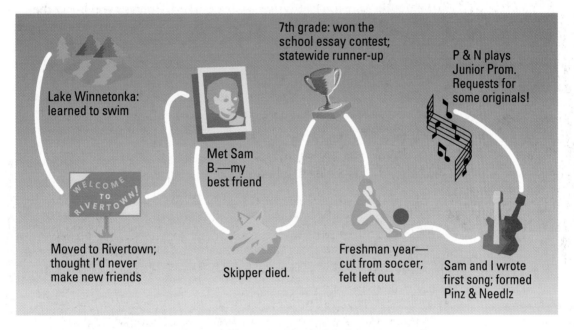

Once you sketch a life map, you'll want to look for the patterns that connect the events. Such patterns connect events the way a road links one town to another on a map. For example, the student who drew the map above might notice that the low points in his life have inspired him to do things that led to success. In your own writing, you might want to focus on the connection between two or more events.

• JOURNAL ACTIVITY •
Try It Out

Sketch your life map. Find and describe a pattern among the highs, lows, and turning points of your life road. List the specific events that are part of that pattern.

Readers' Reactions

As you write about events from your life map, you will discover new insights about yourself and events in your life. You may decide you'd like to share some of your discoveries with others. Before formally presenting your work by publishing it or reading it aloud, you might want to ask a small group to read and respond to it. A group's purpose is not to evaluate your experiences, but rather to let you know whether what you've written expresses what you want to say. The script below shows the kind of conversation you and your readers might have.

WANDA, THE WRITER: Do you think I gave too much information about the first driving lesson? Is it boring?

ANDY: Some of these details about what the teacher told you to do and how confused he made you are funny. They make the story come alive.

BARBARA: One thing I liked was that this reminded me of the time when I was learning to drive. But I don't like the ending. I don't know why.

ANDY: I disagree. I think the ending is really good, but it takes too long to get into the story.

WANDA: Do you think I should cut the first couple of paragraphs? I wondered whether people needed that information to understand what comes later.

Exchanging ideas can improve anyone's writing. If you decide to share your writing with your friends, listen to their feedback carefully. Write down all responses; even if you disagree with some ideas, you might reconsider them as you revise your writing. You will also learn a great deal by giving feedback to others. Remember the following guidelines as you respond to the writing of others and others respond to you.

Guidelines for Groups			
Listen Make eye contact, nod, and tune in to each person as he or she speaks. Take notes and ask questions.	**Respond** Stay on the subject. Be brief. Make it clear that you disagree with ideas rather than people.	**Clarify** If you don't understand what someone else has said, ask for clarification.	**Cooperate** Offer compliments to each member. Give encouraging feedback such as, "I like Joe's suggestion because. . ."

Writer's Choice

The following are some writing options to help you try out what you have learned.

1. Guided Assignment "The events of childhood do not pass, but repeat themselves like seasons of the year," says Eleanor Farjeon.

Farjeon feels that the patterns that shape our lives—overcoming adversity, making friends, developing personal creativity—occur not just once, but over and over throughout different stages of maturity. Follow the steps below to identify and write about a pattern in your life.

- List important events in your life.
- Chart them on a life map.
- Examine the map for a pattern.
- Outline what you plan to say. Describe the pattern in general terms. Then provide details about how this pattern has operated in the past. Finally, explain how the pattern influences you today.
- Write a rough draft.
- Ask a friend or two to read your draft.
- Ask your friends to summarize your draft for you. Their summaries will help you figure out whether you've said what you meant to say.
- Make changes. Write your final version.

PURPOSE   To describe patterns of events in your life
AUDIENCE   Yourself
LENGTH   2–3 pages

COMPUTER OPTION

You may want to include images in your life map. Consider using "clip art," illustrations available on disk that you can electronically paste into your document. These disks can be purchased from software stores and mail order companies. If you have access to a scanner, you can add family photographs or newspaper photos to your life map.

2. Open Assignment Select a topic from the list below, and explore in writing your ideas on this topic. Be sure to include your conclusions about this topic.

- you as a friend
- you as a student
- you as an athlete
- you as a son or a daughter
- you as a citizen
- you in a role of your choosing

3. American History History is not all in the distant past. You have witnessed, at least through newspapers and television, historic events in your lifetime. Many of these events may become important in the history of your community, state, country, or world.

Imagine you are contributing a personal statement to a time capsule being prepared in your community. A time capsule contains contemporary objects and records and is sealed until a specified future time. You have been asked to write a personal reaction to an event that you believe will be important to history. Select a significant or representative event, brainstorm interesting details, and write about your reactions to and opinions of the event.

4. American Literature Think of a book you enjoyed and write a personal statement regarding a character whom you found especially interesting or sympathetic. Possible choices include Huckleberry Finn, Hester Prynne, or Billy Budd, but you may choose any character from a story or novel by an American author. Spend at least ten minutes freewriting (writing—but not evaluating—every thought that occurs to you on a topic) about why that character is especially appealing to you. Use your freewriting notes as the basis for a written statement of the similarities between your life and that of the character you have chosen.

Keeping a Writer's Journal

All the Persons I've Been

Literature Model

Sometimes when I come across an old photograph of myself, particularly one of those taken when I was ten or twelve or thereabouts, I stare at it for a while trying to locate the person I was then, among all the persons I've been, trying to see stretched out down the years the magnetic chain linking the onlooker and the looked at, the gay expectant child and the sober near-adult. If I am successful, and very often I am, the two merge and I recall little snatches of life. Running through the wet grass in the dusk of early evening. My father's vulnerable smile as I walked down the aisle on graduating from kindergarten. . . .

Joan Frances Bennett,
Members of the Class Will Keep Daily Journals

What triggers Bennett's memory of her kindergarten graduation?

Both Joan Frances Bennett (above) and naturalist Loren Eiseley (below) used journals to jot down impressions, whether distant memories or thoughts and feelings of the moment.

Literature Model

Last evening the largest house centipede I have ever seen died peacefully on our bathroom rug. . . . Like two aging animals who have come into a belated understanding with each other, we achieved a mutual tolerance if not respect. He had ceased to run with that flowing, lightninglike menace that is part of the horror of centipedes to man; and I, in my turn, ceased to drive him away from the woolly bathroom rug on which his final desires had centered.

Loren Eiseley, *The Lost Notebooks of Loren Eiseley*

What features of this journal entry tell you that these are the personal reflections of a scientist?

The Journal as Springboard

Many writers store impressions and bits of information in journals to use as they write. When novelist F. Scott Fitzgerald overheard the intriguing comment "He wants to make a goddess out of me and I want to be Mickey Mouse," he wrote it in a notebook. The same words later came out of the mouth of a character in his story "On Your Own."

Other writers, like Louisa May Alcott, have returned to journal entries written years before to comment on their earlier views. For example, when Alcott's publisher asked her to write a book for girls, she wrote in her journal, "I don't enjoy this sort of thing. Never liked girls or knew many, except my sisters; but our queer plays and experiences may prove interesting, though I doubt it." Years later, following the tremendous success of her novel *Little Women*, Alcott wrote "Good joke" beside this passage.

The impressions you record in your journal might seem insignificant when you write them. Two, ten, or forty years from now, however, these impressions may hold more importance.

This journal excerpt by Japanese exchange student Mutsumi Hirai will preserve Mutsumi's initial impressions of the United States long after she ceases to find American ways remarkable.

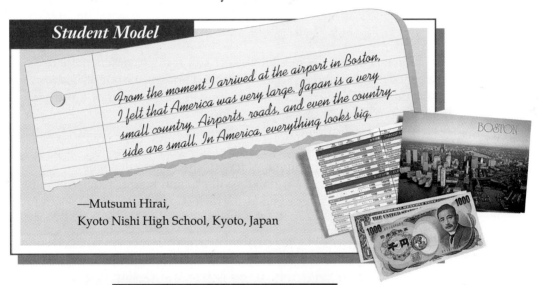

Student Model

From the moment I arrived at the airport in Boston, I felt that America was very large. Japan is a very small country. Airports, roads, and even the country-side are small. In America, everything looks big.

—Mutsumi Hirai,
Kyoto Nishi High School, Kyoto, Japan

• JOURNAL ACTIVITY •
Try It Out

Look around your classroom and make rapid notes for twenty minutes about what you feel and think. Use your immediate environment as a stimulus, but write about anything that comes to mind. Don't stop until the twenty minutes are up. Then read your notes. Which ones do you find most surprising?

A Book of Your Own

What you write in your journal is up to you. You might report observations, record impressions in poetry, or invent characters and situations for a short story. Several possible journal responses to a street musician are illustrated below.

Street Musician

Nonfiction
More and more people seem to be performing on the streets these days.

Poetry
Strong, sweet,
Singing, drumming,
Lyrical, rhythmical,
Ringing, strumming,
Street song.

Fiction
Playing music always took Edward's mind off the stress and turmoil of his life.

Whatever you call it—a journal, a diary, a daybook, or a log—a journal will express your own sensibilities. It can be a bound book with a lovely cover, a spiral notebook, a looseleaf binder, or a stack of index cards. Write every day: perhaps the first thing in the morning, maybe the last thing at night, or during a few private moments in the middle of the day.

Some people write in a subway car late at night; others write on screened porches at dawn. Henry David Thoreau, author of *Walden*, sometimes scribbled notes while floating in a canoe; author Gertrude Stein often wrote during airplane trips.

Your journal can include your thoughts and ideas, lists, titles, outlines, first sentences, sketches and photographs, ticket stubs, diagrams, quotations, newspaper clippings, letters, interesting dialogue, or notes. As novelist and essayist Virginia Woolf explains below, a journal can be that desk drawer of your mind into which you put everything you want to keep.

Literature Model

How would you describe the kind of diary Woolf wants to have? What other kinds of diaries or journals might one keep?

What sort of diary should I like mine to be? Something loose knit and yet not slovenly, so elastic that it will embrace anything, solemn, slight or beautiful that comes into my mind. I should like it to resemble some deep old desk, or capacious hold-all, in which one flings a mass of odds and ends without looking them through.

Virginia Woolf, *A Writer's Diary*

Writer's Choice

The following are some writing options to help you try out what you have learned.

1. Guided Assignment   Dag Hammarskjold, former secretary-general of the United Nations, kept a journal he called "the book my days are writing." Write in your journal for five consecutive days as directed below; try writing in at least three different locations during those five days.

- On the first day include a list, such as a list of all the pleasant sounds you've heard that day.
- On the second day, write a paragraph about a topic that interests you, and then write a poem, or words and phrases for a poem, about the same subject.
- On the third day, draw a diagram that illustrates a relationship or process in your life.
- On the fourth day, record a conversation you had or overheard.
- On the fifth day, ask and answer a question such as "What makes a person successful?"

At the end of five days, read your journal. Discuss with others in your class what you have learned about journal writing. What techniques did you like best? Where and when did you most enjoy writing?

PURPOSE   To record thoughts and impressions in a variety of forms
AUDIENCE Yourself
LENGTH   3–5 pages

2. Open Assignment   Choose a topic from the list below and use it as the basis for a journal entry. Devote at least one page in your journal to the topic you choose.

- an old photograph of yourself
- an animal or insect you have seen
- an article in a newspaper or magazine
- a person you don't know very well but find intriguing
- a subject of your choice

3. Art   Look at the painting on this page. Imagine that you are standing near the people in the painting and can hear what they are saying. In your journal, describe your impressions of the children and the scene. As you write about the painting, notice whether it triggers any memories of your own childhood, thoughts about a child you know, or reflections about childhood in general. Follow this train of thought and allow yourself to freewrite or simply list ideas and phrases for at least ten minutes. Think about how you might use these notes to write a longer piece of nonfiction, poetry, or fiction.

Marie Bashkirsteff, *A Meeting*, c. 1883

So Much to Learn, So Little Time!

"My arms are breaking off from lugging all these books."

"I stayed up all last night cramming for the chem exam."

"Parker's midterm was really tough. It was like he expected us to memorize the lectures!"

Textbooks, supplementary readings, labs, lectures—so much to learn. How do you begin to sort through all this material to decide what you really need to study?

A learning log is a kind of journal that helps you understand what your personal strengths and weaknesses are. Here's an example of a log entry.

Student Model

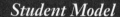

I have just spent another 45 minutes in trigonometry. We had a quiz on probability today. I went into class uncertain whether I understood combinations and permutations because I have been absent for most of the unit, but everything worked out and I did very well. . . . Doing well on the tests should be a good indication of how well I understand the material. Sometimes, though, I fall into the trap of thinking that I can get by without doing my homework. I wish that I could get rid of this recurring laziness. The assigned homework is usually not very long or difficult, but it is hard to do when it just seems like busy work.

Peter Ivaska, Evanston Township High School, Evanston, Illinois

What insights might Peter gain from this passage in his learning log?

In the learning log entry above, Peter evaluates his progress and considers his strengths and weaknesses in trigonometry class. A learning log lets you step back from your schoolwork to analyze what you know, and it allows you to examine from several different angles material you find unclear. By assessing where you are in your learning, you can get more out of the time you spend studying.

Raising the Percentages

Within two weeks most people forget 80 percent of what they have learned. No wonder students panic when exam time rolls around. However, if you keep a learning log, you'll have several strategies for increasing the amount of information you retain.

In a learning log you can grapple with the facts and concepts introduced in your classes. It is only when you become actively involved with facts and concepts by testing and using them that real learning takes place.

You can use a learning log in many ways. A log can help you decide how to focus your study time by sorting out what you know and don't know. A list like the one to the right can help you prepare for a chemistry lab, research a history paper, or study for a literature exam.

Another learning log technique is to project yourself into a situation and imagine how you would be affected by it. For instance, you might rephrase the review question "What were the ramifications of the cotton gin on the southern economy?" by asking yourself, "If I had been a southern farmer in the early nineteenth century, how would buying a cotton gin affect my operations?"

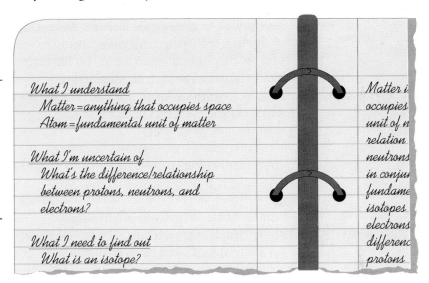

You can keep your learning log in a separate binder or notebook. You can also incorporate your log into your regular notebook. Use the back, or left-hand, page to comment on, question, paraphrase, or discuss the note on the facing right-hand page. You can also divide each page of your notebook in half. Use one half of the page for notes, the other half as a learning log.

• JOURNAL ACTIVITY •
Try It Out

Use one learning log technique to explore a difficult concept from a recent class. You might focus on the most important points, think about how the problem is relevant to you, condense information, or debate an issue.

What Clicks for You

Once you know what you need to learn, it's helpful to understand how you learn best. Experiment with a variety of learning log techniques, including the ones below. You'll find out which help you most.

- Evaluate progress in a class. Assess strengths and weaknesses.
- Write a dialogue in which you take turns arguing for and against an idea you find confusing or intriguing.
- Try explaining to a child what you have been studying.
- Make up your own essay test for a class. Answer one of the questions yourself.

Another way to improve your learning is to analyze how you process information. You probably use one of three basic learning styles: visual, auditory, or tactile. Visual learners do best when they can read or see things in front of them. Auditory learners prefer to hear an explanation of what they are trying to learn. Tactile learners benefit from actually handling and manipulating material. For example, tactile learners might use blocks or folded paper to better understand concepts in geometry. Many people use a combination of learning styles, but most people find that one style dominates.

Experiment with the three learning styles, and record the results in your learning log to better understand your learning strengths and weaknesses. One way to get started is to reserve a section in a notebook for each of your subjects. Then set up a schedule to write in the log on a regular basis. At first you might simply keep track of your progress in each class, dating each entry. Next you might try working in each section for a few minutes at a time, writing whatever comes to mind. You may achieve insights like those illustrated below.

Tactile Learner
The best way for me to learn is to get my fingers on the keys and play the piece over and over.

Auditory Learner
The best way for me to learn a song is to listen to recordings and hear the way other musicians play the piece.

Visual Learner
The best way for me to learn a song is to study the sheet music.

Writer's Choice

The following are some writing options to help you try out what you have learned.

1. Guided Assignment Look through your textbooks and find one in which headings are used to organize the information. In your learning log, use the following procedure to study for an exam in that subject:

- Make an outline of the chapter or unit using the headings.
- Leave several blank lines under each heading you write.
- Read the chapter.
- Without looking back at the book, write beneath each heading a paragraph or a few sentences explaining the significance of each heading.

PURPOSE To use a learning log to study for a test
AUDIENCE Yourself
LENGTH 2–3 pages

COMPUTER OPTION

You may wish to keep your learning log on a computer. Create subdirectories or folders for different classes. Store comments and questions about each class in separate files within the appropriate subdirectory or folder.

2. Open Assignment In your learning log, write a question about something that has puzzled you in one of your classes. Choose from these classes:

- American literature or history
- chemistry or physics
- algebra or trigonometry
- another class you are taking

Review the learning log techniques described earlier in this lesson. Decide which technique is most likely to help you answer the question that puzzles you. Vary these techniques to answer the question you are trying to understand. Work through the question, noting in your learning log your successes and failures in finding a reasonable answer.

3. Driver's Education If you are taking driver's ed, use your learning log to "practice" difficult maneuvers. For example, if parallel parking gives you trouble draw a diagram of two parked cars. Then use a piece of paper to rehearse the moves required to park your car between them. In your learning log, list the steps that were required to move your car into the desired position.

4. Music Cellist Yo Yo Ma says that one of the techniques he used to learn music as a child was to play a piece through mentally before going to bed each night. If you take music lessons, participate in a band or orchestra, or sing in a choir or chorus, try the following exercises to determine how you learn best.

- Play a song through once. (Don't play from memory.) Next, close your eyes and for a full minute visualize yourself playing a passage from the piece. Then play the song through again.
- Repeat the above process with a different song of equal difficulty, but instead of visualizing yourself playing, "hear" the complete song in your mind, and then play it through again.
- Finally, with yet a different song of equal difficulty, play the song through once and then, without using your instrument, duplicate the motions necessary to play the music. Then play the song through.

When you are finished, explain in your learning log which method worked best for you and what this might indicate about your learning style.

Don't Call; Send Letters!

People don't write letters as often as they once did. It seems easier to phone, yet it may take less time to write a letter than it does to make a phone call. Letters bring pleasures not offered by telephone conversations: letters provide the recipient with something to hold and reread. Letters are a form of personal writing that allows both the writer and the recipient an opportunity for insight and understanding.

Student Model

Dear Sarah,
It's so sad how we used to write to one another every other week, and now only once every four or five months. I guess as we got older we also got much busier. . . . Still, I miss not having my best friend, Short Legs, here to share everything with me.

I played tennis again this year, and my partner in one doubles was Mary Trujillo. I know you remember Mary. She is still a clown and a good friend. . . . We did really well this season, and went to the state tournament that was held here in Pueblo. We made it to the second round and lost to a team we should have beaten. Isn't that always the story? Oh well! This summer, I am going to take private lessons from the coach at Cheyenne Mountain High School. . . .

What about you? What are you going to do this summer? I know you have been in some successful plays this year that you need to tell me about. . . . I know you're busy too, but try to respond soon. I'll be thinking about you!

Love always,
"Mish"

Michelle Eddy, Centennial High School, Pueblo, Colorado

How does Michelle express her feelings about Sarah in the first paragraph?

What is the purpose of Michelle's last paragraph?

Audience and Purpose

Once you move beyond purely private writing, you need to think about audience. Who are you writing for? Are you writing for a friend as Michelle was? Michelle tailored her letter for Sarah alone. The letter describes Michelle's memories of her old friend. Even when Michelle wrote about her present life, she described people Sarah knew.

You may not always know your audience as well as Michelle knew Sarah. Even if you are writing for people you have never met, however, you should try to anticipate your audience's interests and depth of knowledge about your topic. For example, if Michelle had been writing to someone she didn't know, she would have provided more background details about each person mentioned in her letter.

Just as you use different expressions and tones of voice when talking with friends than you do when talking with a grandparent, so the language and tone of your letters will also depend on your audience. Even though you might write letters covering some of the same topics to your friend and your aunt on the same day, each letter will have to be a completely fresh and original writing project. You can't write a letter to a friend and then quickly revise it to make it a suitable thank-you note for your aunt. Though there may be some topics that may interest both your aunt and friend, you'll find that much of *what* you write about, as well as *how* you write it, will be influenced by your audience. This diagram illustrates the way Michelle's choice of topics may change for a letter to a friend and a letter to her coach.

Letter to a friend
- Friendship
- Tennis partner
- Feelings about tournament loss

Elements in common
- The state tournament
- Plans to take private lessons

Letter to tennis coach
- Schedule for lessons
- Tennis skills to be improved

Your *purpose* in writing should be clear to both you and your audience. For example, you may decide that your purpose in writing is to inform, persuade, entertain, narrate, or describe. Michelle probably had several purposes in writing to Sarah: to rekindle that old spark of friendship and to get Sarah to fill her in on what has been happening in her life.

• JOURNAL ACTIVITY •

Think It Through

Make notes on two letters you want to write to two different people. List the topics you would cover in each letter. Put a check by the topics you would mention in both letters.

Recording a Relationship

A letter may contain a funny story, an engaging description of a person or place, or a heated defense of a political or ethical position. But no matter what it says, a good letter begs for an answer. Perhaps that is why so many relationships have been preserved through the regular exchange of letters. These letters between American writers Zora Neale Hurston and Fannie Hurst, written in the 1940s, are an example.

Literature Model

What does Hurston say to convince Hurst that her offers of help are sincere?

Dear, dear Friend,
I cannot tell you how shocked I am to hear that you have been ill at all, let alone being in a hospital! I have never conceived of you as either ill nor ailing. I see you always swirling the waving veils of space like a spear of flame.

Now what can I do about it? Do you need me in any way? I am at your feet and at your service. There is nothing I would not do for my benefactor and friend. You know that I can type now. I can cook as always, [and] I can do many more things than I could when you scraped me up out of the street. If there is anything that you feel I could do to please you, you must let me know. I should pay back for all that I have received somehow. . . .

Most devotedly,
Zora

Literature Model

How does Hurst respond to Hurston's concern?

Dear Zora:
Thank you for your warm and understanding letter. In this torn and harassed world, the stability of friendship is about the only staff of life we have left.

I am just about emerging from my fantastic convalescence and hope that you will soon be in New York so that I can prove to you that I am back in my seven league stride.

Are you doing a book? I hope so.

I am on a second draft of a fat novel. The illness interfered horribly, but I am about to resume work. . . .

Thine,
Fannie Hurst

Writer's Choice

The following are some writing options to help you try out what you have learned.

1. Guided Assignment Write a short letter to a relative or friend telling about a recent experience and your feelings about it. Follow these steps:

- Brainstorm a list of recent events in your life. Select one that shows what your life is like and how you feel about it.
- Write a rough draft of your letter. Use a warm, conversational tone.
- Reread the letter. Look for places where you want to add information or take information out. Correct any errors in spelling, grammar, or punctuation.
- If you wish, mail the letter.

PURPOSE   To describe an experience in your life
AUDIENCE   A friend or relative
LENGTH   2–3 pages

2. Open Assignment Imagine you are a character in a book you have read or in a movie you have seen. Write a letter to another character in the book or movie. Write on a topic from the list below.

- a gift or service you have received from the other character
- recent accomplishments related to a hobby or volunteer work
- your memories of the last time you saw the character
- a topic of your choosing

3. Art Imagine that while on vacation you saw the scene in the photograph on this page and decided to describe it to a friend or relative. Decide to whom you are going to write, and then think about the following questions: Where would you see this scene? What would you be doing when you saw this scene? What thoughts or emotions might this scene spark in you? Use your answers to these questions to draft a letter that describes your vacation and the moment when you saw the scene.

Marc Riboud, *Kwangsi Province*, 1965

Writing a College Application Essay

Mental Toughness

You might not think at first that a college essay is a form of personal writing. It is addressed to the members of an admissions review panel whom you have never met. Yet your essay, if it is to succeed, must be personal. Your goal is to reveal your own distinctive personality in written form. Look at the way Anna Strasburg brings her involvement in an extracurricular activity to life in the essay below. Note also the way Anna uses the activity to reveal personal strengths that are valuable in many other areas of life.

Student Model

"*S*wimmers up, take your mark, BANG (the Gun Shot)." Splash! I am in the water now and my heart is racing. One lap completed; nineteen more to go. Boy, nineteen laps. Four hundred fifty yards. I have to think about something. Sometimes I sing fifties' songs; or if I am especially hungry I'll think about a yummy hamburger with everything on it. No, wait, I need to concentrate on my stroke and breathing. Is the girl in the lane next to me gaining? Faster, faster! Good, lap nine. I can hear people screaming; they're counting on me. I have to do well.

I've spoken in front of hundreds of my peers in school assemblies, talked to the entire teaching staff, and led cheers before an audience of thousands. I shouldn't be nervous having a friendly swim competition with five other girls with fewer than 200 people watching, but I am. This type of stress to win goes way beyond the amount of practice time one puts in . . . it has to do with a toughness—not physical, but mental.

I am one of the few people the coaches do not have to beg to swim the 500. This is not because I am an exceptional swimmer (my times are just above average in our league). It is because I have the mental toughness to take things to the very end. . . .

Anna Strasburg, Quartz Hill High School, Quartz Hill, California

The essay focuses on a single talent: swimming.

What does Anna say to convince college officials that she has the mental toughness needed to complete college?

Who Are You?

Deans of college admissions say the essay is the part of the application they most enjoy reading. A well-written essay breathes life into the application form's numbers and blanks. While few students have been admitted to a school because of their essay alone, a well-written essay can help you stand out from all the other applicants with similar grades, test scores, and extracurricular activities. Your essay must be something that only you could have written.

Some colleges will ask a specific question that you are to answer at length. Others will simply ask you to "tell us a little about yourself." Either way, the point of the essay is to get you to express something about what makes you unique.

Before you rush into the essay, take a look at your topic—yourself—from different angles. You might start by probing feelings about events or accomplishments in your life. More ideas will emerge if you consider a second angle. How would a friend describe you? How has your family influenced you? The checklist above offers other questions to guide your exploration.

A laundry list of accomplishments won't create an interesting essay. One way to focus your writing is to select one activity or image to illustrate your unique personality. Anna used a swimming competition to show her mental toughness, the character trait she decided to highlight. Anna might have used notes like these to plan her essay.

Qualities to emphasize
— perseverance; mental toughness
— ability to perform under stress
— ability to perform before a crowd
— ability to set and achieve goals

Activity that portrays qualities
— swimming, not only competitive, but distance

How to portray
— stream of consciousness; thoughts that keep me going

• JOURNAL ACTIVITY •

Think It Through

List four accomplishments of which you are proud. Next to each one, list any traits, such as initiative, perseverance, or creativity, that you used to achieve it. Then write a paragraph describing one of the achievements and why you are proud of it. What activities or images can you think of that could help you illustrate these traits and achievements?

Calvin and Hobbes

by Bill Watterson

Putting the Pieces Together

Even if you're much older than six, don't let your application essay run on and on. Once you've written your essay, reread it to be certain each detail makes an important point. You want your essay to sound as fresh and spontaneous as a good conversation. Replace inflated vocabulary with simple words that say the same thing. Aim for clear language that draws attention to what you say, not how you say it.

Literature Model

My father has always said that I have "brain surgeon hands," probably because they're rather large with fingers so long and thin that my school ring has to be held on with masking tape. . . .

When I was a child, these hands curled themselves around a crayon to scrawl my first letters; they clutched at the handles of a bicycle, refusing to trust my training wheels; they arched delicately over my head in pirouettes and slid, wriggling, into softball gloves. . . . These hands once plunged deep into the pinafore pockets of my candy-striped uniform, emerging to write messages and lab orders, punch telephone numbers, steady syringes. . . .

Someday, these hands will grip forceps and retractors, tense and slick; they will rake through my hair with fatigue as I sit in library carrels studying graphs and figures. Someday soon, they will hold a daisy-adorned diploma from Lincoln School, and they will hold again, as they have in the past, trophies and book awards and certificates. I have confidence that they will become the hands of an M.D., with the power to heal and comfort. . . .

Joanne B. Wilkinson, from *100 Successful College Application Essays*

What does Joanne tell the admissions committee that might convince them of her commitment to a career in medicine?

Does Joanne expect the road to career success to be easy? How can you tell?

Writer's Choice

The following are some writing options to help you try out what you have learned.

1. Guided Assignment   Some colleges and universities, knowing how hard it is for students to write about themselves without being given a topic, create a structure for the essay by asking students to answer a question or comment on a specific subject. The sentence below is one that has been used as an essay topic by Williams College:

Comment on an experience that helped you to discern or define a value that you hold.

List three values you hold. Beside each value, jot down notes about an experience that has shaped this value for you. Use these notes to decide which experience you will write about. List details about the experience you have selected. Include as many specific details as possible about what happened as well as about how you behaved or responded to the experience. Using these notes as a guide, write an essay that fulfills the requirements of the essay topic.

PURPOSE   To present a self-portrait for a college admissions committee
AUDIENCE   College admissions personnel
LENGTH   2 pages

2. Open Assignment   Write a college application essay that reveals something about yourself, using one of the following topics:

- how a summer or after-school job changed you
- how you are different from other students
- how you overcame a handicap, shortcoming, or obstacle to achieve something
- how your family has influenced you
- an experience that destroyed your idealism about a certain person or institution
- a topic of your choice

COMPUTER OPTION

If you use a computer to write your essay, store each draft in a separate file. This will free you to be ever more creative in your writing, knowing that if you go too far in any one draft, the earlier version has not been destroyed.

3. American Literature   Answer the following item as if it were an essay topic for a college application:

List the books you have read during the last twelve months. Which one has had the greatest influence on your life? Why?

After listing the books you have read in the past year, note the ones that you found yourself thinking about. What form did your thoughts take? Did you think about one of the characters? Have you found yourself in a situation similar to one in the book? Did you gain knowledge from the book that has helped you understand the world or society better? Have you been influenced in your activities as a result of reading the book? These and similar questions can help you think about the ways a book may have influenced you.

4. Cooperative Learning   Each member of a small group should write a topic for a possible college application essay on a slip of paper and pass it to the person on his or her right. Each student will list details and examples that could be used in an essay on the topic he or she has received and pass it on to the next person. Each student will then write an opening paragraph using at least one detail or example and then pass it on to the last person, who will read the topic and discuss, with the group as a whole, how well it fulfills the topic it is meant to address.

I Read; Therefore, I Think.

"That book helped me understand what was going on."

"I had never thought about it that way before."

Responding to what you read by writing about it, whether positively or negatively, helps you remember and understand what you've read. Writing about what you've read, like writing down your thoughts in a journal or learning log, is a form of personal writing that organizes your thoughts and reactions. Below you'll see how one reader responded to an article that began like this:

> Patricia Szymczak was 36 years old when she decided to pursue a quest she had contemplated since childhood: finding her mother. . . . She knew the woman's name and hometown from a 1953 Illinois adoption decree, obtained when she turned 18 from her adoptive mother. Szymczak called the local post office, found a retired mailman, and got him talking about the family—*her* family. She contacted old neighbors, who led her to friends. Some had seen the woman, who now lived out of state, at a recent high school reunion.
>
> . . .The long search ended with a three-hour call from a pay phone. By the end of the conversation, it was after midnight on the second Sunday in May. Patricia Szymczak smiled and wished her newfound relation a happy Mother's Day.
>
> —Elizabeth Taylor, "Are You My Mother?" *Time* magazine

The writer begins this response by asking and then answering a question. What other questions could be asked to begin a response to this article?

Model

I really enjoyed this article. It started me thinking: Is it a good idea for an adoptee to search for his or her birth parents? It seems that you never know what you might turn up, so why not leave well enough alone? On the other hand, you may be able to answer questions about yourself that would otherwise be forever unresolved. The article basically says that each case is unique. Many people are happy that they went to the trouble to locate their birth parents. Searches don't always end happily, however.

Responding as Readers

Reading is not a passive activity. The more involved you are in what you read, the more you benefit from it. A *reader-response journal*, a notebook in which you record your reactions to books and articles, can be a tool for staying involved in your reading.

A reader-response journal is a place where, after reading, you can store striking facts, inspiring quotes, emotional responses, and questions to ask the author. You can also record your changing ideas on topics as you increase your knowledge and understanding.

If you do not have an immediate response to what you read, a second reading can often reveal patterns and ideas you may have missed. Your ideas need not be organized or developed like those in the model on page 30; they are simply kernels you can later decide to explore and develop. This sample from a reader-response journal illustrates one reader's reactions to the article on adoptees searching for their parents.

<u>Quotation or paraphrase from text</u>
When she turned 18, she obtained her adoption decree from her adoption mother.

<u>What text makes me think of</u>
This made me wonder how adoptive parents feel about their children searching for their birth parents.

The author used Mother's Day to represent the happy reunion.

Mother's Day might mean different things to different people. But for those who can't be with their mothers and for those who don't even know them, it may bring sadness.

Szymczak obviously spent a lot of time and money trying to track down her birth mother.

Szymczak's drive to make a connection with her birth parents must have been powerful. I wonder why the connection was so important to her?

• JOURNAL ACTIVITY •
Think It Through

Examine a work of nonfiction that affected you strongly in either a positive or negative way. Quote or paraphrase information from the work and then respond to it by asking one question about the topic and answering it.

More Creative Responses

You can carry your responses to nonfiction even further. A fuller, more creative response will expand your understanding of the material and allow you to learn more about yourself. The article excerpted below, for example, may inspire a variety of responses. Even students without step-siblings have enough familiarity with complex family relationships to want to respond to an article on this topic.

> Anyone whose parents have divorced and remarried will know what I'm talking about. . . . You need maps, calendars, and a collection of used airline tickets to make any sense out of [my family]. Heather and I lived in Tennessee with my mother and stepfather. We were *from* California—which is where my father and stepmother lived. My stepfather's first wife also lived in California with their four children, Mike, Tina, Angie, and Bill, my step-siblings.
> Confused? So was I.
> . . . How do you separate out all of your feelings about divorce, remarriage, and these strangers who are supposed to be your family? You can't. But you can try to see your stepbrothers and sisters as people. . . . Figure out who they are, not just the role they play in your circumstances, [and] chances are you'll have an easier time understanding them. They've seen the same kinds of hard times that you have and will probably share similar feelings. . . .
>
> —Ann Patchet, "Step-Siblings," *Seventeen* magazine

Your response to such an article might be straightforward or complex. Whatever its form, your response will deepen your understanding, and you will continue the interaction between yourself and the writer whose work you have read. The chart below provides examples of responses. If you want to learn more about a topic, for example, you could write a research paper. A desire to supplement what you have read with further information could stimulate a second article with a different emphasis. A strong emotional response may inspire a poem or a play.

If you read an article such as the one above, you might . . .			
Write a research paper on the same topic:	**Write a poem or notes for a poem:**	**Write a second article with a different emphasis:**	**Write a play or script:**
"What is the contemporary family really like? How many children live with stepparents and siblings from a previous marriage?"	"My stepsister called. Jealousy, again. Somehow when the phone rings I can tell who it is."	"Money is an issue in any family. But when stepchildren are involved, the issue becomes even more complicated."	"**Ursula:** I hate you! I always will. [turns back to John] **John:** Is it me you hate? Or the fact that your parents are divorced?"

Writer's Choice

The following are some writing options to help you try out what you have learned.

1. Guided Assignment Read a feature article in a newspaper or magazine about proposed health-care reforms, and then write an essay that responds to it. Structure your essay by including a summary of the main point of the article, a statement about whether you agree or disagree with the proposed reforms, and three facts or reasons supporting your position.

PURPOSE Explore reactions to a piece of nonfiction
AUDIENCE Yourself
LENGTH 1–2 pages

2. Open Assignment Imagine you are part of a panel that has been asked to make a presentation about one of the topics below. This panel identifies local problems and attempts to present them in a compelling and convincing manner to the local government of your town or city.

- handicapped access to public buildings
- solid waste disposal
- local public recreation facilities
- noise from local industry or air traffic
- a topic of your choice

Look up articles in a magazine index such as the *Readers' Guide to Periodical Literature* or *Infotrak*. Read at least one magazine article on the topic you've chosen. Respond to the article by writing a poem, a short story, an analysis, a report, or a speech that you could present as your contribution to the panel.

3. Theater Arts Imagine that you have been asked to write a one-act play that will provide entertainment and information to attendees at a conference on an issue you care about. Read two or three nonfiction magazine articles about the topic. Create two characters who represent different views on the topic, and then write a

dialogue in response to the articles. One of the characters should express views that are essentially your views; the other character should present an opposing opinion. Be as fair as possible in presenting both points of view, but make it clear which opinion you find most valid. Perform the skit for your class with help from another student.

COMPUTER OPTION

If you have access to a computer or word processor, you may find it useful in writing and printing a script. The word-processing program probably allows you to create lines with a hanging indent. This feature lets you put the speaker's name on the left, while all the dialogue that the character speaks indents to the right of the name. Printing dialogue using hanging indents makes it easier for actors to identify and memorize their lines.

4. Cooperative Learning Working in a small group, read a magazine or newspaper article about changes in family relationships. Discuss the article for a few minutes, and then respond to it in writing. Select one of these methods for your response or choose another way of responding to the article.

- write a poem or phrases for a poem
- suggest another article on the same topic with a different emphasis
- list characters and a possible situation for a play about the topic
- list questions to be answered in a research paper
- write a journal entry explaining why you find this topic interesting or imporant

Discuss the similarities and differences in your responses.

On Fiery Wing

Literature

"On Remembering the Beara Landscape"

Lakes and rivers, lovely scenery,
Parks and skies, mountain greenery,
A lovely day awaiting.
Away we drive through lonely roads,
Late Fall played a tune on our motor car,
We laughed and sang as we sped along,
Pores open wide along polar jaws.
A possie occurred riding,
Along lonely laneways speeding,
A herd of cattle steaming,
Which brought us to a halt.
A paper passed on an ethereal, rapier-like
    wind,
A song bird flew on fiery wing,
Over hill and dale clouds billowed,
Dancing the dance of golden dreams.

—*Christy Nolan*

Poetry packs meaning into a few words. Poets choose words carefully to express their ideas clearly. Christy Nolan, an Irish writer and painter with cerebral palsy—lacking enough muscle coordination to write with his hands—typed with a stick attached to his head. Yet, when he wrote the poem above at age eleven, he thought each word was worth the effort.

First Impressions

We respond in many ways to what we read and hear. Sometimes we're moved to tears; other times, we are more analytical. You can use personal writing to understand and explore your responses to poetry. Following are two responces to Nolan's poem.

The first student really liked the poem and was inspired to write a few lines of poetry that used one of Nolan's images.

> **Model**
>
> I really like the way Christy Nolan puts certain words together.
> A song bird flew on fiery wing—Nolan
>
> My cat flew at the fiery jay,
> The jay laughed raucously from its high perch—Me

The second student was less enthusiastic. Notice, however, that this writer isn't satisfied by simply saying she doesn't like the poem as much as others do. She searches for reasons for her response.

> **Model**
>
> Today we read Christy Nolan's poem, "On Remembering the Beara Landscape." I enjoyed it, but I was not as swayed by it as some people seemed to be. I know that Nolan was only eleven when he wrote it, but I still think it's a little too childlike. For instance, the opening lines about "lovely scenery" and "mountain greenery" are pretty predictable.
>
> I do like some of the lines, though. I especially enjoy this line even though I don't have any idea what it means:
> Pores open wide along polar jaws
> Goose bumps maybe?

What does this writer dislike about Nolan's poem? What does this writer like about the poem?

Each person who reads a poem will respond to it in a different way because every reader brings his or her own expectations and experiences to the poem. There is no "right" way to respond to poetry. The important thing is to tune in to the feelings the poem awakens in you.

• JOURNAL ACTIVITY •
Try It Out

Write your own response to "On Remembering the Beara Landscape." Allow your response to reflect feelings the poem awakens in you. You may either write a creative piece of your own, using the poem as inspiration, or find examples in the poem to explain your reaction.

Spinning Off from the Poem

You can move past your immediate, emotional reactions to a poem and enrich your responses even further. Here are a few ways to do this.

If you read a poem about a trip to the countryside, you might . . .

Write an essay:	Write a journal entry:	Research the poet:	Write a poem:
"This poem is full of words connoting graceful movement. . . ."	"This poem reminded me of a country drive my family made years ago."	"Christy Nolan succeeded in expressing himself despite his disorder. . . ."	"Sand and grass, pale pink shells and gray-green tendrils . . ."

Below, Curran Walker's responses to Christy Nolan's poem show how you can expand on your response to a poem. In his first response, Curran wrote his own poem, using images that came to mind as he read Nolan's poem. He then expanded his first response into fiction.

Student Model

*T*he crisp cool air stirs before a storm.
From atop the mountain meadow, I saw clouds forming.
A horse and rider trotted through the cool, fall air
   before a mountain storm.
The wind soared across meadow and wood, whistling
   along its way.
Leaves fluttered and fell to earth as the wind danced
   among the trees.

Student Model

*L*eaves fluttered to earth. Nathaniel buttoned his coat while he watched the dark towering clouds coming in over the mountain. He shivered. As he guided his horse, Blue, down the mountain, the sky grew black. Wind soared across meadow and wood, whistling along its way. Then lightning flashed and thunder boomed like a thousand cannons. His horse broke into a dead run down the side of the mountain. After what seemed like an eternity to Nathaniel, he regained control of Blue—only to find that he was in unfamiliar surroundings.

Curran Walker, Austin High School, Austin, Texas

Writer's Choice

Pieter Brueghel, *The Fall of Icarus*, 1564

The following are some writing options to help you try out what you have learned.

1. Guided Assignment Read "I Hear America Singing," by Walt Whitman. Respond to the poem by recording your impressions; describing images that come to mind as you read it; and using the imagery from your response to write a poem, story, song, or play.

PURPOSE To explore responses to poetry
AUDIENCE Yourself
LENGTH 1–2 pages

2. Open Assignment Respond to a poem of your choice in one of the following ways:

- Write a poem that expresses your feelings in response to the poem you read.
- Describe in your own words the content of the poem.
- Explain what the subject of the poem has to do with your life.

3. Cooperative Learning The painting on this page inspired W. H. Auden to write "Musée des Beaux Arts." Read and discuss Auden's poem in a small group. One person in the group should respond to the poem by writing another poem; one should write an essay about the relationship between the painting and the poem; one should research the myth of Icarus and relate it to the painting; and one should write a journal entry responding to the poem, the painting, or both. After all group members have read everyone else's responses, discuss what you have learned.

Writing About Literature: Responding to Poetry **37**

LORENE CARY

from

BLACK ICE

Black Ice, *published in 1991, is the story of a bright, young African-American girl who in 1972 entered a celebrated boarding school that had been all male and had begun recruiting girls and minority students. In this autobiographical selection, she is confronted with a variety of unfamiliar experiences. Whether learning to play basketball or finding out that there are actually pills that will help asthmatics, she is jolted into examining and reexamining her experience. Lorene Cary's vivid memoir lets us see her life at St. Paul's School through her mind and heart as well as through her eyes.*

Fumiko met me on the way to soccer.

"Do you play basketball?" she wanted to know.

"Nah." I felt rough in her presence, square-fingered, and loud.

"I like basketball. In Japan, I played a *lot* of basketball. Don't you play at all?"

"A little bit. I don't shoot so well."

"I can teach you! It's easy. I'll teach you." She looked at her watch. "Come on. We have time."

In the gymnasium we heard the commotion below in the locker rooms. Fumiko ran to the wall behind the basket where a few balls lay beside each other. She picked one, dribbled it, and then passed it to me. She ran onto the court, and I passed it back to her. She shot the ball. It headed toward the basket in a low arc and dropped through.

She ran hard to retrieve her own rebound. There could have been four girls after her, as hard as she ran. She snatched the ball out of the air and then leapt to make a lay-up. It hit the backboard softly and fell through the hoop. Then she passed me the ball.

I hesitated and passed it back. She thrust it at me. I caught the pass, chest-high. She threw it as perfectly as a diagram, harder than my old gym teacher, and with no effort I could see.

I did not want to play. I wanted to watch. But she seemed intent on teaching me. Her intelligence and force were as obvious as her athleticism. I had seen none of it before, because I'd been so eager to assume her need for me.

"Hold like this," Fumiko said. She stood behind me in order to position not just my fingers but my arms as well. She pushed me with her body. I was confused. Her language had been so delicate that I hadn't expected the shove.

I shot. The ball bounced off the rim.

"Hah!" Fumiko zoomed down the key for the rebound and rocketed another pass to me. I caught it. My palms tingled. This time she told me to dribble to the basket. She followed me close. Her body was so close and new that I dropped the ball. She laughed.

John N. Robinson, *Reclining Woman*, 1976

Out of the corner of my eye I watched her as we walked to soccer practice. "You are really good." I felt ashamed for having thought of her as a geisha girl. I had done to her what I suspected white people did to me. She did not answer me. I did not repeat myself. It would've been too much like amazement; after all, the girl had told me that she could play.

Green fields stretched out before us. Two soccer fields lay end to end. A line of white paint on the grass divided them, and the four goals lined up like giant white wickets. Beyond them were clay tennis courts and a gravel track. Football fields hid behind a stand of trees at the end of the track. Big and small boys ran past us toward the far fields. Fumiko broke into a run, too, and I trotted along. By the time we got there, I was out of breath.

We flung ourselves onto the damp grass to lounge in the sun with the other girls.

"Have you people finished your laps already?" The voice behind us was blunt, the pronunciation lippy and controlled. Miss Breiner, the modern-languages teacher, appeared in pastel-colored shorts and knee socks. She was one of the few women at the school who wore makeup. "Four laps. Four laps, please, so we can get started."

I could not help but stare at the field. It was as big around as a Philadelphia city block. I knew people who would get in their cars and *drive* that far. The other girls groaned dramatically and started running. I couldn't do it. I'd die.

"Excuse me, Miss Breiner," I said. This would look like shirking, I knew. Her powder-blue eyes studied a clipboard.

"Yes," she said without looking up.

"My parents wrote to the school this summer to tell them that I have asthma."

"I see," she said looking at me. "I know a couple other girls here who have asthma. Do you take medication? Do you have pills?"

Behind me I heard the thunder of distant cleats. "No." I didn't know there *were* pills for asthma. "But I use an inhaler when I need to."

Miss Breiner was finished regarding me. I could see myself in those blue eyes: a robust black girl talking about asthma and didn't even have pills. "Do what you can," she said. "You may find that the exercise will actually help your asthma."

I fell in. What had started as a pack stretched into a column nearly a quarter lap long. Ahead of me girls talked to each other as they ran. One sprinted to sneak up behind another and give her ponytail a yank. Ponytails flashed in the sun. Striding legs stretched out before me like a movie. My breath came so fast now that I had to concentrate as if to break through some partition stretched across my lungs. It

R. Delaunay, *The Runners*, 1925

had to be some failing of mine. I was breathing too fast, that was it. I'd slow it down and let the air go deeper. But then I began to wheeze, and the long, lithe girls in front of me were coming up behind me now, passing me. How had I dropped so far behind? I pumped my legs as hard as I could.

"Do not cut corners. Do not cut corners." Miss Breiner's voice caught me out. She'd be watching me now, for sure.

My arms flailed. I'd never run so far in my life. What were those pills? The top of my body swung from side to side, and none of it, the pumping or flailing or desperate prayer, pushed me forward.

When everyone else finished, I slunk into the huffing group. I was gulping at the air. It came into my lungs in teaspoonsful. One girl asked me if I was all right. I nodded. It cost too much air to talk.

Then practice began. We passed and kicked and chased the ball. It changed direction in an instant. It was tyrannical, capricious. At the end of practice we did little sprints. Fumiko won most of them. After practice she grinned at me. Her face was flushed and happy.

"I can't do this every day, Fumiko," I said as we walked to Simpson.

In my room I sat on the bed and sucked at my inhaler. The medicine spread through my chest like warmth blown in through tiny copper wires. I thought hard about how to handle this soccer business, and decided to get to practice early in order to do laps before Miss Breiner appeared. After two slow ones, I could quit without being suspected—and still have time to get my wind back before practice. . . .

About forty minutes was allotted in the community schedule for bathing and dressing before class at 5:15. At first, eighth-period class seemed cruel and redundant. We carried with us the fatigue of the day but also, much as I hated to admit it, the weary refreshment of exercise. Our teachers, tired from their own classes and sports, seemed less critical and demanding. I felt less competitive. I had made it through another day, and dinner was imminent. Night was coming, and the dark pushed us closer together.

For Discussion

1. Think about a situation that required you to learn or do something that you weren't particularly good at. How did it make you feel? How did your reactions compare with Cary's?

2. Like Cary, have you ever been ashamed to find out that your assumptions about another person were unfounded? How did your relationship with the person change after you made this discovery?

Readers Respond

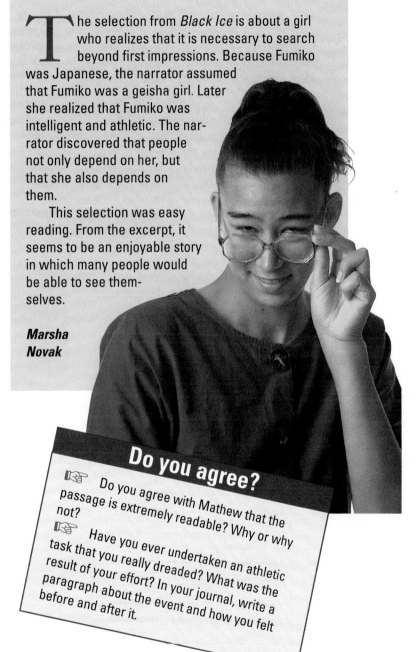

The selection from *Black Ice* is about a girl who realizes that it is necessary to search beyond first impressions. Because Fumiko was Japanese, the narrator assumed that Fumiko was a geisha girl. Later she realized that Fumiko was intelligent and athletic. The narrator discovered that people not only depend on her, but that she also depends on them.

This selection was easy reading. From the excerpt, it seems to be an enjoyable story in which many people would be able to see themselves.

Marsha Novak

I liked the use of a first-person speaker. The passage became much more interesting because the reader was able to get inside the speaker's head and learn her true feelings and emotions (e.g., "I felt ashamed . . ."). The passage is extremely readable.

Mathew Isaac

Do you agree?

☞ Do you agree with Mathew that the passage is extremely readable? Why or why not?

☞ Have you ever undertaken an athletic task that you really dreaded? What was the result of your effort? In your journal, write a paragraph about the event and how you felt before and after it.

Writing Process in Action

A Slice of Life

In the selection from *Black Ice* (pages 38–42), Lorene Cary offers us a snapshot of herself as a sixteen-year-old trying to deal with an alien environment. This personal narrative not only allows us to observe her learning to play basketball and running laps, it puts us right into her tennis shoes. We can almost feel her palms tingle as she catches a pass or hear her wheezing and gulping as she runs. Through the mature writer's careful balance of narration, description, and reflection, we come close to knowing what it felt like to be sixteen-year-old Lorene Cary.

In this assignment you have a similar task—to allow your readers to step into an episode from your life. By writing a personal narrative in which you reflect on the meaning of a particular event, you will offer others a slice of your life.

• Assignment •

CONTEXT	Your college board review course provides the opportunity for you to practice writing essays for your applications. This time you are asked to write about a particularly meaningful experience. The topic is loosely defined: you may write about an event you had a strong reaction to or a situation that affected your attitudes or values. Above all, your essay should convey the real you.
PURPOSE	To write a personal narrative essay in which you communicate your perceptions of who you are
AUDIENCE	A college admissions panel or a job application review board
LENGTH	2–3 pages

1. Prewriting

Several good narrative essay topics are probably lurking in your writer's journal. If these don't pan out, try creating a life map like the one illustrated in Lesson 1.1, or use the techniques explained in Lesson 2.2 to activate your memory. You don't have to have climbed a mountain or have met a famous person in order to write a compelling essay. As you can see in *Black Ice*, simple and ordinary experiences can be just as revealing as dramatic events. What's important is that the experience has deep meaning for you and that you can re-create both the incident and your feelings about it so your readers can experience it, too.

While some of the details about the event you choose will leap out of your memory as fresh as when they occurred, others may be hazy. Try closing your eyes and imagining yourself back in time, going through the experience. Start at the beginning of the event or, even earlier, with the situation that gave rise to it. Proceed slowly, reflecting on all your reactions. Consider these questions, and jot down notes in response to them:

- How did my surroundings look, smell, sound, and feel?
- What were my emotions at the time?
- What were my feelings about the incident after I had some time to reflect?

The more specific details you can provide, the more successful you will be in enabling your readers to live the experience with you.

As you've recalled details, especially reactions and emotions, a deeper meaning of your experience may have begun to crystallize. You don't need to find a world-shaking insight; focus on a simple realization that is important to you. For example, the African-American narrator of *Black Ice* suddenly recognizes the dangers of stereotyping: in thinking of the Japanese student Fumiko as a geisha girl, she says, "I had done to her what I suspected white people did to me," and she is ashamed of her prejudice. Questions such as the following will help you uncover the significance of the event you have chosen to write about:

- How did the experience change me?
- What did I learn about myself?
- What did I learn about other people, human nature, or life in general?

2. Drafting

The selection from *Black Ice* begins by plunging you immediately into the action; it introduces the narrator and her friend through dialogue. You can use a similar technique to open your personal narrative, or you might begin with the background information that readers need to know to understand your experience. Alternatively, you might raise a question that your story and your reflections about it will answer, or you could offer a provocative, attention-grabbing statement about the situation.

Clearly, the natural order for the events of a narrative is chronological: what happened first, second, third, and so on. For dramatic impact, however, you might start at the culminating event and then flash back to reveal the sequence of events that led up to it. Keep in mind, too, that you can combine different methods of organization. Although Cary's narrative is primarily chronological, she uses spatial order to describe the layout of the campus. Transitional words and phrases, such as *then, this time, after, as we walked, now,* and *what had started* signal the sequence of events, while *stretched out before us, end to end, beyond, behind,* and *toward* clarify position in space.

During drafting, think about your tone or voice. As Lesson 1.5 points out, the readers of a college application essay want to "meet" the person behind the words, the distinct personality that is all your own. How do you want your audience to perceive you and your attitude toward your experience? Do you want to sound casual and friendly or distant and formal? Should your approach be comic or serious? Remember, your tone also conveys your attitude toward your audience. Be careful not to patronize or talk down to your readers, but also beware of sounding flip or disrespectful.

Decisions about tone will help you determine what you say and how you say it. In the dialogue from *Black Ice*, for example, the narrator comes across as serious, abrupt, and shy. Her description of the basketball game is also clipped and direct, with few flourishes.

> *I hesitated and passed it back. She thrust it at me. I caught the pass, chest-high. She threw it as perfectly as a diagram, harder than my old gym teacher, and with no effort I could see.*
>
> *I did not want to play. I wanted to watch. But she seemed intent on teaching me. Her intelligence and force were as obvious as her athleticism. I had seen none of it before, because I'd been so eager to assume her need for me.*

Cary's powers of observation and imagination are revealed when she compares Fumiko's pass to a diagram, and she shows her sensitive, introspective side when she compares her stereotyping of Fumiko to her own probable effect on her white classmates. Although drafting is not the place to stew over word choice and sentence structure, do consider tone as you flesh out your details with images, comparisons, and concrete words. Listen as you write dialogue to see that you've captured the liveliness of everyday talk.

Finally, conclude your draft by reflecting on your experience and the meaning it has for you. In the excerpt from *Black Ice* that you read, Lorene Cary weaves many of her insights into the story. In the concluding pages of her memoir, however, she offers a perspective on her experience at St. Paul's and on her title *Black Ice*. You might do a similar appraisal in your conclusion, tying your title or an image or incident from your introduction to the lesson you learned or the general truth you gleaned from the event.

3. Revising

Although the changes and improvements you make to your essay during revising are ultimately your own decision, it helps to know what impact your narrative has on others. Ask a classmate to read your draft using the guidelines in Lesson 1.1 and to respond to questions such as the following:

1. Do you have a sense of actually being involved in the experience described? Which details make the events, people, and places real?
2. Do you have a sense of the writer's personality and voice? Is the tone appropriate to the topic and purpose? Are there any words or images that interfere with a consistent tone?
3. Are thoughts and feelings sufficiently described? Do they reflect conclusions and interpretations about the importance of the experience to the writer?

4. Do the introductory and concluding paragraphs successfully perform their functions?
5. Are the methods of organization that have been used appropriate to the topic and purpose of the essay?
6. Are transitional words and phrases needed anywhere to smooth the flow of ideas?

Consider your classmates' comments carefully, and discuss any you don't understand. Make the revisions you think are appropriate. Then make a clean copy, and consider that draft as objectively as you can. Continue revising until you're satisfied with your essay.

4. Editing

After you've perfected the content and structure of your essay, it's time to take one final look at the mechanics. Read with a critical eye to eliminate any errors in grammar, usage, punctuation, and spelling. Remember, your purpose is to submit this essay as part of a college application; you want the admissions panel to get a positive impression of your skills. The editing checklist in Lesson 2.10 will help make your hunt for errors more systematic.

5. Presenting

Consider storing your personal narrative in a safe place until you begin applying to colleges. You may find that it can serve as the basis for a number of college application essays. You don't have to wait until next year to try out the effect of your personal narrative, however. People usually enjoy reading about and identifying with the experiences of their peers, so share your essay by submitting it to your school literary magazine or one of the many magazines for high school readers.

Criteria

1. *Focuses on an experience that had significance for you and conveys meaning*
2. *Explores your thoughts and feelings as well as the events*
3. *Describes in specific, sensory detail the events, people, and places involved*
4. *Uses organization appropriate to the topic and purpose*
5. *Reflects your personality and your unique voice*
6. *Follows standards of grammar, usage, and mechanics*

• Reflecting •

In his introduction to *Inventing the Truth: The Art and Craft of Memoir,* William Zinsser comments on his own writing process:

> . . . *When I started writing my chapter I was half paralyzed by the awareness that my parents and my sisters were looking over my shoulder, if not actually perched there, and would read whatever version of their life came out of my typewriter. . . . Since then, reading the memoirs of other writers, I've always wondered how many passengers were along on the ride, subtly altering the past.*

How many passengers were along on your ride as you wrote your personal essay? How did they affect what you wrote? Do you think they would be surprised by your interpretation of the event? What new insights did you gain by the very process of reliving and writing about this particular event? Make notes about your writing in your writer's journal.

Portfolio & Reflection

Summary

Key concepts in personal writing include the following:

- Personal writing can lead to self-discovery.
- A life map is one technique for finding personal writing topics.
- Other students can provide constructive criticism that will aid the writing process.
- Use a journal to record impressions.
- Use a learning log to discover problem areas in your school work and to improve the quality of time spent in studying.
- Personal letters can express the writer's personality and appeal to the reader's interests.
- A college application essay should convey the unique personality of the writer.

Your Writer's Portfolio

Look over the personal writing you have done during this unit. Select two pieces of writing to put into your portfolio. Each piece should demonstrate that you have worked with one or more of the preceding concepts. In other words, look for a piece of writing that does one or more of the following:

- is based on personal writing topics you discovered by creating a life map
- results from constructive criticism by other students
- is based on impressions and ideas that you recorded in a journal entry
- helps you discover problem areas in your school work or improve the way you study
- expresses your personality and appeals to your reader through a personal letter
- conveys your personality for a college application essay

Reflection and Commentary

Write one page that demonstrates that you understand what this unit asked of you. Use your two selected pieces of writing as evidence while you consider the following numbered items. Respond to as many items as possible. Label the page "Commentary on Personal Writing," and include it in your portfolio.

1. What did you discover about yourself through personal writing?
2. How did a life map help you select or develop a topic for personal writing?
3. What constructive criticism helped you revise a piece of writing?
4. What impressions or ideas did you record in a journal?
5. What improvements in the way you study did you make as the result of using a learning log?

Feedback

If you had a chance to respond to the following student comment, what would you say or ask?

I discover things about myself when I write because usually I relate the assigned topic to my own life. I can't always say what I feel when I'm talking, but when I write, it comes out freely.

Janine M. Paolucci, Brentwood High School,
Brentwood, New York

The Writing Process

A Fresh Look

Pablo Picasso, *Three Musicians*, 1921

Where Her CHARACTERS Come From

"I don't need readers to fall off their chairs laughing. What I want is for them to say, 'This happened to me; this is a reflection of my life.' In fact, I have a reader who says she looks forward to the Sunday paper to see what aspect of her life I'm going to unveil that day."

Cartoonist Barbara Brandon, creator of "Where I'm Coming From"

A s a child, Barbara Brandon earned her allowance by coloring in silhouettes and putting dots and borders on the cartoons drawn by her father. "These things take a lot of time but not much skill," Brandon explains, "so my father paid me to do them." Brumsic Brandon Jr.'s nationally syndicated cartoon, "Luther," detailed the adventures of an African American inner-city child from 1969 to 1986.

Constructing a Cartoon

1. Listening for Topics   **2. Picturing the Words**   **3. Making It Just Right**

F O C U S

Like writing, cartooning often involves gathering ideas, preparing drafts, and revising for clarity and effectiveness.

Barbara Brandon later followed her father's example. She made history in 1991 when her weekly comic strip, "Where I'm Coming From," leaped from the pages of the *Detroit Free Press* into national syndication. Brandon was the first African-American woman whose comic strip was syndicated nationally outside of the black press.

Brandon's early cartooning efforts had won high praise, but the magazine that had planned to print her cartoon folded before her first strip ran. Brandon's next magazine job, as a fashion and beauty writer at *Essence,* put her cartooning efforts on hold for five years. In 1989 "I finally got my chance," says Brandon. "The *Detroit Free Press* wanted a black cartoonist, and they asked my father if he

knew of one. Dad said to me, 'Are you just going to talk about it, or are you going to do it?' So I did it."

In her father's footsteps: Brumsic Brandon's cartoon, "Luther," served as a model for Barbara's work. Can you see the artistic resemblance between this strip and the ones on the following pages?

1. Listening for Topics

Brandon keeps a pad of paper near her bed and also carries a notebook around so she can jot down possible topics and pieces of dialogue for her strip. Whenever the cartoonist forgets her notebook, she has to ask herself, "Now, where did I write that idea down?"

Brandon gets most of her ideas for dialogue from the things people say, so she has to listen carefully when her friends talk. "I have friends who are open and honest with me, and that's great for my humor," she says. "I egg them on, and what they say ends up in my strip."

The cartoonist also admits to being an incurable eavesdropper. "My ears perk up when I hear people, especially men, talking about relationships."

Occasionally, getting ideas involves more than just listening. Brandon often goes out of her way to join a conversation to stimulate comments that may later appear in the cartoon. She says, "Even if I don't know the person I've overheard, I'll often engage in a conversation. I'll say, 'You said this; does that mean that?' "

By listening, observing, and reflecting, Brandon discovers the many points of view that appear in her comic strip. "I put down what I see," the cartoonist explains. "My own particular point of view is pretty open-minded and understanding, but I can actually identify with parts of all my characters."

2. Picturing the Words

In many cartoons, words are subordinate to the visual gags. But with Brandon, the words always come first. Like a writer, Brandon has to consider her relationship with her audience: Will her readers understand the strip? Will they relate to it? As she writes, she follows a main idea. She creates a certain mood—sometimes humorous, sometimes serious or ironic.

"First, I put down an idea and try to come up with dialogue to make that point," she says. "Then I ask myself which of my characters would say these things. How one character might react is not the same as how another might."

After choosing her characters and writing a rough draft of the dialogue, Brandon begins sketching. "I come up with the [facial] expressions to go with the words," she says. Brandon keeps a file on her recurring characters, including flighty Nicole and solid, dependable Judy (shown below), the lovesick Cheryl, and the socially conscious Lekesia.

"If I do a particular facial expression, I might want to use it again," the artist explains. "If I have it on file, I can . . . just alter a few lines."

Brandon began with twelve characters but has pared down her cast considerably—just as a writer might edit out characters in a novel or a play. "I used to create a new character every time I did a strip," she recalls, "but my editors in Detroit said it's better to use the same characters so the reader can get used to them. . . . I have about nine characters now."

INTERFACE **Study the cartoon below. From your impressions of the two characters, write a short piece of dialogue between the two. Either continue the conversation that is in the cartoon, or start them in a new discussion.**

Before and after: the strip on the right is the revised version of the one on the left; the revision includes changes in the faces and the lettering.

3. Making It Just Right

Brandon draws four to eight cartoons, then begins revising. "I never have liked anyone to look over my shoulder, so I don't really use people as sounding boards," she says. But Brandon does ask her roommate to check for spelling errors before she sends her strips to the *Detroit Free Press*.

Before her work was accepted for national syndication, Brandon spent one year on a trial contract. Under this arrangement, the cartoonist would send the syndication company as many as eight strips a month in pencil. "They would tell me which ones they liked and which ones they didn't," she says. "If I thought their criticism was something I could learn from, I'd listen. If I thought they were wrong, I'd try to make my point

more clearly. By the time I put ink on the cartoon, it had changed."

For example, to prepare the cartoon above for national syndication, Brandon revised the cartoon of Cheryl discussing her boyfriend, Maurice. "I showed more hand expressions and made the lettering stronger," says the cartoonist. "I also emphasized things differently, making the 'I' into box letters rather than underlining it. I think the cartoon looks better now."

INTERFACE **You are Brandon's syndication editor. Study the two versions of the strip shown above. Then draft a note to Brandon evaluating her revision. Is it successful? Why or why not? Should she make further changes?**

ON ASSIGNMENT

1. Humorists such as Barbara Brandon often find material in the situations that involve themselves and their friends or in remarks they've overheard. Imagine you are the cartoonist for your school newspaper. Carry a notebook around for a week and jot down notes about experiences such as your conversations in the lunchroom or on the bus. At the end of the week, choose one humorous situation and develop it into a funny anecdote or cartoon that you can present to your class. Be sure to change names and withhold identifying information that might embarrass a particular student.

2. **Literature Connection**
   In Brandon's cartoons you can count on Nicole to be empty-headed, Lekesia to be socially aware, Cheryl to care only about having a boyfriend, and Judy to be there whenever Nicole has a problem. Look at the comic strips you usually like to read and think about the personality traits of the characters. Then write descriptions of characters you might want to include in a cartoon series of your own. In a line or two, describe each character's personality and appearance.

3. **Cooperative Learning**
   In a small group, compile a book of collected comic strips. Decide on a theme for the book. The cartoons you select will relate to the theme—for instance, school, politics, food, pets, or a wry look at life. Bring in cartoons you find in magazines, newspapers, cartoon anthologies, or books about cartooning. As a group, choose the cartoons that best fit your theme, and decide on a logical order in which they will appear. Brainstorm a name for your book, and work together to compile it and to design a cover.

Case Study: Creating Cartoons   **55**

Two Steps Forward, One Step Back

Scribble, scribble. Rip. Crumple. Swivel and shoot. Scribble, scribble. Rip. Crumple. Swivel and shoot.

Writers make great basketball players. We are armchair Michael Jordans, spending hour after hour crumpling up sheets of paper and taking target practice at the trash basket across the room. Always critical of our work, we throw out more writing than we keep.

Literature

You do not write well right away, and if you're going to get anything done at all you have to blurt out something. And it's going to be bad. And to sit there and do something that's bad all day long is unpleasant—but when you've done this enough, you have the so-called rough draft. And at that point, when I do have a draft—something's on paper, and it's really miserable . . . I can work on it and make it better, and I relax a little, and I get a little more confident when I'm in that second, third phase, or however many times it takes.

Author John McPhee, interviewed by Terry Gross
at WHYY-FM for National Public Radio's "Fresh Air"

Two-way traffic ahead

Fog Area

A Road Map for Writers

If you want to build a radio-controlled plane, you can send away for a kit complete with materials and instructions for assembling it. Follow the steps, and—*voilà!*—an airplane, just like the one on the box. You cannot, however, buy a kit for building a play, a letter, or a short story. If you could, your writing would sound like everyone else's, and who would want to read it? Even a formula novel has the unique imprint of its individual author. When you write, your own mind, methods, temperament, and interests will make your writing unique.

Writing always involves some exploring. As you put your thoughts on paper, new ideas may emerge that lead you in unexpected directions. Like all writers, however, you move through a series of stages to create a finished product. Understanding the writing process, from prewriting through presenting, will help you know how to proceed, whether that means taking two steps forward or one step back.

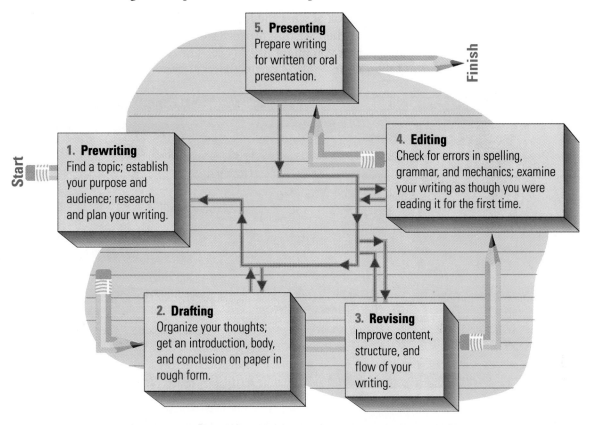

The illustration above shows that you cannot find a shortcut from start to finish, but you can follow many possible paths. You may choose a path that leads to a dead end. Or, you may make a discovery that opens up new directions. At any point, you may decide to return to the prewriting stage. Even as they are revising or editing, successful writers frequently return to previous stages to clarify or expand their thinking.

Doing It Your Way

There are as many ways to write as there are books in a library. Some writers like quiet; some like noise. One writes a dozen drafts; another writes two. Each applies a unique mix of discipline and creativity to writing. As you write, you'll discover what works best for you.

Finding out what others say about their writing can also help you understand your own. Look at what the following writers say about how they write, and compare their writing processes with yours. Pay special attention to strategies that you might like to use. Think about what works best for you and then *try it.*

How Professionals Write

Vladimir Nabokov
I have rewritten—often several times—every word I have ever published. My pencils outlast their erasers.

Katherine Anne Porter
If I didn't know the ending of a story, I wouldn't begin. I always write my last line, my last paragraphs, my last page first.

Anthony Burgess
I don't write drafts. I do page one many, many times and move on to page two. I pile up sheet after sheet, each in its final state, and at length I have a novel that doesn't—in my view—need any revision. . . . Revising is done with each page, not with each chapter or the whole book.

How Students Write

Nina E. Molumby *Evanston, Illinois*
I usually write a first draft in a spiral notebook and make changes on paper. Later I move to my computer. I try to find a quiet room where I can spread out. The time of day doesn't matter as long as I have the inspiration to compose on paper.

Michelle Eddy *Pueblo, Colorado*
I write from my heart. I write what I feel and then go back and revise.

Neelesh Chopdekar *Edison, New Jersey*
Once a good introduction is complete, the rest just flows naturally.

Melissa Frohreich *Bay Shore, New York*
I write about 1,000 rough drafts about completely different things; then, at about three in the morning, inspiration hits me.

Erik Nagler *Aurora, Colorado*
I wait until eleven o'clock the night before it is due before I start writing. Panic usually takes over for inspiration.

Writer's Choice

The following are some writing options to help you try out what you have learned.

1. Guided Assignment Several middle school students are visiting your high school and have called you in as an expert on writing at the high school level. You agree to give them a short talk about your own writing process. Recall several writing assignments you've completed during the last year. Keeping these assignments in mind, ask yourself the following questions:

- Does your approach to writing differ depending on what kind of writing you're doing? How?
- Do you follow a set pattern? Do you do any prewriting, or do you usually start writing "cold"?
- What aspects of writing do you find easiest? Most difficult?
- In what kind of setting do you usually write?
- Which of your writing habits are useful and which are not?
- How do you think you could improve your approach to writing?

Jot down any thoughts that come to mind. Then write an informal outline, incorporating the points you would like to make in your talk.

PURPOSE   To describe your writing methods
AUDIENCE   Middle school students
LENGTH   1–2 pages

2. Open Assignment The editor of your newspaper wants you to write for its new column, "Student Voices." This week, the column is a how-to article for children in elementary school. Your piece should help children deal with a real problem, such as

- how to deal with peer pressure
- how to get through (fourth, fifth, sixth, seventh) grade
- how to get better grades
- how to get along with a brother or sister in the same school

Choose one of these topics or another of your own choice. During prewriting, take notes either from your own experiences or from research. Write a draft of your article. If you get stuck, you can go back to prewriting to choose a new topic or to gather more material.

3. Art Imagine that the print below has been chosen as the cover for a composition textbook and you have been asked to write a paragraph about it for inclusion in the book. What does the image suggest to you about the writing process? What ideas does it inspire that might be useful to students using the textbook? Draft the paragraph. Your writing should engage the interest of both teachers and students.

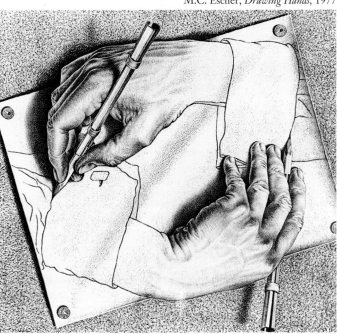

M.C. Escher, *Drawing Hands*, 1977

Prewriting: Finding Ideas

Follow That Thought!

> **1. Prewriting**
> Find a topic; establish your purpose and audience; research and plan your writing.

Start

Get lost.

That's right. Go ahead and get lost. When you're stumped for a topic, let your mind wander and your imagination roam. Sometimes the most unspectacular subject or the most ordinary object can lead you to parts unknown. Eliza Miller started writing about her alarm clock and then, without stopping, followed her thoughts from one idea to another. This strategy, known as freewriting, can help you find writing ideas.

Student Model

With what kind of observations does the writer begin her freewriting? Why?

What associations does the writer make to get from the subject of her alarm clock to Newton and Einstein?

My alarm clock is small and black. It beeps eight times in a row, tiny shrill beeps, then pauses for a second or two and does it again. I put it across the room on my bookcase so I have to get out of bed to shut it off. Even so, I still oversleep. Somehow my sleep-mind rationalizes getting back in bed every single morning, even though I know I will fall back asleep: It's okay, I'll just lie here for ten minutes and not fall asleep. . . . It's too cold to go to school. . . . I have to finish my dream. . . . It's probably Saturday anyway. It's strange the things your mind will think up when it's still asleep. The other day I woke up thinking about math; I don't know why. It seemed to me that I had invented a whole new theory of mathematics. I suddenly understood everything. I was like Einstein or Newton or Pythagoras or any of those amazing mathematicians, and my theory would change everything and make it possible for people to do something impossible, like fly or read minds. I finally woke up all the way and realized I was wrong. There is nothing so disappointing as waking up after a wonderful dream and finding yourself back in your cold room and reality, and it's 7:15 and you have only ten minutes before you have to be out the door.

Eliza Miller, Concord Academy, Concord, Massachusetts

What Should I Write About?

For Eliza and most writers, getting started is the hardest part. Some days no ideas come at all. Freewriting can help you find ideas and write about them more fluently. Writing starters, such as those on the right, can get you going. Try creating your own list of starters.

Writing topics can also come from observing the world. Pay attention to the man sitting on his porch as you pass on your way home. Think about why you didn't like a TV show. Study the way a person walks against the wind or fights with an umbrella. Now compose a list of writing ideas from your observations. When you settle on a topic, explore it. Making a tree can give you different ways to think about your topic.

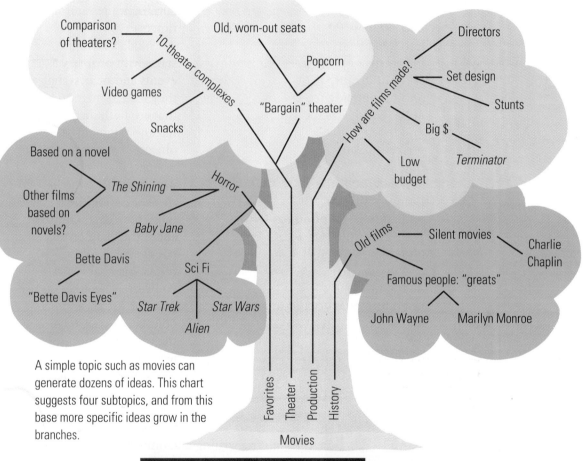

A simple topic such as movies can generate dozens of ideas. This chart suggests four subtopics, and from this base more specific ideas grow in the branches.

• JOURNAL ACTIVITY •
Try It Out

In your journal, try freewriting about an unusual idea. Start on your own, or fill in the blanks of this question: "What if _____ were _____?" Let your imagination run wild.

Turning Lead into Gold

Writing topics don't have to be unusual. Great literature has been inspired by everyday occurrences in the lives of average people. So what is the source of the alchemy that magically turns the ordinary into the extraordinary? You are. The most mundane events can be made new when seen through your unique perspective. On the left is one such personal vision of a very familiar topic: summertime.

Nikki Giovanni starts with ordinary events and objects, but they lead to memories that are both disturbing and poignant. The objects of summer represent the safety and well-being that the speaker of her poem longs for. As you think about the feelings this poem evokes in you, remember that when you write, the way you describe events and objects can transform the most common subject into your own vision.

Look over the details of the topic that you have explored through freewriting and drawing tree diagrams. Choose those details that will lead your readers to envision the topic from your unique perspective. By using these details in your writing, you can take a common topic such as summertime and turn it into a thoughtful and perceptive draft that could only have been written by you.

> ### Literature Model
>
> I always like summer
> best
> you can eat fresh corn
> from daddy's garden
> and okra
> and greens
> and cabbage
> and lots of
> barbecue
> and buttermilk
> and homemade ice-cream
> at the church picnic
> and listen to
> gospel music
> outside
> at the church
> homecoming
> and go to the mountains with
> your grandmother
> and go barefooted
> and be warm
> all the time
> not only when you go to bed
> and sleep
>
> Nikki Giovanni,
> "Knoxville,
> Tennessee"

The poet begins by describing items and events of everyday life.

What does this poem tell you about the other seasons of the year in the speaker's life?

Writer's Choice

The following are some writing options to help you try out what you have learned.

1. Guided Assignment   In the poem on page 62 by Nikki Giovanni, the speaker gives readers a perspective on her life by telling about some common places, things, and events of her childhood. Choose one of the starters below to get you thinking about events in your own life and to inspire five minutes of freewriting:

- I always love Thanksgiving best . . .
- The weirdest thing I've ever seen was . . .
- I was never so embarrassed as when . . .
- What people don't know about me is . . .
- My most peaceful moments are . . .

Look over your freewriting for a topic, serious or amusing, which you think could become the basis of an essay or poem. Then write a draft of your essay or poem. If you're not happy with how your writing is going, don't hesitate to go back to your prewriting sample to find a slightly different focus. You can also freewrite on a new topic and write another draft. Finally, revise and edit your work and submit it to your student literary magazine.

PURPOSE   To amuse or entertain using your personal experiences
AUDIENCE   Readers of a student magazine
LENGTH   1–2 pages

2. Open Assignment   You have just been promoted to the position of editor of a famous magazine, and you have less than one hour to come up with ten good topics to assign to your staff for the next issue. You decide to make a tree diagram to generate ideas. Your magazine specializes in articles on one of the following:

- current events
- fashion
- sports
- technology
- food
- another area of your choice

Make at least four branches and include as many details as possible. Fill a page. You may also freewrite for five minutes on your topic.

Next, test the strength of one of your assignments by writing at least three paragraphs about that topic. If you get stuck while drafting, return to your diagram or freewriting to find a different aspect of your topic on which to focus.

COMPUTER OPTION

If you're a fast typist, a computer may help you in freewriting. By typing, you can keep up with the thoughts that come to mind, more so than if you're writing by hand. Don't stop to check your spelling, however, and don't worry about margins. Just keep thinking and typing. Afterward, you may find a section of your freewriting that you want to save and work with. Copy it into a new file in which you'll begin your first draft. But save your entire file of freewriting in case you want to go back to it for ideas.

3. Home Economics   Challenge yourself to take an everyday subject and use it as the basis for an unusual piece of writing. Brainstorm a list of everyday activities that you might do at home—cleaning the kitchen, making cookies, building a bookshelf, or sewing clothes. Use freewriting or tree diagraming to explore the significance of these activities in your life. Do these actions have certain good or bad associations for you? Do they represent something larger and more meaningful in your life? Do they lead you to any conclusions about other people's lives or life in general? Draft a few paragraphs based on your ideas. Don't forget that things that are nostalgic or funny to you may strike a chord in your readers, too.

Prewriting: Questioning to Explore a Topic

Good Question . . .

BUD: You know, strange as it may seem, they give base-ball players peculiar names nowadays. On the St. Louis team Who's on first, What's on second, I Don't Know is on third.

LOU: That's what I want to find out. I want you to tell me the names of the fellows on the St. Louis team.

BUD: I'm telling you. Who's on first, What's on second, I Don't Know is on third.

LOU: You know the fellows' names?

BUD: Yes.

LOU: Well, then, who's playin' first?

BUD: Yes.

LOU: I mean the fellow's name on first base.

BUD: Who.

LOU: The fellow's name on first base for St. Louis.

BUD: Who.

LOU: The guy on first base.

BUD: Who is on first base.

LOU: Well, what are you askin' me for?

BUD: I'm not asking you. I'm telling you. Who is on first. . . .

LOU: [Trying to be calm.] Have you got a first baseman on first?

BUD: Certainly.

LOU: Well, all I'm tryin' to find out is what's the guy's name on first base.

BUD: Oh, no, no. What is on second base. . . .

Bud Abbott and Lou Costello, "Who's on First?"

Forget it, Lou. To get the answers you want, you have to ask the right questions. The same goes for writers. The answers you get are only as good as the questions you ask. Writing ideas often begin as questions in the writer's mind: Why is the fishing so poor this year? What would I change about my school if I could? As writers focus and research their topics, they continue to ask questions and gather information.

What's Your Question?

Different questions serve different purposes, and knowing what kind of question to ask can be as important as knowing how to ask it clearly. Personal questions ask about your own responses to a given topic. They help you explore your own experiences and tastes. Creative questions ask you to compare your subject to something that seems very different, or to imagine that you are observing your subject from someone else's point of view. Such questions can expand your perspective on a subject. Analytical questions ask about structure and function: How is this topic constructed? What is its purpose? These questions help you evaluate and draw conclusions. Informational questions ask for facts, statistics, or details. When you get stuck at some point in your writing, maybe the answer is really a question.

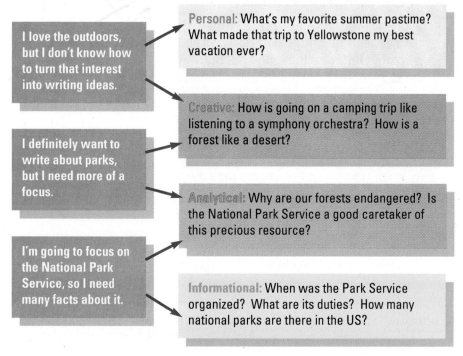

I love the outdoors, but I don't know how to turn that interest into writing ideas.

Personal: What's my favorite summer pastime? What made that trip to Yellowstone my best vacation ever?

Creative: How is going on a camping trip like listening to a symphony orchestra? How is a forest like a desert?

I definitely want to write about parks, but I need more of a focus.

Analytical: Why are our forests endangered? Is the National Park Service a good caretaker of this precious resource?

I'm going to focus on the National Park Service, so I need many facts about it.

Informational: When was the Park Service organized? What are its duties? How many national parks are there in the US?

Questions like these can help you take a subject that intrigues you and turn it into a topic that you can write about.

• JOURNAL ACTIVITY •
Try It Out

Choose a simple object or idea that you know something about—a sneaker, your locker, your favorite car, swim meets—and write at least ten good questions that could help you explore it as a writing topic. Include questions that are personal, creative, analytical, and informational.

Good Questioning, Good Writing

Just as you use questions to get started, you can also question your text as it emerges. For example, if you were to write, "The woman rose from the table and walked to the window," you might ask yourself: "What does the table look like? What does the woman see out of the window? Does she walk quickly or slowly?" With the right questions you can generate infinite depth and detail.

The excerpt below by Estela Trambley is from a short story about an old Mexican peasant woman, Lela. As you read, keep in mind that to develop this scene the writer had to ask many questions: "What did Lela see next? How does it feel to pick up sand? To sleep with a fever?"

Literature Model

What happens to someone in free-fall? The writer envisioned Lela's lungs filling with air.

What questions might the writer have asked herself in order to describe the sand in this part of the story?

How would Lela react to this crisis? The writer had to ask questions like this to develop the details in this passage.

She lost her footing and fell down, down over a crevice between two huge boulders. As she fell, her lungs filled with air. Her body hit soft sand, but the edge of her foot felt the sharpness of a stone. She lay there stunned for a few minutes until she felt a sharp pain at the side of her foot. Somewhat dizzy, she sat up and noticed that the side of her foot was bleeding profusely. . . . She looked up at the boulders that silently rebuked her helplessness; then she began to cry softly. She had to stanch the blood. She wiped away her tears with the side of her sleeve and tore off a piece of skirt to use as a bandage. As she looked down at the wound again, she noticed that the sand where she had fallen was extremely crystalline and loose. It shone against a rising moon. She scooped up a handful and looked at it with fascination. "The sand of the gods," she whispered to herself. She took some sand and rubbed it on the wound before she applied the bandage. By now, she felt a burning fever. She wrapped the strip of skirt around the wound now covered with the fine, shining sand. Then she slept. But it was a fitful sleep, for her body burned with fever. Half awake and half in a dream, she saw the sands take the shapes of happy, little gods. Then, at other times, the pain told her she was going to die. After a long time, her exhausted body slept until the dawn passed over her head.

Estela Portillo Trambley, "The Burning"

Can you imagine what this passage would be like if the writer had settled for a more limited description of a woman falling and injuring her foot? Questioning yourself about the world around you can yield a surprising amount of striking detail.

The following are some writing options to help you try out what you have learned.

1. Guided Assignment You are a summer intern on your local paper, and your assignment is to write science articles that will appeal to other high school students. Your first topic is space travel. You can write about fictional aspects of your subject, such as stories, movies, and television programs that deal with space travel; about any real-life space exploration with which you are familiar, such as the first landing on the moon; or about your own thoughts and feelings on the subject.

Write three questions on space travel in each category—personal, informational, analytical, and creative. Look over your questions and find a specific story idea that you would like to write about. Then write a short article on the topic you've chosen, using freewriting or brainstorming to help you get started. As you write, continue to ask questions to create vivid detail.

PURPOSE To inform or entertain readers about high-interest space topics
AUDIENCE High school readers of a daily newspaper
LENGTH 1–2 pages

2. Open Assignment A foreign exchange student is coming to stay with you in a couple of months, and she has asked you to write to her about American activities and customs. Draft a detailed letter to her about one of the following topics or a topic of your own choice:

- country music
- wildlife
- fashion
- basketball
- education

Edward Hopper, *Cape Cod Evening* (detail), 1939

Ask yourself at least one question from each of the four categories on page 65 to narrow the focus of your topic. As you work, think about what your foreign friend would be most interested in. Once you've chosen your topic, make a second list of questions, this time to help you explore your topic and discover greater levels of detail. Finally, use your notes to write a lively letter of one or two pages.

3. Art Study the painting at the top of this page. Develop four good questions about it. Start with broad questions about the painting to help you think about the colors, content, and texture of the piece. Then choose one aspect of the painting to describe in detail. Write a second series of questions about your chosen topic, using as many of the kinds of questions on page 65 as you can. Finally, write a two-page discussion of the aspect of the painting that you chose.

Barking Up the Right Tree

How would the dog's story change if the mailman told it to his fellow workers? Writing for dog readers, Zeek spins a dog-bites-man story that appeals to dog fears and dog imaginations. Zeek knows his audience. As a writer, that's part of your job: to tailor your words to your readers, be they two-legged or four-legged.

Call of the Calf
by Zeek

I sensed the mailman's fear as he opened the gate. It was like a warm stench in the air--So thick you could cut it with a knife. Suddenly, I felt myself growing dizzy--as if the fear was some powerful drug. The entire yard began reeling. And then I heard his soft, plump calves begin calling to me: "Zeeeeeeeeek... Zeeeeeeeek... bite us, Zeeeeek... biiiiiiiite uuuusss..."

For Whom and Why?

Every day, you face an avalanche of written words. The ones that grab your attention are those aimed squarely at you. Good writers know for whom they're writing.

Before you begin any writing task, you must, like Zeek, know your audience. When prewriting, decide whether your topic is appropriate for your readers. Would dogs be interested in a mailman story? Sure. Would they read a report on high-value postage stamps? No, but a stamp-collectors' club would.

You must also pin down your purpose for writing. As a writer, you will usually select one central purpose: to describe, to explain, to persuade, or to narrate. Once you've decided, really reach out to your readers. For example, if you set out to persuade your readers to elect Carla to the student council, make every sentence grab a vote. If you want to describe a white-knuckle roller-coaster ride, describe your sensations of terror.

Throughout the writing process, take care to use ideas and language that are appropriate for your audience and your purpose. If you write a speech on your town's founders for your history class, you might include lively anecdotes and use informal language. If you're speaking to the local historical society on the same subject, you would probably speak more formally. You would choose more sophisticated anecdotes, as well as information and language that presume more than a basic knowledge of the topic.

Creating a chart like the one on the next page can assist you in determining possible audiences and purposes. Looking at the chart, think about the pros and cons of writing about video games for different audiences and purposes. Writing for your peers would be fun, although they probably don't need much persuading to try a new game. Adults who do not play video games may not be interested in the history of video games; that topic may be better suited to a younger audience. Trying to convince parents that video games are worthwhile is the most challenging of your purposes.

Let's say you decide to go for the challenge, thinking that you may even publish your piece in the school newsletter for parents. Be sure to present your reasons in an orderly manner for maximum effectiveness. The following model is an example of the sort of piece you may decide to write.

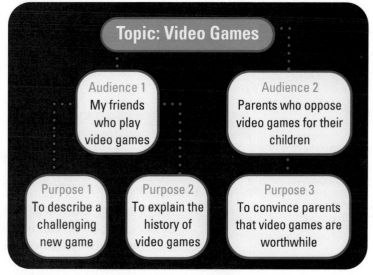

Topic: Video Games

Audience 1
My friends who play video games

Audience 2
Parents who oppose video games for their children

Purpose 1
To describe a challenging new game

Purpose 2
To explain the history of video games

Purpose 3
To convince parents that video games are worthwhile

Model

*P*arents, before despairing that your son or daughter plays video games, consider these arguments on behalf of the sport.

Video games have redeeming qualities that you may have overlooked. They are not only fun, but they also require quick thinking, good reflexes, and keen hand-eye coordination. With practice, virtually anyone can excel at video games. They thus offer an opportunity for friendly, healthy competition. Playing these games can strengthen self-esteem and confidence. Most important, video games force the player to concentrate and to perform well under pressure.

Take some time out to visit a video arcade and to savor the experience of video games. Perhaps you'll gain a new skill; certainly you can count on having a great time.

Find examples of how the writer tailored the language to suit his audience.

• **JOURNAL ACTIVITY** •
Try It Out

Choose a topic of your own, perhaps a favorite hobby or pastime. In your journal, create a chart like the one above in which you list three possible audiences and four possible purposes for the topic you've chosen.

Different Tastes

If you think writing is shaped mostly by its topic, think again. Below, two authors write about the same topic, breakfast cereals. The detail, tone, and language they use are quite different because their audiences and purposes are different.

From reading the first sentence, who do you think is the writers' intended audience and what is the writers' purpose?

What is the tone of this paragraph? How would you describe the choice of words?

What is Erma Bombeck's purpose in writing this piece? What clues can you find in the first sentence to support this purpose?

Literature Models

Cooked cereals are excellent, because the B vitamins stay right there in the water, and the lysine is not destroyed. Besides, could anything be more satisfying than hot, whole-grain porridge? With sliced bananas, raisins or dates, dried apricots or nuts, hot cereal can be mouthwatering to even the pickiest little one. I always thought it had to be sweetened, but try it with Better-Butter. Milk is traditional, but buttermilk and cottage cheese both go well with hot cereal.

Laurel Robertson, Carol Flinders, and Bronwen Godfrey,
Laurel's Kitchen: A Handbook for Vegetarian Cookery and Nutrition

I told the kids I had had it and there would be no more new cereal brought into the house until we cleaned up what we already had. . . . Eventually we polished off every box, only to be confronted with the most important decision we had ever made as a family: the selection of a new box of cereal.

I personally favored Bran Brittles because they made you regular and offered an African violet as a premium.

One child wanted Chock Full of Soggies because they turned your teeth purple.

Another wanted Jungle Jollies because they had no nutritional value whatsoever.

We must have spent twenty minutes in the cereal aisle before we decided on Mangled Wheat Bits because "when eaten as an after-school snack, will give you X-ray vision."

Erma Bombeck, *Aunt Erma's Cope Book*

Notice the difference in the tone of these two passages. The purpose of the first selection is to teach those who know less than the authors; therefore the writers address their audience as instructors. The purpose of the second selection is to entertain a family audience. Erma Bombeck makes us think, "Has she been eavesdropping at the kitchen door during breakfast?" When you write, the details and language you choose will help determine how you come across to your audience.

The following are some writing options to help you try out what you have learned.

1. Guided Assignment You are a member of the marketing department of a large food manufacturing company. Your company is developing a new line of carbonated "health juices" derived from different kinds of vegetables—green pepper, zucchini, and so on. Your boss wants to design an ad campaign that will appeal to teen-agers, and he assigns the task to you as the one closest in age to the potential market.

Write a memo to your boss suggesting a marketing strategy. Your memo should include the names of the drinks, their packaging, slogans, and overall appeal.

Explain in your memo how each aspect of your plan will be tailored to the tastes of your audience. Remember that your purpose is to make the drink attractive to your market.

Pablo Picasso, *Carafe, Jug and Fruit Bowl*, Summer 1909

PURPOSE To design a marketing strategy for a new product
AUDIENCE Teen-agers
LENGTH 2–3 pages

2. Open Assignment Imagine that you've been in an auto accident in which you were forced to swerve your parents' car to avoid a deer crossing the road. The deer is fine; the car is not. Write one sentence expressing your purpose in writing about the accident for each of these audiences:

- the local SPCA (Society for the Prevention of Cruelty to Animals)
- your parents upon seeing the car
- the investigating police officer
- your best friend
- a reporter from the local newspaper

Then choose one audience, and keeping your purpose in mind, write a short essay about the accident. Make sure that the content, language, and tone are appropriate for your audience.

3. Art You are a guide in a famous art gallery in the year 3000. One of the masterpieces that you discuss on your tour is the painting above. Prepare your comments about this painting for two of the following potential audiences: children from the local elementary school, a group of students visiting from another solar system, your own classmates, and intelligent but artistically ignorant robots. Write about 200–250 words for each audience, tailoring your remarks to suit the interests and backgrounds of your audiences.

A Thousand Brushstrokes, One Impression

Claude Monet,
Bridge at Argenteuil,
1874

If you stand close to this painting, you see thousands of tiny brush-strokes, like tiny chips of colored glass. As you step back, the specks of color blend and take shape, and you begin to see the water shimmering in the sunlight and the boats on the water. A good writer, like an impressionist painter, selects and combines a multitude of details to create a picture that conveys a single vivid impression.

An Eye for Detail

Many painters use two techniques that are crucial to observation. One is to take the time to note small details, instead of settling for a passing glance. The other is to study a subject from many perspectives: look at the back of a statue, observe a house in the morning and evening. Claude Monet, a famous French impressionist painter, painted the same haystack again and again to study it in different lights.

Sometimes when you write you will find one or the other technique appropriate to your purpose. In the following excerpt, Alice Munro describes a woman named Flo. Notice the way the writer places details in this paragraph to create an overall impression not unlike a verbal painting.

*F*lo at this time must have been in her early thirties. A young woman. She wore exactly the same clothes that a woman of fifty, or sixty, or seventy, might wear: print house-dresses loose at the neck and sleeves as well as the waist; bib aprons, also of print, which she took off when she came from the kitchen into the store. This was a common costume at the time, for a poor though not absolutely poverty-stricken woman; it was also, in a way, a scornful deliberate choice. Flo scorned slacks, she scorned the outfits of people trying to be in style, she scorned lipstick and permanents. She wore her own black hair cut straight across, just long enough to push behind her ears. . . .

Alice Munro, "Royal Beatings"

> *Is Flo a conformist or a nonconformist? What details in the text support your answer?*

> *The writer observes not only what Flo wears, but what she doesn't wear, which is just as significant.*

A richly observed description like the one above doesn't happen by accident but by methodical thinking about the subject. When you observe a person or scene, try to develop your powers of observation. Use your sense of sight, as Munro does; use your other senses as well: hearing, smell, touch, taste. This most basic level of observation involves physical, sensory details. Below are basic observations of sensory details noted during a traffic jam.

Sights, colors
- cobalt blue hatchback, driver on a car phone
- hot red pickup piled precariously with granite blocks
- huge turquoise truck in middle of intersection
- bright clear blue sky
- pedestrians heedlessly weaving through cars to cross street

Sounds
- strangely subdued, no horns
- brakes squeaking
- truck gears grinding impatiently
- voices of two cab drivers discussing last night's game

Other
- exhaust stinging nostrils
- heat from sun beating on car tops
- aroma from nearby bread factory

• JOURNAL ACTIVITY •
Try It Out

In your journal, write down as many sensory details as possible of a scene that you've observed. Choose from your notes to create a list of those observations that support one clear idea.

Choosing Details

The longer and more carefully you look at something, the more you're bound to see. Go beyond simple sensory details to detect more about a person or a situation. For instance, if you were to return to the traffic jam example from the previous page and spend more time watching and analyzing the scene, you might be able to make the following observations.

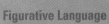

Associations
- Where we used to live, drivers were rude.
- What if you were about to have a baby and had to get to the hospital?
- Like that 2-hour jam coming back from Sox game.
- Dad says driving through Lincoln Tunnel is like smoking a pack of cigarettes—wonder how healthy the air is out here?

Other Perspectives
- Wish I could hop from car top to car top.
- From sky, looks like a checkerboard of cars.
- Should have taken the bypass.

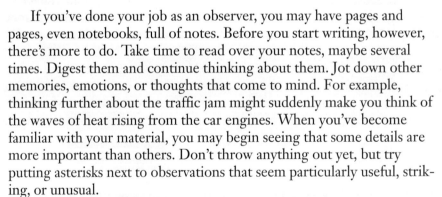

Emotions, impressions
- Sense of camaraderie, good-natured resignation.
- Driver of hatchback looks cool, oblivious to it all.
- I hate being stuck behind a truck; can't see what's causing the jam.
- Bread smell makes me even more impatient to get home and eat.
- Irony: cars speed us up; traffic slows us down.

Figurative Language
- Woman's drooping hair looks like a wilted salad.
- Like a stadium crowd trying to move through a turnstile.

If you've done your job as an observer, you may have pages and pages, even notebooks, full of notes. Before you start writing, however, there's more to do. Take time to read over your notes, maybe several times. Digest them and continue thinking about them. Jot down other memories, emotions, or thoughts that come to mind. For example, thinking further about the traffic jam might suddenly make you think of the waves of heat rising from the car engines. When you've become familiar with your material, you may begin seeing that some details are more important than others. Don't throw anything out yet, but try putting asterisks next to observations that seem particularly useful, striking, or unusual.

You might also go back to your subject on another day or at another hour to make further observations. Return to the scene of the traffic jam at sunrise or on a rainy or snowy day to contrast the atmosphere.

Think of the details you collect as your raw material. Just as a painter starts with all of the colors and brushes needed to depict a particular scene, you must gather all of the descriptive materials you can to paint a sharp and vivid word-picture for your reader.

The following are some writing options to help you try out what you have learned.

1. **Guided Assignment** You are going to produce a one-act play about your life. The story will take place in a room in which you have spent considerable time, such as your bedroom, the kitchen, a classroom, a gymnasium, a library, or a restaurant. Your set designer needs to know what the place looks like in order to construct an accurate replica. Write a memo describing the place in as much detail as you can. Record impressions and associations to bring your description to life. Consider how the place looks from different perspectives: from outside the room looking in or at night.

PURPOSE   To describe a place using vivid details
AUDIENCE   Set designer
LENGTH   1–3 paragraphs

COMPUTER OPTION

If your computer is equipped with drawing and painting software, you can use this feature to make a schematic—a visual outline, diagram, or rough drawing—of the scene you're describing. Drawing a schematic can be a prewriting tool to jog your memory about a place. Or it can be used in the presenting stage of the writing process to accompany your written description.

2. **Open Assignment** A famous movie director has decided to film the climactic scene of a new movie on teen-agers in your town. The scene will be one of the following: a confrontation between the two main characters, a romantic scene, or the discovery of important evidence for a mystery. Your job is to choose a setting for one of these scenes and to decide what time of day and what time of year will be most effective. You might consider the following:

- your backyard
- a cemetery
- a crowded shopping mall
- a wedding at a local church or synagogue
- a bus or train station

First, observe the scene of your choice and list as many sensory details as you can at two different times of day. Record your impressions and your associations. Then try to imagine the scene at a different time of the year, and see what new details begin to surface. Choose a specific time of day and year, and write a memo to the movie director describing the scene as you envision it.

3. **Cooperative Learning** Your high school has just adopted a sister school in Russia. The students at the Russian school are very curious about how an American school operates and what American students are like. You and a group of your classmates have been asked to write an essay describing an aspect of the social life in your school. You choose the lunchtime scene in your cafeteria.

Assign each member of your group one of the senses: taste, smell, sight, sound, and touch (including temperature). During one lunch period, go to the cafeteria and take notes on your assigned sense. Meet again and read your notes to the other members of your group. Ask one another a variety of questions to help you develop your notes and add details. If necessary, go back to the cafeteria for another session of observation.

Finally, each member will write a page-long description of the cafeteria from the perspective of his or her assigned sense. One member will decide on the best order for the description; one will read the essays through for consistency; a third and a fourth will type the descriptions and correct for errors, and the fifth will write an introduction.

Drafting: Achieving Unity

Making Your Point

Student Model

*T*here is an uncontrolled killer in the oceans of the world. Each year it destroys thousands of innocent and unknowing mammals. In fact it can annihilate any marine animal that comes in contact with it. The name given to this murderer is plastic. It is a manmade substance which has been carelessly thrown into the oceans for many years. Each year ships haphazardly discard fourteen billion pounds of waste into the waters of the world. The National Academy of Sciences estimates this rate to be more than 1.5 million pounds of refuse each hour of the day. Thankfully the paper is able to decay and the glass and metal usually sink, but plastic does not decay or sink. By accumulating and floating on the water, plastic turns into a killer.

Heather Ann Sweeney,
William V. Fisher Catholic High School, Lancaster, Ohio

What is the main point of this paragraph? Why do you think the student waits until the end of the paragraph to express it?

Heather's opening paragraph sustains its main idea: plastic kills. Starting with the metaphor "uncontrolled killer," each sentence supports this idea with words such as "annihilate," "murderer," "carelessly," and "haphazardly" and with the repetition of "killer" in the last line. Although the main idea is not explicitly stated until the last sentence, the paragraph is unified. All the details and sentences support the main idea.

Finding a Focus

The main idea, or focus, of your paragraph or essay determines which details, facts, and examples you include in that piece of writing. That's why it is so important to be very clear about your main idea. You should be able to express this idea in a topic sentence when you write a paragraph, or in a thesis statement when you write an essay.

If you are having trouble expressing your main idea, one strategy is to look at your prewriting notes and allow it to emerge from your specific details. Perhaps Heather followed this process as she started to write about the problems of plastics in our environment. Heather's prewriting notes might have included the data in the diagram below: sensory and concrete details, reasons, facts or statistics, and examples or incidents. In clarifying her main idea, she would have thought about what her data suggested as well as what would be most likely to interest her readers.

Plastics

Sensory and Concrete Details	Reasons	Facts or Statistics	Examples or Incidents
• dirty plastic bottles washed ashore on a clean beach • plastic cup left in a beautiful park • cries of baby porpoise struggling to break free of plastic containers	• Plastic is more of a hazard than paper because plastic does not readily decay. • Mammals are more likely to encounter plastic than metal because plastic floats.	• Plastic takes hundreds of years to decay. • Americans throw out billions of tons of plastic every year. Ships discard 14 billion pounds of waste annually.	• landfill overflowing with plastic • a dolphin, head trapped in a round piece of plastic, dies of starvation plastic rings from soda cans strangle seagulls

Thesis Statements
1. The use of plastics in industry is a modern phenomenon.
2. Irresponsible disposal of plastic destroys natural beauty.
✔ 3. Discarded plastic kills sea mammals.

After examining these details, Heather would have rejected the first thesis because it did not fit her data. The second thesis could be supported by the data, but the general reader would already know a great deal about the topic. Moreover, if Heather's intention was to strongly affect her readers' feelings, the third thesis was a better choice. Much of the data supported this thesis, the subject was less widely known, and the details about sea mammals would have a great emotional impact.

Once you've pinned down a thesis statement, some of your details will become irrelevant, as in the example above. Other data may be missing, so you will have to return to prewriting and do more research on your topic.

• JOURNAL ACTIVITY •
Try It Out

Make a diagram like the one above for a topic such as basketball, sneakers, or shopping malls. List at least three possible controlling ideas, and circle the one that seems best suited to the information.

Letting Go of Irrelevant Details

One of the most difficult aspects of writing is deciding what to leave out. If you include information that does not support your main idea, your essay will be less effective. The following writer returned from vacation eager to write about the startling moment of his encounter with a moose. As he read his notes below, he crossed out those items that didn't support his main idea, jotted down questions about others, and wrote in new relevant details.

Rowboats on Lake Azisgahos
Will the image of the rowboats set up the encounter well?
~~A moose can weigh up to 1800 lbs.~~
Sunrise on the lake *Will it help my story to start by establishing time of day?*
Thick brown fur, matted, coarse
Antlers that stretched nearly six feet across
Brown fuzz on the antlers
~~Even in August, cold nights~~
Until now Bullwinkle was my only idea of a moose
Funny, but will this distract the reader from the mood?
Big brown eyes *Too sweet—huge brown eyes?*
~~Also saw two deer the day before~~

Such choices can be painful. The Bullwinkle comment was one of the writer's favorites, but he had to admit that it didn't fit in. As he continued to work, other ideas began to surface. He continued the process of deleting and adding details until the writing felt right.

Model

*I*t was just after sunrise, and the mist was rising on the lake. Several early-risers in rowboats were gently bobbing on the quiet lake, fishing for their breakfasts. Suddenly, I heard hoofbeats like muffled thunder in the meadow. The moose's massive frame burst from the forest, and he stopped, as surprised to see me as I was to see him. His thick brown fur was matted and coarse. His antlers stretched six feet across, like a giant crown lit by the glow of the early sun. I was close enough to see that they were covered in soft fuzz. His huge brown eyes darted right and left, looking for escape. I felt afraid, but also—strangely—glad; I was standing face to face with the grandeur of nature. Steam blew from the moose's nostrils. He gave a great bellow and turned suddenly, heading back into the forest.

Writer's Choice

The following are some writing options to help you try out what you have learned.

1. Guided Assignment You are a freelance writer who specializes in writing about movies. Two different magazines have asked you to write an article about a movie produced especially for children. The first magazine is for children aged seven to twelve; the second is a parents' magazine.

Brainstorm about a children's movie you have seen recently or remember well. You might also create a diagram like the one on page 77. Then consider your two audiences. What would appeal to each? Choose a main idea for each article that is suitable to your audience. Then look at your notes and select the material that would be appropriate for each article. Some of the details in your notes will be appropriate for both articles, some for one or the other, and some for neither.

Write an introductory paragraph for each of your articles. Then list under each introduction the main details, facts, images, and ideas you will use. Make sure each item supports the main idea and is suitable for its audience.

PURPOSE	To select appropriate material for two articles with the same subject but different controlling ideas
AUDIENCES	Children and parents
LENGTH	2–3 pages

2. Open Assignment Write an article for the "Animal Life" column of a school newspaper. Choose from the following topics or come up with an idea of your own:

- the problems of pet ownership in the city or country
- silly pet tricks
- how to avoid encountering wild animals when hiking
- raising farm animals

Keep in mind your main idea, or thesis, as you draft. Revise your writing for unity by eliminating any details, phrases, or sentences that do not support your thesis.

COMPUTER OPTION

A word processor can make revising easy. Not only can you quickly delete unnecessary text, but you can also store your deletions for safekeeping. This is helpful if you change your mind and want to restore the text later, or if you want to use it in some other section, chapter, or writing assignment. Try creating a new document called "Leftovers," "Garbage," or "Trims." Whenever you delete a chunk of text that you may want to hang on to, copy it into this new document. Make sure you save the document immediately.

3. Cooperative Learning Bring to class a draft of a piece of writing you are working on. In groups of four, exchange your drafts. As you read another group member's draft, evaluate the draft for overall unity. Write down two or three questions that will help the writer revise the draft to make it more unified.

Assign to each student in your group one of the types of data illustrated in the diagram on page 77. Read through the draft a second time, this time evaluating it for its use of the type of data you are assigned to look for. Write two or three more questions to help the writer better incorporate this type of data. Pass the draft to another group member.

When all members have read each draft, return the drafts to their writers. Read over the questions that other members have written in response to your draft. As a group, discuss what you have learned from these questions and from evaluating the drafts. Then, rewrite your draft, incorporating your responses to the questions.

Drafting: Organizing an Essay

Piecing It Together

The array of supporting details, reasons, facts, and examples that you have collected for an essay may look to you a little like the collage on the left: a collection of bits and pieces of information, suggestive of several ideas but all very diffuse. Don't go to pieces. A variety of techniques is available that can help you order your mass of material. The following chart defines five common organizing techniques.

Kurt Schwitters,
Opened by Customs,
1937–38

Common Organizing Techniques	
Compare and Contrast	Shows similarities and differences between two objects, persons, or incidents.
Order of Importance	Presents details in order of increasing (or decreasing) significance or scope.
Pro and Con	Presents first positive, then negative aspects of a product or course of action.
Spatial Order	Shows the details of a scene, object, or person according to their relative positions.
Chronological Order	Describes an event or a process in sequence as it occurs over time.

Choosing the Best Order

Imagine that you are writing an essay to present to students in your school. Your general topic is "garbage." How would you choose the right organizing technique? A good strategy is to let your purpose determine the way you order your material. If the data you have selected support your main idea, choosing an appropriate organizing technique can be simple. See page 78 on unity. The following chart demonstrates how different purposes and data lend themselves to different organizing techniques.

Selecting an Appropriate Organizing Technique

Purpose: To explain that Americans generate much more garbage than people in other countries do.

Data: Statistics on landfills, including kinds and amounts of garbage generated in the United States and in other countries.

Organizing Technique: Compare and Contrast

Purpose: To make a compelling argument that disposal of garbage is extremely expensive.

Data: The cost of disposal of a variety of products including glass (expensive), paper (very expensive), waste water (exorbitant).

Organizing Technique: Order of Importance

Purpose: To give a balanced view of the difficulties and rewards of being a garbage collector.

Data: Details and examples of the problems of the job; details and examples of the benefits of the job.

Organizing Technique: Pro and Con

Purpose: To write a description of a landfill that emphasizes its size and diverse content.

Data: Details of visit to local dump: description of the layers of landfill, from underground to the highest "hills"; description of landfill observed from left to right and from foreground to horizon.

Organizing Technique: Spatial Order

Purpose: To provide clear instructions on making toys from trash.

Data: Suggestions for appropriate material such as empty containers and paper; examples of toys that can be made; descriptions of each step in constructing several such toys.

Organizing Technique: Chronological Order

Sometimes you will find that you need to use a combination of organizing methods. For example, if you wanted to show not only that Americans produce more garbage than people in other countries but also that the amount of garbage has been increasing every year, you would choose a combination of compare and contrast and chronological order.

• JOURNAL ACTIVITY •
Try It Out

Create a chart on the topic "high school." Brainstorm three different purposes for writing about this topic. Include the kinds of data to be used and the best organizing technique for each.

Writing an Essay

What did you do when you first looked at the collage on page 80? Many people would stand back to get a sense of the picture as a whole. Then they would come closer and examine the collage, piece by piece. Finally, they would stand back again to see how the collage struck them once they were familiar with its various elements.

The way that a viewer examines a collage is not very different from the way a writer approaches writing an essay. Normally, when you write an essay, you start with the big picture, the essay's main idea. Next, you present your material piece by piece. You end by stepping back for a final overview. Each of the three parts of your essay—the introduction, the body, and the conclusion—has its own unique function and contributes to the overall picture you create.

Introduction
- How can I get my reader's attention?
- How can I introduce my main idea?
- What tone do I want to set?

Body
- How can I develop and support my idea?
- How can I organize my writing?
- How can I tie my ideas together?

Conclusion
- How can I create a strong last impression?
- What is the best way to bring this writing to a close?

Getting Off to a Good Start   In the opening scenes of *Raiders of the Lost Ark*, intrepid archaeologist Indiana Jones narrowly escapes a giant rolling boulder, poisoned darts, and flying spears in a hair-raising flight. Director Steven Spielberg brings you to the edge of your seat even before the title appears. He knows how to seize your attention and set the stage for the next ninety minutes of danger and suspense.

Like the opening scene of a well-directed movie, the introduction to a written work should capture your audience's attention and show where the writing is going. As author John McPhee puts it, an introduction "ought to shine like a flashlight down into the whole piece." An effective introduction will engage the audience, present the main idea, or thesis, and establish the tone and organizing strategy for the rest of the piece.

The Heart of the Essay   The body of your essay presents your supporting material in an order appropriate to your thesis and purpose. Once you have selected an organizing technique, divide your argument into logical sections. As a rule, you will present each section in one or more paragraphs.

The first paragraph of each section should contain a topic sentence. Use supporting details—examples, statistics, quotations from one or more authorities—to amplify or reinforce the topic sentence, and be careful to include only details that are essential to your thesis.

As you move from one topic to the next, remember to take your reader with you. Transitional words such as *first, second, therefore,* and *as a result* can help your reader follow your argument. Longer essays may require transitional paragraphs to sum up the points made so far and introduce the next topic. Keep in mind that your paragraphs should follow an orderly sequence. As the chart on page 81 shows, the precise order that you choose will depend on your purpose and data.

The End   More than merely restating points already made, the strongest and most effective conclusions are those that leave the reader with a new way of seeing the point. If the body of your essay is long and complicated, you may need to summarize or restate your main ideas in your concluding section. But do so in a way that puts your subject in perspective. Shorter essays may not require a repetition of all of the key points, but instead may conclude with an anecdote, a concluding analysis, a pithy quotation, or a striking fact that you've withheld until the end for dramatic effect.

The following paragraph is taken from an essay that asserts that television is harmful to society. In the essay, the writer makes three main points: that there is too much sex and violence on TV, that TV stifles creativity, and that TV gives viewers a false sense of reality. Then he concludes with the following paragraph.

Student Model

*I*n short, television is hurting our society more than it is helping it. The general consensus of authorities suggests that although television can be a valuable tool it is not being used as such. Dr. Neil Postman said, "Words, not visual images, are still the coin of the realm for serious culture." There is much to be learned from television, but one must remember not to become completely absorbed. One should watch television with an inquisitive mind and never become complacent.

Matthew Asbury, Claremont Northeastern High School, Batavia, Ohio

In what ways does this conclusion go beyond mere summarizing?

• JOURNAL ACTIVITY •
Think It Through

In your journal, copy the conclusion of a magazine essay that you find effective. Write a paragraph explaining how the conclusion both sums up and gives a new perspective on the subject of the essay.

Putting It All Together

When Ellen Goodman, a newspaper columnist, had the tape deck stolen from her car, it prompted her to write a humorous essay on the subject. Writing for an urban audience, she hooked her readers with a snappy anecdotal introduction.

What indications does Goodman give you in the first paragraph that this will be a humorous piece?

Literature Model

*L*et me begin this tale of urban crime with a small piece of family lore. My father was a man so intent on believing in an honest world that he wouldn't, on principle, lock the car. I don't mean the doors to the car. I mean the ignition.

For this particular principle he was well rewarded, or should I say targeted. During one brief period in the early sixties, our car was driven off no less than three times.

I, however, have always considered myself relatively (to him) street-smart, somewhere between savvy and paranoid. Nevertheless, last week I got ripped off and it was, everyone seems to agree, my own fault.

Where did I go wrong? you ask. I blush to confess this, but I was foolish enough to actually be the owner of an automobile radio with a tape deck.

Ellen Goodman, "Confessions of a Tape-Deck Owner"

The body of the essay details the matter-of-fact reactions of various friends to Goodman's tale of woe: "Indeed, one colleague suggested that having a tape deck in a car was in and of itself a form of entrapment." Goodman also describes the pieces of dubious advice she received: "You will never have a car stripped down by others, I have been informed, if you do it yourself." She ends her essay with a wry, decisive conclusion.

Literature Model

*W*ith all this advice, I now face two alternatives. I can chuck the music and the illusion that someday I will spend my commuting hours learning French. Or I can spend $550 for the protection of my right to hear a $5.95 tape.

Of course, I have another thought, that I don't even say out loud: Maybe the thief will be caught and the audio system returned. I guess that's the sort of fantasy you'd expect from someone who'd put a tape deck in a city car.

The essay feels finished. Why?

Writer's Choice

The following are some writing options to help you try out what you have learned.

1. Guided Assignment   In "Confessions of a Tape-Deck Owner," Ellen Goodman ridicules modern life by "confessing" to old-fashioned values. Write a short essay in which you poke fun at your own behavior or attitudes. You might select topics such as your driving habits, TV-watching, eating habits, or table manners. After you've chosen a topic, create a list of points you want to include. Think about your introduction: Would an anecdote be effective? A personal experience? Decide on an organizing technique that seems best for your subject, but keep in mind that you can choose another during drafting if the technique you choose doesn't work well.

PURPOSE To amuse your readers
AUDIENCE Readers of your school newspaper
LENGTH 1–2 pages

2. Open Assignment   You have taken a summer job working for the marketing director of a well-known company. Your job is to evaluate how the company's latest line will appeal to high school students. Choose from the list of new products below, or come up with your own:

- disposable cameras
- books on tape
- inflating basketball shoes
- portable three-inch television sets

Develop a short report for your boss about the pros and cons of the new line for high school students. Use an organizing structure that supports your purpose and audience.

3. Art   The painting below, *Vega-Tek*, has been displayed in your school's main lobby. Write one of the following for publication in your school newspaper:

- an essay objecting to the painting's style, subject, or appropriateness
- an essay supporting the painting and explaining its meaning, as you see it, to those who object to it

During prewriting, consider the style, content, theme, and colors of the painting and use your observations as your data. How suitable will it be for students? Then refer to the chart on page 81 to choose a suitable organizing technique.

Victor Vasarely, *Vega-Tek*, 1969

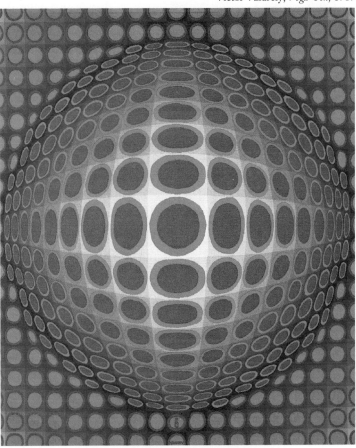

I Don't Follow . . .

In the 1930 comedy *Duck Soup*, Groucho Marx plays Rufus T. Firefly, the new leader of Freedonia. At his first meeting with his cabinet, Firefly plays jacks on the conference table. Then he asks whether there is any new business to take up.

> FINANCE MINISTER: How about taking up the tax?
> FIREFLY: How about taking up the carpet?
> FINANCE MINISTER: I still insist we must take up the tax!
> FIREFLY: He's right. You've got to take up the tacks before you can take up the carpet.
> FINANCE MINISTER: I give all my time and energy to my duties and what do I get?
> FIREFLY: You get awfully tiresome after a while.
> FINANCE MINISTER: Sir, you try my patience!
> FIREFLY: I don't mind if I do—you must come over and try mine sometime.

The lines of this dialogue are linked by puns, or plays on the way the words sound. That's why the finance minister is so confused—just as Firefly intends him to be. If your intention is to communicate with your reader or listener, however, your sentences and paragraphs must be related in a more logical manner.

Making Connections

Coherent writing is writing that develops connections between one sentence or paragraph and the next. Sentences and paragraphs must be arranged in a clear, logical order so that the thought flows smoothly from one sentence to another and from one paragraph to another. You observe many of the rules of coherence automatically when you speak or write: "*Mary* said it was nice out. *She* told me not to bring a sweater" (pronoun reference). "*First*, make sure you have all your ingredients. *Then* you can begin to cook" (transition). "*I asked you* to take out the garbage. *I asked you* to clean up your room. *I asked you* to look after your sister. What did you do? You watched television!" (repetition).

Notice in the passage on the next page how Merry Carlton creates a coherent story of her family's reaction to an intruder.

My dad rushed downstairs for ammunition. Meanwhile, my aunt staggered from her room to investigate the commotion. When she saw the bat, she sprinted wildly to her room to get a flowered shower cap so that the bat could not get caught in her hair. My father was doing his own mad sprint back up the stairs, now armed with my brother's fencing helmet and two tennis racquets. One of the racquets was mine. My brother stood and refereed Dad's "bat-minton" game.

The bat's sonar enabled him to dodge my dad's swings with the tennis racquet. Dad cursed in frustration. I wanted to curse when I saw what he was doing to my tennis racquet. We heard Dad's feet smooshing into cushions as he galloped from chair to bed to chair. We heard the thuds and smacks of the racquet as it crashed into door frames and lamps. And we heard my aunt's yelps of encouragement and advice to my dad. Finally there was a triumphant yell. My fearless father had vanquished the "winged invader."

Merry Margaret Carlton, Princeton High School, Cincinnati, Ohio

How to Make Writing Coherent	
Transitional words	"Meanwhile" . . . "When she saw" . . . "Finally"
Logical organization	Sequential reactions of dad, aunt, brother, and narrator
Sports language and imagery	"mad sprint," "fencing helmets," "tennis racquets," "refereeing," "'bat-minton'"
Pronoun reference	"my aunt . . . she," "my father . . . he," "the racquet . . . it"
Repetition	"sprinted . . . sprint," "Dad cursed . . . I wanted to curse," "We heard . . . We heard . . . And we heard . . ."

• JOURNAL ACTIVITY •
Try It Out

Look at a piece of your own writing. Note all of the connections in a passage, using the chart above as a reference. Then write an evaluation of the coherence of the piece.

Invisible Threads

Readers don't usually stop to think about why the passage they're reading is coherent. But they'll certainly notice if it's *not* coherent.

> Our high school was named Hoover after Herbert Hoover. Every fall the parking lot became a lake. I caught an eight-pound carp and kids would go fishing. Someone called the newspaper in Portland. A photographer showed up one day and someone wrote about it. A lot of the editors are very old.

A few connections are suggested here, but none are clear. The sense of the paragraph seems murky. Is the parking lot the school's? Why did someone call the newspaper? What is the "it" that someone wrote about? How are the editors and the photographers related? Now, consider the following passage from a novel by David James Duncan, noting the subtle connections.

Literature Model

One of the images that ties this paragraph together is the juxtaposition of unlike objects, such as a parking lot and a lake. What other incongruities do you observe?

Our high school was named Hoover, after Herbert, but we called it "J. Edgar" to capture the spirit of the place. Whoever designed the J. Edgar parking lot didn't know much about Oregon; every fall the lot became a lake. One spring I stocked the lake with an eight-pound carp that lived in there for three weeks before someone spotted it feeding by a stalled-out Studebaker. Word got around; kids chased it and fished for it, but it was a strong, smart old fish; somebody called the Portland newspaper—they ran an AP photo of the lot and a write-up in the sports section by one of the senile but tenured editors that the paper was renowned for. This editor calls his column "The Fishing Dutchman." In the column he accounted for the carp's presence by noting the existence of a three-season sewer ditch a quarter mile away; he theorized that the fish, one flooded night, half swam, half crawled its way overland to the J. Edgar parking lot. He then, for the tenth time in the history of his column, went on to say that to cook a carp you broil it on a cedar shingle till it turns golden brown, then throw away the carp and eat the shingle.

David James Duncan, *The River Why*

What examples of repetition and transitional phrases can you find in this paragraph? See page 210 for a list of transitional words.

Although Duncan's writing appears to be rambling and impressionistic, each sentence follows from the one before, and every transition and reference is immediately clear. When you write, check your work to be sure you achieve clear and logical connections.

The following are some writing options to help you try out what you have learned.

1. Guided Assignment In one or two paragraphs, write a description of a place you have visited in the past year. Begin by brainstorming details and observations about the place, using a cluster diagram if you wish. Then put your material together in the most coherent way that you can, making sure that each sentence follows from the previous one.

Then, trade your description with another person. Using the chart on page 87 as a guide, write down suggestions that your partner might use to make his or her piece of writing more coherent. When you have traded descriptions again, use your partner's feedback to rewrite your own description into a model of coherence.

Franz Marc, *Little Blue Horse*, 1912

PURPOSE To describe a familiar place coherently
AUDIENCE Yourself
LENGTH 1–2 paragraphs

2. Open Assignment You are a television screenwriter who writes scripts for a family situation comedy. You want to base your next episode on a very funny event that originally happened in your own family. Write a short summary of the event for the producer of the comedy to get his or her reaction to your idea. Make your rendition of the episode as smooth as you can by using the techniques for achieving coherence in the chart on page 87.

3. Art Coherent writing is essential not only for effective descriptive writing but also for clarity in any communication. Imagine that you work in a day-care center for preschoolers, and the director of your center is considering hanging a print of the above painting in the playroom. You either agree or think the painting should be hung in the arts and crafts room. Write a memo to your employer explaining your position. You will need to order logically your comments about the painting and use clear transitions. Choose appropriate pronouns when you refer to specific elements of the painting.

4. Chemistry Observing the rules of coherence is essential to writing clear technical instructions. Imagine that you are a student assistant in your chemistry class, and you are asked to guide a student who has missed a lab assignment through the steps of an experiment your class has done recently. Using the chart on page 87 as a guide, describe in a page-long essay the steps your classmate must follow to do the experiment correctly.

A Second Opinion

Richmond, Virginia, 1904: A dust-covered package arrives from your good friend Jack London in San Francisco. It is a handwritten copy of a chapter from his new novel The Sea Wolf. *Would you kindly have a look at it, he asks? He's not quite happy with it, and he values your opinion. Please return the manuscript via rail, as the boat transport takes three months and he needs to get the book to his publisher soon.*

If you had read this problem chapter, do you think you'd have realized you were taking part in the making of a classic American novel? Famous writers through the centuries have tried out their new creations on wives, husbands, golfing buddies, other writers, and total strangers. They valued the advice of their peers—even if they didn't always like the advice they received.

An Extra Set of Eyes

Peer reviewing is equally helpful for the not-yet-famous. You cannot be fully objective about your own work; you become too attached to the words you've labored over. In addition, your mind is always filling in the gaps between what you wrote and what you meant. A good reviewer can help by approaching your work with an unbiased mind.

Peer reviewers can read your writing silently, or they can listen to you read it aloud. Feedback from the review will help the writer most if the writer and reviewer follow the tips below.

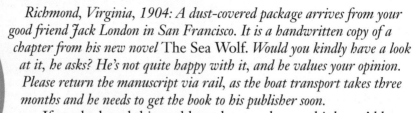

Tips for Peer Reviewers
Your goal is to bring out the writer's best work. The writer will respond better if you begin with praise rather than criticism. Ask questions to help you understand the writer's intention and meaning. Direct criticism at the writing, not the writer. Be constructive; suggest specific solutions. "What if you tried . . . " or "Would it be stronger if you . . . " are better than "This doesn't work."

Tips for Writers
Another pair of eyes can give you fresh insights into your writing. To make the process most productive, question any comments you don't understand and solicit suggestions for how to fix problems. Take careful notes. Listen with an open mind, but remember that in the end you make your own decisions about what and how much to change.

What to Look For

If you are asked to review someone's writing, start by reading the piece all the way through without commenting in order to judge its overall effect. Were you excited, bored, saddened, or entertained? Writers can't possibly find that out on their own. You can provide such feedback.

Next, go through the piece one or more times, jotting down comments in the margins or on a separate piece of paper. Avoid vague remarks such as "This is good" or "This needs a lot of work." Instead, point out specific places where you lost the train of thought or where your interest flagged. If you cannot understand a section or you are unsure of why the writer uses certain evidence or language, ask. Questions are often as helpful as comments.

As you read to help the writer revise, don't be concerned with misspelled words or grammar problems. Those issues can be dealt with later. Now is the time to be concerned with the content, coherence, and flow of the writing. The checklist on the right reviews some items to look for as you read.

When you take notes on your reviewer's comments, keep in mind that every person will react a little differently to what he or she reads. Getting a couple of people's reactions to your writing can help give you various perspectives on your work. What one person doesn't catch, another might. The very words you're reading now were read and commented on by dozens of readers—writers, editors, teachers, business executives, graphic designers, and photo researchers. Their combined insights helped to improve the writing in this book.

If one peer editor likes your work and another doesn't, consider all the comments and choose those you find most helpful. Ultimately, the final decisions are yours.

Peer Reviewer Checklist

1. What are your favorite parts? Why?
2. What do you think is the weakest part? Why?
3. How does the writing make you feel?
4. Does the opening make you want to keep reading?
5. Is the main idea, or thesis, clear? Do all sentences and paragraphs support it? If not, which ones don't?
6. Are there enough details, reasons, facts, and examples to support the thesis? If not, can you ask questions to elicit new supporting details?
7. Are you able to follow the writer's story or argument easily?
8. Are the word choices effective? Are verbs strong ? Are nouns concrete?
9. Is the ending strong?

• JOURNAL ACTIVITY •
Think It Through

Reread the peer reviewer checklist above. Copy the checklist into your journal, grouping together overall questions about the piece, questions about specific sections, and questions about language. Refer to the list when evaluating your own or others' writing.

A Cooperative Effort

In peer reviewing, writer and reviewer have the same goal: to work together to improve the piece of writing. Here's a sample draft complete with written peer responses.

Is this paragraph necessary? If you could identify Miller as the owner at the end, you might delete it. I think the cobwebs sentence is a stronger opening.

Driving past a barn in the small New Hampshire town, my friend and I saw a gleam of chrome, so we stopped to find the owner. Mr. Miller was delighted to show us the car as he'd been trying unsuccessfully to sell it for months.

Do you need "from many years past"? Cobwebs and dust suggest the many years.

Underneath the cobwebs and the dust from many years past sat the 1958 Cadillac. Faded light blue and white paint covered a slightly rusty body, easy to fix with some fiberglass and Bondo. Above the dirty, flaking front bumper a pair of chrome-bevelled headlights stared, eyes of a once majestic beast. A large gold eagle perched proudly on the hood. Inside, the car smelled musty. The worn white leather interior was home to many of the barn animals that had crawled through the minor floor rot. A large white dashboard housed many perfect, simple controls.

You could go into more detail here. I would like to "see" some of the controls. Nice description of the engine noises!

I gave the key a turn and the car turned over, sputtered and finally caught, sending the 503-cubic-inch engine into a frenzy of knocks and pings. The old unused valves made a loud *tick! tick!* After talking to Miller, we settled on a $500 price. It was a bargain for a car that could be restored to look as it did coming off an assembly line in 1958.

General comments: This description really makes me picture this old car, but I'm not sure about the thesis. Do you want to emphasize the car's value or its age and decay? You use many strong details that appeal to the senses, and the ending makes me think that you really respect the car. Maybe you could emphasize that. You could also add dialogue for variety.

Writer's Choice

The following are some writing options to help you try out what you have learned.

1. Guided Assignment Your class has been asked to write inspiring articles about childhood for a children's magazine. You decide to begin your article with a reminiscence of the best day, week, or year of your childhood. Start by jotting down notes of your memories. Use those notes to create a draft that is full of detail, characters (if applicable), and anecdotes. Then exchange drafts with a classmate.

Respond to your classmate's piece in the same way that the reviewer responded to the model on page 92. Use the checklist on page 91 to provide guidelines for your comments. Has the writer used strong details to make the episode come to life? Do you feel as if you have lived through this time with the writer? Why or why not? Can you understand why this time was so special to the writer?

On the basis of the peer review of your work, revise your own piece. Then exchange your papers again and discuss the changes. How do you both think that your writing has been improved through the process? How could each of you have made your comments more helpful?

PURPOSE To use peer review to assist you in writing a short article about your childhood
AUDIENCE Your classmates; children
LENGTH 2 pages

2. Open Assignment You are on the staff of a health magazine for teens. Write a two- or three-page article on one of the following topics or one of your own choosing. The article can be humorous or serious.

- high school students and stress
- the dentist's chair
- pets and your health
- television and your health
- spring fever

Use the checklist on page 91 to review and revise your *own* work. When you're satisfied with your work, exchange articles with a fellow staffer. Review each other's work according to the checklist, and revise your article based on this review.

COMPUTER OPTION

If you and your peer reviewer have access to word processors with split-screen capabilities, you can use a split screen for more effective peer reviewing. Format the draft onto the left side of the monitor, and use the right side to write comments and suggestions at the appropriate places. Don't forget to point out the sections that you liked, as well as those you didn't like.

3. Cooperative Learning Form a peer editing team with three other students. Each of you should make a copy of a writing assignment you have written for English or another subject. Assign each member one area to focus on in the revision: unity, coherence, supporting details, and language. The group should brainstorm a list of questions for each reviewer to use.

Make enough copies of your paper for all members of your group. Review each other's writing, and return the papers to their authors. Afterward, discuss these questions as a group:

- What did you learn from your peers' reviews of your writing that you might not have realized if you had reviewed it yourself?

- What did you find difficult about reviewing another's work? Did you enjoy it? Why or why not?

- Did reviewing another's work give you insights into your own writing? What did you learn?

Editing and Presenting: Completing Your Essay

The Finishing Touch

DETROIT, MICHIGAN: This sports car just came off the assembly line with a price tag of over $25,000. But wait: the bumper sags slightly, a rear hubcap is dented, a side mirror is loose, and the finish is dull. Despite the high-tech engineering, plush upholstery, powerful stereo, and fiery paint job, the car isn't ready until the details are right. In industry, such attention to detail is called quality control.

Reading for Detail

Quality control applies as much to your writing product as to any other product. If you don't get the details right, your job isn't finished. To produce high-quality work, you've got to get tough on your writing.

If you assume the work contains errors, you'll find them. If you assume the writing is perfect, you may not notice the mistakes. You might try the approach of the English poet Samuel Butler.

Literature Model

*T*hink of and look at your work as though it were done by your enemy. If you look at it to admire it you are lost. . . . If we look at it to see where it is wrong, we shall see this and make it righter. If we look at it to see where it is right, we shall see this and shall not make it righter. We cannot see it both wrong and right at the same time.

Samuel Butler, *The Note-Books of Samuel Butler*

Giving Butler's hard look to your own writing comes when you edit and proofread to check the details of grammar, mechanics, and spelling. Editing refers to issues of paragraph and sentence construction, including grammar and transitions. Proofreading has to do with word-level issues, such as capitalization, punctuation, and spelling. Both kinds of quality control are essential to good writing. One cannot list every possible writing error, but the checklist below covers the kinds of errors writers are most likely to make.

After revising and before presenting any piece of written work, you should read it at least twice, first to edit and then to proofread. You may find that by the second or third reading, you have become so familiar with the writing that your eyes skim over spelling mistakes, mentally correcting them as you go. If this happens to you, try this proofreading trick: read backward, word by word. This will force you to look at each word out of context, and you'll be more likely to see mistakes. Be careful, however; you'll miss errors involving possessives and usage.

To polish your writing, try putting the piece aside for a day or two. When you read your writing after being away from it , you will often catch errors you have missed. You might also try reading your piece aloud.

Just as peer reviewing can help you revise writing, peer editing and proofreading can help you polish your work. Most of us recognize others' errors more readily than we do our own. That misspelled word may not look wrong to you, but someone else might spot it immediately.

Editing and Proofreading Checklist

Editing

✔ Do all verbs agree with their subjects?

✔ Do pronouns agree with antecedents?

✔ Are the point of view and tense consistent?

✔ Are there any fragments or run-ons?

✔ Is the writing redundant or wordy?

✔ Are all words used correctly?

Proofreading

✔ Are all necessary words capitalized?

✔ Is punctuation clear and correct: end punctuation, commas, semicolons, apostrophes, quotation marks?

✔ Are numbers treated correctly?

✔ Are all words spelled correctly?

• JOURNAL ACTIVITY •
Think It Through

Start your personal editing and proofreading checklist by reviewing several pieces of writing and noting errors. List specific words that you commonly misspell or misuse. Keep your checklist handy and add to it as you notice other patterns in your writing.

Editing Thoroughly

In the publishing industry, editors and proofreaders check preliminary pages for errors before books are printed. Professional proofreaders have developed a code for indicating corrections. Here are a few of the most common symbols. When you proofread, use a different color ink from that of your draft. Red shows up especially well. Circle any small punctuation marks you add so you won't miss them later.

Proofreading Symbols		
∧ insert something	∼ reverse letters or words	... let it stand as it was
# add a space	⌒ close up space	(under something crossed
¶ begin a new paragraph	M make this letter lower	out)
ℒ delete	case	C capitalize

A sample of a well-edited, well-proofread piece of writing follows. Editing corrections are shown in blue; proofreading corrections in red.

> ### Model
>
> ¶Watching maggie take her first steps is
> a "hoot and a holler," as mom would say.
> First, she hoists herself up to her
> little tiny feet by pulling with all its
> might on the edge of the couch or chair.
> Once up right, she looked around to make
> sure you are watching, and then she grins.
> She turns herself toward the center of
> the room and takes that first step
> still one hand planted on "home base."
> Then, she purses her lips and let go,
> lifting her feet awkwardly and throwing
> her wait toward your outstretched arms.
> She looks like Frankenstein's monster.
> Giggling all the way, hoping she'll make
> it to you before she tumbles.

Details Count

You've spent time prewriting, drafting, revising, editing, and proof-reading. Now take time to make your writing look as good as it reads.

Name and date in upper right-hand corner

Five-space indent at the beginning of paragraphs

Title centered, no quotation marks

Jazmyne Fuentes
September 22, 1992

Unbroken Chains

Clear typing (or printing) with erasing done neatly

    I insisted on carrying the basket, which appeared to contain some canned food and oatmeal. He carried a pail of coffee and led the way through a damp, lumpy field toward the unlit barn where he and his fellow farmhands were spending the night.
    As he pushed open the door, I asked, "What about a can opener for the vegetables?"
    "The cans are empty," he said softly, as the scent of animals and men in close quarters smothered us. "They're for drinking the coffee."

1-inch margin on left, 1 1/2-inch margins on bottom, top, and right

If you're preparing a piece of writing for your teacher or for a publication, be sure to find out whether a certain format is preferred and follow the instructions to the last detail. If the choice is yours, follow the guidelines above, or come up with your own creative ideas appropriate to the piece. For longer pieces, you may want to include a cover sheet, dedication page, or other features such as a table of contents or index. Illustrations, photocopied pictures, charts, and graphs can all contribute to the look and the content of the piece.

The suggestions on this page apply whether you're writing by hand, typing, or using a word processor. A word processor also lets you

change   type   STYLES   and   type   <u>sizes</u>

to give your paper a professional look. Don't go overboard with clever devices, though; keep the text clean and easy to read.

• JOURNAL ACTIVITY •
Try It Out

Test yourself on proofreading symbols by copying them onto note cards or a piece of paper. Then close your book and explain the meaning of each one.

What's in a Title?

When *I'm OK, You're OK* hit the bookstores in the late 1960s, it sold thousands of copies. Had it been titled *Improving Your Human Relationships* or *Getting Along with Others*, it might not have soared to the top of the best-seller list.

A good title can reach right out from the bookshelf and grab you. How it does that depends on the purpose of the work. Some titles are whimsical teasers, like *Zen and the Art of Motorcycle Maintenance*, or Tom Wolfe's *Kandy-Kolored Tangerine Flake Streamline Baby*. The title of Stephen King's thriller *Misery* is simple, true to the content of the book, and hauntingly effective.

Good titles often convey a sense of the content of the work without giving away too much. A twist of language can often be effective if not overdone: alliteration ("The Flower-Fed Buffaloes"), rhyme and rhythm (*Tinker, Tailor, Soldier, Spy*), and word plays (an article on designer baby clothes called "Gucci, Gucci, Goo"). Even among nonfiction works titles can be grabbers. *50 Simple Things You Can Do to Save the Earth* leaves little to the imagination in terms of the book's content, but is sure to pique the interest of readers who care about the environment.

The search for a title, whether it comes at the beginning, middle, or end of the writing process, can cause you to think more deeply about the work and to find its central or main idea. Warning: if a title continues to elude you, it could mean that the piece lacks a strong focus. You may have to back up a step or two in the writing process and rethink your work.

Tempting

A Few Good Voices in My Head by Ted Solotaroff

Steal This Book by Abbie Hoffman

Me by Katharine Hepburn

Intriguing

A Thief of Time by Tony Hillerman

A Hitchhiker's Guide to the Galaxy by Douglas Adams

Humorous

"Shut Up!" He Explained by William Noble

Welcome to the Monkey House by Kurt Vonnegut Jr.

If Life Is a Bowl of Cherries, What Am I Doing in the Pits? by Erma Bombeck

Dramatic

Death of a Salesman by Arthur Miller

Guess Who's Coming to Dinner? by William Rose

Twelve Angry Men by Reginald Rose

One Flew Over the Cuckoo's Nest by Ken Kesey

Borrowed

Go Tell It on the Mountain by James Baldwin

Rosencrantz and Guildenstern Are Dead by Tom Stoppard

All the King's Men by Robert Penn Warren

The following are some writing options to help you try out what you have learned.

1. Guided Assignment Imagine that you are applying for a summer job on a well-known magazine. You have to submit a sample of your writing on any subject, and it has to be letter perfect. Choose something that you are working on for one of your classes today or, if such a piece is not available, something that you have written in the past year. Read the paper through once; think about editing issues, using the checklist on page 95 as a guide. Then read the piece again; this time proofread carefully, referring to the same chart and using the proofreading symbols on page 96.

If you haven't done so already, decide on a strong title for the piece. Then follow the guidelines on page 97 for presenting an essay, and write, type, or print your piece. If you are working on a computer, you may want to use one or two different fonts or sizes, but don't overdo it.

Finally, proofread your paper one more time, looking for typing errors and checking for neatness.

PURPOSE To get a summer job on a magazine
AUDIENCE The managing editor
LENGTH 3–5 pages

2. Open Assignment Choose one of the following topics or come up with one of your own, and freewrite about it for fifteen minutes. Then, trade your freewriting with another writer, and treat the pieces as if they were ready to be edited and proofread. Use the proofreading symbols on page 96 to make corrections.

- mosquitoes
- bowling
- country music
- rain forests
- being ticklish

Marisol, *Working Women*, 1987

3. Art Study the sculpture *Working Women* on this page; note its personality, tone, and style. Then, imagine that the figures in this sculpture come to life, and write a two- to-five-page short story for a fantasy magazine about what they do and what happens to them. Create a plot in keeping with the characters of the two individuals, as you perceive them. Revise your writing for unity and coherence. Then edit and proofread your work carefully. Exchange papers with a partner, and review each other's work for errors in spelling, grammar, punctuation, and presentation.

The Curtain Rises

Literature

Laura: Well, I do—as I said—have my—glass collection—
Jim: I'm not right sure I know what you're talking about. What kind of glass is it?

Laura: Little articles of it, they're ornaments mostly! Most of them are little animals made out of glass, the tiniest little animals in the world. Mother calls them a glass menagerie! Here's an example of one, if you'd like to see it! This one is one of the oldest. It's nearly thirteen.

[Music: "The Glass Menagerie." He stretches out his hand.]
Oh, be careful—if you breathe, it breaks!

Jim: I'd better not take it. I'm pretty clumsy with things.

Laura: Go on, I trust you with him! *[She places the piece on his palm.]* There now—you're holding him gently! Hold him over the light, he loves the light! You see how the light shines through him?

Jim: It sure does shine!

Laura: I shouldn't be partial, but he is my favorite one.

Jim: What kind of a thing is this one supposed to be?

Laura: Haven't you noticed the single horn on his forehead?

Jim: A unicorn, huh?

Laura: Mmmm-hmmm!

Jim: Unicorns—aren't they extinct in the modern world?

Laura: I know!

Jim: Poor little fellow, he must feel sort of lonesome.

Tennessee Williams, *The Glass Menagerie*

The passage above is from the last scene of the famous play *The Glass Menagerie*. If you were asked to write an essay about one of the main characters, Laura, how would you go about it? How would you analyze Laura's character? How would you formulate a thesis and draft your essay? This lesson will show you how the writing process can help.

Looking at Character

When you analyze a piece of literature, you cast your net wide to assemble your own collection of responses and ideas. Begin your analysis of a character by freewriting or by creating a cluster diagram to identify his or her traits. This diagram shows how you might begin thinking about the character of Laura.

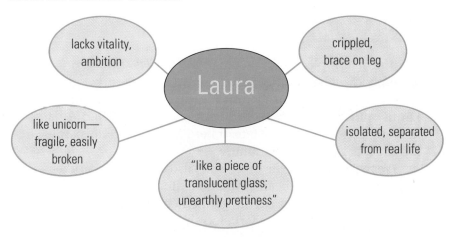

If you want to push your thinking further, you can create another chart, talk about the topic with a friend, or ask yourself questions:

- Do you like the character? Why or why not?
- What adjectives best describe the character?
- What actor or actress might you choose to play the role?
- How is the character related to the theme of the play?

Now study your prewriting notes, and write a one-sentence thesis statement that can guide the organizing and drafting of your analysis. Try to develop your thesis statement from a simple fact to an insight into the function or motivation of the character. For example, if you were writing about Laura in *The Glass Menagerie*, your notes might lead you to the initial thesis: "Laura is like her glass menagerie: fragile, easily broken, and delicate." A more developed thesis might be: "Laura represents the trapped, overprotected woman of her era, as fragile and easily broken as her glass menagerie." Or you might take your thesis in another direction, as Jennifer Simon does in her essay on the next page.

• JOURNAL ACTIVITY •

Think It Through

In your journal, list all the techniques you can think of to generate ideas about a character. Then write down the advantages and disadvantages of each method.

Drafting Your Essay

Once you've formulated a thesis statement, follow the same steps Jennifer followed in her essay on Laura below. Jennifer chose her strongest supporting details and selected an appropriate method of organization. As she wrote, she considered her audience: How much did her readers already know? Finally, she revised and edited her essay.

Student Model

How has Jennifer developed the simple thesis on page 101 to deepen her analysis of Laura?

Which of the details in the diagram on page 101 does Jennifer use to support her thesis?

How much does Jennifer assume her audience knows?

Notice that Jennifer uses elements other than the plot, such as lighting and stage directions, to support her position.

Laura, a crippled young woman in *The Glass Menagerie*, embodies the fragility of her family. Like her prized glass collection, Laura is slightly unreal, delicate, and easily broken. Laura cannot survive real life any more than her delicate glass unicorn. Her fate, and the fate of her glass menagerie, parallels the breakdown of her family.

We meet Laura in the first scene, listening to her mother reminisce about past beaus. Amanda, illuminated in the spotlight, describes the myriad of "gentlemen callers" she had as a girl. Laura remains in the dark, too shy and withdrawn to follow in her mother's footsteps.

As the play continues, we see that Laura exists in a fantasy world, doing nothing except take care of her glass animals. She is trailed by a piece of circus music, "The Glass Menagerie," which underscores the unreality of her life. When Laura's brother Tom has a raging argument with Amanda, Laura stands in a bright spotlight, speechless, as if she were watching an act in the ring of a circus. She is only an audience, never a participant, in life.

The fate of Laura and her family mirrors that of the glass menagerie. At first, the glass pieces are in fine condition. Laura cares for her menagerie almost obsessively, and the family clings together in much the same fashion. During Amanda and Tom's fight, a piece of glass breaks, sparking the family's descent. Later, when Jim arrives, Laura looks "like a piece of translucent glass touched by light." She shows him a piece of her collection, really a piece of herself, but as they dance the glass unicorn is accidentally broken. Soon after, Jim, likewise, breaks Laura's heart. This final blow completes the disintegration of Amanda's hopes for her daughter. Laura, the menagerie, and the dream have all been shattered.

Laura's tragedy is the core of Williams's play. Her delicacy, fragility, and shyness symbolize the death of a family.

Jennifer Simon, Newton North High School, Newton, Massachusetts

Writer's Choice

The following are some writing options to help you try out what you have learned.

1. Guided Assignment Actors express their characters' personalities through costuming, makeup, and hair-styling as well as acting. Recall a play you have read recently. If you were a designer, how would you write a recommendation to a director about the costuming of the main character? First, brainstorm some details, using the chart below.

Name of Character	Act 1	Act 2 (etc.)
Predominant colors		
Kind of clothes		
Shoes		
Jewelry		
Hairstyle		
Makeup		
Accessories		

Then write a memo describing how you would dress and make up the character in each act or scene to show how the character develops or evolves as the play progresses.

PURPOSE To express your assessment of a character through costuming
AUDIENCE Director of a play
LENGTH 1–2 pages

2. Open Assignment Imagine that you are chosen to direct one of the following one-act comedies or one comedy of your choice for a theater production at your high school. Your first job is to hold auditions for the play's main character. To help you evaluate the student actors, you need to have a good understanding of the character. As you read the play, imagine how the character would stand, speak, and move. Then use the writing process described in the last ten lessons to write an analysis of the play's main character.

- *The Public Eye* by Peter Shaffer
- *The Bald Soprano* by Eugene Ionesco
- *The Boor* by Anton Chekov
- *Once Around the Block* by William Saroyan
- *The Man in the Bowler Hat* by A. A. Milne
- *Pullman Car Hiawatha* by Thornton Wilder

3. Speech Effective speech writing often involves assuming a voice that may or may not be similar to your own. Imagine that you are a speech writer for a character in one of your favorite plays, and you're writing a speech on a subject that would be of interest to your character. If you had chosen Laura, the heroine of *The Glass Menagerie*, for instance, you might have her speak about love or family relationships. Keeping in mind your character's opinions, personality, and way of speaking, write a speech in your character's idiom and style.

COMPUTER OPTION

When you are writing a draft for any of the assignments on this page, use the "copy" feature of your word-processing program to preserve your first draft as you work to improve your writing. Try following these steps:

1. Save your first draft when it is complete.
2. Make a copy of your draft, either as a new file or a new page of your existing file.
3. Name this copy "Draft 2."
4. Continue to rework your draft. Each time you complete a new version, save and copy that version as you did the first.

If you follow this procedure, you will always have a record of your initial ideas, as well as a record of the changes you made as you revised.

ANNIE DILLARD

from

aN aMERICAN CHILDHOOD

*Memories, especially of childhood, can spark powerful pieces of writing. In this
selection from her 1987 book,* An American Childhood, *Annie Dillard reflects on her youth by
focusing on memories of her mother. Through her vivid anecdotes, Dillard reveals the ways in
which her mother helped shape her into the adult she is now.*

One Sunday afternoon Mother wandered through our kitchen,
where Father was making a sandwich and listening to the
ball game. The Pirates were playing the New York Giants at
Forbes Field. In those days, the Giants had a utility infielder named
Wayne Terwilliger. Just as Mother passed through, the radio announcer cried—with undue drama—"Terwilliger bunts one!"

"Terwilliger bunts one?" Mother cried back, stopped short. She
turned. "Is that English?"

"The player's name is Terwilliger," Father said. "He bunted."

"That's marvelous," Mother said. " 'Terwilliger bunts one.' No
wonder you listen to baseball. 'Terwilliger bunts one.' "

For the next seven or eight years, Mother made this surprising
string of syllables her own. Testing a microphone, she repeated, "Terwilliger bunts one"; testing a pen or a typewriter, she wrote it. If, as
happened surprisingly often in the course of various improvised
gags, she pretended to whisper something else in my ear, she actually
whispered, "Terwilliger bunts one." Whenever someone used a

French phrase, or a Latin one, she answered solemnly, "Terwilliger bunts one." If Mother had had, like Andrew Carnegie, the opportunity to cook up a motto for a coat of arms, hers would have read simply and tellingly, "Terwilliger bunts one." (Carnegie's was "Death to Privilege.")

She served us with other words and phrases. On a Florida trip, she repeated tremulously, "That . . . is a royal poinciana." I don't remember the tree; I remember the thrill in her voice. She pronounced it carefully, and spelled it. She also liked to say "portulaca."

The drama of the words "Tamiami Trail" stirred her, we learned on the same Florida trip. People built Tampa on one coast, and they built Miami on another. Then—the height of visionary ambition and folly—they piled a slow, tremendous road through the terrible Everglades to connect them. To build the road, men stood sunk in muck to their armpits. They fought off cottonmouth moccasins and six-foot alligators. They slept in boats, wet. They blasted muck with dynamite, cut jungle with machetes; they laid logs, dragged drilling machines, hauled dredges, heaped limestone. The road took fourteen years to build up by the shovelful, a Panama Canal in reverse, and cost hundreds of lives from tropical, mosquito-carried diseases. Then, capping it all, some genius thought of the word Tamiami: they called the road from Tampa to Miami, this very road under our spinning wheels, the Tamiami Trail. Some called it Alligator Alley. Anyone could drive over this road without a thought.

Hearing this, moved, I thought all the suffering of road building was worth it (it wasn't my suffering), now that we had this new thing to hang these new words on—Alligator Alley for those who liked things cute, and, for connoisseurs[1] like Mother, for lovers of the human drama in all its boldness and terror, the Tamiami Trail. . . .

When we children were young, she mothered us tenderly and dependably; as we got older, she resumed her career of anarchism.[2] She collared us into her gags. If she answered the phone on a wrong number, she told the caller, "Just a minute," and dragged the receiver to Amy or me, saying, "Here, take this, your name is Cecile," or, worse, just, "It's for you." You had to think on your feet. But did you want to perform well as Cecile, or did you want to take pity on the wretched caller?

During a family trip to the Highland Park Zoo, Mother and I were alone for a minute. She approached a young couple holding hands on a bench by the seals, and addressed the young man in dripping tones:

1. **connoisseurs** (kän´ə sʉrz´): experts in a special field
2. **anarchism** (an´ər kiz´m): resistance to government or codes of behavior that limit individual liberty

"Where have you been? Still got those baby-blue eyes; always did slay me. And this"—a swift nod at the dumbstruck young woman, who had removed her hand from the man's—"must be the one you were telling me about. She's not so bad, really, as you used to make out. But listen, you know how I miss you, you know where to reach me, same old place. And there's Ann over there—see how she's grown? See the blue eyes?"

And off she sashayed, taking me firmly by the hand, and leading us around briskly past the monkey house and away. She cocked an ear back, and both of us heard the desperate man begin, in a high-pitched wail, "I swear, I never saw her before in my life. . . ."

Mother's energy and intelligence suited her for a greater role in a larger arena—mayor of New York, say—than the one she had. She followed American politics closely; she had been known to vote for Democrats. She saw how things should be run, but she had nothing to run but our household. Even there, small minds bugged her; she was smarter than the people who designed the things she had to use all day for the length of her life.

"Look," she said. "Whoever designed this corkscrew never used one. Why would anyone sell it without trying it out?" So she invented a better one. She showed me a drawing of it. The spirit of American enterprise never faded in Mother. If capitalizing and tooling up had been as interesting as theorizing and thinking up, she would have fired up a new factory every week, and chaired several hundred corporations.

"It grieves me," she would say, "it grieves my heart," that the company that made one superior product packaged it poorly, or took the wrong tack in its advertising. She knew, as she held the thing mournfully in her two hands, that she'd never find another. She was right. We children wholly sympathized, and so did Father; what could she do, what could anyone do, about it? She was Sampson in chains. She paced.

She didn't like the taste of stamps so she didn't lick stamps; she licked the corner of the envelope instead. She glued sandpaper to the sides of kitchen drawers, and under kitchen cabinets, so she always had a handy place to strike a match. She designed, and hounded workmen to build against all norms, doubly wide kitchen counters and elevated bathroom sinks. To splint a finger, she stuck it in a lightweight cigar tube. Conversely, to protect a pack of cigarettes, she carried it in a Band-Aid box. She drew plans for an over-the-finger toothbrush for babies, an oven rack that slid up and down, and—the family favorite—Lendalarm. Lendalarm was a beeper you attached to books (or tools) you loaned friends. After ten days, the beeper sounded. Only the rightful owner could silence it.

She repeatedly reminded us of P. T. Barnum's dictum: You could sell anything to anybody if you marketed it right. The adman who thought of making Americans believe they needed underarm deodorant was a visionary. So, too, was the hero who made a success of a new product, Ivory soap. The executives were horrified, Mother told me, that a cake of this stuff floated. Soap wasn't supposed to float. Anyone would be able to tell it was mostly whipped-up air. Then some inspired adman made a leap: Advertise that it floats. Flaunt it. The rest is history.

Fairfield Porter, *Early Morning*, 1966

She respected the rare few who broke through to new ways. "Look," she'd say, "here's an intelligent apron." She called upon us to admire intelligent control knobs and intelligent pan handles, intelligent andirons and picture frames and knife sharpeners. She questioned everything, every pair of scissors, every knitting needle, gardening glove, tape dispenser. Hers was a restless mental vigor that just about ignited the dumb household objects with its force.

Torpid[3] conformity was a kind of sin; it was stupidity itself, the mighty stream against which Mother would never cease to struggle. If you held no minority opinions, or if you failed to risk total ostracism[4] for them daily, the world would be a better place without you.

Always I heard Mother's emotional voice asking Amy and me the same few questions: Is that your own idea? Or somebody else's? "*Giant* is a good movie," I pronounced to the family at dinner. "Oh, really?" Mother warmed to these occasions. She all but rolled up her sleeves. She knew I hadn't seen it. "Is that your considered opinion?"

---

3. **torpid** (tôr´pid): sluggish
4. **ostracism** (äs´trə siz´m): banishment or exclusion from a group

---

She herself held many unpopular, even fantastic, positions. She was scathingly sarcastic about the McCarthy hearings while they took place, right on our living-room television; she frantically opposed Father's wait-and-see calm. "We don't know enough about it," he said. "I do," she said. "I know all I need to know."

She asserted, against all opposition, that people who lived in trailer parks were not bad but simply poor, and had as much right to settle on beautiful land, such as rural Ligonier, Pennsylvania, as did the oldest of families in the finest of hidden houses. Therefore, the people who owned trailer parks, and sought zoning changes to permit trailer parks, needed our help. Her profound belief that the country-club pool sweeper was a person, and that the department-store saleslady, the bus driver, telephone operator, and house-painter were people, and even in groups the steelworkers who carried pickets and the Christmas shoppers who clogged intersections were people—this was a conviction common enough in democratic Pittsburgh, but not altogether common among our friends' parents, or even, perhaps, among our parents' friends.

Opposition emboldened Mother, and she would take on anybody on any issue—the chairman of the board, at a cocktail party, on the current strike; she would fly at him in a flurry of passion, as a songbird selflessly attacks a big hawk.

"Eisenhower's going to win," I announced after school. She lowered her magazine and looked me in the eyes; "How do you know?" I was doomed. It was fatal to say, "Everyone says so." We all knew well what happened. "Do you consult this Everyone before you make your decisions? What if Everyone decided to round up all the Jews?" Mother knew there was no danger of cowing me. She simply tried to keep us all awake. And in fact it was always clear to Amy and me, and to Molly when she grew old enough to listen, that if our classmates came to cruelty, just as much as if the neighborhood or the nation came to madness, we were expected to take, and would be each separately capable of taking, a stand.

For Discussion

1. What do you think it would have been like to grow up with a mother like Dillard's? Explain.

2. In what ways does the mother remind you of an influential person in your own childhood? In what ways do these memories reveal how the person affected your life?

Readers Respond

This literature selection was funny when the writer talked about the things her mother said. I would love to have a mother with that sense of humor. It would be fun to challenge her. The writer didn't seem to enjoy her mother.

Becky Byer

Through everything Dillard said, I was able to visualize what her mother would be like. What I remember most clearly from the selection is the part where the mother plays the joke on that poor couple. Although I sympathized with the couple, the joke did make me laugh. It was a good example of the mother's strange sense of humor. Almost everyone has a mother and can see his or her mother in Dillard's mother.

David Alonzo

Do you agree?

☞ Do you agree with Becky that Dillard did not seem to enjoy her mother? What passages influenced your response?

☞ Do you think that almost everyone can see aspects of his or her mother in Dillard's mother? Explain your answer in your journal.

Writing Process in Action

"Terwilliger Bunts One"

Memories. Often they begin as hazy outlines, sparked by sights, sounds, and smells. For the selection from *An American Childhood* (pages 104–108) perhaps Annie Dillard's memory was sparked by seeing a baby in a drawstring gown or by hearing a sportscaster announce a successful bunt. During the writing process, such memories can germinate and grow.

Imagine that an editor has decided to publish a collection of essays based on memories of young writers. In this assignment, you'll write an essay to submit to this editor. In the process, you'll think about what makes your childhood unique and how it has shaped the person you are now.

• Assignment •

CONTEXT An editor sends this notice to your school:
American Childhoods: A Collection of Essays by Young Writers
   We are seeking essays that recall American childhoods. The memories can be happy or sad, everyday or extraordinary. Your essay should be something that no one else could possibly have written. It should be specific and lively, and give insight into what you have become as a young adult.

PURPOSE To write an essay that recalls one aspect of your childhood and shows how that experience helped shape the person you are today

AUDIENCE Teachers, psychologists, parents, teen-agers

LENGTH 3–4 pages

---

1. Prewriting

Your task is broadly defined by the editor's notice, but it's up to you to limit your topic and define your purpose. After all, you can't possibly include everything you remember about growing up. First, open up your imagination and think about possibilities. Flip through an old photo album to spark your memory. How about that time your tie caught fire on the birthday candles? Talk to relatives or friends and compare their memories with yours. Make a list of possible topics, from Aunt Eleanor to your treehouse to those crazy Thanksgiving dinners. At this point, don't rule anything out. Remember as much as you possibly can. Then push yourself to remember more.

From your list of possibilities, choose two or three that interest you most. It may help to ask yourself questions such as these:

- Which topics spark a rich variety of memories?
- Which topics have a direct relationship to who I am now?
- Which topics will other people relate to most readily?

Now explore your choices. Lessons 2.2, 2.3, and 2.5 demonstrate a variety of ways to do just that. For example, freewriting, listing, or clustering can help you gather details. To explore your grandmother's attic, for example, you might make a cluster including sights, sounds, and smells you recall. To dig deeper, use one idea from your original cluster, such as *cedar chest*, as the center of another cluster. Open that chest to find details such as *wedding dress, cracked photos, embroidered doilies.* As Dillard was gathering notes for her essay, she didn't just stop at "Mother designed new tools." She dug into her memory to find the sandpaper on the kitchen drawers, the cigar-tube splint, the Lendalarm. The more specific your details, the more vivid your writing will be.

After gathering as many notes as time allows, commit to a topic and begin to formulate a purpose. Annie Dillard chose to focus on a person: her mother. You could, too, or you could consider options such as these:

- **Focus on a place:** a backyard, a basement, a playground, a neighborhood store. You might show how a place changed as you grew up, or how it stayed the same as you grew and changed.
- **Focus on an experience:** you won the spelling bee, you broke your leg, your grandfather died. A story full of dialogue and description can give your readers insight into who you are.
- **Focus on an object:** your rocking horse, a favorite doll, your first watch. Why did you value a particular object so much? Things are often symbols that keep their significance even though we change.

Don't just choose a topic; choose a purpose as well. Write a one-sentence statement telling what you want your essay to say about you. Reread your notes, circling or highlighting items that support your purpose. Add more. Then pat yourself on the back; getting started is now behind you.

2. Drafting

Some writers create formal outlines, while others scrawl lists. Whatever your taste, make some written plans before you draft. Consider the following questions:

- **How will my essay begin?** Dillard hooks her readers with a repeated experience—"Terwilliger bunts one"—that includes crisp dialogue and vivid details of sights and sounds.
- **Where will my essay go, and how will it get there?** How many paragraphs or parts will it have? How will each part contribute to the whole? Dillard's essay is divided into sections separated by spaces. Each section is, in a sense, a mini-essay with its own topic: Mother's love of unusual language, Mother's love of verbal challenges, her joke on the couple at the zoo, her love of inventions, her love of minority opinions. Each section is self-contained yet contributes to the essay's purpose: to show Mother's strong appreciation for individualism. You can also experiment with the size and nature of the building blocks of your essay.

- **How can I enliven my essay with dialogue or quotes?** Notice how much mileage Dillard gets out of three words:

  "Terwilliger bunts one?" Mother cried back, stopped short. She turned. "Is that English?"
  "The player's name is Terwilliger," father said. "He bunted."
  "That's marvelous," Mother said. "'Terwilliger bunts one.' No wonder you listen to baseball. 'Terwilliger bunts one.'"

- **Where and how should I use description?** Dillard uses it sparingly but effectively: Mother "addressed the young man in dripping tones."
- **How will my essay end, and how will this ending affect my reader?** In her last sentence, Dillard tells us what her mother's often outrageous behavior was designed to do: to create children who, in the face of classmates' cruelty or national madness, could and would "take a stand." Look at Lesson 2.6 for more suggestions about endings.

Once you've mapped your essay, start writing. Remember that you can always go back to prewriting if you discover gaps. Even if you discover that you detest your topic, you can begin again.

3. Revising

Often, the best first step of revising is to do nothing: put away your draft, at least overnight. When you return, look at it with the fresh eyes of a critic. Then ask yourself broad questions:

- Does every paragraph serve the larger purpose?
- Does each paragraph flow naturally into the next?
- Is there enough description for the reader to picture and feel my experiences?
- Is the dialogue believable and meaningful?
- Is it clear how this experience helped shape the person I am today?

Once you're satisfied with the big picture, read your draft aloud. Sharpen word choices. Combine sentences or break up long ones. Delete passages that are too vague, too sentimental, or even remotely dishonest. Take out anything that's redundant, weak, or irrelevant. Be tough. And never forget your purpose.

Of course, your purpose might change. One writer started out to show how wonderful her older brother had been as she was growing up, but somewhere between prewriting and drafting, she realized that most of her memories were frightening and gray, not happy and rosy. Her "revising" involved a complete rewriting; her writing process became a valuable and somewhat painful exercise in self-discovery. Writing can do that if you allow it.

Add new details as they jump into your memory. Perhaps during revision Dillard added specific details of the Tamiami Trail, an extra example of Pittsburghisms, or the entire anecdote about the couple beside the seals. Don't stop adding just because you've finished drafting.

When you're satisfied with your revision, ask a peer reviewer to read your draft. In this case, it would be best if the reviewer didn't share your memories, so that he or she can be objective. Refer to Lesson 2.9 for specific suggestions about the peer-reviewing process.

4. Editing

Most writers arrive at the editing stage with a sigh of relief: the hard work is behind them; now, it's polish on the car. You know, however, how important that shiny finish can be to the impression you make driving down the street! Use the editing and proofreading checklists in Lesson 2.10 to check your work for errors. Peer editing is invaluable; it's often difficult to spot your own mistakes.

Be particularly careful with dialogue. An overlooked quotation mark can completely muddle a sentence and make your reader stop. You want the editor of *American Childhoods* to read smoothly, from your title to your zinger ending, without once hesitating over a dangling modifier or a misspelled word.

Criteria

1. *Focuses on a significant aspect of your childhood and shows how you were shaped by that experience*
2. *Uses specific details, including dialogue, to bring the memory to life*
3. *Uses organization appropriate to topic and purpose*
4. *Is unified and coherent, with an engaging introduction and powerful conclusion*
5. *Follows the standards of grammar, usage, and mechanics*

5. Presenting

Choose a title that performs two functions: to hook interest and to suggest your essay's purpose. It may help to use one of your best images in your title, one that captures the spirit of your essay. Dillard's essay is really a chapter of a book. What would be a good title for the selection you read?

Also remember that the editor of *American Childhoods*—or of any other publication to which you decide to submit your essay—will be swamped with manuscripts. Make yours shine. If you are writing by hand, copy your essay neatly on clean paper. If you are typing or word processing, make the format of your essay pleasing to the eye. Even as the editor picks your piece from the pile, he or she is unconsciously making a judgment based simply on your essay's appearance.

• Reflecting •

By now, those recollections that began as hazy outlines should be sharply defined pictures, alive with color and detail. Your writing process—really a discovery process—has pushed your memory to its limits and produced an essay that shows something important about your growing up. Stop and reflect upon what you've done. What prewriting strategies helped you to unlock your memories? During the drafting and revising stages, how did you push your imagination to include more specific details? During the process what did you recall that you hadn't remembered when you began? Based on your answers to these questions, write some specific and encouraging advice to yourself in your writer's journal.

Portfolio & Reflection

Summary

Key concepts of the writing process include the following:

- Writing is a five-stage process in which the writer can return to an earlier stage whenever necessary.
- Prewriting techniques such as questioning, brainstorming, freewriting, and clustering help generate ideas, as well as determine audience and purpose.
- Drafting includes developing a thesis, providing supporting evidence, selecting an organizing strategy, and effectively employing transitions, pronouns, and repetition.
- Revising can be aided by peer review.
- Editing means correcting grammar and mechanics to polish your piece.
- Presenting means sharing your writing.

Your Writer's Portfolio

Look over the writing you have done during this unit. Select two pieces of writing to put into your portfolio. Each piece should demonstrate that you have worked with one or more of the preceding concepts. In other words, look for a piece of writing that does one or more of the following:

- results from a return to an earlier stage of the writing process
- grows out of prewriting techniques
- addresses a specific audience and purpose
- supports a clearly stated thesis with appropriate evidence and organization
- reflects a peer's review in its revision
- reflects meticulous editing

Reflection and Commentary

Write one page that demonstrates that you understand what this unit asked of you. Use your two selected pieces of writing as evidence while you consider the following numbered items. Respond to as many items as possible. Label the page "Commentary on the Writing Process," and include it in your portfolio.

1. When did you go back to a previous stage in the writing process? Which stage did you find most difficult? Most helpful? How would you approach the process differently in the future?
2. What prewriting technique did you use to develop your topic? Do you think another technique would have been more effective?
3. If you had written for a different audience, what changes would you have made?
4. Which evidence best supported your thesis? What evidence did you leave out?
5. What revisions were in response to peer comments? What questions could you have asked your peer reviewer so that his or her comments would have been more helpful?
6. What techniques did you use to edit and proofread? Were they effective?

Feedback

If you had the chance to respond to the following student comment, what would you say or ask?

I usually write my best late at night when it is quiet. I think it is because writing is a very personal thing.

James Chan, Brentwood High School, Brentwood, New York

Descriptive Writing

Mysteries and Clues

René Magritte, *Time Transfixed*, 1938

Discovery in the Digs

"Did such and such happen so many years ago? What is the evidence to prove that it happened? Deduction is as important to this profession as it is to a detective in a detective story."

Dr. Richard "Scotty" MacNeish,
archaeologist

The mystery engaging Scotty MacNeish and his associate, Jane Libby, is this: When did people first appear in the New World? For years, archaeologists maintained that human beings migrated across the Bering Strait within the last 14,000 years. But in 1991, under MacNeish's direction, the Massachusetts-based Andover Foundation for Archaeological Research excavated an important site in New Mexico. What MacNeish's crew unearthed at Orogrande cave suggested to them that people may have lived and hunted on this continent as far back as 39,000 years ago.

Writing About Archaeology

COLLECTING THE EVIDENCE 1

EXAMINING THE CLUES 2

UNRAVELING THE MYSTERY 3

F O C U S

Descriptive writing requires strong observation skills as well as precise, informative word choices.

Libby recalls the excitement of the discovery: "Our crew chief at Orogrande came bounding over the ridge, yelling, 'Hey, look at this!' and Scotty said, 'Wow!' It was the toe bone of an extinct horse. From then on we knew we had a very old cave."

As the dig proceeded, the crew uncovered what MacNeish believes are stone tools, a spear-point, remains of a fireplace, and most important, a human palm-print in clay. MacNeish and many fellow archaeologists find these artifacts to be convincing evidence of an earlier human presence on the continent. Some of his col-leagues, however, are not so sure. The Orogrande discovery has sparked a "battle royal" in archaeological circles, MacNeish says. But this highly respected archaeologist relishes the con-flict. "I started in 1936," he says, "so I have about 7,000 days in the field, but I'm not tired yet.

"I'm still in the center of controversy, still fighting with my colleagues," he adds, "and I'm enjoying every minute of it."

Artifacts like this one don't look significant to most people, but to an archaeologist they are full of informative detail.

1. Collecting the Evidence

Jane Libby accompanies Mac-Neish on his digs, edits his scholarly papers, and writes a newsletter describing the foundation's archaeological work to friends and contributors, some of whom are not archaeologists. A skilled writer and editor, Libby spent her childhood rummaging around the ruins of an old building on her farm, digging up handmade nails and pieces of wooden buckets. Now she scrutinizes clues that as a novice she might have ignored.

"The first day I worked in the field," Libby recalls, "a well-trained archaeologist dumped a pail of dirt onto the screen, shook the screen to get the extra dirt off, and said,

'Look, there's a piece of pottery. There's another—and another.' And I said, 'How can you tell? It all looks like rocks to me.' But after a while, I could do the same thing. The more artifacts you see, the more easily you recognize them. Of course, the main theory we operate under is: 'If in doubt, bag it.' "

MacNeish explains why archaeologists pay strict attention to tiny details. "We got an ancient fingerprint on a piece of clay the size of a peanut. If somebody hadn't had sharp eyes, this baked clay would have been discarded as dirt. You have to know what you're looking for and, when you recognize it, to realize its significance."

MacNeish (below) and his crew found thousands of artifacts at the New Mexico digs, including the arrowhead and other artifacts shown here.

2. Examining the Clues

Every year since 1985, a crew of six to eight people led by MacNeish has spent winter months at archaeology sites in New Mexico, where mild temperatures make digging possible. The crew excavated hundreds of artifacts at the Orogrande site before making the big find.

The crew excavates one-meter-square areas at a time, making notes about the soil, digging conditions, and features such as burials and fireplaces. Each artifact is carefully measured and mapped before being collected for later analysis. In the evenings back at camp, crew members write detailed descriptions from their notes.

"You have to remember that you destroy the evidence as you excavate a square," Libby says. "You want to describe everything you see and do, so it will mean something to somebody else."

"We have all sorts of forms we fill out," Libby explains. The arti-

facts might be studied by other scientists months later, "so it becomes very important to describe things well."

Like police work, archaeology often requires specialized scientific analysis to evaluate the evidence. "The day of the lone-wolf archaeologist who did everything himself is gone," says MacNeish. "To prove our case that people arrived in the New World thousands of years earlier than previous estimates, it is going to take a lot of experts from a number of disciplines, each trying to make his or her point.

"For example," MacNeish continues, "we've sent the fingerprint to the head of the fingerprint division of the Ontario provincial police. And a doctor with laser printing will blow up the print so we can really see it, with its sweat pores and all."

The top picture shows part of an excavated cave. The chalkboard resting against the cave wall tells the location; tags on the wall identify layers from various time periods. The artifacts shown here are bagged and labeled with identification numbers.

Documents from the dig: photos, map, and notebook containing descriptions of sites and artifacts, as well as MacNeish's published reports on the findings.

3. Unraveling the Mystery

Once the scientific evidence is gathered, documented, and evaluated, MacNeish begins writing his report. "My work often takes some pretty heavy editing," the scientist admits. That's where Libby comes in. Incorporating his responses to her questions and comments, "I rewrite it and then it gets corrected again," MacNeish says, "so there may be two or three versions before the final one goes to the printer."

News of the Orogrande discovery spread quickly, and many groups and publications called upon MacNeish to share his findings. In writing for fellow archaeologists, he had to follow the strict guidelines used in his profession.

"Long before I sit down and start writing," MacNeish explains, "I make a very thorough outline of exactly what I'm going to write. I start by defining the problem or purpose of the article or monograph. Next I describe the methodology I used to collect and analyze the data. Then I talk about the data

and how they relate to the problem." Finally he draws a conclusion from the data: "Either they show that I've solved the problem or that I have other problems still to be solved."

Writing informal speeches or articles for the popular press challenges the archaeologist in a different way. MacNeish explains: "When I think about popular writing, I want a lead paragraph that gives all the sensational and interesting data first. Then, of course, I'm hoping that people will read the rest of it.

"If I'm giving a popular speech, I'll describe the interesting aspects of archaeology—the exciting finds and the funny incidents such as having the wheel of our jeep roll past as we drove along or waking rattlesnakes in the back of a cave."

INTERFACE *In what specific ways would writing for archaeologists differ from writing for general publications like the science section of a newspaper?*

ON ASSIGNMENT

1. Archaeologists like Scotty MacNeish and Jane Libby excavate a site in layers. The upper layers contain the most recent artifacts, and deeper layers reveal older objects. Excavate a catch-all drawer in your house, describing the objects you find at the different "levels" of the drawer.

2. **Literature Connection**
   In the opening scene of Sir Arthur Conan Doyle's *The Hound of the Baskervilles*, Dr. Watson ponders a walking stick that a mysterious visitor left on Sherlock Holmes's floor. Here's how Watson describes the stick:

   It was a fine, thick piece of wood, bulbous-headed, of the sort which is known as a "Penang lawyer." Just under the head was a broad silver band, nearly an inch across. "To James Mortimer, M.R.C.S., from his friends of the C.C.H." was engraved upon it, with the date "1884." It was just such a stick as the old-fashioned family practitioner used to carry—dignified, solid, and reassuring.

   Holmes, of course, makes a brilliant deduction about the stick's owner.

   From this description, write a summary of your deductions about the owner. Check the story for the answer.

3. **Cooperative Learning**
   Divide into groups of four. Have a member of each group bring in a strange object. Exchange objects with other groups so no object is in a group with its owner. Within your group, study one object and take turns describing it, trying to guess its function. Individually, write a description and identification of the object. Then read your descriptions to the class to see whether members arrived at similar or different conclusions. Finally, have the owner identify the item.

Creating Vivid Description

The Vague Perfume of Piñon

The mysterious death of an old man leads Navaho detective Joe Leaphorn to the Grand Canyon at twilight. When a scream echoes through the dark canyon, the detective freezes to listen for sounds of the person or animal in the distance.

Literature Model

Here, two hundred feet below the earth's surface, the air moved down-canyon, pressed by the cooling atmosphere from the slopes above. Leaphorn heard the song of insects, the chirping of rock crickets, and now and then the call of an owl. A bullbat swept past him, hunting mosquitoes, oblivious of the motionless man. Once again Leaphorn became aware of the distant steady murmur of the river. It was nearer now, and the noise of water over rock was funneled and concentrated by the cliffs. No more than a mile and a half away, he guessed. Normally the thin, dry air of desert country carries few smells. But the air at canyon bottom was damp, so Leaphorn could identify the smell of wet sand, the resinous aroma of cedar, the vague perfume of piñon needles, and a dozen scents too faint for identification. The afterglow faded from the clifftops.

Tony Hillerman, *Listening Woman*

Hillerman appeals to the senses of touch, hearing, smell, and sight in his description.

Why do you think Hillerman includes so little in the way of visual description?

Hillerman puts you at the bottom of the Grand Canyon and lets you sniff the air, feel the coolness, and hear the insects. He tells you exactly where you are—two hundred feet below the earth's surface. He also tells you about Leaphorn. The sensory description is filtered through Leaphorn's senses ("Leaphorn heard," "Leaphorn became aware," "Leaphorn could identify"). His perceptions help you imagine the scene and show you how detective Leaphorn senses his world through his skin, nose, and ears. In this lesson, you'll learn how to organize your own descriptive writing and bring it to life.

Picking an Approach

Whether you are describing the Grand Canyon or your own backyard, you need to decide how to organize the details. Imagine the following three people arriving at the scene of a crime and describing what they see in these different ways.

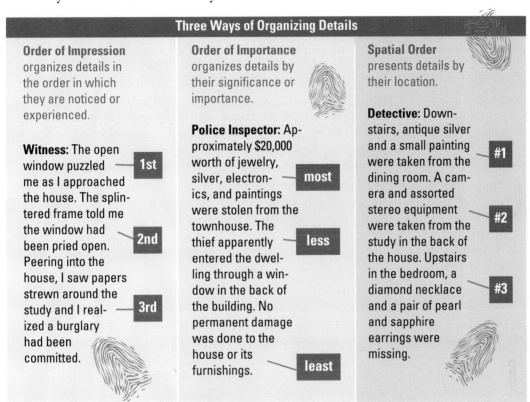

Three Ways of Organizing Details

Order of Impression organizes details in the order in which they are noticed or experienced.

Witness: The open window puzzled me as I approached the house. The splintered frame told me the window had been pried open. Peering into the house, I saw papers strewn around the study and I realized a burglary had been committed. [1st] [2nd] [3rd]

Order of Importance organizes details by their significance or importance.

Police Inspector: Approximately $20,000 worth of jewelry, silver, electronics, and paintings were stolen from the townhouse. The thief apparently entered the dwelling through a window in the back of the building. No permanent damage was done to the house or its furnishings. [most] [less] [least]

Spatial Order presents details by their location.

Detective: Downstairs, antique silver and a small painting were taken from the dining room. A camera and assorted stereo equipment were taken from the study in the back of the house. Upstairs in the bedroom, a diamond necklace and a pair of pearl and sapphire earrings were missing. [#1] [#2] [#3]

Each of these people has described his or her observations in a different order. If you were the witness, you probably would describe them in the order in which you noticed things—the order of impression. The police inspector highlights the value of the stolen items using order of importance. The detective, on the other hand, must pinpoint locations of stolen items. Spatial order can also be very effective if you want your readers to feel as if they are moving through space or if you want to create the sense of a room or a landscape unfolding.

Revising Tip

In the revising stage, think about the objects in your description and ask yourself questions such as, "What kind?" "What color?" "How big?" "How does it sound / feel / smell?"

• JOURNAL ACTIVITY •
Think It Through

Reread the model by Tony Hillerman on page 122. List in your journal all the words and phrases that grabbed your attention. Note the method of organization used in this passage.

Order of Impression

When you want to create a "you are there" feeling in your writing, use order of impression. Because it presents the narrator's changing reactions, order of impression has greater drama and urgency than does either spatial order or order of importance.

Model

I knew I was late for rehearsal as I tugged open the heavy metal fire door. But as I entered the theater I felt like I was entering a tomb. As my eyes adjusted to the darkened auditorium, I realized that no one, absolutely no one, was there. The spotlights lit the vacant stage with a harsh white glare. I squinted up at the empty projection booth. My "Hello?" was met by eerie silence. I ran up on the stage, the wooden boards creaking loudly under my feet. The heavy black curtain was drawn. The freshly painted scenery stood in place. Pages of a script were scattered about the stage.

What is the narrator's initial impression as she enters?

The description is organized to reflect the narrator's impressions and her reactions in response to the situation.

In the model above, the writer's use of order of impression allows the reader to identify with the narrator and to discover things as the narrator discovers them. At the end of the passage, you may be feeling the same confusion and discomfort as the narrator. This technique engages the reader and makes the reader feel involved in the action. You may want to continue reading to find out what's going to happen next and to find out why the theater appears abandoned. Can you think of other ways this description might have been organized to create different reactions in a reader?

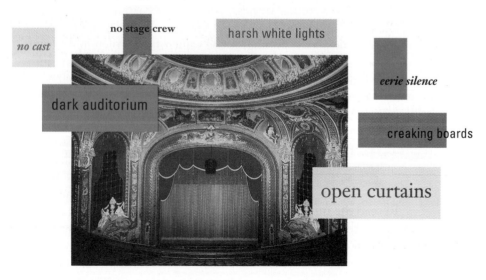

no cast

no stage crew

harsh white lights

eerie silence

dark auditorium

creaking boards

open curtains

Writer's Choice

Winslow Homer, *The Gulf Stream*, 1899

The following are some writing options to help you try out what you have learned.

1. Guided Assignment   Imagine you work for an insurance company that insures art. Your job is to visit museums and describe paintings for your company's records. List the details that make the painting on this page interesting and distinctive. Then decide how you will order the details you have listed. Describe the painting so that someone who has never seen it will recognize it upon seeing it for the first time.

> PURPOSE   Document the painting for insurance purposes
> AUDIENCE   Insurance company officials
> LENGTH   1–2 pages

2. Open Assignment   Imagine you are writing a mystery story for children. Choose one of the following scenes as the setting for your story,

and write a vivid description designed to get readers interested right away. Use one of the methods of organizing details discussed in this lesson.

- the wreck of a sunken ship
- the home of an eccentric junk collector
- a newly discovered planet
- a hurricane or its aftermath
- a scene of your choosing

3. Theater Arts   Imagine you are a theatrical director. Think of a play that you would like to stage, and then write a one- to two-page memo describing the setting for one scene from the play to your set designer. Describe exactly how you want the stage set to look. Use a method of organizing details that seems most appropriate to you. Be sure to include colors, textures, and sizes.

Fiery Red or Cherry Red?

Picture a glamorous woman driving a red convertible. Is the car fiery red or cherry red? Now imagine her nail polish. Is it screaming red, ruby red, or blood red?

A writer pays special attention to colors, smells, sounds, and textures. The real challenge lies in conveying these sensations in writing. Note the use of sensory details in the passage below.

Literature Model

Down a dark passageway I slowly descended, groping my way between ancient stone walls. Before me, a guide carried a lamp that bobbed in the gloom and cast flickering shadows on the cold walls. With each hesitating step, I was penetrating farther into the Tomb of the Leopards, an Etruscan crypt deep in a lonely hillside in Italy. . . .

We soon reached the bottom of the passageway, and I blinked in the dim lamplight, peering anxiously ahead while my eyes adjusted to the subterranean darkness. For a moment I could distinguish nothing more than three stone walls of what looked like a plain little chamber. But then, as I stood watching, it happened.

The chamber exploded with color—vivid color. Bright, startling reds and yellows, emerald greens, and deep azure blues swam into view before me. And as I continued to watch, the room magically began to come alive.

Judith E. Rinard, *Mysteries of the Ancient World*

Rinard's concrete details appeal to senses of touch and sight.

What sense is emphasized in the final paragraph?

Archaeologist Judith Rinard uses sensory details to draw us into the splendor of the tomb. A less precise writer might have said, "It was a cold, dark tomb until you saw lots of colorful drawings on the walls." But a dedicated archaeologist, like a detective or a writer, constantly practices and develops the art of description. Notice how Rinard contrasts the darkness in the first paragraphs with the startling colors in the last paragraph.

At the Bus Station

You don't have to be an archaelogist or detective to observe and use sensory details in your writing. Pretend for a moment that you are in a large urban bus station, bombarded with sensations.

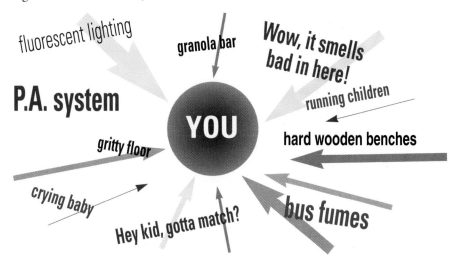

As you look for settings and incidents to use in your writing, ask yourself questions such as, "What is most striking here?" and "What does this remind me of?" and "How could I express this sensation in my writing?"

If you want your writing to be vivid, get specific! "The garbled blare of the P.A. system" tells a reader far more about what you heard than any vague complaint about noise.

Sharpening the Focus			
Perception	**Focus**	**Sharper focus**	**Sharpest Focus**
• Touch	• floor texture	• gritty underfoot	• rough as sandpaper
• Smell	• bus fumes	• noxious odor	• gives me a headache
• Sound	• P.A. system	• loud noise	• garbled blare
• Sight	• fluorescent lighting	• weird, sterile glow	• skin looks greenish
• Taste	• granola bar	• sort of stale	• nuts are rancid

• JOURNAL ACTIVITY •
Try It Out

Use your journal to record sensory details you observe in your classroom. As you note each impression, sharpen the focus by taking it another step or two, as shown in the graphic organizer above. Include at least two observations for each of your five senses.

Revising for Effect

Noting details is only one part of the writer's job. Equally important is the task of selecting and arranging details to achieve the effects you want.

After reading the first draft of the bus station description below, the writer decided the beginning was too abrupt. The writer also decided to elaborate on the lighting.

How does the revised beginning improve on the opening of the first draft?

Model

As soon as I opened the grimy glass door, the bus station began its assault. The first thing I thought was, "Wow, it smells bad in here!" I thought it was from the bus fumes. ~~Then there was the gritty floor and~~ that weird *fluorescent* lighting. There were lots of crying babies and little kids running around. I couldn't understand the garbled blare of the P.A. system. The last time I was there, I was eating a ~~stale~~ granola bar, and this guy came up ~~to me~~ and said, "Hey kid, gotta match?" Well, I don't carry matches so he was out of luck. I just shook my head and he walked away to ask someone else. I sat on those lousy wooden benches for about an hour until my bus came. *made everyone look green. No one looked cheerful at that bus station. We all looked like victims of some new strain of the flu.*

The writer included additional details to emphasize the effects of poor lighting. How does the final sentence of the revision make the paragraph easier to understand?

Even strong sensory details, if simply piled up one on top of another, can numb your reader. Have you ever been bored silly because someone couldn't resist showing you every single picture of a recent family vacation? Writers also are tempted to provide too much information. It's smarter to pick a few good details and let these carry the description.

The following are some writing options to help you try out what you have learned.

1. Guided Assignment   Imagine you work for a restaurant designer. Your job is to describe a fast-food restaurant and the activities that occur in it so that the designer can decide on renovations. Create a cluster diagram for the restaurant. Create five legs, each labeled with one of the senses, and then list as many sensory details as you can in circles that branch out from each of the senses.

Decide whether you want to arrange details in order of impression, order of importance, or spatial order. You may want to refer to page 123 for examples of these methods of organization. Then draft your description.

PURPOSE   To describe a restaurant using sensory details

AUDIENCE   A restaurant designer

LENGTH   1–2 pages

2. Open Assignment   Imagine you are an urban planner. You want to improve one of these sites in your community:

- a park
- a shopping center or retail district
- a complex of government buildings
- an empty lot
- a site of your choice

Use sensory details to describe for the planning board of your local government the site as it is and as it could be.

3. Chemistry   Use sensory details to describe a recent chemistry experiment (for example, "the hissing acid sent up an innocent-looking white vapor that smelled like scorched hair"). Write your description as if it were part of a letter to a friend. Emphasize your own perceptions, rather than trying to describe the experiment so someone else could perform it.

4. Cooperative Learning   Working in a group of four, divide the painting on this page into quadrants. With each group member taking responsibility for one quadrant, observe the painting for one full minute. Then close your book and list the details you recall from your section. After you have exhausted your memories, open your books and look at the picture again. Help each other add to the lists and sharpen your descriptions. Imagine yourselves within the painting and describe any smells, sounds, sights, and textures you might perceive. Using your own observations and those of other group members as a prewriting organizer, write a one- to two-page description of the painting using as many sensory details as possible.

Thomas Hart Benton, *July Hay*, 1943

Creating a Mood

Touchdown!

The mood at a football game can swing from despair to elation with a single touchdown. One minute you may be huddled under a blanket, grimly aware of the raw autumn cold. A moment later you're on your feet cheering, enjoying the invigorating fall air.

a crisp fall day

red and blue jackets in the bleachers add festivity to the field

shouts of the fans

a knot of black-and-yellow players surges forward over the line

dozens of feet pound the dry turf

Below is a description of the overall feeling, or mood, of another game. How does mood in the paragraph below differ from the mood established in the photo?

The lack of time, the player's injury, and bad weather establish the mood of this description.

What specific words in this description create the overall mood of despair?

Model

The two-minute warning blared rudely across the field. Our star running back was out with a sprained ankle and we were down by ten points. The gloomy gray sky dropped a chilly rain on the band members, who seemed more intent on keeping their instruments dry than on tuning up for the fight song. I couldn't tell whether the wet, bedraggled cheerleaders were crying or wiping raindrops from their eyes.

Building Mood

Mood can pervade any scene. Writers use mood to alert readers about how to read what's on the page, just as background music in a movie lets us know when the stranger on the street is likely to be good news or bad. When you write, you create mood by choosing particular details and the language you use to describe them.

Some descriptions may require stronger moods than others, depending on your purpose. Do you want your readers to get a sense of excitement as you describe the music during halftime? You can use words like "trill," "crash," and "jumping." Do you want to convey serenity? Words like "gentle," "wafted," and "familiar" may do the job. Here are some of the ways a writer could describe a high school band at halftime to convey a variety of moods. As you read each sample, think about the mood the writer is trying to evoke.

Glee As the bright notes of the march filled the air, sunshine glinted on the golden horns, and the fluffy plumes of the band members' hats dipped and swayed like birds strutting in time to the music.

Disappointment Some winced at the off-key groans of the new French horn player.

Amusement Fans chuckled as a trombone player made a less than graceful turn and knocked the hat off the player in front of him.

Serenity The gentle strains of the Alma Mater, so familiar to the home fans, wafted over the clipped green field.

Excitement A tremendous trill of the horns, a crash of the cymbals, and the crowd jumped to its feet.

• JOURNAL ACTIVITY •
Think It Through

Analyze the descriptions in the chart above. List words and phrases that evoke mood in each example. Then suggest who might use each mood in a description of the band. For example, the athlete who has just scored a touchdown might feel elation that would affect the way he perceived the music.

Shifts in Mood

Sometimes you will want to convey more than one mood in a piece of writing. Changing the mood of a description can alert readers to a change in feeling toward the subject being described or alert readers to a shift in the action. For example, in the passage below, N. Scott Momaday creates one mood to describe his grandmother's house when she was alive; his description of her house after her death evokes a mood that is quite different. As you read his description, think about the mood he creates in the two paragraphs. What feelings do the paragraphs evoke in you?

Literature Model

What mood does Momaday establish in the first paragraph?

Once there was a lot of sound in my grandmother's house, a lot of coming and going, feasting and talk. The summers there were full of excitement and reunion. . . . The aged visitors who came to my grandmother's house when I was a child were made of lean and leather, and they bore themselves upright. They wore great black hats and bright ample shirts that shook in the wind. They rubbed fat upon their hair and wound their braids with strips of colored cloth. Some of them painted their faces and carried the scars of old and cherished enmities. They were . . . full of jest and gesture, fright and false alarm. They went abroad in fringed and flowered shawls, bright beadwork and German silver. They were at home in the kitchen, and they prepared meals that were banquets. . . .

What details and language signal the change in mood?

Now there is a funeral silence in the rooms, the endless wake of some final word. The walls have closed in upon my grandmother's house. When I returned to it in mourning, I saw for the first time in my life how small it was. It was late at night, and there was a white moon, nearly full. I sat for a long time on the stone steps by the kitchen door. From there I could see out across the land; I could see the long row of trees by the creek, the low light upon the rolling plains, and the stars of the Big Dipper. Once I looked at the moon and caught sight of a strange thing. A cricket had perched upon the handrail, only a few inches away from me. My line of vision was such that the creature filled the moon like a fossil. It had gone there, I thought, to live and die, for there of all places, was its small definition made whole and eternal. A warm wind rose up and purled like the longing within me.

N. Scott Momaday, *The Way to Rainy Mountain*

Presenting Tip

When you present your writing by reading it aloud, you can create or emphasize a mood with vocal techniques such as a lowered voice, a drawn-out phrase, or increased speed.

Writer's Choice

The following are some writing options to help you try out what you have learned.

1. Guided Assignment   Imagine you are a screenwriter looking for ways to help a movie director create a particular mood in a film script. Find a park, restaurant, or gym where you can sit and write. Go there at two different times of day. For example, you could visit a park in the morning, when mothers with strollers crowd the walks, and then again in the late afternoon when the paths whiz with roller blades and bikes. You might visit a restaurant during the lunch rush and then again at 4:30 P.M. when there are few customers. You could observe a gym during the heat of a basketball game and then again an hour after the game has ended and the gym is deserted. Note the differences in light and sounds and in the types of people or the way they behave. Decide on the mood that each visit suggests and then brainstorm a list of nouns, verbs, and adjectives that you might use in creating each mood. Finally, draft a description of each mood you've found in your setting.

> PURPOSE   To create a mood in writing by describing a place
>
> AUDIENCE   Movie director
>
> LENGTH   2 pages

2. Open Assignment   Imagine you are a short story writer and wish to convey a particular mood by describing one of the following places. Try an unlikely combination (for example, serenity at a rock concert or despair at the beach).

- a rock concert
- a religious service
- a family reunion barbecue
- a beach
- a dentist's chair
- a place of your choosing

Once you have selected the setting and mood, use a cluster diagram like the one on page 143 to brainstorm words that will convey your mood. Then draft your description.

COMPUTER OPTION

If you have a word processor, you might like to use the cut-and-paste feature to organize your description. For example, you might find it effective to build gradually to a mood by starting with subtle details. You may find, on the other hand, that beginning your description with a strong statement of mood and following with supporting details works better. The cut-and-paste feature will let you move sentences around to see what works best.

3. American History   Think about an event in American history that evoked strong feelings. For example, the inauguration of Abraham Lincoln as president stirred a mixture of emotions. Imagine that you are a journalist writing a feature story for a local newspaper. Describe the event, evoking the mood that is most likely to strike a chord with your audience. Use descriptive words and phrases to convey the mood.

4. Cooperative Learning   Working in a group of four, choose a setting you know well. This might be a local park, diner, or shopping area. Think of four different moods. Each member of the group should choose one of the moods, and then each should write a couple of paragraphs describing the setting your group has chosen to convey the mood you have selected. Read your descriptions aloud to one another. As each person reads, other members of the group will list either the nouns, verbs, or adjectives and adverbs used. After all four descriptions have been read, compare the lists and discuss the word choices used to create different moods.

From Lean & Mean to Sweet & Petite

It may be easy to convince someone that a person is lean or petite. These physical features are obvious. But what about how mean or sweet people are—their personalities? How can you convey in writing the essence of another person? This is an example of the way a high school student could describe a favorite teacher. How does the writer portray the teacher's personality?

Model

Mr. Kowalski should have been a weight lifter or a football player. Instead he's my driver's ed teacher. His frame is so big he can hardly fit behind the teacher's desk. His arms look as hard as metal beams under his pushed-up shirt sleeves. His bristly crew cut adds to the "tough guy" look.

Actually, "Mr. Ski" is a riot. He really likes teaching and has a way of putting things that makes kids remember, like, "Don't brake for the birds; they'll take off on their own." He tells great stories about his days in the Marines. If anyone complains about an assignment, he says, "Lemme tell ya what they do with whiners in boot camp." There are always a bunch of students talking to him about cars or engines or anything. Mr. Kowalski is a friend as well as a teacher.

Why do you think the writer begins with a physical description?

How does the writer show that " 'Mr. Ski' is a riot"?

A character sketch is a quick profile that reveals personality and physical appearance. Answer these questions when prewriting a character sketch:

- How does the person look, move, and speak?
- How does the person behave toward others?
- How do others react to this person?
- What character traits does the person have?
- What anecdotes and examples would illustrate these traits?
- What overall impression should my description convey?

Zeroing in on a Person

We know the people around us through their appearance and behavior. Over time, we also learn their values and beliefs. A successful character sketch conveys values, beliefs, and personality through the external evidence of appearance and behavior.

Behavior: hangs out with Janet M. and Marty B., babysits brother after school, volunteers in literacy program, swims every day, reads mystery novels.

Appearance: curly black hair, gray eyes, big smile, pierced ears. Wears pink.

Underlying Personality: adores little brother, wants to attend an all-women's college, believes honesty is her most important trait, can't stand to see animals suffer.

Some parts of your sketch may relate basic information, such as "the man was nearly eighty years old." Other parts may use physical description to reveal behavior or personality. If you tell your readers that someone has "sunburned, muscular arms," for example, you suggest someone who works outside.

Be careful that you don't trap yourself or your readers into easy conclusions, however. To some, a soft voice implies shyness, yet a small voice may result from a small voice box; gray hair can imply old age or stress, or it may simply be a genetic trait. People defy stereotypes. Some football players dance to keep fit; not all grandmothers enjoy needlepoint. If you find yourself stereotyping someone's personality, dig a little deeper.

Editing Tip

When editing a character sketch, refer to Unit 17 of Grammar, Usage, and Mechanics to be sure that you have used pronouns correctly.

• JOURNAL ACTIVITY •
Think It Through

How do you appear to others? Brainstorm a list of physical characteristics, behaviors, and beliefs and attitudes to create a multi-layered diagram of your own character based on the diagram above.

Clues to Character

You can add to what you know about a person by looking at pictures and reading old letters and diaries. Clues to a person's character may include a watch, a piece of jewelry, a musical instrument, or other things the person may have treasured and saved.

Grandmother was the youngest of five girls who sang together.

She wore this shawl the day she married grandfather, a violinist.

She loved opera and musical comedy.

She wrote to her mother every week when she and grandfather were performing.

Objects like those above can also enhance a written character sketch. Notice how Maya Angelou uses possessions like "printed voile dresses," "flowered hats," and "gloves" to convey character.

Literature Model

Angelou begins by describing how Mrs. Flowers looked.

What does Angelou mean by this sentence?

What is Angelou's attitude toward Mrs. Flowers? How do you know?

Mrs. Bertha Flowers was the aristocrat of Black Stamps.... She was thin without the taut look of wiry people, and her printed voile dresses and flowered hats were as right for her as denim overalls for a farmer. She was our side's answer to the richest white woman in town.

Her skin was a rich black that would have peeled like a plum if snagged, but then no one would have thought of getting close enough to Mrs. Flowers to ruffle her dress, let alone snag her skin. She didn't encourage familiarity. She wore gloves too.

I don't think I ever saw Mrs. Flowers laugh, but she smiled often. A slow widening of her thin black lips to show even, small white teeth, then the slow effortless closing. When she chose to smile on me, I always wanted to thank her. The action was so graceful and inclusively benign.

She was one of the few gentlewomen I have ever known, and has remained throughout my life the measure of what a human being can be.

Maya Angelou, *I Know Why the Caged Bird Sings*

Writer's Choice

The following are some writing options to help you try out what you have learned.

1. Guided Assignment Sort through your memories for a truly colorful character. For example, you might think of a favorite aunt or uncle, a teacher or coach, or a neighbor who entertained you. Jot down your memories of this person, including what you know of his or her physical appearance and ways of thinking, speaking, and moving. Decide what attitude or impression you want to convey and select the details that will best convey your attitude toward or impression of the person. Use the phrases and images you have selected from this prewriting exercise to draft a character sketch and revise and edit it for clarity and impact.

PURPOSE To convey a character
AUDIENCE Someone who has never met the person being described
LENGTH 1 page

COMPUTER OPTION

You can use a word-processing program to revise the organization of your character sketch. Separate files will allow you to arrange and rearrange details for the best effect. You could also try putting a statement summarizing your attitude toward the person at both the beginning and the end of the paragraph to see which works better.

2. Open Assignment Imagine you have been asked to nominate someone for an award for generosity, sense of humor, or personal integrity. Use the following list to select a person you know that you want to nominate for a particular quality. Write a character sketch to convince the judges that your nominee is especially generous, has a great sense of humor, or is rich in personal integrity.

- a family member
- a neighbor
- a pastor, priest, or rabbi
- a teacher
- a work associate
- a friend
- anyone you choose

3. American History Imagine that you are having a dinner party that includes the following guests from America's past: President Theodore Roosevelt, President Abraham Lincoln, Harriet Beecher Stowe, Susan B. Anthony, Chief Sitting Bull, Tecumseh, Harriet Tubman, Booker T. Washington, W. E. B. DuBois, Thomas A. Edison, Benjamin Franklin, Dolley Madison, President Andrew Jackson, and Mark Twain.

Decide which two of these people are your guests of honor, and write a memo to your butler that includes a brief character sketch of the guests of honor so that he will know how to recognize them and talk to them. Conclude by explaining why these two people should or should not be seated next to each other at the party.

4. Cooperative Learning In groups of four, select a well-known person you would all like to know more about. Assign one member responsibility for describing the person's appearance, a second responsibility for describing the person's behavior, and a third responsibility for describing the person's personality. Each member should research the aspects for which he or she is responsible. The group will agree on the main idea to be conveyed and the fourth member will pull together the information gathered by the other members into a character sketch. One member of the group will present the sketch to the rest of the class and ask the class to guess who the sketch describes and the purpose of the sketch.

Describing an Event

No Time to Think

Have you ever fallen or had an accident and found it difficult to explain what happened? Sometimes you can only say, "It all happened so fast!" Notice how Sue Grafton packs the continuous action of such an event into the following descriptive passage.

Literature Model

How do words like "behind," "straight," "rearview," "forward," and "back" help the reader understand the event?

Grafton uses strong, active verbs in this passage. Identify some of them.

B ehind me, the Dodge had made a U-turn and was now accelerating as it headed straight at me again. I ground at the starter, nearly singing with fear, a terrified eye glued to my rearview mirror where I could see the pickup accumulating speed. The Dodge plowed into me, this time with an impact that propelled the VW forward ten yards with an ear-splitting BAM. My forehead hit the windshield with a force that nearly knocked me out. The safety glass was splintered into a pattern of fine cracks like a coating of frost. The seat snapped in two and the sudden liberation from my seat belt slung me forward into the steering wheel. The only thing that saved me from a half-rack of cracked ribs was the purse in my lap, which acted like an air bag, cushioning the blow.

Sue Grafton, *G Is for Gumshoe*

Grafton's account of the collision describes each step in the action. Readers can follow the sequence of events as the Dodge hurtles toward the VW because every incident is portrayed as it is witnessed by the narrator sitting in the front seat of the stalled VW.

Choosing a Vantage Point

Because events involve time and motion, they are sometimes harder to describe than static scenes. Writers need to dissect an event into a logical sequence of clearly linked actions and reactions. The vantage point from which those actions are witnessed must be clear and consistent in order for the reader to follow what's happening.

Thoughts and Impressions from Different Vantage Points

Neighbor in street:
Is person at window OK? Will he jump? Others in house? Pets out? Will it spread to other houses? What is coming over the firefighters' radio? The firefighter looks hot. The street is closed off. Should I do anything?

Firefighter:
How best to get man down? Others in house? Wind direction could be a problem. Origin of fire? Will it spread? Send for more units? How's the water pressure? Paramedics here? Are there combustibles?

Person at the window:
Choking fumes. Smoke burns my eyes. Too high to jump? Get out on sill? Do I have time to save anything?

Imagine spotting a roaring fire over the rooftops in your neighborhood. You run toward the scene. You hear fire engines. You see your neighbor's house ablaze. How close can you get? How close do you want to get?

It all depends on why you're there. If you intend to rescue a friend, you may need to pound on the door. If you want to interview the firefighters for a story, you'll want to stand near the truck. If you just want to watch the fire being put out, standing across the street may offer the best perspective.

Choosing a vantage point in writing is like finding a place to stand at the scene of a fire; it selects and limits the details available to you. You should, therefore, determine your purpose in writing before choosing your vantage point. Do you simply want the reader to know what has happened? Or do you want the reader to feel involved in the action as it is happening? Are you trying to create a particular reaction to the events described? Fear? Anger? Delight? You have many options.

> ## Drafting Tip
>
> As you draft a piece, be sure to alert the reader when you shift vantage points. Begin a new paragraph, or say something like "Meanwhile, at Sue's house . . ."

• JOURNAL ACTIVITY •
Think It Through

Think of an event you described in a way that was different from the way someone else described it. It might have been an accident, a party, an athletic event, even a scene from a movie. List in your journal some reasons why you think your impressions might have differed.

Testing Your Description

It's easy to garble an account of an event. Time gets confused; the vantage point jumps around; information is left out. You've probably heard people recounting events in such a confusing manner that you had to keep interrupting to ask questions. However, your readers can't interrupt you with questions. Look at this model to see what to avoid.

Model

*T*he thief rummaged in the drawers for valuables. Before that, he disarmed the burglar alarm. When he found nothing in the dining room, he went into the back bedroom. When he saw the police car pull up in front of the house, he grabbed the earrings and slithered out the back window, leaving a thin trail of blood on the white carpet.

Keep these questions in mind when you describe an event:

- Is my vantage point clearly defined and consistent?
- Can I see, hear, smell, taste, or touch the things I describe from my vantage point?
- Is the passage of time logical and believable?

Diona Haley demonstrates how to use different, yet clearly defined and consistent, vantage points.

Student Model

*A*s the man lingered between life and death, his wife's cries were drowned out by that word no one wants to hear. "Flatline!" "Get the pads, set it at three hundred. Ready, clear!" A long pause. "Again at five hundred!" Another pause. "We're losing him. Once more, ready, CLEAR!"

The doctors didn't realize what was going on in his seemingly lifeless brain. His sixteenth birthday, the red car. Graduation, college, his job. His wife. Thirty long beautiful years. Where did it go? Why didn't he make his life more meaningful, enjoy it, and not take it for granted? . . . Why didn't he tell his wife how much he really loved her? Wait, it doesn't have to be this way. Fight it! You can do it, fight!

"We got him!" A big sigh of relief, then the bustling resumes. "Good job, Doctor, he gets another chance now."

Diona Haley, Centennial High School, Pueblo, Colorado

The following are some writing options to help you try out what you have learned.

1. Guided Assignment Imagine that you were driving a car over a bridge during an earthquake. *Life* magazine has asked you to write about your experience. Develop a list of details that are consistent with your vantage point to describe the earthquake. As you draft your account, be sure readers can follow each incident through time and space. In revising your draft, use specific nouns, active verbs, and strong modifiers.

PURPOSE To describe a natural disaster as an eyewitness
AUDIENCE Readers who have never been in an earthquake
LENGTH 1–2 pages

2. Open Assignment Pretend that you are on a trip around the United States. Write a letter to a friend back home describing one of the following events you have seen:

- a rodeo in Montana
- surfing on the California coast
- colonial artists at work in Williamsburg, Virginia
- a show at Sea World in Orlando, Florida
- white-water rafting in Colorado
- your choice of a similar event

Select an appropriate vantage point and make sure that you make movement through time and space clear to the reader.

Thomas Eakins, *Between Rounds*, 1899

3. Art What do you think is happening in the painting on this page? It all depends on your vantage point. Write three brief descriptions of the events in the painting. One should be from your vantage point as a student in the present looking at a work of art. The second should be from the vantage point of one of the men in the boxing ring, either the boxers themselves or one of the referees. The third should be from the vantage point of the reporter or one of the spectators. Be sure you maintain a consistent vantage point within each account.

Describing an Event   **141**

Gloomy and Decayed

In the first act of *Sherlock Holmes*, playwrights Arthur Conan Doyle and William Gillette hint that something fishy is going on at Edelweiss Lodge. Madge Larrabee, "a strikingly handsome woman, but with a somewhat hard face" waits anxiously in the drawing room. When Forman, a servant, enters with the evening paper, Madge snatches it and searches for an item.

Edward Gorey,
The Listing Attic, 1954

Literature

*A*s if not seeing the print well she leans near light, and resumes reading with the greatest avidity. FORMAN *quietly shuts the door. He stands at the door looking at* MADGE *as she reads the paper. This is prolonged somewhat, so that it may be seen that he is not waiting for her to finish from mere politeness. His eyes are upon her sharply. . . . She finishes and angrily rises, casting the paper violently down. . . . Sees* FORMAN, *calms herself at once. Just as* MADGE *turns,* FORMAN *seems to be coming into room.*

Arthur Conan Doyle and William Gillette, *Sherlock Holmes*

Elements of Dramatic Mood

The scene above takes place only a few minutes into the play, yet already the audience knows what sort of play to expect. The "gloomy and decayed house," a character who has a "somewhat hard face," and a scene in which two characters are obviously trying to deceive each other lead the audience to expect a play of suspense.

Later when Sherlock Holmes forces Madge and her husband to produce Alice Faulkner, music and dialogue heighten the tension.

Literature

*P*athetic music, very p.p. (pianissimo, or very soft)
A pause—no one moves.
[*Enter* ALICE FAULKNER. *She comes down a little—very weak* ➡

—looking at LARRABEE, *then seeing* HOLMES *for first time.*]
    [*Stop music.*]
    HOLMES [*on seeing* ALICE *rises and puts book on mantel. After a brief pause, turns and comes down to* LARRABEE]: A short time since you displayed an acute anxiety to leave the room. Pray do not let me detain you or your wife—any longer.
    [*The* LARRABEES *do not move. After a brief pause,* HOLMES *shrugs shoulders slightly and goes over to* ALICE. HOLMES *and* ALICE *regard each other a moment.*]
    ALICE: This is Mr. Holmes?
    HOLMES: Yes.
    ALICE: You wished to see me?
    HOLMES: Very much indeed, Miss Faulkner, but I am sorry to see— [*placing chair near her*] —you are far from well.
    ALICE [*a step.* LARRABEE *gives a quick glance across at her threateningly and a gesture of warning, but keeping it down*]: Oh no—[*Stops as she catches* LARRABEE's *angry glance.*]
    HOLMES [*pausing as he is about to place chair and looking at her*]: No? [*Lets go of his chair.*] I beg your pardon—but—[*Goes to her and takes her hand delicately—looks at red marks on her wrist. Looking up at her.*] What does this mean?
    ALICE [*shrinking a little. Sees* LARRABEE's *cruel glance*]: Oh—nothing.

Arthur Conan Doyle and William Gillette, Sherlock Holmes

Prewriting Tip

Music can be one of the strongest elements in a dramatic production. When prewriting an essay on mood in drama, you may want to begin by analyzing the contribution of the music.

If you wanted to describe the mood in *Sherlock Holmes*, you might begin with a chart like the one below. Such a chart lets you isolate and analyze elements contributing to the mood of a play.

Mood (Suspenseful)				
Dialogue	**Characters**	**Action**	**Music**	**Setting**
"You are far from well.... What does this mean?"	woman with a hard face; man with angry looks	Holmes examines marks on Alice Faulkner's wrist	pathetic as Alice Faulkner enters	decayed and gloomy house

• JOURNAL ACTIVITY •
Try It Out

    What kind of mood is set by the theme music or opening credits of a popular television show or movie? Write about the music, type, images, lighting, sights, or other elements that create the mood of this program or movie.

Analyzing Mood

Jennifer Spiher analyzed mood in "The Final Hour," an episode from the old radio mystery drama series known as *The Shadow*. "The Final Hour" is the dramatic story of the efforts of Lamont Cranston, also known as the Shadow, to exonerate Jim Martin, who faces the death penalty for a crime he never committed. With only three hours until the scheduled execution, the Shadow races the clock to save Martin.

Analyzing the elements that contribute to mood in a play can help a writer focus and organize an essay. For example, which sound effects have the biggest impact in "The Final Hour"? How do the sound effects make the listener feel? What is the effect of the repetition of these sounds?

Notes like those below helped Jennifer organize her thoughts and decide which elements to emphasize and which to eliminate from her essay. What element seems to be most important?

Student Model

Where does Jennifer summarize her analysis of the mood of this play? Do you find this effective? Why or why not?

Jennifer gives examples of each element that she has identified as contributing to mood: character, dialogue, and sound effects.

Are there any elements that Jennifer does not discuss that you would have included? Which ones?

"The Final Hour" is a dramatic play which was broadcast over radio in 1954. The playwright, Jerry McGill, creates a feeling of suspense for the reader. Defined by Webster as a state of uncertainty or anxiety, suspense is conveyed through the characters, dialogue, and sound effects of this play. The main character, Lamont Cranston's alter ego, the Shadow, is a good example of suspense as created through characters. The word "shadow" compels the reader to envision dark corners and lurking figures, thus helping to produce a sense of apprehension. Another example is Sam Walker. His frantic actions at Barton's Tavern on the night Jim Martin is to be executed convey to the reader a sense of uncertainty as to Jim's fate. . . . This feeling of urgency is also produced by the constant ticking of the clock in Sam's house. Finally, by repeating the phrase "final hour," in the dialogue Jerry McGill causes the reader to recall Jim Martin's predicament and to feel anxiety.

Jennifer Spiher, Rangeview High School, Aurora, Colorado

Sound effects — which have biggest impact?
— footsteps
— slamming cell door
— ticking clock . . .
clock ties into title!
Final Hour/passing time
Emphasize idea of repetition
~~Another mention theme song?~~
Importance of the word "shadow"

Writer's Choice

1. Guided Assignment Imagine that you hope to become the drama or film reviewer for your local newspaper. You are told that you are one of three finalists, and that the job will be given to the writer who does the best job of describing the mood of a dramatic production. Watch a play, movie, or TV show, taking notes on the elements that create a certain mood. For example, frantic violin music may heighten tension. Exaggerated shadows can create a sense of foreboding. Write an essay analyzing the mood of the production you have watched, beginning with a general statement followed by supporting details.

> **PURPOSE** To describe the mood of a dramatic production
>
> **AUDIENCE** Editors of your local paper
>
> **LENGTH** 2 pages

2. Open Assignment Plays often have more than one mood. For example, the mood in the first act of a play may be upbeat, but in the second act, the mood may be one of frustration. The mood may also vary from scene to scene. Tragedies, especially, may include comic elements to alleviate the overall mood of despair.

Read one or two scenes from *The Glass Menagerie*, *Death of a Salesman*, *The Crucible*, or *Our Town*. Select one element from the list below and then analyze the way this element changes to create different moods.

- character
- setting
- sound
- dialogue
- an element you choose

Imagine that your school has decided to stage this play. You have been asked to write notes for the theater program. Use your analysis of the element above for an essay discussing the mood of the play.

3. American Literature Edgar Allan Poe was a master at creating mood. He believed a work should have a single effect and that all elements should work toward that effect. Read one of Poe's short stories, such as "The Masque of the Red Death," "The Pit and the Pendulum," or "The Tell-Tale Heart." Imagine that you want to be hired to adapt the story for a television production. Write a letter to the producer discussing the mood of the story and the techniques Poe uses to create that mood. Explain how you would create that mood if you were adapting the story for television. Describe how specific elements such as music, lighting, and scenery would contribute to the mood of the production.

COMPUTER OPTION

If you have access to a word processor with an outlining feature, you could rough out your letter in advance and then fill in the details.

4. Cooperative Learning In a small group, brainstorm a list of seven or eight moods you might observe in a play, such as anger, suspense, comedy, or excitement. Then have three people in your group improvise a scene of a couple being served dinner at a restaurant. After about a minute have someone in the "audience" call out one of the moods. The players should then, without breaking character, change their dialogue, tone of voice, actions, and body postures to suggest that mood. Repeat this process with a different group of players, continuing to call out different moods every couple of minutes until either the list or the players are exhausted. Then discuss the improvisations. Each member of the group should write a review of the performances given by the other performers. Assess which moods were most successfully created and why.

ELIZABETH ENRIGHT

the Signature

With a background in art, Elizabeth Enright (1909–1968) established herself as an illustrator of children's books and a writer of short stories. In the following story, "The Signature," Enright draws a striking portrait of a strange city and an alienated character mystified by both her surroundings and her own identity.

The street was wide and sloped gently upward ahead of me. It was paved with hardbaked dust almost white in the early-afternoon light, dry as clay and decked with bits of refuse. On either side the wooden houses stood blind to the street, all their shutters closed. The one- and two-story buildings—some of them set back a little; there was no sidewalk—had door yards with dusted grass and bushes, but many of them stood flush to the road itself with nothing but a powdered weed or two for grace. All of the houses had an old, foreign look, and all were unpainted, weather-scoured to the same pale color, except for the eaves of some which had been trimmed with wooden zigzags and painted long ago, like the crude, faded shutters, in tones of blue or red.

The sky was blanched[1] with light, fronded with cirrus, unemphatic; just such a sky as one finds near the sea, and this, in addition to the scoured, dry, enduring look of the town, persuaded me that an

---

1. **blanched** (blanchd): made pale

ocean or harbor must be somewhere near at hand. But when I came up over the rise of the road, I could find no furred line of blue at any horizon. All I could see was the great town—no, it was a city—spread far and wide, low lying, sun bleached, and unknown to me. And this was only one more thing that was unknown to me, for not only was I ignorant of the name of the city, but I was ignorant of my own name, and of my own life, and nothing that I seized on could offer me a clue. I looked at my hands: they were the hands of a middle-aged woman, coarsening at the joints, faintly blotched. On the third finger of the left hand there was a golden wedding ring, but who had put it there I could not guess. My body in the dark dress, my dust-chalked shoes were also strangers to me, and I was frightened and felt that I had been frightened for a long time, so long that the feeling had become habitual—something that I could live with, in a pinch, or, more properly, something that until this moment I had felt that I could live with. But now I was in terror of my puzzle.

I had the conviction that if I could once see my own face, I would remember who and what I was, and why I was in this place. I searched for a pane of glass to give me my reflection, but every window was shuttered fast. It was a season of drought, too, and there was not so much as a puddle to look into: in my pocket there was no mirror and my purse contained only a few bills of a currency unknown to me. I took the bills out and looked at them; they were old and used and the blue numerals and characters engraved on them were also of a sort I had never seen before, or could not remember having seen. In the center of each bill, where ordinarily one finds the pictures of a statesman or a monarch, there was instead an angular, spare symbol: a laterally elongated diamond shape with a heavy vertical line drawn through it at the center, rather like an abstraction of the human eye. As I resumed my walking I was aware of an impression that I had seen this symbol recently and often, in other places, and at the very moment I was thinking this I came upon it again, drawn in chalk on the side of a house. After that, watching for it, I saw it several times: marked in the dirt of the road, marked on the shutters, carved on the railing of a fence.

It was this figure, this eye-diamond, which reminded me, by its persistence, that the eye of another person can be a little mirror, and now with a feeling of excitement, of possible hope, I began walking faster, in search of a face.

From time to time I had passed other people, men and women, in the street. Their dark, anonymous clothes were like the clothes of Italian peasants, but the language they spoke was not Italian, nor did it resemble any language I had ever heard, and many of their faces had a fair Northern color. I noticed when I met these people that the answering looks they gave me, while attentive, were neither inimical[2] nor friendly. They looked at me with that certain privilege shared by kings and children, as if they possessed the right to judge, while being ignorant of, or exempt from, accepting judgment in return. There is no answer to this look and appeal is difficult, for one is already in a defensive position. Still, I had tried to appeal to them; several times I had addressed the passers-by hoping that one of them might understand me and tell me where I was, but no one could or would. They shook their heads or lifted their empty hands, and while they did not appear hostile, neither did they smile in answer to my pleading smiles. After they had passed I thought it strange that I never heard a whisper or a laugh or any added animation in their talk. It was apparently a matter of complete indifference to them that they had been approached in the street by a stranger speaking a strange language.

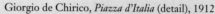

Giorgio de Chirico, *Piazza d'Italia* (detail), 1912

2. **inimical** (in im′i k′l): unfriendly or hostile

Knowing these things I thought that it might be difficult to accomplish my purpose, and indeed this proved to be the case. The next people I met were three women walking together; two were young and one was middle-aged. I approached the taller of the young women, for her eyes were on a level with my own, and looking steadily into them and coming close, I spoke to her.

"Can you tell me where I am?" I said to her. "Can you understand what I am saying?"

The words were a device. I expected no answer and got none of any sort. As I drew close she looked down at the ground; she would not meet my gaze. A little smile moved the corners of her lips, and she stepped aside. When I turned to her companions they also looked away, smiling. This expression on other faces might have been called embarrassment, but not on theirs. The smile they shared seemed noncommittal, secretive, knowledgeable in a way that I could not fathom, and afterward I thought it curious that they had shown no surprise.

For a long time after that I met no one at all. I met no cat, no dog, no cabbage butterfly; not even an ant on the packed, bald dust of the road, and finally rejecting its ugliness and light I turned to the left along another street, narrower and as graceless, and walked by the same monotony of weather-beaten houses. After a few minutes I heard a sound that halted me and I stood listening. Somewhere not far away I heard children's voices. Though their words were foreign they spoke also in the common tongue of children everywhere: voices high, eruptive, excited, sparked with the universal jokes, chants, quarrels of play; and here, listening to them, my memory stirred for the first time—a memory of memory, in fact. For whatever it was that nearly illuminated consciousness was not the memory itself, but a remnant of light which glowed on the periphery of the obstacle before it: a penumbra.[3]

Where are the children, I thought; where are they? With great urgency and longing I set out in the direction of their voices, determined to find them and in doing so to find something of myself. Their voices chattered, skipped, squabbled like the voices of sparrows, never far away, but though I turned and hunted and listened and pursued I could not find them. I never found them, and after a while I could not hear them either. The ghostly light of memory faded and was extinguished, and my despair rose up in darkness to take its place.

The next person I met was a man, young and dark-browed, and when I confronted him and asked my questions, it was without hope.

---

3. **penumbra** (pi num´brə): the partly lighted area surrounding the complete shadow of a body during an eclipse; a vague or borderline area

I knew he would not meet my look, or let his eyes show me my longed-for, dreaded face. Yet here I was wrong; he stood before me without speaking, but the gaze with which he answered mine was so intense and undeviating that it was I who dropped my eyes and stepped aside. I could not look, and soon I heard him going on his way.

I had been walking a long time, and the light was changing; the sun was low and full in my face. West, I said to myself; at least I know west, and I know that I am a woman, and that that is the sun. When the stars come out I will know those, too, and perhaps they will tell me something else.

After a while I sat down on a wooden step to rest. I was struck by the silence of the city around me, and I realized this was because it was a city of walkers who walked on dust instead of on pavements. I remembered that I had seen no mark of a wheel on any road, and that nothing had moved in the sky all day except for a few birds in flight.

A breath of dry wind crept along the dust at my feet, and, far away, a noise of knocking started, a sound of stakes being driven into the ground with a wooden mallet. Desolate, reiterated, it sounded as though somewhere in the city they were preparing a gallows or a barricade. Too tired and dispirited to move I sat there listening to the double knock-and-echo of each blow. A few people passed me on their way home, each of them giving me the glance of casual appraisal I had seen so often. Doors opened and doors closed, the sun went down, and soon the street was still again and the knocking stopped. Where would I sleep that night, or find a meal? I neither knew nor cared.

One by one the stars came out on the deepening sky, perfect, still, as if they were really what they seemed to be—calm ornaments for hope, promises of stillness and forever.

I looked for Venus, then Polaris, then for Mars. I could not find them, and as the stars grew in number, coming imperceptibly into their light, I saw with slow-growing shock that these were not the stars I knew. The messages of this night sky were written in a language of constellations I had never seen or dreamed. I stared up at the brand-new Catherine wheels,[4] insignias, and fiery thorn crowns on the sky, and I do not think that I was really surprised when I spied at the zenith, small but bright, a constellation shaped like an elongated diamond, like the glittering abstraction of a human eye. . . .

It was just at this moment, before I could marshal or identify my thoughts in the face of such a development, that I heard a sound of trees, wind in the leaves of trees, and I realized, irrelevantly it

4. **Catherine wheels**: fireworks displaying wheels with projecting spikes

Giorgio de Chirico, *Piazza d'Italia*, 1912

seemed, that in all my walking in this city—how many hours, how many days?—I had not seen a single tree, and the sound of their presence was as welcome as the sound of rain is after a siege of drought. As I stood up it occurred to me that neither had I seen one child among all the strangers I had met, that though I had heard the children I had not been able to find them, and now to all the other fears was added the fear that the trees, too, would magically elude me.

The street was dark, though light was glimmering through the cracks of the closed shutters. What was left of sunset, green as water, lay on the western horizon. Yet was it really western? In a sky of new stars, was it not possible and in fact probable that what I had believed to be the sun was not really Sun at all? Then what were the compass points, what were the easts and wests of this city? And what would I find when once I found myself?

I heard the beckoning of trees again and as if they were the clue to sanity, I ran along the street in the direction of their sound. I turned a corner, and there, ah yes, there were the trees: a grove of tall, dry, paper-murmuring trees that grew in a little park or public garden where people were walking together or sitting on the dusty grass. At the center of this park or garden there was a great house of stone, the first stone building I had seen all day. It was lighted from top to bottom; the lights of its long windows twittered in gold among the small leaves of the trees, and a door stood open at the head of a flight of steps.

I passed many people on the path, but now I did not look at them or ask them questions. I knew that there was nothing they could do for me. I walked straight to the steps and up them and through the door into the lighted house. It was empty, as I had expected, a great empty ringing house, but there was a splendor about it, even in its emptiness, as if those who had left it—and left it recently—had been creatures of joy, better than people and gayer than gods. But they, whoever they were, had gone. My footsteps sounded on the barren floor, and the talk of the loiterers outside, the foreign talk, came in the windows clearly on the night air.

The mirror was at the end of the hall. I walked toward it with my fists closed, and my heart walked, too, heavily in my chest. I watched the woman's figure in the dark dress and the knees moving forward. When I was close to it, I saw, low in the right-hand corner of the mirror, the scratched small outline of the eye-diamond, a signature, carved on the surface of the glass by whom, and in what cold spirit of raillery? Lifting my head, I looked at my own face. I leaned forward and looked closely at my face, and I remembered everything. I remembered everything. And I knew the name of the city I would never leave, and, alas, I understood the language of its citizens.

For Discussion

1. In what ways is this a satisfying or unsatisfying story? How does it compare with other mystery or science-fiction tales that you have read?

2. What do you find is the most disturbing feature of the world Enright creates? How would you react to this feature if you were the main character in the story?

Readers Respond

I have always been a sucker for mystery. The scene I remember best is the last scene, when the woman in the story looked into the mirror. The story still has my attention because I'm trying to figure it out! I would recommend this to a friend, mainly to see if my friend could make heads or tails of the ending.

Marsha Novak

This selection was very metaphorical and very universal. Enright comments that all of us are born as nameless, faceless individuals carving our own identity. If we fail to find this identity, we are doomed to our worst fate—isolation. I found this selection captivating and thought-provoking. I wonder: Have I found my identity?

Mathew Isaac

Did you notice?

☞ Did you notice that the ending could be interpreted in more than one way? How did you interpret the ending? Did it change your response to the story as a whole?

☞ Freewrite an answer to this question in your journal.

Writing Process in Action

Flung into an Alien Land

Who is this woman? Where has she found herself, and why is she there? Why can't she remember who she is? Why is she frightened, hopeless, and despairing? These are some of the questions that haunt readers of "The Signature" (pages 146–152). With deft strokes of description, Elizabeth Enright launches both her narrator and her readers on a mysterious quest. You're invited to do the same in this assignment—to involve your audience so intensely in your description that they want to know more.

• Assignment •

CONTEXT You have a terrific idea for a story that you would like to see produced as a television movie. Rather than writing a complete screenplay, you have decided to send several producers a brief description that will evoke the setting, paint a portrait of the main character, and reveal a bit of the central conflict. You are hoping that this sketch will arouse their curiosity and spark their interest in seeing more of what you have in mind.

PURPOSE To create a description of a character and a setting that establishes personality, mood, and conflict

AUDIENCE Several television producers

LENGTH 1–2 pages

---

1. Prewriting

If an idea for a character, setting, and conflict doesn't dance off the page as you read the assignment, don't be concerned. Subjects for your sketch are all around you—in your common everyday experiences, in your hopes and dreams, or in your reading. Tap into your memory by freewriting or clustering, or jump-start your imagination by asking yourself *what if* questions: What if you awoke one day to find that you had turned into an enormous animal? What if there really were time machines that you could travel in? What if people could live under the sea?

As you play with various combinations of setting, character, and conflict, keep in mind what you're after. For example, you'll want your location to serve as more than just background. In "The Signature," the unknown city with its dusty, graceless streets and its old, shuttered houses establishes a mood that affects the character and acts as an element of the conflict. The setting almost becomes another character in the story.

The street was dark, though light was glimmering through the cracks of the closed shutters. What was left of sunset, green as water, lay on the western

horizon. Yet was it really western? In a sky of new stars, was it not possible and in fact probable that what I had believed to be the sun was not really Sun at all? Then what were the compass points, what were the easts and wests of this city? And what would I find when once I found myself?

Like the main character, we feel that if we can "read" the descriptive details and figure out where the woman is, we will have solved the mystery.

You will also need to get to know your main character. While you may not wish to reveal everything to your readers, this person should be so clear in your mind that you understand not only what he or she might think or do in a particular situation but also how others are likely to react to that person's looks, actions, and personality.

Although your sketch will not include a plot summary, you will need to suggest the struggle experienced by the character. This conflict can be inner turmoil about an issue, external discord with other people, or a combination of the two. In her search for her own identity as well as the identity of her surroundings, the woman in "The Signature" confronts her deepest feelings as she contends with forces beyond her control.

Once you have a workable idea, it's time to generate the details that will bring your sketch to life. For example, what does your main character look like? Although Elizabeth Enright expends most of her effort on revealing her character's reactions, notice how she weaves in a few important physical details.

I looked at my hands: they were the hands of a middle-aged woman, coarsening at the joints, faintly blotched. On the third finger of the left hand there was a golden wedding ring, but who had put it there I could not guess.

This description of the woman's hands intensifies the mystery and helps reveal the character's struggle to define herself.

Now think about the setting in which your character will operate. What does the setting look like? What sensory details will create vivid images for my readers? When does the action take place? Is the specific year or season important to the conflict? Cluster, brainstorm, or freewrite to collect as many concrete details as you can. Try making a sensory-details chart in which you categorize your details by sight, sound, smell, taste, touch, and hearing. Lessons 3.1 and 3.2 can help you find and refine your details.

Finally, you need to make some decisions about point of view, which determines what your readers will know and how they will find it out. If you use a first-person narrator and the personal pronoun *I*, as Elizabeth Enright does, you can establish a sense of immediacy and intimacy. With third-person point of view, you refer to the main character by name and by *he* or *she*, and essentially provide an invisible observer. Depending on the effects you wish to achieve, the third-person narrator can be close to the main character, witnessing the action through his or her eyes and privileged to that character's thoughts and feelings, or the narrator can be an objective and distant relater of events. Lesson 3.5 can help you find a suitable point of view.

2. Drafting

As you draft the opening of your sketch, give your readers enough information to pull them immediately into the situation. You can present the main character engaged in an action that establishes the conflict, you can create atmosphere by describing the setting, or you can use engaging dialogue to reveal the situation.

Remember, for this sketch you will be concentrating primarily on description to reveal character, conflict, and setting. Consider carefully the order in which you will present your descriptive details. Whether you use order of impression, order of importance, spatial order, or some combination of these three methods, be sure that your approach is well suited to your purpose and to your audience. Reread the material about organization in Lesson 3.1, and revisit the literature selection to see how Enright leads her audience on a trip through the unknown city on the unknown planet. Notice that in addition to using spatial order and order of impression, Enright also makes us aware of the passage of time.

Although drafting should be a fluid process in which you get ideas down on paper without pausing to polish, this is also a good time to think about choosing vivid details and using evocative comparisons to bring the setting and character to life. Lessons 3.2 and 3.3 suggest strategies to help you sharpen your focus. Simile, metaphor, personification, and analogy can create eloquent mental images, as when Enright describes the chattering, skipping, squabbling voices of children that are like the voices of sparrows.

Finally, draft a conclusion that leaves your readers wanting more. Unlike a complete narrative that must have its loose ends tied up, your sketch might end with a provocative question, a suggestive interpretation, a detail that stimulates the imagination, or a cliffhanger that leaves the reader wondering what will happen next.

3. Revising

Revising, which literally means "re-seeing," gives you the chance to take a fresh look at your ideas and details, their relationships and arrangement, and the degree to which they work or don't work together. Use the strategies in Lessons 2.7, 2.8, and 2.9 or the questions below to help you evaluate what you've written.

First look at content:

- Does the sketch fulfill my purpose? Have I established clear portraits of setting, mood, character, and conflict?
- Are my details concrete and vivid? Do they support the central impression I want to create? Have I evoked all five senses?
- Is my use of simile, metaphor, personification, or analogy fresh and striking? Have I overwhelmed my readers with too many comparisons? Is the sketch clear and straightforward, or is it confusing?

Now look at structure:

- Are my introductory paragraph and my concluding paragraph effective? Do these paragraphs convey my purpose for writing and arouse my readers' curiosity and interest?
- Have I chosen an effective point of view and used it consistently? Would I achieve a more powerful description by changing the point of view of the narrator?
- Does my method of organization support and enhance my purpose for writing the sketch?

4. Editing

Even a graphic and imaginative sketch will lose its impact if it's littered with incorrect grammar and usage, misleading punctuation, or misspelled words. Take the extra time and energy necessary to polish your writing. The strategies in Lesson 2.10 will help you to polish your work until it glows. You may also wish to enlist the aid of a classmate to act as a peer editor.

5. Presenting

If you think your sketch is good television-movie material, collect the names of some producers that appear in the credits at the end of shows. Write a letter to accompany your description, explaining why you believe you have a fresh, dramatic approach that will appeal to the public.

If you're not quite certain you're ready for prime time, test the audience appeal of your sketch by submitting it to the school literary magazine, using it as the basis for a short story, or turning it into a screenplay that you and several classmates work together to videotape.

Criteria

1. Uses description to create mood, reveal character, and suggest conflict
2. Employs concrete and vivid language to evoke the five senses
3. Uses simile, metaphor, personification, or analogy to enhance description
4. Employs a method of organization appropriate to the purpose
5. Uses unity and coherence to create a clear impression
6. Follows the standards of grammar, usage, and mechanics

• Reflecting •

Now that you've exercised a variety of your descriptive muscles, so to speak, think about how successful you were with each of the purposes of descriptive writing outlined in the assignment: sketching the personality of a character, creating mood through setting, and establishing or revealing conflict. Which type of description came most naturally to you? Which provided the greatest challenge?

Shift gears for a moment, and think about which descriptive techniques you use successfully in your everyday conversation: How do you use description when you tell what the new student teacher is like, relate an anecdote, persuade a friend to give you a ride home, or give directions to your house? Can you see any overlap between your descriptive writing skills and your descriptive conversational skills? How can you use the techniques of each to enhance the other?

Portfolio & Reflection

Summary

Key concepts in descriptive writing include the following:

- Descriptive details can be organized by spatial order, order of importance, or order of impression.
- Direct observation is a primary means of collecting sensory details.
- Mood is the emotional quality or atmosphere of a description.
- A character sketch conveys a strong impression of a person through details about appearance and personality characteristics.
- In describing an event, a writer must maintain a consistent vantage point and arrange details by space, time, or importance.

Your Writer's Portfolio

Look over the descriptive writing you have done during this unit. Select two pieces of writing to put into your portfolio. Each piece should demonstrate that you have worked with one or more of the preceding concepts. In other words, look for a piece of writing that does one or more of the following:

- organizes vivid description by spatial order, order of importance, or order of impression
- results from direct observation as the primary means of collecting sensory details
- employs concrete nouns, precise adjectives, and active verbs to create mood
- conveys a strong impression of a person through details about appearance and personality characteristics
- uses a consistent vantage point and arranges details by space, time, or importance

Reflection and Commentary

Write one page that demonstrates that you understand what this unit asked of you. Use your two selected pieces of writing as evidence while you consider the following numbered items. Respond to as many items as possible.

Label the page "Commentary on Descriptive Writing," and include it in your portfolio.

1. Where did you use spatial order, order of importance, or order of impression to create a single dominant impression?
2. What sensory details did you collect through direct observation?
3. List the concrete nouns, precise adjectives, and active verbs you used to create mood in a description.
4. What details of physical appearance and personality characteristics did you use to create a strong impression of a person?
5. What vantage point did you maintain in describing an event? Did you arrange details by space, time, or order of importance?

Feedback

If you had a chance to respond to the following student comment, what would you say or ask?

The hardest thing is to paint the picture in your mind on the paper. I just try to be as detailed as I can to get the picture across.

Rick Greaver, Quartz Hill High School,
Lancaster, California

Narrative Writing

Eyewitness to History

George Catlin, *Catlin Painting
the Portrait of Mah-to-toh-pa-Mandan,* 1857/69

MORE THAN A Baseball Story

"Everybody likes a story. It gives a much greater impact to the subject matter. And in terms of retention, narrative writing is much more effective than any other kind of history writing I've seen."

Samuel Regalado, professor of history,
California State University, Stanislaus

Professor Sam Regalado grew up in a Mexican American family that took baseball seriously. In the 1950s, before Regalado can remember, his uncle Rudy played with the Cleveland Indians; he would be a valuable source of contacts during Regalado's later research into baseball history. The Regalados often traveled from their home in Los Angeles to the barrio league games that were popular in the Southwest following World War II. In border towns in and near Mexico, the family watched and participated in the Sunday afternoon games. "I had cousins in Texas I might not have otherwise seen if not for those baseball trips," Regalado recalls.

As a graduate student in history at Washington State University in Pullman, Washington, Regalado presented a paper on barrio baseball to a sports history conference. One of his listeners was the editor of *Baseball History*. He invited Regalado to submit his paper for publication in the magazine.

Writing About History

1. Talking to Sources   2. Planning and Writing   3. Soliciting Criticism

FOCUS

Narrative writing is especially well suited to history, which contains all the elements of good storytelling.

The paper that so impressed the editor was written as a narrative. "To reach an audience you have to do more than just state facts," says Regalado. "Narrative writing allows you to build a scenario based on the data you've uncovered. In this way you set the stage for a complete understanding of what you're discussing."

To tell his story, Regalado used elements of narrative writing such as setting and character. Although many characters appeared in the paper, Regalado began and ended his story with Manuel "Shorty" Perez. Telling the story through a person "adds a human element that makes the writing more effective," says the historian. "I never knew Shorty, but my piece was based on stories from those who did know him."

Regalado set his story in "rocky, uneven baseball diamonds, with gopher holes dotting the outfield." Instead of electric organs playing "Take Me Out to the Ballgame," barrio baseball featured mariachi bands performing Mexican music. "It's important to place your reader in the world of your topic. We're not just talking about baseball here. People should come away from the article with an appreciation not only for the game, but for what it's like to be involved in Hispanic society."

INTERFACE *If you were going to write a narrative history of your school, what "character" might you choose to feature?*

Regalado charts the history of barrio baseball through one player, Manuel "Shorty" Perez (above, second from left).

1. Talking to Sources

Regalado prepared to write his paper by immersing himself in the topic. "I read a variety of secondary materials—materials written after the fact, such as general texts and biographies," he says.

After surveying these secondary sources, Regalado gathered primary sources. "These are oral histories or contemporary sources such as newspaper articles written without the benefit of hindsight. Primary sources, such as interviews with people who were there at the time, add a lot of color to what you're writing about."

Regalado had to do a certain amount of "detective work" in researching the story of the heroes of barrio base-

ball. "I focused my attention on Los Angeles," the author recalls. "I went to university libraries to find out who carried small local newspapers. As I began to look at that time period, certain names kept appearing. I looked up these people, or their relatives if they'd passed away. Often they had scrapbooks or referred me to other people who knew them."

Regalado used a tape recorder to interview his subjects. He explains, "If you listen to people's inflections very carefully, it brings a human element into your writing."

INTERFACE *If you were interviewing someone for a historical narrative, why might you take notes in addition to or instead of taping the interview?*

Below, some of the sources for Regalado's work: clippings from the sports pages of newspapers throughout the Southwest, as well as old photographs and other documents. The uppermost photo shows a mariachi band playing at a barrio-league game. Below it is a team photo of the renowned Forty-Sixty team, whose name represents the age range of the players.

NORTHEAST SPORTS

Tiger Cage Classic minitourney this weekend

Regalado at his campus office: Like many writers, he prefers to write his first draft by hand before transferring it to his computer for revising.

2. Planning and Writing

Regalado's narrative began with a rough outline. He continually revised as he conducted his research.

"I always bring my outline to each interview," the author points out. "While I'm interviewing somebody, I'm thinking in terms not only of what the person is saying, but also where I am going in my outline. And after I transcribe my interviews, I begin to fuse them into my outline. Pretty soon, I can look at my outline and say, 'OK, this person's interview would be great at this point.'"

Like many writers, Regalado prefers to begin writing with just pencil and paper. "For many years I've been a proponent of writing longhand." But when he's ready to revise and edit, Regalado works on a computer.

"I realize a lot of people don't have access to computers," the historian notes. "But they make such a big difference in terms of easing the editing process and introducing new ideas."

great quote – use it!

3. Soliciting Criticism

After writing his paper, Regalado asked his professors and fellow graduate students to critique his writing. He found their comments "invaluable—exceedingly important," and he followed many of their suggestions. "Of course, it's up to you to decide whether or not these warrant attention," he notes. "Ultimately, you're the writer; you're the one who knows what you are trying to say."

Regalado's paper eventually appeared in *Baseball History* under the title "Baseball in the Barrios." His editors requested only minor revisions before publishing the article, but one editor did suggest that Regalado do further research to draw parallels to other ethnic cultures. "It was a great suggestion," he recalls. "It enhanced my understanding of varied societies within the framework of American history."

Today, as a professor himself, Regalado still asks colleagues for constructive criticism of his writing. He says, "I think that everyone's writing can always use improvement. I'm still learning, and I suspect I probably will for a number of years."

seball in the Barrios:
in East Los Angeles
Since World War II

SAMUEL REGALADO

unday in 1954 or maybe even 1955. It did not
most Sundays were just about the same for
ez. He and his wife usually awoke early for an
d then drove back to their home situated in the
can quarter in East Los Angeles—better known
er a large breakfast, consisting of eggs, chorizo,
slipped into a pair of worn-out baseball knickers
jersey decorated with a sponsor's name writter
ith the help of his son, he loaded up the car wi
quipment, which might contain one very pri
and headed off in the direction of some recre
onfines of the neighborhood.[2]
Shorty's neighborhood were primitive a
onds, with gopher holes dotting the outfiel
t damage it too badly playing soccer the d
ky his team might have been scheduled
n linked batting cage, but, of course,
go" section of town. Shorty would
wever, to find that the scheduled fie
ess for a backstop. It did not both
d conditions seemed to characteriz
untered during the past decade wh
e 50,000 Mexicans entered the
on Mexican Americans alread
e "American dream."[3] While

ISSN 0884-9501

BASEBALL HISTORY

SUMMER 1986/$6.00

ON ASSIGNMENT

1. Choose an event in sports history that you can research through secondary and primary sources: for example, the Olympics, a World Series, or some local event. After you have studied your topic and narrowed your focus by reading secondary sources, gather primary sources such as newspaper and first-person accounts. If possible, interview someone who can give you his or her own personal story.

    Write a brief historical narrative that weaves together the elements you've researched. Include a vivid setting and at least one memorable character.

2. **Literature Connection** Much sports writing is exposition rather than narration. Look in sports magazines, in the sports sections of newspapers, or in reference books to find an article that you can rewrite as a short narrative. Make sure the article you find has information such as characters and setting that are essential to good storytelling. If you cannot find one article containing these elements, use information from two or three sources. Do not try to relate all the information contained in the article, but select details that add to your story.

3. **Cooperative Learning** Work in groups of four or five to produce a book of sports history. Decide whether you want to focus on your school's history, on college sports, or on professional sports lore. Brainstorm possible topics.

    If your focus is your own school, choose members to interview coaches, players, and alumni about their experiences. If your topic is college or pro sports, you may want to narrow your focus to the story of a particular league, team, or player.

    Choose one or two students to find information on the topics, two students to write short narratives on at least two aspects of your topic, and two more members to find accompanying artwork and to present the narratives in an attractive book.

Real-life "Characters"

When Russell Baker spins a story, he doesn't invent his characters; he observes them. His stories are the real-life narratives of history. A journalist and author of the column "The Observer," Baker tells fascinating tales about political figures he has met in his broad travels. One of Baker's colorful characters, the crime-fighting Tennessee senator Estes Kefauver, comes to life in the narrative below. The story takes place on the campaign trail, during Kefauver's bid for the 1956 Democratic presidential nomination.

Literature Model

He was a big, long, thick log of a man who moved in a dreamy, stiff-jointed walk as though he had no knee joints. His public manner was gentle, folksy, down-home. Getting out of his chartered Greyhound at a central Florida prayer meeting, he stood at the front step, rigid as a cigar-store Indian, and let the people come to him to shake that famous hand, and murmured a little something to each.

"Ah'm Estes Kefauver and Ah'm runnin' for president. Will you he'p me? . . ."

To test my theory that he was punch-drunk with fatigue and so groggy he was running on pure reflex, I got in the handshaking line one day to test his reactions. I had been on the Greyhound with him for three or four days. Earlier that day I had been one of four people who chatted with him over lunch at a Cuban restaurant in Tampa. I thought he might crack wise when he found me waiting for my handshake, but there wasn't a flicker of recognition in those eyes when I laid my hand in his paw and said, "An honor to shake your hand, Senator."

Looking through me at something five thousand miles away, he said, "I hope you're going to he'p me," then dropped my hand and reached for the next one.

Russell Baker, *The Good Times*

Baker brings Kefauver to life with imagery: "big, long, thick log of a man" instead of "tall and solidly built."

Why does Baker use the word "paw" here? What does it tell us about Kefauver?

What does Kefauver's mechanical response indicate?

Portraying Real-Life Characters

Adventure, mystery, humor, heroism—history can be every bit as compelling as a good movie or novel. A fictional narrative is a story from a writer's imagination; it contains events, or plot, and it involves characters. The story is set in a specific place and time, or setting, and told from a particular point of view. Nonfiction narratives, such as history and biographies, are about events that really happened, but they also contain plot, characters, setting, and point of view, and can be just as full of action and human interest as fiction.

Real-life characters are at the heart of any historical narrative. They are the people who make history; their actions arise out of their personalities and circumstances, and these actions drive the plot. How you portray these characters can make the difference between a narrative that reads like an encyclopedia and one that is lively and entertaining. When you're writing about real life, you'll want to display these characters vividly for your readers.

Baker uses several strategies to reveal the character of Estes Kefauver. Each method aids Baker's twin purpose: to show Kefauver's "folksy, down-home manner" and to suggest his grogginess and fatigue. The chart below gives you a menu of strategies you can use for developing characters in a narrative.

Prewriting Tip

Use the observation techniques on pages 134–135 to collect details about characters. Then use only those details that will have the most impact.

Strategies for Revealing Character	
Physical Description	"He was a big, long, thick log of a man who moved in a dreamy, stiff-jointed walk."
Character's Own Thoughts or Words	"'Ah'm Estes Kefauver and Ah'm runnin' for president. Will you he'p me?'"
Character's Actions	Anecdote about Kefauver not recognizing Baker after having had lunch with him.
Writer's Opinion	"He was punch-drunk with fatigue and so groggy he was running on pure reflex."

• JOURNAL ACTIVITY •
Think It Through

Sometimes physical description alone can reveal a great deal about a character. In your journal, list as many elements of physical description as you can, such as clothes, hairstyle, walking, tone of voice, way of dressing, even scent. How could you use each of these physical characteristics to reveal something about a character's personality?

Using Vivid Description

When you describe someone, you can give a general statement: "Bob is soft-hearted and impractical." Or you can demonstrate that person's nature through specific observations: "Bob can't pass a musician on the street without giving away all his change, and so he never has a quarter for the telephone." A description that shows what a character is like can have more impact than one that merely tells you what to think. Consider this description of a famous writer.

Literature Model

When Louis Auchincloss chooses to be stiff and formal—which is rare—he can be imposing. He is 61 years old, looks 15 years younger, is six feet tall, weighs a trim 170 pounds, has deep-set dark brown eyes and the sort of patrician nose one associates with, say, the American eagle. There is, in fact, something quite birdlike about the way Louis can turn to look at someone. His head swivels leisurely, magisterially, as if his neck were scarved in rich plumage; his eyelids lower slowly, then rise, providing pause enough for feathers to settle, and when he speaks he *pronounces*.

C. D. B. Bryan, "Under the Auchincloss Shell"

Vivid language shows rather than tells: "turns" has become "swivels."

Bryan could have simply ended the Auchincloss description at the word "eagle." But that would only have told you how Auchincloss looks. In the extended comparison, the writer shows you Auchincloss as he turns to look at someone. Auchincloss actually becomes an eagle in this passage.

Showing and telling can work well in combination. Notice how the Auchincloss description uses both.

Ways of Revealing Character	
Telling	**Showing**
"stiff and formal"	"nose [like] the American eagle"
"imposing"	"head swivels leisurely, magisterially"
"birdlike"	"neck … scarved in rich plumage" "eyelids lower slowly, then rise, providing pause enough for feathers to settle"

Using Dialogue

Talk, talk, talk. That's how we get to know people. We exchange ideas; we notice people's gestures and their ways of speaking. We try to figure out whether what they're saying is what they're really thinking. Using conversation, or dialogue, is a good way to bring characters to life. Dialogue lets readers form opinions about characters as they "listen in."

In the model below, Jennifer Beyersdorf introduces the main character of her narrative through dialogue. As the narrator tries to match her Uncle Larry's enthusiasm for his stodgy new car, you almost feel as though you are overhearing a real conversation.

Editing Tip

When you quote from an actual conversation, you may not want to include everything that was said. Use ellipses to indicate the omissions you make. See page 664 on use of ellipses points.

Student Model

"It's great Uncle Larry, really—great." (Is he serious?)
"Thanks, Jen. It's pretty weird for me, you know. I've never even had a car with a backseat; now I've got room for seven plus a luggage rack. We'll be thankful for the room, though, once the baby arrives."

"Yeah, I guess you're right." (He's serious.) I scan the minivan's fake wood trim as Uncle Larry rubs the last of the Turtle Wax onto the fender. "So what are you gonna do with your RX-7?" I ask, casually. "I'll be sixteen next month, you know. I'd really hate to see that car leave the family."

"Nice try, Jen, but your dad would kill me. Besides, I think you should get something bigger for your first car—maybe drive Grandpa's old Granada for a while."

I laugh; Uncle Larry doesn't. "You're serious?"

"Yeah, why not? It's big and safe, and it won't let you go too fast, just what you need."

Jennifer Beyersdorf, Northville High School, Northville, Michigan

Notice the beginning of a second, internal dialogue, the narrator's thoughts.

What does the writer reveal by using the word "casually" here?

Take a moment to consider what this dialogue has revealed about Uncle Larry. You know he's expecting a baby; you see that he is staid and practical. The writer could have told you these things; instead, she lets you find them out through the dialogue.

• JOURNAL ACTIVITY •
Try It Out

What if Uncle Larry were the opposite of staid and practical? Rewrite the dialogue accordingly. You may have to modify the narrator's words to make the dialogue realistic.

Rounding Out Your Characters

A person's actions can reveal a great deal, and so can the opinions of observers. In the remainder of the "Uncle Larry" narrative that began on the previous page, Jennifer weaves anecdotes from the past with observations of the present into a character study of her uncle.

Student Model

The narrator is also a character. What does her opinion of Uncle Larry tell us about her?

I sigh and study my uncle's face. He doesn't look any older, but he surely is acting weird. In fact, ever since he married Aunt Kimberly I've noticed a change in his personality: a gradual loss of coolness accompanied by a rapid increase in nerdiness. In fact, lately he's reminded me of Dad.

Before he got married, Uncle Larry used to pick me up from school in his red Mazda. We'd cruise the San Diego Freeway to Grandma and Grandpa's; he always used to blast rock music out the window. Then he'd put the top down and give me an extra pair of sunglasses—"We're cool, Jen, we're cool."

What does this anecdote tell us about the "old" Uncle Larry?

And sometimes we'd walk to Turmaline Hill, the best surfing park in Pacific Beach. Uncle Larry knew everyone's name down there. He "knew how to surf before he knew how to walk" is what he told everyone. Since he hurt his knees skiing last year, he hasn't gone down as much, but I still ask him to take me. I know how he loves the ocean.

We'd sit on the red clay rocks overlooking the beach and watch his wetsuited friends for hours. Once, Grandma came looking to tell us we'd missed dinner. So we went to Jack-In-The-Box for 39-cent tacos. We tried skipping family meals about four or five times after that, but Grandma caught on.

The narrator rounds out her character description with other people's opinions of her Uncle Larry.

As I look at him now, waxing his minivan with suburban glee, I wonder what could've happened. Marriage I guess. Grandma's thrilled that "Larry's finally taking responsibility for his life." And Mom and Dad say Aunt Kimberly's really made him grow up. All I know is that I haven't been to Turmaline Hill since the wedding.

Uncle Larry stands up and examines his project. "Looks mighty nice, huh Jen? Finished just in time for dinner."

The writer returns to dialogue to reveal both characters and their current relationship.

"Yup—wouldn't want to be late," I mumble, but he's already turned and doesn't hear me. I pick up the spilled can of Turtle Wax and carefully screw on the lid.

"Hurry up, Jen," he calls back. "After dinner we'll ride out to Turmaline Hill and watch the surfers."

But somehow I know it won't be the same.

The following are some writing options to help you try out what you have learned.

1. Guided Assignment Imagine that the painting on this page is an illustration for a narrative about a real person who survived (or perhaps did not survive) a tornado. You are a reporter assigned to write the narrative to accompany the picture.

Focusing on one person as your main character, freewrite about the picture. What has happened, is happening, and will happen? What might your character be saying? What are the important details of physical description? What do the details reveal about your character?

Select ideas from your freewriting to write a narrative about what happened to your character. Use at least two of the strategies listed on page 167. When you revise your story, ask yourself: Have I used the best details from my freewriting? Do I show as well as tell about my character? Ask a classmate to read your story and judge whether your character seems real.

PURPOSE   To write an illustrated human-interest story for a local magazine

AUDIENCE   Local community

LENGTH   1–2 pages

2. Open Assignment Imagine that a famous person has come to your school to give a talk—a sports star, an actor or musician, a political leader, or any celebrity you know something about. You have promised to write a letter describing that person's visit to one of the following:

- a classmate who was at home sick
- a relative who lives in another country
- a grandparent

Using physical description and at least one other strategy from the chart on page 167, write several paragraphs about this celebrity's visit to your school. Remember that your description will be different for different audiences.

3. Cooperative Learning A TV network news program has introduced an award called "Person-of-the-Week: The High School Choice." This week they have asked your school to choose someone to be the national person-of-the-week and to support the choice with a narrative that shows the person's character.

Meet in a small group to choose someone in the news you would like to be person-of-the-week. Then assign each member a different source for information on your choice: a newspaper account, a magazine profile, an appearance on an evening news broadcast, an article your subject has written, or a speech he or she has given. Meet again to compare notes and discuss the most striking details of physical description, actions, and so on. Using your combined information, write individual narratives about your subject.

John Steuart Curry, *Tornado Over Kansas*, 1929

Writing a Biographical Sketch

Split Personalities

As a gift to visitors who won her favor, Queen Elizabeth I of Britain used to hand out miniature portraits of herself. They depicted Elizabeth as she wanted to be remembered: regal, formal, and bejeweled. But official court paintings do not tell the whole story. On this page, you have three "portraits" of the queen: two in paint and one in words. At first glance, they seem contradictory. Yet each shows a real side of "Good Queen Bess."

Nicholas Hillard, *Queen Elizabeth I*, c. 1600

What does this anecdote reveal about the queen's personality?

What purpose does this unflattering portrait serve in the narrative?

Literature Model

Allegorical portrait of Queen Elizabeth I, English School, c. 1600

Bare-headed and wearing a breastplate, she rode along the lines of men escorted only by the Earl of Leicester, the Earl of Ormonde bearing the sword of state, and a page who carried her white-plumed helmet. She had dismissed her bodyguard for, as she was presently to say, she did not desire to live to distrust her faithful and loving people. Such fear was for tyrants. . . .

Her dazzled and adoring amateur army did not see a thin, middle-aged woman with bad teeth and wearing a bright red wig perched on the back of an enormous white gelding. Instead they saw the personification of every goddess of classical mythology they had ever heard about, every heroine of their favorite reading, the Bible. They saw Judith and Deborah, Diana the Huntress and the Queen of the Amazons all rolled into one. But they also saw their own beloved and familiar queen.

Alison Plowden, *Elizabeth Regina*

Imagine you want to write a biographical sketch of Queen Elizabeth. You can't address every aspect of her life. You'll have to make choices, just as the artists who painted the pictures above chose certain ways to depict her. This lesson will show you ways to make those choices.

Narrowing Your Subject

Before you can write even a short essay, you need to know a great deal. A good way to begin a biographical sketch is by reading about your subject. You might use an encyclopedia or general biographical reference, such as *Current Biography, Contemporary Authors, Men and Women of Science,* or *Dictionary of American Biography.*

Next, ask yourself questions that will help you narrow the focus of your biographical sketch. Do you want to cover Elizabeth's whole life? Should you focus on her personality? Her historical significance? Her main claims to fame or interesting sidelights?

To answer these questions, try freewriting or completing a cluster diagram that explores the topics further.

Prewriting Tip

As you research, write notes on index cards. Be sure to record the source on each card.

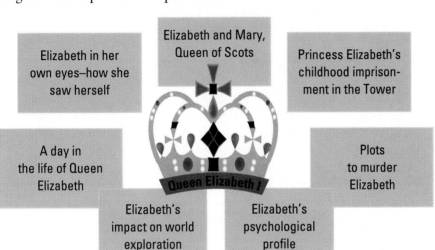

Elizabeth and Mary, Queen of Scots

Elizabeth in her own eyes–how she saw herself

Princess Elizabeth's childhood imprisonment in the Tower

A day in the life of Queen Elizabeth

Queen Elizabeth I

Plots to murder Elizabeth

Elizabeth's impact on world exploration

Elizabeth's psychological profile

Choose a topic to focus on, such as Elizabeth's childhood. Now you need an "angle." As you continue to read, think about what aspect of Elizabeth's character you want to reveal: Harsh, clever politician? Vulnerable child? Unforgiving relative? Visionary? You will find that you need to examine different sources for each angle. For example, a sketch on Queen Elizabeth as vulnerable child imprisoned in the Tower of London would require information from an autobiography, childhood diary, or biography. To learn different ways of organizing your information into an essay, see pages 76–79.

• JOURNAL ACTIVITY •
Think It Through

The diagram above can be adapted for other historical figures, contemporary sports stars, or someone you know. Construct such a diagram for a subject of your choice. Where might you find information on each of your topics?

Keeping and Discarding

Many writers are packrats. Once they've found a fact, they simply can't throw it away. When you have narrowed the focus of your story, be ruthless about discarding unnecessary information. Ask yourself these questions about each incident and detail you could use: Does it show the side of my character I have chosen to reveal? Is it striking? Will it capture my audience's imagination? If you are having trouble answering these questions, you probably haven't fully clarified the focus of your story.

In the model below, the author chose to depict a side of his subject not often seen. He presents a young Richard Nixon in love with his future wife, Pat. His is a giddy, puppy love, undaunted by Pat's repeated rejections. Notice how the writer carefully selects just the right details to shed light on the personality of young Nixon. Nothing is extraneous.

Literature Model

Morris chooses an incident from Nixon's young, schoolboy days to reveal an unknown side of Nixon's character.

Pat's comment makes Nixon more vulnerable and human than most readers would expect.

How does the friend's observation make us feel toward Nixon? How is this detail consistent with the other details Morris presents?

Is this last bit of information surprising? What does it reveal about the older Nixon that we might not have known?

That spring of 1938 Nixon asked [Pat] repeatedly for dates. Turned down always on weekends and often during the week, he began showing up at her rooms unannounced in the evening to take her on drives or walks through the hillside blocks around the college. Pat thought him "a bit unusual," as she told a friend soon after their meeting, and continued to put him off. When she tactfully excused her own indifference by remarking lightly that she was a vagabond or gypsy, Nixon wrote her affectionate little notes addressed to "Miss Vagabond" or "My Irish Gypsy." When she pointedly arranged a date for him with her roommate, he agreed readily to go, and through the evening talked only about Pat. "He chased her but she was a little rat," said one of her friends who watched it unfold. The notes were soon interspersed with his own romantic poetry, verse she later described as having a "mysteriously wild beauty." Within weeks of their meeting, he even composed a song for her. It was one of the two compositions, along with "Rustle of Spring," . . . that he still knew by heart more than thirty years later—and picked out on the White House grand piano the night he moved in.

Roger Morris, *Richard Milhous Nixon*

Morris could have mentioned Nixon's intense political aspirations or given evidence of Nixon's drive for success, but he does not. He focuses only on Nixon's boyish romanticism. When you write a portrait, try to choose the right details and let them speak for themselves.

Writer's Choice

The following are some writing options to help you try out what you have learned.

1. **Guided Assignment** Hal Holbrook has just hired you as his research assistant. Holbrook, who brought Mark Twain alive in his famous one-man show, *Mark Twain Tonight*, wants you to help him create a new Mark Twain special. Read and take notes on an encyclopedia article about Mark Twain. Next, narrow your topic to one aspect of his life such as his frontier boyhood, his adventures as a riverman, or as a prospector. What side of Mark Twain should Holbrook present? You may have to go back to the library to get more information on your topic from a biography or personal writings.

Look over your notes and choose details that you think will help Holbrook bring this aspect of Mark Twain to life on stage. Before you write your sketch, write an informal outline showing how you would weave the material together. See pages 76–79 for instructions on organizing and outlining. Write your narrative sketch. When you revise, ask yourself: Are all the details relevant? Will the incidents I've described hold an audience's attention?

PURPOSE   To describe an aspect of Mark Twain's life in a biographical sketch
AUDIENCE   Famous character actor
LENGTH   2–3 pages

2. **Open Assignment** You are a teen-ager in another time. To inspire you to work harder at your studies, your tutor has told you to write a sketch about someone your age who has an unusual hobby or a special talent.

Luckily for you, you just happen to live next door to an unusual young person named Leonardo da Vinci or Wolfgang Amadeus Mozart or Charlotte Brontë or Marie Sklodowska (one day to be Marie Curie) or someone equally interesting. Find out about that person's childhood and youth, his or her experiences, activities, and personality. Then write a two-page essay telling the story of your neighbor's early life.

COMPUTER OPTION

As you take notes, you can create note cards on your computer. Type the information with a boldface heading. Then box it so it looks like a note card. Organize your notes just as they would appear if they were actually on cards. Some software programs, such as HyperCard, are made for this purpose. As you write your sketch, you can copy information from your note cards directly into your draft.

3. **Cooperative Learning** You and a group of students are on the editorial board of your high school literary magazine, and you have decided to call the next issue "Family History." To start, you will write a collection of biographical sketches of people in your own families. As a group, discuss the angle you would like to have for these portraits: Do you want to take long views of their lives or short views of significant events? Do you want to focus on actions they took that influenced you strongly? Have one student make up a list of basic questions to ask family members. Review the questions as a group, and have another student make up a questionnaire.

Using the completed questionnaire from a family member, each student will write a short narrative with the agreed-upon focus, and make copies so that everyone in the group can read all the sketches. Then discuss the portraits as a group: Do they share the same angle? What order would be most effective for presenting? Assign one member to write an introduction to the collection on a computer, another to proofread, and another to design a cover.

Structuring the Long Narrative

Charting the River of Life

Some events are emblazoned in our memories. We never forget those huge occurrences, happy and tragic—a move to a new town, a new school, a first love, an award, the loss of a friend—that launch us on a new course in our lives.

Former slave Sojourner Truth led a life that took many unexpected turns as she became a crusader in the antislavery and women's movements. Here is one such turning point.

> **Literature Model**
>
> A lone, for none of the others would face the mob of young men, Sojourner walked to the top of a small hill on the meeting ground and began to sing. Her deep, melodious voice carried far, and the troublemakers turned and ran toward her as if to pull her down and silence her. As they approached, she stopped singing and asked them: "Why do you come about me with clubs and sticks? I am not doing any harm to any one." Disarmed by her tranquillity, they answered that they would not hurt her: "We came to hear you sing. Sing to us, old woman. Talk to us, old woman. Tell us your experience."
>
> Surrounded by the roughnecks, Sojourner spoke to them and answered their questions. She even made them laugh. And they evidently enjoyed her singing, for they threatened bodily harm to anyone who might interrupt her. Finally she stopped and said to them: "Children, I have talked and sung to you, as you asked me; and now I have a request to make of you: Will you grant it?" They assured her of their good will, and she asked them to leave in peace after she sang just one more song. True to their word, the men dispersed after hearing her sing, silently and without further trouble.
>
> This experience marked an important stage in Sojourner's life, demonstrating the character traits that would carry her triumphantly through hostile confrontations in future years.
>
> Victoria Ortiz, *Sojourner Truth: A Self-Made Woman*

What words and phrases does the writer use in the first paragraph to show us that this is a perilous moment in her subject's life?

Notice Sojourner Truth's diction: it is almost biblical and gives power to her speech.

What do the others learn about Sojourner Truth in this incident? What does she learn about herself?

The Big Picture

Sojourner Truth's life had many such turning points. One way to understand the overall direction of her life is to construct a time line. Time lines give you the big picture and help you see trends; they also allow you to focus on specific periods and put events into context. Start with the beginning and ending dates—birth and death; next, identify the major turning points. Then insert details and look at the big picture.

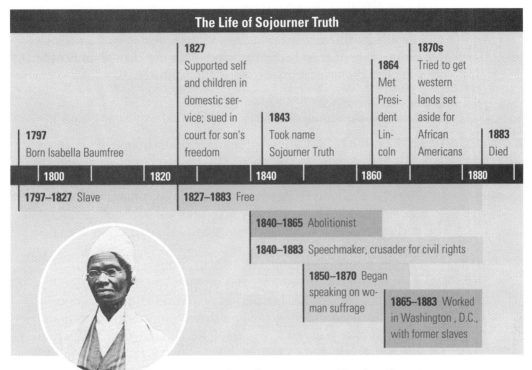

The Life of Sojourner Truth

1797 Born Isabella Baumfree

1827 Supported self and children in domestic service; sued in court for son's freedom

1843 Took name Sojourner Truth

1864 Met President Lincoln

1870s Tried to get western lands set aside for African Americans

1883 Died

1800 — 1820 — 1840 — 1860 — 1880

1797–1827 Slave

1827–1883 Free

1840–1865 Abolitionist

1840–1883 Speechmaker, crusader for civil rights

1850–1870 Began speaking on woman suffrage

1865–1883 Worked in Washington, D.C., with former slaves

The time line for Sojourner Truth tells not only what happened in her life, but it also gives you a sense of the forces driving her. Before you write a narrative, think about the big picture, or theme, and express it in a thesis statement. For instance, if you were writing about Sojourner Truth, you might say that she was a fighter from an early age. This theme will guide you as you give your narrative both unity and coherence.

Presenting Tip

Besides being a prewriting aid, a colorful and well-organized time line can be a thought-provoking illustration for a biographical narrative.

• JOURNAL ACTIVITY •
Try It Out

Develop a time line for the life of someone in your family. Block out the main chapters from birth to the present, and insert important events. Look for patterns in the time line, writing in your journal any insights you gain into forces that have driven your subject's life.

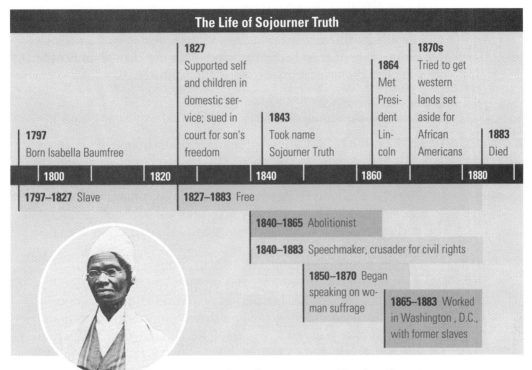

Shaping the Narrative

The themes you observe in a person's life will determine how you tell the story. Structure the body of your narrative chronologically, but don't include everything. Put in those events and details that best support your image of your subject; summarize or omit less relevant incidents. When you revise, look for repeated incidents or images to use as connecting threads throughout. Conclude with a particularly characteristic anecdote, image, or perhaps a personal reflection.

In the following excerpts from a narrative, the author uses her grandmother's different styles of dress to shape her story. Notice how Obachon's style of dress becomes a symbol for the changes in her life, showing her gradual acceptance of her new culture.

Literature Model

What is a "picture bride"? What do you imagine Obachon wore in the picture sent to her prospective husband?

What remnants of Japanese habit does Obachon maintain during this period of her life?

In the third chapter of her life, Obachon wore Western dresses. What other indications of her assimilation into Western culture does the narrator give?

The story comes full circle as Obachon's granddaughter wears the kimono Obachon wore as a girl.

She came to Hawaii as a "picture bride." In one of her rare self-reflecting moments, she told me in her broken English-Japanese that her mother had told her that the streets of Honolulu in Hawaii were paved with gold coins, and so encouraged her to go to Hawaii to marry a strange man she had never seen. . . . She grew silent after that, and her eyes had a faraway look.

She took her place, along with the other picture brides from Japan, beside her husband on the plantation cane-fields. . . . I remember her best in her working days, coming home from the canefields at "pauhana" time. She wore a pair of faded blue jeans and an equally faded navy-blue and white checked work shirt. A Japanese towel was wrapped carefully around her head, and a large straw "papale" or hat covered that. . . .

Having retired from the plantation, she now wore only dresses. She called them "makule-men doresu," Hawaiian for old person's dress. They were always gray or navy-blue with buttons down the front and a belt at the waistline. Her hair, which must once have been long and black like mine, was now streaked with grey and cut short and permanent-waved. . . .

She once surprised me by sending a beautiful "yukata" or summer kimono for me to wear to represent the Japanese in our school's annual May Day festival. . . . I have often wondered, whenever I look at that kimono, whether she had ever worn it when she was a young girl.

Gail Y. Miyasaki, "Obāchan"

Writer's Choice

The following are some writing options to help you try out what you have learned.

1. Guided Assignment You will assist a biographer in writing your life story for a book on unusual high school students. Using Sojourner Truth's time line on page 177 as a guide, create your own time line. Study the events to understand how and why they occurred. Decide which aspects you wish to emphasize, which time periods you can gloss over, and what background information to include. Then write a sketch of the major trends and shape of your life.

PURPOSE To assess your life story
AUDIENCE A biographer
LENGTH 1–2 pages, plus completed time line

COMPUTER OPTION

Would you like to produce a graphic version of the time line of your life? You can use a drawing software program to create your time line. If you want to print it on a laser printer, neighborhood print and copy shops may let you do so for a small fee.

2. Open Assignment A former teacher asks you to present the life story of a person to his or her class, which is studying biography. Select one of the following people or someone else, and research to create a time line of his or her life. You might use a general reference work, newspapers, interviews, or your memories.

- Barbara Jordan
- Squanto
- Sting
- Michael Jordan
- a grandparent

Use your time line to guide you in writing a two-page narrative.

3. Business Education Write a rags-to-riches narrative about a famous person in business who started with nothing and made it big. Take as your subject one of the following people:

- Lee Iacocca
- Ray Kroc
- Levi Strauss
- Steven Jobs
- Bill Gates
- Ben and Jerry

Find out as much as you can about your subject's life, career, and successful business. Sketch a time line of your subject's life, and use it to help draft your story.

4. Cooperative Learning You are part of a team of reporters for your school newspaper, and you are profiling a worker in your school. Assign each member one chapter of your subject's life: childhood, schooling, career, and so forth. Each member prepares questions on his or her topic. Then interview your subject, either in a "press conference" or one-on-one. Listen carefully, ask follow-up questions, and take good notes. A tape recorder can be helpful for recording events.

Sketch a time line showing the important events in your assigned time period. Then meet as a group and analyze the time lines, highlighting major events, transitions, and turning points. Look for a strong organizing principle or repeated image that will give unity to your profile. Does your subject love film? Turn his story into a movie review.

When you have agreed upon a theme, write a few paragraphs on your time period. Then choose one member of your group to compile the sections, two to revise, and a fourth to type up the profile. Submit the profile to your school paper.

But What Does It Mean?

If you were to take a poll asking students to name the most dreaded question on a literature exam, the number one response would probably be, "State the theme of. . . . " Many people expect to find a single, correct answer to this question hidden like buried treasure in an X-marked spot. Such answers do not exist. As a matter of fact, the richer the work, the less likely you are to come up with exactly the same gleaming nugget of meaning as your fellow hunters. Just look below at how a number of well-respected literary scholars express the theme of Herman Melville's novel *Moby-Dick*.

Moby-Dick is a book about man's attempt to understand and interpret his world.

Michael T. Gilmore, Introduction to *Twentieth Century Interpretations of* Moby-Dick

Moby-Dick. . . . Of course he is a symbol.
Of what?
I doubt if even Melville knew exactly. That's the best of it.

D. H. Lawrence,
Studies in Classical American Literature

Moby-Dick . . . is, fundamentally, a parable on the mystery of evil and the accidental malice of the universe.

Lewis Mumford, "Moby-Dick as Poetic Epic"

Which of these writers is correct? They all are—as long as they can support their ideas with evidence from the novel.

What Is Theme?

Theme is the controlling idea of a story or novel. A particularly rich and complex work may have several complementary themes, all reflecting the author's world view and insight into the human condition. The theme is seldom stated directly; consequently the treasure-hunt approach to finding it hardly ever works. Instead the theme permeates the entire work. The more familiar you are with the story or novel as a whole, the better your chances of determining its theme(s).

First Impressions After seeing a movie with friends, you probably say what you think about it. In some cases, however, you may be puzzled. Your conversation may begin with the question "What did you think of the characters?" and move to "The son: he's a mystery" and "How does the father feel about him?" or "But it wasn't her fault." You can take the same approach to stories you read. If you feel comfortable with a work after reading it, try freewriting to express your ideas immediately. If not, try writing a cluster diagram like the one on the right to help sort out your thoughts.

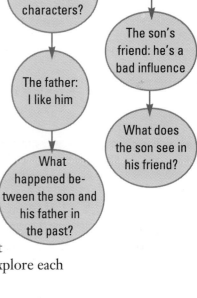

Gathering Evidence When you analyze a narrative to determine its theme, be sure to consider all the elements: not only character, but also setting, plot, and point of view. In a well-crafted work, all of these should reflect the theme. The questions below suggest some ways you can explore each narrative element to write about theme.

Determining Theme	
Setting	Is it hostile or friendly? What mood does it create?
Characters	Who are the most likeable characters? The least? Why? Who "wins" and who "loses"? Why?
Plot	What sort of actions lead to success? To failure? Do the characters instigate the action, or do things happen to them?
Point of View	Who tells the story? Can you trust the narrator's opinion? Does anyone seem to speak for the author?

Look at your answers and think about what rules govern the world of this narrative and how these rules could apply to ourselves or to a specific time and society. Perhaps these rules apply to human life in general. Try to express your understanding of the theme in a sentence or two.

• JOURNAL ACTIVITY •
Think It Through

Set up questions like those in the diagram above for a story or novel you've read recently. You may want to refine the headings in the left column as well as create new questions in the right column.

Drafting Tip

When you write your essay, you will probably state the theme in the opening paragraph. Make sure you have expressed the theme in a full sentence. Love is a subject; "Love conquers all" a theme.

Supporting Your Theme

Now treat your statement of theme as if it were a hypothesis. Can you prove it? In other words, can you support it with evidence from the story? Go back to your notes on plot, character, setting, and point of view. You might want to take another look at the narrative, too. Do your observations of the elements of the story support your theory?

In the model below, notice how the writer assembles evidence from setting, character, and plot to support the theme "things are not always what they seem."

Student Model

Notice how the writer develops her statement of the theme to make it apply to all of us.

Which narrative elements are introduced as evidence in this paragraph?

Why is it important that Mrs. Wang recognize the Japanese soldier's hunger?

Remember that a narrative can have more than one theme. What secondary theme does this analysis of Mrs. Wang's personality suggest?

Though provincial, Mrs. Wang has seen enough of the world to know that things are not always what they seem. In "The Old Demon," Pearl S. Buck reminds us that we must be like Mrs. Wang, open to new things, hesitating to judge until we have seen for ourselves. Perhaps then we can understand our enemies, and overcome our ignorant hatred.

The river, which Mrs. Wang first thought was her greatest threat, is actually "full of good and evil together." In the end, it is a weapon capable of saving her country. Similarly, Mrs. Wang learns that the Japanese are not "large, coarse foreigners," but young men, real people who can be hurt and loved. In fact, Mrs. Wang at first thinks the downed soldier is Chinese. When some Chinese soldiers come along and ask her why she is feeding a Japanese soldier, she replies, "I suppose he is hungry too."

Just as the river and the Japanese are not what they first seem to be, neither is Mrs. Wang the ignorant old fool she first appears to be. In the beginning, Mrs. Wang declares that she doesn't believe in the Japanese, that the war "was not real and no more than hearsay since none of the Wangs had been killed." She seems to be a lady rooted in her narrow beliefs, refusing to believe what she hasn't seen. Yet it is this very naïveté that makes her so wise. She does not carry hatred for people and things she does not know. In both her encounter with the soldier and the river, she shows her ability to change. Not only does this sort of attitude open her to new experiences, but ultimately it gives her the courage for her final sacrifice. She understands that the evil river can also contain good, and that she, in her old age, can still serve a vital purpose. She dies a wise, fulfilled woman.

Brenda Marshall, Newton North High School, Newton, Massachusetts

The following are some writing options to help you try out what you have learned.

1. Guided Assignment You have just started working for an editor of a publishing house, and you are asked to write the book jacket copy for a novel. You need to give a succinct statement of the novel's main idea, and at the same time introduce the key elements of the story in a way that will entice a reader to buy the book. Choose a novel that you've read recently or that made a strong impression on you. You may wish to reread the narrative before embarking on this assignment. Use a cluster and chart (see page 181) to help you identify the theme and the narrative elements that support the theme. State the theme in one complete sentence.

Thomas Eakins, *Max Schmitt in a Single Scull,* 1871

Now look back over your notes. What details would best bring the central idea of the novel to life? Starting with your statement of theme, draft your jacket copy.

Revise your draft to make sure that your first sentence is well supported. Eliminate any irrelevant details. Do any points need further support? Edit your work carefully, making sure that all your references to the novel are accurate.

PURPOSE   To write an attention-getting book jacket
AUDIENCE   Potential novel readers
LENGTH   1–2 pages

2. Open Assignment Read one of the following very short stories or one of your own choosing, and write an essay similar to the model on page 182. Express the theme in a few sentences, develop it to apply to all of us, and then support your theme with evidence from the story.

- "A Day's Wait," Ernest Hemingway
- "The Story of an Hour," Kate Chopin
- "The Blanket," Floyd Dell
- "The Day the Sun Came Out," Dorothy M. Johnson

3. Art Meet with a group of classmates and look carefully at the painting on this page. Appointing a secretary to take notes, discuss the painting as if it were a narrative. What is its setting and mood? Who are the characters? Imagine the painting as a moment frozen in time, and speculate about the plot: What is happening now? What might happen next? Finally, what is the artist's point of view? Does he seem involved in his subject or distant from it? Brainstorm other relevant questions.

Have the secretary read the notes of your discussion. Then write individual statements of the theme, using one or two complete sentences. On the same sheet of paper, list at least three examples supporting your theory. Return to the group, read your statement of the theme aloud, and speaking from your notes, present your supporting evidence. After each group member has spoken, discuss the differences and similarities in your interpretations of the painting.

Writing About Literature
Responding to Narrative Poetry

A Blend of Song and Story

How do you feel when you read a poem? If you are at a loss, if you don't know what to think, or if you're sure that what you do think couldn't possibly be right, you're not alone. But you don't have to react this way.

Think about how you respond to other art forms. Do you sing or dance to songs on the radio? Have you ever tried to copy a famous painting or sculpture? When you read a good book, do you go right back to the library to find another work by the same author? Can you and your friends have endless conversations about movies or TV shows? These are natural responses to works of art. Believe it or not, you can become just as comfortable reacting to a poem.

The stanza below sets the scene for the 1877 surrender of Joseph, chief of the Nez Percé, to Colonel Miles and General O. O. Howard. Their combined forces had chased Chief Joseph's people away from their sacred homeland in Oregon to clear the way for farmers and gold prospectors.

> At late afternoon, light failing, Howard
>   Is called, with his brass, to the buffalo robe that
>   Lies black against snow. Up from the dry
>   Brown gravel and water-round stones of the Eagle,
>   Now going snow-white in dryness, and up
>   From the shell-churned
>   Chaos of camp-site, slowly ascends
>   The procession. Joseph, not straight, sits his mount,
>   Head forward bowed, scalp lock with otter-skin tied.
>
> Robert Penn Warren, from "Chief Joseph of the Nez Percé"

It's the end of the day. Winter, too—end of the year. End of Joseph. Cold, dry, bleak place. No life. Seems to fit in with what's happening.

What does "water-round" stones mean? Made smooth by water? How about "shell-churned"?

How does your response to this stanza compare to the response shown in the notes? This stanza may seem different from other poetry you've read. In fact, it is part of a book-length narrative poem. Like a narrative in prose, it has characters, setting, point of view—and an amazing story to tell.

Listening to the Poem

Even though it is usually longer than most lyric poems, a narrative poem is accessible because it tells a story. When you read a narrative poem, start by just enjoying the story. Along the way, try listening to the music of the poem. The sound of poetry is always important: Listen for rhythm and the repetition of sounds, as in rhyme or alliteration. Poetry is often more concentrated than prose. The poet may leave out details that would be considered necessary in a prose story. Every word is carefully chosen for its impact. Below, the story of Chief Joseph's surrender continues.

> Joseph draws in his mount. Then,
> As though all years were naught in their count, arrow
>   straight
> He suddenly sits, head now lifted. With perfect ease
> To the right he swings a buckskinned leg over.
>   Stands.
> His gray shawl exhibits four bullet holes.
>
> Straight standing, he thrusts out his rifle,
> Muzzle-grounded, to Howard. It is
> The gesture, straight-flung, of one who casts the
>   world away.

Joseph rises to meet his fate—pride, dignity. Four bullet holes—was he badly hurt? "Straight-flung" sounds defiant, yet he's above it all somehow.
Story shocking and sad, makes me angry. But (strangely) it's also inspiring—he has such grace and stature.

A group of people watching a movie may all respond differently. One might react to the setting ("I'd love to live there"), another to a character ("I can't stand the nurse"). One may be engrossed in the plot ("There are so many twists and turns!"); another may hum the soundtrack all evening. All of these are legitimate responses, as well as starting points for delving deeper into the elements of the movie.

When you read a poem, try out all of these responses, and any others that you feel, and see where they lead. Trust your instincts the way you do with other kinds of art. One way to get ideas flowing is by freewriting in a learning log, such as the ones you see next to these models. See pages 18–21 for instructions on writing a learning log.

Revising Tip

If you think that your essay lacks sufficient supporting evidence, go back to your first learning log for your earliest impressions. You may have overlooked a strong detail in your first draft.

• JOURNAL ACTIVITY •
Try It Out

Choose a narrative poem. As you read, jot down your impressions in your journal. Write the line numbers from the poem next to your comments.

Expressing Your Response

After you have let your thoughts about a poem run freely, try to articulate them. Talk about the poem with your classmates or your teacher. If you have questions about the story, you may want to get more background information. For example, after you read this poem, you might want to find a biography of Chief Joseph or do historical research into the flight of the tribe and the events that followed the surrender. Finally, try to get something on paper. You could recast the narrative into a play or a short story. You might create a realistic or abstract painting of one moment of the story, such as the opening scene described on page 184. You might want to set the words to music. Or you might write a response essay such as the one below.

Model

Reading Warren's narrative poem, one wonders if it is as much about the deceptiveness of words as it is about Chief Joseph and his people. "But what is a piece of white paper, ink on it?" Chief Joseph says, speaking of the broken treaty between his people and the white settlers. Later, when the extent of the deception has become clear, Chief Joseph cannot speak at all. It is almost as if he has ceased believing in words, or at least in his ability to use them: "Oh, Who will speak! cried the heart in my bosom/Speak for the Nimipu, and speak Truth!"

I guess that is the reason Warren wrote this poem, to speak Truth for the now-silent tribe of the Nez Percé. Warren seems to actually adopt the rhythm of a Native American dialect when he says:

> The salmon leaps, and is the Sky-Chief's blessing.
> The Sky-Power thus blessed the Nimipu
> And blessed them, too, with
> The camas root, good to the tongue, in abundance.

Significantly, the language seems very spare, unembellished, as if Warren, like Chief Joseph, does not trust the language he uses: "muzzle-grounded, " "straight-flung." Each word shows a careful choice.

Even Warren finally finds words to be inadequate. At the end of the poem, he and a friend visit the site of the Indian warrior's surrender to General Miles over a hundred years ago. "We went," he writes, "and did not talk much on the way."

Unlike an essay on theme, a response essay expresses the personal feelings and thoughts of the reader. What can you see in the first paragraph of this model that shows it is a response essay?

What response did you have to Chief Joseph's language?

Writer's Choice

The following are some writing options to help you try out what you have learned.

1. Guided Assignment Imagine you are a screenwriter who wants to interest a producer in a movie version of a narrative poem. (*Camelot* was one such venture.) Read or reread a narrative poem, and then choose a part of the poem that could be a good opening for a film. Recast this section of the narrative as the opening scene of a film.

First, identify briefly the setting, characters, plot, point of view, and theme. Add details that you might need to use in your script: description of the scene for the stage sets, details on the characters' appearances for costume and makeup, dialogue (directly from the poem if possible, or invent dialogue). Then write your script. Stay as close to the facts and feelings of the original poem as you can.

PURPOSE   To write an engaging script for the opening scene of a movie
AUDIENCE   A movie producer
LENGTH   3–4 pages

2. Open Assignment Your school is putting on a dramatic version of one of the following narrative poems or a poem of your choice. You are interested in auditioning for one of the parts. To help you prepare, you need to understand your character thoroughly and think the way he or she thinks. Read the poem carefully. Then imagine how you would react to the poem as your character, and write a response essay from his or her point of view.

- "The Other Pioneers," Roberto Salazar
- "The Lady of Shalott," Tennyson
- "The Centaur," May Swenson
- "Two Tramps in Mud Time," Frost

3. Music Do you like to listen to or sing folk songs? Many folk songs are actually narrative poems set to music. Brainstorm a list of folk songs with narrative lyrics, from older songs, such as "John Henry" or "Scarlet Ribbons" to contemporary ballads by Bruce Springsteen or Bob Dylan. Look for records or tapes of the songs. After you have listened to recordings of at least four different songs, freewrite about them: Which one do you like best? Which one least? Why? How does the music enhance the words of the poem? How does the performer interpret the poem? Finally, put your reactions to one of the songs into a short response essay.

4. Cooperative Learning You are a cartoon scriptwriter for a famous animation company, and you want to produce a version of Alfred Noyes's narrative poem "The Highwayman" for today's audiences. Meeting with a group of animation experts, you discuss a modern setting, contemporary characters, and a different ending for your cartoon. The hero might be a race-car driver who "came driving, driving, driving . . .", or a rock musician, "jiving, jiving, jiving . . . ." You might recast the poem entirely with animals or cartoon characters.

When you have agreed upon your comic version, assign one member to write a description of the characters, another of setting, and another of storyline. Then review the elements, and have a fourth member write an introductory overview of your cartoon drama.

A fifth member can put the sections together and revise the draft for clarity and consistency.

COMPUTER OPTION

When dividing tasks among the members of a group, it can be helpful to copy your section onto a floppy disk. Then the student assigned to put all of the pieces together can transfer all the information onto his own computer and rework the entire draft.

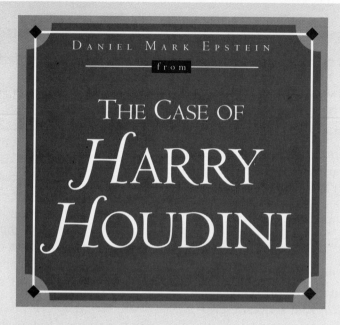

DANIEL MARK EPSTEIN

from

THE CASE OF
HARRY HOUDINI

It's easy to pull a rabbit out of a hat. It's not so easy, though, to make a ten-thousand-pound elephant disappear on a brightly lit stage with no trapdoor. But this and other miraculous feats were just part of Harry Houdini's repertoire. This excerpt from Epstein's essay unlocks some secrets, while acknowledging that the lock on some may never be picked.

As he had done in America and England, Houdini began his tour of Germany with a visit to police headquarters. The Dresden officers were not enthusiastic, yet they could hardly refuse the magician's invitation to lock him up. That might suggest a crisis of confidence. And like their colleagues the world over, the Dresden police viewed Houdini's news clippings as so much paper in the balance with their locks and chains. Of course the Dresden police had no more success than those of Kansas City, or San Francisco, or Scotland Yard. Their manacles were paper to him. The police chief reluctantly signed the certificate Houdini demanded, but the newspapers gave him little coverage.

So on his opening night at Dresden's Central Theater, Houdini arranged to be fettered in the leg irons and manacles of the Mathilde-gasse Prison. Some of the locks weighed forty pounds. The audience, packed to the walls, went wild over his escape, and the fact that he spoke their language further endeared him. If anything could have held him captive it would have been the adoring burghers of Dresden, who mobbed the theater for weeks. The manager wanted to buy out Houdini's contract with the Wintergarten of Berlin, so as to hold him over in Dresden, but the people of Berlin could not wait to see the magician.

Houdini arrived in Berlin in October of 1900. The first thing he did was march into the police station, strip stark naked, and challenge the jailors. They could not hold him. This time Count von Windheim, the highest ranking policeman in Germany, signed the certificate of Houdini's escape. The Wintergarten was overrun. The management appealed to the theater of Houdini's next engagement, in Vienna, so they might hold him over an extra month in Berlin. The Viennese finally yielded, demanding an indemnity equal to Houdini's salary for one month. When the magician, at long last, opened at the Olympic Theater in Paris, in December of 1901, he was the highest paid foreign entertainer in French history.

But meanwhile there was big trouble brewing in Germany. It seems the police there had little sense of humor about Houdini's peculiar gifts, and the Jew had quickly exhausted what little there was. In Dortmund he escaped from the irons that had bound Glowisky, a notorious murderer, beheaded three days before. At Hanover the police chief, Count von Schwerin, plotted to disgrace Houdini, challenging him to escape from a special straitjacket reinforced with thick leather. Houdini agonized for one and a half hours while von Schwerin looked on, his jubilant smile melting in wonder, then rage, as the magician worked himself free.

The cumulative anger of the German police went public in July of 1901. Inspecter Werner Graff witnessed Houdini's escape from all the manacles at the Cologne police station and vowed to end the humiliation. It was not a simple matter of pride. Graff, along with von Schwerin and other officials, feared Houdini was weakening their authority and inviting jailbreaks, if not other kinds of antisocial behavior. So Graff wrote a letter to Cologne's newspaper, the *Rheinische Zeitung*. The letter stated that Houdini had escaped from simple restraints at the police headquarters, by trickery; but his publicity boasted he could escape from restraints *of any kind*. Such a claim, Graff wrote, was a lie, and Houdini ought to be prosecuted for fraud.

Though he knew the letter was nonsense, the magician could not ignore it, for it was dangerous nonsense. If the police began calling him a fraud in every town he visited, Houdini would lose his audience. So he demanded that Graff apologize and the newspaper publish a retraction. Graff refused, and other German dailies reprinted his letter. Should Harry Houdini sue the German policeman for libel? Consider the circumstances. Germany, even in 1901, was one of the most authoritarian states in the world. Houdini was an American, a

Jew who embarrassed the police. A libel case against Graff would turn upon the magician's claim that he could escape from *any* restraint, and the courtroom would become an international theater. There a German judge and jury would try his skill, and, should they find it wanting, Houdini would be washed up, exiled to play beer halls and dime museums. Only an artist with colossal pride and total confidence in his methods would act as Houdini did. He hired the most prominent trial lawyer in Cologne, and ordered him to sue Werner Graff and the Imperial Police of Germany for criminal libel.

There was standing room only in the Cologne *Schöffengericht*. The judge allowed Werner Graff to seek out the most stubborn locks and chains he could find, and tangle Houdini in them, in full view of everyone. Here was a hitch, for Houdini did not wish to show the crowd his technique. He asked the judge to clear the courtroom, and in the ensuing turmoil the magician released himself so quickly no one knew how he had done it. The *Schöffengericht* fined the astonished policeman and ordered a public apology. So Graff's lawyer appealed the case.

Two months later Graff was better prepared. In the *Strafkammer*, or court of appeals, he presented thirty letters from legal authorities declaring that the escape artist could not justify his advertisements. And Graff had a shiny new pair of handcuffs. The premier locksmith of Germany had engineered the cuffs especially for the occasion. Werner Graff explained to the judge that the lock, once closed, could never be opened, even with its own key. Let Houdini try to get out of these.

This time the court permitted Houdini to work in privacy, and a guard led the magician to an adjacent chamber. Everyone else settled down for a long wait, in a chatter of anticipation. They were interrupted four minutes later by the entrance of Houdini, who tossed the manacles on the judge's bench. So the *Strafkammer* upheld the lower court's decision, as did the *Oberlandesgericht* in a "paper" appeal. The court fined Werner Graff thirty marks and ordered him to pay for the trials as well as a published apology. Houdini's next poster showed him in evening dress, his hands manacled, standing before the judge, jurors, and a battery of mustachioed policemen. Looking down on the scene was a bust of the Kaiser against a crimson background, and a scroll that read: "The Imperial Police of Cologne slandered Harry Houdini . . . were compelled to advertise 'An Honorary Apology' and pay costs of the trials. By command of Kaiser Wilhelm II, Emperor of Germany."

Now this is surely a wondrous tale, like something out of the *Arabian Nights*, and it will seem no less wonderful when we understand the technique that made it come true. In 1901, when Houdini took on the

Imperial Police, he was not whistling in the dark. By the time he left America at the end of the nineteenth century he had dissected every kind of lock he could find in the New World, and whatever he could import from the old one. Arriving in London, Houdini could write that there were only a few kinds of British handcuffs, "seven or eight at the utmost," and these were some of the simplest he had ever seen. He searched the markets, antique shops, and locksmiths, buying up all the European locks he could find so he could dismantle and study them.

Then during his Berlin engagement he worked up to ten hours a day at Mueller's locksmith on the Mittelstrasse, studying restraints. He was the Bobby Fischer of locks. With a chessmaster's foresight Houdini devised a set of picks to release every lock in existence, as well as *any he could imagine*. Such tireless ingenuity produced the incandescent light bulb and the atom bomb. Houdini's creation of a theatrical metaphor made a comparable impact on the human spirit. He had a message that he delivered so forcefully that it goes without mentioning in theater courses: humankind cannot be held in chains. The European middle class had reached an impressionable age, and the meaning of Houdini's theater was not lost upon them. Nor was he mistaken by the aristocracy, who stayed away in droves. The spectacle of this American Jew bursting from chains by dint of ingenuity did not amuse the rich. They wanted desperately to demythologize him.

It was not about to happen in the German courtroom. When Werner Graff snapped the "new" handcuffs on Houdini, they were not strange to the magician. He had already invented them, so to speak, as well as the pick to open them, and the pick was in his pocket. Only a locksmith whose knowledge surpassed Houdini's could stop him; diligent study assured him that, as of 1901, there could be no such locksmith on the face of the earth.

What else can we understand about the methods of Harry Houdini, born Ehrich Weiss? We know he was a superbly conditioned

athlete who did not smoke or take a drop of alcohol. His straitjacket escapes he performed in full view of the world so they could see it was by main force and flexibility that he freed himself. He may or may not have been able to dislocate his shoulders at will—he said he could, and it seems no more marvelous than certain other skills he demonstrated. Friends reported that his toes could untie knots most of us could not manage with our fingers. And routinely the magician would hold his breath for as long as four minutes to work underwater escapes. To cheapen the supernatural claims of the fakir Rahman Bey, Houdini remained underwater in an iron box for ninety minutes, as against the Egyptian's sixty. Examining Houdini, a physician testified that the fifty-year-old wizard had halved his blood pressure while doubling his pulse. Of course, more wonderful than any of these skills was the courage allowing him to employ them, in predicaments where any normal person would panic.

These things are known about Houdini. The same tireless ingenuity, when applied to locks and jails, packing cases and riveted boilers; the same athletic prowess, when applied at the bottom of the East River, or while dangling from a rope attached to the cornice of the *Sun* building in Baltimore—these talents account for the vast majority of Houdini's exploits. As we have mentioned, theater historians, notably Raymund Fitzsimons in his *Death and the Magician*, have carefully exposed Houdini's ingenuity, knowing that nothing can tarnish the miracle of the man's existence. Their accounts are technical and we need not dwell on them, except to say they *mostly* support Houdini's oath that his effects were achieved by natural, or mechanical, means. The Houdini problem arises from certain outrageous effects no one has ever been able to explain, though capable technicians have been trying for more than sixty years.

Let us briefly recall those effects. We have mentioned the disappearing elephant. On January 7, 1918, Houdini had a ten-thousand-pound elephant led onto the bright stage of the Hippodrome in New York City. A trainer marched the elephant around a cabinet large enough for an elephant, proving there was space behind. There was no trap door in the floor of the Hippodrome, and the elephant could not fly. Houdini ushered the pachyderm into the cabinet and closed the curtains. Then he opened them, and where the elephant had stood there was nothing but empty space. Houdini went on with his program, which might have been making the Hippodrome disappear, for all the audience knew. A reporter for the *Brooklyn Eagle* noted: "The program says that the elephant vanished into thin air. The trick is performed fifteen feet from the backdrop and the cabinet is slightly elevated. That explanation is as good as any." After Houdini stopped making elephants disappear, nineteen weeks later, the trick would

never be precisely duplicated. . . .

In the Houdini Museum at Niagara Falls, Canada, you may view the famous *Mirror* handcuffs. If you are a scholar you can inspect them. In March of 1904 the London *Daily Mirror* discovered a blacksmith who had been working for five years to build a set of handcuffs no mortal man could pick. Examining the cuffs, the best locksmiths in London agreed they had never seen such an ingenious mechanism. The newspaper challenged Houdini to escape from them. On March 17, before a house of four thousand in the London Hippodrome, a journalist fastened the cuffs on Houdini's wrists and turned the key six times. The magician retired to his cabinet onstage, and the band struck up a march. He did not emerge for twenty minutes. When he did, it was to hold the lock up to the light. Remember that most "Challenge" handcuffs were regulation, and familiar to Houdini. He studied the lock in the light, and then went back into the cabinet as the band played a waltz.

Ten minutes later Houdini stuck his head out, asking if he could have a cushion to kneel on. He was denied. After almost an hour Houdini came out of the cabinet again, obviously worn out, and his audience groaned. He wanted the handcuffs to be unlocked for a moment so he could take off his coat, as he was sweating profusely. The journalist denied the request, since Houdini had never before seen the handcuffs unlocked, and that might give him an advantage. Whereupon Houdini, in full view of the four thousand, extracted a penknife from his pocket and opened it with his teeth. Turning the coat inside out over his head, he shredded it loose with the penknife and returned to the cabinet. Someone called out that Houdini had been handcuffed for more than an hour. As the band played on, the journalists of the *Daily Mirror* could taste the greatest scoop of the twentieth century. But ten minutes later there was a cry from the cabinet and Houdini leaped out of it, free, waving the handcuffs high in the air. While the crowd roared, several men from the audience carried Houdini on their shoulders around the theater. He was crying as if his heart would break.

For Discussion

1. What response did you have to the *Mirror* handcuffs episode? Why do you think you responded this way?

2. If you could ask Houdini about one of his performances, which one would it be and why?

Readers Respond

I remember the parts about how Houdini unlocked the handcuffs and how all the Germans were trying to prove he was a fraud, but failed. By using words and phrases like "Houdini . . . tossed the

manacles on the judge's bench," Epstein makes the accusers look like fools.

Becky Byer

The things that Harry Houdini did were phenomenal. I believe that anyone would be interested in a person who was able to accomplish such magic tricks. Houdini's persistence is also an inspiration. A person who gives up when something gets tough could learn a lesson from Houdini. He had the courage to rise to any challenge. That is something that everyone should have. With hard work and strong will, anything can be done. I think that is the message of this reading. It was a joy to read this.

David Alonzo

Do you agree?

☞   Do you think that Houdini's persistence should serve as an inspiration to others? What qualities did Houdini have that are available to everyone?

☞   In your journal, copy words and phrases that Epstein uses to characterize Houdini and his enemies. Then, write a paragraph describing how these words and phrases affected your reaction to Epstein's essay.

Writing Process in Action

Wonder of Wonders

Daniel Mark Epstein was not yet born when Harry Houdini was circling the globe and dazzling audiences, but Epstein is still able to tell Houdini's story with all the richness of a first-hand account. In the excerpt from "The Case of Harry Houdini" (pages 188–194), Epstein's skill as a writer and his keen interest in his subject have brought Houdini back to life—as if by magic. What's more, Epstein has made the magician a significant historical figure, not merely an entertaining spectacle. By placing Houdini in his historical context, Epstein not only narrates but interprets the famous tricks and escapes. Of course he wants you to remember the disappearing elephant and the underwater escapades. But it is the image of the manacles tossed on the judge's bench that points to the writer's serious purpose: to show that Houdini's life contained a message of hope, that "humankind cannot be held in chains."

In this lesson you'll have an opportunity to write a narrative about a subject that amazes you as much as Houdini amazes Epstein. Like Epstein, you will turn your subject upside down and inside out in search of details that will amaze your readers and lock your writing firmly in their memory.

• Assignment •

Context   You have decided to enter a local TV station's "The Wonder of Wonders" essay contest for high school juniors. According to the rules, contestants are to write a narrative about an astonishing and inspiring person. The focus may be the person's character or a particular achievement or event. The narrative must be based on personal experience, research, or a combination. No fictional narratives will be accepted.

Purpose   To write a narrative about a person you find astonishing and inspiring

Audience   A panel of high school juniors

Length   3–6 pages

1. Prewriting

What do you find wonder-ful? In other words, what or who in your experience has left you full of wonder? As you were reading this assignment, a person or an achievement may have popped immediately to mind. If so, you can begin exploring your topic for details right away. If not, review Lesson 2.2 for start-up help. In particular, you might try freewriting in response to the following: "The most astonishing person I've ever met is . . ." or "The most amazing achievement I've ever heard of is . . ." Your topic needn't be showy and spectacular. Revealing what is extraordinary about what seems ordinary can also be dramatic. For example, "the girl next door" may run a program for disadvantaged children, be a sky-diving champion, or be the best friend a person could ever have. On the other hand, you, like Epstein, might be inspired by a figure from history and how that person exemplified or altered an era.

Once you have a general idea of what you want to write about, you'll need to narrow your focus. Ask yourself questions such as these:

- What do I find wonderful about this person?
- What is truly significant: one achievement or the entire life?
- What is the scope of influence of this person or achievement: family? neighborhood? local? worldwide? historic?
- Why am I amazed or impressed?
- What else do I want to know about this person or this achievement?

Now search your topic for specifics that will breathe life into it. Notice how Epstein uses specific detail to make you, the reader, part of Houdini's astonished audience. He tells you, for example, that Houdini made not a huge but a "ten-thousand pound" elephant disappear, not just anywhere but on "the bright stage" of the Hippodrome in New York City. Specifics like these pull you into the action and make you feel as if you are there. Remember that ideas in narrative writing need support as much as ideas in persuasive writing. If you say that something is exciting, use concrete and vivid words to show what makes it exciting. Here, in addition, you are attempting to convince your reader of the legitimacy of a conclusion you have reached, so the vividly rendered events of your narrative serve as your proof. Look at Epstein's methods again. He doesn't just say that the German police were afraid of Houdini's power to make them look foolish; he proves it with an extended example of Inspector Werner Graff's desperate effort to discredit the great magician.

Creating a large pool of details and examples now will make the drafting stage of the writing process easier and more enjoyable. Therefore, let your mind run free. This is the time to get thoroughly acquainted with your topic, which may mean doing some library research, interviewing people, or observing some process unfold. Lesson 2.5 offers several strategies for improving your observation skills and for choosing the most effective details. With your purpose and audience in mind, select the most relevant and vivid details from your pool.

2. Drafting

The word *draft* comes from the Middle English *draught*, meaning to draw or pull. Now is the time for pulling together the details you have collected— and others that occur to you as you draft—into a unified and coherent whole.

Because you are writing a narrative, you will be dealing with all or most of the following elements: character, dialogue, setting (time and place), action or plot, point of view, and tone. This list may sound intimidating, but as you probably already know, narrative is the most natural mode of writing. Storytelling is a part of everyday life. To help you ease into your story, look over

Lessons 2.6, 2.7, and 2.8 for an in-depth review of organizing your narrative and of giving it unity and coherence. Then look at Lessons 4.1 and 4.2 to refresh your memory on character development.

Given your purpose, what structure or organization will hook your readers and keep their attention? Epstein uses one that is tried and true: he keeps the reader in suspense. To do so, he strategically withholds important information and details. Not until midway through the narrative does Epstein reveal that Houdini was "the Bobby Fischer of locks," devising picks for all known locks "as well as any he could imagine." Even this remarkable revelation fails to explain the disappearance of the elephant and the escape from the *Mirror* handcuffs. An intriguing question tickles the back of the reader's mind: What is the ultimate source of Houdini's astounding ability? This keep-them-guessing approach works especially well in narrative writing.

Before deciding on the most effective structure for your narrative, formulate a thesis statement and write it down. It will probably be similar to your original idea, which included showing how a certain person or achievement is wonderful. This is your controlling idea; let it guide you through the decisions that lie ahead. Next, construct a time line as discussed in Lesson 4.3, and flesh out this "skeleton" with carefully chosen details from your prewriting notes and with any new images and ideas that occur to you. Then experiment with different, non-chronological arrangements. Consider starting your narrative with the ending rather than the beginning. Consider, too, creating suspense by building up to a climax or by unfolding your story slowly, as Epstein does.

After you have played with two or three structures, choose the one that best fulfills the promise of your thesis. Then reread the prompt for this assignment so that it's fresh in your memory, and start writing!

3. Revising

At this stage of the writing process, you must treat your work as if someone else has written it. A peer reviewer can help you achieve objectivity. For guidance in using peer review, see Lesson 2.9. Ask a classmate to read your narrative and to evaluate your work using the criteria in the prompt. This strategy may prove especially useful here as your specified audience is a panel of high school students.

Even if you have the benefit of a peer response, be sure to do your own evaluation, using the following questions as a guide. Then, allowing your draft to "rest" for a day or two, make the necessary revisions.

- Are my characters believable? Are their motivations clear? Is my dialogue relevant and accurate?
- Is my setting sufficiently detailed? Have I bridged gaps in time and place?
- Is the action easy to follow? Have I made cause-and-effect relationships clear?
- Is my point of view consistent? Would a different point of view be more effective?

- Is my language fresh? Have I avoided clichés and vagueness?
- Is the tone consistent and appropriate? Do I need to turn the volume up in some places and down in others?
- Is my title an attention-getter? Does it reflect my thesis?

Above all, ask yourself if your work has unity and coherence:

- Is my controlling idea really in control?
- Do my sentences and paragraphs flow smoothly?
- Have I said all I wanted to say—no more, no less?

4. Editing

Now is the time to look for trouble, to get picky. During revising, you were concerned with larger questions of content and structure. When you edit, you will be concerned with issues of sentence and paragraph construction and of mechanics. Refer to Lesson 2.10 for checklists to help you produce a reader-ready work. Most writers find that making several passes through their work assures a better product. On your first pass, look for such problems as fragments and run-on sentences and inconsistent verb tenses. On your second and third passes, check spelling and punctuation. If your narrative contains dialogue, pay particular attention to quotation marks and paragraph indentions.

Criteria

1. Uses narrative to show why a particular person or achievement is wonderful and has significance
2. Makes the characters vivid through physical description, believable action, and dialogue
3. Orders the details of plot so as to hold the reader's attention
4. Uses appropriate tone and word choice
5. Is unified and coherent
6. Follows standards of grammar, usage, and mechanics

5. Presenting

Would you consider Houdini a magician if he had never performed a magic act in public? Similarly, a writer is not truly a writer until he or she has risked the response of an audience. Consider having a friend, teacher, or family member read your narrative. Encourage your reader to make marginal notations or to discuss the impact of your writing. Then consider using the responses you get to refine your narrative even more. Eventually, you may find that your polished version will be perfect for a college application.

• Reflecting •

Houdini was wonderful because he could create the *nothing* of empty space from the hefty *something* of a ten-thousand-pound elephant. You have created a wonder of your own. You have made *something* out of *nothing*. You have taken the empty space on a blank sheet of paper (and perhaps a sense that you had "nothing" to say) and created a narrative worth sharing, a piece of writing that brings a story to life while revealing a great deal about you, its creator. Think about this magical process of creation and all its stages. In this piece, what were your special tricks of the trade? Can they be duplicated in other kinds of writing? For you, where does the technique end and the special magic of the creative process begin?

Portfolio & Reflection

Summary

Key concepts of nonfiction narrative writing include the following:

- Description, vivid language, dialogue, and anecdote bring characters to life.
- To write about a theme, you must examine all the elements of a narrative: plot, character, setting, and point of view.
- A biographical sketch must have a focus supported by relevant details.
- A time line organizes narrative elements chronologically.
- Identifying recurring themes and images in your subject's life can strengthen the coherence of your narrative.

Your Writer's Portfolio

Look over the narrative writing you have done during this unit. Select two pieces of writing to put into your portfolio. Each piece should demonstrate that you have worked with one or more of the preceding concepts. In other words, look for a piece of writing that does one or more of the following:

- uses vivid description, dialogue, and anecdote
- grows out of research done on a historical person
- uses details tailored to the focus selected
- is illustrated by a timeline
- is shaped by the recurring themes and images in the subject's life
- determines the theme of a narrative by examining all the narrative elements
- responds to a narrative poem

Reflection and Commentary

Write one page that demonstrates that you understand what this unit asked of you. Use your two selected pieces of writing as evidence while you consider the following numbered items. Respond to as many items as possible. Label the page "Commentary on Narrative Writing," and include it in your portfolio.

1. Did you use one technique more than any other to portray your subject in a character study? Which additional techniques could you have used to make your character seem more alive?
2. If you were to write for a different audience, how might you change the focus of your character study or biographical sketch?
3. If one of your selections is a biographical sketch, where did you go for information on the subject? Did you use one kind of source or many? What kind of information would have strengthened your sketch?
4. What theme or image did you choose to shape your narrative?
5. If you were to choose a different theme or image, what details would you omit? What new ones would you add?

Feedback

If you had a chance to respond to the following student comment, what would you say or ask?

I enjoy the way [narrative writing] lets me be creative and develop feeling.

Keri Thomas, Quartz Hill High School, Quartz Hill, California

Expository Writing

Here and Now

Richard French, *City Number Eleven*, 1991

When the World Wants to Know

"You have to understand something technical yourself if you're going to explain it to someone else. You need to think of ways to make it understandable—through an analogy, a visual image in words."

Shelley Lauzon, director of public information,
Woods Hole Oceanographic Institution

F or Shelley Lauzon (LOOZ ahn), the phones started ringing at 7:30 A.M. on September 1, 1985, and didn't stop for days. Was it true? reporters wanted to know. Had the *Titanic* been found?

Touted as the unsinkable luxury liner and the fastest ship in the world, the *Titanic* met disaster in 1912 on its maiden voyage from England to the United States. At 11:40 P.M. on April 14, the luxury ship struck an iceberg south of Newfoundland and sank with about 1,500 people aboard.

Now, news broke that the *Titanic* had been found on the ocean floor about one thousand miles east of Massachusetts. A joint U.S.–French expedition led by Dr. Robert Ballard, a geologist with the Woods Hole Oceano-

Explaining the Discovery

1. Gathering Information

2. Writing about Technology

3. Assembling the Booklet

FOCUS

Effective expository writing gives the reader a logical step-by-step path through new information.

graphic Institution in Massachusetts, had discovered the broken ship in pitch black, near-freezing water 12,000 feet deep. Shelley Lauzon, spokeswoman for Woods Hole, was the world's source of information about the institution, the mission, and the discovery.

"We were on a test cruise," says Lauzon. Scientists aboard a Woods Hole research ship, the *Knorr,* were trying out a new vehicle called *Argo,* equipped to take video pictures and still photos of the ocean floor. The fifteen-foot-long *Argo,* submersible to a depth of 2.5 miles, was towed behind the *Knorr.* Scientists on the *Knorr* controlled *Argo*'s depth and viewed its video pictures on a TV monitor.

"We had to test the *Argo* in very deep water," Lauzon says, "and the *Titanic* was supposedly in very deep water, so it was a perfect object for *Argo* to look for." At 1:00 A.M. on September 1, the crew got its first glimpse of the *Titanic*'s boilers 12,000 feet below.

Lauzon was swamped with phone calls from around the world. Requests for information came from news media, students, and people whose relatives had died on the *Titanic.*

Lauzon's first job was handling the flood of media requests. "I taped interviews with Ballard and others for the press," she says. "We airlifted a shipment of film off the ship and mass-produced information—hundreds of press kits, thousands of images."

Lauzon also faced a growing pile of letters from people all over the world. What was the best way to give them the information they wanted? "A booklet," she says. "It was a fairly inexpensive way for us to spread the word."

1. Gathering Information

"There were obvious things people wanted to know about"— the *Argo,* the *Knorr,* and the history of the *Titanic,* Lauzon recalls. The public especially wanted to see *Argo*'s pictures of the sunken ship. Lauzon decided to publish a booklet twenty to twenty-four pages long.

First Lauzon outlined subjects she wanted to include in the booklet. She decided she would need to generate about eleven short articles plus several pages of photographs of the *Titanic* and of the *Knorr*'s homecoming.

"I had the basic information about Woods Hole, and I'd gathered information on the *Knorr* and other aspects of the expedition for the press," Lauzon says. But other subjects needed more research. For example, Lauzon called the Titanic Historical Society for information on the sunken luxury liner. She spent hours gathering facts about the *Argo,* one of more than 350 projects continually under way at Woods Hole.

Lauzon's research yielded a stack of papers about two feet tall. "I went through it all, read it, and decided what was important for a brief overview of the whole project," she says. When she got to technical material about the *Argo,* she found lots of engineering terms that she didn't understand. She was certain that much of her audience wouldn't understand them either.

"I circled all the things I could not understand, and I met with the engineer and said, 'OK, what does this mean? Is there another phrase we can use so people can understand?'"

For instance, Lauzon worked with the engineer to find a way to explain the low-light-sensitive film used to capture pictures of the *Titanic.* "I asked what ASA the film was"—that is, what film speed was used to shoot the photos— "because the public buys film and is used to asking for 400 ASA or 1000 ASA." Lauzon says. "Well, this film was equivalent to 200,000 ASA! It can almost take pictures in the dark," she says.

Lauzon needed to convey a great deal of information clearly—from historical facts about the Titanic *to an explanation of the film used to photograph the ship in extreme darkness. From the murky image above, experts identified part of the ship's anchor chain.*

2. Writing About Technology

Since her office hadn't yet bought computers, Lauzon wrote her first drafts in longhand. She kept her pieces short, about two hundred to four hundred words.

"Most of the work went quickly," Lauzon says. "The short piece on the *Argo,* about 350 words, took only a few hours. It went fast because once I understood the technical information, I could translate it into popular English."

Lauzon edited her articles in longhand, too. "I edited on the piece of paper I wrote on," she explains. Lauzon moved paragraphs around and worked to make her explanations clear and simple.

Once Lauzon had a draft she liked, she typed the article and sent it to the appropriate Woods Hole experts—technical subjects, for instance, went to engineers for review. "The engineers made sure that whatever was written was technically accurate," she says. Once experts reviewed the text, Lauzon made any changes they called for and typed a final draft.

INTERFACE *You're the editor of a general-interest science magazine. A writer wants to do an article for you on the latest bicycle technology. What guidance might you give for making the writing clear to readers with little technical knowledge?*

Expository writing is strongest when the writer keeps in mind the visuals that will accompany the text. Then the visual and verbal elements will work together, as in Lauzon's booklet below, to help the reader understand the subject.

ARGO — A New Tool for the Ocean Scientist

ARGO — the vessel that carried Jason on his quest for the Golden Fleece. ARGO — the system of cameras, sonars and television that helped find the TITANIC. ARGO — a new generation of exploration tools for the ocean scientists.

ARGO, developed at the Woods Hole Oceanographic Institution with funds provided by the Office of Naval Research, is part of a larger system for ocean bottom research. It is a unique tool to acquire wide angle film and television pictures while flying 50-100 feet above the sea floor, and can also zoom in for detailed views. In the future, ARGO will carry JASON, a robot vehicle under development that can inspect features close-in and collect limited samples. When combined with sonar to map the sea floor from the ship, we shall have an unprecedented ability to explore the mysteries of the ocean bottom. The unmanned systems can operate 24 hours a day, doing the basic reconnaissance necessary for JASON or manned exploration in research submersibles like the Deep Submergence Vehicle ALVIN, owned by the U.S. Navy and operated since 1964 by the Woods Hole Oceanographic Institution.

ARGO has been specially designed to operate in the rugged terrain of undersea mountain ranges. The towed sled, capable of operating to depths of 20,000 feet (98% of the ocean floor is within 20,000 feet of the sea surface), is 15 feet long, 3.5 feet tall and 3.5 feet wide and weighs about 4,000 pounds. It has one forward looking, one down looking and one down looking telephoto television camera in the front end with strobes and other incandescent lighting to illuminate the ocean floor in the rear section, assisting the operator aboard ship to minimize obstacle contact on the bottom.

This new tool, built largely with components which are commercially available but integrated by Institution personnel with specially developed software and cable systems, was designed to enhance man's ability to explore the ocean floor. Dr. Robert Ballard, leader of the Deep Submergence Laboratory which developed ARGO, is a geologist who has spent most of his career investigating the Mid-Ocean Ridge, the largest single feature on the earth's surface, some 45,000 miles long and covering more than 20% of the globe. Since the first detailed exploration of the Mid-Atlantic Ridge, part of the system of ridges which make up the Mid-Ocean Ridge, began in 1973 (and in which Dr. Ballard was a participant), scientists have managed to accumulate only 120 miles of data in twelve years. In the first scheduled scientific use of ARGO in December 1985, Dr. Ballard and his colleagues covered nearly 120 miles of the East Pacific Rise in just 20 days.

With its enhanced images and its ability to operate in the dangerous undersea mountain ranges, ARGO will find many more uses. Geologists and geophysicists will be able to explore large areas and inspect smaller features at close range. Biologists will be able to conduct surveys of seafloor populations. Geochemists will use ARGO for studies in the newly discovered hot vents where chemicals spew forth from within the earth to support unique forms of marine life.

This dramatic engineering tool for finding the R.M.S. TITANIC will enhance the world in general, and ocean exploration in particular, that we are...

ANGUS (Acoustically Navigated Geological Underwater Survey)

ANGUS (Acoustically Navigated Underwater Survey) was the first unmanned search and survey system developed by the Woods Hole Oceanographic Institution more than a decade ago. It was designed to work primarily in extremely rugged volcanic terrain to depths of 20,000 feet, within reach of 98% of the ocean floor. As a result, its various subsystems are mounted within a heavy-duty steel frame capable of withstanding a jarring head-on collision with vertical outcrops of rock. ANGUS has made more than 250 voyages. It's motto: "Takes a lickin but keeps on clickin."

Unlike many other survey systems, ANGUS maintains continuous visual contact with the sea bed, flying 30-50 feet above the bottom. Contained within its 12-foot-long frame are three large-capacity 35mm...

...ment system which transmits the temperature of the water through which... Also on the frame is a down-looking... meters to the surface the height of... bottom, permitting the person "flying" the vehicle aboard ship to maintain the altitude by letting cable in or out.

Electronic strobe lights used to illuminate the bottom permit ANGUS to be flown higher and further than conventional deep sea photo systems. Large area photos are typically taken at 20-second intervals providing a generous photo coverage.

ANGUS is used on a standard ½-inch trawl wire found on most oceanographic ships and is a highly portable system in sea-going containers. Once a lowering has been completed, generally 12 hours or so, the film can be processed aboard ship using warm...

3. Assembling the Booklet

With the text complete, Lauzon was ready to choose photographs and lay out the pages. One of her toughest jobs was narrowing down the fifty-plus *Titanic* photos to a representative sample. Lauzon settled on twenty-eight images: haunting pictures of the ship's bow; bedsprings lying on the ocean bottom; the crow's nest, from where the fatal iceberg was first spotted.

Lauzon sketched out each page of the brochure on a sheet of paper 8 1/2 by 11 inches. Then she photocopied the photographs and pasted them in position, creating a mock-up of the final product to review with key members of the Woods Hole staff. "At that point we had to make sure we weren't omitting any information that might be crucial," Lauzon says. Once everyone gave the nod, Lauzon sent her layouts and text to the printer with an order to print 25,000 copies.

Since Lauzon completed the *Titanic* booklet, the *Argo* has gone on to other research projects, such as photographing and mapping long stretches of the East Pacific Rise, the boundary between the North American and Pacific crustal plates. What *Argo* finds may help geologists predict earthquakes.

Even now, however, the *Argo*'s first discovery holds a special fascination for many people. Says Lauzon: "To this day, six years later, there is not a day that goes by that my office doesn't receive a request about the *Titanic*."

INTERFACE **You're a newspaper reporter covering a new deep-sea expedition. The project uses remote-controlled vehicles to photograph the ocean floor at a depth of 20,000 feet. Write a lead sentence that conveys to your readers how deep the vehicle dived.**

Lauzon acted as writer, editor, and designer on the Titanic *project. She laid out her pages in a way that would make technical information as clear as possible.*

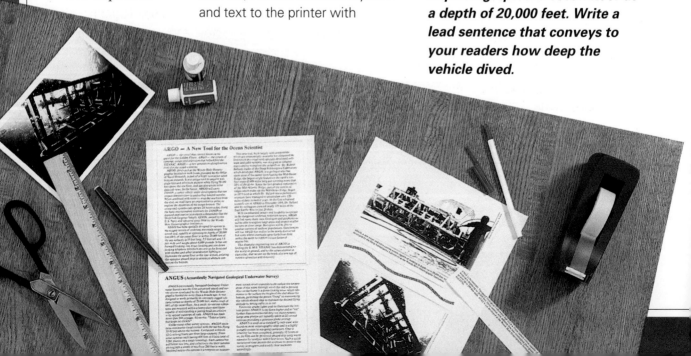

ON ASSIGNMENT

1. Read an encyclopedia entry on an interesting technical subject, such as the space shuttle, biomedical engineering, or electric cars. Write a critique of the entry. Was the explanation clear and interesting? What techniques made it effective? If the explanation was unclear, what would improve it?

2. **Literature Connection**
   Scan several magazines that present technical information to a general audience—magazines such as *Popular Science, Popular Mechanics,* and *Prevention.* Assemble half a dozen examples of vivid, clear technical writing, and organize them into a "how to" book on technical writing. Compose a list of technical writing tips for your reference book, listing the techniques you learned from the articles.

3. **Cooperative Learning**
   Organize a small group to investigate any current technology that interests you—camcorders, videodiscs, fiber optics, or other items. As a group, brainstorm the subject you want to study. Assign members to find various kinds of information about your topic, such as descriptions, diagrams, photos, and charts. Pool your information, and choose the most interesting images for a poster. Choose one member of the group to write a brief explanation of how the technology works. Other members should review the writing for clarity. On a piece of paper, sketch a design for your poster. Then paste in text and images according to your design.

Working Chimps

> *What concrete example does Begley use to bring this topic to life?*

Literature Model

*T*he chimps at the St. Louis Zoo . . . work for a living: they poke stiff pieces of hay into an anthill to scoop out the baby food and honey that curators cache away inside. Instead of idly awaiting banana handouts, the chimps get to manipulate tools, just as they do in the wild. . . .

As species become extinct at a rate unparalleled since the Cretaceous era . . . zoos are striving to make their settings match their new role as keepers of the biological flame. Since 1980 the nation's 143 accredited zoos and aquariums have spent more than $1 billion on renovation and construction, much of it going to create habitats that immerse both animals and visitors in the sights, sounds, feel, and smell of the wild.

Sharon Begley, "Wilder Places for Wild Things," *Newsweek*

The chimpanzees in the St. Louis Zoo work for a living. Sharon Begley begins the passage above with this intriguing statement and then proceeds to explain it. In doing so, Begley uses expository writing, writing that explains or informs.

Planning Your Writing

When you write an expository essay, you first want to select a topic that interests you. Say you choose for your topic not the protection of animals as Begley does, but the destruction and possible extinction of certain animal species such as the African elephant. You know that huge herds of elephants once covered the rolling African savannas, but today the demand for ivory has destroyed half of that elephant population.

Once you've selected a topic, you want to decide how to approach it. What kind of question do you want to ask and explore with your readers? Do you want to explain what caused this problem? Do you want to propose a solution?

Ivory Trade		
Question	Type of Expository Writing	Strategy
1. What is the process by which ivory smugglers transport tusks out of Africa?	Process Explanation	uses step-by-step organization to explain how something happens, works, or is done
2. What has caused the African elephant population to decline?	Cause and Effect	identifies the causes and/or effects of something and examines the relationship between causes and effects
3. How do ivory substitutes compare with ivory in different uses?	Compare and Contrast	examines similarities and differences to find relationships and draw conclusions
4. How can the African elephant be saved from extinction?	Problems and Solutions	examines aspects of a complex problem and explores or proposes possible solutions
5. Would an international ban on the sale of ivory end poaching?	Building a Hypothesis	uses patterns of facts to offer explanations or predictions and then tests the hypothesis

The chart above lists some types of expository writing that you might use to discuss the destruction of African elephant populations. Each question in the first column requires a different type of expository writing. For example, in response to the first question, you can write a paragraph that explains the process by which ivory is smuggled out of Africa.

Answering many of these questions will involve using the same information but will lead to different types of organization and writing. Whichever question you choose, the knowledge and interests of your audience will influence the details you select to support your explanations. This cube shows how the choice of details for two cause-and-effect paragraphs varies depending on the audience.

Topic
Ivory Trade

Audience
Ivory consumers

Details
1. Thousands of elephants cruelly killed for ivory.
2. Elephant populations near extinction.
3. Elephants crucial to African ecosystems.

Audience
Scientists

Details
1. African elephant population dropped from 1.3 million to 625,000 between 1979 and 1989.
2. Seventy-two percent of elephant families in a recent study were lacking adult females.

• JOURNAL ACTIVITY •
Think It Through

Imagine you are writing a paragraph about the African ivory trade for U.S. lawmakers. What information from the boxes above would you delete? What information would you add? Why?

Effective Transitions

Although including the right kinds of details in your expository writing is important, it is just as important to show the relationship between the details. Simply writing detail after detail will leave you with a choppy, unclear paragraph, even if the details are arranged logically. A paragraph like this one takes your reader on a bumpy ride:

> ### Model
>
> That ivory bracelet you just couldn't resist threatens the very existence of elephants in Africa. Mature elephant populations have been virtually wiped out. Poachers kill more and more young adults and juveniles. Elephant families have been destroyed. The killings have disrupted the elephants' breeding patterns.

You can't tell how the ivory bracelet in the first sentence threatens elephants.

Transitional words help make the relationships among ideas clear. Note these commonly used transitions and the relationships they show:

Time: *after, always, before, finally, first, immediately, later, meanwhile, now, sometimes, soon, until*

Place: *above, ahead, around, below, down, far, here, inside, near, next to, opposite, outside, over, parallel, there, under, vertically, within*

Order of Importance: *first, former, latter, primarily, secondarily*

Cause and Effect: *as a result, because, by, so, then, therefore*

Comparison and Contrast: *but, even more, however, just as, like, on the other hand, unlike*

Example: *for example, for instance, namely, that is*

Revising Tip

When you revise your paragraph, make sure it is as clear as possible. Weed out information that doesn't contribute to or support the topic sentence.

Now read the revised model with transitions added:

> ### Model
>
> That ivory bracelet you just couldn't resist may be the end of a cruel and illegal process that threatens the very existence of elephants in Africa. In many regions, mature elephant populations have been virtually wiped out by ruthless poachers seeking large tusks for ivory. Therefore, poachers now kill more and more young adults and even juveniles to get the same amount of ivory. Because of the slaughter, the elephants' breeding patterns have been disrupted. As a result, females bear fewer offspring, shrinking the population even more.

What transitions and links make the relationships between the facts in this paragraph easier to understand?

Writer's Choice

The following are some writing options to help you try out what you have learned.

1. Guided Assignment   You have been asked to explain what a zoo is to a group of small children who are about to visit a zoo for the first time. Write an expository paragraph that will serve as the basis for your talk. You will want to explain not only what the children are going to see when they get to the zoo but also why we have zoos and what role they play. Ideally, you will mention features of a specific zoo with which you are familiar. As you plan your paragraph, select details that are appropriate for your audience. Be sure to include transitions that will help your audience understand the relationships between the details in your paragraph.

PURPOSE   To explain what a zoo is
AUDIENCE   Small children visiting a zoo for the first time
LENGTH   1 paragraph

COMPUTER OPTION

If you use a computer to complete this Guided Assignment, you may want to triple-space a printout of your first draft. The extra space between the lines will make it easier for you to write comments about your work and then revise your draft.

2. Open Assignment   You have just begun a summer job as a tour guide in your town or city or at a nearby tourist attraction. You must write out the tour you will give orally. Write one or more expository paragraphs informing visitors about one of the following sites:

- a historic home or estate
- a cathedral, church, or synagogue
- a park, wilderness, or recreation area
- a museum or historical society
- a historic or public site of your choice

To plan your writing, brainstorm details that will make your tour interesting to teen-age tourists. Once you have selected appropriate details, place them in a logical order. Be sure to use effective transitions to tie the details of your paragraphs together.

3. Algebra   Write an expository paragraph telling a sixth grader how to find the value of a in $2ab = 10a - 2$ when $b = 4$.

Pay close attention to transitions and make the explanation as clear as possible for your audience.

4. American History   Imagine that you are a colonist living in Massachusetts in 1773. You participated in the Boston Tea Party by dressing up as a native American Indian, painting your face, and dumping British tea into Boston Harbor. Although you know that this action was illegal and that you might have chosen other forms of protest, such as boycotting British products, you feel that your behavior was a justifiable protest of British tax policies. You also feel that since colonists can't vote for members of the British Parliament, Parliament should not be allowed to tax the colonists. Furthermore, taxes on colonists have recently increased, and you feel that unless you mount a clear protest, British policies will become only worse.

You have received a letter from a relative in Philadelphia who has heard rumors about the Boston Tea Party. Your relative is worried that you might get into trouble and that your activities might make the situation for American colonists worse than it already is. Write a short letter explaining other forms of protest that you considered and why you decided to participate in the Boston Tea Party. As you plan your letter, keep in mind that your relative is concerned about the possibility of war. Include transitions to link the details and ideas of your explanation together.

Explaining a Process

Here's How It Works

If you've ever followed instructions for assembling a kit, sewing a blouse, or operating unfamiliar equipment, you know how important it is that the process be explained clearly and simply. In the model below, Marcus Romero explains how to make an essential piece of football equipment.

Student Model

One of the football player's most important pieces of protective equipment is a mouth guard. This is one piece of equipment that must be made to fit the person who will use it. The first step in making a mouth guard is to select a mouth piece that is the correct size. . . . The next step is to fit the mouth piece to your mouth. To do this, you'll need to heat a pot of water. While the water is boiling, dip the plastic mouth piece in the water for ten to fifteen seconds. Immediately remove the mouth piece from the water and place it in your mouth. The plastic will be warm, but it isn't hot enough to burn your mouth. Bite down on the mouth piece and suck the excess water out of it. Then remove it from your mouth, spit out the water, and run the mouth piece under cold water. . . .

Marcus Romero, Saint Bonaventure High School, Ventura, California

If you want to make a mouth guard, what is the first thing you do after selecting a mouth piece of the correct size?

Romero explains a fairly simple process that requires steps to be performed in a certain order. In the passage below, John McPhee presents a far more complex process involving years of interaction between rivers and rock to create the whitewater rapids of the expansive Grand Canyon.

Literature Model

Rapids and waterfalls ordinarily take shape when rivers cut against resistant rock and then come to a kind of rock that gives way more easily. This is not the case in the Grand ➡

Canyon, where rapids occur beside the mouths of tributary creeks. Although these little streams may be dry much of the year, they are so steep that when they run they are able to fling considerable debris into the Colorado [River]—sand, gravel, stones, rocks, boulders. The debris forms dams, and water rises upstream. The river is unusually quiet there—a lakelike quiet—and then it flows over the debris, falling suddenly, pounding and crashing through the boulders. These are the rapids of the Grand Canyon, and there are a hundred and sixty-one of them.

John McPhee, *Encounters with the Archdruid*

What is the first step in the process McPhee describes?

The Basic Steps

Explaining a process is harder than it seems. Try teaching a beginner how to shoot a foul shot in basketball. Where do you stand? How do you hold the ball? To explain a process in writing, think through the steps and arrange them in order. After drafting, work through the steps to make sure you've distilled the process in a way your audience can understand. The chart below can guide your writing.

Prewriting
Research the process by reading, watching others, or performing it yourself. Analyze the separate actions or steps necessary to complete the process.

Drafting
Arrange the steps in chronological order. Break one step into two if more detail is needed. Leave out unnecessary steps.

Revising
Reread the explanation. Make sure that you've included all necessary details and signaled separate steps with transition words. Reorder steps as needed.

• JOURNAL ACTIVITY •
Think It Through

Think of a simple process you perform, such as checking messages on an answering machine or operating a microwave oven. List in your journal the steps involved in this process.

Sizing Up the Audience

As you plan your composition, think about who your audience will be. What do they already know about the process you are explaining? How much detail are they likely to want or understand? Will your explanation use unfamiliar terms that you need to define? The excerpt below, explaining how bicycle derailleur gears work, comes from a book that describes the workings of a wide range of machines for people with little technical background.

Drafting Tip

As you draft your explanation, use analogies to give a clear picture of a complicated process.

Literature Model

The chain connecting the pedals of a bicycle to the rear wheel acts as a belt to make the wheel turn faster than the feet. To ride on the level or downhill, the rear-wheel sprocket needs to be small for high speeds. But to climb hills it needs to be large so that the rear wheel turns with less speed but more force.

Derailleur gears solve the problem by having rear-wheel sprockets of different sizes. A gear-changing mechanism transfers the chain from one sprocket to the next.

David Macaulay, *The Way Things Work*

This simple explanation gives readers a basic understanding of a process, using vocabulary that most readers can understand. Notice how the explanation below provides more thorough information using technical terms such as *chainwheel* and *freewheel* that the first writer found unnecessary. This excerpt comes from a book written for serious cyclists who may want to work on their bicycles themselves.

Literature Model

The basic derailleur system uses a combination of two sprockets (called chainwheels) on the front where the pedals are joined, and five sprockets (called the freewheel) at the rear attached to the wheel. To utilize all of the potential gear variations, a method to move the chain from sprocket to sprocket was developed. Using a control lever, the rider can move the derailleur which in turn forces (derails) the chain to adjacent sprockets.

Denise M. de la Rosa and Michael Kolin,
Understanding, Maintaining, and Riding the Ten-Speed Bicycle

The following are some writing options to help you try out what you have learned.

1. Guided Assignment   Pay phones operate differently around the world. In some countries, you wait for the party you are calling to answer before inserting your money. The party on the other end can't hear you until you pay for the call. Imagine you are writing a brochure for foreign visitors to your town. Your brochure will include directions on how to use pay phones in your region.

List the information you need to include. Then order the steps involved and write a draft. Make any necessary revisions.

PURPOSE   To explain how to operate a pay phone
AUDIENCE   Foreign visitors with a good understanding of written English
LENGTH   1–3 paragraphs

2. Open Assignment   Imagine you belong to a club that offers inexpensive workshops to raise money for charity. As a member of the club, you have been asked to offer a short workshop demonstrating a useful skill. Prepare by writing an essay explaining the skill to someone who knows little about it. Choose a skill from the following list. List what you know about the process, place the steps in order, and then write an explanation for each step. After drafting your essay, read it to a friend to see whether the explanation makes sense. Revise your essay on the basis of your friend's comments.

- how to shoot a foul shot
- how to balance a checkbook
- how to change a bicycle tire
- how to apply eye makeup

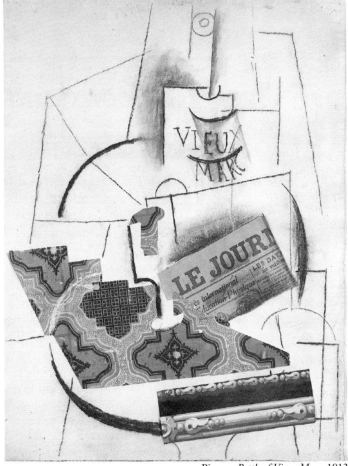

Picasso, *Bottle of Vieux Marc*, 1912

- how to use a word processor to cut and paste text
- any process you know well and would like to teach to someone else

3. Art   The picture on this page combines drawing and collage, a process in which bits of paper and other material are pasted down to form a design.

Imagine you are an artist teaching one of your students how to make a collage. Prepare for this assignment by making a collage of materials you choose. As you work note the steps you follow. Then write out an explanation of the process you used to make a collage.

Analyzing Cause-and-Effect Connections

Cartoons and Satellites

Literature Model

What's up, Doc? Animation, that's what. And that was-cally wabbit Bugs Bunny, who celebrated his 50th birthday in 1990, is only part of animation's exciting comeback. Animation seems to be everywhere. For the first time in 30 years, many movie theaters are running cartoon shorts before live-action motion pictures. . . . And on television, "The Simpsons," the first prime-time weekly animated TV series on a United States network in 20 years, has consistently ranked among the top-rated programs. . . .

One explanation for the animation boom is the high quality of the artwork in the new cartoons and features. Thanks in part to computers, animation has never looked better. Another reason is the appeal animation has for the large chunk of the U.S. population known as baby boomers—people born between 1945 and 1964—who grew up with TV cartoons and who are now looking for entertainment they can enjoy with their own children.

But the biggest reason for the revival of animation, once scarcely seen outside Saturday morning television, is financial reward. . . . When they are successful, . . . [cartoons] can be as profitable as the most popular live-action movies. By late 1990, more than 30 full-length animated motion pictures were in production around the world.

John Canemaker, "Once Again, 'Toons' Are Tops,"
The 1991 World Book Year Book

Many writing assignments will ask you to explain the connections between an event and its causes or consequences. To do this, you will need to determine what those cause-and-effect relationships are and to communicate them clearly to your readers.

Cause-and-Effect Relationships

John Canemaker shows how several causes led to one event, the resurgence of animation. The top panel of the diagram below illustrates this type of cause-and-effect relationship.

In other cases, one event can have several effects. For example, when the Soviet Union launched the first orbiting satellite, *Sputnik*, in 1957, the U.S. government reacted in three ways. Fear of Soviet technical domination led the Eisenhower administration to step up the arms race, to begin its own space program, and to increase funding for science research and education. The middle panel of the diagram illustrates these multiple effects of the *Sputnik* launch.

Still another kind of cause-and-effect relationship is the causal chain, in which one event affects the next, as in a line of falling dominoes. In the bottom panel of the diagram one sees that an increased demand for lobster leads to overfishing. The decrease in the number of lobsters, which are the natural predators of sea urchins, in turn causes an increase in the number of sea urchins.

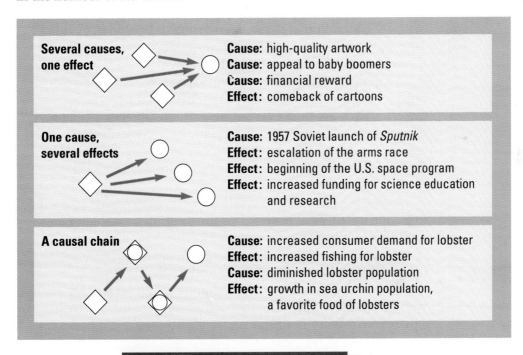

Several causes, one effect

Cause: high-quality artwork
Cause: appeal to baby boomers
Cause: financial reward
Effect: comeback of cartoons

One cause, several effects

Cause: 1957 Soviet launch of *Sputnik*
Effect: escalation of the arms race
Effect: beginning of the U.S. space program
Effect: increased funding for science education and research

A causal chain

Cause: increased consumer demand for lobster
Effect: increased fishing for lobster
Cause: diminished lobster population
Effect: growth in sea urchin population, a favorite food of lobsters

• JOURNAL ACTIVITY •
Think It Through

Think of other examples for each of the three kinds of cause-and-effect relationships shown above. Copy the diagram for each type of relationship into your journal and provide new cause-and-effect labels for each type of relationship.

The Cause-and-Effect Essay

Editing Tip

As you edit a cause-and-effect essay, be sure that your verb tenses clearly reflect the order of events.

Writers help their audience understand events by explaining connections to other events. When you write a cause-and-effect essay, make certain that the events you write about have a true cause-and-effect relationship. Just because one event follows another doesn't mean it was caused by the earlier event. For example, people once believed they needed to perform rituals to stop a solar eclipse. We now know, however, that an eclipse will end no matter what we do or don't do.

By connecting causes and effects, a writer shows patterns that simplify a jumble of events. In the model below, William S. Ellis helps readers understand the modern city by combining elements of two of the three basic cause-and-effect relationships shown on page 217.

Literature Model

How many causes are discussed in this model? How many effects?

*T*his is a magical time in the evolution of America's urban landscapes, a time of bold (for better or worse), fresh architecture and computer-driven engineering, and a time too of a new generation of skyscrapers rising to be clad in clouds over major cities across the country—Minneapolis, even, and Los Angeles with its ill-defined downtown.

All of this is happening at a time when, paradoxically, organized opposition to construction of sunlight-blocking towers is stronger than ever before. It is too late, however, to reverse the reality that the skyscraper has become the logo for urban development in America; from King Kong to Donald Trump, it has bridged the 20th century with its indestructible, prodigious presence.

Draw a diagram to represent the cause-and-effect relationships described in this paragraph.

Today's skyscraper is a creation of economics and the need to escape the press of horizontal crowding. With raw land in midtown Manhattan now costing more than entire buildings a few decades ago, it is not surprising that developers are looking upward rather than outward. And (in the right place, in good times) a prestigious new building can attract tenants who will happily pay more than a thousand dollars for each square foot of lofty floor space they occupy.

William S. Ellis, "Skyscrapers: Above the Crowd," *National Geographic*

Notice that in his opening discussion of the reasons for the evolution of America's urban landscape, Ellis mentions three causes. Then he takes one of those causes, a new generation of skyscrapers, and discusses it as an *effect* with several causes of its own. In essence, Ellis presents a causal chain in reverse.

Writer's Choice

The following are some writing options to help you try out what you have learned.

1. Guided Assignment Make a list of the reasons you think music videos are popular with teen-agers. Then imagine you have been asked to write an article explaining the popularity of music videos among teen-agers for your school's Parent-Teacher Association newsletter. Using the model for multiple causes leading to a single effect in the top panel of the diagram on page 217, plan your essay. As you draft your essay, use transitions that show cause-and-effect relationships. As you revise your essay, make sure that all the details you use contribute to the main idea of the essay.

PURPOSE To explain the appeal of music videos
AUDIENCE Parents of teen-agers
LENGTH 1–2 pages

2. Open Assignment A local weather forecaster has asked you to supplement television weather reports with an explanation of the causes and effects of weather patterns. These explanations will be presented during the evening news and must be comprehensible and interesting to the average television viewer.

Select and research one of these types of weather: snow, hurricanes, drought, freezing rain, or a weather system of your choice. Start by creating a cause-and-effect diagram and include any transitions needed to help listeners understand the cause-and-effect relationships. Then write an essay explaining the causes and effects of this type of weather.

3. Cooperative Learning Mathew Brady, one of the earliest American photographers, traveled with the Union army to capture the

Culver Pictures, Inc.

Civil War with his camera. The Brady photograph on this page shows four members of the Union army, probably taken in about 1863.

Working in a small group, assign one character in the photograph to each group member. Noting details of posture, facial expression, and dress, create a personal background for your character, extending back to 1855. Write down the chain of events that caused you to become involved in the war. Then, in one page, explain how the war has affected your life and your feelings about slavery and states' rights.

As a group, discuss the characters' perspectives. Then, together write a two- to three-page script for a play that illustrates causes and effects discussed in each character profile.

Writing an Essay to Compare and Contrast

· APPLES and ORANGES ·

EDIBLE
WARM COLOR
ROUND SHAPE
SIMILAR SIZE
CONTAIN SEEDS
GROW ON TREES
GOOD FOR JUICE
NAMES BEGIN WITH VOWEL
SIMILAR PESTICIDE TREATMENT
UNSUITABLE FOR MOST SPORTS

Apples and Oranges

As you can see from the cartoon to the left, almost any two objects—even apples and oranges—can be compared. Everyone knows that apples and oranges are different; the trick is to find the ways in which they are similar. This cartoonist was able to find many ways in which apples and oranges are alike, though some are more humorous than serious.

Dalia Bichay wrote the essay below about engagement practices in Egypt and the United States. Notice that Dalia includes both similarities and differences in her discussion.

Student Model

Why do you think Dalia explains American customs before informing her audience about Egyptian practices?

American couples celebrate their engagement and marriage differently from couples in my homeland, Egypt. Here in the United States, in most cases, a couple dates for a while until they decide to get married. They then announce their engagement to their families. In the Egyptian culture, men and women cannot date without a chaperon until they decide to marry. To formalize their engagement, the man must ask the woman's parents, while his parents are present, for their daughter's hand in marriage. If the parents do not agree to the engagement, the relationship between the two must end.

In the United States, during the engagement friends and relatives often throw a wedding shower for the bride, while the groom is given a bachelor's party. In Egypt, a wedding shower is held for the couple. Both American and Egyptian showers feature music, food, and gifts, but the Egyptian shower has one special item on the night's agenda. The table where the bride and groom sit has a bowl of mud, placed there by one of their parents, with a candle in it. This bowl is blessed by a priest who then draws a cross with the mud on ➡

both the man's and the woman's forehead. This shared cross symbolizes their holy unity.

In each culture, the man and woman marry in a wedding ceremony. An American wedding lasts about half an hour to an hour. The Egyptian wedding lasts anywhere from one to two hours. In both cultures, couples are united by a kiss at the end of the ceremony.

Dalia Bichay, Quartz Hill High School, Quartz Hill, California

What comparison between ceremonies in the two cultures concludes Dalia's essay?

A compare-and-contrast essay allows you to give more information than an essay that simply defines one subject. For example, you can clearly define frozen yogurt by saying it has the same consistency as soft ice cream but it contains less fat. It would be much more difficult to define frozen yogurt—or almost anything else—without referring to similar or different items.

Shaping Your Essay

The thesis statement of a compare-and-contrast essay expresses the essential differences and similarities between two subjects. The thesis gives the essay a shape, much as the concept of a constellation leads you to see the linkage among some stars while regarding other stars as extraneous to the pattern. As a result, the thesis statement determines what information belongs in the essay.

The thesis statement of Dalia Bichay's essay, for example, is that Egyptian engagement and wedding customs are more formal than American customs even though they share a common goal. Therefore, Dalia included only information about dating practices, the process of getting engaged, and the actual marriage ceremony in Egypt and the United States. She did not include information about, for example, schools, styles of dress, or child-rearing practices because information on these topics was not related to her thesis. Nor did she include information on dating in Brazil or weddings in China.

• JOURNAL ACTIVITY •
Think It Through

Select two places you know well to compare and contrast. Jot down some ideas for a thesis statement about how these subjects may be compared and contrasted. List some elements that these places have in common; then list some elements that are different.

Sorting the Elements

In the model below, Joseph Weizenbaum explains the differences and similarities between two types of computer programmers. Writers rarely follow a rigorous organizational pattern in comparing and contrasting two subjects; Weizenbaum, however, generally discusses first one type of programmer and then a second type of programmer.

Literature Model

Weizenbaum states his thesis near the beginning of the passage and then proceeds to assemble evidence.

How may the compulsive programmer be distinguished from a merely dedicated, hard-working professional programmer? First, by the fact that the ordinary professional programmer addresses himself to the problem to be solved while the compulsive programmer sees it mainly as an opportunity to interact with the computer. The ordinary computer programmer will . . . do lengthy preparatory work, such as writing and flow diagramming, before beginning work with the computer itself. . . . He may even let others do the actual console work. . . .

How has the thesis influenced Weizenbaum's choice of details in these paragraphs?

Unlike the professional, the compulsive programmer cannot attend to other tasks, not even tasks closely related to his program, while not actually operating the computer. He can barely tolerate being away from the machine. But when he is forced by circumstances to be separated from it nevertheless, he has his computer print-outs with him. He studies them, he talks about them to anyone who will listen, though no one can understand. Indeed, while in the grip of his compulsion, he can talk of nothing but his program. But the only time he is, so to say, happy is when he is at the computer console.

Joseph Weizenbaum,
"Science and the Compulsive
Programmer," *Partisan Review*

Professional Programmer

- Goal is to solve a problem
- Allows others to operate the computer
- Can attend to other aspects of his work

All Programmers

- Work with computers
- Skilled and hard-working

Compulsive Programmer

- Views problem as a chance to interact with computer
- Cannot attend to other aspects of his work
- Happy only when working at the computer

Before you write an essay to compare and contrast, you need to decide how to sort your information. This Venn diagram offers one way to explore the similarities and differences that were presented in the model above. Notice that similarities appear in the area where the circles overlap.

Sketching It Out

There are two basic ways of organizing a compare-and-contrast essay. The chart below illustrates both kinds of organization.

Feature Approach: Egyptian courtship

Feature 1 (Engagement)
U.S.:   occurs after a period of dating
Egypt: begins a dating relationship

Feature 2 (Wedding Shower)
U.S.:   for woman only
Egypt: for both man and woman

Feature 3 (Wedding)
U.S.:   lasts 1/2 – 1 hour, ends with kiss
Egypt: lasts 1 – 2 hours, ends with kiss

Subject Approach: Computer programmers

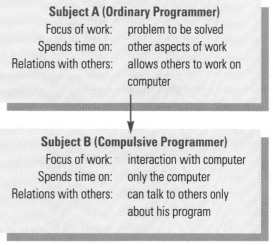

Subject A (Ordinary Programmer)
Focus of work: problem to be solved
Spends time on: other aspects of work
Relations with others: allows others to work on computer

Subject B (Compulsive Programmer)
Focus of work: interaction with computer
Spends time on: only the computer
Relations with others: can talk to others only about his program

Dalia organizes her essay on Egyptian marriage/courtship practices by feature. First she compares and contrasts engagement practices in both cultures, then wedding showers, and finally wedding ceremonies. With a feature approach to organization, you move back and forth between each subject (in Dalia's case, the United States and Egypt) while discussing each feature.

Weizenbaum's discussion of computer programmers is organized by subject rather than by feature. The subjects of his comparison are ordinary programmers and compulsive programmers. Weizenbaum begins by briefly characterizing each type. Then he discusses the attributes, or features, of each programmer in greater detail. With this organization a writer lays a foundation by describing one subject and then describes the second subject in relation to the first. Neither the feature nor subject approach is necessarily better than the other; purpose, topic, thesis, and personal preference determine the method that is better for each essay.

Drafting Tip

As you begin writing comparisons, you might want to refer to the Usage section of this book for more information on indicating degrees of comparison.

• JOURNAL ACTIVITY •
Try It Out

Create a chart or Venn diagram to compare and contrast two appliances or products you use regularly. For example, you might compare and contrast a toothbrush with a hairbrush, a toaster with a toaster oven, or a television with a radio.

Achieving Coherence

Revising Tip

When you revise, check to make sure your comparisons and contrasts are clearly stated and in logical order.

How do you pull these features and subjects together into a clear and cohesive composition? Carefully chosen transitional words and phrases will show the relationships between features and will also improve the flow of your writing. See page 210 for a list of transitional words. Another technique that lends coherence to writing is repetition of key words and phrases. Repetition creates a link between ideas in your essay. Notice how Douglas Adams repeats forms of the words "compete," "survive," and "introduce" in the model below.

Adams begins by explaining what it is he intends to compare and contrast.

Which transitional phrase at the beginning of the second paragraph helps you understand the significance of the information that follows?

Which transitional phrase alerts you that Adams is about to contrast his second subject with his first?

Literature Model

An endemic species of plant or animal **is one that is native** to an island or region and is found nowhere else at all. **An exotic species is one that has been introduced** from abroad, and a disaster is usually what results when this occurs.

The reason is this: continental land masses are big. They support hundreds of thousands, even millions, of different species, **each of which is competing** with one another **for survival.** The sheer ferocity **of the competition** is immense, and it means that the species that do **survive** and flourish are mean little fighters. They grow faster and throw out a lot more seeds.

An island, **on the other hand,** is small. There are far fewer species, and **the competition for survival** has never reached anything like the pitch that it does on the mainland. Species are only as tough as they need to be, life is much quieter and more settled, and evolution proceeds at a much slower rate. **This is why** you find on Madagascar, for instance, species like the lemurs that were overwhelmed eons ago on the mainland. Island ecologies are fragile time capsules.

So you can imagine what happens when a mainland species gets **introduced** to an island. **It would be like introducing** Al Capone . . . to the Isle of Wight—the locals wouldn't stand a chance.

Douglas Adams, *Last Chance to See*

In this excerpt, Adams explains the role of natural competition on a continent and then contrasts that with the role of competition on an island. You can review commonly used transitions and the relationships they indicate by referring to Lesson 5.1, page 210. By repeating certain key ideas, and linking them with transitional phrases, Adams makes it easy to follow and understand his explanation.

The following are some writing options to help you try out what you have learned.

1. Guided Assignment

Imagine that you work in the public relations department of *either* an association of movie theater owners *or* an association of cable television operators. Make a Venn diagram comparing and contrasting watching a movie at a theater and watching a movie on TV. Pattern your diagram after the one on page 222 of this lesson.

Alan Berner, *A Day in the Life of America*

Then write an essay comparing and contrasting watching a movie in a theater and watching one at home. The essay will inform people of the pleasures or convenience of watching movies in a theater *or* of watching movies on television at home.

PURPOSE   Explain the advantages of watching movies in a theater *or* at home

AUDIENCE   People who have stopped going to movie theaters *or* people who do not subscribe to cable television

LENGTH   1–2 pages

2. Open Assignment

Imagine students in your school have started a consumers' newsletter aimed at high school students in your region. This newsletter will contain articles that compare and contrast products and services students use or might use. You have been asked to contribute an article. Write an article for fellow students comparing and contrasting one of the following:

- racing bikes versus trail bikes
- hightops versus running shoes
- two restaurants
- cassette tapes versus compact discs
- two shopping malls
- two products of your choice

3. Cooperative Learning

Working in a small group, look at the photograph on this page. Take notes as the group orally compares and contrasts the occupational risks, benefits, and responsibilities of the two men in this photograph. Then each of you will select one feature for a compare-and-contrast essay (for example, opportunities for exercise or possibilities for career advancement) about these two men. After each student has written a paragraph comparing and contrasting the jobs of the two men in terms of the feature he or she has selected, combine the information in the paragraphs into a single compare-and-contrast essay. Decide whether a subject approach or a feature approach is better for your material.

Unlocking Gridlock

Have you ever been so stuck in traffic that you began to wonder whether you'd ever get home again? The number of cars on the road multiplies significantly each year as Americans opt for the convenience and comfort of a private car instead of the efficiency of car pools and public transportation. Convenience and comfort have their costs, however, and traffic congestion is just one of the prices you pay.

Literature Model

R emember when getting there was half the fun? When driving was a breeze and flying was a cinch? No longer. Gridlock has gripped America, threatening to transform its highways and flyways into snarled barriers to progress. . . .

The congestion, which is certain to grow worse in the coming decade, is hampering Americans' cherished mobility and changing the way they travel and do business. Instead of boasting "I Get Around," the tune they are wailing nowadays is "Don't Get Around Much Anymore." Consider:

The Detroit Tigers baseball team lost an important asset last week when its newly hired outfielder, Fred Lynn, failed to qualify for postseason play. Reason: he got caught in a traffic jam. Lynn was playing in Anaheim, Calif. . . . when he accepted Detroit's offer late Wednesday afternoon. But to qualify for the playoffs under league rules, he had to join the team, then in Chicago, by midnight. The Tigers chartered a jet for Lynn . . . but rush-hour congestion reportedly stretched his 35-minute drive to an hour and 15 minutes. That proved a costly delay: Lynn's plane did not reach Chicago airspace until 12:10 A.M.

Stephen Koepp, "Gridlock!" *Time* magazine

How does the writer pull you into the article ?

A colorful example of how a traffic jam affected one man helps readers identify with the problem.

Weighing the Problem

Suppose you want to write about the problem of traffic congestion. First gather information from a range of sources to answer such questions as: What is the nature and extent of the problem? What are the causes of the problem? How does the problem affect people, the environment, and the economy? What would happen if nothing were done about the problem? You may have to do some library research to answer these questions. See Unit 7 for additional information on how to research a topic.

Different kinds of information can help you explain dimensions of a problem. Personal anecdotes can help your readers relate a problem to their own lives. Statistics, on the other hand, allow you to present an overview of a problem, as shown in the chart below.

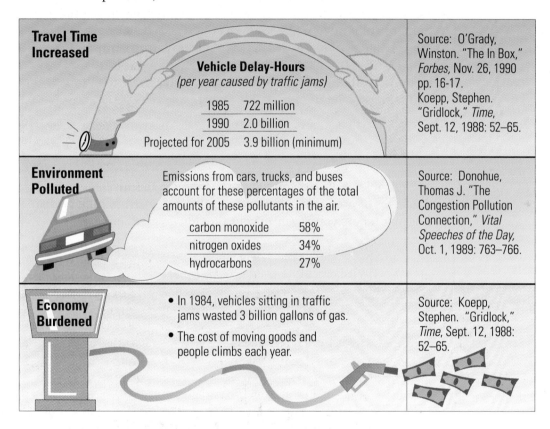

Travel Time Increased	**Vehicle Delay-Hours** *(per year caused by traffic jams)* 1985 — 722 million 1990 — 2.0 billion Projected for 2005 — 3.9 billion (minimum)	Source: O'Grady, Winston. "The In Box," *Forbes*, Nov. 26, 1990 pp. 16-17. Koepp, Stephen. "Gridlock," *Time*, Sept. 12, 1988: 52–65.
Environment Polluted	Emissions from cars, trucks, and buses account for these percentages of the total amounts of these pollutants in the air. carbon monoxide — 58% nitrogen oxides — 34% hydrocarbons — 27%	Source: Donohue, Thomas J. "The Congestion Pollution Connection," *Vital Speeches of the Day*, Oct. 1, 1989: 763–766.
Economy Burdened	• In 1984, vehicles sitting in traffic jams wasted 3 billion gallons of gas. • The cost of moving goods and people climbs each year.	Source: Koepp, Stephen. "Gridlock," *Time*, Sept. 12, 1988: 52–65.

• JOURNAL ACTIVITY •
Try It Out

Spend at least ten minutes freewriting in your journal about a social problem that interests you. Then brainstorm a list of ways to explain the problem.

Presenting Solutions

Your first step in writing about a problem may be to explain how it affects people. But writing about problems and solutions goes beyond simply explaining the problem and its dimensions. This type of expository writing also presents solutions. Jennifer Hudgins presents her solution to the problem of traffic congestion in the paragraph below.

Student Model

*T*he most practical solution to traffic congestion is to reduce traffic by encouraging people to use mass transit and car pools. . . . To encourage people to use mass transit systems, companies who supply employees with company cars and pay for parking fees should instead pay for employees' bus, train, or subway fare. Another incentive is to restrict more freeway lanes to high-occupancy vehicles. During morning rush hour on Interstate 350 in Virginia, two high-occupancy lanes carry about 33,000 commuters, slightly more than four regular lanes, yet in only one-fifth as many vehicles.

Jennifer Hudgins, Penn Manor High School, Millersville, Pennsylvania

Most problems have many solutions. Examine the advantages and disadvantages of proposed solutions carefully and systematically. A chart like this might help you organize your thoughts.

Table of Solutions		
Possible Solution	**Advantages**	**Disadvantages**
1. Build more highways	• reduces congestion immediately	• eats up land • encourages more traffic
2. Improve mass transit	• transports many people efficiently • reduces pollution • reduces need for parking	• trains and buses don't always take people where they need to go
3. Give tax or road toll incentives to car pools	• encourages commuters to car pool, reducing the number of cars	• car pools can be inconvenient

By listing each solution with its advantages and disadvantages, you can see that while each of these solutions offers some relief to the problem of traffic congestion, none of them can solve the problem completely. Be realistic when you explain solutions.

Writer's Choice

The following are some writing options to help you try out what you have learned.

1. **Guided Assignment** You have been asked to contribute to a report on traffic congestion being prepared by the planning board of your local government. Your job is to report on traffic congestion or hazards in a particular location in your community. Note the times and nature of the congestion or hazards. You may supplement your observations with statistics from this lesson. Propose two or more possible solutions to the traffic problem you have identified. Describe some of the advantages and disadvantages of each proposed solution.

PURPOSE	To explain about a local traffic problem and recommend a solution
AUDIENCE	Officials of a local planning board
LENGTH	2–3 pages

2. **Open Assignment** Analyze the issue of cutting education programs to balance budgets. You may use examples from your local community or research information about school systems in other regions or nationwide. Imagine that you are going to write a letter to the editor of a newspaper or magazine explaining the problem and proposing one or more solutions. Write from the perspective of one of the following:

- a parent with three children in the public schools
- an official facing reelection in the next six months
- a retired person whose grandchildren live in another city
- a teacher whose contract may not be renewed
- an ambitious high school student who hopes to enter a competitive premedical program
- a perspective of your choice

COMPUTER OPTION

Before you draft your letter for the Open Assignment, outline details on your computer. Many word-processing programs include a feature that creates a skeleton draft while you create an outline. As you come up with new ideas for your letter and enter the changes on your outline, the draft changes simultaneously. After you have completed your outline, "flesh out" your skeleton draft. Then use the cut-and-paste feature on your computer to help you revise and edit the draft.

3. **Speech** Working with one other student, scan recent issues of newspapers and news magazines to identify and learn about a social problem or issue that interests both of you. Develop a table of solutions similar to that shown on page 228. Decide what groups of people are in a position to bring about change. Each of you should then write a short speech to be presented to one or more of the groups who can implement a solution. Conclude each speech with a recommendation about a solution.

4. **American Literature** Many American authors have written about social problems. Upton Sinclair, John Steinbeck, James Baldwin, Harper Lee, Joseph Heller, Grace Paley, and Bobbie Ann Mason are examples. Review a work of fiction you have read that deals with a social problem. Imagine that you are a character in the novel or short story and write an informative essay discussing one of the social problems that affects you in the book or story. Propose some possible solutions. Assess the advantages and disadvantages of each solution you propose and tell the author which solution or combination of solutions you think would be most effective.

Using Time Lines and Process Diagrams

Words Aren't Everything

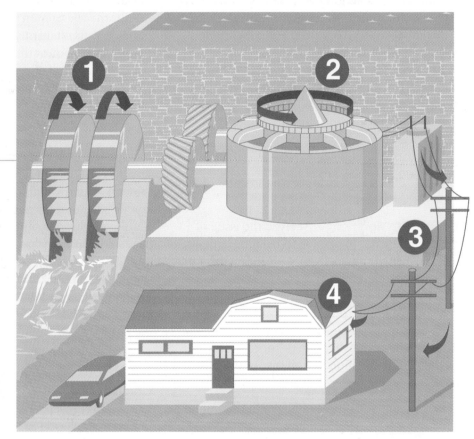

Producing Electricity

1. *Flowing water pushes the turbines' panels, forcing them to rotate.*
2. *Magnets in the generator turn the force of rotation into electrical energy.*
3. *Transmission lines carry electric current in to the house.*
4. *Switches and outlets provide access to electricity.*

If you've ever had to explain how to run a computer program, you know how difficult it can be to reduce a complex series of steps to simple terms. A drawing like the one on this page, however, makes a complex process—in this case, producing electricity—easy for your audience to grasp. Very few words need accompany the drawing to convey how this generator functions. Time lines and process diagrams are other kinds of graphic depictions that present events, processes, and complicated relationships in a form that can be easier to understand than they would be through words alone.

The Time Line in Action

Seeing one time line doesn't mean you've seen them all. Often time lines highlight important events. However, you can construct time lines to organize many types of data. You can use arrows to connect events linked by cause-and-effect relationships. You can also group events using brackets or color to illustrate stages in a person's life. The time line for Sojourner Truth on page 177 illustrates use of a time line.

A time line can also make comparisons and contrasts. You might compare the development of printing in China to the development of printing in Europe. You could place one set of dates above the time line, the other below. The following time line also makes a comparison, but in a different way. The dates above the time line highlight "firsts" for women in education. The percentages below the time line compare and contrast the overall enrollment of women and men in colleges and universities.

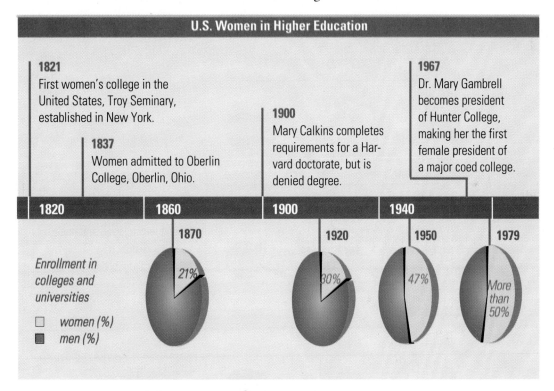

U.S. Women in Higher Education

1821
First women's college in the United States, Troy Seminary, established in New York.

1837
Women admitted to Oberlin College, Oberlin, Ohio.

1900
Mary Calkins completes requirements for a Harvard doctorate, but is denied degree.

1967
Dr. Mary Gambrell becomes president of Hunter College, making her the first female president of a major coed college.

1820   1860   1900   1940

1870   1920   1950   1979

Enrollment in colleges and universities

☐ women (%)
■ men (%)

21%   30%   47%   More than 50%

• JOURNAL ACTIVITY •
Think It Through

Think of two events that you would like to compare and contrast. Make notes in your journal about the ways that you might use a time line to illustrate some point of comparison or contrast between the events.

Showing a Process

A time line can help you show the order of events by tying them to dates. Sometimes, however, you will want to portray the sequence of activities that go into a process. A process diagram will help you portray such a sequence. You don't have to be a talented artist to sketch the major activities in a process. Notice how the process diagram below supports and enhances the explanation of how to use a flywheel rowing machine.

How to Use a Flywheel Rowing Machine

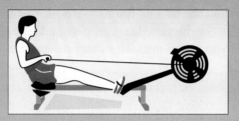

Step 1
Place feet under straps and adjust for comfortable fit. Grasp handlebar and extend legs. Bring handlebars into chest.

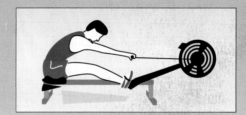

Step 2
Extend arms, lean forward from hips keeping back straight, and bend knees to pull seat forward.

Step 3
Extend legs to slide seat back. Lean backwards from hips. Pull handlebars into chest.

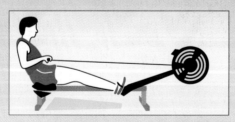

Step 4
Repeat steps 2 and 3 without stopping. Step 3 should be three times faster than step 2.

The process diagram above combines pictures and text in a step-by-step format to make a fairly complex process comprehensible to a reader, even one who has never before used or seen a flywheel rowing machine. Such a diagram can enhance an explanation of almost any process.

Writer's Choice

The following are some writing options to help you try out what you have learned.

1. Guided Assignment You have been asked to teach an exercise routine to a group of students your age. You can decide to teach a routine that involves a machine or special equipment, a routine that utilizes yoga or stretching, or a routine that involves dance or gymnastic skills.

Imagine that the night before your presentation, you sprain your ankle. Since you can't demonstrate the routine as you normally would, you decide to write the steps involved in the routine and present it orally with a large process diagram to accompany your presentation. Write the steps of your routine and create a poster-sized process diagram to accompany it. Present your routine to your class or a smaller group.

PURPOSE To present orally an exercise routine
AUDIENCE High school students
LENGTH 1–2 pages of text accompanied by a poster-sized process diagram

2. Open Assignment Select a familiar process from the list below. Write a how-to paragraph that explains how to perform the process.

- how to feed and groom a particular type of animal
- how to obtain a driver's license in your state
- how to videotape a television program
- how to cross-country ski
- how to perform a process of your choice

After writing your paragraph, create a process diagram to illustrate the tasks involved. Begin by dividing the process into simple steps. Sketch the equipment and actions required to complete each step. Make sure that the steps follow one another logically and that you do not omit any essential information.

3. Chemistry Select a chemistry experiment that you have performed in a chemistry lab this year. Imagine that you have been asked to teach this experiment to another group of students. List the steps involved in the experiment. Then create a process diagram that portrays the steps of the experiment. Use the diagram as part of an essay that explains the purpose of the experiment and what you learned from it.

4. American History Imagine that you have been asked to make an oral presentation to a history club in your town or city about the causes that led to a historical situation. Possible topics include the process of ratifying the U.S. Constitution, causes of the Civil War, or events leading to woman suffrage (right to vote). Construct a time line that shows the stages that led up to the notable event. Then write an oral report explaining the causes of the historical situation. Be sure to cover all the events included on your time line. Present your report to your class or a small group, using your time line to illustrate your talk.

COMPUTER OPTION

You can store facts and dates you may want to use for the American history time line in your computer. You can type each piece of information, give it a heading, and box it so it looks like a note card. You can then work on and organize your boxed computer notes just as you would note cards, adding, deleting, and rearranging facts and dates. When you've finished collecting information and are ready to prepare your time line, you can simply call up your boxes of data and plug them into the time line as you are constructing it.

Arsenic and Iced Cherries

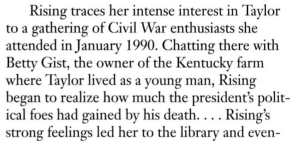

Abraham Lincoln was the first president of the United States to be assassinated—or was he? Zachary Taylor died on July 9, 1850, sixteen months into his term as twelfth president. He fell ill after consuming large quantities of iced cherries and cold milk at the dedication of the Washington Monument on a very hot Fourth of July. Although most historians believed that Taylor died of a stomach ailment, Dr. Clara Rising, former humanities professor at the University of Florida and a historical novelist, found the suddenness of his illness suspect in a man of robust health.

Rising traces her intense interest in Taylor to a gathering of Civil War enthusiasts she attended in January 1990. Chatting there with Betty Gist, the owner of the Kentucky farm where Taylor lived as a young man, Rising began to realize how much the president's political foes had gained by his death. . . . Rising's strong feelings led her to the library and eventually to a Gainesville-based forensic pathologist, Dr. William Maples. She showed him contemporary accounts of Taylor's five-day death agony, which had been ascribed to cholera morbus, a catch-all phrase then used to describe a variety of intestinal illnesses. Maples said that it sounded more like "a classic case of arsenic poisoning."

Newsweek, July 1, 1991

Rising realized that Taylor, a southerner who opposed the extension of slavery and who wanted to bring California and New Mexico into the Union as free states, posed a threat to proslavery factions. The more she studied the case, the more she began to think that Taylor had been poisoned by his political opponents.

Developing a Hypothesis

Questions about the causes of Taylor's death prompted Dr. Rising to develop a new hypothesis to explain the facts of the president's death. You might build a hypothesis to explain a foreign policy decision in a history paper or a chemical reaction in a lab report. Whether used to explain the past or predict the future, hypotheses allow you to find explanations and solve mysteries. The chart below portrays the steps required to build a hypothesis and the way Dr. Rising carried them out.

Building a Hypothesis				
Step 1 Identify what you are trying to explain.	**Step 2** Collect data and consult experts.	**Step 3** Compare and contrast data to identify patterns or trends.	**Step 4** Decide on most reasonable hypothesis based on the data.	**Step 5** Test conclusion for acceptance, modification, or rejection.
Asked what caused Taylor's death.	*Researched historical accounts. Consulted forensic pathologist and historians.*	*Considered arsenic poisoning, stomach ailment, and other explanations.*	*Selected arsenic poisoning as best explanation of data.*	*Had Taylor's remains tested for traces of arsenic.*

The first step in building a hypothesis is to decide on the question you want to answer. Dr. Rising wanted to find the cause of Taylor's death.

Once you have collected your facts and expert opinions, either through research, observations, or interviews, examine them for patterns or trends. Dr. Rising noted, after consulting historical records and a forensic pathologist, that Taylor's death resembled that of someone who had been poisoned. She also noted that Taylor's political opponents benefited from his death. These observations led to the hypothesis that Taylor was poisoned by his political enemies.

The final step is to test your hypothesis. Dr. Rising tested hers by having Taylor's remains analyzed for arsenic. Since no appreciable levels of arsenic were found, it seems that Taylor died of natural causes after all. Dr. Rising, however, did not feel she had wasted her time. "We found the truth," she said. "The truth also contains the fact that his political enemies benefited from his removal, whether they removed him or not." Dr. Rising understood that a well-thought-out hypothesis, even if disproved, provides a framework for examining, organizing, and testing evidence.

Prewriting Tip

As you research a tentative hypothesis, keep these two questions in mind: What do you want to prove? What do you need to do to prove it?

• JOURNAL ACTIVITY •
Try It Out

You return home to find papers strewn all over your living room. The window in the living room is open. In your journal, explain how you would follow the steps outlined above to formulate and test a hypothesis.

Presenting Your Data

Once you have selected the hypothesis that offers the best explanation for your question, you need to present your thoughts in a logical and coherent manner. State your hypothesis in a thesis statement. This statement should be part of an introductory paragraph that suggests how and why your topic and thesis are important.

Develop your explanation in the body of your essay by supporting each point with specific examples, facts, or expert testimony where appropriate. Use transitional words and phrases to direct your readers from one idea to the next. (See pages 210 and 224 in lessons 5.1 and 5.4 for further discussion of transitional words and phrases.)

Finally, summarize your main points in your concluding paragraph. Draw a conclusion by evaluating the evidence you've assembled or by expressing a judgment or a realization. In the example below, Edward T. Hall, an expert in the science of proxemics (how people use the space around them) develops one aspect of his hypothesis that Arabs and Americans have difficulty understanding each other because they have very different ideas about how space should be used.

Literature Model

What assumption do Americans make about Arab conversational style?

How do many Arabs interpret American conversational patterns?

One mistaken American notion is that Arabs conduct all conversations at close distances. This is not the case at all. On social occasions, they may sit on opposite sides of the room and talk across the room to each other. They are, however, apt to take offense when Americans use what are to them ambiguous distances, such as the four- to seven-foot social-consultative distance. They frequently complain that Americans are cold or aloof or "don't care."...

Arabs are involved with each other on many different levels simultaneously. Privacy in a public place is foreign to them. Business transactions in the bazaar, for example, are not just between buyer and seller, but are participated in by everyone. Anyone who is standing around may join in. If a grownup sees a boy breaking a window, he must stop him even if he doesn't know him. Involvement and participation are expressed in other ways as well. If two men are fighting, the crowd must intervene....

Perceiving the world differently leads to differential definitions of what constitutes crowded living, different interpersonal relations, and a different approach to both local and international politics....

Edward T. Hall, "The Arab World," *The Hidden Dimension*

The following are some writing options to help you try out what you have learned.

1. Guided Assignment You are an Australian journalist whose job is to explain the following facts about American television-viewing habits to readers of an Australian magazine for teen-agers.

Edward Hopper, *Gas*, 1940

- Female teen-agers watch an average of 23 hours of television per week.
- Women aged 18–34 watch about 29 hours of television per week.
- Women aged 55 and over watch an average of 41 hours of television per week.

Follow the steps on page 235 to formulate a hypothesis that would explain these facts. What additional information would allow you to test your hypothesis? Write an essay presenting your hypothesis. Explain that further information is needed to test the hypothesis.

PURPOSE   To present a hypothesis that explains American television viewing habits

AUDIENCE   Readers of an Australian magazine for teen-agers

LENGTH   1–2 pages

2. Open Assignment You are a detective. The painting on this page is evidence in a case you are investigating. Formulate a hypothesis about who the man in this painting is and what he is doing. Present your hypothesis to your clients by following the steps in this lesson. Use details of dress, posture, and setting to support your hypothesis.

3. Cooperative Learning You are a market researcher for a large corporation that sells a variety of products for people in different age groups. Your company wants you to determine the best television programs and time slots for reaching likely buyers of each of their products.

Working in a small group, formulate a question about age-related viewing behavior for which you would like to develop a hypothesis. For example, is *Murphy Brown* especially popular with viewers aged 30–39? Do people aged 20–29 watch *The Simpsons* more than any other program? During what hours are people in the 50 and older age group most likely to be watching television?

Each member of your group will interview four people of different ages to determine their television viewing behavior. Divide your subjects into 5 age groups: 10–19, 20–29, 30–39, 40–49, and 50 and older.

Compile and analyze your data to test your hypothesis. Then follow the steps for presenting a hypothesis outlined on page 236 of this lesson. Each member of the group will draft, revise, and edit his or her own essay.

Writing About Literature

Comparing and Contrasting Two Authors

A New Machine

Progress of Cotton: No. 6, Spinning depicts the textile machines of nineteenth-century American industry.

Can you find and paraphrase Emerson's thesis statement?

What, according to Emerson, is the effect of specialization of labor?

But a man must keep an eye on his servants, if he would not have them rule him. Man is a shrewd inventor and is ever taking the hint of a new machine from his own structure, adapting some secret of his own anatomy in iron, wood and leather to some required function in the work of the world. But it is found that the machine unmans the user. What he gains in making cloth, he loses in general power. There should be temperance in making cloth, as well as in eating. A man should not be a silk-worm, nor a nation a tent of caterpillars. . . . The incessant repetition of the same hand-work dwarfs the man, robs him of his strength, wit, and versatility, to make a pin-polisher, a bucklemaker, or any other specialty. . . .

Ralph Waldo Emerson, "Wealth"

For centuries, workers have worried that labor-saving machinery would replace human laborers. Ralph Waldo Emerson, writing in the latter half of the nineteenth century, worried that machines would rob people of far more than their jobs.

Analyzing Similarities and Differences

Who has won Emerson's battle between people and machines? Does the conflict continue? The writer of the following model wanted to analyze how visions of technology have changed by comparing and contrasting Emerson's view of the new machines of his era with Tracy Kidder's view of one of the newest machines of our own era, the computer. Read the selection by Kidder on page 246, and then look at the way the writer of the model below begins an essay to compare and contrast the work of these two writers. Notice that her first paragraph discusses the similarities between the two writers.

Model

Technology has always promised a new world. From the first steam locomotive to the latest electronic gadget, industry experts have predicted better, easier, more efficient living. Along with those who glorify the results of technology, however, are those who question the value of better and faster machines. Ralph Waldo Emerson and Tracy Kidder, writing over a century apart, see both the positive and the negative aspects of technological change. Although they view different machines from different perspectives, both urge caution in allowing technology to dominate our lives.

Ralph Waldo Emerson, writing in the second half of the nineteenth century, takes a serious approach to textile machinery in the almost zealous tone of a social reformer. He speaks of machines as servants needing supervision, lest they come to rule their creators. Emerson worries that technology "unmans" users, absorbing their power. Kidder, on the other hand, approaches his subject with the air of an investigator. He questions and observes, comparing what he reads and hears with what he sees. To him it seems that computers have delivered neither the harm they threatened nor the benefits they promised.

What is the thesis statement in this model?

How, according to this writer, are Emerson and Kidder similar? How are they different?

• JOURNAL ACTIVITY •
Try It Out

Think about two short stories that might be compared and contrasted. Write the titles of the stories in your journal. Note one way in which they are similar and one way in which they are different.

What Sets Them Apart

Although Emerson and Kidder treat a common theme, they are far from identical in the way they discuss it. Writing in different centuries, about different technologies, the writers take very different approaches to their subject, as can be seen in the following chart.

Basis of Comparison or Contrast		
Feature	1st Subject: Emerson	2nd Subject: Kidder
Time	1876	1981
Technology	textile machinery	computers
Position	opposed: criticizes industrialization, sees few advantages	open-minded: presents arguments for and against
Tone	exhorting	reflective
Imagery	natural: silk worms, caterpillars, ant-hills	technological: machines
Word Choice	derogatory: "unmans," "loses," "incessant," "dwarfs," "robs"	qualifying: "almost," "perhaps," "maybe," "not always" some technical: "cybernetics," "chronocentrism," "artificial intelligence"
Theme	Machines should not supersede people.	Machines have advantages and disadvantages. They are neither as dangerous nor as powerful as people think.

Editing Tip

As you edit, be sure that the adjectives and adverbs you use to compare the selections are in the comparative, not the superlative, degree.

You can use the features listed in the chart above to compare and contrast many different pieces of nonfiction writing. Of course, in comparing and contrasting other pieces of writing, you may wish to add or delete categories of comparison. For example, if you are comparing two pieces of writing written only a few years apart, "time" may not be an important category. "Where" the author lived—a rural setting, an urban setting, this country, a foreign country—may play an important role, however, as may the author's gender or ethnic identity.

Imagine that this chart includes an additional category: "Impact on Reader." In this category, you would answer the questions: How did you react to this piece of writing? Why?

Writer's Choice

The following are some writing options to help you try out what you have learned.

1. Guided Assignment As a classroom aide in the local junior high school, you write a monthly curriculum supplement. One month you are asked to write an essay about how fiction expresses common human emotions and experiences. Choose short stories that have similar subjects but represent different periods or cultures. Create a Venn diagram (page 222) or a comparison/contrast chart (page 240) to examine the similarities and differences of the literary elements. Then draft an essay in which you explain how different writers using different techniques can express similar views on a subject. Organize your ideas in a feature-by-feature approach or a subject approach.

PURPOSE   Explain how two works of fiction from different periods or cultures can reflect similar experiences and emotions
AUDIENCE   A class of junior high school students
LENGTH   2–3 pages

COMPUTER OPTION

Before submitting your essay for publication, you might want to use your computer's spelling checker to double-check your work. Remember, however, that you cannot rely on an electronic spelling checker to catch all of your errors. If in misspelling a word, you create another word (for example, typing *week* instead of *weak*), your software will not be able to detect the error.

2. Open Assignment Find two different reviews of one of the following items:

- a musical recording
- a book
- a concert
- a movie
- an art exhibit
- a play
- an event or production of your choice

Think about the ways the reviewers agree and disagree with each other's opinions. Look as well at the differences and similarities in the way they write. Use a chart similar to the one shown in this lesson on page 240 to organize your ideas. Write an essay comparing and contrasting the two reviews for your school newspaper.

3. Journalism Find two different accounts of the same event in different newspapers or news magazines. Read each account carefully, and then construct a chart similar to the one shown in this lesson on page 240. Use the chart to decide how the two articles are similar and how they are different. Fill in the chart and then write an essay comparing and contrasting the two articles.

4. American Literature When discussing contemporary authors, critics often compare a newer or lesser-known writer with a better-known writer to convey to readers just how good they think the lesser-known writer is. Humorist Garrison Keillor, for example, has often been compared to Mark Twain.

Read essays or stories by two American humorists, such as Garrison Keillor, Mark Twain, James Thurber, Robert Benchley, Dave Barry, Bill Cosby, Alice Kahn, Molly Ivins, Lynda Barry, or Calvin Trillin. Use a chart like the one used in this lesson on page 240 to compare and contrast different elements of the two stories or essays. Then write an essay comparing and contrasting the two pieces. Be sure that your essay has a controlling idea as described in lesson 5.4. Do you like one piece better than the other? If so, try to determine why that might be the case.

"If Ever Two Were One. . ."

The valentine on the left, like the first of the two poems below, was created over three hundred years ago. The second poem, written less than twenty years ago, also discusses love, but from a very different perspective.

To My Dear and Loving Husband

If ever two were one, then surely we.
If ever man were loved by wife, then thee;
If ever wife was happy in a man,
Compare with me, ye women, if you can.
I prize thy love more than whole mines of gold
Or all the riches that the East doth hold.
My love is such that rivers cannot quench,
Nor ought but love from thee, give recompense.
Thy love is such I can no way repay,
The heavens reward thee manifold, I pray.
Then while we live, in love let's so persevere[1]
That when we live no more, we may live ever.

Anne Bradstreet

In Retrospect

Last year changed its seasons
subtly, stripped its sultry winds
for the reds of dying leaves, let
gelid drops of winter ice melt onto a
warming earth and urged the dormant
bulbs to brave the
pain of spring.

We, loving, above the whim of
time, did not notice.

Alone. I remember now.

Maya Angelou

[1] *Pronounced "pur sev' ər" in the seventeenth century*

Scratching the Surface

What's your reaction to these two poems? Explaining your reaction to poetry and other forms of literature is another form of expository writing. Sometimes reading a poem may ignite a barrage of feelings and memories. Other times you may need to read a poem a second or third time before your reactions begin to surface. By exploring your responses, you can find personal meaning in what you read. Here are some basic questions to pose to uncover your likes and dislikes.

Exploring Responses to Two Poems

- Which poem did you prefer? Why?

- What did you like least about either poem?

- Which poem matches your own experiences or observations? In what way?

- Which ideas in the poems do you agree or disagree with?

- What is the most memorable image or idea from each poem?

- Which words or phrases in the poems did you find interesting or beautiful?

Once you have explored your taste in poetry, you can dig deeper for meaning. In the following model, the writer begins to compare and contrast Bradstreet's and Angelou's approaches to poems about love.

Model

*B*oth writers use poetry to explore the nature of love. The speaker in Bradstreet's poem views love as immortal, even transcending the deaths of the lovers. Angelou's speaker, on the other hand, sees love as transient, like the seasons. Ironically, however, it is after love has died that the speaker in Angelou's poem is able to notice the life around her.

Drafting Tip

When drafting an essay about a poem, be sure that you provide a quotation from the poem to back up every statement you make about the poem.

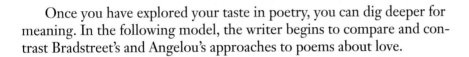

• JOURNAL ACTIVITY •
Think It Through

Do you prefer Bradstreet's formal, rhythmic style or Angelou's less structured, modern language? How does the language of these poems affect the way you respond to them? Record your responses to these questions in your journal.

Digging Deeper

Once you have responded to the poems on an emotional level, you can approach them from an intellectual perspective. Bradstreet and Angelou do not achieve their effects accidentally. Both poets employ a variety of tools, such as meter, rhyme, sound effects, line length, and imagery. By comparing and contrasting these poetic ingredients, you'll experience these poems more fully. Your own pleasure will increase when you understand how each poet used the tools and techniques of poetry to convey her message.

Basis of Comparison or Contrast		
Features	**1st Subject: Bradstreet**	**2nd Subject: Angelou**
Time	American colonial	Modern day
Form and meter	12 lines, iambic pentameter, rhymed	10 lines, free verse
Imagery	Images of wealth: gold, riches of the East	Natural images: changing seasons, dying leaves, melting ice, dormant bulbs
Figurative language	Metaphors of trade: "prize," "recompense," "repay," "reward" Metaphor of thirst: "rivers cannot quench"	Metaphors of the natural world: changing seasons, melting ice, warming earth, growing bulbs
Characterization of love	Love is of great value	Love is changeable, natural
Speaker	Addresses her husband	Speaks to herself
Tone	Intimate, celebratory	Pensive, somewhat sad
Conclusion	Perseverance in love while we live will bring us immortality after death.	Love is a state that removes lovers from the concerns of daily life but not forever.
Overall effect	Love is the most valuable thing on earth and one should maintain it at all costs.	Love is transitory, yet the experience of loving and ceasing to love is natural and healing.

You can combine the method for responding to poetry shown on page 243 with the chart on this page to develop an essay that compares and contrasts two or more poems. Starting with your own emotional response to poetry can help you decide what to look for when you begin an intellectual analysis.

Writer's Choice

The following are some writing options to help you try out what you have learned.

1. Guided Assignment   From a literature textbook or anthology, select two poems that share some common elements. Use the guidelines below to help you plan an essay comparing and contrasting these two works.

- Use the questions in the checklist on page 244 to help you determine your emotional responses to the poems.
- Begin your analysis by making a chart for such literary elements as tone, speaker, imagery, conclusion, and overall effect.
- To compose your thesis statement, look through your notes to find patterns. Formulate a generalization about the points of comparison or contrast you discover.
- When you write an essay to compare and contrast, you can choose the way you want to present your ideas. You can compare and contrast the poems feature-by-feature, or you can organize your material by subject, discussing first one poem and then the other. In either case, use transitions to connect your points.
- Refer to or quote from the poems to illustrate your points.

PURPOSE   To compare and contrast two poems
AUDIENCE   Your teacher and classmates
LENGTH   2–3 pages

2. Open Assignment   Choose two or three poems by the same author. Look for a single topic (such as nature or loneliness) in the poems, and compare and contrast the treatment of that topic in the two poems. Fill out a chart similar to the one in this lesson to begin comparing and contrasting the poems. Develop a thesis about the ways in which the poems are similar and different, and let your thesis deter-

mine what aspects of each poem you will discuss. Finally, write an essay comparing and contrasting the two or three poems. Be sure to organize your essay by either subject or feature.

COMPUTER OPTION

Although it is helpful to quote directly from the poems you are discussing when writing about poetry, there will be times when you will want to paraphrase or describe a poem without actually quoting it. But finding the exact word to express the subtle variations in meaning used by poets can be a frustrating task. Many word-processing programs include an electronic thesaurus that can suggest words with the same overall meaning but with subtle differences in connotation, tone, or usage.

3. Cooperative Learning   Select two dramatic poems, such as "Danny Deever" by Rudyard Kipling and "The Death of the Hired Man" by Robert Frost. In a small group, read the poems aloud, assigning different speaking parts to different members of the group. Have one member read the part of the narrator. Read the poem to yourselves silently and then read it aloud two or more times so each student becomes familiar with his or her lines. Discuss the questions in the box on page 243.

In your group, discuss what differences and similarities you noticed between the poems. Adapt the chart in this lesson to suit these poems and their dramatic elements. Fill out the chart together. Then work alone to write essays comparing and contrasting the two poems.

After writing your essays, read your thesis statements aloud to each other. How were your responses to the poems similar or different?

TRACY KIDDER

from

The SOUL OF A NEW MACHINE

Ever since their inception in the late 1940s, computers have aroused the anger, fear, and excitement caused by any major innovation. In this selection, Tracy Kidder and a friend attend a computer fair, the National Computer Conference (NCC), at the New York Coliseum in New York City. As he reflects on the event, Kidder takes a realistic view of the changes in society that have resulted from computerization.

Norbert Wiener coined the term *cybernetics* in order to describe the study of "control and communication in the animal and the machine." In 1947 he wrote that because of the development of the "ultra-rapid computing machine, . . . the average human being of mediocre attainments or less" might end up having "nothing to sell that is worth anyone's money to buy." Although Wiener clearly intended this as a plea for humane control over the development and application of computers, many people who have written about these machines' effects on society have quoted Wiener's statement as though it were a claim of fact; and some, particularly the computer's boosters, have held the remark up to ridicule—"See, it hasn't happened."

Since Wiener, practically every kind of commentator on modern society, from cartoonists to academic sociologists, has taken a crack at the sociology of computers. A general feeling has held throughout:

that these machines constitute something special, set apart from all the others that have come before. Maybe it has been a kind of chrono-centrism, a conviction that the new machines of your own age must rank as the most stupendous or the scariest ever; but whatever the source, computers have acquired great mystique. Almost every commentator has assured the public that the computer is bringing on a revolution. By the 1970s it should have been clear that *revolution* was the wrong word. And it should not have been surprising to anyone that in many cases the technology had served as a prop to the status quo. The enchantment seemed enduring, nevertheless. So did many of the old arguments.

"Artificial intelligence" had always made for the liveliest of debates. Maybe the name itself was preposterous and its pursuit, in any case, something that people shouldn't undertake. Maybe in promoting the metaphorical relationship between people and machines, cybernetics tended to cheapen and corrupt human perceptions of human intelligence. Or perhaps this science promised to advance the intelligence of people as well as of machines and to imbue the species with a new, exciting power.

"Silicon-based life would have a lot of advantages over carbon-based life," a young engineer told me once. He said he believed in a time when machines would "take over." He snapped his fingers and said, "Just like that." He seemed immensely pleased with that thought. To me, though, the prospects for truly intelligent computers look comfortably dim.

To some the crucial issue was privacy. In theory, computers should be able to manage, more efficiently than people, huge amounts of a society's information. In the sixties there was proposed a "National Data Bank," which would, theoretically, improve the government's efficiency by allowing agencies to share information. The fact that such a system could be abused did not mean it would be, proponents said; it could be constructed in such a way as to guarantee benign[1] use. Nonsense, said opponents, who managed to block the proposal; no matter what the intent or the safeguards, the existence of such a system would inevitably lead toward the creation of a police state.

Claims and counterclaims about the likely effects of computers on work in America had also abounded since Wiener. Would the machines put enormous numbers of people out of work? Or would they actually increase levels of employment? By the late seventies, it appeared, they had done neither. Well, then, maybe computers would eventually take over hateful and dangerous jobs and in general free

---

1. **benign** (bi nīn´): beneficial

people from drudgery, as boosters like to say. Some anecdotal evidence suggested, though, that they might be used extensively to increase the reach of top managers crazed for efficiency and thus would serve as tools to destroy the last vestiges[2] of pleasant, interesting work.

Dozens of other points of argument existed. Were computers making nuclear war more or less likely? Had the society's vulnerability to accident and sabotage increased or decreased, now that computers had been woven inextricably into the management of virtually every enterprise in America?

Wallach and I retreated from the fair, to a café some distance from the Coliseum. Sitting there, observing the more familiar chaos of a New York City street, I was struck by how unnoticeable the computer revolution was. You leave a bazaar like the NCC expecting to find that your perceptions of the world outside will have been altered, but there was nothing commensurate in sight—no cyborgs, half machine, half protoplasm, tripping down the street; no armies of unemployed, carrying placards denouncing the computer; no TV cameras watching us—as a rule, you still had to seek out that experience by going to such places as Data General's parking lot. Computers were everywhere, of course—in the café's beeping cash registers and the microwave oven and the jukebox, in the traffic lights, under the hoods of the honking cars snarled out there on the street (despite those traffic lights), in the airplanes overhead—but the visible differences somehow seemed insignificant.

Computers had become less noticeable as they had become smaller, more reliable, more efficient, and more numerous. Surely this happened by design. Obviously, to sell the devices far and wide, manufacturers had to strive to make them easy to use and, wherever possible, invisible. Were computers a profound, unseen hand?

In *The Coming of Post-Industrial Society,* Daniel Bell asserted that new machines introduced in the nineteenth century, such as the railroad train, made larger changes in "the lives of individuals" than computers have. Tom West liked to say: "Let's talk about bulldozers. Bulldozers have had a hell of a lot bigger effect on people's lives." The latter half of the twentieth century, some say, has witnessed an increase in social scale—in the size of organizations, for instance. Computers probably did not create the growth of conglomerates and multinational corporations, but they certainly have abetted it. They make fine tools for the centralization of power, if that's what those who buy them want to do with them. They are handy greed-extenders. Computers performing tasks as prosaic as the calculating

2. **vestiges** (ves´ti jz): traces

David Em, *Transjovian Pipeline*, 1979

of payrolls greatly extend the reach of managers in high positions; managers on top can be in command of such aspects of their businesses to a degree they simply could not be before computers.

Obviously, computers have made differences. They have fostered the development of spaceships—as well as a great increase in junk mail. The computer boom has brought the marvelous but expensive diagnostic device known as the CAT scanner, as well as a host of other medical equipment; it has given rise to machines that play good but rather boring chess, and also, on a larger game board, to a proliferation of remote-controlled weapons in the arsenals of nations. Computers have changed ideas about waging war and about pursuing science, too. It is hard to see how contemporary geophysics or meteorology or plasma physics can advance very far without them now. Computers have changed the nature of research in mathematics, though not every mathematician would say it is for the better. And computers have become a part of the ordinary conduct of businesses of all sorts. They really help, in some cases.

Not always, though. One student of the field has estimated that about forty percent of commercial applications of computers have proved uneconomical, in the sense that the job the computer was bought to perform winds up costing more to do after the computer's arrival than it did before. Most computer companies have boasted that they aren't just selling machines, they're selling *productivity*. ("We're not in competition with each other," said a PR man. "We're in competition with labor.") But that clearly isn't always true. Sometimes they're selling paper-producers that require new legions of workers to push that paper around.

Coming from the fair, it seemed to me that computers have been used in ways that are salutary,[3] in ways that are dangerous, banal[4] and cruel, and in ways that seem harmless if a little silly. But what fun making them can be!

A reporter who had covered the computer industry for years tried to sum up for me the bad feelings he had acquired on his beat. "Everything is quantified," he said. "Whether it's the technology or the way people use it, it has an insidious ability to reduce things to less than human dimensions." Which is it, though: the technology or the way people use it? Who controls this technology? Can it be controlled?

Jacques Ellul, throwing up his hands, wrote that technology operates by its own terrible laws, alterable by no human action except complete abandonment of technique. More sensible, I think, Norbert Wiener, prophesied that the computer would offer "unbounded possibilities for good and for evil," and he advanced, faintly, the hope that the contributors to this new science would nudge it in a humane direction. But he also invoked the fear that its development would fall "into the hands of the most irresponsible and venal of our engineers." One of the best surveys of the studies of the effects of computers ends with an appeal to the "computer professionals" that they exercise virtue and restraint.

For Discussion

1. How do you feel about using personal computers? Do they intimidate or fascinate you?

2. Generally speaking, do you think computers have improved or worsened the way we live? Explain your answer.

---

3. **salutary** (sal´yo͞o ter´ē): beneficial
4. **banal** (bā´n'l; bə nal´): dull because of overuse; commonplace

Readers Respond

I found Kidder's style of writing appealing. He had an upbeat approach to the influence of computer technology. He explained his subject matter as an observer.

If I had written the selection, I might have displayed some more of my own opinion toward the subject.

Michelle Kalski

I disagreed with Kidder's opinion of computers, or what I feel his opinion is. He seemed to dislike them. I felt it was unfair that whenever he mentioned a good quality about computers, he counter-attacked with a bad quality, but not vice-versa. I did like his use of quotes. I found his quotations of Norbert Wiener especially fascinating.

Arthur Housinger

Do you agree?

☞ Do you think the selection would have been more effective if Kidder had offered more of his own opinions on the subject? Why or why not?

☞ Is it your impression that Tracy Kidder dislikes computers? In your journal, explain how evidence from the selection supports your impression?

Writing Process in Action

On the Cutting Edge

You've just logged onto your voice-recognition computer and have begun to write up yesterday's lab report using a special pen applied directly to the screen. Nearby, another student simulates dissecting a frog by using *virtual reality:* a computer, touch-sensitive gloves, and special goggles that project images of the simulated work. Does this sound like a science-fiction version of the biology lab of the future? It really isn't; the devices that will make these tasks possible are now the cutting edge of technology. We're living in the midst of the same kind of rapid technological change that Tracy Kidder writes about in the selection from *The Soul of a New Machine* (pages 246–250).

In his discussion of the so-called computer revolution, Kidder provides a balanced look at what computers have and have not done. You have a similar task in this assignment: to weigh the advantages and disadvantages of various technological advances as you analyze how a particular piece of equipment could benefit your school.

• Assignment •

CONTEXT   The board of directors of a local corporation has offered to donate equipment to your school. They need to know what sort of high-tech equipment would be of most benefit to your particular school. Price is no object, within reasonable limits. The principal has asked your class to write individual proposals explaining what would best serve the school population.

PURPOSE   To write an essay analyzing and explaining what piece of equipment would be most beneficial to your school

AUDIENCE   The board of directors of a corporation

LENGTH   1–2 pages

---

1. Prewriting

Would students' writing improve if they had a computer lab? Have students and teachers been yearning for an on-site physical fitness club? Would high-tech science equipment for the physics lab be preferable to an audio-visual studio for the drama department? While you probably have some excellent ideas of your own about what the corporation should donate, the old adage "Two heads are better than one" still applies. Try brainstorming with your classmates: list everything you can think of, from practical, everyday needs to pie-in-the-sky daydreams. Consider taking an informal poll of students, teachers, and administrators. The more ideas you collect, the more objective your recommendations can be.

Once you assemble your "wish list," evaluate the advantages and disadvantages of the possibilities, and eliminate the most far-fetched ideas. Lesson 5.5 can help you chart the pros and cons. Clustering, brainstorming, or making a tree diagram will also help you to narrow the field. Finally, to zero in on your final choice, use the strategies for analyzing a problem (any deficiencies your school is currently experiencing) and presenting solutions (a gift of equipment) that are demonstrated in Lesson 5.5.

Once you've made your selection, you need to show your corporate benefactors why it's the best choice. Suppose you've decided that the science department needs an electron microscope. What does the corporate board of directors need to know about this piece of equipment? What, in fact, do you know about it? If you can't write a brief explanation of how the technology works, do some research to find out. Don't get bogged down in technical details, but try to understand the overall process.

Next try charting, clustering, or freewriting to focus on the major effects you think the equipment would have in your school. Use the questioning techniques explained in Lesson 2.3, interview the head of the science department, or survey other local high schools to see whether they have an electron microscope. At this stage, include both the positive and negative effects of acquiring this equipment. You want to be sure you've chosen the best option. Notice how Kidder thinks through the effects of computers: "They have fostered the development of spaceships—as well as a great increase in junk mail. . . . given rise to machines that play good but rather boring chess, and also, on a larger game board, to a proliferation of remote-controlled weapons in the arsenals of nations."

Although you may be tempted to take all of the material you've gathered and begin molding it into your proposal, stop and consider two other important issues: purpose and audience. Review your information with your specific purpose and your particular audience in mind. As you reread your notes, ask yourself questions such as these:

- What do my readers need and want to know?
- What impression do I want to convey about this equipment and our need for it?
- What will help the board of directors select my recommendations over those of my classmates?

If you can answer these questions, you're ready to create the thesis statement that will guide your draft and to select the details that you will include. If you can't, return to any of the prewriting techniques to generate the answers.

Finally, consider the method or methods of organization that will best help you accomplish your purpose and impress your audience. The excerpt by Tracy Kidder begins with the liveliest issue followed by the most crucial one. Kidder generally follows this order of impression throughout the selection. However, he also cites advantages and disadvantages of the computer revolution. In addition, Kidder uses comparison and contrast to set forth the claims and counterclaims of proponents and critics of computers. Unlike Kidder, you are acting as an advocate for the purchase of a particular piece of equipment. While order of importance is the most obvious choice, it is not the only one. Like Kidder, you might use comparison and contrast to show how the equipment will improve the quality of education at your school. Again, refer to the problem-solution strategies covered in Lesson 5.5.

2. Drafting

Because you are writing a proposal, you want to focus the attention of your audience immediately on the type of equipment that best suits your school's needs and why. Therefore, your introduction should contain a clear thesis statement, although you needn't open with this sentence. You might consider beginning with a startling statistic to attract attention, an anecdote that illustrates the school's need for the equipment, or a rhetorical question directed to your audience. You can also build to your thesis statement in two paragraphs, as Kidder did, by using a quotation and providing background information.

As you draft the body paragraphs of your proposal, keep your audience and purpose in mind. Define terms your readers may not understand, and, if necessary, include a brief explanation of how the equipment works. Don't forget to describe your school and analyze its needs. Use transitional words and phrases to signal changes in content or focus within and between paragraphs so that your readers can follow the development of your argument. Although you don't want to belabor each word at this stage, do consider word choice and tone. Because you want your recommendation to be regarded as the objective result of a serious and thoughtful analysis, don't overstate your case. You may want to take another look at how Tracy Kidder uses qualifying words such as *perhaps*, *maybe*, and *almost*.

Finally, you need to draft a concluding paragraph that is more than simply a mechanical reiteration of what you've already stated. While your conclusion should reemphasize the main points of your essay, it should also interpret their meaning or explore their implications. A strong conclusion gives you a final opportunity to drive your recommendation home, so you may want to save a particularly good quotation or anecdote for last.

3. Revising

Nearly all writers agree that it's easier to revise in stages than to try to change everything at once. Use the revising guidelines in Lesson 2.9, or evaluate from the standpoints below.

Check for clarity:

- Have I fulfilled my purpose and satisfied my goals?
- Is my thesis statement clear and well supported?
- Have I defined terms and provided background information?

Check for unity:

- Do all of my details contribute to my purpose?
- Do I need to weed out any irrelevant details or to add details to make a stronger case?

Check for coherence:

- Do my introductory and concluding paragraphs contain a clear statement of my recommendation?
- Are the methods I've chosen to organize my material the most effective ones for my topic, purpose, and audience?
- Do transitions reinforce the flow of my ideas?

4. Editing

Errors in grammar, usage, punctuation, and spelling distract your readers, who are likely to focus on the mistakes rather than the content. Don't let errors detract from what you've accomplished during the other stages of the writing process.

Like revising, editing is best performed in stages. Use the guidelines in Lesson 2.10 to ensure that your proposal will receive the serious attention that it deserves.

5. Presenting

Criteria

1. Analyzes and explains how a piece of high-tech equipment would benefit your school
2. Explains how the equipment works
3. Analyzes your school's needs and shows how the equipment would meet those needs
4. Uses vocabulary and organization suitable to the purpose and audience
5. Is unified and coherent
6. Follows the standards of grammar, usage, and mechanics

Many businesses and organizations are extremely supportive of education and even receive tax benefits for donating equipment to schools. Investigate some of the corporations in your area, and send your proposal to the appropriate executives of several companies. Your recommendations may help to put your school on the cutting edge of technology.

• Reflecting •

Toward the end of the selection, Tracy Kidder quotes a computer industry reporter, and then offers some ruminations about technology and control.

"Everything is quantified," [the reporter] said. "Whether it's the technology or the way people use it, it has an insidious ability to reduce things to less than human dimensions." Which is it, though: the technology or the way people use it? Who controls this technology? Can it be controlled?

Now that you've analyzed how a particular piece of equipment might affect your school, think about how important it really is to the students. Will it improve the quality of their lives? Will it really improve education? Finally, think about how the process of writing about the technology deepened your understanding of both the issue and the process of understanding the issue. Note which techniques and stages of the writing process gave you the most insight and helped you to clarify your thoughts.

Portfolio & Reflection

Summary

Key concepts in expository writing include the following:

- An expository paragraph consists of a topic sentence supported by appropriate details.
- Writing to explain a process requires ordering the steps of the process.
- Expository writing can be used to explain cause-and-effect relationships.
- Transitions and repetition of key ideas can lend coherence to expository writing.
- Essays to compare and contrast can be organized by subject or by feature.
- Expository writing can be used to analyze problems and present solutions.
- Time lines and process diagrams can enhance expository writing.
- Expository writing can support a hypothesis.

Your Writer's Portfolio

Look over the expository writing you have done during this unit. Select two pieces of writing to put into your portfolio. Each piece should demonstrate that you have worked with one or more of the preceding concepts. In other words, look for a piece of writing that does one or more of the following:

- supports a topic sentence with details
- presents the steps of the process in chronological order
- explains a cause-and-effect relationship
- uses transitions and repetition of key ideas
- compares and contrasts by subject or feature
- analyzes a problem and presents a solution
- uses a time line or process diagram
- presents and supports a hypothesis

Reflection and Commentary

Write one page that demonstrates that you understand what this unit asked of you. Use your two selected pieces of writing as evidence while you consider the following numbered items. Respond to as many items as possible. Label the page "Commentary on Expository Writing," and include it in your portfolio.

1. What details did you use to support a topic sentence in an expository paragraph?
2. In explaining a process, how did you organize the steps of the process?
3. What cause-and-effect relationship did you explain?
4. What transitions and repeated key ideas did you use for coherence?
5. What was the thesis of an essay you wrote to compare and contrast? Did you organize the essay by subject or feature?
6. What problem did you analyze? What solutions did you present?
7. Did a time line or process diagram enhance your writing?
8. What hypothesis did you present and support in your writing?

Feedback

If you had a chance to respond to the following student comment, what would you say or ask?

I like writing because I'm not always able to get my point across when in class. The hardest thing about writing is organizing my ideas.

Dannie Etienne, Brentwood High School,
Brentwood, New York

Persuasive Writing

At the Podium

E. L. Henry, *Electioneering in a Country Town* (detail), 1913

A Plea for the Rights of
NATIVE ANCESTORS

"You lose credibility by being shrill, emotional, or one-sided in your presentation, even though you are an advocate. You preserve a lot of your credibility by being as dispassionate as you can. The best advocacy is to lay out your position and let the reader draw her or his own conclusions."

Walter R. Echo-Hawk

Walter Echo-Hawk got an unusual phone call in 1986. A Sioux woman at a small Kansas college was asking Echo-Hawk to come to Kansas to address the issue of a farmer who had unearthed the remains of 160 Native American dead and had put them on display for tourists. "The Native community there was concerned about the situation," says Echo-Hawk, a staff attorney for the Native American Rights Fund in Boulder, Colorado. In response to the situation, Native leaders had decided to hold a seminar "about the ethical, legal, and scientific interests in such a display."

Echo-Hawk addressed the seminar in Kansas. But as he explored the situation, he stumbled upon a surprising fact: "As it turned out those 160 men, women, and children from a 600-year-old burial ground in Kansas were my own ancestors," Echo-Hawk explains. "I'm a member of the Pawnee tribe. . . . The dead were ancestors to present-day Pawnee, Wichita, and Arikara tribes. I was retained to represent the

Writing the Speech

1. Identifying the Audience

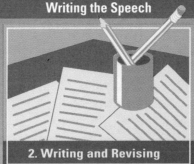

2. Writing and Revising

3. Presenting the Speech

FOCUS

Like persuasive writing, persuasive speeches use facts and sound opinions to support a well-structured argument.

three tribes to try to secure reburial of these dead."

Echo-Hawk won the Kansas case in 1989, bringing the issue, and Echo-Hawk himself, into the national limelight. The attorney became a leader of a nationwide lobbying effort to seek protection of Native ancestral remains and cultural objects. Bought, stolen from burial grounds, and taken from battlefields for decades, an estimated 2.5 million Indian dead were held in America's museums, universities, and historical societies. Showcases and vaults held sacred artifacts as precious to the tribes as the original Constitution is to the United States.

On one side of the dispute were institutions seeking to retain the collections for study. Many scientists feared the loss of these remains, a key source of knowledge about where Native Americans originated and migrated. On the other side were Native peoples seeking to reclaim the remains of their ancestors. "I determined that our opponents had more political clout than we did," says Echo-Hawk. "And the way to offset that clout was through public education." Through writing and speaking, he would make his case to as many people as would listen.

1. Identifying the Audience

As a spokesman for the Native cause in this bitter debate, Echo-Hawk received an invitation from the Montana and Alberta archaeological societies to speak at their joint meeting in May 1990.

"The Montana legislature had considered and rejected a bill to protect Indian graves," says Echo-Hawk. "The Montana Archaeological Society wanted to look into this issue. There are many Indian tribes in Montana; those large reservations take up most of the state. The archaeologists realized they had to work with the tribes, so they wanted to learn more. This was the only invitation I had ever received to address archaeologists directly on this issue."

In thinking about an approach for his speech, Echo-Hawk assumed that his audience of scientists would be opposed to the Native cause. He also knew that policy makers from the National Park Service would be on hand to hear the Native view as they considered the future of their collections of Native artifacts.

"You have to write for your audience," Echo-Hawk explains. "It directs your whole organization, tenor, and style." With this tough audience in mind, the lawyer decided to make an emotional appeal to the audience's humanity, supported with an argument based on facts and clear reasoning.

After considering his approach, Echo-Hawk constructed an outline "to organize my thoughts and lay out the points I wanted to make." The main points of his argument were these: First, the nation's laws and policies protect graves and cemeteries and guarantee every person a decent burial. Second, these laws had not been applied consistently to Native people, resulting in serious human rights violations. Third, society's attitude toward Native rights was changing fast, and it was time for scientists to join the mainstream.

Efforts to restrict the work of archaeologists worry many members of the profession. They cite the vast contributions to human knowledge made by archaeologists. Echo-Hawk understood this concern as he prepared to address his audience.

INTERFACE *You have been asked to give a speech to a group of people who might not be receptive to your point of view. Describe the opening of your speech: How will you capture your audience's attention?*

2. Writing and Revising

Now Echo-Hawk was ready to write—to "fill in the outline and create a first draft." Avoiding complex legal issues, he based his appeal on "universal values concerning treatment of the dead to make the point that this was a basic human problem shared by all humanity regardless of race—not a Native American issue but a universal thing."

Echo-Hawk stressed the human, not the scientific, side of the issue. "Instead of protecting Native dead as human beings," he notes, "law and social policy treat them as 'property,' 'archaeological resources,' 'scientific data or specimens,' . . . or just plain 'booty' for private collections."

He cited the research of scholars to assign responsibility for mistreatment of the dead. "Historians have documented the many facts and circumstances under which these dead were taken by government agents, soldiers, pot hunters, and other private citizens, museum collecting-crews, and scientists."

Echo-Hawk concluded by naming museums and historical societies that had repatriated human remains and sacred objects, and called upon the scientists to "stand up for the human rights of the very people they study."

It took Echo-Hawk about a day and a half to draft his forty-five-minute presentation, editing as he went. "You have to remember that

for five years I had been working in this area and I was very versed in the law and facts, so I didn't need to do any independent legal research. I also do a lot of writing in my job, so I write pretty fast."

After setting aside his draft for a day or two, he returned to it with a fresh eye and edited it one last time. "You have to work on it, polish it, fine-tune it, and make it something you can be proud of," he says.

INTERFACE *You are the head of a committee in your community to prevent a local developer from building an office park in an environmentally sensitive area, such as a park, a forest, or wetlands. Outline the key points of a speech you would deliver to local leaders, petitioning them to set aside the land to protect it from development.*

Tourist sites such as the one advertised above are found throughout the country. To many Native Americans, such displays of ancestral remains and sacred artifacts are offensive and sacrilegious.

3. Presenting the Speech

More than 250 archaeologists, anthropologists, U.S. government officials, and Native tribal leaders from the United States and Canada gathered for the conference May 3–6, 1990 at Waterton Lakes National Park in Alberta, Canada. With his speech in hand, Echo-Hawk addressed his audience, reading some parts and improvising others, using his prepared remarks as notes.

Echo-Hawk was surprised by the response of his audience. "People were genuinely receptive to what I had to say," he recalls, saying he thought the historical part of his paper was especially convincing. Later, Echo-Hawk talked one-on-one with people at the conference. "I think we were able to change a few minds."

After the conference, the attorney continued his effort to gain passage of a repatriation bill. Later that year President George Bush signed into law the Native American Grave Protection and Repatriation Act, which requires all federal agencies and federally funded museums to return certain Native remains and objects upon request by tribes. Says Echo-Hawk: "It's probably the most important human rights law ever passed for Indian people."

ON ASSIGNMENT

1. As presidential, local, or school election campaigns near, listen to a political speech by a candidate and write a one-page evaluation of the speech. Consider questions such as these: What issues did the candidate discuss? What main points were made? What was the individual's most persuasive argument? Did that argument persuade you to agree with the candidate? Why or why not?

2. **Literature Connection**
   Choose a historic or modern political speech from an anthology such as *A Treasury of the World's Great Speeches* or *A Treasury of Great American Speeches.* Write a brief paper explaining the issue involved in the speech you chose, and describe how the speaker structured the presentation to persuade listeners. For instance, did the speech use humor, or was it serious? What kinds of evidence— statistics, examples, historical data—did it employ to support the opinions

expressed? Did the speaker use personal experiences or anecdotes to bring the subject to life?

3. **Cooperative Learning**
   In a group of four students, brainstorm to come up with a controversial issue of interest, such as increased funding for space exploration, on which to write a persuasive speech. Individually, familiarize yourself with your topic by doing some general reading about it in magazines or

newspapers. Then meet as a group, and give yourselves ten minutes for each member to write an opening paragraph for a persuasive speech on the topic.

Consider whether you want to open with an anecdote, a statistic, a slice of humor, or simple and strong reasoning. Read your openings aloud, and discuss their effectiveness. Identify techniques that made the openings interesting, clear, and persuasive.

Case Study: Speech **263**

Writing to Persuade

A Bird of a Different Feather

When it came to choosing a national bird, Benjamin Franklin cried *fowl!* The eagle, he asserted, is a feathered villain "of bad moral character" that robs food from other birds and is too cowardly to defend its territory. In a letter to a friend more than two hundred years ago, Franklin suggested an alternative: the turkey.

Literature Model

*T*he Turk'y is . . . a true original native of America. Eagles have been found in all Countries, but the Turk'y was peculiar to ours; the first of the Species seen in Europe being brought . . . from Canada, and serv'd up at the wedding table of Charles the Ninth. He is, though a little vain and silly, it is true, but not the worse emblem for that, a Bird of Courage, and would not hesitate to attack a Grenadier of the British Guards, who should presume to invade his Farm Yard with a *red* Coat on.

Benjamin Franklin, letter to Mrs. Sarah Bache, January 26, 1784

Light-hearted as this passage is, it can serve as a model for any effective persuasion. In persuasive writing, the writer tries to make the reader accept a specific claim or opinion. Like Franklin, persuasive writers state their positions clearly. They back up their positions with facts, reasons, and examples, and then choose a presentation that is designed to appeal to their particular audiences.

Stating Your Case

At some time or another you will have your own case to make—to your boss, your parents, maybe even your political constituents. It may be tongue-in-cheek, like Franklin's argument for turkeys, or it may be more serious. You may be running for public office, writing an editorial opposing hazardous waste-disposal practices, or simply arguing with a friend about something you believe in.

You must construct a strong argument if you wish to persuade your listener. An argument is the presentation of your opinion, logically supported by evidence: concrete details, facts or statistics, examples, and reasons. First, express your position clearly in a thesis statement.

Sample Thesis Statements		
Not So Good	**Coming Along**	**Right On**
In a democracy all citizens are allowed to participate.	*Democratic rule requires participation; therefore, everyone should vote.*	*Low voter turnout is undermining our democracy; we must encourage greater participation through voter information.*
Not an opinion, just a statement of fact.	Vague; sounds like a platitude.	Well-defined position, specific solution.

To test your thesis, summarize the opposing view: *Voting doesn't really make a difference because all candidates are basically alike.* Or: *Distributing voter information will not increase voter participation.* If you cannot state an opposing view, you probably do not have a strong point to make.

Once you state your thesis, you need a strategy for presenting your supporting evidence. Two common strategies are outlined below. One begins with a punch; the other saves its persuasive power for the end.

Drafting Tip

Increasing order of importance can fail if you don't hold the audience's attention until the end. A catchy introduction and strong middle are essential to this strategy.

Decreasing Order of Importance

Thesis: The school year should be lengthened to 11 months.

Argument:
- ✔ **U.S. students are falling behind those in other countries.**
- A longer school year would help parents who work.
- More time in school would keep kids out of trouble.

Increasing Order of Importance

Thesis: Everyone should donate blood regularly.

Argument:
- Donations take very little time.
- Fears of contagion are unfounded.
- ✔ **Your donation could save someone's life.**

• JOURNAL ACTIVITY •
Think It Through

In your journal, describe a time when you used one of these strategies to make a request of your parents, a teacher, or a friend. How well did the strategy work for you? How would you make the same request now?

Know Your Audience

In 1852 the antislavery crusader Frederick Douglass was asked to give a Fourth of July speech. The holiday was a time of jubilation for the seventy-six-year-old nation. If Douglass had opened with harsh words and bitter antislavery rhetoric, he might have antagonized his audience. Instead, he began with patriotic words that most would find inspiring.

Notice how Douglass works to create a sense of community between himself and his audience.

Literature Model

*T*he signers of the Declaration of Independence were brave men. They were great men, great enough to give frame to a great age. It does not often happen to a nation to raise, at one time, such a number of truly great men. . . . They were statesmen, patriots and heroes, and for the good they did, and the principles they contended for, I will unite with you to honor their memory.

Frederick Douglass, Fourth of July Oration, July 5, 1852

Prewriting Tip

Make a list of your audience's characteristics: their likes and dislikes, their biases. Keep these in mind when crafting your argument.

Gradually, however, Douglass's message shifted to the subject of slavery. "Washington could not die till he had broken the chains of his slaves," he said. Then he delivered the real gist of his argument: "What, to the American slave, is your Fourth of July? I answer: a day that reveals to him, more than all other days in the year, the gross injustice and cruelty to which he is the constant victim. To him, your celebration is a sham; . . . your sounds of rejoicing are empty and . . . heartless; your shouts of liberty and equality, hollow mockery."

Because Douglass understood his audience and the occasion of his speech, his argument began with statements that his listeners would easily accept and then moved to ones that might challenge them.

Least controversial assertion	The nation was founded on ideals of freedom and justice.
More controversial assertion	Slavery makes the Fourth of July celebration meaningless.
Most controversial assertion	The practice of slavery is cruel and unjust.

Writer's Choice

The following are some writing options to help you try out what you have learned.

1. Guided Assignment It's Saturday morning, and your brother is still asleep. You decide to borrow his car to go to your friend's house. He probably will not be happy about what you have done. Beginning with statements with which he will most likely agree, write a note in which you try to persuade him not to be upset with you. Remember that to win him over your opening comments must take into account his preferences and state of mind. You might find it helpful to brainstorm a list of possible reasons for your action and rank them from least controversial to most controversial. Then draft your note.

> **PURPOSE** To persuade your audience to accept a controversial position
>
> **AUDIENCE** Your older brother
>
> **LENGTH** 1–2 pages

2. Open Assignment Concerned by falling test scores during the last ten years, your local school board decides to take one of the following actions:

- lengthen the school day by 1 1/2 hours
- lengthen the school year by one month
- restrict off-campus privileges
- reduce the number of games each sports team plays

Choose one of the alternatives above and write a persuasive essay for or against the action. You may take the position of a school board member or of a student with strong feelings about the measure.

3. Art The magazine cover on the right shows a woman sewing the button on her husband's shirt as he eats breakfast. What kind of family life does it portray? Does it differ from family life today?

Make notes on your reactions to the cover and on issues it raises in your mind. If possible, interview two people who lived through the 1930s, 1940s, and 1950s, and ask them whether they think the cover accurately portrays family life during that time period. How have families changed since then? Write a thesis statement expressing your position on the roles men and women should have in the family today. Then draft a persuasive speech to present to your classmates. Use the cover, as well as your interviews and other research, to support your position.

Life magazine cover, 1925

$1000.00 PRIZE CONTEST—(INQUIRE WITHIN)

Life

Commuters' Number

JAMES MONTGOMERY FLAGG

FEBRUARY 12, 1925   *The 8:15—or Bust!*   PRICE 15 CENTS

Sifting Fact from Opinion

Wheat and Chaff

By the 1830s, the Cherokee homelands in the southern Appalachians were in jeopardy. Under pressure from Georgians who wanted to move west into the gold-rich land, President Andrew Jackson decided that the Cherokee must go. Privately, Jackson told a Georgia congressman, "Build a fire under them. When it gets hot enough, they'll move." Publicly, Jackson said the forced removal of the Cherokee was for their own welfare. He offered these "facts."

Jackson refers to "established fact" but offers no proof; this statement is simply opinion.

What is the purpose of these authoritative-sounding phrases?

Literature Model

I t seems now to be an established fact that [the Cherokee] cannot live in contact with a civilized community and prosper. Ages of fruitless endeavor have at length brought us to a knowledge of this principle . . . no one can doubt the moral duty of the Government of the United States to protect and if possible to preserve and perpetuate the scattered remnants of this race which are left within our borders.

President Andrew Jackson, address to Congress, 1835

Contrast Jackson's statement with a speech by John Ridge, a prominent Cherokee leader. Ridge's speech describes, clearly and factually, how his people adapted their culture to the white society around them.

Literature Model

Y ou asked us to throw off the hunter and warrior state: We did so. You asked us to form a republican government: We did so, adopting your own as a model. You asked us to cultivate the earth, and learn the mechanic arts: We did so. You asked us to learn to read: We did so. You asked us to cast away our idols, and worship your God: We did so.

John Ridge, address to Georgia state officials, 1832

Ridge lists specific, verifiable facts to support his conclusion that the Cherokee had a right to stay.

Opinions in Disguise

The case of the Cherokee illustrates the importance of evaluating evidence in conflicting political claims. Recognizing the difference between fact and opinion can help bring us closer to the truth as well as guide us in using facts and opinions appropriately in writing. Follow the guidelines below to help you determine whether the "facts" you read and hear are actually opinions in disguise.

Revising Tip

Using repeated patterns of words can add emphasis in persuasive writing, as Ridge does in the speech on page 268.

Recognizing Facts and Opinions	
Recognizing Facts	**Recognizing Opinions**
Can the statement be verified? Facts can be proven or measured; you can check them in an encyclopedia or other reference works compiled by experts. Sometimes you can observe or test them yourself.	**Is the statement based on personal preference or belief?** Often, although not always, opinions contain phrases such as "I believe" or "in my view" and are open to interpretation.

The following hypothetical situation is typical of many issues in the news that challenge citizens to sift facts from opinion.

"City in Danger of Burning," reads the headline. The head of the city firefighters' union maintains that recent cutbacks in personnel threaten the safety of residents. Fires could burn out of control, he says, if firefighters are not rehired.

Pressed by reporters for a response, the mayor says that the union leader—her opponent in the upcoming mayoral election—is trying to capture the headlines and smear her. The mayor dismisses the claims as mere opinion, not fact.

If you're a reporter covering the uproar, how will you make sense of this situation for your readers? If you're a citizen, how will these claims affect your voting decision? The challenge is to sort fact from opinion.

To resolve the dispute between the two mayoral candidates, you might check city records to measure the firefighters' response time for emergency calls. A sharp drop in the number of calls handled promptly after the layoffs will support the union leader's statement. If no change has occurred, however, you might judge the claims to be scare tactics.

• JOURNAL ACTIVITY •
Try It Out

Clip a newspaper article on a controversial subject. Paste it into your journal. Then use two colored markers, one to indicate facts and the other to indicate opinions.

Judging the Value of Fact and Opinion

To evaluate the strength of an argument, you need to do more than distinguish between fact and opinion. You also need to determine that the facts are relevant and that they tell the whole story. Return to the example of the firefighters on page 269. What if the mayor tried to answer her opponent's claim by distributing the results of a poll showing that most city residents supported the layoffs of firefighters? No one can deny the results of the poll. The support of city residents for the layoffs, however, has no bearing on whether the city is adequately protected.

Opinions, as well as facts, should be evaluated carefully. Many opinions are no more than hearsay, instincts, or hunches. Such uninformed opinions do not constitute strong evidence. Informed opinions, based on facts and on the experiences of eyewitnesses or experts, carry the most weight. If you can identify the source of an opinion and evaluate how reliable it is, you will become a more discerning reader; you will also be able to choose the best evidence to use in your own writing.

Return once more to the example of the firefighters and evaluate the range of opinions illustrated below.

Prewriting Tip

In researching evidence to support your argument, gather as many facts as you can. You can select the strongest facts later, during drafting.

Reporter:
Statistics show that it takes firefighters an average of two minutes longer to answer calls than it did before the layoffs. But these delays probably were due to the unusually large number of fires this month. I don't see any cause for alarm.

Consultant:
I evaluate fire departments around the country to see whether cities are properly protected. Based on my research and experience, I can say with certainty that the recent layoffs have placed the city at risk. I recommend that at least fifty firefighters be rehired immediately.

City Resident:
Seventy-five firefighters were laid off last month, and I don't see the city going up in smoke. Obviously the layoffs were a good idea.

Writer's Choice

The following are some writing options to help you try out what you have learned.

1. **Guided Assignment**   Some animal-rights activists believe that no wild animals should be held captive, either in zoos and circuses or as working animals. They view these practices as cruel and unnatural. Below is an opposing view by animal trainer Vicki Hearne.

> In Africa, 75 percent of the lions cubbed do not survive to the age of two. For those who make it to two, the average age at death is ten years. Asali, the movie and TV lioness, was still working at age twenty-one. . . . For orangutans in the wild in Borneo and Malaysia, the life expectancy is thirty-five years; in captivity, fifty years. The wild is not a suffering-free zone or all that frolicsome a location.

This quotation appeared in *Harper's*. Prepare an imaginary letter to the editor of the magazine arguing either for or against keeping wild animals in captivity. First, write a thesis statement. Then create some faulty evidence to "support" your position: at least one opinion expressed forcefully enough to appear to be a fact, two irrelevant facts, and two uninformed opinions. Choose one of the two methods on page 265 for organizing your evidence, and draft your letter.

PURPOSE	To persuade readers by using faulty evidence
AUDIENCE	Readers of a general-interest magazine
LENGTH	1 page

2. **Open Assignment**   Choose one of the following thesis statements or one of your own, and write a brief persuasive essay for the "Students Speak" column of a high school newspaper. Make sure to support your thesis statement with relevant facts and informed opinion.

- Because of diminishing funds, high school sports programs should be cut and more funds allocated to academics.
- Young people should be required to spend one year doing community service jobs such as delivering food to the poor, tutoring illiterate adults, or planting new forests.
- School administrators should have the right to randomly search students' lockers.

COMPUTER OPTION

Statistics are a persuasive type of factual evidence. You can use computer functions to help you gather, analyze, and present data clearly. In the open assignment, for instance, you might present statistics showing that funding for high school sports has been declining over the last five years. Then you might argue against further cuts that would eliminate many sports programs altogether. This kind of information lends itself to presentation in tables, charts, or graphs that you can construct using spreadsheet software and some word-processing programs. Line graphs are particularly effective for showing increases or decreases over time. Pie charts are good for showing percentages.

3. **Cooperative Learning**   In groups of three, role-play a job interview. One student, the applicant, should be prepared to answer questions about his or her job history, education, and qualifications. The second student, the interviewer, will draft six to eight good questions to gather facts from which to form an opinion of the applicant. The third student will take notes and write a one-page report that will persuade his or her company to hire or not to hire the applicant. The writer should support opinions with facts from the interview. Then switch roles to repeat the activity so that each student plays each role.

The force of gravity is equal to the square root of . . .

Kid Stuff

As a toddler, you probably conducted your own scientific experiments: flinging your spoon to the floor to hear it crash, stacking building blocks and then knocking them down, observing ants working busily on their anthills and spiders on their webs. Pretty simple stuff, right? Not really. The speaker quoted below argues that much of our mental development occurs at the spoon-dropping age. To make his point, he reveals a surprising fact about our physical development.

Literature Model

Most of a child's growth has occurred before the age of sixteen. As a matter of fact, it's a little awesome to realize that all of us had attained one-half of our mature height by the time we were two-and-one-half years old. That's right. If you're six feet tall now, you were already three feet tall when you were two and one half.

Irving B. Harris, address to City Club of Cleveland, December 15, 1989

Continuing the analogy between physical and mental development, Harris asks: If you wanted to increase children's height, would you spend money to improve the diet of sixteen-year-olds? No. The money would go toward better diets for the very young. Likewise, he says, to increase children's mental development, we must spend money to improve education at the youngest ages, when mental growth is most rapid.

Types of Evidence

The wider your range of supporting evidence, the stronger your argument. Harris has begun with a persuasive analogy, but an analogy alone doesn't give enough strength to his argument. To persuade his listeners, he needs well-substantiated, convincing facts about mental development. In the excerpt on the next page, Harris goes on, using other types of evidence to back up his claim.

Literature Model

Professor Benjamin Bloom [of the University of Chicago] pointed out that human intelligence . . . grows at a decelerating rate. His research showed that by the age of four, more than one-half of our intelligence is in place. . . . T. Berry Brazelton, a respected pediatrician at Harvard, says he can tell by examining a nine-month-old infant whether that infant is likely to make it in school or fail in school, simply by observing how that child approaches very simple tasks, like playing with blocks.

Harris uses both statistics and expert opinion to bolster his argument.

A variety of facts and opinions leads to Harris's conclusion: "Programs that attempt to radically improve children's health, education, and overall well-being must start very early."

When you build a persuasive argument, each kind of evidence you use adds a different kind of support to your position (see page 77 on types of evidence). Factual information and concrete details, such as statistics, observations, scientific reports, and historical precedents, are especially convincing because they are verifiable. Opinions, while not verifiable, are effective if they are from a respected authority. Examples, anecdotes, and analogies can bring your subject to life or put it in a new perspective. Reasons guide your audience through the logic of your position.

Collecting mountains of evidence, however, doesn't guarantee that you'll have a strong argument. As you read and gather evidence for your argument from books, newspapers, interviews, and television, you need to judge the quality of the information. The questions on the right can help you analyze your evidence.

Checklist for Evaluating Evidence

- Does the evidence come from a reliable, qualified, unbiased source?
- Is the evidence consistent with what you know to be true or with what authorities on the subject agree to be true?
- Does the evidence address all sides of the issue, taking all objections into account?
- Is the evidence up-to-date?

• JOURNAL ACTIVITY •
Think It Through

Carefully read a persuasive article in a newspaper or magazine, such as an editorial, a letter to the editor, an op-ed article, or an arts review. State the opinion expressed in the article; then list the evidence used. Refer to the questions above as a guide. Is the evidence sound?

Handling the Opposition

When writing an argument, be your own devil's advocate. If you anticipate people's objections to your view, you can try to head off or answer those objections. A good strategy for handling opposition is to make concessions—to admit that some point in your argument is weak or to agree with some part of your opponent's argument. Such honesty often strengthens rather than weakens your case.

Eleanor Roosevelt used this strategy effectively in a 1954 speech in support of the United Nations. President Franklin Delano Roosevelt had worked for the creation of the U.N. in the 1940s. In the 1950s, however, the U.N. was widely ridiculed as weak and ineffective. Nations that had cooperated during World War II and had worked together to form the U.N. had become deadlocked enemies. Eleanor Roosevelt chose to defend the United Nations by meeting its critics head-on.

Drafting Tip

Unity is essential for effective persuasive writing. Make sure that every piece of evidence you include is relevant; extraneous data will weaken an argument.

Roosevelt's first statement acknowledges the complaints against the U.N.

Why does Roosevelt begin her argument with facts everyone can agree on?

What evidence does Roosevelt use to make her case?

She concedes "failures," but turns this failure into part of her proposed solution.

Literature Model

You hear people say, "Why hasn't the United Nations done this or that?" The United Nations functions just as well as the member nations make it function, and no better or worse. And so the first thing to look at is, I think, the kind of machinery that was set up, and what it was meant to do.

Now we have to go back in our minds to the time when the [U.N.] was first planned. At that time the war was not over, and this was a dream, and everybody accepted it as a dream—an idea to set up an organization, the object of that organization being to keep peace. . . .

[The founding nations] had co-operated during the war; they believed that they were going to go on co-operating after the war. That was one of the great myths of the centuries.

They also believed that this organization they were setting up was to be an organization to maintain peace, not to make peace. Peace was going to be made, and then this organization would help to maintain it. What happened, of course, was that peace has never been found. And so this organization, which was not set up to meet certain questions, has had questions brought to it that were not in mind at the beginning.

. . . When we look upon the failures in the United Nations, we should not be disheartened, because if we take the failure and learn, eventually we will use this machinery better and better. We will also learn one important thing, and that is, no machinery works unless people make it work.

Eleanor Roosevelt, speech for the U.N. Seminars, Brandeis University, 1954

The following are some writing options to help you try out what you have learned.

1. Guided Assignment You are a student representative to a special school board committee on dress codes in your high school. The following excerpt from an article in *Forbes* (September 17, 1990) is submitted for the committee's consideration.

A growing number of schools are enacting dress codes or even requiring uniforms. The trend is healthy. Uniforms are democratic. No one need feel any the less because he or she can't afford the latest in shoes, shirts, jackets, jewelry or whatever. . . . Kids can concentrate more on their studies than on what's fashionable—at least during school hours. Uniforms help establish a sense of discipline, without which there is no education. . . . [T]here's an added bonus: less crime. There have been a growing number of incidents of students' committing violence against other students, stealing expensive jackets or fancy sweaters. Dress codes or uniforms quickly smother such violence.

Write a critique of the position given above for the committee. First, identify the kinds of evidence used. What kinds of evidence are not used? Then evaluate the evidence, using the checklist on page 273 as a guide. Are you convinced? Why or why not?

PURPOSE To persuade for or against uniforms in high schools by evaluating supporting evidence

AUDIENCE School board members

LENGTH 2 pages

Junius Allen, *Metropolis*, 1932

2. Open Assignment As a reward for your work as a summer intern, a local TV station has asked you to write and deliver a one-minute editorial on one of the following topics or one of your choice: high school students involved in sports must maintain a C average; humane societies should destroy abandoned animals; congressional terms should be limited.

You may argue for or against any of these statements. Support your argument with several types of evidence and try to anticipate the objections of local viewers.

3. Art You have been chosen to address your classmates at the dedication of the above painting donated to your school in honor of Earth Day. What feelings does the painting evoke in you? Use them to develop a position on an environmental issue. Do research on industrial pollution, including scope of problem, progress made, and problems still to be addressed. In your speech support your position by drawing on your reactions to the painting and your research.

What Happened?

The scenario is straight out of a science-fiction movie: Giant meteorite strikes earth, setting the planet afire. Volcanoes erupt, tsunamis crash into the continents. . . . In the moments following the impact of an object ten kilometers in diameter, experts believe, a blast wave similar to that of a nuclear explosion would destroy everything within several hundred kilometers, its intense heat and winds combining to set wildfires, perhaps even a global inferno.

National Geographic, June 1989

Based on evidence uncovered in the late 1980s, many researchers conclude that the scenario described above—a giant meteorite colliding with the earth—occurred about 66 million years ago. The meteorite theory has aroused keen interest. Some scientists suggest that the cataclysmic impact devastated the earth's ecosystems and caused the sudden mass extinction of the dinosaurs.

Yet this meteorite theory is based on mere scraps of evidence: rock samples from around the world. No human beings were around to witness such an event; no one can go back in time to see what happened, and measure the effects. So how can scientists be sure their conclusions are reasonable?

Inductive Reasoning

Scientists often use what is called inductive reasoning. With induction, one assembles a series of facts and finds a relationship between them that can be stated as an overall conclusion, or a generalization. The chart on the next page shows how inductive reasoning led scientists to conclude that the earth was hit by a meteorite.

Scientists had speculated about a meteorite impact for years, but the idea was not widely accepted. The iridium discovery has persuaded many scholars to take this theory seriously, although some scientists are still skeptical.

We rely on inductive reasoning for much of our knowledge. We cannot test whether the sun will rise in the east and set in the west every day, but we can state with reasonable certainty that it will do so. You don't have to conduct tests on all ten fingers to figure out that if you place any one of them on a hot stove, it will get burned. Fortunately, you need experience that sensation only once; you can then generalize about the effect of a hot stove on all fingers.

In all of these examples, the argument proceeds logically from limited facts or observations to a broader statement. Your inductive argument will hold up only if the evidence you use is accurate and the conclusion follows reasonably from the evidence. Be sure you have your facts straight. Then check your reasoning by asking yourself: How might I attack this conclusion? Could I draw another logical conclusion from this evidence? A correct inductive argument will meet the criteria below.

Revising Tip

Persuasive arguments will seem more objective when presented in the third person. Avoid using the first person *I* unless you are stating an opinion.

Inductive Reasoning Checklist

✓ **Is the conclusion consistent with other known facts?**
For instance, the meteorite collision is thought to have occurred at the precise time that dinosaurs suddenly disappeared from the earth. That something wiped out the dinosaurs at the time of the meteorites fits nicely with the theory of a cataclysmic impact.

✓ **How large was the sample from which the evidence was drawn?**
The iridium was found in several widely separated locations on earth, a fact that scientists say is significant.

✓ **Does the evidence apply to the whole group it claims to represent?**
All of the rock containing the iridium was of the same age; as far as we know, iridium exists in all meteorites.

• JOURNAL ACTIVITY •
Try It Out

Your friend is an excellent basketball player; she is also good at tennis, volleyball, softball, and football. Construct a chart like the one at the top of this page in which you use inductive reasoning to draw a conclusion about your friend.

Pitfalls of Inductive Reasoning

Conclusions reached through inductive reasoning are not foolproof. Using evidence improperly can lead to a problem in inductive reasoning called a hasty generalization. This error in reasoning occurs when your conclusion goes further than the evidence permits.

Hasty generalizations can lead to stereotyping. Stereotypes of people can be dangerous; they are often inaccurate. Suppose, for instance, that the only drummers you had ever seen were boys. You might reason inductively that only boys play drums. The reasoning is incorrect because you have not examined a large enough sample. If you look at a larger number of drummers, as in the entire photo to the left, you can see that many girls play drums as well.

Of course, most people probably wouldn't stereotype drummers this way. Nevertheless, real-life stereotyping does occur frequently. People stereotype certain ethnic or religious groups, erroneously concluding that all of the members of a particular group behave in a particular way. Stereotyping can be both harmful and insulting.

Avoid stereotyping by limiting your generalizations. Unless you are certain that something is true of every member of a group, don't use absolute terms such as *all* or *everyone*. You might say, "*Most* teen-agers like going to parties" rather than "*All* teen-agers like going to parties." In addition, make your sample as large and as representative as possible. Don't claim, "Most students in our school are good athletes" unless you have measured the athletic ability of more than half the students. Most important, avoid stereotypes that describe all members of a group as alike. Such generalizations deny people's individuality and diversity.

Looking at a small sample, you conclude that all drummers are boys.

Looking at a larger sample, you see that drummers are both boys and girls.

Deductive Reasoning

In the 1970s, residents of Love Canal, in Niagara Falls, a suburb of Buffalo, New York, discovered to their horror that their community was built on top of a former landfill containing highly toxic chemical waste. The discovery led most residents to abandon their homes. The Love Canal area became a ghost town ringed with fences and "Danger" signs. What was the reasoning of the people who left?

Generalization: Toxic chemical waste is dangerous to humans.

 is

Fact: Love Canal is located on top of a layer of toxic waste.

 is

Conclusion: Love Canal is a dangerous place to live.

 is

Editing Tip

During editing, check for pronoun-antecedent agreement. To follow your line of reasoning, a reader must know to what pronouns refer. See pages 565–590 on pronoun usage.

This reasoning is called deductive reasoning. Deductive reasoning begins with a generalization, and then arrives at a conclusion about a specific situation. You use deduction all the time without realizing it. When you take a bite of a banana, how do you know that you will like it? You know that you like bananas; you know that this piece of fruit is a banana; you deduce that you therefore will like this piece of fruit.

In essays or speeches, deduction may be difficult to identify. Susan B. Anthony used two deductive arguments to make her case in her famous 1873 speech for woman suffrage. All persons living in this country are citizens, she asserted.

Literature Model

The only question left to be settled now is: Are women persons? And I hardly believe any of our opponents will have the hardihood to say they are not. Being persons, then, women are citizens; and no State has a right to make any law, or to enforce any old law, that shall abridge their privileges.

Susan B. Anthony,
"On Woman's Right to Suffrage," 1873

Citizens	have the right to vote.
Women	are citizens.
Women	should have the right to vote.

• JOURNAL ACTIVITY •
Try It Out

Construct two charts, one illustrating incorrect inductive reasoning for the conclusion "All birds can fly," the other illustrating correct deductive reasoning for "A turkey has wings."

Pitfalls of Deductive Reasoning

When you reason deductively, you start with a general statement about a group—for instance: *All dogs have four legs.* You then identify someone or something that belongs to that group: *Rover is a dog.* Finally, by deduction, you attribute the characteristic of the group to that member: *Therefore, Rover has four legs.*

You must be careful, however, in constructing such an argument. The following reasoning would be incorrect: *Dogs have four legs; Rover has four legs; therefore Rover is a dog.* In fact, Rover could be a hippopotamus or a muskrat or any other four-legged creature.

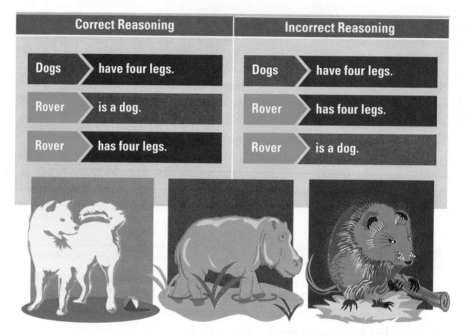

Correct Reasoning		Incorrect Reasoning	
Dogs	have four legs.	Dogs	have four legs.
Rover	is a dog.	Rover	has four legs.
Rover	has four legs.	Rover	is a dog.

One additional note of caution: your deduction may be logically constructed, but your conclusion may still be false. If any statement in your argument is not true, the entire deduction becomes questionable.

Consider the following line of reasoning: *To attract top-notch students, a school needs a good science program; our school wants to attract top-notch students; therefore, we need to improve our science program.* Not everyone may agree with your first assumption. Must we have a good science program in order to attract top-notch students? In this case, your reasoning is well constructed but the conclusion is not necessarily true.

Most arguments use both inductive and deductive logic. For instance, if you were trying to dissuade someone from trying a crash diet, you could cite studies linking crash dieters with weight gain to prove inductively that such diets are ineffective. You could also cite studies linking such diets with depression, eating disorders, anemia, and an increased incidence of colds. Then you could use the amassed evidence to *deduce* that crash dieting can threaten one's health.

Writer's Choice

The following are some writing options to help you try out what you have learned.

1. Guided Assignment Compared to employers in other industrialized countries, U.S. employers give their employees relatively little vacation time. Imagine that a bill is proposed in Congress that would require companies to give all full-time employees at least three weeks of vacation per year. You are either the owner of a small company or a union representative, and you must write a persuasive letter to a congressional representative urging passage or rejection of the bill.

Use inductive reasoning to structure your argument. Begin by examining the evidence in the fact sheet below about vacation policies in other countries and the effects of those policies. Then form a generalization that supports your view. When you write your draft, select and organize the evidence so that your letter is as persuasive as possible.

- The average American full-time worker works 40 hours per week and gets 11 official holidays and just over 2 weeks of vacation. (Those who have worked fewer than 5 years at a job get less vacation.)
- Among major industrial countries, only the United States gives more vacation time to those with seniority.
- The average British and French worker works 39 hours per week and gets 8 official holidays and 5 weeks of vacation.
- The average German worker works 38 hours per week and has 10 holidays and 6 weeks of paid vacation.
- The average Japanese worker works 42 hours per week, has 20 holidays a year, and is entitled to over 3 weeks of vacation per year (but usually takes only 2).
- The Japanese used to work on Saturdays, but this is gradually being phased out.

- In the United States, unionized companies tend to have more vacation time.
- The United States has the highest standard of living in the world.
- In assembly-line jobs, every hour worked adds to productivity.
- Productivity might decline if Americans had more vacation time.

PURPOSE To persuade your audience to support or oppose increasing the amount of vacation time for American workers

AUDIENCE The congressional representative for your district

LENGTH 2 pages

2. Open Assignment Your school is considering launching a new work-study program that will allow juniors and seniors to go to school for half a day and go to an outside job during the other half. You are a student in the school, and you want to circulate a petition urging the administration to approve the proposed program. Draft a cover letter to state your case and persuade students to sign. Use inductive or deductive reasoning. For instance, you might want to make an inductive generalization based on the experiences of working students you may know, or you might find national statistics on students who work and use deductive reasoning to apply those figures to your school.

COMPUTER OPTION

Use the design functions on a word processor to make your cover letter grab students' attention. Try making a huge banner headline with catchy wording. You can also use illustration software to design an emblem or logo for your cause—for example, a page of a calendar torn into two halves, signifying the half-school day/half-workday proposal.

Something Fishy

Red herring is a smoked fish, a favorite food of the British for centuries. This odoriferous little fish was once used to train fox-hunting dogs to follow the trail of a scent. People who were opposed to fox hunting sometimes dragged a red herring across the fox trail. The dogs, confused by the scent, would veer off after the red herring, losing the scent of the fox.

Faulty Reasoning

What do smelly fish have to do with writing? In persuasion, a red herring is a statement that diverts attention from the issue at hand. Red herrings appear frequently in politics. A congressional representative attacked for irregular attendance might, in defending himself, launch into a discourse on his charitable work. Charity is fine, but it doesn't excuse all the missed meetings.

Red herrings are an example of faulty reasoning. Intentionally or unintentionally, they creep into what we write and speak. Such faulty arguments are called logical fallacies. By learning to recognize logical fallacies, you will strengthen your own persuasive writing, and you will be less likely to fall prey to others' attempts to confuse your thinking.

Circular Reasoning In another common fallacy, circular reasoning, an argument appears to lead to a logical conclusion but merely takes you back to where you started. The statement *Michael Jordan is a great basketball player because he has so much talent* sounds true enough. To say, however, that talent makes Jordan great is just another way of saying that he is a great basketball player. The statement doesn't prove anything; it merely repeats the point in different words.

The danger of circular reasoning is that we can fool our audience—even ourselves—into believing we have sup-

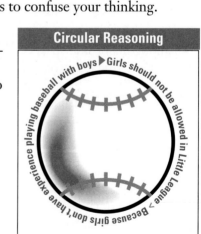

Circular Reasoning

Girls should not be allowed in Little League ▷ Because girls don't have experience playing baseball with boys ▷

The reasoning fails: Girls cannot get that experience unless they're allowed to play.

ported our position when we have just talked in circles, as shown in this speech by a fictitious Secretary of Defense.

Model

I have been proud to oversee the administration of our nation's space program, and I believe the Department of Defense should continue directing this program. As you all know, the department has been involved in every aspect of space research and development, from the efforts of the nation's first astronauts in the 1950s to the secret military missions of the space shuttle today. During this period, the Defense Department has been headed by such famous figures as General Buhrl and General Donnelly.

Based on this record, it is clear that research and systems development of our nation's crucial space program should go forward under the direction of the Defense Department.

The military should direct research and development in the space program because . . .

. . . the military has always directed research and development in the space program.

Revising Tip

If you or a peer editor finds a passage confusing, always study the logic. Write the key points of evidence in an outline or chart to check for fallacies.

Circular reasoning usually becomes apparent the longer you look at it. If you are not sure about an argument, try making a list of the evidence offered. In the example above, the speaker's only evidence to support his claim that the military should run the space program is that the military has always run it, and that the military has been headed by famous people.

Bandwagon Reasoning   Bandwagon reasoning, another kind of faulty reasoning, gets its name from the era when important political candidates rode through towns in parades that included a wagon full of musicians. Local politicians would jump on the bandwagon to show their support for the candidate. Today, "jumping on the bandwagon" means doing something because everyone else is doing it. When you try to persuade your parents to let you go to a party "because everyone else is going," you are using bandwagon reasoning.

• JOURNAL ACTIVITY •
Think It Through

How would you diagram an argument that uses a red herring? In your journal, write a passage that uses this faulty reasoning, and then devise a diagram to represent it.

Oversimplification

In 1952 the United States government conducted atomic bomb tests above-ground in Nevada. In early 1953 the country experienced an unusually large number of tornadoes. Many people were convinced that the nuclear tests caused the tornadoes, even though there was no evidence to link the two phenomena.

Cause and Effect   If you assume that since one event preceded another it caused the other, you fall prey to a cause-and-effect fallacy. Such reasoning is an example of oversimplification, which is another form of logical fallacy.

The cause-and-effect fallacy often enters into political discourse. For example, the political party in office takes credit for peace and prosperity during its administration, even though previous officeholders may have set the stage for such conditions. Similarly, President Herbert Hoover was blamed for the Great Depression, which began shortly after he took office, even though the conditions for the economic crisis had been brewing long before Hoover's time.

The cause-and-effect fallacy often stems from superstition, ignorance, or wishful thinking. The following time line shows how events related chronologically can lead people to such misguided reasoning.

February 1992: The Springfield Stilts win their twelfth consecutive state high school basketball championship.	**July 1992:** Springfield High completes construction of a new gymnasium.	**September 1992:** Enrollment at Springfield High reaches an all-time high.	**November 1992:** The Stilts get new uniforms.	**February 1993:** The Stilts fail to win a thirteenth championship title.
February	**May**	**August**	**November**	**February**
1992				**1993**

Springfield was devastated by the Stilts's loss of the thirteenth state title. Some people claimed that replacing the old "lucky" uniforms and gymnasium caused the defeat. Some said it was the unlucky number *thirteen* that was responsible for the loss. Others felt that the increased enrollment brought bigger crowds to the games, heightening the players' nervousness. Virtually no one reasoned that the Stilts lost because they were outplayed by a better team.

Either/Or   Comedian Groucho Marx, posing as a doctor, takes a patient's pulse and says, "Either this man is dead or my watch has stopped." This scenario illustrates another kind of oversimplification called the either/or fallacy.

Either/or reasoning assumes that there are only two alternatives and ignores other possible explanations. You sometimes hear this fallacy used deliberately, as a form of hyperbole or overstatement. "Either come down from that tree or you'll break your neck!" is another way of saying, "If you don't come down, you'll break your neck." A mother who says that to her child might concede a third possibility—that the child could stay in the tree without getting hurt—but she uses the either/or wording to give her command more impact.

One of the most celebrated examples of the either/or fallacy is the conclusion of Patrick Henry's speech to the Virginia Convention of Delegates in 1775. Urging his fellow citizens to war against the British, he said: "Is life so dear, or peace so sweet, as to be purchased at the price of chains and slavery? Forbid it, Almighty God! I know not what course others may take; but as for me, give me liberty, or give me death!"

Before the United States had decided to enter World War II, Dorothy Thompson, a well-known American journalist, gave a less-often quoted but similarly impassioned speech urging her countrymen and women to enter another war. Notice how she sets up what appears to be an either/or fallacy in order to show that, in this case, it is no fallacy.

Drafting Tip

To avoid oversimplifying, don't be afraid to note other viewpoints in your text. A well-constructed argument will persuade people that your view is superior to others.

Literature Model

*E*very nation on this globe and every individual on this globe will presently learn what a few have always known: that there are times in history when the business of one is the business of all, when life or death is a matter of choice, and when no one alive can avoid making that choice. These times occur seldom in history, these times of inevitable decisions. But this is one of those times.

Before this epoch is over, every living human being will have chosen, every living human being will have lined up with Hitler or against him, every living human being will either have opposed this onslaught or supported it. For if he tried to make no choice that in itself will be a choice. If he takes no side, he is on Hitler's side: if he does not act that is an act—for Hitler.

Dorothy Thompson, May 2, 1941

How does Thompson prepare her audience for the choice she feels they have to make?

Thompson asserts that we have only two choices: oppose Hitler or support him.

Thompson refutes those who would object to this logic as a fallacy by arguing that there are no alternatives. Do you agree or disagree? What alternatives could you suggest?

• JOURNAL ACTIVITY •
Think It Through

Think of a time when someone you know used the either/or fallacy to put pressure on you, and describe it in your journal. How did it make you feel? Was it convincing? Were you able to counter the fallacy with an alternative?

Spotting Errors in Reasoning

If you outline your argument and check its validity carefully during prewriting, you will probably be able to avoid most logical fallacies. Nevertheless, it pays to double-check your reasoning as you revise, as the writer does in the model below.

Model

Strong introduction—keep.

Compared with people from other nations, Americans know next to nothing about cultures outside their own. This ignorance leads to intolerance and misunderstandings. One place to begin eliminating the problem is in schools. Why not in <u>our</u> school?

Circular reasoning.

I propose that we launch a student exchange program. Such a program will involve the entire student body, ~~because all students will participate~~. Teachers and parents will also enjoy contact with visiting students.

Faulty cause and effect? There may be other reasons for dropout rates in those schools. Besides, it's a red herring.

The chance to study abroad will be an incentive for studying foreign languages and world history. Exchange students will return with stories that will inspire others to participate. ~~In addition, statistics show that in schools that have adopted exchange programs, the dropout rate has not increased, as it has elsewhere.~~

Either/or fallacy: either my proposal or isolation. Not true.

I urge you to adopt my proposal, so we may begin the exchanges next year. ~~Without such a program, our students will grow up in isolation.~~ Students deserve the opportunity to learn more about their world.

The following are some writing options to help you try out what you have learned.

1. **Guided Assignment** It is the mid-1800s, and you are a young man who has gone west to make your fortune mining gold. After a year of hard work, you have saved enough money to bring your brother and his family to join you in California. Your brother, however, does not want to move. He sends you his objections in the following telegram.

NOT SURE WE WILL LIKE CALIFORNIA BECAUSE WE'VE NEVER LIVED THERE STOP WHY WON'T YOU COME HOME STOP HAVEN'T I ALWAYS BEEN A GOOD BROTHER TO YOU STOP DON'T YOU LOVE YOUR FAMILY STOP IF WE MOVE OUT WEST WE'LL NEVER COME BACK STOP MARY'S BROTHER NEVER CAME BACK STOP EVERYONE SAYS GOING TO CALIFORNIA IS BAD LUCK STOP CAROLINE AND JIMMY MOVED TO CALIFORNIA LAST YEAR AND THEIR HOUSE BURNED DOWN STOP YOUR LOVING BROTHER

Send him a telegram in return, pointing out his errors in reasoning. Telegrams are expensive, so make every word count.

> PURPOSE To persuade your brother to join you in California by exposing his logical fallacies
> AUDIENCE Your brother
> LENGTH 1 page

2. **Open Assignment** You have been asked to speak to your local parent-teacher association as part of a program to air student views on education. Choose one of the topics below or another controversial topic on education. Brainstorm a list of reasons to support your position, and then write a draft of your speech. During revision, check for logical fallacies.

- Do school boards or parent groups have the right to decide what books should be allowed in school libraries?

- Should all high school students be required to take courses in music and art?
- Should high school students be required to perform a certain number of hours of community service as part of their social studies curriculum?

3. **Art** Study the colored engraving below. What does it suggest to you about fashion and fashion-conscious people? Do you agree or disagree with this view? What effects does the emphasis on fashion in our society have on individuals and on groups of people? Write a letter to the editor of a men's or women's fashion magazine, stating what you believe to be the advantages or drawbacks—or both—of being fashion conscious. Be especially alert to the bandwagon fallacy as you write.

Red Tennis Player, c. 1885

Writing and Presenting a Speech

Unforgettable Words

In 1963 President John F. Kennedy traveled to what was then West Berlin, Germany. He saw the twenty-six-mile Berlin Wall, erected by the communist government of East Germany to keep its people from fleeing to the West. The divided city of East and West Berlin symbolized the division between totalitarianism and democracy. More than half of West Berlin, expectant and highly charged, had gathered to hear how the young American president would identify with their plight. Kennedy did not disappoint them.

Literature Model

*T*wo thousand years ago the proudest boast was *Civis Romanus sum.* ["I am a citizen of Rome."] Today, in the world of freedom, the proudest boast is *Ich bin ein Berliner.* ["I am a Berliner."]

There are many people in the world who really don't understand, or say they don't, what is the great issue between the free world and the communist world.

Let them come to Berlin!

And there are some who say in Europe and elsewhere we can work with the communists. . . .

Let them come to Berlin!

. . . When this city will be joined as one. . . the people of West Berlin can take sober satisfaction in the fact that they were in the front lines for almost two decades.

All free men, wherever they may live, are citizens of Berlin, and therefore, as a free man, I take pride in the words *Ich bin ein Berliner!*

President John F. Kennedy, address to the citizens of West Berlin,
June 1963

The ecstatic crowd erupted. The wall has since fallen, but Kennedy's speech remains a classic of oratory.

Writing a Speech

The President's speech writer, Ted Sorensen, knew what words would persuade the people of West Berlin that Kennedy was on their side, and Kennedy knew how to deliver those words. To get from Sorensen's typewriter in Washington to Kennedy's windy platform in Berlin, however, even this great speech had to go through the steps of the writing process.

If you have to give a speech, use prewriting techniques to help you find a topic and position, reflect on audience and purpose, and come up with strong reasons and evidence. When you draft your speech, organize your material in a way that will be most persuasive. Decide how much of your speech you want to write down and how much, if any, you want to give spontaneously. Some people are naturals at public speaking; they may enjoy the informality of an improvised speech. Others prefer to deliver a fully written speech. Either way, it's a good idea to have a well-thought-out opening for your talk, so your first words will be powerful.

The chart below presents some pointers for effective speaking.

Revising Tip

Tape record your speech and listen to it, taking notes on tone and rhythm. Use your notes to help you revise your speech; then record the speech again.

Aspects of Speaking	Tips
Length How much time are you allotted? Have you practiced your speech aloud, timing it?	*Take it easy: People often rush their words when they're nervous.*
Audience What is the mood of your listeners? Their background? Attitudes?	*Create rapport: Humor is often a good way to win over an audience.*
Tone Do you want your speech to sound casual, emotional, serious?	*Choose suitable language: In an informal speech you may use contractions and slang.*
Rhythm Dr. Martin Luther King Jr. made four words immortal by repeating them: "I have a dream."	*Repetition of words or phrases can make your speech memorable: "Let them come to Berlin!"*

• JOURNAL ACTIVITY •
Think It Through

If you were running for a school government office and had to give a speech to your classmates, which of the aspects above do you think would cause you the most difficulty? In your journal, jot down the aspect and two possible solutions.

Say It with Pictures

Words are not a speechmaker's only tools of persuasion. Visual images such as charts, diagrams, and photos can be dramatic and extremely convincing. Sometimes you can use visuals to strengthen your point; other times you can convey an idea more clearly in a diagram or picture than in words. The visuals on this page both underscore and develop ideas in the model.

Presenting Tip

Practice delivering your speech before a mirror. Try using gestures and body movements for emphasis at key points in your speech. Make your gestures natural.

Student Model

Many people don't recycle because they think it is just as expensive to recycle goods as it is to make items from new materials. This is not true. Not only is recycling less expensive, but it also provides the recycler with a small profit. And not only does recycling cost less, it saves energy as well. For example, even though bauxite (the material from which aluminum is made) is earth's most abundant metal, it is expensive to mine and refine. It takes 95 percent less energy to make aluminum cans from recycled ones than from aluminum ore. The energy saved from recycling one aluminum can is enough to keep a 100-watt light bulb burning for 3 1/2 hours! Likewise, paper made by recycling consumes half the energy needed to process new paper. And by recycling 43 newspapers, you will save one mature tree.

Darin R. Anderson, Wynford High School, Bucyrus, Ohio

RECYCLED U.S. ALUMINUM CANS

50 bil.	
40 bil.	
30 bil.	
20 bil.	
10 bil.	
1 bil.	

1972 1980 1985 1989 1990

It takes an entire forest—over 500,000 trees—to supply Americans with their Sunday newspapers every week.

Writer's Choice

The following are some writing options to help you try out what you have learned.

1. **Guided Assignment** Read the following excerpt from *Time* magazine.

> Law-and-order is the longest-running and probably the best-loved political issue in U.S. history. Yet it is painfully apparent that millions of Americans who would never think of themselves as lawbreakers, let alone criminals, are taking increasing liberties with the legal codes that are designed to protect and nourish their society.

Author Frank Trippett cites graffiti, jaywalking, speeding, littering, tax cheating, and illegally loud radios as examples of an increase in "scofflaws"—people who disregard the law. The trend, he says, has severe consequences.

Write a persuasive speech arguing for or against Trippett's position. Are we indeed all scofflaws, and does this threaten law and public safety? If so, how? Or is the issue blown out of proportion? Use evidence from your own behavior or behavior you have observed in others. Consider your audience as you revise. Finally, practice your delivery.

PURPOSE To persuade your audience that scofflaws are or are not a serious problem
AUDIENCE Your class
LENGTH 2 minutes

2. **Open Assignment** The president has just appointed you to be the new secretary of education. Prepare a five-minute speech to a national parent-teacher conference arguing for funding a problem you wish to tackle. Choose one of the topics below or one of your own. Create visuals to accompany your speech.

- College tuition continues to rise, while government assistance for it has shrunk. Increasingly, lower- and middle-income students cannot afford college.
- Scores on the Scholastic Aptitude Test have declined significantly over the past 20 years. In 1991, scores on the verbal portion of the test reached a record low.

COMPUTER OPTION

Proofreading is especially important in speeches because you don't want to stumble over a misspelled or omitted word. If you prepare your speech on a word processor, use the spell checker. Double- or triple-spacing will make your text easier to read aloud.

3. **Cooperative Learning** Poems can often be as persuasive as prose. Have one student read aloud the Langston Hughes poem below.

Harlem
What happens to a dream deferred?

Does it dry up
like a raisin in the sun?
Or fester like a sore—
And then run?
Does it stink like rotten meat?
Or crust and sugar over—
like a syrupy sweet?

Maybe it just sags
like a heavy load.

Or does it explode?

As a group, discuss the meaning of this poem, written in 1951. What "dreams" do all people have a right to today? How does Hughes express the urgency of his dream? Divide your group into pairs. One student in each pair will be the reader of the Hughes poem; the other will be the coach. When each pair is satisfied with the reading, the readers will present the poem to the group. All group members will orally compare and contrast the two deliveries.

Dear Editor . . .

Model

Dear Editor:
Whose idea was it to endorse Joe Graft for reelection? If you had simply walked outside and opened your eyes, you couldn't help but see what's happened here since His Majesty was elected mayor.

Let's take a look at what he's done to help the town of Dillard. The streets are full of holes the size of the Grand Canyon. The playgrounds should have "Danger: Keep Out" signs on them. And how about that eyesore at the end of Nice Street? I'm ready to go out and rent a wrecking ball and rip down that hideous old house myself!

Mayor Graft can't get involved in these matters, of course. He's too busy signing new tax bills and playing golf with his pals at the country club. To his credit, however, he did spend thousands of taxpayer dollars for that so-called sculpture in front of City Hall. That's the ugliest piece of junk I've ever seen!

Graft is the worst mayor Dillard has ever had! Wake up to the facts, *Dillard Daily Snooze.*

A Concerned Citizen

Where has the writer used name calling and insults? What effect would these have on readers?

Exaggeration and unsupported opinions obscure legitimate issues. What needs to be done that Graft did not do?

Planning Your Letter

The letter above represents a good way not to get published. Editors are often swamped with letters. They read or scan them once, and the ones that are unclear or fanatical go directly into the wastebasket. If you want to influence or affect a course of events rather than merely spout off, your letter must be reasonable, well written, and credible, not to mention legible.

Unlike a speech or a debate, a letter depends solely on the strength of written words to express an opinion or to prompt people to action. Most publications have limited space, so there's no room for a long treatise. To compose a letter that is pithy, convincing, and publishable, do the necessary prewriting tasks. Use freewriting, brainstorming, and clustering to explore an issue. Next, develop a thesis statement that identifies a problem and, if appropriate, a proposed solution.

Most important, get your facts straight. Do a little homework to uncover some relevant data that readers may not know. To support your point, use concrete details, facts or statistics, examples, and sound reasons. The illustration below gives an example of how to collect evidence, highlight the strongest points, and come up with a method for organizing the evidence persuasively.

Thesis
The dilapidated house at the end of Nice Street is an eyesore: it should be restored and turned into a museum of local town history.

Notes
1. House built 1798 by town founder Millard Dillard
2. Quirky: has hidden staircases, secret rooms, unexpected windows and gables: unusual 18th-century architecture
3. Bad shape: weeds, peeling paint, cracked windows
4. Dillard High School Community Service

Club is looking for a worthy project
5. Architect and contractor will donate services
6. Vacant since Josephine Dillard died there in 1971
7. Neighbors want it torn down
8. Reports of wails, bangs, and odd noises at night

Strategy
Describe situation: condition of house
Propose solution: restoration
Reasons for restoring: architectural, historic value
Solving obstacles to restoration: donated labor

• JOURNAL ACTIVITY •
Think It Through

In your journal, make a checklist of the features of a good letter to the editor. Then read and evaluate some letters in your local newspaper. Were you persuaded by the writer's point of view? Why or why not?

Editing Tip

During editing, make sure you consistently use the first person singular "I" in your letter. Proofread your letter so it will make a good impression.

A Better Letter

Once you've stated your thesis and assembled and organized your evidence, writing the letter can be fairly straightforward. As you revise your letter, pay attention to your tone. Even the most logical, well-supported argument can be ineffective if the tone is disrespectful, unpleasant, or too casual.

Model

The opening will catch the interest of the editor as well as that of the paper's readers.

The writer acknowledges the problem and offers a solution. What elements contribute to a reasonable tone?

The facts in this paragraph support the writer's opinion, and they are believable because they are based on research.

How does the writer anticipate possible objections?

Dear Editor:
Hauntingly beautiful, perhaps—but not a haunted house!

Some neighbors claim they hear strange sounds at night from the old Dillard house at the end of Nice Street. Others complain that with the foot-high weeds, teetering fence, and peeling gray paint, the place might just as well be haunted. Now the Nice Street Neighborhood Association is pressuring the city government to bulldoze the old house.

The house has been empty since 1971, and it certainly has become a dilapidated eyesore. But I don't believe that it is haunted, and I don't believe that tearing it down is the answer. This once-grand house is an important structure in this town's history. It could easily be made into a spacious and beautiful museum.

Many of our citizens recognize that Dillard needs a town museum. In fact, the Clarion Historical Society has been talking about building a town museum for some time now. Why not restore this remarkable old house?

I have researched the old records at City Hall and discovered that the house was built in 1798 by our town founder, Millard Dillard. The house has a number of unusual architectural features, such as hidden staircases leading to secret rooms, rare amethyst-glass windows, and unexpected gables. It pains me to think of bulldozing the hidden history and quirky charm of this historic eighteenth-century mansion.

Restoring the house would not cost the city much more than tearing it down. Architect Nick Coven and the Lockley Construction Company have offered to donate their time and material to help restore the house. The Community Service Club at Dillard High School is willing to contribute labor.

Let's preserve the heritage of our city and make Dillard House into a museum we can all be proud of!

Sincerely,
Sam Citizen

Writer's Choice

Ant Farm, *Cadillac Ranch*, c. 1974

The following are some writing options to help you try out what you have learned.

1. Guided Assignment Read the following data from a 1991 study of smoking and high school students that was conducted by the Centers for Disease Control in Atlanta:

- Of those surveyed, 36 percent had smoked or chewed tobacco in the previous month.
- 13 percent were frequent smokers (smoking on at least 25 of 30 days).
- 41 percent of twelfth-graders had used tobacco in the previous month.
- 18 percent of twelfth-graders were frequent smokers.
- Tobacco use is higher among boys than girls because boys use chewing tobacco.
- Cigarette smoking among boys and girls is nearly the same.

Use these data about teens and tobacco to form a thesis statement for a persuasive letter to the editor of a magazine for teen-agers.

Consider the following questions: What do these figures suggest to you? How do they relate to your own observations and knowledge? How would you define the problem of teen-age smoking? Brainstorm a list of possible solutions to the problem you've identified. Draft your letter, making sure to include some of the data above to support your opinion. Use the letter on page 294 as a guide to writing a letter that is attention-getting but reasonable.

PURPOSE To persuade teen-agers to accept your point of view on smoking

AUDIENCE Readers of your school newspaper

LENGTH 1 page

2. Open Assignment Write a letter to the editor of two different kinds of publications, choosing one of the topics below or one of your own:

- recycling paper goods
- colleges' athletic scholarships
- nuclear energy

You might address letters on the first topic to an environmental magazine and to a lumbering association. Make sure the tone of your letter is appropriate to each audience. Research your topic to find supporting evidence.

3. Art The picture above is more than just a landscape; it's a work of art, according to the group that designed it. The artists belong to a San Francisco collective called Ant Farm. In 1974 this group partially buried ten 1950s-era Cadillacs along famous Route 66 near Amarillo, Texas. The exhibit is intended to challenge what people think of as art. Draft a letter to the editor of an art magazine, giving your opinion of the value of this exhibit. Is it art? Why or why not? Should government funds be used for such projects? You may want to research what art critics have said about avant-garde landscape art and use authoritative opinion to support your position.

Writing a Letter to an Editor **295**

Writing About Literature
Evaluating a Speech

Wake Me When It's Over

After church one day, the pastor of a small Ohio congregation went up to one of his parishioners and reprimanded him.

"I saw you napping during the sermon today," the minister said.

The man replied: "I was awake when I came in."

If the audience is snoring, the speaker isn't doing a good job. A good speaker—whether minister, professor, politician, or business executive—will catch and hold the attention of the audience.

When you evaluate a speech, consider these questions: In what frame of mind did the speaker find the audience—expectant, bored, hostile? How did the speaker leave the audience—thoughtful, enthusiastic, yawning? Did the speech accomplish its purpose?

Saturday Evening Post cover, 1946

The Strength of Ideas

Skilled orators often have rallied their audiences to support worthy causes and high ideals. Other equally persuasive speakers have manipulated public opinion by appealing to emotion instead of reason. If you learn to examine carefully what you hear before responding to it, you are less likely to be manipulated. You must look at the content of the words and separate it from the emotional appeal.

Although speeches are more than essays read aloud, the written text of a good speech will still have many of the same features that apply to writing a persuasive essay.

Analyzing the Text of a Speech	
Purpose	Can you identify the main point of the speech?
Credibility	Are the ideas and arguments well supported and believable?
Appropriateness	Do the language and ideas suit the audience and occasion?
Coherence	Can you easily follow the ideas or points of the speaker?
Interest	Do the ideas hold your attention?
Variety	Does the speech incorporate anecdote, opinion, and facts?

In 1976 Texas Representative Barbara Jordan was selected to be the keynote speaker at the Democratic National Convention. She was the first African American to receive this prestigious honor. Jordan is a highly respected speaker. Said a colleague: "When Barbara Jordan speaks, those within hearing listen."

Literature

A lot of years have passed since [the first Democratic party convention in] 1832, and during that time it would have been most unusual for any national political party to ask that a Barbara Jordan deliver a keynote address—but tonight, here I am. And I feel notwithstanding that past that my presence here is one additional bit of evidence that the American Dream need not forever be deferred.

Now that I have this grand distinction, what in the world am I supposed to say? I could easily spend this time praising the accomplishments of this party and attacking the Republicans, but I do not choose to do that. I could list the many problems which Americans have. . . . and then I could sit down and offer no solutions. But I do not choose to do that either. The citizens of America expect more. . . .

We are a people in a quandary about the present. We are a people in search of our future. We are a people in search of a national community. . . . The great danger that America faces [is] that we will cease to be one nation and become instead a collection of interest groups: city against suburb, region against region, individual against individual. . . .

If that happens, who then will speak for America? Who then will speak for the common good? . . . There is no law that can require the American people to form a national community. This we must do as individuals and if we do it as individuals, there is no President of the United States who can veto that decision.

Barbara Jordan, address to Democratic National Convention, 1976

Jordan knows her audience expects her to criticize the Republicans and list the nation's problems, so she begins by stating what she is not going to talk about.

Note the solemn and dignified language and tone, in keeping with the occasion.

• JOURNAL ACTIVITY •

Try It Out

Use the criteria at the bottom of page 296 to evaluate the content of a speech in print, either in a newspaper or in a collection of well-known speeches.

Powerful Presentation

A good delivery of a speech can convey qualities that the written text alone cannot. In reviewing Barbara Jordan's address to the Democratic National Convention, reviewers noted that the speaker's personality shone through her words.

Literature Model

*I*t was the second keynote address, by U.S. Rep. Barbara Jordan of Texas, that generated the only excitement. It is almost a pity that the competition was so feeble, because the speech itself was far and away the best political address that any of us are liable to hear in the Bicentennial election year.

Jordan's integrity, sincerity, faith, common sense, and passionate—rather than emotional—commitment to what this country is all about tower so far above the main candidates that it is indeed a pity that she is not a candidate herself. Not since Franklin Roosevelt has either political party had an adherent with more rights to a podium—she is one of the very few Americans who should be allowed to make speeches. Jordan dropped all clichés; she spoke as an American rather than a party hack, and she even quoted a Republican president.

Donald Morris, *Houston Post*, July 15, 1976

Good speakers use a variety of techniques to enhance their delivery and make their speeches more effective, as shown in the chart on the left. How important is a good delivery? An anecdote about one of the most famous American history speeches of our time provides a useful lesson. When Lincoln delivered his Gettysburg Address, many reviews were critical. "Anything more dull and commonplace it would not be easy to produce," wrote the *London Times*; "dishwater" and "silly," wrote Democratic editors.

We will never be sure why Lincoln's speech was not immediately recognized for its greatness. Lincoln was not the most polished of orators, however, and on that day in November, he spoke after one of the most celebrated orators of the time, Edward Everett. Perhaps Lincoln's delivery seemed unexciting, compared to that of the more dramatic Everett. Ironically, Everett's speech is rarely reprinted; the text of Lincoln's Gettysburg Address has survived as one of the most eloquent speeches in American history.

Clear, loud, natural tone of voice

Effective rhythm, pacing, and pauses

Powerful Presentation

Believable style— sincere, honest

Tone to match the text and occasion

Effective use of facial expressions and gestures

The following are some writing options to help you try out what you have learned.

1. Guided Assignment   Read the Gettysburg Address by Abraham Lincoln. Most encyclopedias contain the speech, or a librarian can help you find a copy. If you were a reporter covering the address for a local Gettysburg newspaper, how would you evaluate the speech? Imagine how Lincoln might have delivered the speech and how the audience might have reacted. Then write a newspaper article on the address, including both your overall reaction to the speech and descriptions of audience response. During prewriting, take separate notes on the text and the delivery. Use the charts on pages 296 and 298 to guide you in your evaluations.

PURPOSE   To evaluate both content and presentation of a political speech
AUDIENCE   Readers of a Gettysburg newspaper in 1863
LENGTH   1–2 pages

2. Open Assignment   Read one of the following speeches or a speech of your own choosing. A librarian can help you locate both these and other speeches. Write an essay evaluating the speech you select. Include an evaluation of the use of oratorical devices such as repetition, pacing, and rhythm.

- Patrick Henry's "Give me liberty or give me death" speech
- any speech by Frederick Douglass
- Elizabeth Cady Stanton's keynote address at the first Women's Rights Convention
- John F. Kennedy's "I am a Berliner" speech
- Martin Luther King's "I have a dream" speech

3. Cooperative Learning   In groups of four, brainstorm important issues at your school that would make appropriate topics for a persuasive speech. Then divide into two teams. Each team will jointly write a single speech. Agree on a topic from the brainstorming list (teams can choose the same topic or different topics). Then have one partner of the team write the opening and closing of the speech, and the other write the body of the speech. Work together to revise the speech, keeping in mind that the other team will be your audience. Collaborate on visuals, if appropriate. Choose one team member to deliver the speech.

Each team can then serve as the audience for the other team. The team that is acting as the audience should listen to the speech, one member taking notes on content, the other on presentation. After each speech, hold a five-minute discussion to share the audience's impressions with the speech writers. After both speeches have been given, each member should write a review of the other team's speech. The reviews should be at least one page long. Include references to the content and delivery.

4. American History   Obtain from the library a tape recording of Martin Luther King Jr.'s "I have a dream" speech or any other important speech from U.S. history. Listen to the speech and freewrite about your reactions to it. Then listen to the speech again, taking further notes about specific devices the speaker uses. Finally, write an essay evaluating the speech, focusing on the speaker's delivery.

COMPUTER OPTION

One possible problem in writing about speeches is the tendency to repeatedly write, "She said . . . She said . . ." You can use the word-search function of your word processor to locate this repeated phrase, as well as repetitions of the speaker's name. Then you can find ways to vary your sentences as you revise your writing.

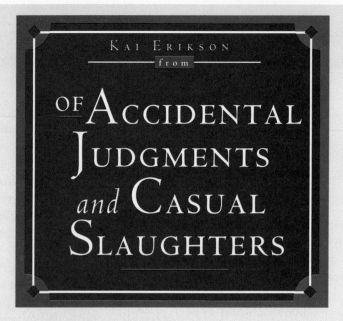

KAI ERIKSON

from

OF ACCIDENTAL JUDGMENTS and CASUAL SLAUGHTERS

Are important decisions always deliberately made, or do things—even terrible things—sometimes "just happen"? At the end of Hamlet, *Horatio laments the "accidental judgments" and "casual slaughters" that have proved the ruin of his friend Hamlet and Hamlet's country, Denmark. In the following excerpt from a 1985 essay, historian Kai Erikson examines the atomic attacks on Japan during World War II and argues that they may be an all-too-real example of the danger of "accidental judgments."*

The bombings of Hiroshima and Nagasaki, which took place forty years ago this month, are among the most thoroughly studied moments on human record. Together they constitute the only occasion in history when atomic weapons were dropped on living populations, and together they constitute the only occasion in history when a decision was made to employ them in that way.

I want to reflect here on the second of those points. The "decision to drop"—I will explain in a minute why quotation marks are useful here—is a fascinating historical episode. But it is also an exhibit of the most profound importance as we consider our prospects for the future. It is a case history well worth attending to. A compelling parable.

If one were to tell the story of that decision as historians normally do, the details arranged in an ordered narrative, one might begin in 1938 with the discovery of nuclear fission, or perhaps a year later with the delivery of Einstein's famous letter to President Roosevelt. No matter what its opening scene, though, the tale would then proceed along a string of events—a sequence of appointees named, committees formed, reports issued, orders signed, arguments won and lost, minds made up and changed—all of it coming to an end with a pair of tremendous blasts in the soft morning air over Japan.

The difficulty with that way of relating the story, as historians of the period all testify, is that the more closely one examines the record, the harder it is to make out where in the flow of events something that could reasonably be called a decision was reached at all. To be sure, a kind of consensus emerged from the sprawl of ideas and happenings that made up the climate of wartime Washington, but looking back, it is hard to distinguish those pivotal moments in the story when the crucial issues were identified, debated, reasoned through, resolved. The decision, to the extent that one can even speak of such a thing, was shaped and seasoned by a force very like inertia.[1]

Let's say, then, that a wind began to blow, ever so gently at first, down the corridors along which power flows. And as it gradually gathered momentum during the course of the war, the people caught up in it began to assume, without ever checking up on it, that it had a logic and a motive, that it had been set in motion by sure hands acting on the basis of wise counsel.

Harry Truman, in particular, remembered it as a time of tough and lonely choices, and titled his memoir of that period *Year of Decisions*. But the bulk of those choices can in all fairness be said to have involved confirmation of projects already under way or implementation of decisions made at other levels of command. Brig. Gen. Leslie R. Groves, military head of the Manhattan Project, was close to the mark when he described Truman's decision as "one of noninterference— basically, a decision not to upset the existing plans." And J. Robert Oppenheimer spoke equally to the point when he observed some twenty years later: "The decision was implicit in the project. I don't know whether it could have been stopped."

In September of 1944, when it became more and more evident that a bomb would be produced in time for combat use, Franklin Roosevelt and Winston Churchill met at Hyde Park and initialed a brief *aide-mémoire*, noting, among other things, that the new weapon "might, perhaps, after mature consideration, be used against the Japanese." This document does not appear to have had any effect on the conduct of the war, and Truman knew nothing at all about it. But it would not have made a real difference in any case, for neither chief of state did much to initiate the "mature consideration" they spoke of so glanc-

1. **inertia** (in ur´shə): the tendency to keep moving in the same direction

ingly, and Truman, in turn, could only suppose that such matters had been considered already. "Truman did not inherit the question," writes Martin J. Sherwin, "he inherited the answer."

What would "mature consideration" have meant in such a setting as that anyway?

First of all, presumably, it would have meant seriously asking whether the weapon should be employed at all. But we have it on the authority of virtually all the principal players that no one in a position to do anything about it ever really considered alternatives to combat use. Henry L. Stimson, Secretary of War:

At no time, from 1941 to 1945, did I ever hear it suggested by the President, or by any other responsible member of the government, that atomic energy should not be used in the war.

Harry Truman:

I regarded the bomb as a military weapon and never had any doubt that it should be used.

General Groves:

Certainly, there was no question in my mind, or, as far as I was ever aware, in the mind of either President Roosevelt or President Truman or any other responsible person, but that we were developing a weapon to be employed against the enemies of the United States.

Winston Churchill:

There never was a moment's discussion as to whether the atomic bomb should be used or not.

And why should anyone be surprised? We were at war, after all, and with the most resolute of enemies, so the unanimity[2] of that feeling is wholly understandable. But it was not, by any stretch of the imagination, a product of mature consideration.

"Combat use" meant a number of different things, however, and a second question began to be raised with some frequency in the final months of the war, all the more insistently after the defeat of Germany. Might a way be devised to demonstrate the awesome power of the bomb in a convincing enough fashion to induce the surrender of the Japanese without having to destroy huge numbers of civilians? Roosevelt may have been pondering something of the sort. In September of 1944, for example, three days after initialing the Hyde Park *aide-mémoire*, he asked Vannevar Bush, a trusted science adviser, whether

2. **unanimity** (yoō′ nə nim′ ə tē): complete agreement

the bomb "should actually be used against the Japanese or whether it should be used only as a threat." While that may have been little more than idle musing, a number of different schemes were explored within both the government and the scientific community in the months following.

One option involved a kind of *benign strike*: the dropping of a bomb on some built-up area, but only after advance notice had been issued so that residents could evacuate the area and leave an empty slate on which the bomb could write its terrifying signature. This plan was full of difficulties. A dud under those dramatic circumstances might do enormous damage to American credibility, and, moreover, to broadcast any warning was to risk the endeavor in other ways. Weak as the Japanese were by this time in the war, it was easy to imagine their finding a way to intercept an incoming airplane if they knew where and when it was expected, and officials in Washington were afraid that it would occur to the Japanese, as it had to them, that the venture would come to an abrupt end if American prisoners of war were brought into the target area.

The second option was a *tactical strike* against a purely military target—an arsenal, railroad yard, depot, factory, harbor—without advance notice. Early in the game, for example, someone had nominated the Japanese fleet concentration at Truk. The problem with this notion, however—and there is more than a passing irony here—was that no known military target had a wide enough compass to contain the whole of the destructive capacity of the weapon and so display its full range and power. The committee inquiring into likely targets wanted one "more than three miles in diameter," because anything smaller would be too inadequate a canvas for the picture it was supposed to hold.

The third option was to stage a kind of *dress rehearsal* by detonating a bomb in some remote corner of the world—a desert or empty island, say—to exhibit to international observers brought in for the purpose what the device could do. The idea had been proposed by a group of scientists in what has since been called the Franck Report, but it commanded no more than a moment's attention. It had the same problems as the benign strike: the risk of being embarrassed by a dud was more than most officials in a position to decide were willing to take, and there was a widespread feeling that any demonstration involving advance notice would give the enemy too much useful information.

The fourth option involved a kind of *warning shot*. The thought here was to drop a bomb without notice over a relatively uninhabited stretch of enemy land so that the Japanese high command might see at first hand what was in store for them if they failed to surrender soon.

Edward Teller thought that an explosion at night high over Tokyo Bay would serve as a brilliant visual argument, and Adm. Lewis Strauss, soon to become a member (and later chair) of the Atomic Energy Commission, recommended a strike on a local forest, reasoning that the blast would "lay the trees out in windrows[3] from the center of the explosion in all directions as though they were matchsticks," meanwhile igniting a fearsome firestorm at the epicenter. "It seemed to me," he added, "that a demonstration of this sort would prove to the Japanese that we could destroy any of their cities at will." The physicist Ernest O. Lawrence may have been speaking half in jest when he suggested that a bomb might be used to "blow the top off" Mount Fujiyama, but he was quite serious when he assured a friend early in the war: "The bomb will never be dropped on people. As soon as we get it, we'll use it only to dictate peace."

Now, hindsight is too easy a talent. But it seems evident on the face of it that the fourth of those options, the warning shot, was much to be preferred over the other three, and even more to be preferred over use on living targets. I do not want to argue the case here. I do want to ask, however, why that possibility was so easily dismissed.

The fact of the matter seems to have been that the notion of a demonstration was discussed on only a few occasions once the Manhattan Project neared completion, and most of those discussions were off the record. So a historian trying to reconstruct the drift of those conversations can only flatten an ear against the wall, as it were, and see if any sense can be made of the muffled voices next door. It seems very clear, for example, that the options involving advance notice were brought up so often and so early in official conversations that they came to *mean* demonstration in the minds of several important players. If a James Byrnes, say, soon to be named Secretary of State, were asked why one could not detonate a device in unoccupied territory, he might raise the problem posed by prisoners of war, and if the same question were asked of a James Bryant Conant, another science adviser, he might speak of the embarrassment that would follow a dud—thus, in both cases, joining ideas that had no logical relation to each other. Neither prisoners of war nor fear of failure, of course, posed any argument against a surprise demonstration.

There were two occasions, however, on which persons in a position to affect policy discussed the idea of a nonlethal demonstration. Those two conversations together consumed no more than a matter of minutes, so far as one can tell at this remove, and they, too, were off the record. But they seem to represent virtually the entire investment of the government of the United States in "mature consideration" of the subject.

3. **windrows** (wind´rōz´): rows

Jacob Lawrence, *Hiroshima Series, "Family,"* 1983

    The first discussion took place at a meeting of what was then called the Interim Committee, a striking gathering of military, scientific and government brass under the chairmanship of Secretary Stimson. This group, which included James Byrnes and Chief of Staff Gen. George C. Marshall, met on a number of occasions in May of 1945 to discuss policy issues raised by the new bomb, and Stimson recalled later that at one of their final meetings the members "carefully considered such alternatives as a detailed advance warning or a demonstration in some uninhabited area." But the minutes of the meeting, as well as the accounts of those present, suggest otherwise. The only exchange on the subject, in fact, took place during a luncheon break, and while we have no way of knowing what was actually said in that conversation, we do know what conclusion emerged from it. One participant, Arthur H. Compton, recalled later:

Though the possibility of a demonstration that would not destroy human lives was attractive, no one could suggest a way in which it could be made so convincing that it would be likely to stop the war.

And the recording secretary of the meeting later recalled:

Dr. Oppenheimer . . . said he doubted whether there could be devised any sufficiently startling demonstration that would convince the Japanese they ought to throw in the sponge.

Two weeks later, four physicists who served as advisers to the Interim Committee met in Los Alamos to consider once again the question of demonstration. They were Arthur Compton, Enrico Fermi, Ernest Lawrence and Robert Oppenheimer—as distinguished an assembly of scientific talent as could be imagined—and they concluded, after a discussion of which we have no record: "We can propose no technical demonstration likely to bring an end to the war; we see no acceptable alternative to direct military use." That, so far as anyone can tell, was the end of it.

We cannot be sure that a milder report would have made a difference, for the Manhattan Project was gathering momentum as it moved toward the more steeply pitched inclines of May and June, but we can be sure that the idea of a demonstration was at that point spent. The Los Alamos report ended with something of a disclaimer ("We have, however, no claim to special competence. . . ."), but its message was clear enough. When asked about that report nine years later in his security hearings, Oppenheimer said, with what might have been a somewhat defensive edge in his voice, "We did not think exploding one of those things as a firecracker over the desert was likely to be very impressive."

Perhaps not. But those fragments are telling for another reason. If you listen to them carefully for a moment or two, you realize that these are the voices of nuclear physicists trying to imagine how a strange and distant people will react to an atomic blast. These are the voices of nuclear physicists dealing with psychological and anthropological questions about Japanese culture, Japanese temperament, Japanese will to resist—topics, we must assume, about which they knew almost nothing. They did not know yet what the bomb could actually do, since its first test was not to take place for another month.

But in principle, at least, Oppenheimer and Fermi reflecting on matters relating to the Japanese national character should have had about the same force as Ruth Benedict and Margaret Mead reflecting on matters relating to high-energy physics, the first difference being that Benedict and Mead would not have presumed to do so, and the second being that no one in authority would have listened to them if they had.

The first of the two morals I want to draw from the foregoing— this being a parable, after all—is that in moments of critical contemplation, it is often hard to know where the competencies of soldiers and scientists and all the rest of us begin and end. Many an accidental judgment can emerge from such confusions.

But what if the conclusions of the scientists had been correct? What if some kind of demonstration had been staged in a lightly occupied part of Japan and it *had* been greeted as a firecracker in the desert? What then?

Let me shift gears for a moment and discuss the subject in another way. It is standard wisdom for everyone in the United States old enough to remember the war, and for most of those to whom it is ancient history, that the bombings of Hiroshima and Nagasaki were the only alternative to an all-out invasion of the Japanese mainland involving hundreds of thousands and perhaps millions of casualties on both sides. Unless the Japanese came to understand the need to surrender quickly, we would have been drawn by an almost magnetic force toward those dreaded beaches. This has become an almost automatic pairing of ideas, an article of common lore. If you lament that so many civilians were incinerated or blown to bits in Hiroshima and Nagasaki, then somebody will remind you of the American lives thus saved. Truman was the person most frequently asked to account for the bombings, and his views were emphatic on the subject:

It was a question of saving hundreds of thousands of American lives. I don't mind telling you that you don't feel normal when you have to plan hundreds of thousands of complete, final deaths of American boys who are alive and joking and having fun while you are doing your planning. You break your heart and your head trying to figure out a way to save one life. The name given to our invasion plan was "Olympic," but I saw nothing godly about the killing of all the people that would be necessary to make that invasion. I could not worry about what history would say about my personal morality. I made the only decision I ever knew how to make. I did what I thought was right....

Veterans of the war, and particularly those who had reason to suppose that they would have been involved in an invasion, have drawn that same connection repeatedly, most recently Paul Fussell in the pages of *The New Republic*. Thank God for the bomb, the argument goes, it saved the lives of countless numbers of us. And so, in a sense, it may have.

But the destruction of Hiroshima and Nagasaki had nothing to do with it. It only makes sense to assume, even if few people were well enough positioned in early August to see the situation whole, that there simply was not going to be an invasion. Not ever.

For what sane power, with the atomic weapon securely in its arsenal, would hurl a million or more of its sturdiest young men on a heavily fortified mainland? To imagine anyone ordering an invasion when the means were at hand to blast Japan into a sea of gravel at virtually no cost in American lives is to imagine a madness beyond anything even the worst of war can induce. The invasion had not yet been called off, granted. But it surely would have been, and long before the November 1 deadline set for it.

The United States did not become a nuclear power on August 6, with the destruction of Hiroshima. It became a nuclear power on July 16, when the first test device was exploded in Alamogordo, New Mexico. Uncertainties remained, of course, many of them. But from that moment on, the United States knew how to produce a bomb, knew how to deliver it and knew it would work. Stimson said shortly after the war that the bombings of Hiroshima and Nagasaki "ended the ghastly specter of a clash of great land armies," but he could have said, with greater justice, that the ghastly specter ended at Alamogordo. Churchill came close to making exactly that point when he first learned of the New Mexico test:

> To quell the Japanese resistance man by man and conquer the country yard by yard might well require the loss of a million American lives and half that number of British. . . . Now all that nightmare picture had vanished.

It *had* vanished. The age of inch-by-inch crawling over enemy territory, the age of Guadalcanal and Iwo Jima and Okinawa, was just plain over.

For Discussion

1. Does Erikson persuade you to share his viewpoint about the bomb? Identify specific passages that influence your response.

2. What is your reaction to the four options that Erikson says were available to the scientific community and the government? Which option, if any, do you think should have been chosen?

Readers Respond

Erikson claims that a definite decision to drop the atomic bomb was never really made. The people involved in the decision never really weighed all the options. I liked the way Erikson used psychology in talking about history.

Susannah Levine

The point of studying the causes and effects of dropping "the bomb" is not to rehash the horror or play God and dish out blame, but rather to remember these bombings because they remind us of our destructive capabilities. The repercussions from the decision to drop the atomic bomb still ring, and it would benefit everyone to educate themselves about it. Under circumstances of war or confusion, "accidental judgments and casual slaughters" are quite possible. This essay lays out the issues surrounding the bombings and makes an old but important point. We must learn from our mistakes.

Peter Ivaska

Did you notice?

☞ Did you notice the way Erikson used quotations and logic to argue a controversial point? How do you think your reaction to his essay might have been affected if he had simply summarized his points without backing them up in this way?

☞ Erikson takes his title from a passage in Shakespeare's *Hamlet*. Do you think the title is a good one for this piece? Write a brief journal entry to explain your answer.

Writing Process in Action

The 20/20 Vision of Hindsight

As Kai Erikson says, "Hindsight is too easy a talent." Yes, most people are good at figuring out what they should have done or said after the fact. In "Of Accidental Judgments and Casual Slaughters" (pages 300–308), Erikson argues that the question of whether to use atomic force against Japan was never given thorough, "mature consideration." If it had, he implies, the bombs might never have been dropped on Hiroshima and Nagasaki and thousands of innocent people would have been spared. While you may question his conclusion, it's hard to disagree with the judgment that, in general, inadvertent consequences can be avoided if people think carefully before they act. It's also hard to disagree with his reminder that we can indeed learn from history.

Bring Erikson's argument closer to home. Think about the times when you (or someone you know) have done something regrettable, something that backfired, something that turned out in a way you never intended. The assignment below gives you the opportunity to use your talent for hindsight in a persuasive essay that can help others to learn from your experience.

• Assignment •

CONTEXT   Your school has instituted a peer-support group to help freshmen adjust to high school, and you have been invited to speak to a small group about pitfalls to avoid. You are free to choose your subject; however, there are some restrictions: your aim is to *persuade* your audience to think or behave in a certain way, not just to inform them of a wise course of action. Your argument must be based primarily on experience and observation. While you're encouraged to use humor and irony, your overall tone should be thoughtful.

PURPOSE   To persuade your audience to avoid or follow some course of action

AUDIENCE High school freshmen

LENGTH   3–5 pages

---

1. Prewriting

All writers face the same "enemy": the blank page. The only way to subdue this adversary, of course, is to write on it. So, after reading the assignment once again, pick up a pencil and attack. Write the question "What have I (or someone I know) done that I regret and that could serve as a warning to others?" at the top of the page. Then write down *anything* that comes to mind: words, phrases, or sentences. If you "see" an image, sketch it. You may also want to formulate your own questions. Refer to Lesson 2.3 for a discussion of questioning. If this prewriting technique doesn't get results, try clustering or brainstorming. Lesson 2.2 focuses on other useful techniques. Once you've gotten several ideas or snips of ideas to work with, turn two or three of them into situations. That is, make a rough outline of what led up to and what resulted from the climactic event or events.

Now it's time to select your topic and to decide what lesson you want to draw from it. As you proceed, keep two things in mind: your audience and your purpose. Ask yourself which of the situations you've outlined fits the criteria in the assignment. In other words, which one is suitable for a group of freshmen and which one lends itself to persuasion? Remember, you're trying to persuade your audience that what might look like a safe course of action may end in unpleasantness or even disaster. Therefore choose a hazard you think is significant and for which you can offer compelling reasons and supporting details. For example, a warning not to buy a pass for the nonexistent elevator is probably not of enough significance. However, advice not to believe everything you hear from upperclassmen—with the elevator pass as a minor humorous example and your major focus on more serious deceptions— might well be worthwhile.

When you've made your choice of topic, summarize your persuasive purpose in a thesis statement. Lesson 6.1 can help you formulate and test the strength of your thesis. At this point, however, what's more important than the words you use is the conviction you feel and the appropriateness of the topic to your audience.

Lastly, jot down some thoughts on what caused things to go awry. Try drawing a diagram that illustrates what was intended, what actually resulted, and where things went wrong. Use the 20/20 vision of hindsight to *analyze* the sequence of events, to make inferences, and to draw conclusions. Be sure to look at the situation from several different angles, and don't be satisfied with easy answers. This process will tell you a great deal about yourself, too. For example, what caused you to become overwhelmed your freshman year? Was it too many extracurricular activities, as you first thought, or was part of the problem your unwillingness to give up your favorite soap operas? Try turning your new personal insights into sound advice.

2. Drafting

Because every element of your argument hinges directly or indirectly on your thesis statement, write it down and refer to it often as you draft. Your essay is an amplification of this single idea. It's not necessary, however, to state your thesis right away. You have an audience to win first. By planning the organization of your essay before you begin drafting, you can determine the most strategic moment to present your thesis and the most convincing arrangement of your reasons. Refer to Lesson 2.6 for ideas on organization.

Also take a look at how Erikson organizes his essay. His opening is dramatic; he reminds us that Hiroshima and Nagasaki "constitute the only occasion in history when atomic weapons were dropped on living populations." He hints that something about the "decision to drop" is amiss. In the body of his argument he reveals and supports his thesis that no decision in the ordinary sense was ever made and that the danger of such an "accidental judgment" in the future, though possible, is avoidable. Notice how orderly his presentation of the options is, from benign strike to warning shot. Notice, too, how effectively he uses quotations to reinforce the points that make up his argument. You might highlight quotations this way, use the give-and-take of dialogue, or integrate short, quotable phrases into your argument.

Now try mapping out your plan of attack. Make an informal outline or some other kind of list that shows you where you're going in your argument and how you're going to get there. Include at least one piece of supporting evidence (a personal observation, an expert opinion, a quotation, an anecdote, a statistic, an example) for every major point you make. Because you will be generalizing from particular facts and opinions, or reasoning inductively, supporting evidence is especially important. See Lesson 6.4 on the difference between deductive and inductive reasoning and the pitfalls of each.

Once you've completed your outline—however informal—you're ready to begin drafting. For many writers, this is the most enjoyable phase of the writing process. Now is the time to give your thoughts and feelings their freedom. This is not the time to worry about grammar or about being fuzzy or redundant. Just let it out. If you're following your outline, you'll be fine. On the other hand, you'll also be fine if you rework your organization as new and better ideas occur to you.

3. Revising

To be in top form when you revise, you must gain perspective on your writing. One way to do this is to allow at least a day before revising. Another is to solicit opinions of peers about the content and structure of your essay (see Lesson 2.9). Both methods help you achieve objectivity for a tough, thorough revision. Now is the time to evaluate the strengths and weaknesses of your argument, to check the tone for appropriateness and consistency, and to test your writing for unity and coherence. If your essay lacks unity and coherence, your argument will be difficult to follow and unlikely to persuade anyone. Before revising any other aspect of your writing, make sure that all your ideas and supporting details relate to your thesis and that they connect with one another. Lessons 2.7 and 2.8 explain these concepts.

Once you feel secure that your thesis is in control and that the connections between the parts of your essay are clear, ask yourself the following questions:

- Is my opening tantalizing?
- Is my argument tight or are there holes that need filling?
- Are all aspects of the essay in line with my audience and purpose?
- Does my enthusiasm and conviction come through?
- Is my reasoning sound? Have I oversimplified? Have I introduced a red herring? (Lesson 6.5 helps with logical fallacies.)
- Is my organization logical and easy to follow?

- Do I use transitional words correctly?
- Is my language original and vivid?

Give this last question serious consideration. Your choice of words, your similes and metaphors, have the power to persuade. Erikson puts language to work in the service of his argument when he describes the bombings in a poignant image: ". . . all of it coming to an end with a pair of tremendous blasts in the soft morning air over Japan." The juxtaposition of the hard blasts and the soft air remind the reader that innocent people were killed in their sleep. Look for ways to create word-pictures that amplify and underscore your meaning.

4. Editing

The last stage your essay must pass through before it's reader-ready is editing. Make several passes through your work, editing for a different kind of error each time. To do the job right, you'll need a good dictionary and a writer's handbook. First, check your grammar. Do all subjects and verbs agree? Are all sentences complete? Do all pronouns have clear antecedents? Next, check the mechanics of your work, and finally, check your spelling. For a list of editing issues, review the checklists in Lesson 2.10. Don't lose steam when you edit. Doing a half-hearted job now would be like tripping yourself in a race that you're winning.

Criteria

1. _Focuses on an issue or situation of importance to freshmen_
2. _Uses a situation from your own experience or observation to persuade this audience to follow a particular course of action_
3. _Captures the audience's attention immediately_
4. _Is logically argued and well supported with evidence_
5. _Uses humor or irony when appropriate_
6. _Follows the standards of grammar, usage, and mechanics_

5. Presenting

If you continue on through this stage, you may be about to reap one of the primary rewards of writing: seeing your words change someone else's life. Think about who might benefit from reading or hearing your essay. Do you know someone who's in danger of making the mistake you described or of getting caught up in the circumstances you wrote about? Is the issue you tackled one that affects many people at your school or in your community? If so, consider turning your essay into a speech or a letter to the editor of your school or local newspaper. Let others benefit from your experience.

• Reflecting •

It's a safe guess that the very act of writing his essay deepened Kai Erikson's conviction that in the nuclear age we can no longer afford "accidental judgments." The writing process is a process of learning, of experimenting, of struggling, and of conquering. Think about how the process of writing this essay has helped you clarify your thoughts. What has it taught you about yourself, about the dangers of fallacious reasoning or the pleasures of creating an elegant metaphor? Review the process, stage by stage, and jot down your reflections on each stage in your journal. In the end, you will probably convince yourself of the benefits of the writing process!

Portfolio & Reflection

Summary

Key concepts in persuasive writing include the following:

- Persuasive writing supports a claim with a logical argument and relevant evidence.
- Persuasive writing should distinguish between fact and opinion.
- Persuasive writing should avoid errors in inductive and deductive reasoning.
- Logical fallacies include red herrings, circular reasoning, bandwagon thinking, the cause-and-effect fallacy, and the either/or fallacy.
- An effective speech is developed by going through the stages of the writing process.
- A strong letter to the editor includes a clear statement of thesis, accurate and well-organized supporting evidence, and careful attention to tone.
- To evaluate a speech, you must consider the written text as well as the delivery.

Your Writer's Portfolio

Look over the persuasive writing you have done during this unit. Select two pieces of writing to put into your portfolio. Each piece should demonstrate that you have worked with one or more of the preceding concepts. In other words, look for a piece of writing that does one or more of the following:

- backs up a clearly stated claim with appropriate evidence
- appeals to a particular audience
- distinguishes between fact and opinion
- uses a wide range of supporting evidence
- uses correct inductive or deductive reasoning and avoids common logical fallacies

Reflection and Commentary

Write one page that demonstrates that you understand what this unit asked of you. Use your two selected pieces of writing as evidence while you consider the following numbered items. Respond to as many items as possible. Label the page "Commentary on Persuasive Writing," and include it in your portfolio.

1. How did you tailor the argument to appeal to a specific audience? If the piece were written for a different audience, what changes would you make?
2. Did you use one kind of evidence (facts, authoritative opinion, and so forth) more than other kinds in your argument? What other kinds of evidence could you have added to strengthen your position?
3. Where do you use inductive or deductive reasoning? Where, if ever, do you fall into a logical fallacy? If you used the fallacy intentionally, is it effective?
4. Which stage of the writing process worked best? What stage gave you trouble? How will you work differently in future persuasive writing?

Feedback

If you had a chance to respond to the following student comment, what would you say or ask:

The best thing about writing is looking back on earlier pieces and evaluating them. This gives me a sense of accomplishment.

Laurel Pacquaio, Edison High School,
Edison, New Jersey

The Research Paper

Edward Hopper, *Automat*, 1927

Exploring the Unknown

Your footsteps echo through the cave's musty darkness. Your flashlight probes the rock cavern for passages to explore. Some passages will lead to dead ends, forcing you to backtrack. Others will open up into spectacular caverns seen by no one else.

Like exploring a cave, researching a topic can be exhilarating. You're on your own as you choose and explore material to read. You too will make your way along twisting and turning paths as you draft and revise your thoughts, and you can expect to run into dead ends from time to time. The result, however, can be the most satisfying writing that you will do in high school.

Where to Start?

Writing a research paper can feel overwhelming. It doesn't have to immobilize you, however. Before you get lost in the process, break down the project into smaller tasks, and then set a schedule to complete each task. Your schedule might look like this.

The arrows show how you will spend most of your time, but at any stage, you may need to return to a previous stage to rethink your topic, gather more information, or reorganize your ideas.

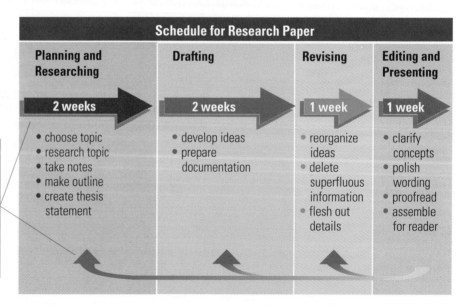

Schedule for Research Paper

Planning and Researching	Drafting	Revising	Editing and Presenting
2 weeks	2 weeks	1 week	1 week
• choose topic • research topic • take notes • make outline • create thesis statement	• develop ideas • prepare documentation	• reorganize ideas • delete superfluous information • flesh out details	• clarify concepts • polish wording • proofread • assemble for reader

Investigate and Limit a Topic

When choosing the topic for a research paper, make sure the topic interests you. To get started, list possible topics. Consider books and television documentaries that you have enjoyed. Classroom discussions may also trigger ideas. Brainstorm ideas with your teacher, family, and friends, too. No matter what the source, make sure you choose a topic that you want to investigate, not a topic someone else thinks is interesting and recommends.

After you choose a topic, determine whether it is too broad for a research paper of the length you are writing. Analyze how your topic can be divided by scanning the tables of contents of books about your topic. You will need to limit your topic until it is neither so broad that you will be writing in generalities nor so narrow that you can't find adequate resources to use.

Stephanie Murray, a student at Westwood High School in Westwood, Massachusetts, is interested in art. Throughout this unit, you will see examples of notes, outlines, and drafts leading to a finished research paper about the art of Grant Wood and of Edward Hopper. You can read Stephanie's finished paper on pages 342–347.

Notice how the following topics about art are narrowed.

Narrowing a Topic		
Too Broad	**Limited**	**Too Limited**
Western art	The theme of man against nature in Western art	Telegraph lines in Western art
Art in the Depression era	Depression era artists Wood and Hopper	Cats in Depression era art

Before you begin your own research, you need to know what you are looking for. Ask yourself questions such as these to clarify your topic and to guide your research: Why is my topic interesting? Why do people care about it? What people or events are integral to it? What caused these events to happen? What are some of the effects of my topic? As you learn more, you can refine your research questions and begin to focus on a central idea for the paper.

Find Information

Researching a topic is not a linear process; undoubtedly you will make more than one trip to the library as you develop your view of your topic. You can conserve some effort, however, by doing background reading before you plunge into gathering sources. Reading about your topic in its larger context will make you more aware of the significance of your topic. For example, if you are writing a paper about railroads in the American West, you need to know what social and economic factors encouraged their development.

When you gather research resources, you will be looking for important facts, interesting statistics, and revealing quotations. Refer to pages 704–711 for the kinds of sources and references available in libraries. Many references cover specific topics. For example, for sources on American art, literature, and culture, you can consult the *Art Index*, the *Humanities Index*, and the *Media Review Digest*, to name a few.

Evaluate Sources   Since you have only a limited amount of time for research, you should carefully evaluate sources before taking notes from them. Some sources may be dated, reflecting obsolete opinions or old technology. Other sources, such as tabloids and propaganda published by radical groups, are unsuitable because of their slanted treatment of topics.

Some of the information you find will be based more on opinion, and some will be based more on fact. If your topic is a controversial one, such as prison reform, read a variety of viewpoints. A broad perspective will enrich your understanding. Also evaluate how an author presents facts. Although an author will certainly have opinions about the facts, blatant bias will hinder an author's ability to present a clear, analytical evaluation. To detect bias in an author or a source, ask yourself the following questions.

Drafting Tip

Use the formats on page 333 to record bibliography data so that when you prepare a list of works cited, the information will already be formatted.

To Detect Author Bias, Ask Yourself . . .

- Does the author fail to give evidence for certain claims?
- Is the author reliable on some points and not others?
- Is the author's scope of vision limited by his or her era, country of origin, or politics?
- Is the author a qualified expert on this subject?
- Does the author's biography indicate a special interest that would prejudice his or her judgment?

As you read further, you may want to review your topic and guiding questions occasionally to be sure that the notes you take are relevant to your paper. While you should be open to taking new directions as you learn more about the subject, don't digress into another area and take notes on material that ultimately you can't use.

Make Bibliography Cards   As you find possible sources for your research, for each source record the full publication information on a three-by-five-inch index card. You will use the information on the cards twice: once to give credit to your source in the body of your paper and once to list your sources at the end of your research paper. Number your bibliography cards so that when you take notes, you can write just the number of the bibliography cards instead of writing out the titles of sources. An example of a numbered bibliography card for Stephanie's research paper is to the right.

If your source is a book, record the author, title, name of the editor or translator (if there is one), edition, number of the volume (if the book is part of a multivolume work), place of publication, name of the publisher, and date of publication. The bibliography card illustrated is for a book.

If your source is a magazine or a newspaper, record the author, title, name of the periodical, series number or name (if there is one), and date of publication.

Take Notes from Sources

Now read your sources more carefully. If a source has useful information, take notes on four-by-six-inch index cards, using one card for each distinct piece of information. On each card record the source's corresponding bibliography card number and the page or pages from which you took information. Number each note card, too. You will use the numbers on your note cards to identify your sources when you draft your research paper.

Take Notes in One of Three Ways   A paraphrase is a restatement of information in your own words. A summary is a brief synthesis of a long passage, or several pages. When you summarize, write down only main ideas and key supporting information. A direct quotation is the exact wording of a source; set it off with quotation marks. Look at the note cards on the following page.

Note that simply stringing together pages of direct quotations is not the same as writing a research paper. To prepare an insightful paper, you will need to understand your sources and weave them together with your own explanations and analysis. Your distinctive writer's voice will make your research paper flow seamlessly from idea to idea.

Presenting Tip

As you take notes, be alert to possible visual aids, such as pictures and diagrams, that will help your readers to understand your ideas.

Prewriting: Planning and Researching   **319**

Wood's farm landscapes are, without a doubt, the most sensuous and passionate works he painted. Mingling eroticism with ecstasy, Wood made the relationship between the farmer and mother earth into a Wagnerian love duet. While mother earth is always the principal protagonist, overwhelming the farmer in scale and vitality, she is always loving and benevolent. In Wood's idyllic farmscapes, man lives in complete harmony with Nature; he is the earth's caretaker, coaxing her to abundance, bringing coherence and beauty to her surfaces.

> Record direct quotations exactly as they appear, including punctuation.

Direct Quotation Note Card

Wood – Rural Themes   Bib. 10
"In Wood's idyllic farmscapes, man lives in complete harmony with Nature; he is the earth's caretaker, coaxing her to abundance, bringing coherence and beauty to her surfaces."
(quotation) page 90

Paraphrase Note Card

Wood – Rural Themes   Bib. 10

Wood paints man as caretaker of the earth, drawing out her abundance and bringing coherence to her surface.
(paraphrase)
page 90

Summary Note Card

Wood – Rural Themes   Bib. 10
Wood's farmscapes his most passionate works
– farmer and mother earth "love duet"
– man as caretaker of the land
(summary)
page 90

> A paraphrase is a restatement of someone else's original idea; in what other ways could you restate this information?

> When you summarize, you synthesize key points and important details.

> The page number of the source is 90; complete information about the source is on bibliography card #10.

As you take notes, consider how ideas interrelate. Note how certain trends or patterns emerge. As your ideas evolve, you may need to take several trips to the library to gather more data for your paper or to fill in gaps.

Avoid Plagiarism An honest writer avoids plagiarism, the use of another writer's words or ideas without giving credit. The first step in avoiding plagiarism is to take notes carefully and to indicate on each note card whether an idea is your own, a paraphrase, a summary, or a direct quotation. If you do not mark your note cards, days later you will not remember whether an idea was yours or was summarized or paraphrased from a research source.

You can plagiarize unintentionally. If you carelessly treat something as a paraphrase or summary when it is, in fact, a direct quotation, you have plagiarized. Paraphrasing someone's ideas too closely, even if you attribute them, is also plagiarism. For instance, if a source's words are "Successful advertising preys on our fear of rejection and desire to be loved" and you paraphrase it as "Successful advertising campaigns pitch to people's fear of rejection and desire to be loved," you have plagiarized, even if you name your source.

You can avoid paraphrasing a source too closely by putting it aside as you take notes. Use your own words as you recall the information that you have just read. Then, after you write your paraphrase, reread the source to ensure that the words you have used are your own and that they accurately reflect the facts and opinions that are presented in the original source.

• ACTIVITIES •
Writer's Choice

1. For each broad topic listed below, list three ideas for appropriately limited topics.

- technology in sports
- women in modern art
- the detective as a figure in American culture
- the motion picture industry

2. Imagine that you will write a research paper on the work of playwright Thornton Wilder. Which of the following sources do you think will be suitable? Which would be most suitable? Why?

- a collection of Thornton Wilder's essays: *American Characteristics*
- the *National Enquirer*
- a videotape of Wilder's *Our Town*
- a television documentary about Wilder
- a *TV Guide* summary of a movie version of his novel *The Bridge of San Luis Rey*
- *The Best American Plays of 1938*
- an interview with Carol Channing, star of the musical *Hello, Dolly!* which was based on Wilder's play *The Matchmaker*

3. "The simplified abstract shapes of [Georgia O'Keeffe's] flowers, bones, mountains, and clouds reveal a classic order hidden in nature."

This quote was taken from page 181 of Charlotte Streifer Rubinstein's book *American Women Artists*. For each of the research paper sentences below, determine whether or not plagiarism has taken place.

- Georgia O'Keeffe's subject matter consisted of natural forms such as flowers, bones, and mountains.
- O'Keeffe took simple natural objects and painted them in an abstract way.
- In natural shapes O'Keeffe found a classic order.
- O'Keeffe painted the classic order that was hidden in nature.

4. Select a topic for your own research paper and write five questions about it. After your teacher approves your topic, prepare your bibliography cards, and be prepared to hand them in to your teacher. Be sure to allow yourself adequate time for taking notes.

Prewriting: Developing an Outline

An Overview First, Details to Follow

People in all fields need ways in which to organize their ideas. Sculptors, for example, make clay models to get an overview of their designs. Computer programmers create flow charts to show the steps in their programs. Writers devise outlines to organize their ideas and information.

Now you will create a working outline to help you to organize your research notes. As you learn more, adjust your outline to reflect your increasing knowledge.

Edward Hopper, *Cape Cod Evening (sketch)*, 1939

Develop an Outline

You can use many methods to arrange your note cards into an outline. You may wish to use a combination of methods—one method for main ideas and another method for supporting details.

Use the other units in this book to explore methods of organization. Unit 3, for example, examines order of importance, order of impression, and spatial order (pages 123–124). Unit 4 illustrates chronological order (pages 176–178), and Unit 5 demonstrates how to explain a process (pages 208–210).

The outline that follows uses another method of organization illustrated in Unit 5, comparison and contrast (pages 220–223). The first page of the outline begins with an introduction and some background information. Then the outline examines the paintings of Grant Wood by contrasting the reality presented in the paintings with the reality of Wood's times. As you can see in the completed research paper on pages 342–347, the paintings of Edward Hopper are similarly examined after those of Wood. Comparison and contrast are then used to highlight the differences between the work of the two artists.

The Art of Grant Wood and of Edward Hopper

I. Wood's time in history

   A. Population moving to cities

      1. Prompted by World War I

      2. Problems with unemployment, etc.

   B. Hard times in rural America

      1. Farm economy depressed ←— *Get more statistics.*

      2. Crash of 1929

      3. Droughts, dust storms, grasshoppers

   C. Economy and national spirit at an all-time low

II. Paradox: between Wood's paintings and his era

   ←— *Move down.*
   A. Wood as spokesman for rural America

   B. Paintings *Spring Turning, Stone City*

      1. Awesomeness of American landscape

      2. Man a small element in picture

      3. No signs of industrialization

   C. Realities of dust bowls and rotting crops

   D. Government policies initially ineffective

      ←— *Unnecessary idea. Delete.*
III. Paradox: theme of community spirit

   A. Paintings *Arbor Day, Dinner for Threshers*

      1. Community spirit

         a. People working together

         b. No signs of industrial progress

      2. Role of women ←— *Get more information.*

         a. Dressed in old-fashioned clothes

         b. Feeding the men after work is done

            (1) Establishment of social ritual

            (2) A simpler America

> *Use Roman numerals for main topics. For subtopics, start with capital letters; continue with Arabic numerals, then lower-case letters, and, finally, Arabic numerals in parentheses.*

> *Historical background information is in chronological order. It gives readers a context in which to understand the information that follows.*

> *Not all ideas need equal development.*

> *Comparison and contrast are used to examine the paradoxes created by the reality shown in the paintings.*

Drafting Tip

When you choose a method of organizing details, think of how they are most logically related to the main idea and to each other.

When you create a formal outline, you may employ several levels of subheadings. If you have subheadings under a subheading, you must have at least two of them (for example, A,1,2;B,1,2,a,b). In addition, all subheadings should be written in parallel grammatical form, either clauses (used in the above outline) or complete sentences.

Alternative Forms of Outlines

Depending on your topic, you may find that other ways of organizing your paper are more helpful than the traditional outline. A tree or cluster diagram, for example, will let you compare different sections of your paper for similarities or parallel developments. If you're using a computer, the software program may have outline capabilities that encourage you to "fill in the blank." Choose the form of organization that helps you best to manage your information and that will be most useful to you during drafting. Remember that as the bulk of your information increases, so will the need to organize it clearly and in detail.

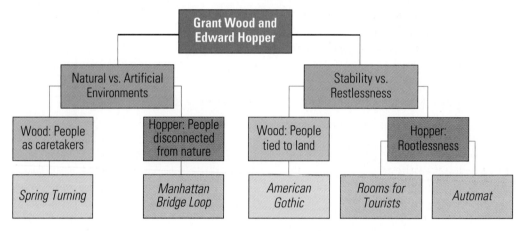

Create and Revise a Thesis Statement

A successful thesis statement does several things: It presents in one sentence the main idea that you will develop in your paper, it explains your perspective on your topic, and it prepares readers to see how you arrived at that perspective. To create a thesis statement, consider the "big picture." Recall the ideas that guided your research, and read the Roman numeral headings of your working outline; they will suggest a main idea. To clarify your perspective on your topic, remember how you answered classmates who asked you what your topic is about. Writing answers to the following questions will also help you to formulate a thesis statement.

Questions Leading to a Thesis Statement

1. What was the central idea that guided my research?
2. What questions did I answer in my research?
3. What significant ideas surfaced during my research?
4. How could my research findings be stated in one sentence?

Thesis Statement

Continue to revise your thesis statement and your outline to reflect the insights you gain from your research and writing. The final polished version of your thesis statement may not emerge until you write the final revision of your paper. Look at how the example thesis statement evolves through a series of revisions.

The wording in the central idea illustrates the sort of obvious, surface observation that you might develop after doing preliminary reading and research about a topic. It is a cornerstone on which research is based.

The first thesis statement is more specific than the central idea, but it's still just a general statement of the differences in subjects of the two painters. The significance of the writer's research is not captured, nor is the writer's approach to the topic revealed. The real value of a first thesis statement is that it can keep a writer from veering off the topic during research and the early stages of drafting the paper.

The first revised thesis statement is more detailed and reveals more of the depth of the writer's research, but the writer's approach to the topic is not clear. Thus, the thesis statement does not seem to make a point and needs further refinement.

The second revised thesis statement succinctly states the topic and writer's unique approach to it. This thesis statement makes a point that readers will expect to be supported in the body of the research paper.

Evolution of a Thesis Statement

Central idea Grant Wood and Edward Hopper painted at about the same time, but their paintings were very different.

Thesis statement While Wood painted scenes of rural America, Hopper dealt with city life.

Revised thesis statement While Wood evoked a simpler era, Hopper portrayed an urban world of loneliness and disconnection.

Revised thesis statement The art of Grant Wood and Edward Hopper reflected the conflict between rural and urban views of American life during the Depression.

• ACTIVITIES •
Writer's Choice

1. Rewrite each of the following into a concise, single-sentence thesis statement.

- The 1960s were a tumultuous time in all aspects of American society. A great deal of artistic energy was devoted to the exploration of nontraditional media. For this reason, it is impossible to identify the one preeminent 1960s novel.

- The frontier has influenced American arts since the country was founded. This influence extends to the present day, even though the actual frontier disappeared long ago.

- Motion pictures generally provide a reflection of the political era in which they are made. This is true whether or not the film deals with contemporary issues or stories.

- Censorship of popular music or the rating of music by standards boards is not necessary and is, in fact, futile. The public will ultimately find a way to buy the music they want and will ignore the music they don't want.

2. Now prepare a working outline and a thesis statement for your own research paper.

Molding Words into Form

Sitting down to write can be hard, even for professional writers. John McPhee admits that once he resorted to using the belt on his bathrobe to tie himself into his writing chair. You may not relish drafting either, but there are easier ways of creating a draft than tying yourself into a chair.

Drafting from an Outline

Before you begin writing, review your outline and note cards, and think about what you want to say. Try arranging your note cards using other methods of organization, and adjust your outline if one of those methods seems more fitting. Be sure that the sequence of your note cards matches your final outline. If the information on some note cards doesn't fit naturally into your outline, put those note cards aside for now. Never throw any note cards away, even if you think you are finished using the information on them. You may need to refer to them as you revise.

When you begin to write, you will learn more about your topic. Holes will begin to emerge in your research notes. When you return to the library to gather more information, your draft should pinpoint the additional information that you need. If you need to make several return trips to the library, don't feel as if you are doing something wrong; professional writers may make five or more library trips to gather information for one article.

In addition to containing the body paragraphs that your outline suggests, your paper will begin with an introduction that includes your thesis statement and will end with a conclusion. Many writers begin by writing the introduction first; others choose to start with the sections that seem easiest to write. If you have trouble writing anything at all, freewrite a page or two without referring to your note cards. Freewriting may help you to develop a tone and a feel for your paper. You can then go back to your note cards and begin to focus your writing.

As you write each section, use your outline as a guide. In the following example, the outline guides the draft without limiting it.

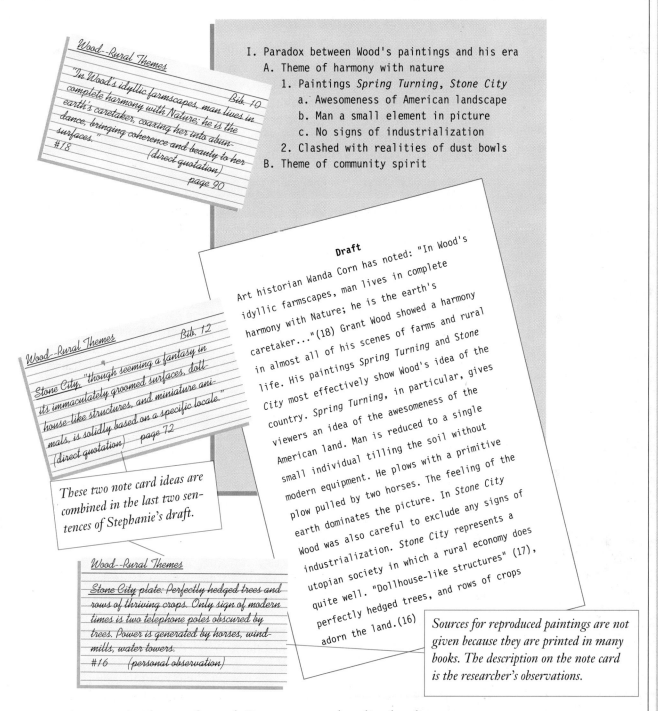

Wood--Rural Themes   Bib. 10

"In Wood's idyllic farmscapes, man lives in complete harmony with Nature; he is the earth's caretaker, coaxing her into abundance, bringing coherence and beauty to her surfaces."

#18   (direct quotation)

           page 90

I. Paradox between Wood's paintings and his era
  A. Theme of harmony with nature
    1. Paintings *Spring Turning*, *Stone City*
      a. Awesomeness of American landscape
      b. Man a small element in picture
      c. No signs of industrialization
    2. Clashed with realities of dust bowls
  B. Theme of community spirit

Wood--Rural Themes   Bib. 12

Stone City: "though seeming a fantasy in its immaculately groomed surfaces, dollhouse-like structures, and miniature animals, is solidly based on a specific locale."

(direct quotation)   page 72

These two note card ideas are combined in the last two sentences of Stephanie's draft.

Wood--Rural Themes

Stone City plate: Perfectly hedged trees and rows of thriving crops. Only sign of modern times is two telephone poles obscured by trees. Power is generated by horses, windmills, water towers.
#16   (personal observation)

Draft

Art historian Wanda Corn has noted: "In Wood's idyllic farmscapes, man lives in complete harmony with Nature; he is the earth's caretaker..."(18) Grant Wood showed a harmony in almost all of his scenes of farms and rural life. His paintings *Spring Turning* and *Stone City* most effectively show Wood's idea of the country. *Spring Turning*, in particular, gives viewers an idea of the awesomeness of the American land. Man is reduced to a single small individual tilling the soil without modern equipment. He plows with a primitive plow pulled by two horses. The feeling of the earth dominates the picture. In *Stone City* Wood was also careful to exclude any signs of industrialization. *Stone City* represents a utopian society in which a rural economy does quite well. "Dollhouse-like structures" (17), perfectly hedged trees, and rows of crops adorn the land.(16)

Sources for reproduced paintings are not given because they are printed in many books. The description on the note card is the researcher's observations.

    As you write the text for each Roman numeral outline heading, consider how the main ideas relate to each other and how details support main ideas. Use strong, logical transitions between ideas; a research paper requires more than just "connecting the dots."

    Be sure to write the number of each note card in your draft as you use it. Later you will replace the numbers with your sources' identification.

Managing Information

As you draft, don't worry about finding the perfect word. Concentrate on sequencing your ideas in the most effective order. You will revise your paper for style and usage later.

If the amount of information that you have gathered is overwhelming, draft your paper one section at a time. You can make connections between sections when you revise. The chart that follows contains other hints for overcoming drafting problems.

Editing Tip

You can combine similar ideas from note cards in the same way that you create compound sentences. Review pages 485–487.

Drafting Problems and Solutions	
Problems	**Solutions**
I can't seem to get a handle on my topic.	Make sure that your thesis statement is clearly focused. Also, try telling someone about your topic to clarify your thinking and to build up your enthusiasm.
I need more information for one section of my paper.	Go back to the library and get it. Neither you nor your readers will be satisfied with your work if it's incomplete.
I'd like to change topics.	Be realistic about how much time you have. Don't start over without discussing it with your teacher.
I feel as if I'm just cutting and pasting the words of other people.	Use direct quotations sparingly; summarize and paraphrase more often. Your paper should reflect your thinking and analysis of what other writers have written plus your own insights.

Drafting an Effective Introduction

A good introduction announces your topic, presents a clear thesis statement, and grabs the readers' interest. You can begin your paper with a pithy quotation, a vivid description, or a little-known fact. You can also ask your readers a question to draw them into your topic.

You might freewrite several introductions before deciding on the best one. You don't need a long introduction; once you have the readers' attention, get on with your paper.

Why is this introduction effective? Read another effective introduction on page 342.

An Introduction
Have you ever experienced the pleasure of biting into a veggie-nut burger, spilling over with guacamole, tomatoes, and sprouts? No? Then you're probably not a vegetarian. Vegetarians are people who choose not to eat meat for political, ecological, biological, or spiritual reasons. These people have changed their life styles to live out their convictions.

Drafting a Conclusion

Your conclusion should recap the main ideas of your paper and create a sense of closure. It might also put your ideas in perspective, describe the significance of your research, or stress the need for further investigation. Make sure it doesn't introduce new or unexplained information that will leave readers dangling. Notice how the following conclusion summarizes the topic and creates a sense of closure.

A Conclusion

Whether for the health of their planet, their fellow creatures, their country, or themselves, vegetarians are setting an example of constructive activism. Vegetarianism may not be for everyone; however, if everyone held the concerns of vegetarians, the results might be more far-reaching than even the most avid vegetarian could hope for.

• ACTIVITIES •
Writer's Choice

1. Freewrite an introduction for three of the thesis statements that follow. Your introduction should include the main points that you would make in a research paper about the topic.

- Because making motion pictures has become a multibillion dollar industry, artistic expression is often sacrificed for big box-office receipts.
- As sculpture has become increasingly abstract, the average art viewer's appreciation and support for sculpture has decreased dramatically.
- Government support of the arts is increasingly under fire from a public that feels its tastes and interests are not being represented.
- Film censorship neither promotes quality entertainment nor protects innocent citizens from the censored material.
- If creative expression in high schools is encouraged through more financial and public support, students will be more focused on creating art that the entire society can enjoy, rather than on committing destructive acts.

2. For each of the pairs of note card sentences below, write a transitional sentence that connects the ideas.

- Television has been labeled a "vast wasteland" with little artistic merit. Many artists today incorporate video into their work.
- Art is very often a reaction against the political status quo. Politicians often use art as propaganda to further their own purposes.
- Many people prefer live theater to movies because theater is "more real." One of the attractions of live theater is that it brings together real people (the actors and the audience).
- Many authors become unhappy when they see how their novels have been made into films. The visual aesthetics of film is fundamentally different from the verbal aesthetics of the novel.

3. Now begin drafting your research paper. Use your thesis statement and outline as guides. Save all bibliography cards and note cards, even those that you think you won't use.

Name That Tune

"They're playing my song." That's been the cry of several famous musicians who have recognized their tune in someone else's release. Famous singers are often sued successfully for recording a hit song without paying royalties to its creator. However, creative ideas are often shared in the music industry. Rap stars routinely use parts of other people's songs through electronic sampling and other methods. This use is perfectly legal, as long as the rapper gives credit to and pays royalties to the original artists.

Similarly, when you write a research paper, your readers will expect you to borrow a certain amount of information from other sources. But when you cite, or name, the sources of the information in your research paper, you avoid plagiarism by giving credit where credit is due.

Documenting Sources

Citing sources, or documenting sources as it is also called, allows you to give credit to the author whose original work you use. In addition, citing your sources allows readers to locate a source if they want to read it in its entirety. In addition to citing books, magazines, and newspapers from which you take information, you must cite interviews, television programs, song lyrics, letters, and dialogue from plays. If you put into words information that is expressed graphically in tables, charts, and diagrams, also cite these sources.

Generally, you will cite your sources each time you use direct quotations, facts and statistics, and the opinions and ideas of others. Of course, you don't need to document every sentence in your paper. You need not document your own ideas, common knowledge, or well-known facts. For example, it's a well-known fact that Grand Coulee Dam is in Washington State, so you would not need to document that information. The chart on the next page illustrates some documentation issues that you might encounter when you draft your research paper.

Type of Information	Is Citation Needed?
"The very long horizontal shape of this picture is an effort to give a sensation of great lateral extent."	**Yes.** Always cite a direct quotation.
The Gothic windows in the background indicate that in the couple's house the values of Christianity are fostered and taught.	**Yes.** Always credit another writer for his or her opinion, even if you agree with it.
Almost every American city would eventually suffer overcrowding, housing shortages, slums, unemployment . . . pollution, and a lack of recreational facilities.	**Yes.** Always credit an author's generalization that is based on his or her own research and analysis.
Wood emphasized the harmonious relationship between man and the land.	**No.** This is a paraphrase of information that can be found in many sources.
By 1920, the bulk of the American population lived in cities with 2,500 people or more.	**Yes.** Always cite statistics that are not well known; doing so enables readers to evaluate the source of the data or to search for further information.
The stock market crashed in 1929.	**No.** The year of the first stock market crash is common knowledge.

Formatting Citations

Borrowed information can be cited in one of three ways: parenthetical documentation, footnotes, or endnotes. Use the method that your teacher prefers. Completing and numbering note cards and bibliography cards carefully as you research your paper will save you frantic moments and return trips to the library when you draft your paper. Providing all necessary information on these cards will also allow you to document your sources easily using any of the three citation formats.

Parenthetical Documentation with a List of Works Cited   The common method of identifying sources is to indicate the source in parentheses within the body of the paper. After each borrowed piece of information, place in parentheses the author's last name and the page or pages from which you took the borrowed information. Give a full description of the parenthetical source in a list of works cited at the end of your paper.

Prewriting Tip

Make sure that each of your note cards identifies its source and the page number(s) from which the information was taken.

Creating parenthetical documentation should be an uncomplicated task. In your draft, you wrote the numbers of the note cards next to the information you used from them. Now, replace the note card numbers with the proper parenthetical documentation. Place the citation as close to the borrowed information as possible so that readers can tell which ideas are being cited. You can improve your paper's readability by placing the citation where pauses occur in the text, such as directly before a period or comma, or between two halves of a compound sentence. Notice the following example:

> "A total of over 31 million cars were sold . . ." (Hobbs 91). Yet the horse-drawn buggy represented the only means of transportation in Wood's art.

Editing Tip

To aid your placement of citations, review the structure of clauses on pages 483–493.

Source	Parenthetical Documentation
One author (Goodrich 70–71).	Documentation shows the author's last name and the numbers of the pages where the information is found. Notice that there is no comma following *Goodrich* and no abbreviation for the word *pages*.
Two or three authors (Barr and Burchfield 55)	For more than three authors, use the last name of the first author, followed by *et al.* and the page number(s): (Jones *et al.* 44–47).
No author ("Waiting" 44)	If no author is listed, use the name of the editor. If there is no editor, use an abbreviated version of the source's title in quotation marks.
Authors listed more than once in the works cited (Pratt, "Modern Art" 99–102)	Use this form if you use more than one source by the same author: the author's name is placed first, followed by a comma; the source's title is abbreviated, and page numbers follow.
Author's name in text (178)	Use this form if you clearly indicate where the material originated: Critic John Davidson claims the artist's style is "unconsidered and blobby" (178).

Works cited entries contain the complete publishing information that you wrote on your bibliography cards. Some of Stephanie's works cited entries follow. Her research paper on pages 342–347 ends with a works cited page. Carefully note the features of the entries. Titles or works of art are in italic type (or underlined if you're using a typewriter). Publishers' names are shortened by abbreviating or deleting unnecessary words like *press* and *company*. Dates of articles are given in the order of day, month (usually abbreviated), and year. Notice also that cited entries contain no page numbers for books, while for articles in anthologies, magazines, and newspapers, entries include the page range of the entire article. In your draft, however, use just the numbers of the specific page(s) from which you take information. For the format of sources that are not covered by the chart, consult your teacher.

Source	Format for Works Cited Entries
A book with one author	Hobbs, Robert. *Edward Hopper*. New York: Abrams, 1987.
A book with two or three authors	Barr, Alfred H., and Charles Burchfield. *Edward Hopper Retrospective*. New York: Museum of Modern Art, 1933.
An author of two or more works cited	Dennis, James M. *Grant Wood*. Columbia: U of Missouri P, 1986. ---. *Grant Wood: A Study in American Art and Culture*. New York: Viking, 1975.
A book with an editor but no author	McCoubrey, John W., ed. *Modern American Painting*. New York: Time-Life, 1970.
A work included in an anthology	Rosenblum, Robert. "The Primal American Scene." *The Natural Paradise: Painting in America 1800–1950*. Ed. Kynaston McShine. New York: Museum of Modern Art, 1976. 165–178.
An encyclopedia article	"Realism." *World Book Encyclopedia*. 1990 ed.
An article in a magazine	Wooden, Howard E. "Grant Wood: A Regionalist's Interpretation of the Four Seasons." *American Artist* July 1991: 58.
An article in a newspaper	Artner, Alan G. "An American Original: The Unique Midwestern Vision of Grant Wood." *Chicago Tribune* 15 Jan. 1984, sec. 10: 15–19.
A television documentary	*Art of the Western World*. Videotape. Annenberg/CPB Collection, 1989.

Use this order, as it applies, for book sources: authors' name(s), title of anthologized work, title of book, name of editor, name of edition, city of publication, publisher's name, and publication date.

Three hyphens replace the author's last name in the author's second entry.

Use this order, as it applies, for periodical sources: authors' name(s), title of article, name of periodical, series number, date of publication, newspaper edition, and page numbers of the complete article.

How to Format a List of Works Cited   The following works cited shows the proper format, indentation, and punctuation. Notice that all entries are alphabetized by authors' names or by title, excluding words such as *A* and *The* at the beginning of titles. Thus, the first entry is a book written by Wanda Corn titled *Grant Wood: The Regionalist Vision*. The title of the book is followed by the city of publication, New Haven (Connecticut); an abbreviation of the publisher, Yale UP, (Yale University Press); and the year of publication, 1983. Consult your teacher for abbreviations of other publishers' names.

The final entry begins with the title of an encyclopedia article because the author is not named. If an encyclopedia article does name an author, treat the name as you would for an author whose work is included in an anthology.

Works Cited

> *Your name and page number go here.*

Corn, Wanda. *Grant Wood: The Regionalist Vision*. New Haven: Yale
  UP, 1983.

> *The first line of an entry is flush left; indent all others five spaces.*

Dennis, James M. *Grant Wood*. Columbia: U of Missouri P, 1986.

---. *Grant Wood: A Study in American Art and Culture*. New York:
  Viking, 1975.

> *For a second entry by the same author, instead of the author's name, use three hyphens, a period, and two spaces.*

Hobbs, Robert. *Edward Hopper*. New York: Abrams, 1987.

McCoubrey, John W., ed. *Modern American Painting*. New York:
  Time-Life, 1970.

> *Double-space all lines and between entries.*

"Realism." *World Book Encyclopedia*. 1990 ed.

Note Numbers with Endnotes   Another way to document sources is with endnotes. Information to be documented is numbered consecutively throughout the paper with a superscript number typed one-half line above the rest of the sentence. These numbers refer to the specific information about the source contained in a list at the end of the paper, on a separate page under the heading "Notes." The references on the notes page contain all of the publishing information that you have written on your bibliography cards. After your first citation of a source, you can refer to it again in another note by using just the author's last name (or last name and abbreviated title of the source, if you are using more than one source by the same author) and a page number.

Endnote Example:
  (in paper)   ". . . isolated and disconnected."[1]

  (in notes)   [1]Gail Levin, *Edward Hopper: The Art
        and the Artist* (New York: W. W. Norton,
        1980) 270.

Note Numbers with Footnotes   A third citation method uses footnotes. Like endnotes, footnotes are marked by superscript numbers in the text. The full documentation references, however, are placed at the bottom (or "foot") of the page containing the borrowed information. Footnotes are seldom used today. Both footnotes and endnotes are typed single-spaced, with the first line indented and a blank line between notes.

You can see that all documentation methods provide the same basic elements of information. Their variation is in their placement in the paper and in the order and punctuation of elements.

Evaluating Your Treatment of Sources

When you took notes, you checked sources for bias and for dated information. When you finish your draft, evaluate how well you have represented your sources. First, make sure that you haven't taken a quotation out of context and thus changed its meaning. For example, suppose a critic had written, "While Grant Wood is unsophisticated and sentimental in his subject matter, his compositions reflect a mastery of modern design." You would misrepresent the author's opinion of Wood's skill if you quoted only the first half of the sentence.

Also, if your topic is a person or persons, make certain that you have accurately portrayed their beliefs. For example, many writers and artists in their youth make bold assertions about their philosophies of life and art, and then alter those ideas as they age. It would be misleading to present a person's brash, immature statement as a lifelong belief.

If you are writing about a controversial subject, make sure you have included a variety of opinions. Presenting only statements from one point of view creates a boring and biased paper. If your topic is controversial, readers will expect you to comment on opposing viewpoints.

You should also strive for a balance of primary and secondary sources. Primary sources are first-hand accounts, such as newspaper articles, interviews, and original documents. Secondary sources are writings about primary sources, such as biographies, literary criticism, and histories. While primary sources will give your paper a sense of immediacy and authority, secondary sources will enrich your paper with the wisdom of perspective and expert analysis.

• ACTIVITIES •
Writer's Choice

1. For each of the following statements on artist Andy Warhol, state whether documentation is needed and why.

- Andy Warhol worked for many years as a commercial artist.
- Silk-screening allowed Warhol to experiment with repetitive images.
- "Warhol seems concerned about our anesthetized reaction to what is put in front of us."
- Warhol himself wrote, "You live in your dream America that you've custom-made from art and schmaltz and emotions just as much as you live in your real one."

2. Write proper entries for a list of works cited for the following sources.

- An article by Robert Morris in the April 1968 issue of Artforum magazine entitled "Anti-Form," on pages 55–58.
- A book, Art on Trial, by Lois Miller, published by Viking Press in New York City in 1991.
- An unsigned article, "Surrealism," in the 1990 edition of Encyclopedia Americana.

3. Now insert the documentation for your research paper in your draft. Also create a draft of your works cited page. Ask for documentation formats not covered in this lesson. Be prepared to hand your draft in to your teacher.

Refining Your Original Work

Grant Wood,
American Gothic, 1930

Great works of art, as well as great research papers, do not spring into existence as perfect and complete. Artists often make changes in their composition by painting out figures, adding more details, and rearranging elements. You should revise the first draft of your paper in the same spirit. Step back from your work, and give it a fresh look as did Grant Wood when he painted *American Gothic*, the painting on this page.

Creating any work, a painting or a research paper, involves a rethinking of the path that the work is to take while keeping a vigilant eye on one's original purpose. Grant Wood's original purpose was to depict a couple whose long faces embodied the long, somber appearance of the American Gothic house. As you determine your paper's future, review its past. Reread your research questions, all versions of your thesis statement, and your outline to ensure that you have not strayed from your original vision.

Revising the Research Paper

After you finish your first draft, be sure to allow enough time to set your draft aside for a day or two before you revise it. By putting some distance between yourself and the drafting process, you'll gain perspective and be better able to notice flaws.

When you revise your paper, you will analyze everything from organization and content to word choices. However, it's nearly impossible to revise both the "big picture" and the details at the same time. It will be faster and easier for you to revise your paper in stages, focusing on only one kind of problem at each stage. First tackle major ideas, next inspect supporting details, then polish tone, style, and individual word choices.

Revision Strategies

Many different strategies can aid you in revision. To check your paper's organization, write a new outline of your first draft. If information is missequenced, you will quickly notice. If a method of organization is not apparent, find out why. Chances are you will need either to reorganize information or to create stronger transitions. You can experiment with different methods of organization by physically cutting apart your draft and resequencing elements.

A good way to test your writing style for smoothness and clarity is to read your draft aloud. Mark awkward passages, breaks in tone, inadequate transitions, and wordy or repetitive sentences.

For another perspective on your work, exchange drafts with classmates. Ask them to point out not only what is wrong with your paper but also what they liked about it. After hearing your readers' comments, you will be better able to determine whether you need to provide more information to clarify some points.

After a first revision, you will probably want to revise your paper a second, or perhaps even a third, time. Using a computer with a word-processing program will speed your revisions by allowing you to cut and paste text electronically. Alternatively, make subsequent revisions easy to read by using differently colored pencils or by writing on self-sticking removable notes.

Revision Checklist

Review the following points as you revise your paper.

✓ **Content and Organization:**
Does the thesis statement reflect the content of the paper?
In what ways could you better organize major ideas?
What irrelevant or repetitious ideas could you delete?
Which of your main points need more explanation?
How could you strengthen transitions between ideas and paragraphs?

✓ **Style:**
Have you varied your sentence structures and used energetic verbs to keep the writing lively?
Have you avoided sophisticated vocabulary that you don't really understand?

✓ **Usage:**
Have you defined technical terms that will be unfamiliar to readers?
For which frequently used words can you substitute synonyms?
Which pronoun antecedents are vague?

✓ **Documentation:**
Do your parenthetical documentation and list of works cited contain all necessary information?

Analyze a Revision

The following research paper has been revised in stages. Notice how the major organizational and content elements are examined first, and then the details are considered.

Editing Tip

Review the rules for capitalizing titles of works and proper names on pages 633–637.

Wood surely "recognized" the influence, but he made the decision to exclude it from his paintings.

Why are these first two sentences more effective when they are combined?

This wording is more specific about how Hopper used it.

Why is "however" set off with commas? For a review of conjunctions and coordinating conjunctions, see pages 425 and 426.

More accurately, the subject is the city or environment of these people.

First Stage of a Revision

While Wood stayed in Iowa and ~~didn't~~ refused to recognize the influence of modern life, Hopper lived in New York city and ~~used it.~~ drew upon it as a subject for his art ~~New York society was obviously very different from Iowa's.~~ The New York city that interested Hopper was not the wealthy "aristocrats," but the working class world of the common man. Edward Hopper showed a different vision of America than Grant Wood did.

Second Stage of a Revision

Edward Hopper ~~showed~~ presented a very different vision of America ~~than~~ from that of Grant Wood ~~did.~~ While Wood ~~stayed~~ remained in Iowa and refused to recognize the influence of modern life, Hopper lived in New York city and drew upon it as a subject for his art. The New York city that interested Hopper, however, was not that of the wealthy "aristocrats," but the working-class world of the common man.

The first revision re-sequences the last sentence, which summarizes the paragraph, as a topic sentence. An obvious point is deleted as superfluous. The second revision employs more vivid verbs and corrects errors in usage and mechanics.

Revising a Paper About American Art and Culture

If you are writing a research paper about the arts or culture, you have some special issues to consider as you revise your paper. For example, make sure that you have explained specialized terms or techniques that will be unfamiliar to your readers. You should also anticipate the confusion that may result from words that take on a specialized meaning when they are used in the context of the arts. For example, there is quite a difference between a romantic composer and a Romantic composer.

Another issue to consider is that of subjective judgment. The merit of a work of art or a social trend is often a matter of opinion rather than one of fact. You may be tempted to state your own opinions, but remember that you are writing a research paper, not an editorial. Words such as "I feel" have no place in an objective analysis. Instead, use the opinions of experts to make your points. To be fair to your subject, though, present criticism from more than one source. Your readers will also appreciate a well-rounded analysis.

• ACTIVITIES •
Writer's Choice

1. Rewrite the following passage so that it's more clear, concise, and well organized. Also correct errors in grammar, usage, spelling, and punctuation.

One subject that for centuries artists have used for inspiration is religion. European art in the Middle Ages was often patronized by the church and people connected with the church. The church of that time had an influence that was pervasive in most aspects of Medieval society. The church has less influence as an institution in current times. Many modern artists are exploring religous themes, even though they may not belong to any formal religion as such. Primitive religious art has attracted many modern artists. Devotion and transcendent striving is being explored by these artists outside of a strict system of doctrine.

2. Revise the following sentences to make them more powerful.
   1. Jazz is sometimes considered the only musical art form that was created solely in America.
   2. More movies are produced in India (almost three times as many) than in the United States.
   3. A legend has grown around Jack Kerouac the writer, due to his freewheeling life style and rejection of mainstream values that were current then.
   4. Some modern artists have looked into the idea of how humanity relates to nature, which is ironic since we grow more removed from the natural world every day.
   5. People watch a lot of TV in America, which affects the way they come to look at other forms of art.
   6. Communication of personal feelings is a big theme among many artists today, but it hasn't always been.

3. Now begin the revision of the paper you've been working on throughout this unit. First consider your paper's content and organization, and then evaluate sentence structure, word choices, punctuation, and documentation.

Editing and Presenting: A Model Paper

Grant Wood,
Stone City, Iowa, 1930

The Importance of the Finishing Touches

Once a painting is finished, an artist wants to be sure the painting is shown to its best advantage. The proper frame, position on a wall, and lighting are all part of the presentation. In the same way, you will want to show your writing to its best advantage by preparing a final copy that is free of errors.

Final Edit Checklist

After typing a final revision of your research paper, you should carefully proofread it for errors in logic, grammar, punctuation, spelling, and typing. Use the following final edit checklist as an aid to your editing and proofreading.

Final Edit Checklist
✓ Read your paper for the first time to check the consistency of your logic and your presentation of information.
✓ Skim your paper to make sure that no information has been omitted or inadvertently missequenced.
✓ Read your paper once just for errors in grammar and usage. Make sure that pronoun references are clear and correct.
✓ Peruse your paper again to be sure all words are spelled and capitalized correctly, especially proper names. Double-check the spellings and accent marks of foreign words and phrases.
✓ Read your paper yet another time to be sure that all parenthetical documentation is in place and that the works cited page is complete.
✓ Read your paper a final time for punctuation errors. Make sure that periods come after internal citations instead of in front of them.

Present Your Paper

Your final paper will include a title page (or a first page that acts as a title page), a body, and a works cited page. In addition, you may wish to use a separate cover for your paper. You may also wish to include visual aids such as copies of works of art, diagrams, time lines, and process charts. Visual aids will give your readers a context in which to consider your paper's information. The model paper presented in this lesson could include photographs of the famous paintings by Grant Wood and Edward Hopper that are discussed in the text.

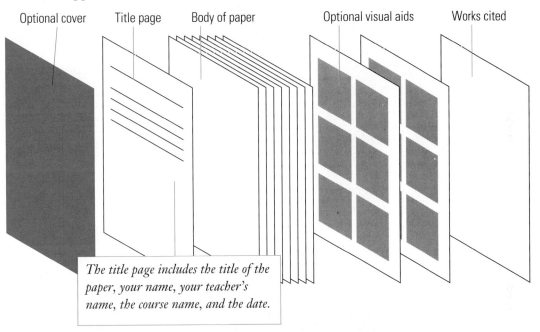

Optional cover   Title page   Body of paper   Optional visual aids   Works cited

The title page includes the title of the paper, your name, your teacher's name, the course name, and the date.

• ACTIVITIES •
Writer's Choice

1. Rewrite the paragraph that follows, correcting the errors in spelling, grammar, and punctuation.

Architecture is an art form that carries with it an enormus amount of technicall requirements. Architects must design structures, that is pleasing to the eye. They must also build structures, that are practical and safe. A third ellement must be considered as well. That is the wishes of the client who finances the project. Constructing buildings that meet all the necessary use and aesthetic requirements also within the budget, is quite a balancing act. Aesthetics must make compromises with functionality. Sometimes successfully, sometimes not. Sometimes state safety requirements, such as a buils-ing's being earthquake-proof, compromise what an architect consider a good design.

2. In the paragraph above, can you find any sentences that can be combined into one or rewritten for parallel construction? Mark these corrections.

3. Prepare and hand in the final version of your research paper.

This research paper was first published by The Concord Review, *a quarterly review of essays by secondary students of history in the English-speaking world.*

A quote from Hopper presents the premise on which the paper is founded.

What is the function of this opening sentence?

Why is this an effective thesis statement?

This sentence incorporates the author's name into the text.

Why is historic background on urban and rural living useful?

Contrasting Images of America:
The Art of Grant Wood and Edward Hopper

The question of the value of nationality in art is perhaps unsolvable. In general, it can be said that a nation's art is greatest when it most reflects the character of its people.

—Edward Hopper (Goodrich 9)

Grant Wood (1892–1942) once claimed that "his greatest inspiration came while milking a cow" (McCoubrey 66). This statement contains truth, for many of Wood's paintings portrayed idyllic country scenes of a bygone era. On the other hand, Edward Hopper (1882–1967) focused on the city as the quintessential reflection of American society. Unlike Wood, Hopper did not try to idealize what he saw. Thus, the art of Grant Wood and Edward Hopper reflected not only the conflict between romanticism and reality but also the conflict between rural and urban views of American life that existed in the decades of the 1920s and the 1930s.

According to historian Richard Hofstadter, "The United States was born in the country and has moved to the city" (23). By 1920 "more Americans lived in cities and towns of over 2,500 people than in the countryside" (Blum 549). "Almost every U.S. city would eventually suffer overcrowding, housing shortages, slums, unemployment, pollution and a lack of recreational facilities" (Weisberger 214). Despite these problems, people kept coming to the cities.

While the American city experienced growth during the 1920s, rural America experienced hard times. "In the early twenties the farm prosperity of the war years had rapidly declined and the rural economy was failing" (Dennis 206). The more crops farmers tried to produce, the less profit they made. By 1929 the economic failure had spread to the cities after the stock market crash. This crash brought the reality of the Great Depression to all sectors of the economy: more than 100,000 businesses failed between 1929 and 1932; the annual income of labor fell from $53 billion in 1929 to $31.5 billion in 1933. Western farmers were also hit extremely hard by "droughts, dust storms and plagues of grasshoppers from 1933 to 1936, which drove many families off their farms into tenancy or migrancy" (Dennis 206). The American economy and national spirit had reached an all-time low during the early years of the 1930s.

Wood emphasized in his art the theme of rural America: ➡

the land, community spirit, and pioneer values. A paradox surrounding Grant Wood's works resulted from the contrast between Wood's choice of themes and the times in which he painted. He portrayed an idyllic rural America during an age when America had become the most powerful industrial country in the world; he painted America as a land of bountiful harvests at a time of dust bowls and deprivation.

Art historian Wanda Corn has noted: "In Wood's idyllic farmscapes, man lives in complete harmony with Nature; he is the earth's caretaker . . ." (90). Grant Wood portrayed this sense of harmony in almost all of his farmscapes. His paintings *Spring Turning* and *Stone City* most effectively illustrate Wood's idea of the country. *Spring Turning*, in particular, conveys the awesomeness of the American land. Wood painted lush, rolling hills, evenly plowed fields, and golden light to celebrate the land. The feeling of the earth dominates the picture; man is reduced to a single small individual tilling the soil. The man in the painting does not work with modern equipment but with a primitive plow pulled by two horses. In *Stone City* Wood was also careful to exclude any signs of industrialization in his rural scene. *Stone City* represents a Utopian society in which a rural economy flourishes. "Dollhouse-like structures" (Corn 72), perfectly hedged trees, and rows of thriving crops adorn the land. Wood revealed only a small hint of industrial America by including two thin lines to represent telephone poles. Yet the poles are barely visible, for they are partially hidden by trees. Water tanks, horses, and windmills provide the energy for the people of *Stone City*. Through his paintings of farmers nurturing fecund woods, Wood emphasized the harmonious relationship between man and the land.

Wood's view of rural America clashed with the realities of the times, however. Actual farm conditions included "dustbowls, droughts, rotting crops, and mosquito-infested fields" (Dennis 206).

A second major theme in Wood's work was community spirit. In his paintings *Arbor Day* and *Dinner for Threshers*, Grant Wood portrayed rural America as a community-oriented society. In *Arbor Day* a wood schoolhouse stands proudly elevated on a green plateau. Communal activity centers around the schoolhouse as people work together to plant a tree in the schoolyard. This rural scene shows no signs of industrialization or urbanization. The tracks in the unpaved dirt road were created not by an automobile but by a horse-drawn buggy. No evidence of telephone poles or electric ➡

What do ellipses indicate?

How can titles of books and works of art be indicated other than by putting them in italic type?

Why is this transition effective?

wires appears in this picture. Instead, a hand-operated pump places the scene in a simpler past.

Wood further turned back the clock in his portrayal of women. In *Arbor Day*, for example, he painted the woman with her hair pulled back, dressed in a long dress that hangs below her ankles. Also, in *Dinner for Threshers*, women are again portrayed dressed in late nineteenth-century attire. The feeling of "community" permeates the work as the women graciously serve their men dinner after they have just finished a hard day of work. According to art historian Wanda Corn, "*Dinner for Threshers* rejoices not just in the fullness of agrarian life, but in the establishment of community and social ritual on the frontier" (104). Men comb their hair and wash before eating dinner. The subject matter of the painting presents an image of a simpler America. A horse and wagon rest in front of the barn, in place of a car. The women cook over a wood stove, oblivious to the advantages of electricity. The sense of simplicity is further enhanced by the colors Wood used to paint this picture. He limits his palette to only five colors: the three primary colors—red, yellow, and blue—and black and white. Wood definitely believes that this spirit of community and family which he portrayed in *Arbor Day* and *Dinner for Threshers* could only survive in a simpler, mainly rural America.

Although Wood painted both *Arbor Day* and *Dinner for Threshers* in the early 1930s, he refused to recognize automobiles, electricity, or even the railroad in these paintings. Art historian Robert Hobbs reminds us that "the total number of car registrations almost tripled during the decades of the twenties. A total of over thirty-one million cars were sold . . ." (91). Yet the horse-drawn buggy represented the only means of transportation in Wood's art.

Similarly, Wood's portrayal of women was out of sync with reality. In the decades of the 1920s and 1930s, Wood presented women wearing long dresses and slaving over primitive stoves to serve men, while in reality, the "new woman had revolted against masculine prerogatives . . . against being treated as a species of property" (Leuchtenburg 159). The hemline on women's dresses rose from ankle to midthigh as "flappers" emerged in the 1920s.

Finally, in his most famous painting, *American Gothic* (Corn 128), Wood exemplified the theme of pioneer values that he felt made America great. In this picture Wood portrayed an elderly Midwestern couple. The man and woman stare straight ahead, sternly. The lines in their faces reflect a hard life; their expressions suggest the Puritan values of ➡

Why do you think Murray might want to include photos of some of these paintings in her paper?

This statistic puts the times into focus.

Why is the word "flappers" in quotation marks? If you don't know, review pages 665–667.

hard work and thrift (Corn 130). There is no doubt that they possess strong rural roots and a stable environment. The man's pitchfork reveals that the couple is tied to the land. A hint of religion permeates the picture. The Gothic windows in the background indicate that in the couple's house the values of Christianity are fostered and taught (Corn 133). In fact, Grant Wood once claimed about the couple in *American Gothic*, "I tried to characterize them honestly. . . . To me they are basically good and solid people" (McCoubrey 66).

Edward Hopper presented a very different vision of America from that of Grant Wood. While Wood remained in Iowa and refused to recognize the influence of modern life, Hopper lived in New York City and drew upon it as a subject for his art. The New York City that fascinated Hopper, however, was not that of the wealthy "aristocrats," but that of the working-class world of the common man.

A paradox, however, also existed in Hopper's portrayal of the city in the 1920s and 1930s. Hopper painted at a time when the building of skyscrapers had escalated, especially in New York. All around Hopper, enormous buildings were going up which "represented a radiant, defiant display of American energy and optimism" (Leuchtenburg 182–183). Yet Hopper chose not to paint this side of the city. He looked beyond the spectacular facade of city life, its tall buildings, crowds, excitement, and glamour. "There are never any crowds in Hopper's pictures, never the hurrying tide of humanity . . ." (Goodrich 68).

In *Approaching a City* and *Manhattan Bridge Loop*, Edward Hopper portrayed a realistic view of urban society. The view in *Approaching a City*, for example, is seen from the eyes of a traveler. The painting invites the viewer down into the depths of the railroad tunnel. Stone buildings loom overhead, their windows forming monotonous rows. Hopper painted this picture in cold colors, reflecting the coldness of urban society. He employed cool tans, charcoal grays, brick reds, and dull blues to give the effect of lack of warmth.

In the painting *Manhattan Bridge Loop*, Hopper presented the city as even more uninviting. The sky is painted a slate blue; steel grays are used to indicate buildings. Contrasting with Grant Wood's *Spring Turning* which celebrates the land, this painting depicts the domination of buildings and the conversion of grass to paved sidewalks. A solitary man, hunched over, walks along the street, his figure lost in the shadows cast by the buildings. He appears insignificant in the midst of these colossal structures. Hopper wanted this picture to ➡

Notice how repeating Wood's name makes the transition to Hopper smoother.

A parallel is drawn between the artists: paradoxes exist in both of their works.

To emphasize the contrast, readers are briefly reminded of Wood's painting.

give the viewer a sense of the vast space of the city: "The very long horizontal shape of this picture," he wrote, "is an effort to give a sensation of great lateral extent" (Goodrich 69).

Hopper tried to reveal a deeper character of urban America: its rootlessness, lack of community, and loneliness. These elements represented a theme in his art. The city's lack of community spirit and the rootlessness of its people is represented in the painting *Nighthawks*. Hopper painted three people sitting at the counter of an all-night diner. The viewer is placed outside the diner, in the dark empty streets, observing people through a glass window. "Many of Hopper's city interiors are seen through windows, from the viewpoint of a spectator looking in at the unconscious actors . . . a life separate and silent, yet crystal clear" (Goodrich 70). *Nighthawks* emphasizes the disconnectedness that exists among people in a city. Although the people in the diner share an intimate environment, they are probably strangers, for they sit looking straight ahead without any signs of communication between them. *Nighthawks* presents a great contrast to Grant Wood's *Dinner for Threshers*. In Wood's painting the viewer sees a warm, personal environment in which people gather together to share food and conversation with one another. The sense of community is as strong in this picture as the sense of separateness is in *Nighthawks*. These two paintings, then, represent not merely differing views of American society, but rather, opposing views.

Along with the theme of lack of community, Hopper also explored the theme of rootlessness in his paintings. In his work *Rooms for Tourists*, for example, Hopper depicted a boarding house, a place where transients could come and go. This house with its advertisement for a room for rent represented a reality about urban life. Many of the people who came to the city were just "passing through" or were people who could not afford to own the kind of homes pictured in Grant Wood's *Stone City*. A room or a tiny apartment was the only "home" the city boarder would ever know.

Finally, loneliness constituted still another major theme in Hopper's art. In his painting *Automat*, a solitary woman sits at a table. She seems to have no roots, no real home, as she sits drinking a cup of coffee in a strange restaurant. The only light is the artificial light which hangs above her. Hopper almost seems to be implying that this world in which she exists was, in fact, an artificial world, man-made and unnatural. The woman herself has no identity; shadows from her hat conceal her face, yet the viewer can ascertain that she is part of the ➡

Why do you think Murray included this quotation in her paper?

Murray interprets the painting but remains objective in her analysis of it.

Why is this contrast effective?

cheapness of urban society. Her top dips low and her skirt rises up. Critic Robert Hobbs has commented that "in his painting of a lonely female, Hopper emphasizes the new 1920s look of short skirts and silk stockings . . . the girl's legs form the brightest spots on the canvas and the viewer is drawn into the uncomfortable position of staring" (72). Hopper's *Automat*, then, presents a great contrast to Wood's *American Gothic* in which the upright Puritanical values of rural America are proclaimed.

Thus, Edward Hopper's works portrayed not only the realities of urban society in the 1920s and 1930s, but also the changes which had taken place in American life during this period. Unlike Grant Wood, Hopper did not turn away from the "uglier," unpleasant sides of American society. According to one critic, "Hopper's work is most decidedly founded, not on art, but on life . . ." (Goodrich 64).

This contrast summarizes the artists' differences.

Through their art Grant Wood and Edward Hopper have presented us with two contrasting views of America in the 1920s and 1930s. Grant Wood's vision of American society as based on simple, solid rural values has survived mainly as a dream. Edward Hopper's vision of American society has, in fact, become a reality. Considered together, Wood and Hopper represent both ends of the spectrum of the Great Depression era.

Why is this conclusion effective?

In your own paper, the list of works cited should be on a separate page.

Works Cited

Blum, John M. *The National Experience: A History of the United States.* New York: Harcourt, 1985.

Corn, Wanda. *Grant Wood: The Regionalist Vision.* New Haven: Yale UP, 1983.

Dennis, James M. *Grant Wood.* Missouri: U of Missouri P, 1986.

Goodrich, Lloyd. *Edward Hopper.* New York: Abrams, 1976.

Hobbs, Robert. *Edward Hopper.* New York: Abrams, 1987.

Hofstadter, Richard. *The Age of Reform.* New York: Knopf, 1955.

Leuchtenburg, William E. *The Perils of Prosperity: 1914–1932.* Chicago: U of Chicago P, 1958.

McCoubrey, John W., ed. *Modern American Painting.* New York: Time-Life, 1970.

Weisberger, Bernard A., ed. *The Family Encyclopedia of American History.* New York: Reader's Digest, 1975.

Portfolio & Reflection

Summary

Key concepts in writing a research paper include the following:

- Prewriting includes selecting a topic, creating bibliography cards, and taking notes.
- A working outline organizes research notes.
- A thesis statement presents the paper's main idea and the writer's perspective.
- Drafting from an outline and note cards forges research notes into an organized framework.
- Research sources are noted within the body of the research paper and detailed at its end.
- Revising a research paper involves resequencing ideas, deleting irrelevancies, and refining wording.
- Editing a research paper involves correcting errors in usage, mechanics, spelling, and documentation.

Your Writer's Portfolio

Look over the research paper you have worked on during this unit, and put it into your portfolio. Your paper should demonstrate that you have worked with the preceding concepts. In other words, your research paper should do the following:

- show your sustained interest in the topic
- demonstrate your ability to locate and correctly use library resources
- employ a method of organization best suited to your topic
- contain a succinct thesis statement
- employ proper documentation of sources
- support assertions with facts
- assemble elements in the correct form

Reflection and Commentary

Write one page that demonstrates that you understand what this unit asked of you. Use your research paper as evidence while you consider the following numbered items. Respond to as many items as possible. Label the page "Commentary on Writing a Research Paper," and include it in your portfolio.

1. During your research and writing, how did your thesis statement change?
2. How does your present attitude toward your topic differ from your attitude when you began your paper?
3. How did you ensure the accuracy of direct quotations and avoid plagiarism?
4. In what ways did your outline aid your paper's organization?
5. Did you make multiple revisions of your paper for content, organization, and form?
6. What assumptions did you make about readers' preexisting knowledge of your topic?
7. What was your greatest problem in writing your paper? How did you overcome it?

Feedback

If you had a chance to respond to the following student comment, what would you say or ask:

Trying to keep focused on the thesis of the paper is the most difficult aspect of writing. This is especially hard during the research stage.

Stephanie Murray, Westwood High School, Westwood, Massachusetts

Style Through Sentence Combining

Frank Stella, *Takht-i-Sulayman 1* (detail), 1967

8 | Style Through Sentence Combining

Grim Realities

You know the feeling. Hunched over your rough draft, you stare at sentences that look like snarled spaghetti. Should you start over? How will you ever untangle the mess? Is there no hope?

Take heart. One approach that has worked for millions of students is sentence-combining practice. This approach helps you learn revising skills such as adding, deleting, and rearranging ideas, which can help you transform sentences into more readable structures. Research on sentence combining indicates that such practice transfers to your real writing and improves its overall quality.

Of course, sentence-combining practice won't extend the deadline for your research paper or cure confused thinking. But if you need help in smoothing out your sentences—improving their readability, variety, and style—here's an approach that deserves your attention.

A Workshop on Style

In this unit, you will find two types of sentence-combining exercises. The first type consists of clusters of short sentences that you will combine into longer ones. The second type, drawn from literature selections in this book, is set up in an unclustered format.

The first type of combining gives you practice in creating descriptive, narrative, expository, and persuasive paragraphs. You can combine each cluster of short sentences into one single sentence, or you can leave a cluster partially combined—or combine two or more clusters together. The idea, always, is to take risks and create the best sentences you can, writing them in your journal or as your teacher directs.

Exercises on facing pages deal with the same topic or situation. Think of these exercises as "bookends" for the writing you will do. After you have combined sentences into paragraphs, your task is to connect the paragraphs into a longer essay or story. Doing so will help you transfer sentence-combining skills to your own writing.

The second type of exercise, drawn from literary passages, invites you to test your skills against those of a professional writer. As you do these unclustered exercises, you will need to figure out the ideas that belong logically together. After you have completed the sentence-combining exercises, you can check your version against the author's original.

By studying the similarities and differences in the two passages, you will learn a great deal about your own style. Sometimes you will prefer the professional writer's sentences. Why, specifically, are they "better" than yours? But sometimes you will prefer your own style. Can you build on this writing skill, trying it out in your own stories and essays? Either way, you learn how to write.

Exploring Your Own Style

Sentence-combining practice helps when you revise your real writing. Why? Because you know that sentences are flexible instruments of thought, not rigid structures cast in concrete. The simple fact that you feel confident in moving sentence parts around increases your control of the writing process.

To acquire this sense of self-confidence—one based on your real competence in combining and revising sentences—you can try strategies like those shown below.

1. *Vary the length of your sentences.* Work for a rhythmic, interesting balance of long and short sentences, remembering that brevity often has dramatic force. Use this knowledge.
2. *Vary the structure of your sentences.* By using sentence openers on occasion—and by sometimes tucking information in the middle of a sentence—you can create stylistic interest.
3. *Use parallelism for emphasis.* Experiment with repeated items in a series—words, phrases, and clauses—to understand how structural patterns work and how you can use them to advantage.
4. *Use interruption for emphasis.* Colons, semicolons, dashes, commas, parentheses—all of these are useful tools in your stylistic tool kit; knowing how to use them well matters.
5. *Use unusual patterns for emphasis.* That you might sometimes *reverse* normal sentence patterns may never have occurred to you, but such a strategy can work—if you know how.

Of course, the whole point of sentence-combining practice is to improve your revising and editing skills. Therefore, when it comes time to rework a draft, it's important to apply what you have learned about combining and revising.

The same holds true when you are responding to the writing of your peers. If you spot a passage that can be improved with stylistic tinkering, simply write SC (for sentence combining) in the margin. This will provide a cue to apply some of the skills learned in the unit.

8.1   Description

Exercise A: Sandwich Shop

Directions   Combine each cluster of numbered items into one or more sentences. Combine clusters, if you wish.

1.1 The sun had faded in the west.
1.2 The air still seemed humid.
1.3 It still seemed thick with heat.
1.4 This was inside the sandwich shop.

2.1 A half-dozen tables jammed the room.
2.2 They had checkered tablecloths.
2.3 They had chrome napkin holders.

3.1 Two boys lounged in a corner booth.
3.2 One ran fingers through his hair.
3.3 His hair was oily.
3.4 The other slouched against red vinyl.
3.5 He sipped a king-size cola.

4.1 A girl stood at the jukebox.
4.2 She chewed pink bubble gum.
4.3 She combed her hair in the reflection.
4.4 Her hair was sun-bleached.
4.5 The reflection was neon.

5.1 Behind a counter were shelves.
5.2 The shelves were cluttered.
5.3 The shelves displayed clever signs.
5.4 The shelves displayed boxes of candy.
5.5 The boxes were dusty.

6.1 The counter itself was glossy white.
6.2 It was worn thin by many elbows.
6.3 It was worn thin by scrubbings.
6.4 The scrubbings were countless.

7.1 A dozen stools stood like sentries.
7.2 The sentries were silent.
7.3 The sentries awaited customers like me.
7.4 The customers might be hungry.

Writing Tip

To create parallel absolutes in cluster 3, change *ran* to *running* and *slouched* to *slouching.* For more on absolutes, see page 471.

Invitation   How do you handle yourself in such a situation? To link "Sandwich Shop" to "Meatball Sandwich," describe the scene that happens next.

Exercise B: Meatball Sandwich

Directions   Combine each cluster of numbered items into one or more sentences. Combine clusters, if you wish.

1.1 The sandwich arrived in a basket.
1.2 The sandwich was split in half.
1.3 The basket was oval-shaped.
1.4 It was lined with wax paper.
1.5 The wax paper was yellow.

2.1 Meatballs filled a loaf of French bread.
2.2 The meatballs were huge.
2.3 The meatballs were juicy.
2.4 The loaf was freshly baked.

3.1 It was smothered in tomato sauce.
3.2 It was sprinkled with grated cheese.
3.3 It smelled of onions.
3.4 It smelled of garlic.
3.5 It smelled of Italian spices.
3.6 The spices were fragrant.

4.1 It was a culinary triumph.
4.2 It was a work of art.
4.3 The work engaged all the senses.

5.1 I eyed it with anticipation.
5.2 My anticipation was mouthwatering.
5.3 I then made my move.
5.4 My move was swift.
5.5 It was unhesitating.

6.1 The tomato sauce was rich.
6.2 It was deliciously thick.
6.3 It was pungent with Old-World flavor.

7.1 Bread complemented the meatballs.
7.2 The bread was crusty.
7.3 It was still warm from the oven.
7.4 The meatballs were succulent.

Writing Tip

Try opening cluster 3 with participial phrases beginning with *smothered* and *sprinkled;* try using a pair of dashes for emphasis in cluster 7.

Invitation   Describe what you notice as you eat the sandwich. Share your text—"Sandwich Shop" plus "Meatball Sandwich"—with a writing partner.

Exercise C: Country Drive

Directions   Combine each cluster of numbered items into one or more sentences. Combine clusters, if you wish.

1.1 Cheryl felt nervous.
1.2 She turned into a lane.
1.3 The lane was asphalt.
1.4 The lane was narrow.
1.5 It led to her employer's estate.

2.1 Her headlights swept past lilacs.
2.2 Her headlights swept past chestnuts.
2.3 Her headlights swept past white fences.
2.4 These were below the hilltop house.

3.1 On both sides were acres of fields.
3.2 The fields were grassy.
3.3 Arabian horses ran safe there.
3.4 Arabian horses ran free there.
3.5 The horses were prize-winning.

4.1 The night air was cool along the ridge.
4.2 The night air was soft along the ridge.
4.3 A summer moon blanched the landscape.
4.4 The landscape was rolling.

5.1 The house held a view of the valley below.
5.2 The house was Georgian-style.
5.3 The view was commanding.
5.4 Lights carpeted the darkness.
5.5 The darkness was velvety.

6.1 Luxury sedans lined the driveway.
6.2 Cheryl parked her car there.
6.3 Her car was well used.
6.4 It was built for economy.

7.1 She had never seen such a house.
7.2 She tried to imagine its interior.
7.3 She tried to imagine what to expect.

Writing Tip

Cluster 3 provides an opportunity to use *where* as a connector. Look for other opportunities elsewhere in this exercise.

Invitation   Using a spatial pattern of organization, describe what Cheryl first sees inside. Link this description to "Chief Executive."

Directions Combine each cluster of numbered items into one or more sentences. Combine clusters, if you wish.

1.1 French doors opened into a dining room.
1.2 The dining room was massive.
1.3 A chandelier hung from the ceiling.
1.4 The chandelier was glittering.

2.1 There stood the company's leader.
2.2 She looked poised.
2.3 She looked regal.

3.1 She was a woman.
3.2 The woman was tall.
3.3 The woman was gaunt.
3.4 She shimmered in a sequin dress.
3.5 The sequins were black.

4.1 One hand was extended in greeting.
4.2 Her mouth was frozen into a smile.
4.3 The smile was waxy.
4.4 She welcomed selected employees.
4.5 Their work was outstanding.

5.1 Her hair was pulled into a knot.
5.2 The knot was tight.
5.3 The knot was smooth.
5.4 This emphasized her diamond earrings.
5.5 The diamonds were emerald-cut.

6.1 Behind her was a table spread with silverware.
6.2 Behind her was a table spread with china.
6.3 Behind her was a table spread with crystal.
6.4 The table was elegant.
6.5 The crystal was imported.

7.1 Everything about her suggested wealth.
7.2 Everything about her suggested power.
7.3 Everything about her suggested privilege.

Writing Tip

To create parallel modifying phrases in cluster 4, try using *with* as a sentence opener and deleting *was* in sentences 4.1 and 4.2.

Invitation Is Cheryl speechless? Does she use a table napkin to blow her nose? Share the text you create with a writing partner.

8.2   *Narration*

Directions   Combine each cluster of numbered items into one or more sentences. Combine clusters, if you wish.

1.1 Dexter carried a backpack.
1.2 It was jammed with books.
1.3 Dexter shuffled into an empty classroom.
1.4 His teacher was correcting papers there.

2.1 She glanced up from her work.
2.2 She smiled at him.
2.3 He made his hesitant approach.
2.4 His forehead was knitted with worry.

3.1 He hunched his shoulders.
3.2 He limped toward her.
3.3 He looked as submissive as possible.
3.4 He looked as deferential as possible.

4.1 She invited him to be seated.
4.2 He folded his hands meekly.
4.3 He studied his running shoes.
4.4 His shoes had untied laces.

5.1 Then he collapsed with a sigh.
5.2 His sigh was audible.
5.3 He bit his lip.
5.4 He watched her conclude a comment.
5.5 He had interrupted the comment.

6.1 His request was well rehearsed.
6.2 It was for a deadline extension.
6.3 He wondered how she would respond.

7.1 She looked up from her work.
7.2 She put down her pen.
7.3 He took a deep breath.
7.4 He returned her gaze.
7.5 He summoned up persuasive skills.
7.6 The skills were from past experience.

Writing Tip

To make an absolute in cluster 2, delete *was* in sentence 2.4. Try a participle (*hunching, limping,* or *looking*) in cluster 3.

Invitation   Narrate the conversation between Dexter and his teacher. Use this dialogue to link "Con Man" to "Act Two."

Directions Combine each cluster of numbered items into one or more sentences. Combine clusters, if you wish.

1.1 Dexter was out of the classroom.
1.2 Dexter sprinted for his locker.
1.3 He would dump his backpack there.
1.4 His backpack was unwanted.

2.1 It thumped his ribs.
2.2 It jostled his ribs.
2.3 He grinned smugly.
2.4 He congratulated himself.

3.1 He slid around one corner.
3.2 He then loped past a teacher.
3.3 The teacher was eagle-eyed.
3.4 The teacher was on hall patrol.

4.1 The bus still stood at the curb.
4.2 It awaited any stragglers.
4.3 Dexter still hoped to make it.

5.1 He slouched against his locker.
5.2 He spun the combination too far.
5.3 He missed the right numbers.

6.1 He muttered under his breath.
6.2 He eyed the dial more carefully.
6.3 He tried once again.

7.1 His friends sauntered by.
7.2 They were urging him to hurry up.
7.3 He jerked the locker open.
7.4 He grabbed a tennis racket.
7.5 He shoved his backpack inside.

8.1 It was then he saw his teacher.
8.2 She was striding down the hall.
8.3 Her hand was lifted to stop him.

Writing Tip

In clusters 5 and 6 try using participles to vary sentence rhythms. In sentence 8.3 delete *was* to create an absolute.

Invitation How does Dexter handle himself? Narrate an effective ending for "Con Man" and "Act Two." Then share your text with a writing partner.

Directions   Combine each cluster of numbered items into one or more sentences. Combine clusters, if you wish.

1.1 Kim hobbled from the floor.
1.2 Her eyes were filled with tears.
1.3 Her mouth was clenched tight.

2.1 Her date found her a chair.
2.2 She collapsed.
2.3 She pulled off her shoe.
2.4 Her shoe was scuffed.
2.5 She inspected the damage.

3.1 A bruise had already formed.
3.2 The bruise was purple.
3.3 The bruise was aching.
3.4 It was just above her toes.

4.1 She shook her head.
4.2 She muttered under her breath.
4.3 She knew her prom night was over.

5.1 Then she put ice on the bruise.
5.2 She watched a football player.
5.3 The football player was manic.
5.4 He was still stomping.
5.5 He was still lunging about.
5.6 He was on the dance floor.

6.1 The dancer clapped his hands.
6.2 He cleared a wide swath.
6.3 No one ventured there.
6.4 It was too dangerous to do so.

7.1 Kim rubbed her foot.
7.2 Her foot was injured.
7.3 Kim felt her anger grow stronger.
7.4 The brute had not even apologized.
7.5 The brute was clumsy.

Writing Tip

By opening with *hobbling* in cluster 1, you create a humorous writing error, a *dangling participle*. For more on this, see page 390.

Invitation   What does Kim think about on the sidelines? Use her thoughts (or her dialogue with her date) as a link to the "Chaperones" exercise.

Directions   Combine each cluster of numbered items into one or more sentences. Combine clusters, if you wish.

1.1 The chaperones shuffled past Kim.
1.2 They shuffled onto the dance floor.
1.3 They were middle-aged.
1.4 The dance floor was crowded.

2.1 The man made a pivot.
2.2 His pivot was sudden.
2.3 The woman followed him.
2.4 Her shoulders bounced in tempo.
2.5 The bounce was light.

3.1 They cocked their heads back.
3.2 They clicked their fingers.
3.3 They snaked through the crowd.

4.1 The man's face was relaxed.
4.2 The man's face was smiling.
4.3 His forehead glistened with sweat.
4.4 His forehead was broad.

5.1 The woman spun beneath his hand.
5.2 The woman followed his lead.
5.3 She then began to improvise.
5.4 She tried a step of her own.
5.5 The step was complicated.
5.6 This caused a small crowd to gather.

6.1 The pair danced in a controlled way.
6.2 They enjoyed each other's company.
6.3 They welcomed each other's steps.

7.1 Off to one side was the football player.
7.2 He had just backed into another girl.
7.3 He crushed her white shoe with his heel.
7.4 Her shoe was slender.
7.5 His heel was wide.

Writing Tip

To create absolutes in clusters 2 and 4, change *bounced* to *bouncing* and *glistened* to *glistening*. For more on absolutes, see page 471.

Invitation   What does Kim do next? Narrate an effective conclusion for "Prom Night" and "Chaperones." Then share it with a writing partner.

8.3 Exposition

Exercise A: How Animals Navigate

Directions   Combine each cluster of numbered items into one or more sentences. Combine clusters, if you wish.

1.1 Many creatures have senses.
1.2 The creatures migrate.
1.3 The creatures forage for survival.
1.4 The senses are astonishingly acute.

2.1 A salmon uses its sense of smell.
2.2 A salmon migrates thousands of miles.
2.3 A salmon returns to its home to spawn.
2.4 A salmon returns to its home to die.

3.1 Sharks detect electrical fields.
3.2 The electrical fields are faint.
3.3 The fields are generated by prey.
3.4 Sharks use this information to attack.

4.1 A homing pigeon sees ultraviolet light.
4.2 A homing pigeon hears wind sounds.
4.3 The wind sounds have low frequencies.
4.4 The sounds are thousands of miles away.

5.1 Honeybees sense subtle changes.
5.2 Bobolinks sense subtle changes.
5.3 The changes are in the earth's magnetic field.
5.4 They use this information to navigate.

6.1 A black desert ant has a unique compass.
6.2 Each of its eyes has eighty lenses.
6.3 Each lens receives polarized light.
6.4 The light is from different points in the sky.

7.1 Savannah sparrows use the stars to navigate.
7.2 The sparrows are night flyers.
7.3 They may also use their sense of smell.

8.1 Many animals have such highly developed senses.
8.2 Our equipment seems simple by comparison.

Writing Tip

In cluster 6 first try a colon followed by a complete sentence. Then try a dash followed by an *each of which* construction.

Invitation   Is intelligence a "sense" that human beings have developed? If so, what purpose might this sense serve? Write a follow-up paragraph.

Exercise B: Genetic Compasses

Directions Combine each cluster of numbered items into one or more sentences. Combine clusters, if you wish.

1.1 Many animals have sensory equipment.
1.2 The equipment is remarkable.
1.3 Others apparently have genetic compasses.
1.4 The compasses provide built-in direction.

2.1 One such animal is the monarch butterfly.
2.2 It migrates by the millions from Mexico.
2.3 It spends the winter there.

3.1 Monarchs look like an orange cloud.
3.2 Monarchs flutter northward each spring.
3.3 The journey to Canada is a long one.

4.1 Along the way the monarchs mate.
4.2 Along the way the monarchs lay their eggs.
4.3 The eggs are laid atop milkweed.
4.4. Along the way the monarchs die.

5.1 Their offspring then take up the journey.
5.2 Their offspring repeat the same life cycle.

6.1 Several generations of monarchs are born.
6.2 Several generations of monarchs breed.
6.3 Several generations of monarchs die.
6.4 A final generation reaches Canada.

7.1 Autumn winds begin to blow.
7.2 The monarchs ingest flower nectar.
7.3 The monarchs get ready to head south.

8.1 The old monarchs are long gone.
8.2 The new monarchs "know" where home is.

9.1 They fly all the way back to Mexico.
9.2 They have never been there before.
9.3 They roost in the trees of their ancestors.

Writing Tip

In cluster 6 try using *after* and *before* as connecting words. Which is preferable if you use *after* in cluster 7?

Invitation Are human beings "programmed" for language just as monarchs are "programmed" for flight? Consider this idea in a follow-up paragraph.

Exercise C: Native American Words

Directions   Combine each cluster of numbered items into one or more sentences. Combine clusters, if you wish.

1.1 English colonists settled the New World.
1.2 This was early in the seventeenth century.
1.3 They encountered a great wilderness.
1.4 It was inhabited by native tribes.
1.5 The native tribes were widely dispersed.

2.1 The native languages contained sounds.
2.2 The settlers had never heard them before.
2.3 They therefore had trouble reproducing them.
2.4 They therefore had trouble spelling them.

3.1 John Smith listened to the Algonquian Indians.
3.2 He tried to capture their word for an animal.
3.3 The animal was small and furry.
3.4 He recorded the sounds as *raughroughcum*.
3.5 He later shortened it to *rarowcun*.

4.1 In 1672 the word was finally printed as *raccoon*.
4.2 This was sixty-five years after Smith's first effort.
4.3 This was a far cry from the native original.

5.1 A similar process occurred for many other names.
5.2 The names included *skunk* (from *segankw*).
5.3 The names included *woodchuck* (from *otchock*).
5.4 The names included *moose* (from *moosu*).

6.1 Others native terms were absorbed intact.
6.2 The terms included *hominy*.
6.3 The terms included *mackinaw*.
6.4 The terms included *moccasin*.
6.5 The terms included *tepee*.
6.6 The terms included *powwow*.

7.1 The colonists learned hundreds of native words.
7.2 They used them to name their new home.
7.3 They used them to enrich their language.

Writing Tip

In cluster 3 try opening with the participle *listening* for sentence variety. In cluster 4 try making an appositive.

Invitation   Many of America's landmarks—thousands of places across the land—bear Native American names. How do you feel about this heritage?

Directions   Combine each cluster of numbered items into one or more sentences. Combine clusters, if you wish.

1.1 Many European languages enriched English.
1.2 Spanish contributed the most words.
1.3 This was during the settling of America.

2.1 Many Americans pushed westward.
2.2 This was after the Mexican War.
2.3 This was during the California gold rush.
2.4 They heard Spanish words of many kinds.
2.5 They adopted them into their vocabularies.

3.1 Among these words were topographical terms.
3.2 The terms included *canyon*.
3.3 The terms included *mesa*.
3.4 The terms included *sierra*.

4.1 They adopted building terms like *adobe*.
4.2 They adopted building terms like *patio*.
4.3 They adopted building terms like *plaza*.
4.4 They also adopted mining words like *bonanza*.
4.5 They also adopted mining words like *placer*.
4.6 They also adopted mining words like *El Dorado*.

5.1 Dozens of ranching words were appropriated.
5.2 These included words like *alfalfa*.
5.3 These included words like *corral*.
5.4 These included words like *bronco*.
5.5 These included words like *stampede*.
5.6 This is not to mention the word *ranch* itself.

6.1 Spanish also gave us the word *cockroach*.
6.2 It is derived from *cucaracha*.
6.3 Spanish also gave us the word *tornado*.
6.4 This occurs only in the United States.

7.1 Even *California* is a Spanish name.
7.2 It literally means "hot oven."

Writing Tip

In cluster 5 put the list of specific examples in the middle of the base sentence, following *words*. Use dashes for emphasis.

Invitation   Many other Spanish words are a part of modern American English. Write about the ones that spring immediately to mind.

8.4 Persuasion

Exercise A: Cheeseburger

Directions   Combine each cluster of numbered items into one or more sentences. Combine clusters, if you wish.

1.1 On the grill sizzles a hamburger.
1.2 The hamburger is plump and rare.
1.3 It is in the Fast-Food Tradition.
1.4 The tradition is American.

2.1 The meat bastes in a puddle.
2.2 The puddle is sputtering.
2.3 The puddle sends up hot showers.
2.4 The showers are greasy.

3.1 Its patty is covered by a bun.
3.2 The patty is quarter-pound.
3.3 The bun traps meat juices.
3.4 The bun traps water vapor.

4.1 A slab of cheese assures added fat.
4.2 It assures added cholesterol.
4.3 The cheese was melted.

5.1 The meat spatters grease.
5.2 The bun is stroked with mayonnaise.
5.3 Mayonnaise is a crowning touch.
5.4 It is rich in egg yolks.
5.5 It is rich in oils.

6.1 A spatula cradles the cheeseburger.
6.2 The spatula is dripping.
6.3 It positions the cheeseburger atop condiments.
6.4 The sandwich is wrapped in foil.
6.5 This is to seal in the juices.
6.6 The flavor is succulent.

7.1 It is then packaged with French fries.
7.2 They have been soaked in more fat.
7.3 This is to provide a dining experience.
7.4 The experience is truly unforgettable.

Writing Tip

In cluster 1 try a pair of adjectives after *hamburger;* in cluster 5 try a dash—plus an appositive that describes *mayonnaise.*

Invitation   To make this introduction more vivid, now describe an unattractive person eating a cheeseburger and fries in a disgusting way.

Exercise B: Fat City

Directions Combine each cluster of numbered items into one or more sentences. Combine clusters, if you wish.

1.1 Fast foods are a major source of fat.
1.2 These include hamburgers.
1.3 These include French fries.
1.4 These include milkshakes.
1.5 The fat is in the American diet.

2.1 Health experts suggest twenty grams of fat.
2.2 This would be a daily average.
2.3 The daily average would be reasonable.
2.4 Fewer grams of fat should be a goal.

3.1 Many hamburgers have thirty grams of fat.
3.2 The hamburgers are commercially prepared.
3.3 Some contain more than thirty-five grams.

4.1 Now add a slice of cheese.
4.2 It has eight grams of fat.
4.3 Now add an order of fries.
4.4 It has eleven grams of fat.
4.5 Now add a chocolate shake.
4.6 It has nine grams of fat.

5.1 The total is hardly good nutrition.
5.2 The total approaches sixty grams of fat.
5.3 This is for a *single* meal.
5.4 It triples the suggested daily quota.

6.1 Such meals are pitched in TV commercials.
6.2 The meals are fat-saturated.
6.3 The commercials are seductive.
6.4 Many of us see them 5,000 times per year.

7.1 Our culture is hooked on a diet.
7.2 The diet emphasizes fast foods.
7.3 Kids today are fatter than twenty years ago.
7.4 Our nation has high rates of heart disease.

Writing Tip

In cluster 3 try *and* or a semicolon (;) to join sentences 3.1 and 3.3. In cluster 7 try connectors like *because, hence, therefore.*

Invitation Write a concluding paragraph that addresses the "Fat City" problem. Then share your text with a writing partner.

Exercise C: Holiday Spirit

Directions   Combine each cluster of numbered items into one or more sentences. Combine clusters, if you wish.

1.1 December 26 is a peculiar occasion.
1.2 It is the day after Christmas.
1.3 Americans go slightly berserk then.

2.1 Parking lots become a snarl.
2.2 Intersections become a snarl.
2.3 The snarl is confused.
2.4 Cars head for shopping malls.
2.5 The malls are jammed with people.

3.1 Shoppers clog the store aisles.
3.2 The shoppers are short-tempered.
3.3 They are trying to exchange gifts.
3.4 They are trying to find bargains.
3.5 The bargains are discounted.

4.1 Most have received gifts.
4.2 The gifts were useless.
4.3 The gifts were ill-fitting.
4.4 They hope to redeem these for credit.

5.1 Such gifts have little or no meaning.
5.2 They were often purchased under duress.
5.3 The purchase was to fulfill obligations.
5.4 The obligations are social.

6.1 Holidays have been commercialized.
6.2 Much junk is dutifully given.
6.3 Much junk is politely accepted.
6.4 Much junk is exchanged with relief.

7.1 What underlies these rituals is guilt.
7.2 The rituals are strange.
7.3 The rituals are gift-giving.
7.4 The guilt is pervasive.
7.5 The guilt is supported by advertising.

Writing Tip

In clusters 5 and 6 try causal connectors—*because, since, therefore, consequently,* and *so.* Make sure to check your punctuation.

Invitation   Describe a personal experience with holiday shopping that you can use to introduce "Holiday Spirit" and "Shopping Spree."

Directions Combine each cluster of numbered items into one or more sentences. Combine clusters, if you wish.

1.1 Merchants look forward to December 26.
1.2 It is always a day for record sales.
1.3 It is a chance to reduce inventories.
1.4 The inventories are unwanted.

2.1 Typically they discount merchandise.
2.2 They reinforce the desire to spend.
2.3 The reinforcement is through advertising.
2.4 The advertising is relentless.

3.1 A "bandwagon effect" is created.
3.2 Shoppers convene for a single purpose.
3.3 The purpose is to buy for themselves.
3.4 The buying is not for someone else.

4.1 The buying spree intensifies.
4.2 Group behavior supports spending.
4.3 Group behavior encourages spending.
4.4 The spending is mindless.

5.1 Many shoppers are sucked into this vortex.
5.2 The shoppers are undisciplined.
5.3 The vortex is consuming.
5.4 They are like moths.
5.5 The moths are drawn to a candle flame.

6.1 They are no longer buying for others.
6.2 The buying is out of guilt.
6.3 They are instead spending on themselves.
6.4 The spending is unashamed.

7.1 December 26 is finally over.
7.2 Credit cards are at their limit.
7.3 The shoppers head for home.
7.4 They feel exhausted.
7.5 They feel strangely depressed.

> **Writing Tip**
>
> In cluster 3 try either a colon or a dash for stylistic emphasis. For more on these punctuation marks, see pages 648–650 and 662.

Invitation Write a concluding paragraph for "Holiday Spirit" and "Shopping Spree." Then share your text with a writing partner.

8.5   *Literature Exercises*

Directions   Scan the sentences below. The unnumbered one comes directly from *Black Ice*, by Lorene Cary. The numbered sentences are adapted from Cary's original. Decide which of the numbered sentences belong together, and combine them in your own way. Then compare your sentences with the originals on pages 38–42.

1. We were in the gymnasium.
2. We heard the commotion below.
3. The commotion was in the locker rooms.
4. Fumiko ran to the wall behind the basket.
5. A few balls lay there.
6. They were beside each other.
7. She picked one.
8. She dribbled it.
9. She then passed it to me.
10. She ran onto the court.
11. I passed it back to her.
12. She shot the ball.
13. It headed toward the basket.
14. It made a low arc.
15. It dropped through.
16. She ran hard to retrieve her own rebound.

There could have been four girls after her, as hard as she ran.

17. She snatched the ball out of the air.
18. She then leapt to make a lay-up.
19. It hit the backboard softly.
20. It fell through the hoop.
21. Then she passed me the ball.
22. I hesitated.
23. I passed it back.
24. She thrust it at me.
25. I caught the pass.
26. It was chest-high.
27. She threw it perfectly as a diagram.
28. She threw it harder than my old gym teacher.
29. She threw it with no effort I could see.
30. I did not want to play.
31. I wanted to watch.
32. She seemed intent on teaching me.

Directions   Scan the sentences below. The unnumbered ones come directly from *An American Childhood*, by Annie Dillard. The numbered sentences are adapted from Dillard's original. Decide which of the numbered sentences belong together, and combine them in your own way. Then compare your sentences with the originals on pages 104–108.

She [Mother] didn't like the taste of stamps so she didn't lick stamps; she licked the corner of the envelope instead.

1. She glued sandpaper to the sides of kitchen drawers.
2. She glued sandpaper under kitchen cabinets.
3. She always had a handy place to strike a match.
4. She designed doubly wide kitchen counters.
5. She designed elevated bathroom sinks.
6. She hounded workmen to build them against all norms.
7. She wanted to splint a finger.
8. She stuck it in a lightweight cigar tube.
9. She wanted to protect a pack of cigarettes.
10. She carried it in a Band-Aid box.
11. She drew plans for a toothbrush for babies.
12. The toothbrush went over the finger.
13. She drew plans for an oven rack.
14. The rack slid up and down.
15. She drew plans for Lendalarm.
16. Lendalarm was the family favorite.
17. Lendalarm was a beeper.
18. You attached it to books (or tools).
19. The books (or tools) were loaned to friends.
20. The beeper sounded after ten days.
21. Only the rightful owner could silence it.

She reminded us of P. T. Barnum's dictum: You could sell anything to anybody if you marketed it right. The adman who thought of making Americans believe they needed underarm deodorant was a visionary.

22. So, too, was the hero.
23. The hero made a success of a new soap.
24. A cake of this stuff floated.
25. Soap wasn't supposed to float.
26. Then some inspired adman made a leap.
27. Advertise that it floats.
28. The rest is history.

Directions   Scan the sentences below adapted from *The Soul of a New Machine*, by Tracy Kidder. Decide which of the numbered sentences belong together, and combine them in your own way. Then compare your sentences with the originals on pages 246–250.

1. Computers were everywhere, of course.
2. They were in the cafe's beeping cash registers.
3. They were in the cafe's microwave oven.
4. They were in the cafe's jukebox.
5. They were in the traffic lights.
6. They were under the hoods of the honking cars.
7. The cars were snarled out there on the street.
8. This was despite the traffic lights.
9. They were in the airplanes overhead.
10. The visible differences somehow seemed insignificant.
11. Computers had become less noticeable.
12. They had become smaller.
13. They had become more reliable.
14. They had become more efficient.
15. They had become more numerous.
16. Surely this happened by design.
17. Something was obvious.
18. Manufacturers wanted to sell the devices far and wide.
19. Manufacturers had to strive to make them easy to use.
20. Manufacturers had to strive to make them invisible.
21. Were computers a profound, unseen hand?

* * *

22. Obviously, computers have made differences.
23. They have fostered the development of spaceships.
24. They have fostered a great increase in junk mail.
25. The computer boom has brought the diagnostic device.
26. The device is known as the CAT scanner.
27. The device is marvelous.
28. The device is expensive.
29. It has brought a host of other medical equipment.
30. It has given rise to machines.
31. The machines play good chess.
32. The machines play rather boring chess.
33. It has also given rise to a proliferation of weapons.

Part 2

Grammar, Usage, and Mechanics

Watching Maggie take her first steps is a "hoot and a holler," as mom would say. First, she hoists herself up to her ~~little~~ tiny feet by pulling with all ~~its~~ *her* might on the edge of the couch or chair. Once upright, she ~~looked~~ around to make sure you are watching, and then she grins. She turns herself toward the center of the room, and takes that first step, ~~still~~ *with* one ... ed on "home base. ... Then, she purses her lips and ... feet akwwa... and throwing her *weight* ~~wait~~ toward ... rms. She loo... like Frankenstein, *and she* giggling ... shell make it ... fore she tumbles.

TROUBLESHOOTER CHECKLIST

- ☐ Sentence Fragment
- ☐ Run-on Sentence
- ☐ Lack of Subject-Verb Agreement
- ☐ Lack of Pronoun-Antecedent Agreement
- ☐ Lack of Clear Pronoun Reference
- ☑ Shift in Pronoun
- ☐ Shift in Verb Tense
- ☐ Incorrect Verb Tense or Form
- ☐ Misplaced or Dangling Modifier
- ☑ Missing or Misplaced Possessive Apostrophe
- ☐ Missing Commas with Nonessential Element
- ☐ Missing Comma in a Series

Part 2 Grammar, Usage, and Mechanics

Troubleshooter

Research on thousands of student papers has identified the errors most frequently made by students and marked by teachers. This Troubleshooter is based on that research and is designed to help you correct these errors.

Use the Table of Contents below to locate quickly a lesson on a specific error. Your teacher may mark errors with the handwritten codes in the left-hand column.

9.1 Sentence Fragment

PROBLEM 1

Fragment that lacks a subject

frag   Michael slipped a length of rope into his pack. Thought it might be useful.

Solution

Michael slipped a length of rope into his pack. He thought it might be useful.

Add a subject to the fragment to make it a complete sentence.

PROBLEM 2

Fragment that lacks a complete verb

frag   The silence was broken by an eerie sound. A loon out on the lake.

frag   Zina pointed toward the west. A golden sun setting on the horizon.

Solution A

The silence was broken by an eerie sound. A loon out on the lake was calling.

Zina pointed toward the west. A golden sun was setting on the horizon.

Add a complete verb or a helping verb to make the sentence complete.

Solution B

The silence was broken by an eerie sound, for a loon out on the lake was calling.

Zina pointed toward the west, where a golden sun was setting on the horizon.

Combine the fragment with another sentence.

Fragment that is a subordinate clause

> frag   Linda returned the novel to the library. Although she had not read the last four chapters.
>
> frag   Jorge owns an antique car. Which he has restored himself.

Solution A

Linda returned the novel to the library although she had not yet read the last four chapters.

Jorge owns an antique car, which he has restored himself.
Combine the fragment with another sentence.

Solution B

Linda returned the novel to the library. She had not yet read the last four chapters, though.

Jorge owns an antique car. He has restored it himself.
Rewrite the fragment as a complete sentence, eliminating the subordinating conjunction or the relative pronoun and adding a subject or other words necessary to make a complete thought.

Fragment that lacks both a subject and a verb

> frag   The chorus sang Kirsten's favorite song. "Misty."
>
> frag   Keisha found the kitten. In her dresser drawer.

Solution

The chorus sang Kirsten's favorite song, "Misty."

Keisha found the kitten in her dresser drawer.
Combine the fragment with another sentence.

Need More Help?

If you need more help in avoiding sentence fragments, turn to 13.9, pages 496–498.

PROBLEM 1

Comma splice—two main clauses separated only by a comma

run-on
> Andres could not attend the meeting, he had a previous commitment.

Solution A

Andres could not attend the meeting. He had a previous commitment.

Replace the comma with an end mark of punctuation, such as a period or a question mark, and begin the new sentence with a capital letter.

Solution B

Andres could not attend the meeting; he had a previous commitment.

Place a semicolon between the two main clauses.

Solution C

Andres could not attend the meeting, for he had a previous commitment.

Add a coordinating conjunction after the comma.

PROBLEM 2

Two main clauses with no punctuation between them

run-on
> Mariko writes poetry one of her poems was recently published.

Solution A

Mariko writes poetry. One of her poems was recently published.

Separate the main clauses with an end mark of punctuation, such as a period or a question mark, and begin the second sentence with a capital letter.

Solution B

Mariko writes poetry; one of her poems was recently published.
Separate the main clauses with a semicolon.

Solution C

Mariko writes poetry, and one of her poems was recently published.
Add a comma and a coordinating conjunction between the main clauses.

PROBLEM 3

Two main clauses with no comma before the coordinating conjunction

run-on
```
Last year Julius won the contest easily but
this year the competition is stiffer.
```

run-on
```
We saw several deer and raccoons were everywhere.
```

Solution

Last year Julius won the contest easily, but this year the competition is stiffer.

We saw several deer, and raccoons were everywhere.
Add a comma before the coordinating conjunction to separate the two main clauses.

Need More Help?

If you need more help in avoiding run-on sentences, turn to 13.10, pages 498–500.

9.3 Lack of Subject-Verb Agreement

PROBLEM 1

A subject that is separated from the verb by an intervening prepositional phrase

agr	The brightness of those colors (please) the baby.
agr	The sources of revenue (has) increased.

Do not mistake the object of a preposition for the subject of a sentence.

Solution
The brightness of those colors pleases the baby.

The sources of revenue have increased.
Make the verb agree with the subject, which is never the object of a preposition.

PROBLEM 2

A predicate nominative that differs in number from the subject

agr	Crossword puzzles (is) his favorite pastime.

Solution
Crossword puzzles are his favorite pastime.
Ignore the predicate nominative, and make the verb agree with the subject of the sentence.

PROBLEM 3

A subject that follows the verb

agr	At the bottom of the stairs (stand) a statue.
agr	Here (comes) the newest members of the cheerleading squad.

At the bottom of the stairs stands a statue.

Here come the newest members of the cheerleading squad.
In an inverted sentence look for the subject *after* the verb. Then
make sure the verb agrees with the subject.

PROBLEM 4

A collective noun as the subject

agr	The audience always (cheer) loudly for that singing group.
agr	The quartet (comes) from several nearby communities.

Solution A
The audience always cheers loudly for that singing group.
If the collective noun refers to a group as a whole, use a singular verb.

Solution B
The quartet come from several nearby communities.
If the collective noun refers to each member of a group individually,
use a plural verb.

PROBLEM 5

A noun of amount as the subject

agr	Fifty dollars (seem) high for that radio.
agr	Three strikes (makes) an out in baseball.

Solution
Fifty dollars seems high for that radio.

Three strikes make an out in baseball.
Determine whether the noun of amount refers to one unit and is
therefore singular or whether it refers to a number of individual
units and is therefore plural.

PROBLEM 6

A compound subject that is joined by and

agr   Sodium and chlorine (combines) to form table salt.

agr   Fish and chips (are) on the menu today.

Solution A

Sodium and chlorine combine to form table salt.
If the parts of the compound subject do not belong to one unit or if they refer to different people or things, use a plural verb.

Solution B

Fish and chips is on the menu today.
If the parts of the compound subject belong to one unit or if both parts refer to the same person or thing, use a singular verb.

PROBLEM 7

A compound subject that is joined by or *or* nor

agr   Neither Ed nor the twins (likes) to travel.

agr   Either the pasta or the fish (are) excellent.

Solution

Neither Ed nor the twins like to travel.

Either the pasta or the fish is excellent.
Make the verb agree with the subject that is closer to it.

PROBLEM 8

A compound subject that is preceded by many a, every, *or* each

agr   Many a boy and girl (have) great ambitions.

When *many a*, *each*, or *every* precedes a compound subject, the subject is considered singular.

Solution
Many a boy and girl has great ambitions.
Use a singular verb when *many a*, *each*, or *every* precedes a compound subject.

PROBLEM 9

A subject that is separated from the verb by an intervening expression

aqr   Carl, as well as Mattie, (love) to swim.

Certain expressions, such as *as well as*, *in addition to*, and *together with*, do not change the number of the subject.

Solution
Carl, as well as Mattie, loves to swim.
Ignore an intervening expression between a subject and its verb. Make the verb agree with the subject.

PROBLEM 10

An indefinite pronoun as the subject

aqr   Each of the students (are) giving a report.

Some indefinite pronouns are singular, some are plural, and some can be either singular or plural, depending upon the noun they refer to. (See page 553 for a list of indefinite pronouns.)

Solution
Each of the students is giving a report.
Determine whether the indefinite pronoun is singular or plural, and make the verb agree.

If you need more help with subject-verb agreement, turn to 16.1 through 16.7, pages 545–554.

9.4 Lack of Pronoun-Antecedent Agreement

PROBLEM 1

A singular antecedent that can be either male or female

ant A good doctor treats his patients considerately.

ant A member may be accompanied by his guest.

Traditionally a masculine pronoun is used to refer to an antecedent that may be either male or female. This usage ignores or excludes females.

Solution A
A good doctor treats his or her patients considerately.

A member may be accompanied by his or her guest.
Reword the sentence to use *he or she*, *him or her*, and so on.

Solution B
Good doctors treat their patients considerately.

Members may be accompanied by their guests.
Reword the sentence so that both the antecedent and the pronoun are plural.

Solution C
A good doctor treats patients considerately.

A member may be accompanied by a guest.
Reword the sentence to eliminate the pronoun.

PROBLEM 2

A second-person pronoun that refers to a third-person antecedent

ant Milena and Sean like volunteer work because it gives you a chance to help others.

Do not refer to an antecedent in the third person using the second-person pronoun *you*.

Solution A
Milena and Sean like volunteer work because it gives them a chance to help others.
Use the appropriate third-person pronoun.

Solution B
Milena and Sean like volunteer work because volunteers have a chance to help others.
Use an appropriate noun instead of a pronoun.

PROBLEM 3

A singular indefinite pronoun as an antecedent

ant   Each of the women finished (their) work quickly.

ant   Neither of the boys remembered to bring (their) lunch.

Each, everyone, either, neither, and *one* are singular and therefore require singular personal pronouns.

Solution
Each of the women finished her work quickly.

Neither of the boys remembered to bring his lunch.
Don't be fooled by a prepositional phrase that contains a plural noun. Determine whether the indefinite pronoun antecedent is singular or plural, and make the noun agree.

If you need more help with pronoun-antecedent agreement, turn to 16.7, pages 553–554, and 17.6, pages 573–574.

9.5   Lack of Clear Pronoun Reference

PROBLEM 1

A pronoun reference that is weak or vague

ref   My article was poorly written, (which) was the result of careless research.

ref   The dry cleaners ruined my new sweater, and (that) annoyed me greatly.

ref   The candidates argued for an hour about details of the budget, and so (it) was boring.

Be sure that *this*, *that*, *which*, and *it* have a clear antecedent.

Solution A
My article was poorly written and contained factual errors, which were the result of careless research.
Rewrite the sentence, adding a clear antecedent for the pronoun.

Solution B
The dry cleaners ruined my new sweater, and their carelessness annoyed me greatly.

The candidates argued for an hour about details of the budget, and so the debate was boring.
Rewrite the sentence, substituting a noun for the pronoun.

PROBLEM 2

A pronoun that refers to more than one antecedent

ref   Shotaro told David that (he) had missed the deadline.

ref   When the chorus performed for the hospital patients, (they) enjoyed themselves.

Solution A
Shotaro told David that David had missed the deadline.
Rewrite the sentence, substituting a noun for the pronoun.

Solution B

The chorus enjoyed performing for the hospital patients.

Rewrite the sentence, making the antecedent of the pronoun clear.

PROBLEM 3

The indefinite use of you *or* they

ref   In many European countries (you) are expected to master English at an early age.

ref   Maria and Suki went to the museum, where (they) have a dazzling display of minerals.

Solution A

In many European countries children are expected to master English at an early age.

Rewrite the sentence, substituting a noun for the pronoun.

Solution B

Maria and Suki went to the museum, where there is a dazzling display of minerals.

Rewrite the sentence, eliminating the pronoun entirely.

If you need more help in making clear pronoun references, turn to 17.7, pages 579–580.

PROBLEM

An incorrect shift in person between two pronouns

> *pro*   They spent their vacation in Glacier National Park, where (you) see remnants of ancient glaciers.
>
> *pro*   I like traveling in the West, where (you) can still find great expanses of unsettled land.
>
> *pro*   One has choices to make in life: (you) can either move ahead or remain in place.

Incorrect pronoun shifts occur when a writer or speaker uses a pronoun in one person and then illogically shifts to a pronoun in another person.

Solution A

They spent their vacation in Glacier National Park, where they saw remnants of ancient glaciers.

I like traveling in the West, where I can still find great expanses of unsettled land.

One has choices to make in life: one can either move ahead or remain in place.

Replace the incorrect pronoun with a pronoun that agrees with its antecedent.

Solution B

They spent their vacation in Glacier National Park, where vacationers can see remnants of ancient glaciers.

I like traveling in the West, where travelers can still find great expanses of unsettled land.

Replace the incorrect pronoun with an appropriate noun.

If you need more help in eliminating incorrect pronoun shifts, turn to 17.6, pages 576–577.

9.7   Shift in Verb Tense

PROBLEM 1

An unnecessary shift in tense

shift t Whenever Alice watches the news, she (paid) particular attention to the weather report.

shift t I dropped my menu just as the waiter (arrives.)

When two or more events occur at the same time, be sure to use the same verb tense to describe each event.

Solution

Whenever Alice watches the news, she pays particular attention to the weather report.

I put down my menu just as the waiter arrived.
Use the same tense for both verbs.

PROBLEM 2

A lack of correct shift in tenses to show that one event precedes or follows another

shift t By the time Enrique called, we (left.)

When events being described have occurred at different times, shift tenses to show that one event precedes or follows another.

Solution

By the time Enrique called, we had left.
Shift from the past tense to the past perfect tense to indicate that one action began and ended before another past action began. Use the past perfect tense for the earlier of the two actions.

Need More Help?

If you need more help with shifts in verb tenses, turn to 15.4, page 528, and 15.6, pages 532–533.

9.8 Incorrect Verb Tense or Form

PROBLEM 1

An incorrect or missing verb ending

tense Three new stores (open) in the mall last week.

tense Have you ever (wish) for a second chance?

Solution

Three new stores opened in the mall last week.

Have you ever wished for a second chance?

Add *-ed* to a regular verb to form the past tense and the past participle.

PROBLEM 2

An improperly formed irregular verb

tense Max (creeped) along behind the hedges looking for the ball.

tense Lawana (lended) me her computer software.

Irregular verbs form their past and past participle in some way other than by adding *-ed*. Memorize these forms, or look them up.

Solution

Max crept along behind the hedges looking for the ball.

Lawana lent me her computer software.

Use the correct past or past participle form of an irregular verb.

PROBLEM 3

Confusion between the past form and the past participle

tense Have you ever (rode) on a monorail?

tense Karen has (drank) the last of the juice.

Solution

Have you ever ridden on a monorail?

Karen has drunk the last of the juice.

Use the past participle form of an irregular verb, not the past form, when you use the auxiliary verb *have*.

PROBLEM 4

Improper use of the past participle

tense	To our dismay it begun to rain hard.
tense	We sung all our favorite songs for the guests.

The past participle of an irregular verb cannot stand alone as a verb. It must be used with the auxiliary verb *have*.

Solution A

To our dismay it has begun to rain hard.

We have sung all our favorite songs for our guests.

Add the auxiliary verb *have* to the past participle to form a complete verb.

Solution B

To our dismay it began to rain hard.

We sang all our favorite songs for the guests.

Replace the past participle with the past form of the verb.

If you need more help with correct verb forms, turn to 15.1, page 521, and 15.2, pages 521–524.

9.9　Misplaced or Dangling Modifier

PROBLEM 1

A misplaced modifier

> *mod*　The woman in the front row (with the red dress) is our new swimming coach.
>
> *mod*　(Cleaned and polished,) Kareem proudly viewed his car.

Modifiers that modify the wrong word or seem to modify more than one word in a sentence are called misplaced modifiers.

Solution

The woman with the red dress in the front row is our new swimming coach.

Kareem proudly viewed his cleaned and polished car.
Move the misplaced phrase as close as possible to the word or words it modifies.

PROBLEM 2

The adverb *only* misplaced

> *mod*　Juana (only) eats mushrooms on her pizza.

The meaning of your sentence may be unclear if the word *only* is misplaced.

Solution

Only Juana eats mushrooms on her pizza.

Juana eats only mushrooms on her pizza.

Juana eats mushrooms only on her pizza.
Place the adverb *only* immediately before the word or group of words it modifies. Note that each time *only* is moved in the sentence, the meaning of the sentence changes.

A dangling modifier

mod (Having lost the directions,) the house was hard to find.

mod (After hiking for hours,) the mountaintop finally came into sight.

mod (Following the recipe carefully,) the soup was easy to make.

Dangling modifiers do not logically seem to modify any word in the sentence.

> **Solution**
>
> **Having lost the directions, we had trouble finding the house.**
>
> **After hiking for hours, Tasha finally saw the mountaintop.**
>
> **Following the recipe carefully, Daryl found the soup easy to make.**
>
> Rewrite the sentence, adding a noun to which the dangling phrase clearly refers. Often you will have to add other words, too.

If you need more help with misplaced or dangling modifiers, turn to 18.7, pages 599–602.

9.10 Missing or Misplaced Possessive Apostrophe

PROBLEM 1

Singular nouns

> *poss*   The (mayors) assistant greeted the delegation.
>
> *poss*   The (actress) dressing room was opulent.

Solution

The mayor's assistant greeted the delegation.

The actress's dressing room was opulent.
Use an apostrophe and an *-s* to form the possessive of a singular noun, even one that ends in *-s*.

PROBLEM 2

Plural nouns ending in -s

> *poss*   The (teachers) lounge is down that corridor.

Solution

The teachers' lounge is down that corridor.
Use an apostrophe alone to form the possessive of a plural noun that ends in *-s*.

PROBLEM 3

Plural nouns not ending in -s

> *poss*   The (mens) tennis team practices at four o'clock.

Solution

The men's tennis team practices at four o'clock.
Use an apostrophe and an *-s* to form the possessive of a plural noun that does not end in *-s*.

PROBLEM 4

Pronouns

> *poss*   Is (everyones) name correctly spelled?
>
> *poss*   The package on the table is (your's.)

Solution A

Is everyone's name correctly spelled?

Use an apostrophe and an *-s* to form the possessive of a singular indefinite pronoun.

Solution B

The package on the table is yours.

Do not use an apostrophe with any of the possessive personal pronouns.

PROBLEM 5

Confusion between its *and* it's

> *poss*   A canyon wren was warbling (it's) melodic song.
>
> *poss*   (Its) wise to take an umbrella.

The possessive of *it* is *its*. *It's* is the contraction of *it is*.

Solution A

A canyon wren was warbling its melodic song.

Do not use an apostrophe to form the possessive of *it*.

Solution B

It's wise to take an umbrella.

Use an apostrophe to form the contraction of *it is*.

If you need more help with apostrophes and possessives, turn to 17.1, page 566, and 21.13, page 671.

9.11 Missing Commas with Nonessential Element

PROBLEM 1

Missing commas with nonessential participles, infinitives, and their phrases

com   Jesse‿obviously pleased‿stood admiring the large mural.

com   My sister‿looking a little anxious‿hesitated before her first dive from the high tower.

com   To be sure‿no one can help you if you will not help yourself.

Solution

Jesse, obviously pleased, stood admiring the large mural.

My sister, looking a little anxious, hesitated before her first dive from the high tower.

To be sure, no one can help you if you will not help yourself.
Determine whether the participle, infinitive, or phrase is truly not essential to the meaning of the sentence. If so, set off the phrase with commas.

PROBLEM 2

Missing commas with nonessential adjective clauses

com   His most recent play‿which was written in just one week‿has won every major award.

Solution
His most recent play, which was written in just one week, has won every major award.
Determine whether the clause is truly not essential to the meaning of the sentence. If so, set off the clause with commas.

Missing commas with nonessential appositives

> *com*   Roberto Morales◦our class president◦will represent us at the convention.

Solution
Roberto Morales, our class president, will represent us at the convention.
Determine whether the appositive is truly not essential to the meaning of the sentence. If so, set off the appositive with commas.

Missing commas with interjections and parenthetical expressions

> *com*   My goodness◦movie tickets have become expensive.
>
> *com*   Elaine said◦I think◦that she would be here by seven o'clock.

Solution
My goodness, movie tickets have become expensive.

Elaine said, I think, that she would be here by seven o'clock.
Set off the interjection or parenthetical expression with commas.

If you need more help with commas and nonessential elements, turn to 21.6, pages 655–657.

9.12　Missing Commas in a Series

PROBLEM

Missing commas in a series of words, phrases, or clauses

↓ com　Yvette packed the basket with enough sandwiches◦ salad◦soup◦and fruit for everyone.

↓ com　Manuel carefully turned the knob◦opened the door◦ and peered into the darkened room.

↓ com　We watched the mouse scamper across the table-cloth◦down a chair leg◦and under the refrigerator.

↓ com　Pat saw the sailboat drifting with the tide◦ riding the waves◦and skimming the blue water.

↓ com　In our trio Neil sings tenor◦Otis sings baritone◦and Tom sings bass.

Solution

Yvette packed the basket with enough sandwiches, salad, soup, and fruit for everyone.

Manuel carefully turned the knob, opened the door, and peered into the darkened room.

We watched the mouse scamper across the tablecloth, down a chair leg, and under the refrigerator.

Pat saw the sailboat drifting with the tide, riding the waves, and skimming the blue water.

In our trio Neil sings tenor, Otis sings baritone, and Tom sings bass.

When there are three or more elements in a series, use a comma after each element, including the element preceded by a conjunction.

If you need more help with commas in a series, turn to 21.6, pages 653–654.

Unit 10 Parts of Speech

10.1 Nouns

A **noun** is a word that names a person, a place, a thing, or an idea.

PERSON	aunt, astronaut, Ramón, daughter-in-law, child
PLACE	universe, village, bedroom, North Carolina
THING	shark, eagle, oak, foot
IDEA	pride, honor, dignity, hope, 1992

A **concrete noun** names an object that occupies space or that can be recognized by any of the senses.

stone   lightning   shout   air   salt

An **abstract noun** names an idea, a quality, or a characteristic.

sadness   hope   anger   clarity   dissonance

Nouns are singular or plural. A singular noun names one person, place, thing, or idea. A plural noun names more than one.

SINGULAR	mask, briefcase, fly, loaf, woman
PLURAL	masks, briefcases, flies, loaves, women

Nouns have a possessive form, which is used to show possession, ownership, or the relationship between two nouns.

SINGULAR POSSESSIVE	PLURAL POSSESSIVE
a **boy's** hat	the **boys'** hats
the **country's** laws	those **countries'** laws
a **woman's** smile	**women's** smiles

Exercise 1

Identifying Nouns   On your paper write each of the twenty nouns that appear in the following paragraph.

Lucy Terry, Poet

[1]According to the scholar Blyden Jackson, a teen-ager named Lucy Terry was the first African-American poet. [2]This claim is based on one short work bearing her name. [3]Born in Africa around 1730, Terry came to America as a slave but was later freed. [4]The poem describes an attack on the French by Indian allies in Massachusetts, her home after her marriage.

Exercise 2

Supplying Abstract and Concrete Nouns   For each concrete noun in items 1–5, write an abstract noun that names an idea with which the concrete noun can be associated. For each abstract noun in items 6–10, write a concrete noun that has the quality of the abstract noun.

SAMPLE ANSWERS   astronaut—fearlessness
darkness—cave

1. athlete
2. thunder
3. roses
4. honey
5. toothache
6. authority
7. truth
8. tranquility
9. sourness
10. guilt

Exercise 3

Completing Sentences with Nouns   On your paper complete each sentence by filling in the blanks with nouns. Be sure that your completed sentences make sense.

1. We discovered four _____ in the old _____.
2. Ramón's _____ to help others wins my _____.
3. A(n) _____ destroyed the _____.
4. The _____ soared high over the _____.
5. The _____ reminded us of _____.

Proper and Common Nouns

A **proper noun** is the name of a particular person, place, thing, or idea.

A **common noun** is the general—not the particular—name of a person, place, thing, or idea.

Proper nouns are capitalized; common nouns are generally not capitalized.

PROPER NOUNS	
PERSON	Richard Wright, Connie Chung, Dr. Jonas Salk, Eric the Red
PLACE	Pasadena, Bering Sea, Nicaragua, White House, Saturn
THING	Society of Friends, *Titanic, Native Son,* Memorial Day, Ford Motor Company
IDEA	Augustan Age, Hinduism, Romanticism, Abstract Expressionism

Exercise 4

Matching Proper Nouns with Common Nouns On your paper match the numbered proper nouns on the left with the lettered common nouns on the right.

1. San Antonio
2. Iroquois
3. Patrick Ewing
4. Clara Barton
5. December
6. *Time*
7. Hawaii
8. *A Raisin in the Sun*
9. Toyota Celica
10. Statue of Liberty

a. month
b. car
c. tribe
d. landmark
e. athlete
f. nurse
g. state
h. city
i. play
j. magazine

Collective Nouns

A **collective noun** names a group.

class	(the) faculty
crew	(the) cast
team	(a) herd (of cows)
congregation	(a) swarm (of bees)

A collective noun may be considered either singular or plural. When a collective noun refers to a group as a whole, it is regarded as singular. When a collective noun refers to the individual members of a group, it is regarded as plural.

SINGULAR	The **jury** has reached a verdict.
	The **cast** includes a small chorus.
PLURAL	The **jury** were unable to agree.
	The **cast** stay at different hotels.

Exercise 5

Identifying Collective Nouns   On your paper list the five collective nouns in the following paragraph.

A Nature Study

¹Unloading their gear, the band of naturalists set up their tents along the river by the entrance to the cave. ²Nearby a flock of mallards rests quietly in the shallows while a swarm of gnats reels overhead. ³The party are eager to conduct their separate studies of different aspects of this cave, which is noted for its numerous bats. ⁴As they begin their exploration, none of the naturalists are disappointed to discover a thriving colony of insect-eating mammals.

Exercise 6: Sentence Writing

Creating Sentences with Nouns   Write five sentences about a close friend. Rely especially on concrete nouns to convey a vivid picture of the person.

Exercise 7: Review

Nouns   On your paper complete each sentence by filling in the twenty blanks with the kinds of nouns specified in italics. Be sure that your completed sentences make sense.

1. _proper_ saw a _common_ near the _concrete_.
2. The _abstract_ of _common_ has always intrigued the _collective_.
3. The _collective_ left their _concrete_ at _proper_.
4. Two _concrete_ stalked a _collective_ of _common_.
5. The young _collective_ spent a long, lazy _common_ on their _concrete_.
6. _proper_ was the best _common_ of his _common_.
7. _abstract_ is a(n) _abstract_.

A good writer chooses nouns that will give the reader a clear and vivid mental image. The writer will avoid vague nouns and use instead words with a precise meaning. Moreover, the experienced writer pays close attention to details, using them to help the reader visualize the particular person, place, or thing being described.

In the following passage from *The Waves*, Virginia Woolf uses nouns effectively to describe sunlight flooding a room:

> Sharp-edged wedges of light lay upon the window-sill and showed inside the room plates with blue rings, cups with curved handles, the bulge of a great bowl, the criss-cross pattern in the rug, and the formidable corners and lines of cabinets and bookcases. Behind their conglomeration hung a zone of shadow in which might be a further shape to be disencumbered of shadow or still denser depths of darkness.

Study the passage above closely, and try to apply some of Woolf's techniques when you write and revise your own work.

1. Whenever possible, use precise concrete nouns rather than general or abstract nouns. Notice that Woolf uses precise nouns to describe the objects that the sunlight illuminates in the room: plates, cups, a bowl, the rug, cabinets, bookcases. By listing these objects, Woolf gives us a clearer picture than she would have had she merely said that the sunlight illuminated "the furnishings." Notice also, however, that in the last sentence Woolf does use general nouns to suggest the mysterious areas of darkness remaining in the room: "zone of shadow," "a further shape," "depths of darkness."

2. Try to choose nouns for the effect of their sound as well as for their meaning. For example, notice how the *b* and *l* sounds in Woolf's phrase "the *b*u*l*ge of a great *b*ow*l*" help accentuate the shape and size of the object.

3. Try to expand single nouns into noun phrases. Notice that Woolf expands the nouns "corners" and "lines" into the phrase "the formidable corners and lines of cabinets and bookcases." This expansion helps her make her point that light reveals the particular nature of general shapes.

Practice the techniques described above by revising the following passage on your paper. As you work, pay particular attention to the italicized words.

> When the *moon* slides above the horizon, everything slowly becomes bathed in *light*. The *field* shimmers, and the *trees* loom larger with their own *darkness*. *Anyone* out at this *time of night* is also washed in the *moonlight*. *Everything* is transformed into *something strange*.

10.2 Pronouns

A **pronoun** is a word that takes the place of a noun, a group of words acting as a noun, or another pronoun. The word or group of words that a pronoun refers to is called its **antecedent.**

> Ralph Bunche received the Nobel Prize for Peace in 1950 while **he** served as director of the United Nations Trusteeship Division. [The pronoun *he* takes the place of the noun *Ralph Bunche.*]

> Both Benito Juárez and Emiliano Zapata affected Mexican history. **Each** is regarded as a national hero. [The pronoun *each* takes the place of the nouns *Benito Juárez* and *Emiliano Zapata.*]

> **Few** remembered to bring **their** notebooks to the lecture. [The pronoun *their* takes the place of the pronoun *few,* which stands for an unidentified group of people.]

There are about seventy-five pronouns in the English language. They fall into one or more of the following categories: personal pronouns, possessive pronouns, reflexive and intensive pronouns, demonstrative pronouns, interrogative pronouns, relative pronouns, and indefinite pronouns.

Personal and Possessive Pronouns

A **personal pronoun** refers to a specific person or thing by indicating the person speaking (the first person), the person being addressed (the second person), or any other person or thing being discussed (the third person).

Like nouns, personal pronouns are either singular or plural.

Personal Pronouns		
	Singular	**Plural**
FIRST PERSON	I, me	we, us
SECOND PERSON	you	you
THIRD PERSON	he, him	they, them
	she, her	
	it	

FIRST PERSON	**We** sent Angela a get-well card. [*We* refers to the people speaking.]
SECOND PERSON	Tell Otis to give **you** the key. [*You* refers to the person being addressed.]
THIRD PERSON	**They** told **her** the good news. [*They* and *her* refer to the people being discussed.]

Pronouns in the third-person singular have three **genders:** *he* and *him* are masculine; *she* and *her* are feminine; *it* is neuter (neither masculine nor feminine).

Among the personal pronouns are forms that indicate possession or ownership. These are called **possessive pronouns,** and they take the place of the possessive forms of nouns.

Possessive Pronouns		
	Singular	**Plural**
FIRST PERSON	my, mine	our, ours
SECOND PERSON	your, yours	your, yours
THIRD PERSON	his	their, theirs
	her, hers	
	its	

Where there are two possessive forms, you use the first before a noun and the second alone, in place of a noun.

USED BEFORE A NOUN   Where is **their** house?
USED ALONE   That house is **theirs.**

Exercise 8

Using Personal and Possessive Pronouns   Improve the following paragraph by replacing the underlined words or groups of words with personal or possessive pronouns. Write your answers on your paper.

Christopher Columbus

¹The reader of this passage may already know a great deal about the explorations of Christopher Columbus. ²But how extensive is the reader's knowledge of the earlier days, before Ferdinand and Isabella gave Columbus Ferdinand and Isabella's support for the four voyages to the New World? ³As schoolchildren the reader and the writer of this passage learned that Columbus was born in 1451 in Genoa, Italy. ⁴Genoa was an important port and trading center, although Genoa had been eclipsed by Genoa's rival city, Venice. ⁵Columbus was the oldest of five children; two brothers helped Columbus on later projects. ⁶Columbus's and Columbus's brothers' father was a wool weaver, and young Columbus worked in Columbus's father's shop. ⁷What is not known is when Columbus made his first sea voyages. ⁸What is the reader's guess?

Reflexive and Intensive Pronouns

To form the reflexive and intensive pronouns, add *-self* or *-selves* to certain personal and possessive pronouns.

Reflexive and Intensive Pronouns		
	Singular	**Plural**
FIRST PERSON	myself	ourselves
SECOND PERSON	yourself	yourselves
THIRD PERSON	himself, herself, itself	themselves

A **reflexive pronoun** refers to a noun or another pronoun and indicates that the same person or thing is involved.

He let **himself** into the house.

We considered **ourselves** honored to be invited.

An **intensive pronoun** adds emphasis to another noun or pronoun.

The cast **itself** chose the play.

They built that cabin **themselves**.

Demonstrative Pronouns

A **demonstrative pronoun** points out specific persons, places, things, or ideas.

Demonstrative Pronouns		
SINGULAR	this	that
PLURAL	these	those

Is **this** the guitar you like?   **These** are the only drums left.
Let me do **that** today.   Bring **those** to me.

Exercise 9

Using Reflexive, Intensive, and Demonstrative Pronouns   Supply the appropriate reflexive, intensive, or demonstrative pronoun for each blank. On your paper write the pronoun, and identify whether it is *reflexive, intensive,* or *demonstrative.* ➡

1. After I read *Spring Moon* by Bette Bao Lord, I wanted to discover for _____ how she came to write this novel about her family's past.
2. The novel _____ is a masterpiece of research into the complex and tumultuous history of China in the twentieth century.
3. _____ is Lord's first novel; her first book was a biography of her sister.
4. _____ are books that touch the reader through rich characterization and absorbing situations.
5. Lord _____ has had an eventful life, both as a child in Shanghai during World War II and as the wife of the American ambassador to China.
6. Her first memories were _____: air-raid sirens, people rushing into shelters, bombs falling during the Japanese invasion of Shanghai.
7. When the Communists took control of China, the Bao family suddenly found _____ immigrants in Brooklyn, New York.
8. In the United States young Bette Bao faced problems that were very different from _____ she had encountered in China.
9. Just learning English must have been a struggle in _____, for Lord has said that to Chinese ears "English sounds like somebody gargling water."
10. Lord's description of _____ as an immigrant child gave me a fresh insight into the courage that people must have as they face the challenges of living in a strange new land.

Interrogative and Relative Pronouns

An **interrogative pronoun** is used to form questions.

who?   whom?   whose?   what?   which?

Who were the winners?
Whom did the drama coach praise?
Whose are these?
What does this mean?
Which of these songs do you like?

Whoever, whomever, whosoever, whichever, and *whatever* are the intensive forms of the interrogative pronouns.

Whatever do you want?

A **relative pronoun** is used to begin a special subject-verb word group called a subordinate clause (see Unit 13).

who	whose	whomever	that	what
whom	whoever	which	whichever	whatever

They praised the writer **who** won the prize. [The relative pronoun *who* begins the subordinate clause *who won the prize*.]

Roots, **which** was filmed for television, was written by Alex Haley. [The relative pronoun *which* begins the subordinate clause *which was filmed for television*.]

Exercise 10

Distinguishing Between Interrogative and Relative Pronouns   On your paper list the interrogative and relative pronouns that appear in the following sentences, and label each of them as *interrogative* or *relative*.

Cleopatra, an Extraordinary Queen

1. Which Egyptian queen was one of the most fascinating women in history?
2. At eighteen Cleopatra, who was of Macedonian descent, became queen of Egypt.
3. The coins that were minted during her reign do not portray her as the beautiful woman of legend.
4. Cleopatra, who was ruthless at times, also cared for her subjects' welfare and won their loyalty.
5. Julius Caesar first met Cleopatra in Alexandria, which was Egypt's capital in the first century B.C.
6. Caesar fell in love with Cleopatra, whose intelligence and charm he found captivating.
7. According to history, which other famous Roman leader loved Cleopatra?
8. Do you think Mark Antony, whom Cleopatra married, wished to be the sole ruler of Rome?
9. Which of Shakespeare's plays tells the story of Cleopatra and Antony?
10. Shakespeare's *Antony and Cleopatra* (1607) is one of several well-known literary works that dramatize the extraordinary story of the legendary leader of ancient Rome.

Indefinite Pronouns

An **indefinite pronoun** refers to persons, places, or things in a more general way than a noun does.

Do you know **anyone** who can run as fast as Jackie? [The indefinite pronoun *anyone* does not refer to a specific person.]

Many prefer this style of jacket. [The indefinite pronoun *many* does not refer to a specific group of people.]

When we opened the box of pears, we found that **each** was perfectly ripe. [The indefinite pronoun *each* has the specific antecedent *pears*.]

Some Indefinite Pronouns			
all	either	much	others
another	enough	neither	plenty
any	everybody	nobody	several
anybody	everyone	none	some
anyone	everything	no one	somebody
anything	few	nothing	someone
both	many	one	something
each	most	other	

Exercise 11: Sentence Writing

Using Pronouns   Write ten sentences about a sport that you enjoy watching or playing with friends. Try to use pronouns from all the categories you studied in this lesson.

Exercise 12: Review

Pronouns   (a) On your paper list in order the twenty pronouns that appear in the following paragraphs. (b) Identify each pronoun as *personal, possessive, reflexive, intensive, demonstrative, interrogative, relative,* or *indefinite.*

A Visit to a Tropical Rain Forest

[1]Everyone on our tour enjoyed the last stop best—El Yunque, which means "The Anvil" in Spanish. [2]This is the second highest mountain in Puerto Rico, only a short drive from San Juan. [3]It is special, however, because of the tropical rain forest that covers its slopes. [4]According to the tour guide, the pre-Columbian natives of the island believed El Yunque was the home of the creator god, Yukiyú, who lived on the mist-enshrouded summit. [5]None of us could imagine a better home for him. ➡

⁶Everyone was amazed to learn that the forest's annual rainfall is in excess of 180 inches, an amount conducive to a profuse variety of plant and animal life. ⁷The guide claimed she herself has identified many of the 250 varieties of trees known to exist in the forest. ⁸Walking the trails, we saw cascading waterfalls, orchids, thirty-foot ferns, and flocks of colorful parrots chattering among themselves. ⁹Whoever said an earthly paradise does not exist? ¹⁰If you ever visit Puerto Rico, be sure you spend an afternoon at El Yunque.

10.3   Verbs

A **verb** is a word that expresses action or a state of being and is necessary to make a statement.

Students **concentrate.**	The test **is** tomorrow.
The teacher **reviewed** the story.	The class **became** noisy.

A verb expresses time—present, past, and future—by means of various *tense* forms.

PRESENT TENSE	We **see** the waves.
PAST TENSE	We **saw** the waves.
FUTURE TENSE	We **will see** the waves.

Exercise 13

Adding Verbs to Make Sentences   On your paper write ten complete sentences by supplying a verb for each of the blanks in the items below.

The Excitement of Hot-Air Balloons
1. The hot-air balloons _____ over the countryside.
2. They _____ colorful against the white clouds.
3. Noticing the balloons, villagers _____ outside.
4. Moving with the wind, the balloons _____ silently.
5. The gathering villagers _____ mesmerized.
6. Do you want to watch us _____ a hot-air balloon?
7. First, you _____ the balloon on the ground.
8. A large fan _____ air into the balloon until it is about half full.
9. The pilot _____ a propane burner, heating the air inside the balloon.
10. Gradually the balloon _____, lifting the basket aloft.

Action Verbs

An **action verb** tells what someone or something does.

Action verbs can express action that is either physical or mental.

PHYSICAL ACTION   The baker **prepared** the cake.
MENTAL ACTION   The baker **studied** the recipe closely.

A **transitive verb** is an action verb that is followed by a word or words that answer the question *what?* or *whom?*

The athletes **obey** their coach. [The action verb *obey* is followed by the noun *coach*, which answers the question *obey whom?*]

An **intransitive verb** is an action verb that is *not* followed by a word that answers the question *what?* or *whom?*

The athletes **obey** immediately without protest. [The action verb is followed by words that tell *when* and *how*.]

Exercise 14

Recognizing Action Verbs   Write on your paper the action verb in each of the following sentences. Indicate whether each action verb is used as a *transitive* or an *intransitive* verb.

The Anasazi

1. The Anasazi, ancestors of many Native American peoples of the Southwest, lived in parts of Colorado, Arizona, New Mexico, and Utah.
2. They first settled there almost two thousand years ago.
3. The ruins of one of their most spectacular settlements survive high on the Mesa Verde, a plateau in Colorado.
4. The earliest Anasazi, skillful basket makers, hunted game for much of their food.
5. Later Anasazi, famous for their exquisite jewelry and pottery designs, also cultivated the land.
6. We know these Native Americans by another name—the Pueblo, from the Spanish word for "town."
7. In time the name Pueblo identified not only the Anasazi themselves but also their descendants.
8. The height of the development of the Anasazi culture occurred between the years 1050 and 1300.
9. Sometime during the fourteenth century the Anasazi left their homes for reasons still unknown.
10. Their legacy, however, continues in the traditions and customs of such peoples as the Hopi and the Zuñi.

Exercise 15: Sentence Writing

Creating Sentences with Action Verbs   Choose five of
the action verbs that you identified in Exercise 14. For each
verb write one sentence.

Exercise 16: Sentence Writing

**Creating Sentences with Transitive and Intransitive
Verbs**   For each of the following action verbs, write two sentences. First, use the verb as a transitive verb. Then use it as an
intransitive verb.

1. ride   **4.** fly
2. spin   **5.** rush
3. plunge

Linking Verbs

A **linking verb** links, or joins, the subject of a sentence (often a
noun or pronoun) with a word or expression that identifies or
describes the subject.

Be in all its forms is the most commonly used linking verb. Forms of
be include *am, is, are, was, were, will be, has been*, and *was being*.

The hiker **is** an expert.   The noise **was** loud.
These trees **are** rare.   The bus **will be** late.

In addition, several other verbs can act as linking verbs.

Other Linking Verbs			
appear	grow	seem	stay
become	look	smell	taste
feel	remain	sound	

Exercise 17

Identifying Action and Linking Verbs   On your paper
write the verb that appears in each of the following sentences.
Then identify each verb as either an *action verb* or a *linking
verb*. ➡

Virginia Hamilton, Novelist

1. Yellow Springs, Ohio, was the childhood home of the author Virginia Hamilton.
2. The southern Ohio area became part of the Underground Railroad system for runaway slaves on their way to freedom in the North.
3. Virginia Hamilton's ancestors lived as slaves in the United States.
4. The setting of *The House of Dies Drear* by Virginia Hamilton is a southern Ohio community.
5. The large old houses of Hamilton's own community were hideouts for slaves during the Civil War.
6. *The House of Dies Drear* tells a present-day mystery story with connections to the period of the Underground Railroad.
7. From early childhood, writing was Virginia Hamilton's strongest ambition.
8. Virginia Hamilton studied at both Antioch College and Ohio State University.
9. Hamilton's husband is an author, too.
10. Before her return to Yellow Springs, Hamilton lived for many years in New York City.

Verb Phrases

The verb in a sentence may consist of more than one word. The words that accompany the main verb are called **auxiliary,** or helping, **verbs.**

A **verb phrase** consists of a main verb and all its auxiliary, or helping, verbs.

Auxiliary Verbs	
FORMS OF *BE*	am, is, are, was, were, being, been
FORMS OF *HAVE*	has, have, had, having
OTHER AUXILIARIES	can, could
	do, does, did
	may, might
	must
	shall, should
	will, would

The most commonly used auxiliary verbs are the forms of *be* and *have*. They enable the main verb to express various tenses.

> She **is talking.**
> She **has talked.**
> She **had been talking.**

The other auxiliary verbs are not used primarily to express time.

> Binh **should be coming.**
> They **might have followed.**
> **Could** Marisa **have sung?**
> I **will stay.**

Exercise 18

Identifying Verb Phrases   On your paper write each verb phrase that appears in the following sentences. (Four of the sentences have more than one verb phrase.) Put parentheses around the auxiliary verbs in each phrase. (Words that interrupt a verb phrase are not considered part of the verb phrase.)

Justice Holmes

1. "We must think things, not words."
2. The above words were spoken by Supreme Court Justice Oliver Wendell Holmes Jr. in 1899.
3. Holmes was still expressing eloquent ideas thirty-two years later, when he was approaching the age of ninety.
4. In 1871, five years after he had graduated from Harvard Law School, Holmes was appointed university lecturer on jurisprudence at that same institution.
5. After he had spent a year in the law office of George Shattuck, Holmes was well prepared for the Massachusetts bar exam.
6. Holmes had by then expressed interest in the position of chief justice of Massachusetts.
7. In 1902 Justice Holmes would move to Washington, D.C., as a member of the Supreme Court.
8. Generations of law students have read, and undoubtedly will continue reading, Justice Holmes's Supreme Court opinions.
9. You might enjoy Francis Biddle's biography, *Mr. Justice Holmes.*
10. According to Justice Oliver Wendell Holmes, the law must be expedient for the community.

Creating Sentences with Vivid Verbs Write five sentences that describe how a particular animal moves. Choose very specific action verbs and verb phrases to convey a vivid sense of movement.

Verbs On your paper write the verb in each sentence in this passage. Identify each verb as an *action* or a *linking verb*. Also identify each action verb as *transitive* or *intransitive*.

All About Broccoli

[1]Broccoli originally grew in Asia Minor. [2]In ancient times it was one of the favorite vegetables of the Romans. [3]Since then it has had a permanent place in Italian cuisine. [4]By the early eighth century cultivation of broccoli extended to England. [5]Americans owe their familiarity with broccoli to nineteenth-century European immigrants. [6]A member of the cabbage family, this bright green vegetable is nutritious and versatile. [7]It can serve as a side dish or as the principal ingredient of a main dish. [8]For example, you might serve broccoli with pasta and oil and garlic. [9]At the grocery store choose only heads with unopened flowers. [10]This flavorful vegetable should be available year round.

Writing Link

Writers use vivid verbs to evoke expressive and clear-cut images. Read the following passage, which opens the short story "A Summer Tragedy" by Arna Bontemps. As you read, pay particular attention to the italicized verbs.

Old Jeff Patton, the black share farmer, *fumbled* with his bow tie. His fingers *trembled* and the high stiff collar *pinched* his throat. A fellow *loses* his hand for such vanities after thirty or forty years of simple life. Once a year, or maybe twice if there*'s* a wedding among his kinfolks, he *may spruce up;* but generally fancy clothes *do* nothing but *adorn* the wall of the big room and *feed* the moths.

Here are some of Bontemps's techniques that you can apply when you write and revise your own work:

1. Use action verbs rather than linking verbs wherever possible. Notice that only one linking verb—*is* contracted to "*'s*"—appears in the passage. All the other verbs express actions that readers can picture. In the second sentence, for instance, the action verb "pinched" is much more vivid than a linking verb would be: consider the difference between "the high stiff collar *pinched* his throat" and "the high stiff collar *was* uncomfortable."

2. Try to use precise action verbs rather than more general verbs. For example, instead of saying "Jeff Patton *handled* or

adjusted his bow tie," Bontemps uses the verb "fumbled." *Fumbled* is more precise and more vivid than either *handled* or *adjusted* would be.

3. Try to replace a group of words with a single action verb. Bontemps could have said that the fancy clothes "*provide food for the moths,*" but he chooses the much stronger action verb "feed" instead.

4. Choose verbs that contribute to the overall feeling or attitude that you want to convey. Bontemps, for example, wants to convey the awkwardness and discomfort a simple farmer feels when he must dress in fancy clothing. Notice how the verbs "fumbled," "trembled," and "pinched" all stress the farmer's awkwardness and discomfort.

Practice these techniques by revising this passage on a sheet of paper. Pay special attention to the italicized words.

Tourists *take enjoyment in* the snowy peaks and sunny beaches that *are on* the island of Hawaii. The island's largest city, Hilo, *creates a surprise for* many visitors. With its stone lanterns and bridges, Hilo *is like* a Japanese city. Nearby Akaka Falls *falls* 442 feet into a beautiful rocky pool. A short distance away *is* Mauna Kea, Hawaii's highest volcano. At Kaimu the black sand that *covers* the beach *appears to glisten* in the ample sunlight. Sunbathers *lie* on the sand, and swimmers *swim* in the warm ocean waters.

10.4 Adjectives

An **adjective** is a word that modifies a noun or pronoun by limiting its meaning.

quiet song	**two** dollars	**that** house
baby turtles	**Korean** cooking	**these** shoes
blue sky	**official** documents	**few** people

You can consider possessive pronouns—such as *my, our,* and *your*—adjectives because they modify nouns in addition to serving as pronouns: *my* dog, *our* dream, *your* accomplishments. Similarly, you can consider possessive nouns adjectives: *Tanya's* vacation.

An adjective's position in relation to the word it modifies may vary.

How **green** the leaves are!
The **green** leaves shook in the breeze.
The leaves are **green.**
Sunlight makes the leaves **green.**
The leaves, **green** as emeralds, shook in the breeze.

Many adjectives have different forms to indicate their degree of comparison.

POSITIVE	COMPARATIVE	SUPERLATIVE
fast	faster	fastest
happy	happier	happiest
beautiful	more beautiful	most beautiful
good	better	best

Exercise 21

Finding Adjectives   On your paper list the twenty-three adjectives in the following passage. Count possessive nouns and pronouns as adjectives in this exercise, but do not count the words *a, an,* and *the.*

Literature: Rainy Mountain

[1]A single knoll rises out of the plain in Oklahoma, north and west of the Wichita Range. [2]For my people, the Kiowas, it is an old landmark, and they gave it the name Rainy Mountain. [3]The hardest weather in the world is there. [4]Winter brings blizzards, hot tornadic winds arise in the spring, and in summer the prairie is an anvil's edge. [5]The grass turns brittle and brown, and it cracks beneath your feet. [6]There are green belts along the rivers and creeks, linear groves of hickory and pecan, willow and witch hazel. [7]At ⇒

a distance in July or August the steaming foliage seems almost to writhe in fire. [8]Great green and yellow grass-hoppers are everywhere in the tall grass, popping up like corn to sting the flesh, and tortoises crawl about on the red earth, going nowhere in the plenty of time. [9]Loneliness is an aspect of the land. . . . [10]To look upon that landscape in the early morning, with the sun at your back, is to lose the sense of proportion.

From *The Way to Rainy Mountain* by N. Scott Momaday

Exercise 22: Sentence Writing

Creating Sentences with Adjectives   Select five of the adjectives from the sentences in Exercise 21. Write five sentences of your own, using each one.

Articles

Articles are the adjectives *a*, *an*, and *the*. *A* and *an* are called indefinite articles. *The* is called a definite article.

INDEFINITE	I wrote **a** poem.
	Luisa wrote **an** essay.
DEFINITE	I wrote **the** poem.
	Luisa wrote **the** essay.

Proper Adjectives

A **proper adjective** is formed from a proper noun and begins with a capital letter.

Federico García Lorca was a **Spanish** writer.
They believe in the **Jeffersonian** ideals of democracy.
Russian is written in the **Cyrillic** alphabet.

The suffixes *-an*, *-ian*, *-n*, *-ese*, and *-ish* are often used to create proper adjectives.

PROPER NOUNS	PROPER ADJECTIVES
Augustus Caesar	Augustan
Brazil	Brazilian
America	American
China	Chinese
Finland	Finnish

Exercise 23

Forming Proper Adjectives   Write a proper adjective formed from each of the following proper nouns. Consult a dictionary if you need help.

1. India
2. Laos
3. Albert Einstein
4. Norway
5. Scotland
6. Venus
7. Chile
8. Japan
9. Bali
10. Peru

Exercise 24: Sentence Writing

Creating Sentences with Adjectives   Write five sentences about a place you have always wanted to visit. Describe the place as vividly as you can. Use a variety of adjectives, including those that describe, classify, identify, and qualify.

Exercise 25: Review

Adjectives   On your paper write the twenty adjectives, including articles, that appear in the following paragraph.

Marianne Moore, American Poet

[1]Some critics consider Marianne Moore the most delightful American poet. [2]Her witty, sharp poems quickly grasp the attention of readers. [3]Her vision is original and precise but rather eccentric. [4]The brilliant and oblique surfaces of her poems are filled with observations of animals and nature. [5]Often she cryptically tosses in mysterious but appropriate quotations from her extensive reading.

Study this description of the Texas desert from *Blue Highways*, William Least Heat-Moon's book about traveling across America. Notice how the italicized adjectives help make the description effective:

> There was nothing *gradual* about the change—it was *sudden* and *clear*. Within a mile or so, the bluebonnets vanished as if evaporated, the soil turned *tan* and *granular*, and *squatty* trees got *squattier* with *each* mile as if *reluctant* to reach too far from their *deep*, *wet* taproots. . . . From the tops of the tableland, I could watch *empty* roadway reaching for miles to the scimitar of a horizon *visible* at every *compass* point. It was *fine* to see the *curving* edge of the *old blue* ball of a world.

Try to apply some of Least Heat-Moon's techniques when you write and revise your own work:

1. Use adjectives to make nouns more specific. Least Heat-Moon's nouns are made more specific by his use of vivid adjectives that describe color ("tan," "blue"), size or shape ("squatty," "deep," "curving"), texture ("granular"), and other physical characteristics ("wet," "empty"). These adjectives all appeal to our senses.

2. Use adjectives to make abstract nouns more concrete. In Least Heat-Moon's opening sentence, for example, the abstract noun "change" becomes concrete and vivid because the adjectives "sudden" and "clear" help us picture it.

3. Keep in mind that not every noun requires an adjective. Notice, for instance, that Least Heat-Moon does not use an adjective to describe the Texas wildflowers known as bluebonnets. There is little need to describe these flowers, since their name in itself gives us a good idea of what they look like.

Practice these techniques by revising the following passage on a separate sheet of paper. Add adjectives where you think they will be helpful, and remove those that you feel are unnecessary.

> Trudging through the town, Carla at first heard nothing but the cawing of a crow. Then from the porch of a house on a side street came the strumming of a banjo. The sound lightened Carla's spirits, and she approached the porch to hear the tuneful music better. Perched on the railing in the darkish shadows was a young male farm boy dressed in overalls and a shirt. Although the banjo, with its neck, seemed cumbersome for the boy, he nevertheless managed to pluck out tune after tune.

10.5 Adverbs

An **adverb** is a word that modifies a verb, an adjective, or another adverb by making its meaning more specific.

In the following sentence you can see how adverbs are used to modify an adjective (*intelligent*), a verb (*leap*), and an adverb (*high*):

Surprisingly intelligent dolphins leap **very high.**

Adverbs tell *when, where, how,* and *to what degree.*

My uncle paid me a visit **yesterday.**
Many birds fly **south** for the winter.
The judge ruled **fairly.**
You have been **exceedingly** kind.

Some adverbs, like adjectives, take different forms to indicate the degree of comparison.

POSITIVE	COMPARATIVE	SUPERLATIVE
sat **near**	sat **nearer**	sat **nearest**
walks **slowly**	walks **more slowly**	walks **most slowly**
sings **badly**	sings **worse**	sings **worst**

An adverb that modifies a verb may be placed in different positions in relation to the verb. An adverb that modifies an adjective or another adverb must immediately precede the word it modifies.

MODIFYING A VERB	**Usually** we will dine there.
	We **usually** will dine there.
	We will **usually** dine there.
	We will dine there **usually.**
MODIFYING AN ADJECTIVE	That restaurant is **very** fine.
MODIFYING AN ADVERB	**Only** seldom do we dine elsewhere.

Negative Words as Adverbs

The word *not* and the contraction *-n't* are considered adverbs. Certain adverbs of time, place, and degree also have a negative meaning.

The dolphin **didn't** leap.   It is **nowhere** near here.
That dolphin **never** leaps.   That fish can **barely** swim.

Exercise 26

Identifying Adverbs   Write the adverb(s) that appear in each of the following sentences. Then write the word or words each adverb modifies. (Remember that adverbs modify an entire verb phrase.)

Traditional Dances of Africa

[1]Though traditional dances are usually designed to entertain, they frequently have religious purposes. [2]For example, tribal priests sometimes dance themselves into a trance. [3]In many cultures dancers have traditionally used masks to represent the spirits of the gods, animals, or ancestors. [4]The Yao and Maku people of Tanzania, for instance, use complex masks of cloth and bamboo, which they gradually elongate to truly astonishing heights to suggest the power of animal spirits. [5]Some dances powerfully reinforce the social structure. [6]While the *oba* (a Yoruba king) dances with very dignified, upright movements, his wives dance more humbly, their upper bodies inclined toward the earth. [7]Dance styles also vary with the environment; for example, the Ijo people, who live by fishing, lean forward from the hips and shift their weight as though balancing unsteadily in a canoe. [8]Obviously gestures from daily life are incorporated into dance movements. [9]These gestures may include a farmer's bend of the knees as he gracefully swings his machete or a fisherman's rotation as he flings his net skyward. [10]Because the traditional arts almost always celebrate communal values, the people generally dance in lines or circles.

Exercise 27

Positioning Adverbs   (a) Rewrite each of the following sentences, using the verb-modifying adverb that appears in parentheses. (b) Then rewrite each sentence again, placing the same adverb in a different position.

Brasília, a Modern Capital for Brazil

1. The idea of building a new capital for Brazil was proposed in 1789. (originally)
2. At the time construction began in the 1950s, Brazilians looked forward to having a modern capital city. (eagerly)
3. The National Congress Building, an immense bowl-shaped structure, sits on a huge concrete platform with two skyscrapers nearby. (boldly) ➡

4. The circular underground cathedral is considered to be the most impressive structure in the city. (actually)
5. Brasília is the most original national capital in the modern world. (certainly)

Exercise 28: Sentence Writing

Using Adverbs   Write ten sentences about a game you have watched or played with friends or teammates. Try to use adverbs from all the categories you studied in this lesson.

Exercise 29: Review

Adverbs   On your paper write each of the twenty adverbs that appear in the following paragraph. Then write the word or words that each adverb modifies.

Athletes and Health

[1]Athletes require carefully planned training programs designed particularly for their own needs. [2]In addition, they must be in tune with their bodies, which quickly respond to overuse. [3]Athletes who are alert to such signs as pain and lack of appetite can undoubtedly save themselves from especially poor performances. [4]Because athletes must take good care of themselves, it is hardly unusual for them to take care of their back, legs, and feet constantly. [5]For example, runners must be very sure that their shoes fit well and are periodically replaced, for all shoes will eventually show signs of wear. [6]Many athletes must confront shin splints, pains along the lower leg that usually result from a muscular problem. [7]Other athletes suffer from sciatica, which is often incorrectly diagnosed as a pulled calf muscle . [8]Athletes find that some back pains are relieved by a regularly followed program of abdominal exercises. [9]They also know that sore muscles are best treated immediately with cold water. [10]For athletes good health is vitally important, and they can never afford to neglect their bodies.

Adverbs are sometimes essential to the meaning of a sentence. Without "south" in "geese fly *south* in autumn," the sentence would take on a different meaning, as would "ostriches do *not* fly" if "not" were omitted. In other cases adverbs are optional, but they can still help "fine tune" your writing. Keep in mind the following techniques when you write and revise your work:

1. Use adverbs to emphasize a point. Notice how Paule Marshall uses the italicized adverbs in the passage from "To Da-duh, in Memoriam":

> . . . She stopped before an *incredibly* tall royal palm which rose *cleanly* out of the ground, and drawing the eye *up* with it, soared *high* above the trees around it into the sky.

Marshall could have omitted all four of the adverbs without altering her basic meaning, but the inclusion of the adverbs stresses her point, that the palm trees are impressively tall.

2. Use adverbs to clarify or qualify information. Study the italicized adverbs in this passage from "The Boy with Yellow Eyes" by Gloria Gonzalez:

> That's why when the stranger *first* arrived, his presence went *almost* unnoticed. It was *only* after he was *still* visible over a period of weeks that others became aware of him.

Here the adverbs "first," "only," and "still" help clarify the time sequence. "Almost," by qualifying "unnoticed," helps Gonzalez avoid an inaccurate generalization.

3. Add subtlety to your writing by using a negative adverb along with a negative adjective or verb to imply that the opposite of what seems to be indicated may be true. Examine the use of the negative adverb "not" along with the negative adjective "useless" in the following passage from Dorothy Canfield Fisher's story "The Bedquilt":

> She had never for a moment known the pleasure of being important to anyone. *Not* that she was *useless* in her brother's family. . . .

By insisting that the woman is *not useless*, Fisher gives us the impression that others do, in fact, regard her as useless. The effect would have been lost if Fisher had written, "she was useful in her brother's family," even though on the surface the words say the same thing.

Apply these techniques as you revise the following passage on a separate sheet of paper. Use the first two techniques by adding adverbs in the places indicated by carets (∧). Employ the third technique with the italicized word.

> The cross-country runner was ∧ *unfamiliar* with the route. She established her pace ∧ while the course wound ∧ along the soft forest floor. Soon ∧ she emerged from the forest shade into the ∧ brilliant heat of the sun as the course continued along a narrow footpath that traversed a ∧ hilly field. It was ∧ later, as she dashed ∧ across the finish line, that the other two racers ∧ caught up with her.

10.6　Prepositions

A **preposition** is a word that shows the relationship of a noun or pronoun to some other word in a sentence.

> The cat is **under** the desk. [*Under* shows the spatial relationship of the desk and the cat.]

> I saw my counselor **before** my first-period class. [*Before* expresses the time relationship between the meeting and the class period.]

> I read your poem **to** them. [*To* relates the verb *read* to the pronoun *them*.]

Commonly Used Prepositions			
aboard	beside	into	through
about	besides	like	throughout
above	between	near	to
across	beyond	of	toward
after	but*	off	under
against	by	on	underneath
along	concerning	onto	until
amid	despite	opposite	unto
among	down	out	up
around	during	outside	upon
as	except	over	with
at	excepting	past	within
before	for	pending	without
behind	from	regarding	
below	in	respecting	
beneath	inside	since	

*meaning "except"

A compound preposition is a preposition that is made up of more than one word.

Compound Prepositions		
according to	because of	next to
ahead of	by means of	on account of
along with	in addition to	on top of
apart from	in front of	out of
aside from	in spite of	owing to
as to	instead of	

Prepositions are found at the beginning of phrases that usually end with a noun or pronoun called the **object of the preposition.**

Eli told me **about the fire.** Sook came here **from Korea.**
Owen sat **opposite me.** All **but Jane** agreed.

Exercise 30

Identifying Prepositions On your paper list the prepositions that appear in each of the following sentences. Remember that some prepositions are made up of more than one word. (The numeral in parentheses at the end of each item indicates the number of prepositions in that sentence.)

Jackson Hole Valley

1. Scenic Jackson Hole Valley lies at the foot of the Teton Mountains. (2)
2. Towering above Jackson Hole, the Tetons have ten peaks that are over ten thousand feet high. (2)
3. According to reports, the first white trapper in Jackson Hole was John Coulter. (2)
4. With the exception of hardy mountaineers who hunted game, early pioneers stayed outside the valley. (3)
5. In the 1880s the first homesteaders became concerned about the survival of Jackson Hole elk. (3)
6. As a result, in 1912 the National Elk Refuge was established within the valley. (3)
7. In addition to the elk problem, there was the question of conservation. (2)
8. By 1929 Congress had established the Grand Teton National Park along the eastern slopes of the Tetons. (3)
9. In the meantime John D. Rockefeller Jr. had begun to acquire acres of Jackson Hole land for public use. (3)
10. Through the intervention of Franklin D. Roosevelt, a 221,000-acre Jackson Hole National Monument was established in 1943. (3)
11. The monument was abolished in 1950, and most of it was added to the Grand Teton National Park. (3)
12. Many Jackson Hole residents were against all outsiders coming into the valley. (2)
13. In spite of protests, only 3 percent of Teton County's land is now in private hands. (3)
14. Aside from these small private holdings, the Jackson Hole area now forms the 310,000 acres of the Grand Teton National Park and is accessible to the public. (3)
15. Flying above Jackson Hole, you see vistas of truly breathtaking splendor. (2) ➡

16. Beyond a doubt, Jackson Hole's lakes and mountains are spectacular. (1)
17. Because of many clear streams, the fishing alone draws a host of visitors. (2)
18. Along the shore of Jackson Lake, a paved campground overlooks the marina of Coulter Bay. (3)
19. Amid the soaring peaks of Mount Moran, Grand Teton, and South Teton lies little Jenny Lake. (2)
20. Throughout Jackson Hole wildflowers carpet summer foothills with a riot of color. (3)

Exercise 31: Sentence Writing

Creating Sentences with Prepositions Choose five prepositions from the lists on page 423. Use each preposition in a sentence, adding adjectives and adverbs wherever necessary.

10.7 Conjunctions

A **conjunction** is a word that joins single words or groups of words.

Coordinating Conjunctions

A **coordinating conjunction** joins words or groups of words that have equal grammatical weight in a sentence.

Coordinating Conjunctions					
and	but	or	nor	for	yet

They stand **and** wait.
Put the boxes in the kitchen **or** in the garage.
We planted tulips, **but** they did not grow.
The door was open, **yet** nobody was home.

Exercise 32

Identifying Coordinating Conjunctions Read the paragraph at the top of the next page. Then, on a separate sheet of paper, write the coordinating conjunction(s) that appear in each sentence. ➡

Kareem Abdul-Jabbar

[1]At the time of his birth in 1947, Ferdinand Lewis Alcindor Jr. was over twenty-two inches long and weighed twelve pounds eleven ounces. [2]By the time he was in sixth grade, the six-foot Lew Alcindor was already playing basketball, but he was too clumsy to be good. [3]The school coach coaxed Lew to stay for practice at the gym until six or seven o'clock most evenings. [4]When he was in the seventh grade, Lew was tall enough (six feet eight inches) to dunk the basketball, and other students grew proud of his ability. [5]Lew won a scholarship to Power Memorial Academy, for the coach there recognized his potential. [6]Lew joined the varsity basketball team as a freshman, yet he was still awkward. [7]With much practice he acquired considerable grace, and he was hailed as the most promising high school player in the country. [8]Lew's basketball career at UCLA was lonely, but it brought many offers from professional recruiters. [9]At the age of twenty-four, Lew Alcindor was a renowned basketball star and was named Most Valuable Player of the National Basketball Association. [10]Now, of course, Lew Alcindor is known as Kareem Abdul-Jabbar, for he changed his name to acknowledge his African heritage.

Correlative Conjunctions

Correlative conjunctions work in pairs to join words and groups of words of equal weight in a sentence.

Correlative Conjunctions	
both . . . and	neither . . . nor
either . . . or	not only . . . but (also)
just as . . . so	whether . . . or

Correlative conjunctions can make the relationship between words or groups of words somewhat clearer than coordinating conjunctions can.

COORDINATING CONJUNCTIONS	CORRELATIVE CONJUNCTIONS
He **and** I should talk.	**Both** you **and** I should talk.
He **or** I should talk.	**Either** he **or** I should talk.
	Neither you **nor** I should talk.
I speak French **and** Chinese.	I speak **not only** French **but also** Chinese.

Identifying Correlative Conjunctions On your paper write both parts of the correlative conjunctions that appear in the following sentences.

Finding Shelter

1. Whether you are lost on a hike or stuck in a disabled car, your life may depend upon finding shelter.
2. Both the severe cold of a snow-capped mountain and the burning heat of a desert require some kind of shelter.
3. In either hot or cold locations it is important to protect oneself from the elements.
4. Tarpaulin shelters are not only quick and easy to put up but also light to carry.
5. A triangular tent can be formed either by leaning a pole into the crook of a tree branch or by lashing two poles together in an X.
6. Just as strong trees can help provide shelter, so can dense brush.
7. A dense stand of either willows or sagebrush makes a fine shelter when their tops are tied together.
8. Should you have neither tarpaulin nor brush, you may be able to find a protected spot along a river bank.
9. Whether a river bank provides safe shelter or presents risks depends upon the incidence of flash floods in the area.
10. In deep snow a simple trench roofed with evergreen branches provides both shelter and insulation from the cold.

Subordinating Conjunctions

A **subordinating conjunction** joins two clauses, or ideas, in such a way as to make one grammatically dependent upon the other.

A subordinating conjunction introduces a subordinate, or dependent, clause, one that cannot stand alone as a complete sentence.

The audience applauded **when** Aretha Franklin appeared on the stage.

Franklin smiled **as** the audience cheered.

Wherever she appears, people flock to see her perform.

As soon as I heard she was coming, I rushed to buy tickets for my whole family.

Common Subordinating Conjunctions

after	as though	provided (that)	until
although	because	since	when
as	before	so long as	whenever
as far as	considering (that)	so that	where
as if	if	than	whereas
as long as	inasmuch as	though	wherever
as soon as	in order that	unless	while

Exercise 34

Identifying Subordinating Conjunctions   Write the subordinating conjunction that appears in each sentence below. Remember that some subordinating conjunctions are made up of more than one word.

An Wang, a Pioneer of the Electronic Age

1. Born in China, An Wang came to the United States in 1945 to study and decided to stay when the Chinese Communists took power soon after.
2. Because he was brilliant and had had practical experience, he breezed through his doctoral studies in applied physics.
3. His breakthrough came when he devised a way to store electronic information on the tiny magnetized iron doughnuts that were used in primitive computers.
4. Although he had only six hundred dollars, An Wang used his savings to set up a small business in 1951.
5. In 1956 his ferrite magnetic memory core brought him a small fortune after IBM began using it in computers.
6. An Wang's invention served as the standard memory-storage device in computers until it was replaced by the semiconductor chip twenty years later.
7. Although his first electronic calculator for scientists sold for sixty-five hundred dollars, it cost much less than a mainframe computer and was easier to operate.
8. His name became well-known in business after the Wang electronic word processor, the first "thinking typewriter," was used successfully in offices.
9. An Wang knew his company would prosper as long as he could design useful machines for science and business.
10. As one of twelve outstanding naturalized American citizens, Wang was awarded the Medal of Liberty when the centennial of the Statue of Liberty was celebrated in 1986.

Conjunctive Adverbs

A **conjunctive adverb** is used to clarify the relationship between clauses of equal weight in a sentence.

Conjunctive adverbs are usually stronger than coordinating conjunctions because they more precisely explain the relationship between the two clauses.

COORDINATING CONJUNCTION	The office was cold, the noise was intolerable, **and** he resigned.
CONJUNCTIVE ADVERB	The office was cold, and the noise was intolerable; **consequently,** he resigned.

The uses of conjunctive adverbs are illustrated by the following examples:

TO REPLACE *AND*	also, besides, furthermore, moreover
TO REPLACE *BUT*	however, nevertheless, still
TO STATE A RESULT	consequently, therefore, so, thus
TO STATE EQUALITY	equally, likewise, similarly

Exercise 35

Using Conjunctive Adverbs   Rewrite each of the following sentences, filling in the blank with an appropriate conjunctive adverb that makes the sentence meaningful. In most cases there will be more than one correct answer.

SAMPLE   Scientists in police laboratories must be experts in one branch of science; _____, they must have common sense.

ANSWERS   Scientists in police laboratories must be experts in one branch of science; moreover, they must have common sense.

Scientists in police laboratories must be experts in one branch of science; furthermore, they must have common sense.

The Police Laboratory

1. Every case that comes to a police laboratory is different; _____, all cases require two basic steps.
2. In criminal cases physical evidence must be identified; _____, it must be matched to an individual.
3. Everybody's fingerprints are unique; _____, the bullets fired by every firearm are marked with unique grooves. ➡

4. Each chemical compound absorbs different wavelengths of light; _____, police scientists can identify the contents of a pill or a liquid.
5. Modern police laboratories make use of computers; _____, the matching of fingerprints takes only minutes.
6. Forged documents are frequent in fraud cases; _____, police laboratories employ document examiners.
7. Professional document examiners can usually match hand-writing samples; _____, they can often match typewriting to a specific typewriter.
8. With ultraviolet and infrared light, document examiners can decipher invisible writing; _____, they can spot erasures and alterations.
9. Police laboratory workers may be most at home behind the scenes; _____, an important part of their job often involves testifying in court.
10. Scientific analysis has helped convict many guilty people; _____, it has also prevented many people from being convicted of crimes they did not commit.

Exercise 36: Sentence Writing

Creating Sentences with Conjunctions Think of a favorite motion picture or television program that you have seen. Write several sentences about the typical characters, events, or setting of the movie or show, using as many conjunctions as possible.

Exercise 37: Review

Conjunctions On your paper replace the blank or blanks that appear in each of the following sentences with a conjunction that makes sense. The kind of conjunction to use is stated in parentheses at the end of each sentence.

The Lost City Meteorite

1. An Oklahoma farmer went looking for a calf; _____ he found a meteor fragment. (conjunctive adverb)
2. _____ the Lost City Meteorite descended over Oklahoma, it was seen as far away as central Nebraska. (subordinating conjunction) ➡

3. _____ the meteorite was descending, a sonic boom was heard all the way from Tulsa to Tahlequah. (subordinating conjunction)

4. _____ was the Lost City Meteorite tracked photographically, _____ its landing place was accurately predicted. (correlative conjunction)

5. The first meteorite fragment was found quickly _____ flown to the Smithsonian Institution. (coordinating conjunction)

6. _____ the photographic tracking was accurate, many airborne meteor particles could be recovered. (subordinating conjunction)

7. _____ the meteor entered the earth's atmosphere at nine miles per second, it slowed to two miles per second at an altitude of eleven miles. (subordinating conjunction)

8. The fireball dropped the 9.85-kilogram meteorite on December 28, 1970; _____, it was not found until six days later. (conjunctive adverb)

9. _____ the original meteorite _____ three others found later by investigators formed a total mass of 17.3 kilograms. (correlative conjunction)

10. _____ scientists tracked the Oklahoma fireball, they had tracked only one meteor by means of photography. (subordinating conjunction)

In this passage from his novel *The Autobiography of an Ex-Colored Man*, James Weldon Johnson uses conjunctions effectively to link ideas. Read the passage, focusing especially on the italicized conjunctions.

> At a very early age I began to thump on the piano alone, *and* it was not long *before* I was able to pick out a few tunes. *When* I was seven years old, I could play by ear all of the hymns *and* songs that my mother knew. I had also learned the names of the notes in both clefs, *but* I preferred not to be hampered by notes. About this time several ladies for whom my mother sewed heard me play, *and* they persuaded her that I should at once be put under a teacher; *so* arrangements were made for me to study the piano with a lady who was a fairly good musician. . . .

Here are some guidelines for using conjunctions when you write and revise your own work:

1. To clarify the relationship between ideas, use a coordinating conjunction other than *and* wherever appropriate. Johnson, for example, uses "but" to clarify the contrast between learning the notes and preferring not to be hampered by them.

2. Try to use appropriate subordinating conjunctions to clarify the relationship between ideas instead of relying only on coordinating conjunctions. Notice how the subordinating conjunction "when" helps clarify the time relationship between the events in the second sentence. Had Johnson merely said, "I was seven years old, *and* I could play by ear . . . ," the time relationship would have been far less clear.

3. Wherever appropriate, replace coordinating conjunctions with conjunctive adverbs in order to clarify relationships and add variety to your writing. In the last sentence Johnson could have used *and* instead of the conjunctive adverb "so," but *so* does a better job of clarifying the cause-and-effect relationship. It also adds variety, since "and" appears in the preceding clause.

Practice these techniques by revising the following paragraph on a separate sheet of paper. Combine the *a* and *b* sentences of each item by using different conjunctions. Avoid *and;* instead, choose conjunctions that clarify the relationship between ideas. (Remember that the conjunction can be placed between the sentences *or* at the beginning of the *a* sentence.)

> (1a) A bonsai tree is considered a work of art. (1b) Unlike a painting or a symphony, the bonsai is alive. (2a) Bonsai artists create what look like miniature trees. (2b) They are actually training young trees to resemble old ones. (3a) To train the tree, the bonsai artist must begin to work in winter. (3b) New spring growth has not yet begun. (4a) The artist carefully prunes off some of the branches and twists the remaining ones. (4b) The plant begins to resemble an older tree. (5a) The art of bonsai originated in Japan. (5b) It is now popular all over the world. (6a) My Aunt Mioshi is an expert on bonsai. (6b) She speaks at garden clubs throughout the country.

10.8   Interjections

An **interjection** is a word or phrase that expresses emotion or exclamation. An interjection has no grammatical connection to other words.

Well, such is life.
Ouch! That hurts.
Ah, that's delicious!
Sh! Be quiet.

Exercise 38

Using Interjections   On your paper fill in the blank in each sentence below with an appropriate interjection from the following list:

oh no	wow	bravo	oh well	hooray
whew	oops	ouch	gee	my

1. _____, I'm sorry I forgot your birthday.
2. _____! You just stepped on my foot.
3. _____! That was the finest performance of that play I have ever seen.
4. _____, how you've grown!
5. _____! I spilled the milk.
6. _____! José Canseco has just hit his second home run of the game.
7. _____! That is the tallest building I have ever seen.
8. _____, we burned the meat loaf, but now we can go out to dinner.
9. _____! It looks as though there has been a serious accident down the road.
10. _____! I'm relieved that the exam is over.

*G*rammar Workshop

Parts of Speech

Set in a coastal town in Colombia, Gabriel García Márquez's novel is about an unrequited love that endures for more than fifty years. In this episode the hero, Florentino Ariza, then a young boy, contemplates sending a letter to Fermina Daza, the girl who becomes the great love of his life but whom he admires from afar. This passage, translated from the Spanish, has been annotated to show the parts of speech covered in this unit.

Literature Model

from LOVE IN THE TIME OF CHOLERA

by Gabriel García Márquez
translated from the Spanish by Edith Grossman

Linking verb ——

Common noun ——

Preposition ——

Possessive pronoun ——

Proper noun ——

Coordinating conjunction ——

Action verb ——

Personal pronoun ——

It was in this innocent way that Florentino Ariza began his secret life as a solitary hunter. From seven o'clock in the morning, he sat on the most hidden bench in the little park, pretending to read a book of verse in the shade of the almond trees, until he saw the impossible maiden walk by in her blue-striped uniform, stockings that reached to her knees, masculine laced oxfords, and a single thick braid with a bow at the end, which hung down her back to her waist. She walked with natural haughtiness, her head high, her eyes unmoving, her step rapid, her nose pointing straight ahead, her bag of books held against her chest with crossed arms, her doe's gait making her seem immune to gravity. At her side, struggling to keep up with her, the aunt with the brown habit and rope of St. Francis did not allow him the slightest opportunity to approach. Florentino Ariza saw them pass back and forth four times a day and once on Sundays when they came out of High Mass, and just seeing the girl was enough for him. Little by little he idealized her, endowing her with improbable virtues and imaginary sentiments, and after two weeks he thought of nothing else but her. So he decided to send Fermina Daza a simple note written on both sides of the paper in his ➡

exquisite notary's hand. But he kept it in his pocket for several days, thinking about how to hand it to her, and while he thought he wrote several more pages before going to bed, so that the original letter was turning into a dictionary of compliments, inspired by books he had learned by heart because he read them so often during his vigils in the park. . . .

    By the time the letter contained more than sixty pages written on both sides, Florentino Ariza could no longer endure the weight of his secret, and he unburdened himself to his mother, the only person with whom he allowed himself any confidences. Tránsito Ariza was moved to tears by her son's innocence in matters of love, and she tried to guide him with her own knowledge. She began by convincing him not to deliver the lyrical sheaf of papers, since it would only frighten the girl of his dreams, who she supposed was as green as he in matters of the heart.

    Adjective

    Adverb

    Reflexive pronoun

    Subordinating conjunction

    Relative pronoun

Grammar Workshop Exercise 1

Identifying Nouns   On your paper identify each of the nouns in the following sentences, which provide background for the passage from *Love in the Time of Cholera*. After each noun write in parentheses *common*, *proper*, or *collective*, depending upon how the noun is used in the sentence.

SAMPLE	A throng of girls strolled toward the Academy of the Presentation.
ANSWER	throng (collective), girls (common), Academy of the Presentation (proper)

1. In Spain and South America in those days, adults supervised young people in public.
2. Escolástica was the chaperone of her niece, a schoolgirl named Fermina Daza.
3. Fermina and her aunt walked more rapidly than the other women in the group going to the academy.
4. Because of a vow, Escolástica dressed in the brown clothes of a Franciscan.
5. In former times the school Fermina attended, the Academy of the Presentation, had accepted only the daughters of aristocratic families.

Grammar Workshop Exercise 2

Using Pronouns Effectively   The following sentences elaborate on ideas suggested by the passage from *Love in the Time of Cholera*. On your paper write the pronoun that makes sense in each blank. Follow the directions in parentheses.

1. Florentino pretended to read so that _____ could catch sight of Fermina. (Use a third-person singular personal pronoun.)
2. _____ was that woman walking alongside Fermina? (Use an interrogative pronoun.)
3. _____ was Aunt Escolástica, the sister of Fermina's father. (Use a demonstrative pronoun.)
4. Escolástica was a stalwart chaperone _____ would not allow any man to approach Fermina. (Use a relative pronoun.)
5. Fermina _____ walked so haughtily that no one could easily approach her. (Use an intensive pronoun.)
6. Florentino had not finished the letter, _____ told of his love for Fermina. (Use a relative pronoun.)
7. Perhaps he felt he had listed _____ of Fermina's virtues but not all of them. (Use an indefinite pronoun.)
8. Florentino asked _____ how he could hand Fermina the letter. (Use a reflexive pronoun.)
9. Florentino thought, "I will ask _____ mother what to do." (Use a first-person singular possessive pronoun.)
10. His mother told him _____: a passionate love letter might frighten Fermina. (Use a demonstrative pronoun.)

Grammar Workshop Exercise 3

Identifying Transitive and Intransitive Verbs   The following sentences contain verbs that appear in the passage from *Love in the Time of Cholera*. For each item write *transitive* or *intransitive* on your paper, depending upon the way the italicized verb is used in the sentence. Then write your own sentence using the verb in the same way it is used in the item.

SAMPLE   Couples often *sit* on park benches.
ANSWER   intransitive
           Elena sits gracefully on the sofa.

1. Young men and women *see* one another at dances.
2. Sometimes the men *walk* with the women for hours.
3. The women *hold* garlands of flowers. ⇢

4. They *keep* small gifts that they give each other.

5. The couples *pass* one another in the park.

6. Those who are courting often *idealize* each other.

7. They *think* of each other constantly.

8. Sometimes they *write* long, ardent letters.

9. One can *inspire* the other with brilliant language.

10. The young people *read* the letters they receive dozens of times.

Grammar Workshop Exercise 4

Writing Sentences with Adjectives   The following sentences are adapted from *Love in the Time of Cholera*. First, identify the adjectives in each sentence. Then, for each sentence in this exercise, write a sentence of your own with an identical structure. Place your adjectives in the same position in which they appear in the sentence in this exercise. Each of your sentences may be about a different subject.

SAMPLE   Florentino began his secret life in an innocent way.

ANSWER   his, secret, innocent
Gemma drew an imaginary winter scene on the frosty window.

1. Fermina wore her long hair in a single braid.

2. Her doelike gait made her seem immune to gravity.

3. The innocent love and romantic longings of her son touched Tránsito Ariza.

4. Would the lyrical sheaf of papers frighten the haughty girl?

5. Fermina might be as innocent as Florentino in tender matters of the heart.

Grammar Workshop Exercise 5

Using Adverbs   The following sentences describe the courtship customs that would have been practiced in the social and historical setting of *Love in the Time of Cholera*. Rewrite each sentence, substituting an appropriate adverb for the phrase in italics. The adverb should express the same idea as the prepositional phrase.

SAMPLE   Courtship had to be handled *with delicacy*.

ANSWER   Courtship had to be handled delicately. ➡

1. By custom young women did not speak *in public* to men.
2. Chaperones guarded their charges' honor *with ferocity*.
3. A wealthy young woman would *in all probability* have many suitors.
4. *According to tradition*, marriages were arranged by the parents of the young people.
5. A young man who acted *with imprudence* might lose his chance to win a young lady.

Grammar Workshop Exercise 6

Using Prepositions　The following sentences elaborate on ideas suggested by the García Márquez passage. Rewrite each sentence, filling in the blanks with a preposition that completes the word or phrase in italics and makes sense in the sentence. There may be more than one preposition that makes sense.

SAMPLE　　Florentino began his vigil every morning _____ *seven o'clock.*

ANSWER　　Florentino began his vigil every morning at seven o'clock.

1. Florentino sat _____ *a shady almond tree.*
2. Once again he saw Fermina walking _____ *Escolástica,* her chaperone.
3. Fermina's natural haughtiness was evident _____ *the way* she held her head.
4. Her oxfords looked _____ *shoes* a man might wear.
5. Her eyes did not wander _____ *the left or right.*
6. She had woven her hair _____ *a thick braid.*
7. She wore a lace mantilla _____ *church* on Sundays.
8. _____ *Florentino's calm manner* his heart was pounding.
9. _____ *several days* he kept adding to his letter.
10. He could recite _____ *memory* every compliment and lofty sentiment in the letter.

Grammar Workshop Exercise 7

Using Conjunctions　The following sentences offer background about Colombia, where *Love in the Time of Cholera* is set. Rewrite each sentence, filling in the blanks with appropriate conjunctions. Follow the directions in parentheses. ➡

SAMPLE	The Spanish colony of New Granada once included what is now Colombia, Ecuador, Panama, _____ Venezuela. (Add a coordinating conjunction.)
ANSWER	The Spanish colony of New Granada once included what is now Colombia, Ecuador, Panama, and Venezuela.

1. _____ the Chibcha people of the Andes once ruled Colombia, their land was taken by Spaniards seeking gold. (Add a subordinating conjunction.)
2. Two Chibcha chieftains, called the Zipa _____ the Zaque, ruled the savannas of preconquest Colombia. (Add a coordinating conjunction.)
3. Bogotá was _____ the main city of the Chibcha _____, later, the capital of Colombia. (Add a correlative conjunction.)
4. _____ Colombia was a Spanish colony, its high government officials had to be born in Spain, according to Spanish law. (Add a subordinating conjunction.)
5. The conquerors would not perform agricultural _____ mechanical labor in the vanquished land. (Add a coordinating conjunction.)
6. The Spaniards who ruled the colony retained their European identity, _____ those who were born locally, the Creoles, saw themselves as true Americans. (Add a coordinating conjunction.)
7. The mestizos, who were of mixed ancestry, were not accepted by _____ the Creoles _____ the Native Americans. (Add a correlative conjunction.)
8. The mestizos were treated as outcasts for many years, _____ they gained recognition from the two other cultures. (Add a subordinating conjunction.)
9. The Spanish rulers were driven out of Colombia _____ they were defeated by Generals Simón Bolívar and Francisco Santander. (Add a subordinating conjunction.)
10. Colombia won its independence in 1821 _____ did not become a unified republic until 1886. (Add a coordinating conjunction.)

Grammar Workshop Exercise 8

Review   Read the brief biography of Gabriel García Márquez. On your paper rewrite the ten sentences that follow it, filling in the blanks with an appropriate word. ➡

Use the directions in parentheses as a guide. You will need to consult the biography in order to fill in some of the blanks properly.

Gabriel García Márquez

Gabriel García Márquez is one of the writers credited with awakening world interest in contemporary Latin American literature. A newspaper reporter turned novelist, García Márquez was born in 1928 in Aracataca, Colombia. He transformed this small Caribbean town into Macondo, the setting for his highly acclaimed novel *One Hundred Years of Solitude*, published in 1967. Told with a journalist's regard for detail, the book is both a family chronicle and a mythical history of a century of turmoil and change in Latin America. It has been praised as one of the great novels of the twentieth century for its imaginative blend of fantasy, fable, and fact. Subsequent major works include *The Autumn of the Patriarch* (1975), *Chronicle of a Death Foretold* (1981), and *The General in His Labyrinth* (1989). García Márquez was awarded the Nobel Prize for Literature in 1982.

1. The novels of García Márquez _____ world interest in Latin American literature. (Add an action verb.)
2. García Márquez was a newspaper reporter who _____ a novelist. (Add a linking verb.)
3. Aracataca, the novelist's _____, is a small town on the Caribbean coast of Colombia. (Add a common noun.)
4. His masterpiece, *One Hundred Years of Solitude*, received _____ acclaim from critics around the world. (Add an adjective.)
5. A native of Colombia who now lives in Mexico City, he writes in _____, but his novels have been translated into numerous languages. (Add a proper noun.)
6. _____ *One Hundred Years of Solitude* has been translated into many languages, its author has become famous worldwide. (Add a subordinating conjunction.)
7. This novel _____ blends fantasy, fable, and fact. (Add an adverb.)
8. García Márquez published four major novels _____ the years 1975 and 1985. (Add a preposition.)
9. In 1982 Gabriel García Márquez won the coveted _____. (Add a proper noun.)
10. Carlos Fuentes of Mexico _____ Julio Cortázar of Argentina have also published world-renowned novels. (Add a coordinating conjunction.)

Proofreading   This passage describes the artist Patricia Gonzalez, whose painting appears on this page. Rewrite the passage, correcting the errors in spelling, capitalization, punctuation, grammar, and usage. There are ten errors in all.

Patricia Gonzalez

[1]Patricia Gonzalez was born in 1958 in Cartagena, Colombia and moved to London when she was eleven. [2]There she studied art, recieving a Bachelor of Fine Arts from the Wimbledon school of Art in 1980. [3]Gonzalez returned to Cartagena to teach; but had trouble adopting to her new life. [4]"I could hardly paint at all", she has said of that time. [5]She returned to England in 1981, and later moved to Texas, her home today.

[6]Gonzalez's imagery, which recall the landscapes of Latin America, is inspired partly by memory, and partly by imagination. [7]Her dreamlike paintings are rich in color and texture. [8]The woman in *Sleep*, barefoot and dressed in red, sleeps amid a tropical landscape. [9]Gonzalez creates the sense that the landscape exists only in the woman's dreams. [10]The hero of *Love in the Time of Cholera* also lives in a fantasy world: he dreams that the girl who he adores will become the love of his life.

Patricia Gonzalez, *Sleep,* **1985**

Parts of Speech

Nouns and Pronouns

[pages 397–400, 402–408]

Identify each underlined word as **(a)** a common or a collective noun, **(b)** a proper noun, **(c)** a personal or a possessive pronoun, **(d)** a demonstrative, an intensive, or a reflexive pronoun, or **(e)** an interrogative, a relative, or an indefinite pronoun.

[1]Anyone [2]who lives in a Chinese-American neighborhood (as [3]I [4]myself do) hears [5]fire-crackers each January or [6]February. [7]This is the event [8]that heralds the [9]Chinese New Year, a traditional [10]holiday that begins the lunar [11]year. In celebration [12]everyone in a [13]family shares symbolic food, such as [14]tangerines, for good [15]luck. [16]Who would have suspected that in [17]China [18]all of the [19]population once celebrated [20]their birthday on the New Year?

Verbs

[pages 408–413]

Indicate whether each of the underlined verbs is **(a)** a transitive verb, **(b)** an intransitive verb, or **(c)** a linking verb.

The Federal Bureau of Land Management [21]is offering thousands of wild burros for adoption. The fee [22]is just seventy-five dollars for an animal that [23]will eat weeds and [24]carry equipment on its back. The burros [25]are not native to the desert; they [26]came to America with the Spanish settlers. As the burros [27]found their way to freedom, they [28]increased alarmingly. Trampling tiny plants and animals, they [29]threaten the desert's ecosystem. To solve the problem, the government [30]must reduce the number of burros running wild.

Adjectives and Adverbs

[pages 415–417, 419–421]

Indicate whether each of the underlined words is **(a)** an adjective, **(b)** an article, **(c)** an adverb modifying a verb, **(d)** an adverb modifying an adjective or another adverb, or **(e)** a negative adverb.

My [31]youngest brother [32]finally saved [33]enough money to buy [34]a guitar. For an [35]extremely long time he could [36]not choose. When he finally picked [37]a [38]handsome maple guitar, he looked [39]completely [40]delighted.

Prepositions, Conjunctions, and Interjections

[pages 423–425, 425–431, 433]

Indicate whether each of the underlined words is used here as **(a)** a preposition, **(b)** a coordinating conjunction, **(c)** a part of a correlative conjunction, **(d)** a subordinating conjunction, or **(e)** an interjection.

[41]Though city dwellers may deal with pollution [42]and crime, the isolation [43]of rural life can be stressful, too. Urbanites may cope better [44]with disrupted friendships, [45]for they often have friendships [46]outside the family [47]in addition to cultural opportunities. [48]Yes, the differences between city [49]and country life are huge, [50]but there are advantages to both.

Writing for Review

Write one paragraph on any subject. In your paragraph underline and identify at least one *noun, pronoun, verb, adjective, adverb, preposition,* and *conjunction.*

Unit 11 | Parts of the Sentence

A **sentence** is a group of words expressing a complete thought.

The *subject* and the *predicate* are the two basic parts of every sentence.

11.1 | Simple Subjects and Simple Predicates

The **simple subject** is the key noun or pronoun (or word or group of words acting as a noun) that tells what a sentence is about.

The **simple predicate** is the verb or verb phrase that expresses the essential thought about the subject of the sentence.

SIMPLE SUBJECT	SIMPLE PREDICATE
Nikki Giovanni	wrote.
Senators	will attend.
Everything	has been discussed.
Traffic	slowed.

The way to find the simple subject is to ask *who?* or *what?* about the verb. For example, in the first sentence above, the noun *Nikki Giovanni* answers the question *who wrote?*

11.2 | Complete Subjects and Complete Predicates

You can usually expand or modify the meaning of both a simple subject and a simple predicate by adding other words and phrases to the sentence.

The **complete subject** consists of the simple subject and all the words that modify it.

The **complete predicate** consists of the simple predicate and all the words that modify it or complete its meaning.

COMPLETE SUBJECT	COMPLETE PREDICATE
The celebrated Nikki Giovanni	wrote delightful poetry.
The two senators from Ohio	will attend a local caucus.
Everything on the agenda	has been discussed by her.
The rush-hour traffic	slowed to a snail's pace.

Identifying Subjects and Predicates   Copy each of the following sentences, and indicate with a vertical line the division between the complete subject and the complete predicate. Then underline the simple subject once and the simple predicate twice.

The National Park System

1. Delighted visitors flock each year to the more than three hundred sites in the National Park System.
2. The National Park System consists of areas of great natural beauty, historic importance, scientific significance, or recreational interest.
3. Yellowstone Park, in Wyoming, Montana, and Idaho, became the first national park in the United States in 1872.
4. Yellowstone is known throughout the world for its hot springs, geysers, and mud volcanoes.
5. The national parks, among them such famous ones as Yosemite and Grand Canyon, are administered today by the National Park Service, a bureau of the Department of the Interior.
6. The National Park Service has developed different categories of national areas of special interest through the years.
7. Areas of historic interest in the system include national monuments, a battlefield site, historic sites, and memorials.
8. The recreational opportunities of future generations of Americans are guaranteed by the National Park System's national seashores and national lakeshores.
9. A staff of thousands—including rangers, naturalists, fire control aides, and historians—maintains the parks.
10. Of all the employees of the National Park System, the rangers have the most contact with visitors.

11.3   Compound Subjects and Compound Predicates

A **compound subject** is made up of two or more simple subjects that are joined by a conjunction and have the same verb.

Both **experience** and adequate **training** are necessary.
Neither the **bus** nor the **subway** goes there.
Crimson, cerise, and **vermilion** are shades of red.

Expanding Subjects (a) Write five sentences. In each one use a simple subject and a simple predicate. (b) Expand each sentence by making the subject compound.

SAMPLE ANSWER   (a) Jackie Joyner-Kersee ran in the Olympics.
(b) Jackie Joyner-Kersee and Carl Lewis ran in the Olympics.

A **compound predicate** (or **compound verb**) is made up of two or more verbs or verb phrases that are joined by a conjunction and have the same subject.

Holograms **amaze** and **fascinate**.
Jerome **will** either **call** or **write**.
The helicopter **hovered** briefly but **landed** almost at once.
Our guests **will arrive** early, **eat** a light meal, and **retire** by ten.

Sentences can have both a compound subject and a compound predicate.

    S   S   P   P
Crocuses and **daffodils** both **herald** and **symbolize** spring.

Exercise 3

Identifying Subjects and Predicates On your paper copy the following sentences. Then for each sentence underline the simple subject(s) once and the simple predicate(s) twice. Note that some subjects and predicates are compound.

Tourist Attractions in Atlanta

1. Tourists and local residents alike enjoy the rich and varied historic sites in Atlanta, Georgia.
2. The birthplace and final resting place of Dr. Martin Luther King Jr., the famous civil rights leader, are in Atlanta.
3. Dr. King was born and raised in a house on Auburn Avenue, now part of the King National Historical District.
4. For many years Dr. King and his father shared the pulpit at the nearby Ebenezer Baptist Church.
5. Tourists can leave Dr. King's birthplace and walk to the Martin Luther King Center for Nonviolent Social Change.
6. There visitors can view Dr. King's tomb and think about the accomplishments of this great man.
7. The Hammonds House and the Herndon Home are also among the city's interesting attractions. ➡

8. In 1910 Alonzo Franklin Herndon, an insurance tycoon and former slave, not only designed but also built the Herndon Home, a mansion in the Beaux Arts style.
9. The Hammonds House features artworks on loan and from the collection of the late Dr. O. T. Hammonds.
10. Atlanta's African-American Panoramic Experience (APEX) Museum treats visitors to an authentic 1905 trolley car.

Exercise 4: Sentence Writing

Expanding Subjects and Predicates   (a) Write five sentences, each with one subject and one predicate. (b) Make the subject and the predicate of each sentence compound.

SAMPLE ANSWER   (a) Television provides entertainment.
(b) Television and radio provide entertainment and disseminate information.

11.4 Order of Subject and Predicate

In English the subject comes before the verb in most sentences. A discussion of some exceptions to this normal word order follows.

1. *You* as the subject is understood rather than expressed in the case of commands or requests.

   [You] **Listen!**   [You] **Carry** it home.   [You] **Please** see me.

2. In order to add emphasis to the subject, a sentence can be written in **inverted order,** with the predicate coming before the subject.

PREDICATE	SUBJECT
Beneath the waves **lay**	an ancient **shipwreck.**
Over the years **had arisen**	many improbable **tales.**

3. When the word *there* or *here* begins a sentence and is followed by the verb *to be*, the predicate usually comes before the subject. (The sentence appears in inverted order.) Be aware that *there* and *here* are almost never the subject of a sentence.

PREDICATE	SUBJECT
Here **is**	the **quilt** for my friend.
There **were**	new **books** on the shelf.

Exercise 5

Recognizing the Order of Subject and Predicate Copy each of the following sentences, draw a vertical line between the complete subject and the predicate, and label each. Then indicate with the letter *C* or *I* those sentences that are either a command (*C*) or written in inverted order (*I*). (Not all sentences will be labeled *C* or *I*.)

SAMPLE ANSWERS

                     P
     | Look at that cherry blossom tree. C

       P   S
     On the tour is | the Senate. I

       P   S
     There are | many reasons for thinking of Washington, D.C., as one of this country's most beautiful cities. I

Washington, D.C.

1. Washington, D.C., has a distinctive atmosphere.
2. Of course, there is the monumental quality of many of its public buildings.
3. Notice the distinctive shape of the Washington Monument.
4. Among the best of the contemporary buildings is the stunning East Building of the National Gallery of Art.
5. Complementing the classic layout of the city are many broad, tree-lined avenues.
6. Ask the tour guide how much of the land is composed of parks.
7. Below street level runs Rock Creek Park, with miles of roadways and bicycle paths.
8. A lack of skyscrapers reinforces the city's sense of openness.
9. Look at the charming Georgian colonial houses in the residential district of Georgetown.
10. The city has left a lasting impression on millions of visitors.

11.5   Complements

A **complement** is a word or group of words that completes the meaning of a verb.

There are four kinds of complements: *direct objects, indirect objects, object complements,* and *subject complements.*

Direct Objects

A **direct object** answers the question *what?* or *whom?* after an action verb.

The action indicated by the verb in a sentence is usually performed by the subject of the sentence. A direct object—someone or something—is the recipient of that action. Nouns, pronouns, or words acting as nouns may serve as direct objects. Only transitive verbs have direct objects.

Estela sold her **typewriter**. [Estela sold *what?*]
Everyone watched the **diver**. [Everyone watched *whom?*]
They understood **what I had said**. [They understood *what?*]
Estela sold her **typewriter** and **radio**. [Estela sold *what?*]

Exercise 6

Identifying Direct Objects   On your paper write the action verb that appears in each of the following sentences. Then list any direct objects.

Faith Ringgold, Contemporary Artist

1. During the 1950s Faith Ringgold studied art and education at the City College of New York.
2. After graduation she taught art classes for many years.
3. Ringgold gained a position as a professor of art at the University of California at San Diego in 1984.
4. A political artist, Ringgold once made a large painting of one hundred human faces, eyes and noses only, of which 10 percent were African American.
5. She sometimes uses very interesting and unusual media, such as life-sized portrait masks of famous people.
6. Her stuffed fabric masks, *The Harlem Series*, portray politicians, athletes, and other famous African Americans.
7. She used these masks as props in dramatic presentations.
8. Ringgold wrote stories for a series of "narrative quilts."
9. These unusual creations contain both text and images on panels sewn together like ordinary quilts.
10. In 1987 Faith Ringgold received an honorary doctorate.

Exercise 7: Sentence Writing

Creating Sentences with Direct Objects   Write five sentences describing how to make or do something. Use action verbs. Identify all subjects, verbs, and direct objects.

Indirect Objects

An **indirect object** answers the question *to whom? for whom? to what?* or *for what?* after an action verb.

In most cases, in order for a sentence to have an indirect object, it must first have a direct object. The indirect object always appears between the verb and the direct object.

Airlines give **passengers** bonuses. [Airlines give bonuses *to whom?*]

The owner reserved **us** a table. [The owner reserved a table *for whom?*]

The committee gave my **project** top priority. [The committee gave top priority *to what?*]

Airlines give **passengers** and **employees** bonuses. [Airlines give bonuses *to whom?*]

Exercise 8

Identifying Indirect Objects   First write on your paper the direct object in each of the following sentences. Then list any indirect objects. (There may be more than one indirect object in a sentence, or there may be none at all.)

The Art of Collage

1. Collage offers the beginner and the professional an especially flexible art form.
2. The maker of a collage simply glues material to a "ground."
3. The use of diverse materials can lend this genre an unusual effect.
4. For example, different types of paper give artists the opportunity to experiment with various textures.
5. Some artists create vivid sensory detail through the imaginative use of multiple textures and layered effects.
6. Some artists give their collages added interest by incorporating three-dimensional objects.
7. The use of paint and ink virtually guarantees both the experienced artist and the novice a way of achieving additional variety and striking effects.
8. Photographs of famous persons often lend collages a social or political import.
9. Abstract works, however, can also evoke powerful feelings.
10. The technique of collage has attracted many famous artists, including Pablo Picasso and Georges Braque.

Exercise 9

Recognizing Direct and Indirect Objects   (a) For each of the following sentences without a direct object, rewrite the sentence on a separate sheet of paper, adding a direct object. (b) For each sentence that already has a direct object, rewrite the sentence, adding an indirect object. (c) Write a *D* above each direct object and an *I* above each indirect object.

Using Computers for Writing

1. The use of computers for schoolwork offers many advantages.
2. With computers students often write more carefully.
3. From time to time, they check for errors.
4. Computers have also allowed greater ease in the correction process.
5. With a special program students can even mail their work electronically.

Object Complements

An **object complement** answers the question *what?* after a direct object. That is, it *completes* the meaning of the direct object by identifying or describing it.

Object complements will be found only in sentences that contain a direct object *and* one of the following action verbs or a similar verb that has the general meaning of "make" or "consider":

appoint	consider	make	render
call	elect	name	think
choose	find	prove	vote

An object complement may be an adjective, a noun, or a pronoun. It usually follows a direct object.

The accident rendered her car **useless**. [adjective]
I called the dog **Dusty**. [noun]
Jeanine considers our house **hers**. [pronoun]
The board named Cho **president** and **treasurer**. [nouns]

Exercise 10

Identifying Object Complements   On your paper write the object complement(s) that appear in the following sentences. (One sentence has two object complements, and one sentence has none.) ➡

Subject Complements

A **subject complement** follows a subject and a linking verb and identifies or describes the subject.

There are two kinds of subject complements: *predicate nominatives* and *predicate adjectives*.

A **predicate nominative** is a noun or pronoun that follows a linking verb and points back to the subject to identify it further.

Cellists are **musicians.**

The soloist for this concert is **someone** from Dallas.

Predicate nominatives usually appear in sentences that contain a form of the linking verb *be*. Some other linking verbs (for example, *become* and *remain*) can also be followed by a predicate nominative.

Those two may be **thieves.**
When did he become **treasurer**?
The candidates remained **rivals** but **friends.**

A **predicate adjective** follows a linking verb and points back to the subject and further describes it.

That cellist is **talented.**

The soloist seemed **thoughtful.**

Any linking verb may precede a predicate adjective.

Rachel's tale sounded **preposterous** to all of us.
The runners looked **exhausted** but **happy.**
His manner was **coarse.**
We became quite **impatient** with the long wait.
I felt **elated.**

Identifying Subject Complements   On your paper write all the subject complements that appear in the following sentences. Identify each as a predicate nominative or a predicate adjective. (Two sentences have more than one predicate nominative or predicate adjective; one sentence has none.)

The Japanese Tea Ceremony

[1]Among twelfth-century Zen monks, drinking tea was a way to stay awake during long periods of meditation. [2]Today the tea ceremony has become a traditional Japanese custom. [3]A teahouse may be a detached structure or a special room in the host's house. [4]The design of a teahouse is simple. [5]Bowing to enter through the three-foot doorway, guests feel humble. [6]A scroll, a flower arrangement, and fragrant incense greet visitors. [7]The special treats served before the ceremony taste exquisite. [8]During the ceremony one feels calm and aware of the surroundings. [9]An admiring examination of the host's teapot and utensils is an important part of the ritual. [10]The *wabi* style of these utensils, plain and simple, has been traditional in Japan since the sixteenth century.

Writing Sentences with Complements   Write four sentences about a natural phenomenon. In each sentence use at least one of the four kinds of complements. Label the complements.

Complements   On your paper write the complements that appear in the following paragraph. Next to each complement write the kind of complement it is.

American Sign Language

[1]American Sign Language (ASL) is the standard language of deaf children of deaf parents. [2]Like spoken languages ASL has its own grammar and syntax. [3]Nonetheless, many linguistic experts give ASL short shrift. [4]They call the language primitive. [5]In fact, users of ASL are capable of great precision and subtle expression. [6]In contrast, Signed English is a simple ➡

system of conventional signs. [7]ASL affords deaf people an efficient means of communication. [8]A hearing learner of ASL can eventually become competent. [9]Only after years of practice, however, can hearing learners achieve proficiency. [10]Few ever become experts.

Writing Link

Varying sentence length and word order is a good way to make your writing interesting. Notice how effectively Maxine Hong Kingston varies sentence length and word order in this fantasy sequence from her book *The Woman Warrior*:

> I leapt onto my horse's back and marveled at the power and height it gave me. Just then, galloping out of nowhere straight at me came a rider on a black horse. The villagers scattered except for my one soldier, who stood calmly in the road. I drew my sword.

Try to apply some of Kingston's techniques when you write and revise your own work.

1. Vary the length of your sentences. Notice that the length of Kingston's sentences varies from four to sixteen words.

2. Occasionally use a very short sentence to stress a point, indicate a change of thought, or clinch an idea. Kingston's sentence "I drew my sword" has an abrupt, clinching effect.

3. To help achieve variety, try inverting the word order of a sentence sometimes, as Kingston does in the second sentence.

Practice these techniques by revising the following passage adapted from *The Woman Warrior*. The original is part of the fantasy sequence you just read. Imagine how Kingston would have combined ideas to create a pleasing variety of sentence lengths. Also decide which sentence would be most effective in inverted order. (Note: An ideograph is a character or symbol in the Chinese language.)

> A white horse stepped into the courtyard. I was polishing my armor. The gates were locked tight. It came through the moon door anyway. It was a kingly white horse. It wore a saddle and bridle. The saddle and bridle had red, gold, and black tassles dancing. The saddle was just my size. It had tigers and dragons tooled in swirls. The white horse pawed the ground. It wanted me to go. The ideograph for "to fly" was on the hooves of its near forefoot and hindfoot.

Grammar Workshop

Parts of the Sentence

The setting of *Main Street* is Gopher Prairie, Minnesota, but as Sinclair Lewis says in his introduction to the novel, the town could be any American town, and "its Main Street is the continuation of Main Streets anywhere." In this excerpt the heroine, a young woman named Carol Kennicott, glumly surveys the little town. The passage has been annotated to show some of the parts of the sentence covered in this unit.

Literature Model

from MAIN STREET

by Sinclair Lewis

When Carol had walked for thirty-two minutes she had completely covered the town, east and west, north and south; and she stood at the corner of Main Street and Washington Avenue and despaired.

Main Street, with its two-story brick shops, its story-and-a-half wooden residences, its muddy expanse from concrete walk to walk, its huddle of Fords and lumber-wagons, was too small to absorb her. The broad, straight, unenticing gashes of the streets let in the grasping prairie on every side. She realized the vastness and the emptiness of the land. The skeleton iron windmill on the farm a few blocks away, at the north end of Main Street, was like the ribs of a dead cow. She thought of the coming of the Northern winter, when the unprotected houses would crouch together in terror of storms galloping out of that wild waste. They were so small and weak, the little brown houses. They were shelters for sparrows, not homes for warm laughing people.

She told herself that down the street the leaves were a splendor. The maples were orange; the oaks a solid tint of raspberry. And the lawns had been nursed with love. But the thought would not hold. At best the trees resembled a thinned woodlot. There was no park to rest the eyes. And since not Gopher Prairie but Wakamin was the county-seat, there was no court-house with its grounds.

She glanced through the fly-specked windows of the ⟹

Labels (left margin):
- Compound predicate
- Simple subject
- Complete subject
- Direct objects
- Indirect object
- Subject complement (predicate adjective)
- Inverted sentence beginning with *there*
- Simple predicate

most pretentious building in sight, the one place which welcomed strangers and determined their opinion of the charm and luxury of Gopher Prairie—the Minniemashie House. It was a tall lean shabby structure, three stories of yellow-streaked wood, the corners covered with sanded pine slabs purporting to symbolize stone. In the hotel office she could see a stretch of bare unclean floor, a line of rickety chairs with brass cuspidors between, a writing-desk with advertisements in mother-of-pearl letters upon the glass-covered back. The dining-room beyond was a jungle of stained table-cloths and catsup bottles.

    She looked no more at Minniemashie House.

Subject complement (predicate nominative)

Complete predicate

Grammar Workshop Exercise 1

Identifying Simple and Compound Subjects and Predicates The following sentences describe the winter storms common to Minnesota, the same ones Carol was concerned about in the passage from *Main Street*. Copy each sentence. Then underline and label the simple or compound subject and the simple or compound predicate. Finally, draw a line separating the complete subject from the complete predicate.

SAMPLE   A heavy snowfall delights children but worries commuters.

                      SIMPLE SUBJECT   **COMPOUND PREDICATE**

ANSWER   A heavy <u>snowfall</u> | <u>delights</u> children but <u>worries</u> commuters.

1. The state of Minnesota usually experiences frigid temperatures and heavy snowfall during the winter.
2. Some winter storms are as strong as hurricanes and can result in extensive destruction.
3. The temperature and the direction of the storm affect the nature of the storm.
4. Sleet occurs early in the season and presents a danger for motorists.
5. Sleet can leave a layer of ice more than an inch thick on every building, tree, street, automobile, and utility wire.
6. An ice storm leaves behind an especially heavy coat of ice.
7. Sleet or ice storms can occur before or after a snowfall.
8. A snowfall after an ice storm increases the thickness and weight of the layer of ice.
9. The first snow can arrive as early as September. ➡

10. Annual amounts of snowfall vary from twenty inches in the southwest sections of the state to seventy inches in the northeast.
11. Late-season storms are not uncommon in Minnesota.
12. A storm in late March of 1966 produced gale winds and eleven inches of snow.
13. The effects of the storm included broken utility poles, impassable roads, and widespread damage to trees.
14. Temperatures below twenty degrees Fahrenheit, winds of thirty-five miles per hour or more, and blowing snow indicate blizzard conditions.
15. Dangerous blizzards can result in winds over fifty miles per hour and temperatures below zero degrees Fahrenheit.
16. The dangers of blizzards include limited visibility, the risk of overexposure to cold, and destruction of property.
17. Travel in blizzards is extremely hazardous because of poor visibility.
18. Most deaths in blizzards result from frostbite and hypothermia.
19. The winds of some blizzards can damage buildings, break windows, and dislodge telephone poles.
20. Smart people stay indoors during a winter storm.

Grammar Workshop Exercise 2

Writing Sentences with Complete Subjects and Complete Predicates   Each of the following partial sentences elaborates on an idea suggested by the passage from *Main Street*. Make each sentence complete by writing on your paper either a complete subject or a complete predicate. Do not repeat the exact wording from the novel. Although there is no single right answer, your sentence should make sense within the context of the passage.

SAMPLE   The two-story brick stores _____.

ANSWER   The two-story brick stores seemed small and
            uninteresting to Carol.

1. _____ depressed Carol.
2. _____ stared back emptily at her.
3. The vast and empty prairie _____.
4. The streets with their broad, straight lines _____.
5. An abandoned iron windmill _____.
6. _____ would roar through the town in winter.
7. The bright orange leaves of the maple trees _____. ➡

8. _____ had been carefully tended by their owners.
9. The tall, shabby Minniemashie House _____.
10. _____ made the hotel singularly unattractive.

Grammar Workshop Exercise 3

Writing Sentences with Compound Subjects and Compound Predicates   Write on your paper a complete sentence answering each of the following questions about the passage from *Main Street*. Do not repeat the exact wording from the novel. Begin your sentence with the subject. When composing your answer, follow the directions in parentheses. Then underline and label the simple or compound subject and the simple or compound predicate. Finally, draw a line separating the complete subject from the complete predicate.

SAMPLE   What two streets met at one corner of Gopher Prairie? (Use a compound subject.)

                       COMPOUND SUBJECT   SIMPLE PREDICATE
ANSWER   <u>Main Street</u> and <u>Washington Avenue</u> | <u>met</u> at one corner of Gopher Prairie.

1. What did Carol do at the corner of Main Street and Washington Avenue? (Use a compound predicate.)
2. What kinds of buildings lined Main Street? (Use a compound subject.)
3. What kinds of vehicles were parked close together along Main Street? (Use a compound subject.)
4. What struck Carol about the land around Gopher Prairie? (Use a compound subject.)
5. What characteristics of the houses made them unfit to stand up to winter storms? (Use a compound subject.)
6. What trees down the street were turning color? (Use a compound subject.)
7. According to Carol, which missing elements of the town would improve its appearance? (Use a compound subject.)
8. What did the Minniemashie House do for visitors? (Use a compound predicate.)
9. What added to the shabbiness of the hotel office of the Minniemashie House? (Use a compound subject.)
10. What gave the dining room of the Minniemashie House an uninviting look? (Use a compound subject.)

Grammar Workshop Exercise 4

Writing Inverted Sentences   The following sentences describe a typical small town of the early twentieth century, the time in which *Main Street* is set. On your paper rewrite each sentence in inverted order, following the directions given in parentheses.

SAMPLE   The American small town is of great interest to many historians. (Begin the sentence with *Of great interest.*)

ANSWER   Of great interest to many historians is the American small town.

1. The similarities among the small towns of turn-of-the-century America were often striking.
(Begin the sentence with *There were.*)
2. A railroad depot was usually right in the center of town.
(Begin the sentence with *There was.*)
3. The railroad tracks ran alongside the main street.
(Begin the sentence with *Alongside the main street.*)
4. The railroad was vital to most towns of that time.
(Begin the sentence with *Vital to most towns of that time.*)
5. Freight and travelers came through the railroad station.
(Begin the sentence with *Through the railroad station.*)
6. Businesses and hotels sprang up near the station.
(Begin the sentence with *Near the station.*)
7. Little effort was expended in matching the architecture of the various buildings.
(Begin the sentence with *There was.*)
8. Attractive displays of merchandise were in many storefront windows.
(Begin the sentence with *In many storefront windows.*)
9. Many kinds of stores were found in a typical town.
(Begin the sentence with *There were.*)
10. The offices of dentists, doctors, and lawyers were located above these stores.
(Begin the sentence with *Above these stores.*)

Grammar Workshop Exercise 5

Writing Sentences with Predicate Nominatives and Predicate Adjectives   The pairs of words that follow are derived from the passage from *Main Street*. For each pair write a sentence that uses the first word as the subject and the ➡

second word as a predicate adjective or a predicate nominative. Do not use Lewis's exact words, and be sure to add more than a verb to each pair. Then indicate whether the second word from the pair is acting as a *predicate adjective* or a *predicate nominative*.

SAMPLE   Main Street, expanse
ANSWER   Main Street was an expanse of mud between
                   sidewalks of dull concrete.
                   predicate nominative

1. Carol, woman
2. Gopher Prairie, town
3. Main Street, uninteresting
4. streets, gashes
5. prairie, vast
6. houses, weak
7. trees, woodlot
8. Minniemashie House, building
9. floor, dirty
10. tablecloths, stained

Grammar Workshop Exercise 6

Writing Sentences with Direct and Indirect Objects

Each of the following groups of words elaborates on an idea suggested by the passage from *Main Street*. Each word is labeled *S* (for *subject*), *DO* (for *direct object*), or *IO* (for *indirect object*). Write a sentence using each group of words, but do not use Lewis's exact wording. Add modifiers and prepositional phrases to your sentences.

SAMPLE   Carol (S), Gopher Prairie (IO), look (DO)
ANSWER   Carol gave Gopher Prairie a long, disappointing look.

1. town (S), Carol (IO), feeling (DO)
2. mud (S), streets (DO)
3. windmill (S), ribs (DO)
4. houses (S), people (IO), protection (DO)
5. trees (S), Carol (IO), comfort (DO)
6. Minniemashie House (S), strangers (IO), lodging (DO)
7. windows (S), view (DO)
8. corners (S), stone (DO)
9. dining room (S), guests (IO), atmosphere (DO)
10. hotel (S), Carol (IO), impression (DO)

Review   The following sentences describe the life of Sinclair Lewis. Rewrite each sentence on your paper, according to the directions that appear after each item. Make sure your answers are complete sentences.

Sinclair Lewis

1. Born in 1885, Sinclair Lewis grew up in Sauk Centre, Minnesota.
   (Add *and later modeled Gopher Prairie after his hometown* to the complete predicate.)
2. To Lewis the atmosphere of Sauk Centre seemed smug.
   (Add *and repressive* to create a second predicate adjective.)
3. Different from any of Lewis's previous works, *Main Street* (1920) was a success.
   (Add *great* as a modifier of the subject complement.)
4. Lewis wrote about various segments of society.
   (Add *novels* so that it functions as a direct object.)
5. In Lewis's novel *Babbitt* the pressures of conformity in the business world allow no room for idealistic pursuits.
   (Add *the title character* so that it functions as an indirect object.)
6. In his novel *Arrowsmith* is found a portrait of corruption among doctors.
   (Rewrite the sentence so that it begins with the complete subject.)
7. In 1926 *Arrowsmith* earned Lewis the Pulitzer Prize.
   (Rewrite the sentence so that *Lewis* becomes the subject and *Pulitzer Prize* becomes the direct object.)
8. While at work on these and other books, Lewis became a hermit.
   (Add *virtual* as a modifier of the subject complement.)
9. Few famous authors were as uneven in their writing as Sinclair Lewis.
   (Rewrite the sentence so that it begins with *There were*.)
10. Nevertheless, Lewis's exceptional ability as a satirist helped him win the coveted Nobel Prize for Literature in 1930.
    (Add *and his powerful talent for mimicry* to the complete subject.)

Proofreading The following passage describes the artist Gustave Moeller, whose painting is reproduced on this page. Rewrite the passage, correcting the errors in spelling, capitalization, punctuation, grammar, and usage. There are ten errors in all.

Gustave Moeller

[1]The United States has a rich tradition of regional art and the midwest was both home and subject for many artists. [2]Many Wisconsin painters were of German heritage. [3]Among them was Gustave Moeller (1881–1931). [4]Born in New Holstein, Wisconsin and educated at art schools in Milwaukee, Moeller refines his technique in New York and in Munich. [5]His paintings, carefully composed and extravegantly colored, depict everyday scenes in his native state.

[6]In *Main Street, Alma,* Moeller gives us a view of an unpreposessing Wisconsin town on a summer day. [7]At first glance the street seems deserted the figures (there are at least seven of them) blend inconspicuosly with the scene. [8]It is not hard to imagine Carol, the heroine of *Main Street,* wandering through a town such as this, with it's modest shops, unpaved streets, and battered fords.

Gustave Moeller, *Main Street, Alma,* 1925

Unit 11 Review

Parts of the Sentence

Subjects and Predicates

[pages 443–447]

Identify the underlined word or words in each of the following sentences as **(a)** a complete subject, **(b)** a complete predicate, **(c)** a simple subject, **(d)** a simple predicate, or **(e)** a compound subject.

1. Several <u>groups</u> of Native Americans lived long ago in the Southwest.
2. One of these groups <u>was the Anasazi</u>.
3. <u>The Navaho word *anasazi*</u> means "ancient ones."
4. The <u>Anasazi</u> flourished for nearly three centuries.
5. Secret <u>ceremonies</u> and religious <u>rites</u> were performed by Anasazi men in underground chambers called *kivas*.
6. The Anasazi's society <u>was</u> a forerunner of Pueblo culture.
7. There are <u>many living Pueblo descendants of the Anasazi</u>.
8. The highly advanced civilization of the Anasazi <u>vanished</u> around A.D. 1300.
9. Severe <u>drought</u> or a bad <u>epidemic</u> may have driven the people away.
10. <u>Throughout Arizona and New Mexico are</u> the sites of the ancient Anasazi settlements.

Complements

[pages 447–453]

Identify the underlined word or words in each of the following sentences as **(a)** a direct object, **(b)** an indirect object, **(c)** an object complement, **(d)** a predicate nominative, or **(e)** a predicate adjective.

11. The Anasazi left their northern <u>settlements</u> behind and resettled in the fertile valleys of the Rio Grande and its branches.
12. Chaco in New Mexico is their largest <u>settlement</u>.
13. The Anasazi built <u>some</u> of their stone or adobe villages on high cliffs in steep-walled canyons.
14. Their extreme height made these villages <u>secure</u>.
15. Many of the Anasazi buildings are <u>huge</u> and resemble apartment buildings.
16. The Spaniards gave the Anasazi <u>buildings</u> a Spanish name.
17. They called these buildings <u>*pueblos*</u>, which is Spanish for "towns."
18. Anasazi pottery was highly <u>distinctive</u>.
19. Typical Anasazi crops were <u>corn</u>, <u>beans</u>, and <u>squash</u>.
20. The Spanish brought this <u>area</u> many new foods.

Writing for Review

Write a paragraph on a topic of your choice. In your paragraph underline and identify at least five of the following: *simple subject, simple predicate, direct object, indirect object, object complement, predicate nominative,* and *predicate adjective.*

Phrases

A **phrase** is a group of words that acts in a sentence as a single part of speech.

12.1   Prepositional Phrases

A **prepositional phrase** is a group of words that begins with a preposition and usually ends with a noun or a pronoun, called the **object of the preposition.**

> I'm going **to the river.** [*River* is the object of the preposition *to*.]

> That river is challenging **for the canoeists.** [*Canoeists* is the object of the preposition *for*.]

See page 423 for lists of common prepositions.

Adjectives and other modifiers may appear between the preposition and its object, and a preposition may have more than one object.

> He looked **across the broad, serene river.** [adjectives added]
> The view was **to the east and the south.** [two objects]

Prepositional phrases may also occur in a sequence of two or more.

> The door **of the car with the skis on top** is scratched. [series of prepositional phrases]

A prepositional phrase usually functions as an adjective or an adverb. When it is used as an adjective, it modifies a noun or a pronoun. When it is used as an adverb, it modifies a verb, an adjective, or an adverb.

> Please use the door **in the rear.** [adjective phrase modifying the noun *door*]

> One **of these doors** is locked. [adjective phrase modifying the pronoun *one*]

> **After work** I will return this faulty lock **to the store.** [adverb phrases modifying the verb phrase *will return*]

> Automatic doors are commonplace **in supermarkets.** [adverb phrase modifying the adjective *commonplace*]

> The old door swings easily **for its age.** [adverb phrase modifying the adverb *easily*]

Open the door **at the head of the stairs.** [adjective phrase modifying the noun *door* followed by an adjective phrase modifying the noun *head*]

Exercise 1

Identifying Prepositional Phrases Write each prepositional phrase that appears in the following sentences. (Some of these sentences have more than one prepositional phrase.)

Thurgood Marshall, Supreme Court Justice

1. In the late 1920s Thurgood Marshall pursued a law career.
2. He was denied admission by one law school because he is an African American, but then he was admitted to Howard University's new law program.
3. Marshall graduated at the top of his class.
4. In 1936 he was hired as an assistant counsel to the NAACP.
5. He filed lawsuits challenging discrimination against African Americans in graduate programs and professional schools.
6. When he argued the case *Brown v. Board of Education*, Marshall challenged the practice of separate-but-equal education for African Americans and whites in the public schools.
7. The Court's 1954 agreement with Marshall's arguments changed the educational system throughout America.
8. Thirteen years later, during the administration of Lyndon Johnson, Marshall became a Supreme Court justice.
9. Throughout his years on the Court, Justice Marshall showed concern for the poor and the unempowered.
10. After twenty-four years of service, he resigned in 1991.

Exercise 2

Identifying Adjective and Adverb Phrases Write the word or words each prepositional phrase in Exercise 1 modifies. Indicate whether each phrase is acting as an *adjective* or an *adverb*.

Exercise 3: Sentence Writing

Expanding Sentences with Prepositional Phrases
Expand the following sentences by adding at least one adjective phrase and one adverb phrase to each. ➡

1. The revelers set off fireworks.
2. Four nurses received awards.
3. Anyone could have seen it.
4. The spaceship transmitted messages.
5. The ruler was broken.

12.2　Appositives and Appositive Phrases

An **appositive** is a noun or pronoun that is placed next to another noun or pronoun to identify or give additional information about it.

An a**ppositive phrase** is an appositive plus any words that modify the appositive.

> My sister **Amelia** sells computer software. [The appositive *Amelia* identifies the noun *sister.*]

> She works for Softwarehouse, **a new retail outlet**. [The appositive phrase, *a new retail outlet*, identifies *Softwarehouse.*]

If an appositive is not essential to the meaning of a sentence, it should be set off by commas.

Exercise 4

Identifying Appositives and Appositive Phrases　Write the appositive or appositive phrase that appears in each sentence. (Two sentences have more than one.)

Notable Sports Figures

1. Tiffany Chin, an Olympic figure skater, turned pro in 1987.
2. Walter Payton, star running back of the Chicago Bears, was nicknamed Sweetness because of his smooth running style.
3. During a 1920 World Series game Cleveland Indians second baseman Bill Wambsganss performed the first unassisted triple play.
4. Tracie Ruiz, a swimmer in the 1984 Olympics, won gold medals in the solo synchronized event and, with her partner, Candy Costie, in the duet synchronized event.
5. One of the most versatile athletes ever was the Native American Jim Thorpe, who won gold medals in the pentathlon and the decathlon in the 1920 Olympics.
6. The golf star Nancy Lopez has been setting records since the 1970s. ➡

7. Bill Greene, the victim of an accidental shooting, became an expert at wheelchair sports.
8. Estelle Caito, an expert softball player, began her ten-year career in 1955 with the Orange Lionettes.
9. Wilma Rudolph, a track star, had been paralyzed as a child as a result of two major illnesses, double pneumonia and scarlet fever.
10. In 1972 the great baseball player Roberto Clemente became the eleventh player in major league history to reach the three-thousand mark in hits.

Exercise 5: Sentence Writing

Writing Sentences with Appositive Phrases   On your paper expand the following sentences by adding an appositive phrase to each one. Be sure to use commas where necessary.

SAMPLE   Mr. Díaz hired me to paint his fence.
ANSWER   Mr. Díaz, my neighbor, hired me to paint his fence.

1. My friend mailed me a postcard from Madrid.
2. The movie we saw last night starred two fine actresses.
3. Mei Ying went to a concert featuring a new rock group.
4. The announcer reported that our team had won the game.
5. Daryl had no trouble winning the race.

12.3   Verbals and Verbal Phrases

A **verbal** is a verb form that functions in a sentence as a noun, an adjective, or an adverb.

A **verbal phrase** is a verbal plus any complements and modifiers.

Verbals include *participles*, *gerunds*, and *infinitives*. Each of these can be expanded into phrases.

Participles and Participial Phrases

A **participle** is a verb form that can function as an adjective.

Present *participles* always have an *-ing* ending. *Past participles* often end in *-ed*, but they can take other forms as well. Many commonly used adjectives are actually participles.

Rising prices are inevitable.

I cut my finger on the **broken** glass.

The **opening** speech detailed many **needed** changes.

A participle that is part of a verb phrase is not acting as an adjective.

PARTICIPLE AS ADJECTIVE The **lost** ship has been recovered.
PARTICIPLE IN VERB PHRASE The warehouse **had lost** a big shipment.

A **participial phrase** contains a participle plus any complements and modifiers.

A participial phrase can function as an adjective, and therefore, like an adjective, it can appear in various positions in a sentence. When it appears at the beginning of a sentence, a participial phrase is followed by a comma.

Preparing for the lunar eclipse, we set our alarm clocks.

The full moon, **suspended in the sky,** was brilliant.

Badly needing sleep but **delighted by the spectacle,** we maintained our vigil.

A past participle may be used with the present participle of the auxiliary verb *have* or *be*. (For more on the *-ing* form of a verb, see Unit 15.)

Having read about the eclipse, we were anxious to see it.

We watched the white light of the moon **being consumed by shadow.**

Exercise 6

Identifying Participles and Participial Phrases Write the participle or the participial phrase that acts as an adjective in each of the following sentences. Then identify the word each one modifies.

George Lucas, an Influential Filmmaker

1. George Lucas achieved international fame in 1977 with his stunning science fiction movie *Star Wars.* ➡

2. Celebrated for its superb special effects and suspenseful story, *Star Wars* is still widely seen and admired.
3. Raised in California, Lucas developed an interest in movies.
4. Having competed against other students, he won a national film competition in 1967 at the age of twenty-three.
5. Lucas's first major success was the popular *American Graffiti* (1973), a film portraying the lives of California teenagers in the 1960s.
6. Lucas worked on *American Graffiti* in two capacities, serving as both coauthor and director of the film.
7. By 1981, having produced *The Empire Strikes Back* and *The Return of the Jedi*, Lucas again proved his great versatility.
8. That year Lucas produced the highly successful adventure film *Raiders of the Lost Ark*, directed by his old friend Steven Spielberg.
9. Many people in the film industry marveled at the huge profits of *Raiders* and the two films succeeding it—*Indiana Jones and the Temple of Doom* (1984) and *Indiana Jones and the Last Crusade* (1989).
10. Freed from dependence upon film studios through his wealth and influence, Lucas can continue to pursue his personal artistic vision.

Gerunds and Gerund Phrases

A **gerund** is a verb form that ends in *-ing* and is used in the same way a noun is used.

> **Training** is essential. [gerund as subject]

> We considered **flying.** [gerund as direct object]

> We should give **speaking** more attention. [gerund as indirect object]

> Do I get credit for **trying?** [gerund as object of a preposition]

> Their passions were **sailing** and **sculling.** [gerunds as predicate nominatives]

> Two skills, **reading** and **writing,** are basic. [gerunds as appositives]

A **gerund phrase** is a gerund plus any complements and modifiers.

> **Actively participating in sports** has many benefits.
> This suit shows **expert tailoring.**

Although both a present participle and a gerund end in *-ing*, they serve as different parts of speech. A present participle is used as an adjective in its sentence, whereas a gerund is used as a noun.

Waiting in line, we grew impatient. [participial phrase]
Waiting in line made us impatient. [gerund phrase]

Exercise 7

Identifying Gerunds and Gerund Phrases   List on your paper the gerunds and gerund phrases that appear in the following sentences. (Three of the sentences have two gerunds or gerund phrases, and one has three.)

New Mexican Tin Working

1. The art of creating decorative tin objects is practiced mostly by Hispanic men and women, long admired as tin workers.
2. After studying and adapting century-old patterns, these artisans begin by expertly cutting a sheet of tin.
3. Making indentations in the tin, or punching, is done with blunt steel or iron tools.
4. Piercing, which requires sharper implements, has the effect of enhancing an object's design.
5. Selling these masterful products is easily accomplished since many people enjoy owning them.

Exercise 8: Sentence Writing

Creating Sentences with Gerunds   Select five of the gerunds that you identified in Exercise 7, and write an original sentence for each one. Make sure you use the *-ing* word as a gerund, not as a present participle.

Infinitives and Infinitive Phrases

An **infinitive** is a verb form that is usually preceded by the word *to* and is used as a noun, an adjective, or an adverb.

The word *to* used before the base form of a verb is part of the infinitive form of the verb, not a preposition.

To exercise is healthful. [infinitive as subject]
No one wishes **to volunteer.** [infinitive as direct object]
Their decision was **to merge.** [infinitive as predicate nominative]

I felt a need **to call.** [infinitive as adjective]

Everyone was prepared **to sacrifice.** [infinitive as adverb]

An **infinitive phrase** contains an infinitive plus any complements and modifiers.

> The lawyers want **to continue working on the case** as long as possible.

> Would you prefer **to sleep until noon**?

> **To speak clearly and slowly** is most important.

Occasionally an infinitive may have its own subject. Such a construction is called an *infinitive clause.*

> Circumstances forced **the gentlemen to duel.** [*Gentlemen* is the subject of the infinitive *to duel.* The entire infinitive clause *the gentlemen to duel* acts as the direct object of the sentence.]

> The teacher asked **Maria to give a speech.** [*Maria* is the subject of the infinitive *to give.* The entire infinitive clause *Maria to give a speech* acts as the direct object of the sentence.]

Note that the subject of the infinitive phrase comes between the main verb and the infinitive. The subject of an infinitive clause always follows an action verb.

Sometimes the word *to* is dropped before an infinitive.

> Please **[to] call.**
> We could have heard **a pin [to] drop.**

Exercise 9

Identifying Infinitive Phrases   Write the infinitive phrase that appears in each of the following sentences. (One sentence has two infinitive phrases.)

Art in Winston-Salem

1. Art has come to play a major role in the cultural life of Winston-Salem, North Carolina.
2. The city has two famous museums known to attract visitors from all over the United States.
3. For those who wish to see nineteenth-century southern decorative art, the Museum of Early Southern Decorative Arts is the place to explore thoroughly.
4. Over the years art lovers who have wanted to learn more about American painting have visited Reynolda House.
5. The Southeast Center for Contemporary Arts (SECCA) was founded to encourage new southern artists. ➡

6. Thus, what people come to view in this gallery is almost exclusively the work of unrecognized artists.
7. Exhibits change constantly, as SECCA never intended to acquire a permanent art collection.
8. Each year, to foster talent, SECCA awards fellowships to seven artists from the southeastern United States.
9. To win one of these fellowships is a great honor.
10. To judge the works of the Southeast Seven artists each year is the job of a group of experts.

Exercise 10: Sentence Writing

Using Infinitives   Write down five action verbs. Then make up a sentence using each verb in an infinitive phrase. Underline the infinitive phrases.

12.4   Absolute Phrases

An **absolute phrase** consists of a noun or a pronoun that is modified by a participle or a participial phrase. An absolute phrase has no grammatical relation to the rest of the sentence.*

*Absolute phrases are also known as nominative absolutes.

An absolute phrase belongs neither to the complete subject nor to the complete predicate of a sentence. It stands "absolutely" by itself in relation to the rest of the sentence.

Its wings badly damaged in the storm, the aircraft crashed.

In some absolute phrases the participle *being* is understood rather than stated.

We took off on schedule, **the weather [being] perfect.**

Exercise 11

Identifying Absolute Phrases   Write on your paper the absolute phrase in each of the following sentences.

1. I spend many hours in the backyard, gardening being my favorite activity.
2. The soil rich in nutrients, everything grows quickly.
3. The radishes and beans having been planted a week ago, I now await the first signs of growth. ➡

4. The plan of my vegetable garden is strictly geometric, everything laid out in neat rows.
5. The flower bed is more informal, the plants arranged mainly by color.

Exercise 12: Review

Verbal Phrases and Absolute Phrases   Write each of the verbal and absolute phrases that appears in the following sentences. (Three sentences have more than one verbal phrase.) Tell whether each is a *participial phrase*, a *gerund phrase*, an *infinitive phrase*, or an *absolute phrase*. (Remember: an absolute phrase has within it a participle or a participial phrase.)

The Hmong

1. Have you ever seen *pandau*, the beautiful cloths stitched by Hmong women?
2. Cutting material in intricate designs and embroidering bold patterns with fine stitches, the Hmong women create their beautiful needlework.
3. Over the past two thousand years the Hmong people have migrated from China, their ancestral home, to settle in the mountains of Vietnam, Laos, and Thailand.
4. Unfortunately, supporting the Americans in the Vietnam War cost many Hmong their homes and lives.
5. Their allies having withdrawn from Vietnam in 1972, the Hmong were forced to flee the area, and the United States began to admit thousands of Hmong refugees.
6. Building a new life in the United States has not been easy for a people with an alien language and culture.
7. One means that Hmong women have discovered for earning money has been the sale of *pandau*.
8. Americans who appreciate fine needlework delight in the textile art embroidered with traditional designs or decorated with scenes from Hmong folk tales.
9. At street fairs and in small shops, the women sell their own *pandau* as well as those sent from sisters and cousins still in Thai resettlement camps.
10. Today the directors of Hmong craft centers work hard to keep the ancient and beautiful art of *pandau* alive in a new country.

Mature writers have at their command a variety of sentence patterns not only to help them express their meaning but also to control the rhythm of their prose. Phrases in particular provide writers with many ways in which to create sentences that are vividly detailed and rhythmically expressive. Try using the following techniques when you write and revise your work:

1. Use phrases that modify, such as prepositional, participial, and infinitive phrases, to add vivid description and detail to your ideas. In this excerpt from *The Women of Brewster Place*, Gloria Naylor uses modifying phrases to expand the statement "Kiswana could see."

> <u>From the window</u> <u>of her sixth-floor studio apartment</u>, Kiswana could see <u>over the wall</u> <u>at the end</u> <u>of the street</u> <u>to the busy avenue</u> that lay just north <u>of Brewster Place</u>. The late afternoon shoppers looked <u>like brightly clad marionettes</u> as they moved <u>between the congested traffic</u>, <u>clutching their packages against their bodies</u> <u>to guard them from sudden bursts of the cold autumn wind</u>.

The many prepositional phrases in the first sentence tell us where Kiswana is and where she is looking. The prepositional, participial, and infinitive phrases in the second sentence help us picture the scene she sees. Notice how Naylor underscores the steady bustle of the scene by piling phrase atop phrase in long rhythmic sentences.

2. Use appositive, gerund, and absolute phrases to elaborate on your basic ideas. In this example from the short story "By the Waters of Babylon," Stephen Vincent Benét expands a three-word sentence by adding two absolute phrases:

> I went carefully, <u>my strung bow in my hand</u>, <u>my skin ready for danger</u>.

Benét's use of absolute phrases allows the reader to imagine a complete and unified action even though the rhythm divides the sentence into three distinct parts. If Benét had written "I went carefully. I held my strung bow in my hand. My skin was ready for danger," the reader would have imagined three separate and consecutive actions. The effect would have been far choppier.

Apply these techniques by revising the following passage on a separate sheet of paper. Combine choppy and awkward sentences by turning some of them into phrases that give the final passage a smooth rhythm. Try to use a variety of phrases: prepositional, participial, infinitive, appositive, gerund, and absolute.

> It was March. The year was 1513. Ponce de León boldly entered Florida's waters. His hopes were as high as the tall ship's mast. The mast was casting its shadow over him. He had been appointed governor of Puerto Rico several years before. He had heard legends. The legends described a fountain. The fountain had miraculous healing powers. He was dreaming of glory. He had left Puerto Rico and sailed far. He had crossed treacherous seas. He had journeyed to Florida's waters. His purpose was that here he would find the Fountain of Youth.

Phrases

The three passages in this Workshop are taken from a classic American novel, *The Red Badge of Courage*. Each passage has been annotated to show how Stephen Crane used the kinds of phrases taught in this unit. The novel is the story of a young man who finds himself caught up in the violence of the Civil War and who faces up to his feelings of self doubt.

Literature Model

from THE RED BADGE OF COURAGE
by Stephen Crane

Participial phrase —

Prepositional phrase —

A house standing placidly in distant fields had to him an ominous look. The shadows of the woods were formidable. He was certain that in this vista there lurked fierce-eyed hosts. The swift thought came to him that the generals did not know what they were about. It was all a trap. Suddenly those close forests would bristle with rifle barrels. Ironlike brigades would appear in the rear. They were all going to be sacrificed. The generals were stupids. The enemy would presently swallow the whole command. He glared about him, expecting to see the stealthy approach of his death.

Infinitive phrase —

He thought that he must break from the ranks and harangue his comrades. They must not all be killed like pigs; and he was sure it would come to pass unless they were informed of these dangers. The generals were idiots to send them marching into a regular pen. There was but one pair of eyes in the corps. He would step forth and make a speech. Shrill and passionate words came to his lips.

The line, broken into moving fragments by the ground, went calmly on through fields and woods. The youth looked at the men nearest him, and saw, for the most part, expressions of deep interest, as if they were investigating something that had fascinated them. One or two stepped with overvaliant airs as if they were already plunged into war. Others walked as upon thin ice. The greater part of the untested men appeared quiet and absorbed. They ➡

Prepositional phrase —

were going to look at war, the red animal—war, the blood-swollen god. And they were deeply engrossed in this march.

Appositive phrase

❧

Some one cried, "Here they come!"

There was rustling and muttering among the men. They displayed a feverish desire to have every possible cartridge ready to their hands. The boxes were pulled around into various positions, and adjusted with great care. It was as if seven hundred new bonnets were being tried on.

Gerund phrase

The tall soldier, having prepared his rifle, produced a red handkerchief of some kind. He was engaged in knitting it about his throat with exquisite attention to its position, when the cry was repeated up and down the line in a muffled roar of sound.

"Here they come! Here they come!" Gun locks clicked.

❧

When the woods again began to pour forth the dark-hued masses of the enemy the youth felt serene self-confidence. He smiled briefly when he saw men dodge and duck at the long screechings of shells that were thrown in giant handfuls over them. He stood, erect and tranquil, watching the attack begin against a part of the line that made a blue curve along the side of an adjacent hill. His vision being unmolested by smoke from the rifles of his companions he had opportunities to see parts of the hard fight. It was a relief to perceive at last from whence came some of these noises which had been roared into his ears.

Absolute phrase

Grammar Workshop Exercise 1

Elaborating Sentences with Prepositional Phrases The following sentences describe an imaginary battle scene. Read through the sentences quickly to get an idea of the scene, and then rewrite each sentence, adding at least one prepositional phrase—an adjective phrase or an adverb phrase—to each sentence. You do not have to describe a scene from the Civil War, as Stephen Crane did; you can imagine any scene that you wish.

SAMPLE   The struggle was over quickly.
ANSWER   The struggle between the men was over quickly.

1. The attack began early.
2. Mist enveloped the valley. ➡

3. Only a few rays penetrated the fog.
4. The men advanced silently.
5. The leader signaled a halt.
6. Suddenly they heard a shout.
7. The enemy had seen them.
8. The men raced forward.
9. They met fierce resistance.
10. Several men fell wounded.
11. Others ran desperately.
12. The enemy outnumbered the men.
13. The men thought they were doomed.
14. Nevertheless, they pressed on.
15. Never had they seen such confusion.
16. The noise was deafening.
17. Fear paralyzed some.
18. Three men led the assault.
19. They fought a pitched battle.
20. The leader was wounded.

Grammar Workshop Exercise 2

Elaborating Sentences with Appositives   The sentences below elaborate upon an idea suggested by the literary passages. Each sentence is followed by a group of words in parentheses. Rewrite each sentence, incorporating the words in parentheses so that they form an appositive phrase. Use a comma or commas to set off the appositive phrase from the rest of the sentence.

SAMPLE   The battle was indecisive.
             (a brief skirmish)
ANSWER   The battle, a brief skirmish, was indecisive.

1. The soldier saw the house.
   (an island of calm in the midst of chaos)
2. The house had an ominous look.
   (a dilapidated clapboard building)
3. Dark shapes obscured the building.
   (the shadows of giant elms)
4. Perhaps the enemy lurked within those shadows.
   (grim soldiers in gray)
5. The soldier felt trapped.
   (a young boy named Henry Fleming)
6. Never in all his life had he felt so frightened.
   (a mere sixteen years) ➧

7. He had a flash of insight.
   (an awful premonition)
8. He and all his fellow soldiers were going to be sacrificed.
   (the entire regiment)
9. Anger swelled within him.
   (an uncontrollable tide)
10. The line advanced through the fields.
    (an unwavering column of blue)

Grammar Workshop Exercise 3

Elaborating Sentences with Participial Phrases   Each of the sentences below elaborates upon an idea suggested by the passages from *The Red Badge of Courage*. Each sentence is followed by another sentence in parentheses. Combine the sentences, changing the sentence in parentheses into a participial phrase. Be sure to place the participial phrase close to the word in the first sentence that it modifies.

SAMPLE   The boy feared the troops.
            (The troops were hiding in the woods.)

ANSWER   The boy feared the troops hiding in the woods.

1. The house had an ominous look.
   (The house was bordering the woods.)
2. The shadows were dense and foreboding.
   (The shadows were engulfing the house.)
3. The boy feared the enemy.
   (The enemy was lurking in the shadows.)
4. He imagined the woods.
   (The woods were bristling with artillery.)
5. The boy shivered.
   (The boy was disturbed by the thought.)
6. He was filled with anger.
   (He was convinced of the futility of his situation.)
7. The generals were going to sacrifice their troops!
   (The generals were commanding the Union Army.)
8. He advanced through the woods.
   (He was casting baleful glances around him.)
9. He resolved to warn his comrades.
   (He was rousing his courage.)
10. He decided he would make a speech to stir the men.
    (He was setting his fears aside.)
11. His comrades would realize the folly of the assault.
    (His comrades were shaken by his words.) ➡

12. His brave resolve soon disappeared.
    (His resolve was diminished by his fears.)
13. The line of Union soldiers advanced steadily toward their opponents.
    (The line was unwavering in the dim light.)
14. Some men marched jauntily.
    (The men were putting on a show of valor.)
15. Others walked stealthily.
    (They were glancing fearfully from side to side.)
16. The men seemed subdued and serious.
    (The men were untested in battle.)
17. The enemy looked like a dull gray river.
    (The enemy was pouring out of the woods.)
18. Suddenly the boy felt a wave of calm.
    (The calm was breaking over him.)
19. His eyes took in the entire scene.
    (His eyes were unobscured by the dust and smoke of battle.)
20. The sounds of battle brought him a curious sense of relief.
    (The sounds were surging toward him.)

Grammar Workshop Exercise 4

Creating Sentences with Gerund Phrases   Each of the items below consists of a question followed by a phrase in parentheses that answers the question. For each item write a sentence that answers the question, using the words in parentheses as a gerund phrase.

SAMPLE   What is patriotic? (defending one's country)
ANSWER   Defending one's country is patriotic.

1. What is part of every soldier's life? (being afraid)
2. What is essential in battle? (having courage)
3. What do few soldiers find easy? (being brave)
4. What is the boy's goal? (warning his fellow soldiers)
5. What do soldiers dread? (being slaughtered)
6. What makes no sense to the boy? (dying needlessly)
7. What seems absurd to him? (obeying blindly)
8. What is every soldier's responsibility? (accepting duty)
9. What is crucial to the boy? (being able to survive)
10. What does the boy find is easier than he thought? (remaining calm)

Elaborating Sentences with Infinitive Phrases   Each of the items below consists of a question followed by a phrase in parentheses that answers the question. For each item write a sentence that answers the question, using the words in parentheses as an infinitive phrase.

SAMPLE   What is the goal of every soldier?
             (to fight bravely and steadfastly)
ANSWER   The goal of every soldier is to fight bravely and
             steadfastly.

1. What has war often threatened?
   (to destroy nations)
2. What did the Civil War almost manage to do?
   (to divide our country)
3. What was a goal of the Confederates?
   (to maintain the Southern way of life)
4. What was the aim of the North?
   (to preserve the Union)
5. What do most history books tend to do?
   (to side with the North)

Elaborating Sentences with Absolute Phrases   Rewrite each of the following sentences, making the words in italics into an absolute phrase.

SAMPLE   *Because war is common,* many children are forced
             to endure it.
ANSWER   War being common, many children are forced to
             endure it.

1. *Since their experience is limited*, children understand
   little about war.
2. Nevertheless, *because they have few choices*, many children live
   in war zones.
3. Children are strongly affected by conflict, *as their minds
   are impressionable.*
4. *Because turmoil has filled their lives*, the children are forced to
   adapt.
5. *Since their resilience is great*, these children often survive
   remarkably well.

Review   Below is a brief biographical sketch of Stephen Crane followed by ten sentences. Use the facts in the sketch to expand the ten sentences, following the guidelines that appear in parentheses at the end of each sentence. Be sure to place the phrases you add close to the word they modify.

Stephen Crane

Stephen Crane was born in Newark, New Jersey, in 1871. He was the fourteenth child of a Methodist minister. When he was a young man, he was restless and rebellious. He studied briefly at Syracuse University in New York. Then he moved to New York City and became a reporter. He worked for several syndicates. At the time he wrote *The Red Badge of Courage*, he was only twenty-one, and he finished it within ten days. The novel describes a young Union soldier's disillusionment with war. Critics praised *The Red Badge of Courage*. They applauded its unflinching realism. Later Crane covered the Cuban front of the Spanish-American War and won praise for his courage. He died in Germany in 1900. The cause of his death was tuberculosis. His clear and ironic prose influenced a generation of authors, among them Ernest Hemingway.

1. Stephen Crane wrote a powerful novel.
   (Add an appositive phrase.)
2. Crane studied at Syracuse University.
   (Add an adverb phrase.)
3. He later became a reporter.
   (Add an adjective phrase.)
4. He wrote *The Red Badge of Courage*.
   (Add an adverb phrase.)
5. The novel describes the disenchantment.
   (Add an adjective phrase.)
6. Critics praised *The Red Badge of Courage*.
   (Add an adverb phrase.)
7. Crane went to Cuba.
   (Add an infinitive phrase.)
8. Crane was not afraid.
   (Add an absolute phrase.)
9. Crane died in 1900.
   (Add an adverb phrase.)
10. His prose influenced many writers.
    (Add a participial phrase.)

Proofreading   The following passage describes the artist Winslow Homer, whose painting appears on this page. Rewrite the passage, correcting the errors in spelling, capitalization, punctuation, grammar, and usage. There are ten errors in all.

Winslow Homer

[1]Winslow Homer (1836–1910) was born in Boston, Massachusets. [2]When he was six his family moved to the nearby town of Cambridge, where Homer learnd to love the outdoors. [3]A precocious child he began drawing at an early age.

[4]For seventeen years Homer worked as a magazine illustrater. [5]His training in illustration, enabled him to bring a clear and unsentimental eye to his art. [6]Perhaps the most famous illustrations that Homer made were of the Civil War. [7]At the time photography was still a primitive art and illustrators like Homer played a valuable role in relaying images of the war to the public.

[8]In 1866 Homer received wide recognition for the painting shown here: *Prisoners From the Front.* [9]Despite the rather static figures, the scene seems real. [10]Steven Crane, like Homer, immortalized the Civil War. [11]Homer, however, witnessed the war firsthand, whereas Crane, born after it ended, relied on secondery reports and his powerful imagination.

Winslow Homer, *Prisoners from the Front,* 1866

Unit 12 Review

Phrases

Identifying Phrases

[pages 463–473]

Tell whether the underlined phrase in each sentence is **(a)** a prepositional phrase, **(b)** an appositive phrase, **(c)** a participial phrase or an absolute phrase, **(d)** a gerund phrase, or **(e)** an infinitive phrase.

1. Known <u>for her plays</u>, Lorraine Hansberry was a committed artist.
2. <u>Writing about social injustice</u> was important to her.
3. She began <u>to write for herself</u> while still in high school.
4. *A Raisin in the Sun*, <u>her first play</u>, won several awards.
5. <u>Her second play having been produced</u>, Hansberry died at the age of thirty-four.

Prepositional Phrases

[pages 463–465]

Tell whether the prepositional phrase in each sentence is acting as **(a)** an adjective or **(b)** an adverb.

6. The phoenix legend began in Egypt.
7. The phoenix, a bird with the power to die and rise again, symbolized the sun.
8. English kings used the phoenix symbol in heraldry.
9. Asian myths detail a bird like the phoenix.
10. The phoenix inspired the *Firebird* ballet of Igor Stravinsky.

Gerund Phrases

[pages 468–469]

Tell whether the gerund phrase in each of the following sentences is used as **(a)** a subject,

(b) a direct object, **(c)** an object of a preposition, **(d)** a predicate nominative, or **(e)** an appositive.

11. Have you ever considered owning your own business?
12. Coming up with a new idea is essential for success.
13. You will not succeed by copying someone else's ideas.
14. Good management, or creating good relationships, is often overlooked by novice business owners.
15. Your major goal must become making your business a success.

Infinitive Phrases

[pages 469–471]

Tell whether the infinitive phrase in each sentence is used as **(a)** a noun, **(b)** an adjective, or **(c)** an adverb.

16. To save money, the mint makes copper-coated zinc pennies.
17. Some people want to restore more copper to the penny.
18. Others feel that phasing out the penny is an idea to consider.
19. To mint a penny costs much more than one cent.
20. The mint wishes penny hoarders would be willing to stop.

Writing for Review

On a separate sheet of paper, write a paragraph on any subject you choose. Include and underline at least one example of each kind of phrase: *prepositional*, *appositive*, *participial*, *gerund*, and *infinitive*.

Unit 13 | Clauses and Sentence Structure

A **clause** is a group of words that has a subject and a predicate and that is used as a part of a sentence.

The two kinds of clauses are *main clauses* (also called *independent clauses*) and *subordinate clauses* (also called *dependent clauses*).

13.1 | Main Clauses

A **main clause** has a subject and a predicate and can stand alone as a sentence.

Every sentence must contain at least one main clause. The sentence below contains two main clauses: clauses that have both a subject and a verb and would express a complete thought if they appeared individually.

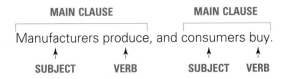

13.2 | Subordinate Clauses

A **subordinate clause** has a subject and a predicate, but it cannot stand alone as a sentence.

A subordinate clause is dependent upon the rest of the sentence because it does not make sense by itself. A subordinate clause needs a main clause to complete its meaning. Subordinating conjunctions or relative pronouns usually introduce a subordinate clause.

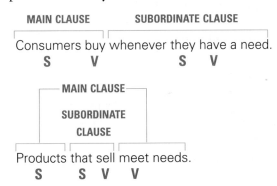

In the first sentence the subordinating conjunction *whenever* introduces the subordinate clause *whenever they have a need.* Even though this subordinate clause has a subject and a predicate, it does not express a complete thought.

In the second sentence the relative pronoun *that* introduces a subordinate clause that comes between the subject and the verb of the main clause. In this case *that* also functions as the subject of the subordinate clause.

Exercise 1

Identifying Main and Subordinate Clauses   Each of the following sentences has a clause that appears in italics. On your paper indicate whether it is a *main clause* or a *subordinate clause.* (Remember that a subordinate clause cannot stand alone as a sentence.)

Shirley Chisholm, Political Pioneer

1. Shirley Chisholm was a congresswoman from New York *who sought the presidential nomination in 1972.*
2. *Chisholm's campaign was notable* because she was the first African-American woman to seek this high office.
3. *Even though her presidential campaign had little chance of success,* Shirley Chisolm considered her bid a serious one.
4. *Because her activities focused attention on important issues,* Chisholm was satisfied.
5. *Chisholm had established another first four years earlier* when she became the first African-American woman to be elected to Congress.
6. Her congressional election followed four years of service in the New York State Assembly, *where Chisholm had gained a reputation for independent thinking.*
7. This independent thinking became obvious to all in Congress *as soon as the freshman representative began her first term in office.*
8. Although her background was in education and she represented an urban district, *Chisholm was assigned to the Agriculture Committee.*
9. After she strongly objected to the inappropriate assignment, *the Democratic leadership was forced to reassign her to a more suitable committee.*
10. This incident exemplified Chisholm's strength of character, *which helped her earn from her constituents the fond nickname Fighting Shirley.*

13.3 Simple and Compound Sentences

A **simple sentence** has only one main clause and no subordinate clauses.

Keep in mind that as long as a sentence has only one main clause, it is a simple sentence. Nevertheless, a simple sentence may have a compound subject or a compound predicate. A simple sentence may also have both a compound subject and a compound predicate. The subject and the predicate of a simple sentence may also be expanded in many ways, such as with the addition of adjectives, adverbs, prepositional phrases, appositives and appositive phrases, and verbal phrases.

Consumers buy. [simple sentence]

Consumers and investors buy. [simple sentence with compound subject]

Consumers compare and buy. [simple sentence with compound predicate]

Consumers and investors compare and buy. [simple sentence with compound subject and compound predicate]

Most serious investors carefully consider alternative uses for their money. [simple sentence expanded]

A **compound sentence** has two or more main clauses.

Although all of the main clauses of a compound sentence are part of the same sentence, each clause has its own subject and its own predicate. A comma, together with a coordinating conjunction (*and, but, or, nor, yet,* or *for*), is usually used to join the main clauses, as in the examples that follow.

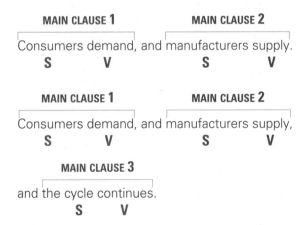

Main clauses may also be joined by a semicolon in place of the comma and the coordinating conjunction.

MAIN CLAUSE **1**

First, demand for a specific product increases;

MAIN CLAUSE **2**

then the price of the product rises.

Exercise 2

Identifying Simple and Compound Sentences   On your paper indicate whether each of the following items is a *simple sentence* or a *compound sentence*. (Remember that a single main clause can have a compound subject and a compound predicate.)

Crocodiles

1. Crocodiles and dinosaurs are related to each other, but crocodiles have survived extraordinary climate changes to the present day.
2. Crocodiles' brains are quite complex, and their hearts are almost mammalian.
3. Full-grown crocodiles can range in length from three to twenty-five feet and can sometimes weigh more than two thousand pounds.
4. A crocodile is strong enough to kill a water buffalo but gentle enough to carry its newly hatched babies between its jaws.
5. A few species of crocodilians prefer to live more or less solitary lives; most, however, prefer to live in sizable communities.
6. Crocodiles usually live in remote places, but hunters greedy for crocodile skins have little trouble discovering them.
7. In many places crocodiles are protected by law but now face another problem.
8. People are moving into and radically changing the crocodile's natural habitat.
9. Engineers dam large rivers, clear once-teeming swamps, and build sprawling new cities to provide habitation for human beings, but this progress spells disaster for the crocodiles in their fight for survival.
10. Have crocodiles survived for about 22 million years only to succumb to the unchecked desires of an increasing human population?

Complex and Compound-Complex Sentences

A **complex sentence** has one main clause and one or more subordinate clauses.

MAIN CLAUSE   SUBORDINATE CLAUSE

Consumers buy fewer goods when prices rise.
   S   V   S   V

SUBORDINATE CLAUSE   MAIN CLAUSE

If they know this, manufacturers can reduce output
  S   V   S   V

SUBORDINATE CLAUSE

when it is necessary to do so.
  S V

A **compound-complex sentence** has more than one main clause and at least one subordinate clause.

SUBORDINATE CLAUSE   MAIN CLAUSE **1**

If production increases, prices may drop, and
  S   V   S   V

MAIN CLAUSE **2**

consumers may buy more.
  S   V

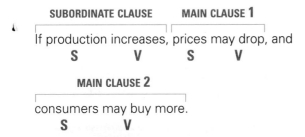

Exercise 3

Identifying Complex and Compound-Complex Sentences Write on your paper the subordinate clause that appears in each of the following sentences. Indicate whether each sentence is *complex* or *compound-complex.*

Plaza of the Three Cultures

1. When the ancestors of the Aztecs migrated to the western region of Lake Texcoco during the fourteenth century, they founded two different cities on neighboring islands.
2. The occupants of the two cities—Tenochtitlán and Tlatelolco—gradually filled in the shallow lake surrounding their islands until the two landmasses were joined. ➡

3. Although Tenochtitlán eventually became the capital of the Aztec Empire, Tlatelolco maintained its independence from the empire.

4. Nevertheless, while the Spanish conquistadors were crushing the Aztec Empire, they destroyed much of Tlatelolco, and the area was eventually absorbed into what is now Mexico City.

5. The Spanish constructed their own buildings, including the Church of Santiago Tlatelolco, on the site where the Aztecs had worshiped their gods.

6. In 1960, over three centuries later, the government of Mexico City began a redevelopment plan that brought new apartment complexes and office buildings to the Tlatelolco area.

7. Construction workers cleared away neglected, dilapidated structures and began to dig the foundations for brand-new buildings, but they soon were greatly surprised by the discovery of ancient stone platforms that were clearly Aztec in origin.

8. Because modern Mexican citizens appreciate the culture and achievements of their Aztec ancestors, the Mexican government has preserved the ancient Aztec ruins for all to appreciate.

9. Today a tourist to Tlatelolco can stand in one place and see evidence of the three cultures—Aztec, Spanish, and modern Mexican—that illustrate Mexico's varied and fascinating history.

10. If you visit the Plaza of the Three Cultures, you can see standing next to one another platforms of Aztec temples, a Spanish church, and modern Mexican apartment and office buildings.

Exercise 4: Sentence Writing

Creating Sentences with Various Structures   On a separate sheet of paper, write a simple sentence. Then rework it, making it into a compound sentence. Now go back to the simple sentence, and rework it to make it part of a complex sentence. Finally, rework your compound sentence, making it into a compound-complex sentence. Refer to the examples on pages 485, 486, and 487 as necessary.

13.5 Adjective Clauses

An **adjective clause** is a subordinate clause that modifies a noun or a pronoun.

An adjective clause normally comes after the word it modifies.

Periodicals **that inform and entertain** often make good reading.

Several writers **whom I admire** contribute to excellent magazines.

Kim enjoys a magazine **whose style is distinctive and modern.**

Both relative pronouns (*who, whom, whose, that,* and *which*) and the subordinating conjunctions *where* and *when* may begin adjective clauses.

I cannot remember a time in my life **when I did not enjoy reading.**

Libraries are places **where many kinds of periodicals can be found.**

The relative pronoun may sometimes be dropped at the beginning of an adjective clause.

The article in this magazine is one **I am sure you will enjoy.** [The relative pronoun *that* has been omitted.]

An adjective clause is sometimes needed to make the meaning of a sentence clear. Such an adjective clause is called an *essential clause*, or a *restrictive clause*. Without the essential adjective clause, the complete meaning of the sentence would not be expressed.

Magazines **that have no photographs** bore me. [essential clause]

Smithsonian is the magazine **that I like best.** [essential clause]

When an adjective clause is not absolutely needed in order to express the complete meaning of a sentence, it is called a *nonessential clause*, or a *nonrestrictive clause*. Always use commas to set off a nonessential clause.

Newspapers, **which I often read,** are interesting. [nonessential clause]

Also informative are newsletters, **which are widely distributed by many organizations.** [nonessential clause]

The relative pronoun *that* usually introduces an essential clause; the relative pronoun *which* introduces a nonessential clause.

Newsmagazines, **which are published weekly,** provide excellent coverage of current events. [nonessential clause]

World events **that have major significance** are thoroughly reported. [essential clause]

Exercise 5

Identifying Adjective Clauses   On your paper write the adjective clause that appears in each of the following sentences. Then write the word that the clause modifies. (In one sentence the relative pronoun has been dropped.)

Pueblo Ceremonial Dances

1. The Pueblo people celebrate occasions in the spring and summer with dances they have been performing in the same way for centuries.
2. These corn dances date from a time when the Pueblo were the only people in the arid southwestern region of the country.
3. Following a designated leader holding a tall symbolic pole, the chorus that will accompany the dancers advances into the plaza.
4. The scores of males who dance wear special jewelry for the occasion and carry ceremonial gourd rattles and sprigs of evergreen.
5. As part of this seasonal ritual of the Pueblo, women and girls carry bunches of evergreen branches and wear impressive wooden headpieces that represent thunder and lightning.
6. The Pueblo dancers circle the musicians, rhythmically shaking the gourd rattles in the air, gently waving ever-green branches, and treading the earth with steps that look deceptively simple.
7. During the ceremonies the rhythms that fill the air are both subtle and complex.
8. At about midday the dancing stops, and food is offered to all who are present.
9. The dances, which in many pueblos are performed first by one group and then by another group, continue until the sun sets.
10. By performing this elaborate ceremony, the Pueblo hoped to ensure sufficient rain for the crops and blessings for those who lived in the pueblo.

Recognizing Essential and Nonessential Clauses For each sentence in the pairs below, write the adjective clause, and then identify it as an *essential* or a *nonessential clause.*

Challenges of the Handicapped

1. **a.** People who are handicapped have impairments of their sensory, physical, or mental faculties.
   b. Handicaps, which may range from mild to severe, can be classified according to three general categories: sensory, motor, or mental.
2. **a.** Most people, who tend to associate physical impairment with mental impairment, react stereotypically and often insensitively to those with handicaps.
   b. People who know handicapped people must take care to see each individual as unique.
3. **a.** Technological innovations in vans, wheelchairs, and electronic equipment have improved the quality of life of those who are handicapped.
   b. The application of new electronic technology to equipment for the handicapped, who make good use of it, is increasing steadily.
4. **a.** New laws have made transportation, which has long been a problem for the physically handicapped, more readily accessible to them.
   b. Physically handicapped people have had to wait too long for transportation that is reliable and inexpensive.
5. **a.** In the past handicapped people were allowed to work only at menial jobs, which offer little mental challenge.
   b. The handicapped are gradually gaining access to jobs that make full use of their abilities.

13.6 Adverb Clauses

An **adverb clause** is a subordinate clause that modifies a verb, an adjective, or an adverb. It tells *when, where, how, why, to what extent,* or *under what condition.*

> **Wherever I go,** I take a magazine. [The adverb clause modifies the verb *take.* It tells *where.*]

> I am happy **as long as I can read**. [The adverb clause modifies the adjective *happy.* It tells *under what condition.*]

I enjoy magazines more **than I usually enjoy a book.** [The adverb clause modifies the adverb *more*. It tells *to what extent*.]

Subordinating conjunctions, such as those listed on page 428, introduce adverb clauses. An adverb clause can come either before a main clause or after it. The first two examples above might have been written in the following manner:

I take a magazine **wherever I go.**
As long as I can read, I am happy.

On occasion words may be left out of an adverb clause in order to avoid repetition and awkwardness. The omitted words can easily be supplied by the reader, however, because they are understood, or implied. Such adverb clauses are called *elliptical adverb clauses*.

Few enjoy reading more **than I [enjoy reading].**
Reading makes me more relaxed **than [it makes] her [relaxed].**

Exercise 7

Identifying Adverb Clauses   On your paper write the adverb clause that appears in each of the following sentences. (Three sentences have more than one adverb clause.)

SAMPLE   For as long as I can remember, I have admired Annie Oakley.

ANSWER   as long as I can remember

Annie Oakley, Sharpshooter

1. Until Annie Oakley came along, sharpshooting had been a rather tame affair.
2. Since Annie's widowed mother was very poor, Annie provided for the family by shooting game birds that she then would sell to hotels and restaurants.
3. When Annie was visiting her sister in Cincinnati, she entered a contest against a champion sharpshooter so that she could earn extra money.
4. After he lost in a close match, the sharpshooter, Frank Butler, fell in love with Annie, and they eventually were married.
5. Frank taught Annie his sharpshooting tricks so that she could join his stage act.
6. Wherever they went, Frank's act was a big success as long as Annie was featured.
7. After Annie was established as a star, Frank retired from the act, though he continued as her manager.
8. Annie attracted many fans because she was entertaining as well as skillful. ➡

9. Because she remembered her own unhappy childhood, Annie befriended orphans, staged charity shows, and paid the bills of many poor families.
10. Although Annie Oakley established sharpshooting records, perhaps her greatest feats were her kind deeds.

13.7   Noun Clauses

A **noun clause** is a subordinate clause used as a noun.

You can use a noun clause in the same ways that you can use a noun or a pronoun: as a subject, a direct object, an object of a preposition, or a predicate nominative.

PRONOUN

Someone left these magazines.
    S

NOUN CLAUSE

Whoever was here last left these magazines.
    S

NOUN

Magazines reflect the values of a society.
    DO

NOUN CLAUSE

Magazines reflect whatever a society values.
    DO

In the examples you have just finished reading, notice that each noun clause forms an inseparable part of the main clause of the sentence. In the second sentence, for example, the noun clause is the subject of the main clause. In the last sentence the noun clause is the direct object of the main clause.

Here are some words that can be used to introduce noun clauses:

how	when	who, whom
that	where	whoever
what	which	whose
whatever	whichever	why

Here are more examples of sentences that contain noun clauses:

Do you know **which magazine is my favorite**? [noun clause as a direct object]

This article is about **how microchips work**. [noun clause as the object of a preposition]

This is **where I get most of my up-to-date information**. [noun clause as a predicate nominative]

At times the relative pronoun is dropped from the beginning of a noun clause.

Hector thinks ***PC Computing* is the best computer magazine on the market**. [The relative pronoun *that* has been omitted.]

Exercise 8

Identifying Noun Clauses   On your paper write the noun clauses that appear in each of the following sentences. (Three of the sentences have two noun clauses each. In one sentence the relative pronoun has been dropped.)

Fireworks

1. Tradition says the Chinese invented fireworks, but this tale has not been proved.
2. What is known by historians today is that explosives were in military use in many countries around the world by the 1300s.
3. By the 1500s victories were celebrated with fireworks, and these fireworks were set off by whoever was brave enough to ignite the explosives.
4. That fireworks continue to be extremely dangerous cannot be denied.
5. Today whoever manufactures or presents fireworks must observe numerous safety procedures.
6. The danger aside, it is easy to see why fireworks of many different kinds are popular.
7. Traditionalists prefer whatever explodes in a radial burst, like the spread of a chrysanthemum.
8. Modern viewers are usually more interested in how loud the explosion is and in how many bursts are included in a cluster of shells.
9. Whoever loves fireworks will want to keep track of when the best fireworks are displayed in celebrations around the world.
10. For example, a good time to see fireworks displays in Mexico is when the country celebrates its National Independence Day.

Using Subordinate Clauses in Sentences   Write four original sentences. In the first, use an adverb clause. In the second, use an adjective clause. In the third, use a noun clause as a subject. In the fourth, use a noun clause as a direct object.

Clauses   On your paper write the subordinate clause that appears in each sentence. Then indicate whether the subordinate clause is (a) an adverb clause, (b) an adjective clause, or (c) a noun clause.

Tulsa, Oklahoma

1. Tulsa, Oklahoma, is called the Oil Capital of the World because more than 850 petroleum companies have headquarters there.
2. The city, which is on the Arkansas River, is the second largest in the state.
3. Although many visitors to the city do not at first realize it, Tulsa is a thriving center of both art and distinguished architecture.
4. Philbrook Art Center, which sponsors an annual competition for Native American artists from both North America and South America, houses an outstanding art collection.
5. Museum goers may find it difficult to decide how they can best spend their time at Tulsa's Gilcrease Institute of History and Art.
6. Although Tulsa has a great many new and distinctive buildings, it has also successfully preserved carefully selected older buildings.
7. The civic center and a unique high-rise Art Deco church are only two of the structures that have received widespread acclaim.
8. The futuristic campus of nearby Oral Roberts University is remembered by all who visit it.
9. That the fountains and shade trees of the new pedestrian mall in Tulsa are special attractions in themselves is quite clear.
10. Many surprises await whoever visits this fascinating and progressive city.

13.8 Four Kinds of Sentences

A **declarative sentence** makes a statement.

> The sun will rise at 6:17 A.M.
> It is already light outside.

The declarative sentence is the kind of sentence used most frequently. You usually end a declarative sentence with a period.

An **imperative sentence** gives a command or makes a request.

> Get up, and take a walk with me.
> Please close the door quietly.

The subject "you" is understood in an imperative sentence. It, too, usually ends with a period.

An **interrogative sentence** asks a question.

> Is anyone else awake?
> Do you think we should wait for the others?

You place a question mark at the end of an interrogative sentence.

An **exclamatory sentence** expresses strong emotion.

> I will *not* hurry!
> What a glorious sunrise there is!

You place an exclamation point at the end of an exclamatory sentence.

Exercise 11: Sentence Writing

Creating Four Kinds of Sentences Write four sentences about a favorite vacation. Use one declarative, one imperative, one interrogative, and one exclamatory sentence.

13.9 Sentence Fragments

In general, avoid sentence fragments in your writing. A **sentence fragment** is an error that occurs when an incomplete sentence is punctuated as though it were a complete sentence.

Look for three things when reviewing your work to detect sentence fragments. First, check for a group of words without a subject. Then look for a group of words without a verb, especially a group that includes a verbal rather than a complete verb. Finally, check to see that a subordinate clause is not punctuated as though it were a complete sentence.

Many times you can correct a sentence fragment by attaching it to a main clause that comes before the fragment or after it. Other times you may need to add words in order to make the sentence complete.

FRAGMENT	Levar and Juanita started hiking on the main trail. **Wanted to explore a remote area of the park.** [lacks subject]
COMPLETE SENTENCE	Levar and Juanita started hiking on the main trail, but they wanted to explore a remote area of the park.
FRAGMENT	They were tired. **The two weary hikers walking for hours.** [lacks complete verb]
COMPLETE SENTENCE	They were tired. The two weary hikers had been walking for hours.
FRAGMENT	To their left they found a faint trail. **Which they followed to the river.** [has subordinate clause only]
COMPLETE SENTENCE	To their left they found a faint trail, which they followed to the river.

There are times when many professional writers use sentence fragments to create a special effect. They might want to emphasize a particular point or portray realistic dialogue. Keep in mind that professionals use sentence fragments carefully and intentionally. In most of your writing, however, including your writing for school, you should avoid sentence fragments.

Exercise 12

Identifying Sentence Fragments   Indicate on your paper whether each of the following numbered items is a *complete sentence* or a *sentence fragment*.

Louis Armstrong, a Jazz Pioneer

[1]Louis Armstrong, known as Satchmo, one of the most famous and beloved figures in American music. [2]Growing up among the brass bands of New Orleans, Louisiana, in the twentieth century's first decade. [3]Armstrong began his musical career singing in a barbershop quartet. [4]As a teen-ager played cornet on riverboats and in New Orleans clubs called honky tonks. [5]Armstrong joined the band of his hero, the jazz cornetist King Oliver, in Chicago in 1922. [6]Switching to the trumpet, Armstrong later formed his own band, the Hot Fives, and made a series of recordings between 1925 and 1928. [7]Which had a profound effect on musicians and jazz enthusiasts alike. [8]After appearing in many films in the late 1930s, ➡

Armstrong quickly became an international star. [9]By the 1950s his winning personality and great talent making him one of the best-known entertainers in the world. [10]When he died on July 6, 1971, the entire world mourned the loss of this great entertainer.

Exercise 13: Sentence Writing

Correcting Sentence Fragments   Revise the preceding paragraph by correcting each fragment. Wherever possible, combine the fragments with other sentences in the paragraph rather than making them into separate sentences.

13.10   Run-on Sentences

Avoid run-on sentences in your writing. A **run-on sentence** is two or more complete sentences written as though they were one sentence.

The following are the three basic kinds of run-on sentences:

1. A **comma splice** is perhaps the most common kind of run-on sentence. It occurs when two main clauses are separated by a comma rather than by a semicolon or a period. In order to correct a comma splice, you can add a coordinating conjunction. Another option is to replace the comma with an end mark of punctuation, such as a period or a question mark, and begin the new sentence with a capital letter.

RUN-ON	Mari and Victor went on a picnic yesterday, they had a wonderful time until it began to rain.
CORRECT	Mari and Victor went on a picnic yesterday**, and** they had a wonderful time until it began to rain.
CORRECT	Mari and Victor went on a picnic yesterday. They had a wonderful time until it began to rain.

2. Another kind of run-on sentence is formed when there is no punctuation between the two main clauses. In order to correct this kind of run-on, you can separate the main clauses with a semicolon, or you can add an end mark of punctuation after the first clause and begin the second one with a capital letter. You can also correct the error by placing a comma and a coordinating conjunction between the two main clauses.

RUN-ON	They brought a large amount of food with them nothing was left over.
CORRECT	They brought a large amount of food with them. Nothing was left over.
CORRECT	They brought a large amount of food with them; nothing was left over.
CORRECT	They brought a large amount of food with them, **yet** nothing was left over.

3. Still another kind of run-on sentence is formed when there is no comma before a coordinating conjunction that joins two main clauses. In order to correct the error, just add the comma before the coordinating conjunction.

RUN-ON	They were looking for a shady spot but they could not find one.
CORRECT	They were looking for a shady spot, but they could not find one.

Exercise 14

Correcting Run-on Sentences Rewrite each of the following sentences, correcting the run-ons. Watch for the three kinds of run-on errors just shown. You may choose from among the several ways of correcting run-ons that you have learned.

The Great Wall of China

1. The Great Wall of China stretches over fifteen hundred miles and it is considered one of the greatest construction projects in history.
2. Its average height is twenty-five feet the structure is fifteen to thirty feet wide along the base and twelve feet wide at the top.
3. Shih Huang-ti, founder of the Ch'in dynasty, feared the nomadic tribes of the north the principal tribe he feared was the Hsiung-nu.
4. He conceived of the Great Wall as a defensive barrier against these tribes but he probably underestimated the cost and danger of the project.
5. In 214 B.C. Shih Huang-ti formed the Great Wall by linking many existing walls, these smaller walls had been built earlier by various local Chinese leaders.
6. The wall features many forty-foot watchtowers these structures facilitated communication across great distances with signals of smoke by day and fire by night. ➡

7. Behind the wall the Chinese established small agricultural settlements, these settlements supported the many troops that defended the wall from enemy attack.
8. The Great Wall was constructed with an array of materials at various points along its length the wall is composed of granite, wood, brick, earth, or masonry.
9. Several times since its completion the wall has been restored, the most extensive rebuilding occurred during the Ming dynasty between 1368 and 1644.
10. Today the Great Wall of China remains a symbol of ancient Chinese history and visitors to China continue to marvel at this extraordinary monument.

Exercise 15: Review

Sentence Completeness   Rewrite the following paragraph, correcting all sentence fragments and run-on sentences.

Carlos Fuentes, Contemporary Author

[1]According to many literary critics, Carlos Fuentes stands as Mexico's most important contemporary author, much of his work deals with the consequences of the Mexican Revolution. [2]Has written such books as *Where the Air Is Clear* and *The Good Conscience*, which criticize aspects of Mexican society. [3]Fuentes has donned several hats during his lifetime he has worked as a diplomat, novelist, playwright, film critic, editor, publisher, lecturer, and university administrator. [4]Because his father was a career diplomat, the family traveled widely and Fuentes learned to speak both English and French at an early age. [5]After attending law school at the University of Mexico, in 1954 helped found an important Mexican literary journal, *Revista mexicana de literatura*. [6]Which he edited for four years. [7]Although master of the short story, essay, and drama, has best displayed his talent in his novels. [8]Many of his novels—notably *The Death of Artemio Cruz* and *Terra Nostra*—show his profound interest in Mexican history and they explore how the nation's past relates to its present. [9]His novel *The Old Gringo* was made into a movie, it is an imaginative examination of the death of the American author Ambrose Bierce. [10]Who disappeared mysteriously in Mexico in 1913, fifteen years before the birth of Carlos Fuentes.

In the following passage from her short story "The Signature," Elizabeth Enright uses a variety of sentence structures. As you read, observe how the changing sentence structures develop a rhythm that helps build suspense.

The mirror was at the end of the hall. I walked toward it with my fists closed, and my heart walked, too, heavily in my chest. I watched the woman's figure in the dark dress and the knees moving forward. When I was close to it, I saw, low in the right-hand corner of the mirror, the scratched small outline of the eye-diamond, a signature, carved on the surface of the glass by whom, and in what cold spirit of raillery? Lifting my head, I looked at my own face. I leaned forward and looked closely at my face, and I remembered everything. I remembered everything. And I knew the name of the city I would never leave, and, alas, I understood the language of its citizens.

Enright effectively uses a variety of sentence structures. Even in this brief passage she uses simple, compound, complex, and compound-complex sentences. Try to apply her techniques to your own writing.

1. Vary the length and structure of your sentences to enliven your writing and to create subtle rhythmic effects. Simple sentences are usually short and can have a quick-paced, abrupt effect. Compound, complex, and compound-complex sentences are often longer and may have a slow, meandering quality. Notice that Enright's passage consistently alternates simple sentences with more complicated structures: simple, compound, simple, complex, simple, compound, simple, compound-complex. The alternating rhythm supports the paragraph's mood of mounting tension and gradual realization.

2. Sometimes the use of an interrogative sentence can heighten dramatic effect. Notice that Enright ends her long fourth sentence as a question. The question not only adds variety but also underscores the narrator's puzzled feelings.

Apply these techniques by revising the following paragraph on a separate sheet of paper. Combine sentences to create a paragraph in which alternating sentence structures achieve a rhythm that builds suspense. Use at least one compound, one complex, one compound-complex, and three simple sentences. Also make one sentence interrogative, exclamatory, or imperative.

In 1916 an explosion swept through a tunnel. The tunnel was part of the Cleveland Waterworks. Many workers were trapped inside. Poisonous gases began seeping through the tunnel. Rescue parties could not enter. The trapped workers were in terrible danger. Then someone remembered Garrett Morgan. Morgan had invented a device called a gas mask. Few people had been interested in buying it. Now his assistance was sought. Morgan brought some of his gas masks to the site of the explosion. Rescuers gingerly donned them. Morgan's device might allow them to enter the tunnel safely .

Grammar Workshop

Clauses and Sentence Structure

The novel from which the following passage is taken is about an unscrupulous social climber, Jay Gatsby, who changes his name, invents a privileged background, and gains admission to an exclusive world. While an army officer during World War I, Gatsby had a brief romance with a southern society girl named Daisy Fay. Years later he tells the story of that romance to his friend Nick Carraway, who is Daisy's cousin. The passage has been annotated to show the types of clauses covered in this unit.

Literature Model

from THE GREAT GATSBY

by F. Scott Fitzgerald

"I can't describe to you how surprised I was to find out I loved her, old sport. I even hoped for a while that she'd throw me over, but she didn't, because she was in love with me too. She thought I knew a lot because I knew different things from her . . . Well, there I was, 'way off my ambitions, getting deeper in love every minute, and all of a sudden I didn't care. What was the use of doing great things if I could have a better time telling her what I was going to do?"

On the last afternoon before he went abroad, he sat with Daisy in his arms for a long, silent time. It was a cold fall day, with fire in the room and her cheeks flushed. Now and then she moved and he changed his arm a little, and once he kissed her dark shining hair. The afternoon had made them tranquil for a while, as if to give them a deep memory for the long parting the next day promised. They had never been closer in their month of love, nor communicated more profoundly one with another, than when she brushed silent lips against his coat's shoulder or when he touched the end of her fingers, gently, as though she were asleep.

He did extraordinarily well in the war. He was a captain before he went to the front, and following the Argonne battles he got his majority and the command of the ⟶

Noun clause — that she'd throw me over

Interrogative sentence — What was the use of doing great things if I could have a better time telling her what I was going to do?

Declarative sentence — On the last afternoon before he went abroad, he sat with Daisy in his arms for a long, silent time.

Adverb clause — before he went to the front

divisional machine-guns. After the Armistice he tried frantically to get home, but some complication or misunderstanding sent him to Oxford instead. He was worried now—there was a quality of nervous despair in Daisy's letters. She didn't see why he couldn't come. She was feeling the pressure of the world outside, and she wanted to see him and feel his presence beside her and be reassured that she was doing the right thing after all.

For Daisy was young and her artificial world was redolent of orchids and pleasant, cheerful snobbery and orchestras which set the rhythm of the year, summing up the sadness and suggestiveness of life in new tunes. All night the saxophones wailed the hopeless comment of the Beale Street Blues while a hundred pairs of golden and silver slippers shuffled the shining dust. At the gray tea hour there were always rooms that throbbed incessantly with this low, sweet fever, while fresh faces drifted here and there like rose petals blown by the sad horns around the floor.

Through this twilight universe Daisy began to move again with the season; suddenly she was again keeping half a dozen dates a day with half a dozen men, and drowsing asleep at dawn with the beads and chiffon of an evening dress tangled among dying orchids on the floor beside her bed. And all the time something within her was crying for a decision. She wanted her life shaped now, immediately. . . .

Compound sentence

Compound-complex sentence

Complex sentence

Adjective clause

Grammar Workshop Exercise 1

Identifying Main and Subordinate Clauses   The following sentences are based on the passage from *The Great Gatsby*. Each sentence contains a clause in italics. Indicate whether the italicized clause is a *main clause* or a *subordinate clause*.

1. *Gatsby was surprised* when he recognized his love for Daisy.
2. *Just before he went off to war,* Gatsby met Daisy.
3. *Daisy loved Gatsby, too,* although he came from a different world.
4. Gatsby didn't head home right after the war *because unexpected events forced him to go to Oxford.*
5. Gatsby hoped *that Daisy would wait for him.*
6. *Daisy didn't understand* why Gatsby couldn't return.
7. She was an eager girl *who couldn't wait long.* ➡

8. *After she had waited for Gatsby for a while*, she felt the pressures of her social world.
9. She returned to her old world, *which was full of fun and flowers and snobbery.*
10. *While Gatsby remained in England*, Daisy danced the evenings away with other men.

Grammar Workshop Exercise 2

Identifying Compound, Complex, and Compound-Complex Sentences   The following sentences are based on the passage from *The Great Gatsby*. On your paper indicate whether each is a *compound*, *complex*, or *compound-complex sentence*.

1. Gatsby spent the last afternoon before he left for the war with Daisy, and he and Daisy had never felt closer.
2. Gatsby was upset when he couldn't return home immediately after the war.
3. Daisy wrote to Gatsby, but her letters, with their sense of despair, only made him worry.
4. The cheerful world of Daisy's society called to her, and Daisy was soon part of it again.
5. Something inside her said that she would not be able to wait for Gatsby's return.

Grammar Workshop Exercise 3

Writing Sentences with Adjective Clauses   The sentences that follow elaborate on ideas from the passage from *The Great Gatsby*. Rewrite each sentence, adding an adjective clause that answers the question in parentheses. Your clause must begin with one of the words listed below, and it must contain a verb. Your sentence should make sense within the context of the passage, but you should not use the exact wording from the passage.

RELATIVE PRONOUNS	who whom whose which that
SUBORDINATING CONJUNCTIONS	when where

SAMPLE	Gatsby was a social climber.
	(What did Gatsby create for himself?)
ANSWER	Gatsby was a social climber who created an imaginary background for himself. ➡

1. Gatsby told his story to Nick Carraway. (Who was Nick Carraway?)
2. Gatsby well remembered a particular fall day. (What happened on that day?)
3. Daisy sat close to Gatsby and felt calm and at peace. (What were Daisy's feelings toward Gatsby?)
4. War took Gatsby away from Daisy. (What did the war do to their romance?)
5. After the war Gatsby was forced to go to Oxford. (What was Gatsby's real desire?)
6. Daisy's letters made Gatsby anxious. (What were the letters like?)
7. Daisy desperately needed Gatsby's presence. (What would his presence do?)
8. Daisy's world was an artificial place. (What could be found in this artificial place?)
9. Every night people in Daisy's world would listen to orchestras. (What did the orchestras do?)
10. Daisy sometimes woke at dawn with her evening dress on the floor beside her. (Which evening dress was this?)

Grammar Workshop Exercise 4

Writing Sentences with Adverb Clauses   The sentences that follow elaborate on ideas from *The Great Gatsby*. Rewrite each sentence, adding an adverb clause that answers the question in parentheses. Your clause must begin with one of the subordinating conjunctions listed below, and it must contain a verb. The sentence should make sense within the context of the passage, but you should avoid the novel's exact wording. There may be more than one correct answer for each item.

SUBORDINATING CONJUNCTIONS

after	as long as	because	if	than	wherever
as	as though	before	so that	when	while

SAMPLE   Daisy and Gatsby felt closest. (When?)

ANSWER   Daisy and Gatsby felt closest as Gatsby was about to leave for the war.

1. Gatsby lied about his background. (Why?)
2. Gatsby and Daisy had a romance. (When?)
3. Gatsby loved Daisy more deeply. (To what extent?)
4. Gatsby became a machine-gun commander. (When?)
5. After the war Gatsby couldn't return home. (Why?) ➡

6. In her letters Daisy sounded nervous. (To what extent?)
7. She might have married Gatsby. (Under what condition?)
8. Daisy saw a cheerful but snobbish world. (Where?)
9. The orchestras played. (When?)
10. Daisy could be faithful to Gatsby. (Under what condition?)

Grammar Workshop Exercise 5

Identifying Noun Clauses   The following sentences describe life during the 1920s, the period in which *The Great Gatsby* is set. On your paper write the noun clauses that appear in the sentences. Two of the sentences have two noun clauses each. In one sentence the relative pronoun before the noun clause has been dropped.

1. In the 1920s the automobile radically changed where Americans went and what they did.
2. Americans could drive their cars to whatever places they pleased.
3. What made the lives of many Americans easier was the widespread availability of electricity.
4. Whoever enjoyed music could now listen to it on electric phonographs.
5. What had once been regarded as shocking behavior became more widely accepted in the 1920s.
6. How men and women dressed showed their new sense of freedom.
7. That many women were suddenly wearing shorter dresses and more makeup led the more staid members of society to feel that the old decorum was gone for good.
8. Whoever had leisure time might attend sports events.
9. Many Americans thought athletic figures like Babe Ruth and Jack Dempsey were heroes.
10. That advertising became widespread was an additional reason for the rapid changes of the 1920s.

Grammar Workshop Exercise 6

Writing Four Kinds of Sentences   On your paper identify each of the following sentences as either *declarative*, *imperative*, *interrogative*, or *exclamatory*. Then rewrite each sentence in the form noted in parentheses. ➡

SAMPLE	Gatsby told Daisy to wait for him. (Rewrite in the imperative form.)
ANSWER	declarative
	"Daisy, wait for me."

1. Nick asked Gatsby to tell the story.
   (Rewrite in the imperative form.)
2. How surprised Gatsby was to find himself in love with Daisy!
   (Rewrite in the interrogative form.)
3. Was Gatsby a great success during the war?
   (Rewrite in the declarative form.)
4. Daisy saw other men and tried to forget about Gatsby.
   (Rewrite in the interrogative form.)
5. Daisy wore a beautiful chiffon dress.
   (Rewrite in the exclamatory form.)

Grammar Workshop Exercise 7

Correcting Sentence Fragments and Run-ons   The following paragraph describes Nick Carraway, the narrator of *The Great Gatsby*. Revise the paragraph, correcting any sentence fragments and any run-ons. The fragments may be corrected by combining sentences, by adding words (such as a subject or a verb), or by changing the form of the verb. The run-ons may be corrected in more than one way.

[1]Nick Carraway was a young man from the Midwest he was the kind of man in whom others often confide. [2]His relatives important people who had made money in the hardware business. [3]Having graduated from Yale and gone to Europe to fight in World War I. [4]Nick came to New York to work in the bond business, he needed a place to live. [5]Convinced by a friend to settle on Long Island, he renting the bungalow next to Gatsby's mansion. [6]Daisy Fay was Nick's second cousin once removed, lived with her husband in a fashionable area nearby. [7]One day Nick drove to her house for dinner, he met her husband, Tom Buchanan. [8]Who was extremely wealthy but unfeeling and arrogant. [9]For Nick this was an important dinner, for it marked the beginning of one of the most momentous summers of his life. [10]Soon Nick getting to know Gatsby and learn about Gatsby's romance with Daisy.

Review   The items that follow describe the life of F. Scott Fitzgerald. Revise each item as indicated in parentheses.

SAMPLE   Fitzgerald was a Midwesterner. He spent much of his adult life in New York, Europe, and Hollywood. (Combine the sentences by turning the second sentence into an adjective clause beginning with *who*.)

ANSWER   Fitzgerald was a Midwesterner who spent much of his adult life in New York, Europe, and Hollywood.

F. Scott Fitzgerald

1. F. Scott Fitzgerald was born in 1896 in Saint Paul, Minnesota. As a teen-ager he was already writing stories, poems, and plays. (Rewrite as a compound sentence.)
2. Fitzgerald met and fell in love with Zelda Sayre, an Alabama belle. He was serving in the army at the time. (Combine the sentences by turning the second sentence into an adverb clause beginning with *while*.)
3. Fitzgerald published his first novel, *This Side of Paradise*, in 1920, the novel described the new style of life of the time. (Eliminate the run-on by creating two sentences.)
4. The novel was a spectacular success. Fitzgerald suddenly became an important man who had both money and reputation. (Rewrite as a compound-complex sentence.)
5. Fitzgerald married Zelda Sayre after the book's publication. She resembled many of Fitzgerald's heroines. (Combine the sentences by turning the second sentence into an adjective clause beginning with *who*.)
6. *The Great Gatsby* (1925) is regarded as Fitzgerald's masterpiece. Did not long support the Fitzgeralds' lavish life style. (Eliminate the sentence fragment.)
7. By the late 1920s Zelda was suffering from a serious mental illness. (Rewrite as an interrogative sentence.)
8. In 1937 Fitzgerald moved to Hollywood. He worked there as a screenwriter in order to pay his debts. (Combine the sentences by turning the second sentence into an adjective clause beginning with *where*.)
9. Fitzgerald died at age forty-four. He was working on *The Last Tycoon*, a novel about Hollywood and America in the 1930s. (Rewrite as a complex sentence.)
10. Fitzgerald once said something. "There are no second acts in American lives." (Combine the sentences by turning the second sentence into a noun clause beginning with *that*.)

Proofreading   This passage describes the artist Guy Pène du Bois, whose painting appears on this page. Rewrite the passage, correcting the errors in spelling, capitalization, punctuation, grammar, and usage. There are ten errors in all.

Guy Pène du Bois

[1]Born in Brooklyn New York, Guy Pène du Bois (1884–1958) was the son of a literary critic. [2]He studied painting at the New York School of Art and later studies on his own in Paris.

[3]Du Bois worked as an Art critic, he also taught painting at a school in New York City. [4]He depicted realistic scenes of everyday life focusing on café society in New York. [5]Mr. and Mrs. Chester Dale Dining Out is typical of many of his paintings: it portrays a small number of people and they have been stylized as if they were mannequins or objects in a still life.

[6]The people in the painting reproduced here has a staid formality in both dress and pose. [7]The figures appear to be carved, out of marble. [8]The painting vividly depicts the elegant society that Jay Gatsby, the hero of F. Scott Fitzgerald's novel *The Great Gatsby*, sought so assiduously. [9]The woman depicted here could be Daisy or any other society woman who reveled in her "twilight universe".

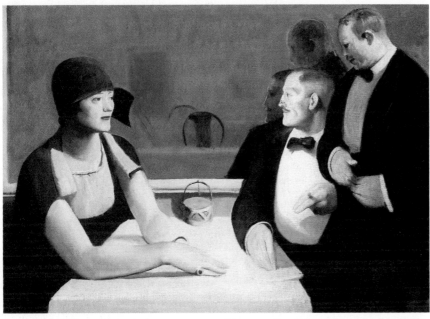

Guy Pène du Bois, *Mr. and Mrs. Chester Dale Dining Out,* 1924

Unit 13 Review

Clauses and Sentence Structure

Clauses and the Sentences They Form

[pages 483–501]

Indicate whether each of the following sentences is **(a)** simple, **(b)** compound, **(c)** complex, or **(d)** compound-complex.

1. Colonial Williamsburg is a section of Williamsburg, Virginia.
2. This area, which was restored, is interesting to visit.
3. Craftspeople work in the shops, and they explain how the colonists did each of their jobs.
4. A master, who owned the shop, might not practice the trade at all, but he or she would hire others to do the work.
5. The colonists respected all the trades; each one was essential.

Kinds of Clauses

[pages 483–495]

Identify the underlined clause in each sentence as **(a)** a main clause, **(b)** an adjective clause, **(c)** an adverb clause, or **(d)** a noun clause.

6. Fairbanks, Alaska, is a city <u>that has severe winters</u>.
7. <u>Summers are quite pleasant</u>, since the days are very long.
8. Fairbanks was founded <u>after gold was discovered there</u>.
9. Gold, <u>which was mined in the early 1900s</u>, caused a boom.
10. <u>That oil has replaced gold as the source of Alaska's prosperity</u> cannot be denied.

Kinds of Sentences

[page 496]

Identify each sentence as **(a)** declarative, **(b)** imperative, **(c)** interrogative, or **(d)** exclamatory.

11. Have you heard about "comfort foods"?
12. Psychologists say that some foods have comforting effects.
13. Some foods are comforting because they evoke good memories.
14. How unfortunate it is that comfort foods are often fattening!
15. To feel good, try drinking some warm milk with honey in it.

Sentence Completeness

[pages 496–500]

Identify each item as **(a)** a fragment, **(b)** a run-on, or **(c)** a complete sentence.

16. Johann Sebastian Bach, one of the world's greatest composers.
17. During his lifetime he was best known as an organist.
18. Born into a musical family, he began music lessons at six.
19. Perfecting the art of polyphony in Baroque music.
20. Bach had twenty children, four sons became famous composers.

Writing for Review

Write a paragraph on a topic of your choice. Use at least one sentence of each kind and a variety of clauses.

Diagraming Sentences

Diagraming is a method of showing the relationship of various words and parts of a sentence to the sentence as a whole.

14.1   Diagraming Simple Sentences

You begin to diagram a sentence by finding the simple subject. Next find the action or linking verb that goes with the subject. Write the subject and the verb on a horizontal line. Separate them with a vertical line.

Trees grow.

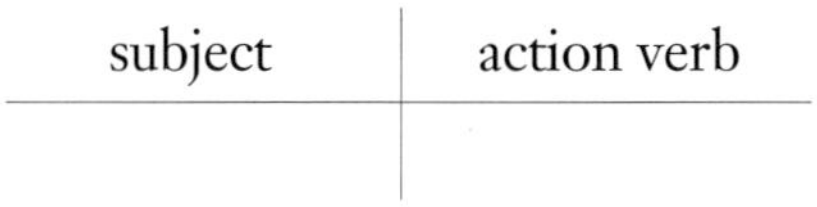

subject	action verb

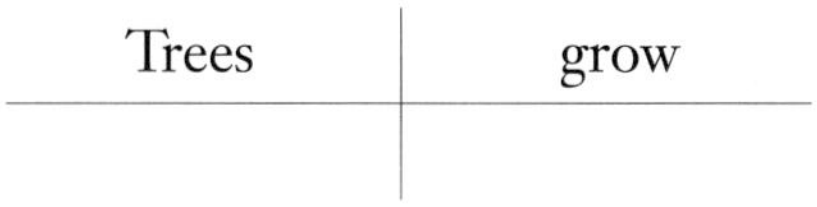

Trees	grow

Adjectives and Adverbs

To diagram a sentence with adjectives and adverbs, follow the model diagram below. Note that you diagram adverbs used to modify verbs in the same way that you diagram adjectives used to modify nouns. Diagram adverbs used to modify adjectives or other adverbs on a separate line, as shown.

The young pine trees grow quite fast.

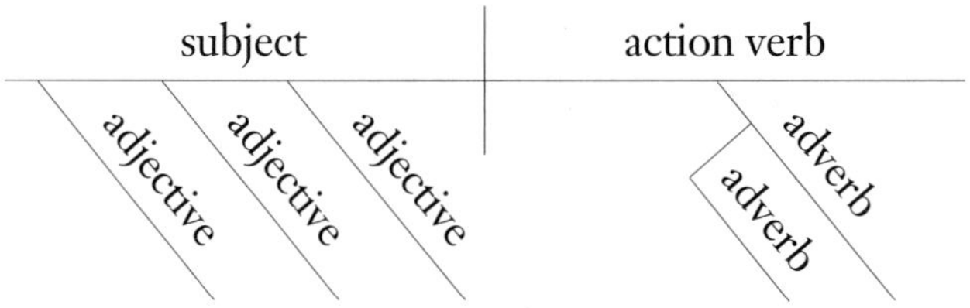

subject	action verb

adjective adjective adjective   adverb adverb

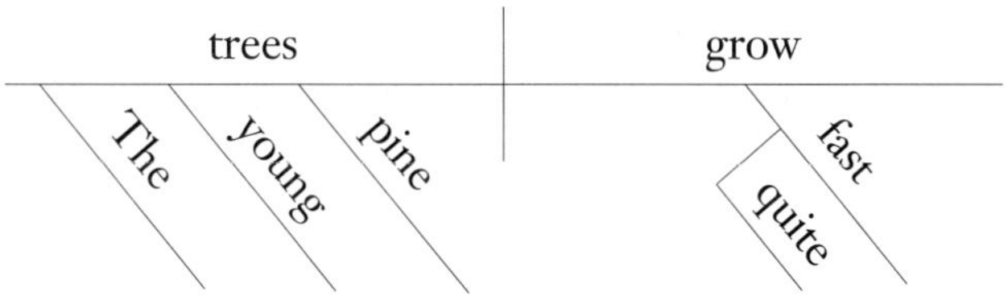

trees	grow

The young pine   fast quite

Direct Objects and Indirect Objects

To diagram a sentence with objects, follow the model.

Trees give us medicines.

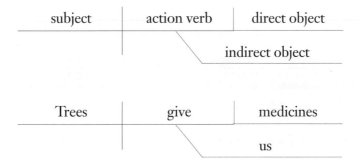

Object Complements

To diagram a simple sentence with a compound subject, a direct object, and an object complement, follow the model.

Designers and carpenters consider hardwoods unsurpassed.

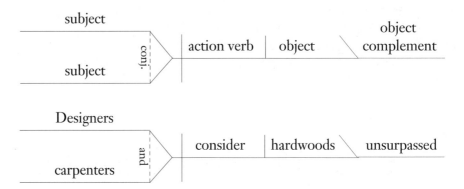

Subject Complements

To diagram a simple sentence with a subject complement (a predicate nominative or a predicate adjective), follow the model.

Trees become timber.

subject	linking verb \ predicate nominative

Trees	become \ timber

Conifers are numerous and will remain plentiful.

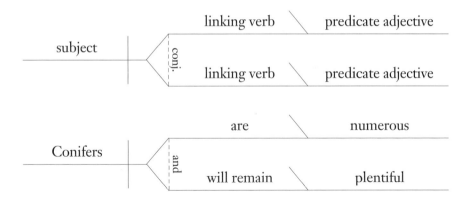

Exercise 1

Diagraming Simple Sentences   Using the preceding models as a guide, diagram the following sentences.

1. The gray forest gradually awakened.
2. New buds tinted the branches green.
3. Hikers and campers considered the weather superb.
4. The longer days gave us more useful hours.
5. The spring breezes were fresh but unpredictable.

14.2   Diagraming Simple Sentences with Phrases

Prepositional Phrases

Place the preposition on a diagonal line that descends from the word the prepositional phrase modifies. Place the object of the preposition on a horizontal line that extends from the diagonal.

Lovers of old buildings spend millions of dollars on renovations.

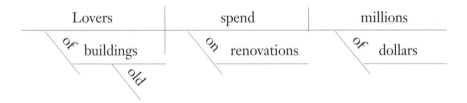

Appositives and Appositive Phrases

Place an appositive in parentheses after the noun or pronoun it identifies. Beneath it add any new words that modify the appositive.

Monticello, the home of Thomas Jefferson, was restored by a private organization.

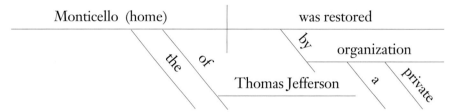

Participles and Participial Phrases

Curve the participle as shown below. Add modifiers and complements.

Researching, one may encounter surprises, discovering scandal in a building's history.

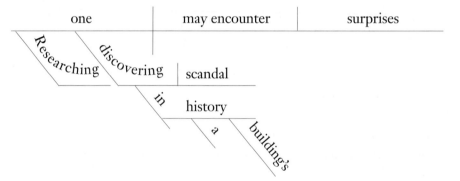

Gerunds and Gerund Phrases

Place a gerund on a "step," and add complements and modifiers. Then set the gerund or the gerund phrase on a "stilt," and position the stilt in the diagram according to the role of the gerund in the sentence.

Finding original plans is a restorer's dream.

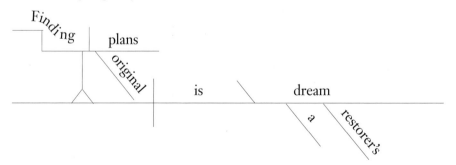

Infinitives and Infinitive Phrases

When an infinitive or an infinitive phrase is used as an adjective or an adverb, it is diagramed like a prepositional phrase. When an infinitive or an infinitive phrase is used as a noun, it is diagramed like a prepositional phrase and then placed on a "stilt" in the subject or complement position.

To perform a restoration project well, you must attempt to re-create something authentically.

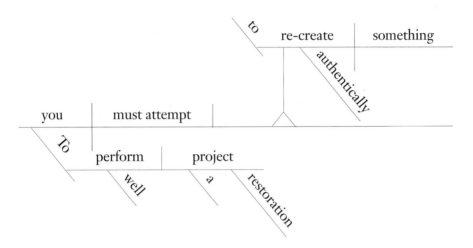

Absolute Phrases

An absolute phrase is placed above the rest of the sentence and is not connected to it in any way. Place the noun or pronoun on a horizontal line. Place the participle and any modifiers on descending lines in the usual manner.

Its exterior freshly painted, the house looked almost new.

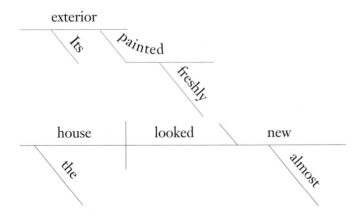

Diagraming Simple Sentences with Phrases   Using the preceding models as a guide, diagram the following sentences.

1. During restoration you should preserve the beams of old buildings.
2. The University of Virginia, an architectural gem, was designed by Thomas Jefferson.
3. A staircase, rising from the street, reached the building's main door.
4. They based the restoration on knowing the original appearance of the house.
5. The cupola, its gold leaf applied, seemed to catch fire in the evening light.

14.3   Diagraming Sentences with Clauses

Compound Sentences

Diagram each main clause separately. If the clauses are connected by a semicolon, use a vertical dotted line to connect the verbs of each main clause. If the main clauses are connected by a conjunction, place the conjunction on a solid horizontal line, and connect it to the verbs of each main clause by vertical dotted lines.

Trial lawyers argue their cases, and juries consider the evidence.

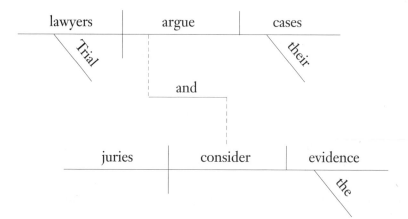

Complex Sentences with Adjective Clauses

Place the main clause in one diagram and the adjective clause beneath it in another diagram. Use a dotted line to connect the relative pronoun or other introductory word in the adjective clause to the modified noun or pronoun in the main clause.

A judge, who presides over trials, rules on procedural matters that may arise.

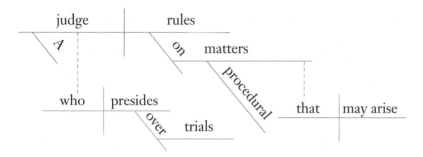

Complex Sentences with Adverb Clauses

Place the main clause in one diagram and the adverb clause beneath it in another diagram. Place the subordinating conjunction on a diagonal dotted line connecting the verb in the adverb clause to the modified verb, adjective, or adverb in the main clause.

Before witnesses testify, they must take an oath.

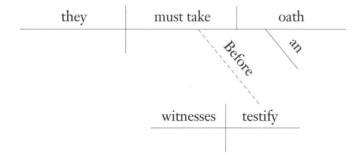

Complex Sentences with Noun Clauses

First decide what role the noun clause plays within the main clause. Is it the subject, direct object, predicate nominative, or object of a preposition? Then diagram the main clause, placing the noun clause on a "stilt" in the appropriate position. Place the introductory word of the clause in the position of the subject, object, or predicate nominative within the noun clause itself. If the introductory word merely begins the noun clause, place it on a line of its own above the verb in the subordinate clause, connecting it to the verb with a dotted vertical line.

NOUN CLAUSE AS SUBJECT

Whatever the witnesses say will influence the jury.

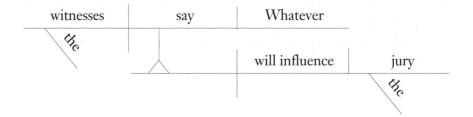

NOUN CLAUSE AS DIRECT OBJECT

Both plaintiffs and defendants hope that juries will believe them.

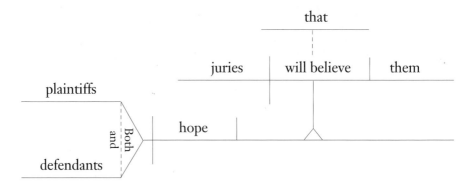

NOUN CLAUSE AS OBJECT OF A PREPOSITION

The jury awards money to whoever wins the case.

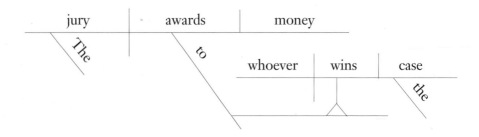

Diagraming Sentences with Clauses   Using the preceding models as a guide, diagram the following sentences.

1. The jury did not believe the final witness's story, or they did not care.
2. Several witnesses whom the attorneys questioned told stories that seemed contradictory.
3. Until sworn statements are introduced, the facts might exist only in written records.
4. That two witnesses contradict each other is extremely common.
5. The oddity is that people see different things in what is a single event.

Diagraming Sentences

Study the sentences below and the accompanying diagram "skeletons." Next, number from 1 to 20 on a separate sheet of paper. Then indicate the place where each word in the sentence should appear in the diagram by matching the letter of each place with the number of the appropriate word. The main verb of each sentence has been placed in the diagram for you and therefore has not been numbered.

Smiling, the magician produced teacups containing two mice in tiny tuxedos.
  1   2   3   4   5   6   7   8   9   10

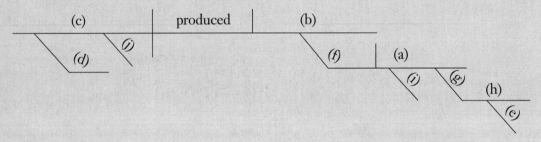

Smiling seemed appropriate when a cat, appearing suddenly, tried to approach.
  11   12   13 14 15   16   17   18 19   20

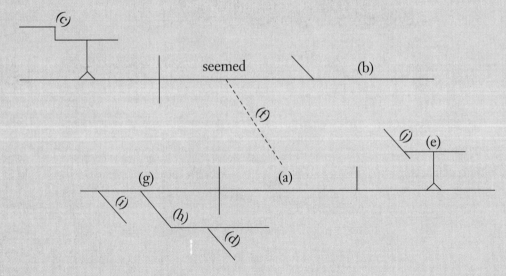

Unit 15 Verb Tenses, Voice, and Mood

15.1 Principal Parts of Verbs

All verbs have four principal parts—a *base form*, a *present participle*, a *simple past form*, and a *past participle*. All the verb tenses are formed from these principal parts.

Base Form	Present Participle	Past Form	Past Participle
walk	walking	walked	walked
fall	falling	fell	fallen
try	trying	tried	tried
speak	speaking	spoke	spoken
be	being	was, were	been

Although the base forms (except for *be*) and the past forms can be used alone as main verbs, the present participle and the past participle must always be used with one or more auxiliary verbs in order to function as the simple predicate.

Dolphins splash. [base or present form]
Dolphins **splashed.** [past form]
Dolphins **are splashing.** [present participle with the auxiliary *are*]
Dolphins **have splashed.** [past participle with the auxiliary *have*]

15.2 Regular and Irregular Verbs

A **regular verb** forms its past and past participle by adding *-ed* to the base form.

Principal Parts of Regular Verbs		
Base Form	Past Form	Past Participle
watch	watched	watched
laugh	laughed	laughed

With some regular verbs there is a spelling change when a suffix beginning with a vowel is added to the base form.

advertise + **-ed** = advertis**ed**
study + **-ed** = stud**ied**
skim + **-ed** = skim**med**

An **irregular verb** forms its past and past participle in some way other than by adding -*ed* to the base form.

Principal Parts of Irregular Verbs		
Base Form	**Past Form**	**Past Participle**
be	was, were	been
beat	beat	beaten
become	became	become
begin	began	begun
bite	bit	bitten *or* bit
blow	blew	blown
break	broke	broken
bring	brought	brought
catch	caught	caught
choose	chose	chosen
come	came	come
do	did	done
draw	drew	drawn
drink	drank	drunk
drive	drove	driven
eat	ate	eaten
fall	fell	fallen
feel	felt	felt
find	found	found
fly	flew	flown
freeze	froze	frozen
get	got	got *or* gotten
give	gave	given
go	went	gone
grow	grew	grown
hang	hung *or* hanged	hung *or* hanged
have	had	had
know	knew	known
lay*	laid	laid
lead	led	led
lend	lent	lent
lie*	lay	lain
lose	lost	lost

*For more detailed instruction on *lay* versus *lie*, see Unit 19.

Base Form	Past Form	Past Participle
put	put	put
ride	rode	ridden
ring	rang	rung
rise*	rose	risen
run	ran	run
say	said	said
see	saw	seen
set*	set	set
shrink	shrank *or* shrunk	shrunk *or* shrunken
sing	sang	sung
sink	sank *or* sunk	sunk
sit*	sat	sat
speak	spoke	spoken
spring	sprang *or* sprung	sprung
steal	stole	stolen
swim	swam	swum
take	took	taken
tear	tore	torn
tell	told	told
think	thought	thought
throw	threw	thrown
wear	wore	worn
win	won	won
write	wrote	written

*For more detailed instruction on *raise* versus *rise* and *set* versus *sit,* see Unit 19.

Exercise 1

Supplying the Correct Principal Part   Complete these sentences with the principal part indicated in parentheses.

Planning Cities

1. Throughout history cities often _____ as small villages. (past form of *begin*)
2. At times some villages spontaneously _____ larger. (past form of *grow*)
3. Enterprising people have always _____ ways to accelerate urban growth. (past participle of *find*)
4. For example, Alexander the Great (356–323 B.C.) _____ seventy new cities in great detail. (past form of *plan*)
5. In modern times the nation of Israel has _____ many new towns on land reclaimed from the desert by means of irrigation. (past participle of *develop*) ➡

6. A number of nations today are _____ urban experiments, new types of cities that meet specific needs. (present participle of *create*)
7. In Europe, Great Britain has _____ one of the leaders in planning new cities. (past participle of *be*)
8. The British have _____ new towns in order to relieve housing shortages and traffic jams. (past participle of *design*)
9. In some instances planned cities have _____ popular with their inhabitants only after many years. (past participle of *become*)
10. Architects and city planners have _____ of many excellent new ways of solving old problems. (past participle of *think*)

15.3 Tense of Verbs

The **tenses** of a verb are the forms that help to show time.

The six tenses in English are the *present*, *past*, and *future* and the *present perfect*, *past perfect*, and *future perfect*.

Present Tense

The present-tense form of any verb other than *be* is the same as the verb's base form. Remember, however, that *-s* or *-es* is added in the third-person singular.

	Singular	**Plural**
FIRST PERSON	I **help**.	We **help**.
SECOND PERSON	You **help**.	You **help**.
THIRD PERSON	She, he, or it **helps**.	They **help**.
	Juanita **helps**.	The children **help**.

	Singular	**Plural**
FIRST PERSON	I **am** honest.	We **are** honest.
SECOND PERSON	You **are** honest.	You **are** honest.
THIRD PERSON	She, he, or it **is** honest.	They **are** honest.
	Juanita **is** honest.	The children **are** honest.

The **present tense** expresses a constant, repeated, or habitual action or condition. It can also express a general truth.

Water **erodes** rock. [not just now but always: a constant action]
Lian **drives** defensively. [now and always: a habitual action]
Steel **is** an alloy. [a condition that is always true]

The **present tense** can also express an action or condition that exists only now.

Clara **seems** interested. [not always but just now]
I **agree** with you. [at this very moment]

The **present tense** is sometimes used in historical writing to express past events and, more often, in poetry, fiction, and reporting (especially in sports) to convey to the reader a sense of "being there."

The applause **continues** as each cast member **steps** forward and **bows.**

The basketball **hovers** on the rim and finally **slips** through the net.

Exercise 2: Sentence Writing

Expressing the Present Tense in Sentences   Write a sentence using each of the following verb forms. The content of your sentence should express the kind of present time indicated in parentheses.

SAMPLE   speaks (now and always)
ANSWER   She speaks Spanish fluently.

1. plays (now and always)
2. tastes (just now)
3. are (always true)
4. accepts (at this moment)
5. walk (always)

Past Tense

Use the **past tense** to express an action or condition that was started and completed in the past.

The spectators **cheered** loudly.
Everyone on the team **swam** well.
We **won** by a big margin.
The victory clearly **was** ours.

With one exception all regular and irregular verbs have only one past-tense form, such as *talked* or *wrote*. The exception—the verb *be*—has two past-tense forms: *was* and *were*.

	Singular	Plural
FIRST PERSON	I **was** strong.	We **were** strong.
SECOND PERSON	You **were** strong.	You **were** strong.
THIRD PERSON	He, she, or it **was** strong.	They **were** strong.

Exercise 3: Sentence Writing

Expressing the Past Tense in Sentences   Write a paragraph using the correct past tense of each of the following verbs:

1. drive
2. begin
3. climb
4. enjoy
5. find

Future Tense

Use the **future tense** to express an action or condition that will occur in the future.

The future tense of any verb is formed by using *shall* or *will* with the base form: *I shall paint; you will sing*.

Hector **will buy** a car.
I **shall finish** my homework.

Other ways of expressing future time do not involve the use of *will* or *shall*. Consider the following options:

1. Use *going to* along with the present tense of *be* and the base form of a verb.

   Hector **is *going to* buy** a car.
   I**'m *going to* do** my homework later.

2. Use *about to* along with the present tense of *be* and the base form of a verb.

   Hector **is *about to* buy** a car.
   I**'m *about to* do** my homework, Mom.

3. Use the present tense with an adverb or an adverb phrase that shows future time.

   Monique **graduates *tomorrow.***
   Monique **graduates *later this week.***

Using Expressions of Future Time Change each sentence below so that the verb(s) are in the future tense. Try to use at least two ways of expressing future time in addition to using *shall* and *will*.

Navaho Sand Painting

1. On Tuesday the director of the Museum of Ceremonial Art in Santa Fe began a three-day demonstration of the Navaho tribe's use of sand paintings in healing ceremonies.
2. During the demonstration a medicine man performed a healing ceremony for a Navaho woman.
3. The ceremony involved the creation of a different sand painting each day for three days.
4. The healer and his assistants prepared various shades of red, yellow, and white powder by grinding sandstone on a stone slab.
5. They ground root charcoal to get black and blue pigments and cornmeal, petals, and leaves to get other colors.
6. With trays of colored sand, the painters worked together each day on an abstract painting based on traditional Navaho mythology.
7. Each worker carefully rubbed sand between the thumb and forefinger and deposited one thin line of color after another onto the painting.
8. Then the patient sat on the finished painting, and the medicine man recited an appropriate chant.
9. The museum director explained that a successful ceremony brought the patient a sense of peace and harmony.
10. At the demonstration's conclusion the medicine man gathered the sandpainting into a blanket and scattered it to the winds.

Exercise 5: Sentence Writing

Expressing Future Time in Sentences Write five statements or predictions about the future. Your sentences may be as realistic or as imaginary as you wish. Remember to vary the ways in which you express future time.

SAMPLE ANSWER   Before too long every home in America is going to have a computer.

15.4 Perfect Tenses

Present Perfect Tense

Use the **present perfect tense** to express an action or condition that occurred at some *indefinite* time in the past.

Use *has* or *have* with the past participle of a verb to form the present perfect tense: *has lived, have eaten.**

> She **has fished** in the Atlantic.
> The birds **have migrated** south.

The present perfect tense is used to refer to past time only in an indefinite way. With this tense adverbs such as *yesterday* cannot logically be added to make the time more specific.

> Richard **has seen** that movie.
> The Ressners **have** often **flown** to Denver.

To be specific about completed past time, you usually use the simple past tense.

> Richard **saw** that movie on Friday.
> The Ressners **flew** to Denver on their vacation.

The present perfect tense can also be used to show that an action or a condition that *began* in the past *continues* into the present. When a verb is used in this way, it is normally accompanied by adverbs of time or adverb phrases.

> Rafael **has studied** art **for many years.**
> The studio **has been** open **since eleven o'clock.**

Past Perfect Tense

Use the **past perfect tense** to indicate that one past action or condition began *and* ended before another past action started.

The past perfect tense is formed with *had* and the past participle of a verb: *had lost, had danced.*

> PAST PERFECT   PAST
> Bernice **had earned** ten thousand dollars before she **resigned.**
> [She earned the money; then she stopped earning it; then she resigned.]

>   PAST   PAST PERFECT
> By the time Ravi **arrived,** all the other guests **had left.** [The other guests began to leave and then finished leaving; Ravi arrived.]

Future Perfect Tense

Use the **future perfect tense** to express one future action or condition that will begin *and* end before another future event starts.

The future perfect tense is formed with *will have* or *shall have* plus the past participle of a verb: *will have met, shall have met.*

In two more laps she **will have run** four hundred meters. [The four hundred meters will be run by the time another future event, the completion of two more laps, occurs.]

By the end of the month, each student **will have submitted** three essays.

Exercise 6

Identifying the Perfect Tenses On your paper write the perfect-tense verb that appears in each of the following sentences. Then identify the verb as *present*, *past*, or *future perfect*. (One sentence contains two perfect tenses.)

Seattle

1. In 1853 Seattle was named for Chief Seattle of the Duwamish and Suquamish tribes, who had agreed to allow settlers to live on his tribes' land.
2. Although Seattle had been a prominent city before 1896, it was not until the gold-rush era that it emerged as the largest city in the Pacific Northwest.
3. Today, with its diverse cultural offerings and its beautiful scenery, Seattle has become a mecca for visitors.
4. In addition, it has long boasted many tourist attractions.
5. One of them, Pike's Place Market, has sold produce, seafood, and all kinds of imported and handcrafted goods to visitors from far and near since it opened in 1906.
6. Once you have crossed Lake Washington by way of the Evergreen Point Bridge, you will have traversed the world's longest floating bridge.
7. The Seattle Space Needle, a 606-foot tower constructed for the 1962 World's Fair, houses a revolving restaurant that has served awestruck tourists for years.
8. The Pacific Northwest Dance Ballet Company will have opened its spring season by the first of March.
9. By May the Seattle Repertory Theatre had staged six plays.
10. By the end of the summer, the Seattle Opera will have performed Richard Wagner's great four-opera cycle, *The Ring of the Nibelung.*

Expressing the Present Perfect Tense in Sentences
(a) Rewrite each of the following sentences, changing the tense of the verb from the past to the present perfect. (b) Add appropriate adverbs or adverb phrases to each of your new sentences to communicate the idea that an action or condition began in the past and continues into the present.

SAMPLE   We wrote term papers.
ANSWER   (a) We have written term papers.
            (b) We have written term papers for the
                past four years.

1. Otis was away on business.
2. The drama club presented skits.
3. I studied Portuguese.
4. Our senators opposed the bill.
5. We visited Yosemite National Park.

15.5   Progressive and Emphatic Forms

Each of the six tenses has a **progressive** form that expresses a continuing action.

The progressive forms consist of the appropriate tense of the verb *be* plus the present participle of the main verb.

PRESENT PROGRESSIVE	They *are* thinking.
PAST PROGRESSIVE	They *were* thinking.
FUTURE PROGRESSIVE	They *will be* thinking.
PRESENT PERFECT PROGRESSIVE	They *have been* thinking.
PAST PERFECT PROGRESSIVE	They *had been* thinking.
FUTURE PERFECT PROGRESSIVE	They *will have been* thinking.

The present and past tenses have additional forms, called **emphatic,** that add special force, or emphasis, to the verb.

The emphatic forms consist of *do* (and *does*) or *did* plus the base form of the verb.

PRESENT EMPHATIC	I *do* agree with you.
	He *does* agree with you.
PAST EMPHATIC	I *did* agree with you.
	They disagreed with your choice of words, but they *did* agree with your idea.

Exercise 8

Using the Progressive and Emphatic Forms   For each of the following sentences, replace each verb in parentheses with the progressive or the emphatic form of the verb that makes sense in the sentence. (Only one of the sentences requires the emphatic form.)

The Progress of Map Making

¹Today I (begin) a study of the history of map making. ²Did you know that when you refer to a modern weather or road map, you (look) at the latest example of a skill that is thousands of years old? ³For some time now scientists (suspect) that in certain rock paintings in Africa, Asia, Europe, and South America, ancient peoples used patterns of lines to represent rivers and roads. ⁴The earliest known maps were made in the Middle East before 2200 B.C.; these clay tablets show rivers, mountain ridges, and cities that (stand) at the time. ⁵Chinese map makers of about 500 B.C. believed that they (live) in a land that covered most of a square world. ⁶Although we no longer have their maps, we (have) reliable accounts of them. ⁷In the far north the Eskimos of Greenland (carve) relief maps of icy coasts out of wood blocks for many years. ⁸Until Europeans first landed on the Marshall Islands in the South Pacific, generations of native islanders (make) maps of sticks, shells, and fibers. ⁹These maps represented the wave patterns that local navigators needed to watch for when they (travel) between the islands. ¹⁰As changing technology provides map makers with new tools, we (see) increasingly detailed and accurate records of our world.

Exercise 9: Review

Understanding the Uses of Verb Tenses   Explain the difference in meaning between the sentences in each of the pairs below. Name the tense(s) used in each sentence.

SAMPLE	(a) He stopped in Juárez to visit his sister.
	(b) He has stopped in Juárez to visit his sister.
ANSWER	In sentence *a* the action occurred and has ended (past).
	In sentence *b* the action occurred in the past and is continuing (present perfect).

1. **a.** Kim and I are planning our visit to Juárez.
   b. Kim and I will be planning our visit to Juárez. ➡

2. **a.** We stayed in El Paso, Texas, just across the river from Juárez.
   b. We have been staying in El Paso, Texas, just across the river from Juárez.
3. **a.** Kim did enjoy the trip to El Paso.
   b. Kim has enjoyed the trip to El Paso.
4. **a.** We were traveling for three weeks.
   b. We have been traveling for three weeks.
5. **a.** Soon we will visit all the nearby Mexican cities.
   b. Soon we will have visited all the nearby Mexican cities.

Exercise 10: Sentence Writing

Expressing Past Time in a Paragraph   Write a paragraph of at least five sentences about an important event in your past. Underline five verbs or verb phrases that you have used. (Remember that the perfect tenses, as well as the past tense, can be used to express past action.)

15.6   Compatibility of Tenses

Do not shift, or change, tenses when two or more events occur at the same time.

| INCORRECT | Teresa **dived** into the pool and **swims** to the other side. [The tense needlessly shifts from the past to the present.] |
| CORRECT | Teresa **dived** into the pool and **swam** to the other side. [Now it is clear that both events happened in the past.] |

Shift tenses only to show that one event precedes or follows another.

| INCORRECT | Because we **hiked** three miles, we **stopped** for a rest. [The two past-tense verbs give the mistaken impression that both events happened at the same time.] |
| CORRECT | Because we **had hiked** three miles, we **stopped** for a rest. [The shift from the past perfect tense (*had hiked*) to the past tense (*stopped*) clearly indicates that the hiking of three miles happened before the hikers stopped to rest.] |

Making Tenses Compatible First find the two verbs that appear in each of the following sentences. Then rewrite each sentence, making the second verb compatible with the first verb.

Alice Walker, Prize-Winning Writer

1. Alice Walker was born in 1944 in rural Georgia, where as the eighth child of sharecroppers she had endured the hardship of poverty.
2. When her brother accidentally shot her with a BB gun, Alice becomes blind in one eye.
3. Because Alice was feeling depressed as a result of the disfiguring injury, she turns to her journal and books as outlets for her emotions.
4. By the time Walker participated in the civil rights movement, she enrolled in Spelman College in Atlanta.
5. When she published her first book, a volume of poetry, she taught at Jackson State University in Mississippi.
6. In this book Walker wrote some poems about Africa, where she traveled as a college junior.
7. In *In Search of Our Mother's Gardens*, Walker pays tribute to the strong, creative African-American woman and is encouraging women to safeguard their own creative legacy.
8. Long after the African-American writer Zora Neale Hurston had died poor and forgotten, Walker discovers her own spiritual kinship with that woman.
9. Before Walker found Hurston's unmarked grave in Florida, she made up her mind to place a tombstone on the site and to write about the experience.
10. Walker has written many novels, including *The Color Purple*, which has won the Pulitzer Prize in 1983.

15.7 Voice of Verbs

An action verb is in the **active voice** when the subject of the sentence performs the action.

> The coach **encouraged** the team.

An action verb is in the **passive voice** when its action is performed on the subject.

> The team **was encouraged** by the coach.

Generally the active voice is the stronger voice. Sometimes, however, the passive voice is preferred or even necessary. For instance, if you do not want to call attention to the performer of an action or you do not know who the performer is, you would use the passive voice.

The book **was returned.** [You may not know who returned it.]

The glass **was broken.** [You may not want to identify the person who broke the glass.]

You form the passive voice by using the auxiliary verb *be* together with the past participle of the verb. The tense of the auxiliary verb determines the tense of the passive verb.

The team **is encouraged** by the coach. [present tense, passive voice]

The team **was being encouraged** by the coach. [past progressive tense, passive voice]

The team **will have been encouraged** by the coach. [future perfect tense, passive voice]

Exercise 12

Changing the Voice of Verbs   In each of the following sentences, change the active voice to the passive or the passive voice to the active.

Confucius and His Teachings

1. People throughout the world study the teachings of the Chinese philosopher Confucius (c. 551–479 B.C.).
2. A doctrine of consideration for others, similar to the golden rule, was taught by Confucius as the basis for all social and political conduct.
3. Followers of Confucius regard duty to parents as the foundation for social order.
4. Moderation in all things, the doctrine of the golden mean, is emphasized in Confucian philosophy.
5. Confucius welcomed students from all social classes.
6. The aristocracy's control over the government was not respected by the philosopher's open-minded policies.
7. Confucius was made provincial governor by the duke of Lu.
8. The nobility of Lu resented many of Confucius's ideas.
9. Before long the men in power forced Confucius into a thirteen-year exile.
10. The *Analects*, a collection of Confucian proverbs and anecdotes, was compiled by Confucius's disciples after his death.

15.8　Mood of Verbs

In addition to tense and voice, verbs also express mood.

A verb expresses one of three **moods:** the **indicative mood,** the **imperative mood,** or the **subjunctive mood.**

The indicative mood—the most frequently used—makes a statement or asks a question. The imperative mood expresses a command or makes a request.

INDICATIVE MOOD	She takes the bus home.
IMPERATIVE MOOD	Take the bus home.

The subjunctive mood, although often replaced by the indicative mood in informal English, has two important uses in contemporary formal English.

1. To express, indirectly, a demand, recommendation, suggestion, or statement of necessity.

We demand [*or* recommend *or* suggest] that she **take** the bus home. [The subjunctive mood drops the *-s* from the third-person singular.]

It is necessary that you **be** home before dark. [The subjunctive mood uses *be* instead of *am, is,* or *are.*]

2. To state a condition or a wish that is contrary to fact. Notice that this use of the subjunctive always requires the past tense.

If she **were** late, she would take the bus home. [The subjunctive mood uses *were,* not *was.*]

They complained to me about the damaged product as if I **were** the one in charge.

I wish that I **were** a genius.

Exercise 13

Using the Indicative and Subjunctive Moods　For each of the following sentences, first determine whether the verb should express the indicative or the subjunctive mood. Then write the sentence, supplying the appropriate form of the verb in parentheses.

A Tennis Lesson

1. My sister Antonia's tennis instructor (teach) people of all ages and levels of ability. ➡

2. Antonia, who practices for an hour a day six times a week, wishes that she (be) an expert player like Chris Evert or Jimmy Connors.
3. I told her, "If I (be) you, I would consider working at least an hour a day on my serve alone."
4. Antonia has learned that in order to hit the ball with a good forehand stroke, it is important that she (prepare) early for the arrival of the ball.
5. Good players are the ones who (shift) their weight forward during the stroke.
6. If my sister is to play her very best game of tennis, it is vital that she (play) on a clay court rather than on a grass court.
7. A good sense of balance (be) absolutely necessary to be a great tennis player.
8. If the net (be) six inches high instead of the regulation thirty-six inches, it would be much easier for me to serve effectively.
9. Antonia (want) me to take tennis lessons from her tennis instructor, too.
10. She thinks if I (be) willing to apply myself, we would make a formidable doubles team in a local tennis tournament next year.

Clarity, grace, and precision are the three qualities that most distinguish an effective writing style. These qualities enable readers to understand what you want to say and to enjoy how you are saying it. One way in which writers develop an effective style is by avoiding any use of the passive voice that may make their sentences unclear, graceless, or imprecise. Here, for example, is a long sentence by the writer Bernard Malamud that has been recast using verbs in the passive voice. Notice how awkward the prose sounds and how difficult it is to follow the action:

> When what *was wanted* done by him to his shoes *was finished* being described by Max, they *were marked* by Feld, both with enormous holes in the soles which he pretended not to notice, with large white-chalk *x*'s, and the rubber heels, thinned to the nails, *were marked* with *o*'s, though he *was troubled* the letters might *have been mixed up*.

Here is Malamud's actual sentence, with the verbs in the active voice. Notice how smoothly the long sentence flows and how easy it is to follow the actions:

> When Max *finished* describing what he *wanted* done to the shoes, Feld *marked* them, both with enormous holes in the soles which he pretended not to notice, with large white-chalk *x*'s, and the rubber heels, thinned to the nails, he *marked* with *o*'s, though it *troubled* him he might *have mixed up* the letters.

The active voice allows us to focus clearly on each character's actions and to follow Feld's movements precisely. Moreover, the sentence has a pleasing, graceful rhythm.

Apply these techniques by revising the following paragraph on a separate sheet of paper. In your revision eliminate the unnecessary use of the passive voice.

> The music known as ragtime is characterized by syncopated rhythms and a cheerful, lilting sound. In the early part of the twentieth century, ragtime was performed all over the United States by solo pianists as well as by ragtime bands. By World War I much of Europe had also been captivated by this uniquely American music. The famous "Maple Leaf Rag" was written by Scott Joplin, one of ragtime's greatest composers. Another Joplin standard, "The Entertainer," was repopularized by *The Sting*, a 1973 movie starring Robert Redford and Paul Newman.

*U*sage Workshop

Verb Tenses, Voice, and Mood

Roots is one man's attempt to reconstruct the history of seven generations of his family. The book begins with the birth in 1750 of Alex Haley's great-great-great-great-grandfather, Kunta Kinte, who was kidnapped from his home in Gambia in West Africa and brought to Maryland as a slave, and ends with the death of Haley's father. In this excerpt Kunta Kinte's mother and other women of the village of Juffure are canoeing down a *bolong*, or canal, to their rice fields. The passage has been annotated to show some of the verb tenses and voices covered in this unit.

Literature Model

from ROOTS

by Alex Haley

Past perfect tense —

It was the planting season, and the first rains were soon to come. On all their farming land, the men of Juffure had piled tall stacks of dry weeds and set them afire so that the light wind would nourish the soil by scattering the ashes.

Past progressive form —

And the women in their rice fields were already planting green shoots in the mud.

Past tense of an irregular verb —

The air was heavy with the deep, musky fragrance of the mangroves, and with the perfumes of the other plants and trees that grew thickly on both sides of the bolong. Alarmed by the passing canoes, huge families of baboons, roused from sleep, began bellowing, springing about and shaking palm-tree fronds. Wild pigs grunted and snorted, running to hide themselves among the weeds and bushes. Covering the muddy banks, thousands of pelicans, cranes, egrets, herons, storks, gulls, terns, and spoonbills interrupted their breakfast feeding to watch nervously as the canoes glided by. Some of the smaller birds took to the air —ringdoves, skimmers, rails, darters, and kingfishers— circling with shrill cries until the intruders had passed.

Past tense of a regular verb —

As the canoes arrowed through rippling, busy patches of water, schools of minnows would leap up together, perform a silvery dance, and then splash back. Chasing the minnows, sometimes so hungrily that they flopped right ⟶

into a moving canoe, were large, fierce fish that the women would club with their paddles and stow away for a succulent evening meal. But this morning the minnows swam around them undisturbed.

The twisting bolong took the rowing women around a turn to a wider tributary, and as they came into sight, a great beating of wings filled the air and a vast living carpet of seafowl—hundreds of thousands of them, in every color of the rainbow—rose and filled the sky. The surface of the water, darkened by the storm of birds and furrowed by their flapping wings, was flecked with feathers as the women paddled on.

As they neared the marshy faros where generations of Juffure women had grown their rice crops, the canoes passed through swarming clouds of mosquitoes and then, one after another, nosed in against a walkway of thickly matted weeds. The weeds bounded and identified each woman's plot, where by now the emerald shoots of young rice stood a hand's height above the water's surface.

— Active voice

— Passive voice

— Correct shift from past tense to past perfect

Usage Workshop Exercise 1

Identifying Principal Parts   The following sentences are based on the passage from *Roots*. Each sentence contains a verb in one of four forms: (a) the base form, (b) the past form, (c) the present participle, or (d) the past participle. At the end of the sentence is a second verb in parentheses. First, identify the form of the verb in italics. Then rewrite the sentence, substituting the verb in parentheses for the italicized verb. Be sure the new verb in the rewritten sentence is in the same form as the original verb.

SAMPLE   The first rains *arrived* late that year. (come)
ANSWER   past form; The first rains came late that year.

1. After the men of Juffure had *piled* dried weeds into stacks, they set them afire. (throw)
2. The women were *starting* their work in the fields. (begin)
3. The villagers always *return* to the same place to plant their rice crops. (go)
4. Kunta Kinte's mother and the other women *journeyed* in their canoes to the rice paddies. (ride)
5. Flocks of birds *sailed* away as the canoes passed. (fly)

Using the Perfect Tenses   Each of the following sentences describes village life in West Africa, the setting for this workshop's passage. On your paper rewrite each sentence, adding the appropriate form of the italicized verb in the place indicated by the caret. Write the verb in the tense indicated in parentheses, using the past participle of the main verb and the appropriate form of the helping verb *have*.

SAMPLE   Village life in West Africa ∧ the same patterns for generations. (present perfect tense of *follow*)

ANSWER   Village life in West Africa has followed the same patterns for generations.

1. Traditionally villages ∧ many generations of an extended family. (present perfect tense of *encompass*)
2. Many West African tribes ∧ Islam for centuries before European colonists arrived. (past perfect tense of *practice*)
3. By early adulthood women ∧ the duties of raising a family and working on a farm. (present perfect tense of *assume*)
4. By the advent of the dry season, the village ∧ adequate food supplies. (future perfect tense of *collect*)
5. By the time the rains end, children and young people already ∧ crops for food. (future perfect tense of *harvest*)

Using the Progressive and Emphatic Forms   The following sentences are based on passages from *Roots* not reproduced in this textbook. On your paper rewrite each sentence, adding the appropriate form of the italicized verb in the place indicated by the caret. Write the verb in the form indicated in parentheses. Use the present participle of the main verb and the appropriate tense of the auxiliary verb *be* or the base form of the main verb and the appropriate form of *do*.

SAMPLE   In 1767 Kunta Kinte ∧ in Gambia. (past progressive form of *live*)

ANSWER   In 1767 Kunta Kinte was living in Gambia.

1. Kunta ∧ the arts of hunting and fighting for many years, and he had become a fine young warrior. (past perfect progressive form of *learn*)
2. In the most dramatic episode of *Roots*, Kunta ∧ from sentry duty in the village fields when four slave traders capture ➡

him. (present progressive form of *return*)

3. Kunta was shipped to Maryland in the fall of 1767; at that time slave ships ∧ thousands of Africans to the United States each year. (past progressive form of *carry*)
4. For the rest of his life, Kunta Kinte ∧ to see his beloved home and family in Gambia. (future progressive form of *yearn*)
5. Kunta never ∧, however; he remained on plantations in Virginia for the rest of his life. (past emphatic form of *return*)

Usage Workshop Exercise 4

Making Tenses Compatible   These sentences are based on the passage from *Roots*. Each sentence has an error in verb tense. On your paper rewrite each sentence, changing the tense of the italicized verb so that the tenses are compatible.

SAMPLE   By the time the rains arrived, the villagers of Juffure already *began* to plant their crops.

ANSWER   By the time the rains arrived, the villagers of Juffure had already begun to plant their crops.

1. As soon as the dry weeds *burned*, the wind scattered the ashes.
2. The women planted rice in the marshy faros, as their ancestors *did* for centuries.
3. Animals *watch* nervously as the women's canoes glided by.
4. Flocks of birds took to the air when the passing canoes *frighten* them.
5. The rice shoots *grew* far above the water's surface by the time the dry season ended.

Usage Workshop Exercise 5

Voice of Verbs   The following sentences describe the writing of *Roots*. First, identify each sentence as being in the *passive voice* or the *active voice*. Then rewrite the italicized portion of each sentence, changing the active voice to the passive or the passive voice to the active.

SAMPLE   *The book was written* by Alex Haley to memorialize the lives of his ancestors.

ANSWER   passive voice; Alex Haley wrote the book to memorialize the lives of his ancestors.➠

1. When Haley was young, *he was told stories by his grandmother about his ancestor Kunta Kinte.*
2. *Only a few facts were known by Haley;* he knew, for instance, that Kunta Kinte had said he lived by a river called "Kamby Bolongo."
3. *Linguists told Haley* that "Kamby Bolongo" might mean "the Gambia River."
4. *Haley was intrigued by the idea;* so he flew to Gambia and traveled to a village where members of the Kinte clan still lived.
5. *There he was told this tale by an elderly storyteller:* a boy named Kunta Kinte had disappeared from the village around 1765, soon after the first slave traders had arrived.

Usage Workshop Exercise 6

Review   The following sentences describe the life of Alex Haley. Rewrite each sentence, following the directions in parentheses.

SAMPLE   Alex Haley inspired many African Americans to trace their family history. (Change the verb to the present perfect tense.)

ANSWER   Alex Haley has inspired many African Americans to trace their family history.

Alex Haley

1. Born in Ithaca, New York, Alex Haley studied education and joins the U.S. Coast Guard in 1939. (Correct the error in the use of verb tense.)
2. During his twenty years with the Coast Guard, Haley writes many adventure stories about the sea. (Change the verb to the past tense.)
3. In 1963 Haley was asked by the African-American politician Malcolm X to work on a book. (Rewrite the sentence in the active voice.)
4. *The Autobiography of Malcolm X* was praised by critics, and the book is still required reading in many black-studies programs. (Change the first verb to the present perfect tense.)
5. Haley had planned to write a book about school segregation in the South but instead spent ten years researching and writing *Roots*. (Change the first verb to the past progressive form.)

Proofreading   The following passage tells about the Senufo people and the carved Senufo door that appears on this page. Rewrite the passage, correcting any errors in spelling, capitalization, punctuation, grammar, and usage. There are ten errors in all.

The Art of the Senufo

[1]The West African peoples known as the Senufo live in the grassy savannas of the northern Ivory Coast (officially known by its French name Côte d'Ivoire) and in Southern Mali. [2]The Senufo tribes who speak four different languages, raise corn and millet, live in thatched, mud houses, and are reknowned marimba players and sculptors.

[3]The art of the Senufo is stylized and elegant. [4]The tribes are famous for their carved wooden masks which were worn during ceremonial dances.

[5]The door shown here once barred the entrance to the shrine of a Senufo secret society. [6]A symbol of the sun flanked by five figures on horseback dominate the central panel. [7]Carvings of animal spirits, including a crocodile, decorates the side panels. [8]The sculptors who created this work were clearly proud of their African heritage Alex Haley, the author of *Roots*, was equally proud of his.

Senufo artists, West Africa, carved wooden door (detail)

Unit 15 Review

Verb Tenses, Voice, and Mood

Principal Parts of Verbs

[page 521]

1. In which of the following items is the underlined participle used correctly to form a complete sentence?

   a. Public television has <u>offered</u> fine programs for years.

   b. PBS recently <u>bearing</u> deep federal budget cuts.

   c. Since federal contributions <u>been</u> shrinking, fund-raising drives have increased.

Regular and Irregular Verbs

[pages 521–524]

For each item indicate the set of principal parts that is correct. (Each set should include the *base form*, the *past form*, and the *past participle*.)

2. **a.** feel, felt, feeled; **b.** get, got, got; **c.** bring, brung, brought
3. **a.** lie, lied, lain; **b.** taste, taste, tasted; **c.** lay, laid, laid

Tense of Verbs

[pages 524–532]

Indicate whether the underlined verb in each sentence is in the **(a)** present tense, **(b)** past tense, **(c)** future or future perfect tense, **(d)** present perfect tense, or **(e)** past perfect tense.

4. By the 1990s *Masterpiece Theatre* <u>had aired</u> for two decades.

5. This popular series <u>has televised</u> dramatizations of many classic novels.
6. *Upstairs, Downstairs* <u>depicted</u> life in Edwardian England.
7. Most television viewers hope that *Masterpiece Theatre* <u>will be broadcast</u> for many more years.

Compatibility of Tenses

[pages 532–533]

8. In which of the following sentences are the tenses compatible?

   a. After it had succeeded in a half-hour format, *The MacNeil/Lehrer Report* expanded to one hour.

   b. Young children watch *Sesame Street* and enjoyed its Muppet characters.

   c. Since they first appeared on *Sesame Street*, the Muppets become big stars.

Voice and Mood of Verbs

[pages 533–536]

Complete each sentence by choosing the appropriate verb.

9. The science program *Cosmos* **(a)** <u>hosted</u>/ **(b)** <u>was hosted</u> by Carl Sagan.
10. If I **(a)** <u>am</u>/**(b)** <u>was</u>/**(c)** <u>were</u>/**(d)** <u>be</u> home, I would watch *Nova*.

Writing for Review

On a separate sheet of paper, write a paragraph relating an incident that happened to you in the past year. Be sure the verbs in all your sentences are used correctly.

Subject-Verb Agreement

A verb must agree with its subject in person and number.

With most verbs the only change in form to indicate agreement takes place in the present tense. You add an *-s* (or *-es*) to the base verb when the subject is in the third-person singular. The linking verb *be* is an exception, however. It changes form in both the present and the past tense.

SINGULAR	PLURAL
She **advises.**	They **advise.**
He **is** there.	They **are** there.
It **was** mysterious.	They **were** mysterious.

When the auxiliary verbs *be*, *have*, and *do* appear in verb phrases, their forms change to show agreement with third-person subjects.

SINGULAR	PLURAL
She **is advising.**	They **are advising.**
She **has left** work.	They **have left** work.
Does he **speak** there?	**Do** they **speak** there?

16.1 Intervening Prepositional Phrases

Do not mistake a word in a prepositional phrase for the subject of a sentence.

The object of a preposition is never the subject of a sentence. Be certain that the verb agrees with the actual subject of the sentence and not with the object of a preposition.

The giant ***tortoise*** of the Galápagos Islands **weighs** more than five hundred pounds. [The subject, *tortoise*, is singular; *of the Galápagos Islands* is a prepositional phrase; the verb, *weighs*, is singular.]

Baby ***tortoises*** around an adult **have** to be careful. [The subject, *tortoises*, is plural; *around an adult* is a prepositional phrase; therefore, the verb, *have*, is plural.]

Exercise 1

Making Subjects and Verbs Agree When Prepositional Phrases Intervene   Find the simple subject in each sentence. Then on your paper write the verb that agrees with each subject. ➡

Chinese-American Scientists

1. In recent decades Chinese Americans in the field of science (has/have) excelled in many areas.
2. The winner of the 1962 Albert Lasker Medical Research Award and of several other prestigious awards (was/were) the notable biochemist Dr. Choh Hao Li, one of the world's foremost authorities on the pituitary gland.
3. In the tenth edition of *American Men of Science,* the list of names (includes/include) not only that of Dr. Li but also those of his three brothers, each distinguished in his own right.
4. Dr. Frances Chew's work on the interactions between plants and insects (consists/consist) of finding out what poisons plants produce to protect themselves from insects.
5. Perhaps the best-known Chinese-American scientists of the twentieth century (is/are) Drs. Tsung Dao Lee and Chen Ning Yang, winners of the 1957 Nobel Prize for physics.
6. The research by these two physicists (was/were) able to disprove a universally accepted law of nature.
7. Because of the work of these men and their collaborator Dr. Chien Shiung Wu, textbooks in science no longer (teaches/teach) that elementary particles in nature are always symmetrical.
8. The discoverer of the subatomic particles known as J and psi (was/were) Dr. Samuel C. C. Ting, who along with Burton Richter won the Nobel Prize for physics in 1976.
9. Katherine Hsu, among other Chinese-American physicians, (has/have) also received special recognition.
10. These considerable contributions to the field of science (has/have) enhanced our understanding of the world.

16.2   Agreement with Linking Verbs

Do not be confused by a predicate nominative that is different in number from the subject. Only the subject affects the number of the linking verb.

> The ***footprints*** in the mud **were** the only clue. [The plural verb, *were*, agrees with the plural subject, *footprints*, not with the predicate nominative, *clue*.]

> My favorite ***breakfast* is** eggs scrambled with onions. [The singular verb, *is*, agrees with the singular subject, *breakfast*, not with the predicate nominative, *eggs*.]

Making Linking Verbs Agree with Their Subjects Find the simple subject in each of the following sentences. Then write on your paper the form of the verb in parentheses that agrees with the subject of each sentence.

Eskimo Carvings

1. As evidenced by Eskimo art, the central element in the life of Eskimos (is/are) the splendors of nature.
2. The lifelike carvings of animals such as birds, seals, and bears (is/are) a popular art form.
3. A popular theme in Eskimo art (has been/have been) creatures from the spiritual world.
4. A favorite medium for carvings (is/are) ivory tusks from walruses.
5. The smooth surfaces of each ivory carving (seems/seem) an invitation to hold each object.
6. Chunks of wood, too, (becomes/become) a delight to the senses.
7. Carved by a skilled Eskimo artist, even the most ordinary objects, such as combs or fish hooks, (is/are) something beautiful and graceful.
8. A more exotic kind of carving (is/are) the masks used in ceremonial dances.
9. Eskimo artifacts from the ancient past (remains/remain) a beautiful and mysterious treasure today.
10. Elegant carvings (has become/have become) part of the proud heritage of the Eskimos.

16.3   Agreement in Inverted Sentences

In an **inverted sentence**—a sentence in which the subject follows the verb—take care in locating the simple subject, and make sure that the verb agrees with the subject.

Inverted sentences often begin with a prepositional phrase. As a result, the object of the preposition may be mistaken for the subject of the sentence. In an inverted sentence the subject always follows the verb.

	V		S
SINGULAR	Beyond the Milky Way **lies** the Andromeda *galaxy*.

	V		S
PLURAL	Beyond the Milky Way **lie** countless *galaxies*.

The words *there* and *here* may also begin an inverted sentence. They are almost never the subject of a sentence.

	V	S
SINGULAR	There **is** one possible ***explanation***.	

	V	S
	Here **comes** my best ***friend***.	

	V	S
PLURAL	There **are** two possible ***explanations***.	

	V	S
	Here **come** my ***friends***.	

In an interrogative sentence an auxiliary verb often precedes the subject. Thus, the subject appears between the auxiliary and the main verb.

	V	S	V
SINGULAR	**Does** that ***man*** **teach** in this school?		

	V	S	V
PLURAL	**Do** those ***schools*** **offer** Latin?		

Exercise 3

Making Subjects and Verbs Agree in Inverted Sentences
Find the simple subject in each sentence. Then write the form of the verb that agrees with each subject.

Computer Games

1. (Does/Do) that woman play computer games?
2. There (is/are) hundreds of computer games available from software developers and amateur programmers.
3. In even the simplest games (lies/lie) the challenge of outwitting a "smart" machine.
4. There (is/are) more complex games that provide both challenge and colorful, high-resolution graphics.
5. Here (is/are) a list of adventures you may have encountered in some of the most popular commercial games.
6. Before you (stretches/stretch) a valley full of magical hazards that your character must master to become a hero.
7. Down the sides of a four-sided well (is/are) falling shapes that you must catch and position on a grid.
8. Within a maze of clues (hides/hide) the identity of the time-traveling thief who has stolen Napoleon's hat.
9. (Does/Do) these games sound familiar to you?
10. With the advent of new technology, there (is/are) a strong probability that games will become even more exciting.

16.4 Agreement with Special Subjects

Collective Nouns

A **collective noun** names a group. Consider a collective noun singular when it refers to a group as a whole. Consider a collective noun plural when it refers to each member of a group individually.

SINGULAR	The ***orchestra* plays.**
PLURAL	The ***orchestra tune*** their instruments.
SINGULAR	The ***family* loves** to travel.
PLURAL	My ***family* take** turns choosing places to visit.

Special Nouns

Certain nouns that end in -*s*, such as *mathematics*, *measles*, and *mumps*, take singular verbs.

SINGULAR	***Measles* is** now an epidemic in my city.

Certain other nouns that end in -*s*, such as *scissors*, *pants*, *binoculars*, and *eyeglasses*, take plural verbs.

PLURAL	These ***binoculars* are** a bargain.
	The ***scissors* were made** in France.

Many nouns that end in -*ics* may be singular or plural, depending upon their meaning.

SINGULAR	***Ethics* is** the branch of philosophy that most interests me. [one subject of interest]
PLURAL	His ***ethics*** in this matter **are** questionable.[more than one ethical decision]

Nouns of Amount

When a noun refers to an amount that is considered one unit, it is singular. When it refers to a number of individual units, it is plural.

SINGULAR	Two ***dollars* is** the fee. [one amount]
PLURAL	Two ***dollars* are** in his pockets. [two individual dollar bills]
SINGULAR	Five ***days* is** an average work week. [one unit of time]
PLURAL	Five ***days* have flown** by. [five individual periods of time]

Titles

A title is always singular, even if a noun within the title is plural.

SINGULAR ***The Adventures of Huckleberry Finn* is** perhaps
Mark Twain's greatest novel.

Exercise 4

Making Verbs Agree with Special Subjects Find the
subject in each sentence, and write on your paper the form of
the verb in parentheses that agrees with the subject.

Michael Jordan, Basketball Superstar

1. The audience (roars/roar) its enthusiasm for Michael
   Jordan each time he steps onto the basketball court.
2. Jordan's statistics (justifies/justify) his fans' reaction.
3. Three years, instead of the usual four, (was/were) all the
   time Jordan felt he should play with his college team, the
   North Carolina Tar Heels.
4. "Gold Medal Winners" (is/are) the title of an article that
   describes how Jordan led the U.S. team to a gold medal in
   the 1984 Olympic games.
5. Thirty-seven points per game (makes/make) an impressive
   year-end average; it was Jordan's in 1988.
6. Jordan's team, the Chicago Bulls, (depends/depend) upon
   one another for inspiration during their grueling season.
7. Five million dollars (is/are) a great deal of money, but many
   think an athlete of Jordan's caliber deserves that salary.
8. Binoculars (helps/help) fans see this brilliant athlete close
   up as he runs, passes, and shoots.
9. While watching Jordan play, the crowd (marvels/marvel)
   at his ability to leap into the air and wriggle past defenders.
10. The public always (enjoys/enjoy) debating among them-
    selves about who is the best basketball player of all time,
    but there is no question that Jordan is among the best.

16.5 Agreement with Compound Subjects

Compound Subjects Joined by And

A compound subject that is joined by *and* or *both . . . and* is plural
unless its parts belong to one unit or they both refer to the same
person or thing.

PLURAL	The *librarian* and the *student* **are reading** in different parts of the library.
	Both **duck** and **chicken** **are** poultry that are found in local markets.
SINGULAR	*Macaroni* and *cheese* **tastes** delicious. [Compound subject is one unit.]
	Her *teacher* and *counselor* **meets** with her daily. [One person is both the teacher and the counselor.]

Compound Subjects Joined by Or or Nor

With compound subjects joined by *or* or *nor* (or by *either . . . or* or *neither . . . nor*), the verb always agrees with the subject nearer the verb.

PLURAL	*Neither* the *adult* *nor* the *children* **are listening.**
SINGULAR	*Either* the *adult* *or* the *child* **is listening.**
	Neither the *adults* *nor* the *child* **is listening.**

Many a, Every, and Each with Compound Subjects

When *many a*, *every*, or *each* precedes a compound subject, the subject is considered singular.

SINGULAR	*Many a* **cook** and **waiter** **works** late.
	Every **man, woman,** and **child** **was** safe.
	Each **adult** and **child** **is listening.**

16.6   Intervening Expressions

Intervening expressions such as *accompanied by, as well as, in addition to, plus,* and *together with* introduce phrases that modify the subject without changing its number. These expressions do not create compound subjects even though their meaning is similar to that of the conjunction *and*.

If a singular subject is linked to another noun by an intervening expression, such as *accompanied by,* the subject is still considered singular.

SINGULAR	*Loyalty,* in addition to common interests, **is** necessary for a lasting friendship.
	The *cook,* as well as the waiter, **works** hard at that restaurant.

Making Verbs Agree with Their Subjects Find the subject in each sentence. On your paper write the appropriate form of the verb in parentheses.

Kitchen Utensils

1. Every chef and gourmet cook (knows/know) that the proper kitchen tool makes any job easier and may make the final product look better as well.
2. Preparing food, as well as serving the meal, often (depends/depend) upon having the correct utensils close at hand.
3. Many an inexperienced cook and homemaker (is/are) surprised by how many utensils are needed.
4. Ham and eggs (is/are) fairly simple to prepare, but you still need the proper utensils, such as a frying pan, a spatula, and a fork.
5. A food processor, which is often accompanied by several different attachments, (makes/make) everything from juices to garnishes.
6. For carving meat, a fork and a sharp knife (is/are) essential to produce smooth, even slices.
7. A kitchen scale together with measuring cups (helps/help) cooks to measure ingredients.
8. A strainer plus colanders of various sizes (is used/are used) to sift flour or shake water from food.
9. Many a lover of fudge or boiled eggs (finds/find) a timer or a stopwatch useful.
10. A grater and a blender (is/are) useful for making delicious soups and sauces quickly.

Creating Sentences with Compound Subjects Write five sentences, each using one of the following items as the compound subject. Make the compound subject agree with a present-tense verb.

1. ham and cheese
2. neither the record nor the tape
3. both the radio and the television
4. Cousin Jaime or my grandmother
5. many a bird and beast

16.7   Indefinite Pronouns as Subjects

A verb must agree in number with an indefinite pronoun subject.

Indefinite pronouns generally fall into three groups.

Indefinite Pronouns			
Always Singular			
each	everyone	nobody	anything
either	everybody	nothing	someone
neither	everything	anyone	somebody
one	no one	anybody	something
Always Plural			
several	few	both	many
Singular or Plural			
some	all	most	none

SINGULAR	***Everyone* wants** a ticket to the concert.
	No one in the group **seems** eager to leave.
PLURAL	***Many*** of the best runners **eat** pasta the night before a race.
	Few of us **believe** in magic.

As you can see from the preceding chart, certain indefinite pronouns can be either singular or plural, depending upon the nouns to which they refer.

SINGULAR	***Some*** of his music **was** quite sophisticated. [*Some* refers to *music*, a singular noun.]
PLURAL	***Some*** of his songs **were** fun to sing. [*Some* refers to *songs*, a plural noun.]

Exercise 7: Sentence Writing

Making Verbs Agree with Indefinite Pronoun Subjects
Write five sentences, each using one of the following indefinite pronouns as the subject. Make each subject agree with a present-tense verb.

SAMPLE	several
ANSWER	Several of the students play piano. ➡

1. everyone
2. many
3. one
4. everything
5. each

Exercise 8: Sentence Writing

Creating Sentences with Indefinite Pronoun Subjects
For each indefinite pronoun listed below, write two sentences.
Use the pronoun as the subject of both sentences. In the first
sentence of each pair, use a singular present-tense verb. In the
second sentence use a plural present-tense verb.

SAMPLE   Most
ANSWER   Most of the water rushes through the canyon.
              Most of the rocks show the smoothing effect of
              the rushing water.

1. some   4. most
2. all   5. none
3. any

16.8   Agreement in Adjective Clauses

When the subject of an adjective clause is a relative pronoun, the
verb in the clause must agree with the antecedent of the relative
pronoun.

The subject of an adjective clause is often a relative pronoun. The
number of the relative pronoun is determined by the number of its
antecedent in the main clause.

The Mexican grizzly is one of the **bears that were thought to be
extinct.**

In the preceding example the antecedent of *that* is *bears*, not *one*,
because *all* the bears, not just the Mexican grizzly, are thought to be
extinct. Since *bears* is plural, *that* is considered plural, and the verb in the
adjective clause, *were*, must also be plural.

The whalebone whale is the only **one** of the whales **that has two
rows of baleen (whalebone) instead of teeth.**

In this example the antecedent of *that* is *one*, not *whales*, because only one kind of whale (the whalebone whale) has two rows of baleen. Since *one* is singular, *that* is considered singular, and the verb in the adjective clause, *has*, must also be singular.

If the expression *one of* appears in the main clause, you must take care to determine whether the antecedent of the relative pronoun is *one*, as in the second example above, or whether it is the following noun, such as *bears* in the first example. When *one of* is modified by *the only*, as in the example about the whales, the antecedent of the relative pronoun is *one*.

Exercise 9

Making Subjects and Verbs Agree in Adjective Clauses

On your paper complete the following sentences by choosing the correct form of the verb in parentheses.

1. The Asian tree shrew is one of the mammals that (is/are) difficult to classify.
2. Akira Kurosawa is the only Japanese director who (has/have) been honored with an Academy Award.
3. Celia Thaxter was one of the few nineteenth-century American poets who (was writing/were writing) primarily for children.
4. Rocky Mountain spotted fever is one of the diseases that (is/are) spread by ticks.
5. Jesse Owens of the United States was the only one of the Olympic competitors who (was/were) able to set six world records in one day.
6. Gloria Estefan is one of the few contemporary music stars who (has/have) successfully combined pop and Latin rhythms.
7. Dwight Gooden is the only one of the major-league pitchers who (has struck/have struck) out at least two hundred batters in each of his first three seasons.
8. Cary Grant was one of the classic Hollywood film actors who (was/were) successful in both comic and dramatic roles.
9. Ella Fitzgerald is one of the great jazz singers of our time who (has popularized/have popularized) so-called scat singing.
10. Martha Graham was one of the innovative choreographers who (was/were) enormously influential in the development of modern dance.

Subject-Verb Agreement   The following paragraph contains ten errors in subject-verb agreement. Locate the sentences with errors, and rewrite those sentences using the correct verb form. (Not every sentence has an error.)

Puerto Rican Celebrations

[1]Puerto Rico, along with many other Caribbean islands, reflect a varied cultural heritage in national and local celebrations. [2]Among the most popular of the Puerto Rican celebrations are Le Lo Lai, a year-round festival that celebrates Puerto Rico's Indian, Spanish, and African heritage. [3]Every man, woman, and child visiting Puerto Rico find some event to enjoy during this celebration. [4]One major tradition handed down from the Spanish culture is the fiestas, or religious festivals, that celebrates each town's patron saint. [5]The music, dancing, parades, and partying connected with a fiesta lasts from one to three days. [6]At these fiestas many a tourist and resident join in dancing the *bomba* late into the night. [7]My family always enjoys the lively spirits and good food found at Puerto Rican fiestas. [8]One of these fiestas, the festival of Santiago, take place in the town of Loíza Aldea. [9]Masks and costumes have been a part of this particular celebration since its origins in Spain. [10]There is also seventy-five to eighty other fiestas celebrated in towns across the island. [11]Twelve days is the traditional length of the Christmas celebration in Puerto Rico. [12]Three Kings' Day (January 6), as well as Christmas Day, is celebrated with feasting and gift giving. [13]Some of the more recent Puerto Rican celebrations includes those associated with national holidays, such as Constitution Day, Luís Muñoz Rivera's Birthday, and Día de la Raza, or Heritage Day. [14]Muñoz Rivera is one of the few Puerto Rican statesmen who is honored with a national holiday. [15]Do these descriptions make you want to attend a Puerto Rican celebration?

When revising your work, you should always check for correct subject-verb agreement. A mistake in subject-verb agreement may mar your credibility and effectiveness as a writer. Keep in mind these guidelines to correct subject-verb agreement:

1. When a prepositional phrase or another expression falls between a subject and its verb, mentally block out the intervening material in checking for agreement.

> . . . A long black *column* of bats *looks* like a tornado spinning far out across the Texas sky.
>
> From "Bats" by Diane Ackerman

2. When a sentence is in inverted order, remember that the subject follows the verb.

> From the fertile fields of Rota, particularly its gardens, *come* the *fruits and vegetables* that fill the markets of Huelva and Seville.
>
> From "The Stub-Book" by Pedro Antonio de Alarcón

3. When the subject is a collective noun, decide whether it refers to the group as a whole or to each member of the group individually. In the former case it is singular; in the latter case it is plural.

> . . . Upon the rebel this *crowd stares*, and the rebel stares back.
>
> From "The Splendid Outcast" by Beryl Markham

> The *mass* of men *lead* lives of quiet desperation.
>
> From *Walden* by Henry David Thoreau

4. When the subject is an indefinite pronoun that can be either singular or plural, decide whether the pronoun refers to a single entity or to several individual entities.

> What though the field be lost?
> *All is* not lost. . . .
>
> From *Paradise Lost* by John Milton

> . . . *All are* gone, the old familiar faces.
>
> From "The Old Familiar Faces" by Charles Lamb

Apply these guidelines in revising the following paragraphs. Make your revision on a separate sheet of paper, and check every sentence for subject-verb agreement, being sure to use the correct form of each verb in your final paragraph.

> Cornfields in my part of rural Pennsylvania is plowed in spring. In the newly turned earth occasionally appears arrowheads, scrapers, and spear points once used by Native American tribes who inhabited the area. Some of the objects comes from many centuries ago; some was carved more recently. The best stones for carving was made of flint or a similar hard but neatly flaking substance. Most arrowheads and other artifacts found today show some damage, since damaged tools and weapons were usually discarded. Near the shores of a local stream sit a cornfield where a Delaware tribe once camped. The tribe no longer live in the area, but some of its history remains recorded in the earth's surface.

*U*sage Workshop

Subject-Verb Agreement

The Country of the Pointed Firs, a novel by Sarah Orne Jewett, is one woman's reflection on a summer spent in a Maine seaside village called Dunnet Landing. In this passage, annotated to show examples of subject-verb agreement covered in this unit, the woman says farewell to the place she has come to love.

Literature Model

from THE COUNTRY OF THE POINTED FIRS
by Sarah Orne Jewett

An inverted sentence introduced by *there* with agreement between a singular noun subject and a singular past form of *be*

An inverted sentence introduced by a prepositional phrase with agreement between a plural noun subject and the plural past form of *be*

There was still an hour to wait, and I went up to the hill just above the schoolhouse and sat there thinking of things, and looking off to sea, and watching for the boat to come in sight. I could see Green Island, small and darkly wooded at that distance; below me were the houses of the village with their apple-trees and bits of garden ground. Presently, as I looked at the pastures beyond, I caught a last glimpse of Mrs. Todd herself, walking slowly in the footpath that led along, following the shore toward the Port. At such a distance, one can feel the large, positive qualities that control a character. Close at hand, Mrs. Todd seemed able and warm-hearted and quite absorbed in her bustling industries, but her distant figure looked mateless and appealing, with something about it that was strangely self-possessed and mysterious. Now and then she stooped to pick something —it might have been her favorite pennyroyal—and at last I lost sight of her as she slowly crossed an open space on one of the higher points of land, and disappeared again behind a dark clump of juniper and the pointed firs.

As I came away on the little coastwise steamer, there was an old sea running which made the surf leap high on all the rocky shores. I stood on deck, looking back, and watched the busy gulls agree and turn, and sway together down the long slopes of air, then separate hastily and plunge into the waves. . . . The little town, with the tall masts of its disabled schooners in the inner bay, stood ⇒

high above the flat sea for a few minutes, then it sank back into the uniformity of the coast, and became indistinguishable from the other towns that looked as if they were crumbled on the furzy-green stoniness of the shore.

The small outer islands of the bay were covered among the ledges with turf that looked as fresh as the early grass; there had been some days of rain the week before, and the darker green of the sweet-fern was scattered on all the pasture heights. It looked like the beginning of summer ashore, though the sheep, round and warm in their winter wool, betrayed the season of the year as they went feeding along the slopes in the low afternoon sunshine. Presently the wind began to blow, and we struck out seaward to double the long sheltering headland of the cape, and when I looked back again, the islands and the headland had run together and Dunnet Landing and all its coasts were lost to sight.

> Agreement between a plural noun subject and the plural past form of *be*; the intervening prepositional phrase does not change the number of the subject.

> Agreement between a compound subject and the plural past form of *be*

Usage Workshop Exercise 1

Making Subjects and Verbs Agree When Prepositional Phrases Intervene   Each of the following sentences describes the scene from the passage from *The Country of the Pointed Firs.* Rewrite each sentence on your paper, following the directions in parentheses. In some cases you will need to change the form of the verb to make the sentence correct; in other cases the verb will remain the same.

SAMPLE   The magical time of summer is ending. (Change *time* to *times*.)

ANSWER   The magical times of summer are ending.

1. The summer visitor to Maine is departing. (Change *visitor* to *visitors*.)
2. Waiting for the steamer, a woman with a suitcase stands on the wharf. (Change *a suitcase* to *suitcases*.)
3. The houses with the apple trees are especially attractive. (Change *houses* to *house*.)
4. Above the houses a gentle hill provides a perfect view. (Move the prepositional phrase so that it comes directly after the subject.)
5. The pastures beyond the houses are visible from the hill. (Change *pastures* to *pasture*.)
6. A walker on the path moves slowly out of sight behind a dark clump of trees. (Change *A walker* to *Walkers*.) ➡

7. Chugging sounds from the rippling waters announce the arrival of the steamer. (Change *waters* to *water*.)
8. The surf on the rocky shore leaps high, shooting spray and salt into the air. (Change *shore* to *shores*.)
9. Near the boat hungry gulls fly noisily back and forth. (Move the prepositional phrase so that it comes directly after the subject.)
10. On a small outer island woolly sheep on the hills graze lazily. (Change *hills* to *hill*.)

Usage Workshop Exercise 2

Making Linking Verbs Agree with Their Subject   The following sentences describe Sarah Orne Jewett's writing. Rewrite each sentence, following the directions in parentheses. If necessary, change the number of the linking verb.

SAMPLE   Jewett's portraits of Maine are treasures. (Change *treasures* to *a treasure*.)

ANSWER   Jewett's portraits of Maine are a treasure.

1. The most important elements in Jewett's stories and books are her characters. (Change *elements* to *element*.)
2. Jewett's best work is a collection of character sketches. (Change *a collection* to *several collections*.)
3. These engaging sketches have become records of a disappearing culture. (Change *records* to *a record*.)
4. The character depiction in *The Country of the Pointed Firs* is a masterpiece. (Change *depiction* to *depictions*.)
5. Her favorite subject is the picturesque villager of coastal Maine. (Change *villager* to *villagers*.)
6. An observer from the outside world frequently appears in Jewett's writing. (Change *An observer* to *Observers*.)
7. In *The Country of the Pointed Firs*, the subject is the reaction of a summer visitor. (Change *reaction* to *reactions*.)
8. The most interesting aspects of the book are the visitor's observations about the residents of Dunnet Landing. (Change *aspects* to *aspect*.)
9. Such small coastal villages are becoming relics of the past. (Change *relics* to *a relic*.)
10. The provincial life of Dunnet Landing remains a reality only in Jewett's book. (Change *life* to *ways*.)

Usage Workshop Exercise 3

Making Subjects and Verbs Agree in Inverted Sentences

Each of the following sentences is based on an idea suggested by the passage from *The Country of the Pointed Firs*. First, write each sentence on your paper, choosing the proper form of the verb in parentheses. Then rewrite each of your sentences in inverted order, making adjustments to the form of the verb if necessary.

SAMPLE   The ships (was/were) beside me on the wharf.

ANSWER   The ships were beside me on the wharf.
              Beside me on the wharf were the ships.

1. The village buildings (clusters/cluster) near the sea.
2. A gentle hill (rises/rise) above the houses.
3. Green pastures (stretches/stretch) beyond the village.
4. The little steamer (sails/sail) on the clear blue waters.
5. Sad farewells (comes/come) with summer's end.

Usage Workshop Exercise 4

Making Verbs Agree with Compound Subjects   Each of the following sentences describes *The Country of the Pointed Firs*. On your paper rewrite each sentence, following the directions in parentheses and making any necessary adjustments to the form of the verb.

SAMPLE   Captain Littlepage appears in Jewett's book. (Add *and Elijah Tilley* to the complete subject.)

ANSWER   Captain Littlepage and Elijah Tilley appear in Jewett's book.

1. The Maine coast is the setting for the novel. (Add *and a small village* to the complete subject.)
2. The town and its people are described by an unidentified summer visitor. (Delete *and its people* from the complete subject.)
3. Her landlady, Mrs. Todd, and a sea captain tell charming tales. (Delete *and a sea captain* from the complete subject.)
4. In fact, every adult in the town has interesting stories to tell. (Add *and child* to the complete subject.)
5. Each story adds to the reader's appreciation of these characters. (Add *and remembrance* to the complete subject.)

Usage Workshop Exercise 5

Making Verbs Agree with Indefinite Pronoun Subjects
The following sentences describe Mount Desert Island, which is located off the coast of Maine. Rewrite each sentence, replacing the indefinite pronoun in italics with the pronoun in parentheses. If necessary, change the number of the verb.

SAMPLE *Everyone* is enjoying Mount Desert Island. (All)
ANSWER All are enjoying Mount Desert Island.

1. *Several* in the group watch the sunrise from Cadillac Mountain. (No one)
2. *Everybody* strolls along the carriage trails. (Many)
3. *Some* of the shoreline is edged with pinkish rocks. (Most)
4. *One* of the boats pulls up lobster traps. (Some)
5. *None* of the lobsters in the trap are undersized. (Each)

Usage Workshop Exercise 6

Review   The following sentences describe the life of Sarah Orne Jewett. For each sentence write the appropriate form of the verb in parentheses.

Sarah Orne Jewett

1. Among the most highly regarded of American regional writers (is/are) Sarah Orne Jewett.
2. In the late nineteenth century some American regional writers (was/were) very popular.
3. Life in particular regions (was/were) captured in fiction.
4. Writers in today's changing world still (tries/try) to preserve vanishing aspects of American culture.
5. Books and stories (is/are) one effective way in which to capture vanishing cultures forever.
6. Neither Jewett's verses nor her tales for children (is/are) as well-known as her sketches about provincial life.
7. One of her favorite activities as a child (was/were) to accompany her father, a physician, on his rounds.
8. From this early experience (comes/come) Jewett's sensitive portrayals of the rural character.
9. Many a Midwesterner and Southerner (has/have) learned about Maine from Jewett's works.
10. Her novels from the late nineteenth century (remains/remain) a kind of album of Maine's people and places.

Proofreading   The following passage describes the artist Edward Hopper, whose work appears on this page. Rewrite the passage, correcting the errors in spelling, capitalization, punctuation, grammar, and usage. There are ten errors in all.

Edward Hopper

[1]Edward Hopper (1882–1967) was born in Nyack, a town twenty-five miles north of New York City. [2]By the time he was a teen-ager, he had developed a keen interest in art. [3]When he was seventeen, he enrolls in the New York School of Art, where painting and illustration was his main fields of study.

[4]For many years Hopper made a living as a magazine illustrator, but creating oil paintings was his real love. [5]His teachers, who Hopper admired considerably, encouraged him to paint the world around him. [6]Hopper took their advise and painted scenes of New England life that included: cityscapes, seascapes, victorian houses and solitery people.

[7]Many of Hopper's images contrasts vivid colors and dramatic lighting with a moody, subdued scene. [8]His figures often seem lonely and melancholy. [9]Like the woman in *The Country of the Pointed Firs*, who gazes at the village she loves, the woman in Hoppers painting surveys the view from her window.

Edward Hopper, *Cape Cod Morning*, 1950

Subject-Verb Agreement

Subject-Verb Agreement

[pages 545–557]

For each sentence indicate the verb that agrees with its subject.

1. A city with the many attractions of New York **(a)** <u>is</u>/**(b)** <u>are</u> rare.
2. The neighborhoods of this city **(a)** <u>contains</u>/**(b)** <u>contain</u> a wide variety of restaurants, shops, and museums.
3. The sounds of Little Italy **(a)** <u>fills</u>/**(b)** <u>fill</u> the air.
4. An interesting place to visit **(a)** <u>is</u>/**(b)** <u>are</u> the streets of Chinatown.
5. The variety of art styles in Soho **(a)** <u>seems</u>/**(b)** <u>seem</u> rich indeed.
6. Soho's many granite and cast-iron buildings **(a)** <u>is</u>/**(b)** <u>are</u> an example of handsome urban architecture.
7. Among the city's urban redevelopment projects **(a)** <u>is</u>/**(b)** <u>are</u> the South Street Seaport Museum.
8. Here **(a)** <u>is</u>/**(b)** <u>are</u> eleven blocks of maritime history.
9. Among the marvels of New York Harbor **(a)** <u>stands</u>/**(b)** <u>stand</u> the Statue of Liberty.
10. Our Drama Club **(a)** <u>visits</u>/**(b)** <u>visit</u> New York as a group every year.
11. Fifty cents **(a)** <u>does</u>/**(b)** <u>do</u> not seem too much to pay for a ride on the Staten Island Ferry.
12. Neither my friends nor my family **(a)** <u>shares</u>/**(b)** <u>share</u> my fascination with subway maps.
13. Many a tourist **(a)** <u>takes</u>/**(b)** <u>take</u> the elevator to the 102nd floor of the Empire State Building.
14. Each of the buildings on this block of Chelsea **(a)** <u>has</u>/**(b)** <u>have</u> been restored.
15. Times Square, in addition to Rockefeller Center, **(a)** <u>attracts</u>/**(b)** <u>attract</u> millions of tourists each year.
16. A group of Dutch colonial buildings, along with other old structures, **(a)** <u>stands</u>/**(b)** <u>stand</u> near the financial district.
17. Mikhail Baryshnikov, as well as the New York City Ballet, **(a)** <u>performs</u>/**(b)** <u>perform</u> at Lincoln Center.
18. New and diverse restaurants are one of the many attractions that **(a)** <u>draws</u>/**(b)** <u>draw</u> tourists to the Upper West Side.
19. Central Park is one of the city's features that **(a)** <u>serves</u>/**(b)** <u>serve</u> both tourists and residents.
20. New York is the only one of the nation's cities that **(a)** <u>has</u>/**(b)** <u>have</u> over seven million residents.

Writing for Review

Write a short description on a subject of your choice. Demonstrate your mastery of subject-verb agreement by including compound subjects and intervening phrases.

Unit 17 Using Pronouns Correctly

17.1 Case of Personal Pronouns

Pronouns that are used to refer to persons or things are called **personal** pronouns.

Personal pronouns have three **cases**, or forms, called **nominative**, **objective**, and **possessive**. The case of a personal pronoun depends upon the pronoun's function in a sentence (whether it is a subject, a complement, or an object of a preposition).

Personal Pronouns			
Case	**Singular Pronouns**	**Plural Pronouns**	**Function in Sentence**
NOMINATIVE	I, you, she, he, it	we, you, they	subject or predicate nominative
OBJECTIVE	me, you, her, him, it	us, you, them	direct object, indirect object, or object of preposition
POSSESSIVE	my, mine, your, yours, her, hers, his, its	our, ours, your, yours, their, theirs	replacement for possessive noun(s)

You can avoid errors in choosing the case of personal pronouns if you keep the following rules in mind:

1. For a personal pronoun in a compound subject, make sure that you use the nominative case.

   Gloria and **I** repaired the fence.
   She and Julius fixed the gate.
   He and **I** mowed the lawn.

2. For a personal pronoun in a compound object, use the objective case.

   Samuel brought Julius and **me** some lemonade.
   He shared some fruit with Gloria and **me**.

Hint: To decide on the correct pronoun in a sentence with a compound subject or object, say the sentence to yourself without the conjunction and the other subject or object.

3. Use the nominative case of a personal pronoun after a form of the linking verb *be*.

> The most skillful gardener was **he.**
> Gloria said that the best supervisor was **I.**
> I said that the best gardeners were **they.**

This rule is now changing, especially in informal speech. When speaking informally, people often use the objective case after a form of the linking verb *be;* they say, *It's me,* or *It was him.* Some authorities suggest using the objective case in informal writing as well, to avoid sounding pretentious. To be strictly correct, however, you should use the nominative case after forms of *be,* especially in your writing.

4. Take care not to spell possessive pronouns with an apostrophe.

> The lawnmower is **hers.**
> The lawn is **ours.**

It's is a contraction of *it is.* Be careful not to confuse *it's* with the possessive pronoun *its.*

> **It's** her book.
> ***Its*** cover is torn.

5. Make sure that you use a possessive pronoun before a gerund (*-ing* forms used as nouns).

> **Your** working late will be helpful.
> We were grateful for **his** playing the piano.

Exercise 1

Choosing the Correct Case Form   For each of the following sentences, choose the correct personal pronoun from each pair in parentheses.

Jamaica Kincaid, Novelist
1. Since Carlos wanted to report on a contemporary West Indian author, (he/him) and (I/me) decided to write about Jamaica Kincaid, who grew up in Antigua.
2. It was (she/her) who wrote *At the Bottom of the River, Annie John,* and *Lucy*—three autobiographical novels about her childhood. ➡

3. (Its/It's) the author's childhood experiences in Antigua that provide the background for each book.
4. (She/Her) and her mother had a very close relationship until Jamaica was nine, when the first of her three brothers was born.
5. What excites Carlos and (I/me) about Kincaid is that lyrical, highly poetic writing style of (hers/her's).
6. An article about Kincaid described for Carlos and (I/me) her move to New York at the age of sixteen to work as an *au pair*, or live-in housekeeper and baby sitter.
7. Many interesting facts came to light as a result of (me/my) reading Kincaid's novel *Lucy*, which describes this period of her life.
8. After Kincaid became good friends with George Trow, a writer for the *New Yorker*, (he/him) and (she/her) attended a West Indian Day parade in Brooklyn.
9. It was (I/me) who found the issue of the *New Yorker* with her description of the event, a discovery that was helpful to Carlos and (I/me).
10. Kincaid's career as a staff writer for this highly respected magazine got (its/it's) start with the publication of this article, which required no editing at all.

17.2   Pronouns with and as Appositives

Use the nominative case for a pronoun that is in apposition to a subject or a predicate nominative.

The first contestants, **she** and **Ramón,** debated well. [*Contestants* is the subject.]

They were the runners-up, **Ramón** and **she.** [*Runners-up* is the predicate nominative.]

Use the objective case for a pronoun that is in apposition to a direct object, an indirect object, or an object of a preposition.

The principal congratulated the winners, **Shiro** and **her.** [*Winners* is the direct object.]

The judge gave the funniest speakers, **Tom** and **her,** a special award. [*Speakers* is the indirect object.]

He had some good words for the scorers, **Grace** and **me.** [*Scorers* is the object of the preposition *for.*]

When a pronoun is followed by an appositive, choose the case of the pronoun that would be correct if the appositive were omitted.

We sisters love skiing. [*We* is the correct form because *we* is the subject of the sentence.]

Uncle Paul gave **us sisters** a set of skis. [*Us* is the correct form because *us* is the indirect object.]

Hint: To choose the correct pronoun, say the sentence aloud without the noun.

Exercise 2

Using Pronouns Correctly with and as Appositives For each of the following sentences, choose the correct personal pronoun from each pair in parentheses.

Early Newspapers

1. (We/Us) student journalists of the modern age have little sense of the history of the newspaper.
2. Our English and journalism teachers, Mr. Gonzalez and (she/her), assigned a joint report on the history of the newspaper industry.
3. It came as a surprise to (we/us) students to learn that the modern newspaper has its roots in an ancient Roman publication, *Acta diurna*, which was posted every day in public and often copied for distribution to distant cities.
4. It was the members of our research group—Jolie, Casey, and (I/me)—who reported on the importance of printing in the development of the modern newspaper.
5. Before the invention of printing, news was disseminated orally or by letters, a fact that fascinated (we/us) researchers.
6. It was two friends from another school, Tomoko Mizumoto and (he/him), who told us that the earliest printed newspapers were really just published newsletters.
7. A reference book found for us by those two librarians, Mr. Biello and (she/her), said that the first modern newspaper was the *Avisa Relation oder Zeitung*, published in Germany in 1609.
8. (We/Us) Americans were surprised to learn that the first newspaper in the colonies was a broadside with the ➡

name *Publick Occurrences*, which was published in Boston as
early as 1690.

9. My uncle, a reporter for his village paper, gave (we/us)
researchers a pamphlet on the history of newspaper journalism.

10. Two people knowledgeable about publishing, (he/him)
and Mr. Gonzalez, said we had collected valuable information for our report.

Exercise 3

Using Pronouns Correctly with and as Appositives   For
each sentence in the following paragraph, choose the correct
pronoun from each pair in parentheses.

Oscar Arias Sánchez, Spokesperson for Peace

[1]In the History Club's discussion of peace in Central
America, the first speakers were two classmates, Kareem and
(she/her). [2]After praising the stabilizing influence of the former
Costa Rican president Oscar Arias Sánchez, they introduced
the next two speakers, Manuel and (I/me). [3]First, we informed
everyone in the audience, fellow club members and (they/
them), of Dr. Arias's brilliant academic career. [4]Then (we/us)
enthusiasts elaborated on Dr. Arias's ongoing efforts to
improve education and economic stability in Costa Rica and to
serve as a peacemaker in Central America. [5]All present,
(they/them) and (we/us), agreed that Dr. Arias was a worthy
recipient of the 1987 Nobel Peace Prize.

17.3   Pronouns After *Than* and *As*

In elliptical adverb clauses using *than* and *as*, choose the case of the
pronoun that you would use if the missing words were fully
expressed.

They arrived at the party earlier than **she.** [The nominative pronoun *she* is the subject of the complete adverb clause *than she
arrived.*]

The play amused our guests as much as **us.** [The objective pronoun *us* is the direct object of the complete adverb clause *as
much as it amused us.*]

17.4   Reflexive and Intensive Pronouns

Take care to observe the following rules in the use of reflexive and intensive pronouns.

1. Do not use *hisself* or *theirselves;* they are incorrect forms. Always use *himself* and *themselves*.

   Paul corrected the error **himself**.
   My parents **themselves** put out the fire.

2. Always use a reflexive pronoun when a pronoun refers to the person who is the subject of the sentence.

INCORRECT	I bought ~~me~~ a book.
CORRECT	I bought **myself** a book.
INCORRECT	He found ~~him~~ a comfortable chair.
CORRECT	He found **himself** a comfortable chair.

3. Do not use a reflexive pronoun unnecessarily. Remember that a reflexive pronoun must refer to the same person as the subject.

INCORRECT	Elsa and ~~myself~~ are going to the mall.
CORRECT	Elsa and **I** are going to the mall.
INCORRECT	Carlos and ~~yourself~~ are invited to the performance on opening night.
CORRECT	Carlos and **you** are invited to the performance on opening night.

17.5 *Who* and *Whom* in Questions and Subordinate Clauses

In questions, use *who* for subjects and *whom* for direct and indirect objects and objects of a preposition.

> **Who** called me yesterday morning? [*Who* is the subject of the verb *called*.]

> **Whom** are you photographing? [*Whom* is the direct object of the verb *are photographing*.]

In questions with interrupting expressions, such as *did you say* or *do you think*, it is often helpful to drop the expression in order to determine whether to use *who* or *whom*.

> **Who** do you think will arrive first? [Think: *Who* will arrive first? *Who* is the subject of the verb *will arrive*.]

Use the nominative pronouns *who* and *whoever* for subjects and predicate nominatives in subordinate clauses.

> Tell me **who** is in charge here. [*Who* is the subject of the noun clause *who is in charge here*.]

> She knows **who** her supervisor is. [*Who* is the predicate nominative of the noun clause *who her supervisor is*.]

> The prize will be given to **whoever** deserves it. [*Whoever* is the subject of the noun clause *whoever deserves it*.]

Use the objective pronouns *whom* and *whomever* for direct and indirect objects and objects of a preposition in subordinate clauses.

> They asked her **whom** she saw at the party. [*Whom* is the direct object of the verb *saw* in the noun clause *whom she saw at the party*.]

> Harding is a president about **whom** I know little. [*Whom* is the object of the preposition *about* in the adjective clause *about whom I know little*.]

> The winner will be **whomever** the people select. [*Whomever* is the direct object of the verb *select* in the noun clause *whomever the people select*.]

In informal speech people generally use *who* in place of *whom* in sentences like this one: *Who did you ask?* In writing and in formal speech, however, it is best to make the distinctions between *who* and *whom*.

Using *Who* or *Whom* in Sentences   On your paper complete the passage below by filling each blank with *who* or *whom*.

Midori, a Prodigious Musical Talent

[1] _____ do you think the critics have hailed as the greatest talent in classical music in the last twenty years? [2]Midori, a young violinist born in Japan, has excited everyone _____ has heard her. [3]Taught by her mother, Setsu Goto, _____ was a professional violinist herself, Midori began playing a tiny violin when she was only three. [4]Dorothy DeLay, _____ musicians worldwide respect as a renowned violin teacher, heard a tape recording of the young violinist and was instrumental in bringing the ten-year-old girl to New York to study at the Juilliard School of Music.

[5]The famous violinist Pinchas Zuckerman, _____ Midori impressed with her playing soon after her arrival in the United States, said that such artists come along only once or twice in a century. [6]During her first year at Juilliard, Midori was heard by the conductor of the New York Philharmonic Orchestra, Zubin Mehta, with _____ she played a brilliant concert on New Year's Eve. [7]_____ do you suppose was more thrilled that night—Midori or her audience? [8]Playing with the Boston Symphony Orchestra when she was fifteen, Midori broke a string; she then walked over to the concert master, _____ handed her his violin; she broke a string on his violin as well, and she finished the piece on a third instrument. [9]After this performance critics knew _____ the next great musical star would be. [10]When I asked my grandparents _____ we were going to hear at the concert on Wednesday evening, I was excited to hear them respond with Midori's name.

Choosing *Whoever* or *Whomever*   For each of the following sentences, choose the correct pronoun from the pair in parentheses.

A Chance to Play with the Professionals

1. (Whoever/Whomever) performs best at the auditions will be offered a summer internship with the orchestra.
2. The orchestra will provide food, lodging, travel ➡

expenses, and master classes for (whoever/whomever) the judges choose.

3. The judges will consider (whoever/whomever) they feel is qualified.
4. (Whoever/Whomever) misses the Friday deadline, however, will have to wait another year.
5. The winner will be (whoever/whomever) the judges feel has played the best.
6. The auditions will be worthwhile (whoever/whomever) wins.
7. The music director will present a plaque to (whoever/whomever) excels.
8. A reporter for our school newspaper will interview (whoever/whomever) she feels will be the most interesting subject for an article about the auditions.
9. Of course, an article will appear in the local newspaper about (whoever/whomever) the judges select.
10. The local newspaper will also photograph (whoever/whomever) wins the competition.

17.6 Pronoun-Antecedent Agreement

An **antecedent** is the word or group of words to which a pronoun refers or that a pronoun replaces. All pronouns must agree with their antecedents in number, gender, and person.

Agreement in Number and Gender

A pronoun must agree with its antecedent in number (singular or plural) and gender (masculine, feminine, or neuter).

A noun, another pronoun, or a phrase or clause acting as a noun may be the antecedent of a pronoun. In the examples that follow, the pronouns appear in boldface type, and their antecedents appear in boldface italic type.

George Eliot published **her** masterpiece, *Middlemarch*, in installments in 1871–1872. [singular feminine pronoun]

Claude's *sisters* sailed **their** catamaran out on the bay. [plural pronoun]

I. M. Pei constructed many of **his** innovative buildings in the Northeast. [singular masculine pronoun]

Rita's *brothers* are respected in **their** business. [plural pronoun]

We should consult this *magazine* for **its** comprehensive article on whales. [singular neuter pronoun]

Dogwoods and *azaleas* are admired in spring for the beauty of **their** blossoms. [plural pronoun]

Traditionally, a masculine pronoun is used when the gender of the antecedent is not known or when the antecedent may be either masculine or feminine.

A good *diver* must practice **his** routines daily.

This rule touches on an area of controversy and changing language, however. Today some people prefer using gender-neutral wording. If you wish to avoid using a masculine pronoun, you can usually reword your sentence in one of the following three ways: (1) by using *he or she, his or her*, and so forth, (2) by making both the antecedent and the pronoun a plural, or (3) by eliminating the pronoun altogether.

A good *diver* must practice **his or her** routines daily.
Good *divers* must practice **their** routines daily.
Good *divers* must practice routines daily. [no pronoun]

Agreement with Collective Nouns

When the antecedent of a pronoun is a collective noun, the number of the pronoun depends upon whether the collective noun is meant to be singular or plural.

The *group* boarded **its** bus promptly at eight. [The collective noun *group* is being used in the singular sense of one unit of persons. Therefore, the singular pronoun *its* is used.]

The *group* bought **their** souvenirs before leaving. [The collective noun *group* is being used in the plural sense of several persons performing separate acts. Therefore, the plural pronoun *their* is used.]

Exercise 7

Making Pronouns and Antecedents Agree   On your paper complete the following sentences by filling each blank with an appropriate possessive pronoun. Then write the antecedent of each pronoun that you supply.

The Attractions of School Theater

1. Anyone who knows my friend Helen will understand _____ devotion to the theater.
2. In ninth grade Mr. Rodriguez, our English teacher, gave ➡

her a small part in one of _____ plays, and she performed the part brilliantly.

3. The entire cast showed _____ enthusiasm for Helen's performance by presenting her with a bouquet of roses on the last day of the show.

4. Since then both she and her boyfriend seem to spend all _____ free time in the theater, either acting or working backstage.

5. Helen has come to believe that an actor must take _____ profession seriously, and she has been studying acting every summer.

6. Set design and lighting are just two aspects of theater that Helen has developed an interest in because of _____ impact on the overall effect of a performance.

7. The three of us have made drama and theater the center of _____ extracurricular lives.

8. From Helen we have learned to read a play before attending one of _____ performances, so that we can judge for ourselves how true the director has been to the playwright's intent.

9. We often noticed that the audience had diverse reactions to a performance and would loudly declare _____ opinions as soon as the curtain had fallen.

10. When I was recently offered the chance to direct a one-act play, I told Helen I would do it only if she agreed to be in _____ cast.

Exercise 8

Making Pronouns and Antecedents Agree   In each of the following sentences, find the personal pronoun and its antecedent. Then revise the sentence in one or more ways to correct the problem in pronoun-antecedent agreement.

Tex-Mex Music

1. A Texan of Mexican descent who enjoys dancing probably counts the *conjunto* and the *orquesta*, two styles of Tex-Mex music, among their favorite types of dance music.

2. Many people find the relaxed folk style and prominent accordion accompaniment of the *conjunto* to his liking.

3. Influenced by American swing, *orquesta* music is especially popular with the sophisticated city dweller who enjoys stylistic diversity in their music. ➡

4. A student of popular music trying to discover who created the *orquesta* will find their answer in the person of Beto Villa, who made many popular recordings in the late 1940s.
5. Fans of Tex-Mex music and of Beto Villa probably also count among his favorite performers Little Joe Hernández, who later revitalized the *orquesta* with infusions of American jazz and rock music.

Exercise 9

Making Pronouns Agree with Collective Noun Antecedents   On your paper complete the following sentences by filling the blank with an appropriate possessive pronoun. Also write the antecedent of each pronoun that you supply.

A Legal Victory

1. The defendant's family found _____ way to the courthouse easily.
2. A group of people left _____ cars in the parking lot behind the courthouse.
3. The audience in the courtroom expressed _____ opinion loudly and clearly.
4. The jury retired to determine _____ verdict.
5. The legal team beamed over _____ victory.
6. The band brought _____ own instruments to the victory party.
7. A class in criminal law wrote _____ term papers on different aspects of the case.
8. Soon a swarm of reporters told the world _____ exciting story.
9. The story's chief attraction was _____ strangeness.
10. Later the crowd voiced _____ various opinions about the verdict.

Agreement in Person

A pronoun must agree in person with its antecedent.

Do not use the second-person pronoun *you* to refer to an antecedent that is in the third person. In order to fix an error in which the second-person pronoun is misused in this way, either change *you* to an appropriate third-person pronoun, or replace it with a suitable noun.

POOR	John and Angela are going to Ravenna, in northern Italy, where ~~you~~ can admire the Byzantine mosaics.
BETTER	John and Angela are going to Ravenna, in northern Italy, where **they** can admire the Byzantine mosaics.
BETTER	John and Angela are going to Ravenna, in northern Italy, where **tourists** can admire the Byzantine mosaics.

When a pronoun has another pronoun as its antecedent, be sure that the two pronouns agree in person. Do not illogically shift pronouns, as between *they* and *you*, *I* and *you*, or *one* and *you*.

POOR	**They** love to walk along the beach, where ~~you~~ can feel the salt spray.
BETTER	**They** love to walk along the beach, where **they** can feel the ocean's spray.
POOR	**I** went to Williamsburg, Virginia, where ~~you~~ can learn how life was lived in colonial times.
BETTER	**I** went to Williamsburg, Virginia, where **I** learned how life was lived in colonial times.

Exercise 10

Making Pronouns and Antecedents Agree in Person
Rewrite each of the following items, eliminating the inappropriate use of *you* by substituting a third-person pronoun or a suitable noun.

English Medieval Plays

1. The audiences of English medieval plays enjoyed the spectacle immensely. They watched the plays outdoors, where you could enjoy the fine weather.
2. The spectators gathered in churchyards. You would often be celebrating a feast day or holiday.
3. Residents of the towns of Wakefield, Chester, York, and Coventry were very fond of medieval plays. You might see many short dramas in the course of a single day.
4. Each guild provided actors for the plays. You would circulate through the town in a wagon, which would serve as a movable stage.
5. In a special kind of performance called mummery, players wore elaborate costumes and masks. You would dance along the streets, enter houses, throw dice with the people, and then move on.

Agreement with Indefinite Pronoun Antecedents

In general, use a singular personal pronoun when the antecedent is a singular indefinite pronoun, and use a plural personal pronoun when the antecedent is a plural indefinite pronoun. (See page 553 for a list of singular and plural indefinite pronouns.)

> **Neither** of the boys in our group wrote **his** own sonnet.
> **Each** of the girls wrote **her** own speech.
> **Several** of my friends presented **their** work.

In the first two examples above, the plural nouns in the prepositional phrases—*of the boys, of the girls*—do not affect the number of the pronouns. *His* and *her* are singular because their antecedents, *neither* and *each*, are singular. In informal speech, people often use the plural pronoun *their* in such sentences.

> INFORMAL   **Neither** of the boys presented **their** speeches.
>   **Each** of them decided on **their** own topic.

When no gender is specified, writers traditionally use a masculine pronoun with an indefinite antecedent.

> **Everyone** should write **his** own research paper.

> **No one** should attempt to begin writing a research paper until **he** has completed his preliminary outline.

This rule, too, is changing as more people come to prefer gender-neutral wording. If you would rather not use a masculine pronoun when the indefinite pronoun may refer to a female, reword your sentence. Try substituting a plural indefinite pronoun for the singular one or eliminating the personal pronoun entirely. Although the use of two pronouns (*he or she, him or her, his or her*) is acceptable, many writers consider such wording awkward.

> **All** the students should prepare **their** own preliminary outlines.

> **Everyone** in the class should prepare a preliminary outline. [no pronoun]

Exercise 11

Making Pronouns Agree with Indefinite Pronoun Antecedents   On your paper indicate which of the following sentences are correct. Then revise each of the incorrect sentences to make it correct. Most of the incorrect sentences can be revised in more than one way. In some cases you will need to change a single word to make a sentence correct; in others you may wish to revise the entire sentence. ➡

Differing Life Styles of Native American Tribes

1. It is well known that each of the Native American tribes had their own way of life.
2. Most of this cultural variety among the Native American tribes had its roots in the diversity of the climate and the terrain of the vast North and South American continents.
3. Several of the tribes in the Southwest made its homes in pueblos, or villages.
4. Almost all of the Pueblo tribes of the Southwest built its homes on mesas.
5. Among the Zuñi, houses were the property of women, and each could sell or trade their home without hindrance from the tribe's leaders.
6. A few of the southwestern tribes earned their livelihood as shepherds.
7. Most of the Pueblo tribes farmed the land, raising corn, beans, and squash as its principal crops.
8. Any of the tribes that relied on hunting and gathering for its sustenance had to travel great distances with every change of season.
9. If most of the time an area received little rain, their residents would be forced to abandon their homes and set out in search of food.
10. Many of the Plains tribes relied on the availability of buffalo for their survival.

17.7 Clear Pronoun Reference

Make sure that the antecedent of a pronoun is clearly stated and that a pronoun cannot possibly refer to more than one antecedent.

Vague Pronoun Reference

You should not use the pronouns *this*, *that*, *which*, and *it* without a clearly stated antecedent.

VAGUE	Gwendolyn Brooks is a talented and accomplished writer, and **this** is apparent from her poetry. [What is apparent from Brooks's poetry? Her writing ability is apparent, but *writing ability* is not specifically mentioned in the sentence.]
CLEAR	Gwendolyn Brooks is a talented and accomplished writer, and **her writing ability** is apparent from her poetry.

VAGUE	In 1906 many buildings in San Francisco burned, **which** was caused by the great earthquake of April 18. [What was caused by the earthquake? A fire was caused, but the word *fire* does not appear in the sentence.]
CLEAR	In 1906 a fire, **which** was caused by the great earthquake of April 18, burned many buildings in San Francisco.
VAGUE	The doctor is examining Sue to see what is wrong with her, and then he will discuss **it** with her. [What will the doctor discuss with Sue? He will discuss the diagnosis, but *diagnosis* has not been mentioned.]
CLEAR	The doctor is examining Sue to see what is wrong with her, and then he will discuss **the diagnosis** with her.

Ambiguous Pronoun Reference

Sometimes a pronoun seems to refer to more than one antecedent. In such cases you should either reword the sentence to make the antecedent clear or eliminate the pronoun.

UNCLEAR ANTECEDENT	When the large dogs approached the small cats, **they** were intimidated. [Which word is the antecedent of *they*? Were the dogs intimidated or the cats?]
CLEAR ANTECEDENT	The large dogs were intimidated when **they** approached the small cats.
NO PRONOUN	When the large dogs approached the small cats, **the dogs** were intimidated.
NO PRONOUN	The large dogs were intimidated by the small cats.

Indefinite Use of Pronouns

The pronouns *you* and *they* should not be used as indefinite pronouns. Instead, you should name the performer of the action. In some cases you may be able to reword the sentence in such a way that you do not name the performer of the action and you do not use a pronoun.

INDEFINITE	When the national anthem is played at a baseball game, **you** should rise.
CLEAR	When the national anthem is played at a baseball game, **the crowd** should rise.
CLEAR	When the national anthem is played at a baseball game, **everyone** should rise.

INDEFINITE	In some neighborhoods **they** pick up the garbage twice a week.
CLEAR	In some neighborhoods **the sanitation department** picks up the garbage twice a week.
CLEAR	In some neighborhoods the garbage **is picked up** twice a week.

Exercise 12

Making Pronoun Reference Clear On your paper rewrite each of the following sentences, making sure that all pronoun references are clearly stated. In some cases you may choose to eliminate the pronoun entirely.

School Sports

1. In most American high schools they offer students a wide range of extracurricular activities, and one of the most popular of these is sports.
2. Rigorous academic classes make heavy demands on students, and this can affect their health and well-being.
3. Girls as well as boys take part in team sports, and they benefit both physically and mentally from a vigorous workout at the end of the day.
4. Unfortunately, in some schools they no longer have a budget for extracurricular sports programs, and the students themselves must organize and meet the expenses of any such programs.
5. Participation in sports also serves to teach students how to get along with one another; when my sister Bernice beat her best friend, Marta, in a race, for example, she succeeded in maintaining their friendship.
6. As field-hockey teammates, Bernice and Marta cooperate rather than compete, which suits them both.
7. When hardworking students play a tough game against another school's team, it can help them in the classroom, for they are likely to feel less tense and therefore can concentrate more fully on their schoolwork.
8. Playing on a team also helps you learn how to work together for the good of the group.
9. When coaches urge players to work as a team instead of playing as separate competing individuals, they know this advice is sound.
10. Sports should be an integrated part of the school experience, and this is evident from the many benefits afforded students.

Pronoun Usage Rewrite each of the following sentences, eliminating any mistakes in the use of pronouns. Each sentence has one error.

African-American Soldiers in the Civil War

1. In Ulysses S. Grant, Abraham Lincoln found him an ally on the issue of allowing African Americans to fight in the Civil War.
2. Both of these men expressed his personal belief that African Americans would make good soldiers.
3. Even after the United States Congress allowed African-American men to enlist in the Union Army, it was not popular among some Northerners.
4. African Americans made up less than 1 percent of the North's population, but this group showed their courage by making up nearly 10 percent of the Union Army by the end of the war.
5. African-American troops fought and died for the first time on June 7, 1863, at Milliken's Bend, Louisiana, which proved their courage and persuaded Union commanders to take them seriously.
6. Colonel Robert Gould Shaw proudly led the all-black Fifty-fourth Massachusetts Regiment, and they bravely attacked Fort Wagner, South Carolina, despite heavy casualties, once again proving the valor of the African-American soldier.
7. Frederick Douglass had campaigned tirelessly for the recruitment of African Americans by the Union Army; it was him who complained directly to President Lincoln about their being paid three dollars less per month than white soldiers.
8. Respect for the courage of these soldiers is redoubled when you think of the dangers of capture; unlike white men, captured African-American soldiers were usually either returned to slavery or immediately shot.
9. The Congressional Medal of Honor is presented to whomever has shown gallantry and courage in conflict with the enemy, at the risk of life and above and beyond the call of duty.
10. No one was more delighted than me to discover that twenty-three African-American soldiers were awarded the Medal of Honor for their bravery during the Civil War.

When you revise your work, be sure that all the pronouns you have used are in the correct form. As you proofread your writing, keep in mind the following guidelines concerning correct pronoun usage:

1. When using personal pronouns as subjects or in compound subjects, be sure to use the nominative case. When using personal pronouns as objects or in compound objects, be sure to use the objective case.

> Gil and *I* got out of the car. . . . *She* seemed no more interested in Gil and *me* than *she* did in anything else around *her.* . . .

From *A Gathering of Old Men* by Ernest Gaines

2. Remember never to use an apostrophe in a possessive pronoun. Keep in mind that *it's* is not a possessive pronoun but a contraction for *it is*.

> Rolling into the wave and savoring *its* lull . . .

From "Voyage" by Carmen Tafolla

> . . . I could say "Elves" to him,
> But *it's* not elves exactly, and I'd rather
> He said it for himself.

From "Mending Wall " by Robert Frost

3. Always use *who* for subjects and *whom* for objects.

> Mrs. Sommers was one *who* knew the value of bargains. . . .

From "A Pair of Silk Stockings" by Kate Chopin

> . . . And therefore never send to know
> for whom the bell tolls; it tolls for thee.

From Meditation XVII by John Donne

4. Remember to use the singular form of a personal pronoun when its antecedent is a singular indefinite pronoun.

> *Each* singing what belongs to *him* or *her* and to none else.

From "I Hear America Singing" by Walt Whitman

Apply your knowledge of pronoun usage by proofreading the following passage. Revise any errors in the use of pronouns as you rewrite the paragraph on a separate sheet of paper.

The actress Madhur Jaffrey, who PBS viewers may know from her cooking series, has published many fine cookbooks over the years. My mother and me especially like *Indian Cooking*, with it's excellent recipes and interesting background information. Everyone in the family has their favorite Jaffrey dish, and for Mom its Goan chicken. Vegetable dishes, more to the liking of my father and I, include potatoes with sesame seeds and Gujarati green beans. Madhur Jaffrey, who grew up in Delhi, India, provides a variety of dishes from many regions of her homeland. For each she includes information about their origins and any unusual ingredients.

Using Pronouns Correctly

Though Langston Hughes made his name as a poet, he also wrote many fine works of nonfiction. In this passage from a memoir, Hughes recalls a trip he made to Mexico City in the mid-1930s and the time he spent there with three aging sisters, the Patiños. The passage has been annotated to show some of the kinds of pronouns covered in this unit.

Literature Model

from I WONDER AS I WANDER

by Langston Hughes

Pronoun in the possessive case

Pronoun in the nominative case used as a subject

Pronoun in the objective case used as an indirect object

The pronoun *they* in the nominative case used as a subject. The pronoun agrees in number with its antecedent, *sisters*.

My last few weeks in Mexico I spent at the Patiño home, because I knew they would feel hurt if I didn't. I went to vespers with them every night in the old church just across the street, lighted by tall candles and smelling of incense. Sometimes I even got up early in the morning to attend mass. And I still cherish the lovely old rosaries they gave me. These sisters were very sweet, kindhearted women. But sometimes I thought their kindness was a little misspent. I was then all in favor of working to change the *basic* economics of the world, while they were engaged in little charities widely dispersed to help various indigents *a little*. From their small income they gave, in proportion, generously—five pesos here, ten there, two to this brother-hood, three to that sisterhood, one peso to one organiza-tion, a peso and a half to another—and regularly each week to the church. Then from their home they had their own little private dispensation every seventh day to the poor of the neighborhood.

This weekly ritual seemed touching, but very futile to me. There were literally thousands of poor people in the neighborhood, since the Patiños lived in the heart of Mexico City, not far from the Zocalo. In our block alone there were perhaps two or three hundred shoeless or nearly shoeless folks. Personal charity for a handful, I felt, was hardly a drop in the bucket for so great a need. But these elderly women had been doing this for years, so I said nothing to discourage them. Every Monday, early in ➡

the morning they would busy themselves, these three sisters, packaging in separate cones of newspapers little cups of beans, a tiny scoop of sugar, perhaps two or three onions, a bunch of grapes or an orange, and a small slice of laundry soap. Several dozen such little packets of each thing they would make. Then from eleven to twelve, just before midday dinner, the poor of the neighborhood would come to receive their gifts. To each who asked, a set of these tiny packets would be given at the door, with a "Bless you, Marianita! . . . Bless you, Luz!" as each filed past with open hands. But the food each got was not enough for even one good meal. And the tiny piece of soap would hardly wash anyone's hands and face more than a day.

But there was among the deserving poor in the neighborhood one woman who must have felt as I did—concerning this small donation—because she always stayed to dinner. After she got her tiny packages, she would squat on the floor just inside the dining-room door, and no one could move her until the three sisters sat down to eat their noonday meal and she was served on the floor, too.

The pronoun *who* in the nominative case used as the subject of *asked*

Agreement in number and gender between the pronoun *she* and its antecedent, *woman*

Usage Workshop Exercise 1

Choosing the Correct Pronoun Case   The following sentences are based on the passage from *I Wonder As I Wander*. For each sentence determine whether the italicized pronoun is used correctly. If it is not, write the pronoun as it should appear. If it is used properly, write *correct*.

SAMPLE   While Hughes was visiting the Patiños, the poet and *them* walked nightly to the old church.

ANSWER   they

1. The house in which Hughes was staying was *their's*.
2. Hughes observed that the kindest people must be *they*.
3. *Him* and the Patiños had different ideas about charity.
4. Although the sisters' generosity was sincere, Hughes wondered about *it's* effectiveness.
5. *Them* distributing little packets of food each week could hardly ease the suffering in the neighborhood.
6. The food that Marianita or Luz received was *hers* alone.
7. The packets did not contain even one meal's worth of food for *they* or their families, however.
8. Hughes decided that *him* and one of the poorest women had the same feelings about the small gifts of food.➡

9. If a truly determined person ever lived, it was *her*.

10. Despite *them* trying to move her out of the dining room, the sisters were forced to serve this woman a meal.

Usage Workshop Exercise 2

Using Pronouns Correctly with and as Appositives

The following sentences are based on a passage from *I Wonder As I Wander* that is not reprinted in this textbook. For each sentence determine whether the italicized pronoun appears in the proper form. If it does not, write the pronoun as it should appear. If it is used properly, write *correct*.

1. The Patiños' house was at times home to both men, Hughes's father and *him*.

2. Of the small gathering, *he* and the Patiño sisters, only he was not dressed in mourning.

3. The four people to whom the will pertained, the Patiños and *him*, sat together silently.

4. The Patiños told Hughes, "*Us* sisters wish to share the estate with you."

5. The Patiños generously suggested to Hughes that the estate be divided among four people, the three sisters and *he*.

Usage Workshop Exercise 3

Using Pronouns After *Than* and *As*

The following sentences are based on a passage from *I Wonder As I Wander* that is not reprinted in this textbook. Each sentence contains an italicized word or group of words. Rewrite each sentence, substituting the correct pronoun for the words in italics.

SAMPLE   Hughes enjoyed no one more than *his Mexican friends*.

ANSWER   Hughes enjoyed no one more than them.

1. These writers and artists relished life as much as *Hughes*.

2. Diego Rivera was probably more famous than *other artists*.

3. Mexicans love few works of art more than *Rivera's murals*.

4. Hughes had never seen anyone as huge as *Rivera*.

5. Hughes also knew Rivera's ex-wife, Lupe; no one was more colorful than *Lupe*.

Choosing *Who* or *Whom*   The following sentences are based on passages from *I Wonder As I Wander* that are not reprinted in this textbook. For each sentence choose the correct pronoun from the pair in parentheses.

1. Hughes's father, (who/whom) Hughes rarely saw, died in Mexico.
2. The father cherished the Patiño sisters, (who/whom) everyone knew had cared for him during his last years.
3. Can you guess (who/whom) inherited the father's estate?
4. He left it to the Patiños, to (who/whom) he owed so much.
5. They tried to share the estate with Hughes, but he refused the offer, knowing (who/whom) needed the money more.

Making Pronouns and Antecedents Agree   The following sentences are about Mexico City, where some of *I Wonder As I Wander* takes place. Each sentence contains an example of pronoun-antecedent agreement. Rewrite the sentences according to the directions in parentheses, changing the pronouns if necessary. You may also have to change the form of the verb.

SAMPLE   Large cities like Mexico City have their advantages and disadvantages. (Change *Large cities* to *A large city*.)

ANSWER   A large city like Mexico City has its advantages and disadvantages.

1. The central core of Mexico City traces its history to Aztec times. (Change *core* to *sections*.)
2. The Aztecs chose an island on which to build their principal city, Tenochtitlán. (Change *The Aztecs* to *Aztec society*.)
3. The achievements of Aztec culture reached their height in Tenochtitlán, now known as Mexico City. (Delete *The achievements of*.)
4. The streets around the Zocalo, a grand plaza, retain their role as the hub of the city. (Change *streets* to *area*.)
5. At the Zocalo an Aztec emperor built two glorious temples for himself. (Change *an Aztec emperor* to *the Aztecs*.)
6. The Spaniards replaced the Aztec temples with a palace and a church of their own. (Change *The Spaniards* to *The Spanish colonial government*.) ⟶

7. Diego Rivera decorated the National Palace with his murals. (Replace *Diego Rivera* with *One of Mexico's great artists*.)
8. Today this city has grown far beyond its original borders. (Add *of millions* after *city*.)
9. Modern manufacturing has brought with it both revenue and pollution. (Change *manufacturing* to *factories*.)
10. Many families in Mexico City find that they must live without electricity. (Change *Many families* to *Many a family*.)

Usage Workshop Exercise 6

Review   The following sentences describe aspects of Langston Hughes's life and work. For each sentence choose the proper pronoun from the pair in parentheses, and write it on your paper.

Langston Hughes

1. Langston Hughes, (who/whom) many associate with the writers of the Harlem Renaissance, was born in 1902.
2. Although (he/him) and the other Harlem Renaissance writers are often regarded as New Yorkers, Hughes himself was born in Missouri.
3. When Hughes was young, his family consisted of three people: his mother, his grandmother, and (he/him).
4. Because of (him/his) leaving his wife soon after their son's birth, Hughes's father was something of a stranger to his son.
5. His father, (who/whom) Hughes saw only occasionally, lived in Mexico for thirty years.
6. Langston Hughes traveled widely and held many jobs, from busboy to war correspondent; few people have led a more varied life than (he/him).
7. He toured Latin America, Europe, Africa, and Asia, and each of these voyages had (its/their) effect on his writing.
8. Few writers were as versatile and prolific as (he/him).
9. (Its/It's) clear that his poems, novels, stories, memoirs, plays, translations, and feature articles have all contributed to his reputation.
10. Of all the Harlem Renaissance poets, it was (he/him) who captured the widest readership outside this country.

Proofreading   The following passage describes the artist Maria Izquierdo, whose painting appears on this page. Rewrite the passage, correcting the errors in spelling, capitalization, punctuation, grammar, and usage. There are ten errors in all.

Maria Izquierdo

¹Born in a small village in the state of Jalisco, Maria Izquierdo (1906–1955) became one of Mexicos outstanding modern painters. ²Although she had little formal training (She studied briefly at the Academy of San Carlos in Mexico City, she had a intuitive grasp of form and color.

³Painting in jewellike tones of blue, rose, yellow, and magenta, Izquierdo depicted scenes of everyday Mexican life. ⁴Peasant women wrapped in black shawls, handmade toys, and circus scenes appears frequently in her work. ⁵Her forms are simple, heavily-outlined, and almost sculptural in their modeling. ⁶Many of her paintings have an otherwordly quality.

⁷The women in *Dos Mujeres con Papaya* (*Two Women with Papaya*) seem strong, capeable, and content. ⁸Its possible to imagine that they resemble the generous Patiño women who Langston Hughes describes in *I Wonder As I Wander.*

Maria Izquierdo, *Dos Mujeres con Papaya*, 1936

Using Pronouns Correctly

Using Personal Pronouns

[pages 565–571]

Indicate the correct personal pronoun.

1. Mike and **(a)** I/**(b)** me run a carpet-cleaning company.
2. The owners of the company are Mike and **(a)** I/**(b)** me.
3. The fees are split between the owners, Mike and **(a)** I/**(b)** me.
4. Aunt Jody gave Mike and **(a)** I/**(b)** me her industrial vacuum cleaner.
5. The vacuum cleaner is as heavy as **(a)** she/**(b)** her.

Who *and* Whom

[pages 571–573]

Indicate the correct pronoun.

6. I wonder **(a)** who/**(b)** whom our next customer will be.

Pronoun–Antecedent Agreement in Number and Gender

[pages 573–576]

Indicate the correct pronoun.

7. The head of the bakers' union has **(a)** their/**(b)** her office downstairs.

Pronoun–Antecedent Agreement in Person

[pages 576–577]

8. In which sentence does the pronoun agree in person with its antecedent?

   a. Before a union declares a strike, it must poll all of the members.

   b. Before a union declares a strike, you must poll all of the members.

Agreement with Indefinite Pronoun Antecedents

[pages 578–579]

9. In which sentence is the agreement between pronouns correct?

   a. Both of the unions asked their members to meet on Thursday.

   b. Each of the unions polled their members.

   c. Only one of the two unions held their annual elections.

Clear Pronoun Reference

[pages 579–582]

10. In which sentence is the pronoun reference clear?

   a. When the campers first met the counselors, they were friendly .

   b. The new campers complained about the food, which made the counselors laugh.

   c. The counselors organized a race, which Lola won.

Writing for Review

Write a paragraph describing your family's activities during a vacation. Use a variety of personal and indefinite pronouns.

Unit 18   Using Modifiers Correctly

18.1   The Three Degrees of Comparison

Most adjectives and adverbs have three degrees: the positive, or base, form; the comparative form; and the superlative form.

The **positive form** of a modifier cannot be used to make a comparison. (This form appears as the entry word in a dictionary.)

The **comparative** form of a modifier shows two things being compared.

The **superlative** form of a modifier shows three or more things being compared.

POSITIVE	Abby is **fast.**
	I ran **slowly.**
COMPARATIVE	Abby runs **faster** than the other runners.
	I ran **more slowly** than my friend.
SUPERLATIVE	Of the three runners, she is the **fastest.**
	I ran **most slowly** of all.

Use the following rules as a guide:

In general, for one-syllable modifiers add -*er* to form the comparative and -*est* to form the superlative.

> small, small**er,** small**est**
> The pianist's hands are **smaller** than mine.
> That is the **smallest** dog I have ever seen.

Spelling changes occur in some cases when you add -*er* and -*est*.

> white, whit**er,** whit**est**
> flat, flat**ter,** flat**test**
> merry, merr**ier,** merr**iest**

With certain one-syllable modifiers it may sound more natural to use *more* and *most* instead of -*er* and -*est*.

> brusque, **more** brusque, **most** brusque
> He is **more brusque** than she.

For most two-syllable adjectives add -*er* to form the comparative and -*est* to form the superlative.

> friendly, friendl**ier,** friendl**iest**
> That kitten is **friendlier** than this one.
> The Siamese kitten is the **friendliest** of the three.

If *-er* and *-est* sound awkward, use *more* and *most*.

> prudent, **more** prudent, **most** prudent
> No one was **more prudent** with money than Victor.

For adverbs ending in *-ly*, always use *more* and *most* to form the comparative and superlative degrees.

> sweetly, **more** sweetly, **most** sweetly
> Of all the birds the nightingale sings the **most sweetly**.

For modifiers of three or more syllables, always use *more* and *most* to form the comparative and superlative degrees.

> talented, **more** talented, **most** talented
> This actor is **more talented** than that one.

Less and *least*, the opposite of *more* and *most*, can also be used with most modifiers to show comparison.

> Earl is **less reflective** than Suki.
> Mark is the **least reflective** person I know.

Less and *least* are used before modifiers of any number of syllables.

Some adjectives, such as *unique*, *perfect*, *final*, *dead*, and *square*, cannot be compared because they describe an absolute condition. However, you can sometimes use *more nearly* and *most nearly* with these adjectives.

> Clara's rug is **more nearly square** than Paul's is.
> That painting is the **most nearly perfect** I have ever seen.

18.2 Irregular Comparisons

A few commonly used modifiers have irregular forms.

Modifiers with Irregular Forms of Comparison		
Positive	**Comparative**	**Superlative**
good	better	(the) best
well	better	(the) best
bad	worse	(the) worst
badly	worse	(the) worst
ill	worse	(the) worst
far (distance)	farther	(the) farthest
far (degree, time)	further	(the) furthest
little (amount)	less	(the) least
many	more	(the) most
much	more	(the) most

Exercise 1

Making Correct Comparisons   Complete the following sentences with the correct degree of comparison of the modifier in parentheses. (The positive degree is used in two sentences.)

SAMPLE	I think Aretha Franklin sings soul _____ than any other recording artist. (well)
ANSWER	better

Aretha Franklin, the Queen of Soul

1. Aretha Franklin is perhaps the _____ female vocalist of all time. (popular)
2. Franklin is well known for her _____ voice. (strong)
3. Because her father was a highly successful minister, Franklin was exposed to _____ gospel singers than another youngster might have been. (talented)
4. _____ than five years after the nine-year-old Franklin began singing in her father's choir, she made her first recording of gospel music in Chicago. (little)
5. After four years of recording only gospel songs, Franklin was encouraged by the singer Sam Cooke to switch to a genre that would be _____ than church music. (commercial)
6. Franklin spent six _____ years with Columbia Records. (disappointing)
7. It was with Atlantic Records that she recorded some of her _____ songs of all, including "Respect" and "Natural Woman." (good)
8. Franklin then rose to fame _____ than anyone could have imagined. (quickly)
9. Franklin, best known for her soul music, has achieved _____ number-one soul hits than anyone else except James Brown. (many)
10. Even so, some people still think she sings the _____ of all when performing gospel songs. (sweetly).

Exercise 2

Making Correct Comparisons   Complete the following sentences with the correct degree of comparison of the modifier in parentheses. (The positive degree is used in two sentences.) ➡

SAMPLE   Lewis believes that James Joyce is _____ to read than any other writer. (difficult)

ANSWER   more difficult

James Joyce, Imaginative Author

1. Many knowledgeable people consider James Joyce the _____ writer of English fiction in the twentieth century. (imaginative)
2. James Joyce utilized _____ new techniques in writing the novel than virtually any other writer of his generation. (many)
3. His short stories are generally _____ than his novels. (accessible)
4. One of his great short stories, "The Dead," explores some of the conflicts in Irish society that arise because the older generation is _____ than the younger generation. (traditional)
5. In this story Joyce _____ presents a number of character types based on real people he knew while living in Dublin. (skillfully)
6. The novel *Ulysses* is considerably _____ in style and narrative technique than Joyce's short stories. (complex)
7. The main character of *Ulysses*, Leopold Bloom, feels that he is one of the _____ men in Dublin. (isolated)
8. Although *Ulysses* is epic in scope, Bloom wanders no _____ than the city limits of the capital. (far)
9. Bloom _____ meets the young Stephen Dedalus, who becomes a surrogate son to him. (finally)
10. Joyce used Homer's epic the *Odyssey* as a prototype for his novel, although the total effect is far different from that of the _____ work. (early)

Exercise 3: Sentence Writing

Creating Sentences That Make Comparisons   Select five of the irregular modifiers from the list on page 592. Write a sentence for each, using the positive and comparative degrees of the modifier. Underline each modifier.

SAMPLE   well

ANSWER   Susan speaks Spanish <u>well</u>, but Marie speaks it <u>better</u>.

18.3   Double Comparisons

Do not make a double comparison by using both *-er* or *-est* and more or most.

INCORRECT	Chimpanzees are ~~more~~ smaller than gorillas.
CORRECT	Chimpanzees are smaller than gorillas.
INCORRECT	That is the ~~most~~ saddest song on the album.
CORRECT	That is the saddest song on the album.

Exercise 4

Correcting Double Comparisons   Rewrite each of the following sentences, correcting the double comparisons.

Gandhi, a Great Leader

1. Many historians judge Mohandas Karamchand Gandhi the single most greatest leader India has ever produced.
2. Because Gandhi's native town could provide only a limited education, it was fortunate that his family moved to Rājkot, where the educational facilities were more better.
3. During Gandhi's teen-age years the discipline demanded by outside authorities was less stricter than the self-discipline imposed by the young man himself.
4. While studying in England, Gandhi found that adapting to Western culture was more harder than his studies.
5. After accepting a job in South Africa, Gandhi found the treatment of Indians there more harsher than anything he had previously encountered.
6. To fight injustice, Gandhi used the principles of civil disobedience and nonviolence, which are more humbler than conventional weapons.
7. In South Africa Gandhi turned his attention to the fact that the most mightiest nation of that era, Great Britain, maintained India as a colony of second-class citizens.
8. Gandhi wanted to dismantle India's caste system and to help the most weakest class of Indians, the untouchables.
9. After being imprisoned by the British government, the great spiritual leader found that one of the most clearest ways to communicate his protest was to cease eating.
10. Although Gandhi did live to see India achieve its independence in 1947, one of the least happiest days of Gandhi's life was the day India was divided into the dominions of India and Pakistan.

18.4 Incomplete Comparisons

Do not make an incomplete or unclear comparison by omitting *other* or *else* when you compare one member of a group with another.

UNCLEAR	New York has more skyscrapers than any city in America.
CLEAR	New York has more skyscrapers than any **other** city in America.
UNCLEAR	Juanita received more prizes than anyone.
CLEAR	Juanita received more prizes than anyone **else**.

Be sure your comparisons are between like things.

UNCLEAR	The salary of a teacher is lower than a lawyer. [The salary of a teacher is being compared illogically with a person, namely, a lawyer.]
CLEAR	The salary of a teacher is lower than **that of a lawyer.**
CLEAR	The salary of a teacher is lower than **a lawyer's.** [The word *salary* is understood after *lawyer's*.]
UNCLEAR	The arms of an orangutan are longer than a chimpanzee. [The arms of an orangutan are being compared illogically with a chimpanzee in its entirety.]
CLEAR	The arms of an orangutan are longer than **those of a chimpanzee.**
CLEAR	The arms of an orangutan are longer than **a chimpanzee's.**

Exercise 5

Making Complete Comparisons   Rewrite each of the following sentences to correct the incomplete comparison in each.

An African Safari

1. On safari in Africa, Henry saw more cheetahs than anyone.
2. Cheetahs are often difficult to spot, since they are more nocturnal than many animals.
3. The cheetah can run faster than any mammal.
4. Its speed of over seventy miles per hour on short runs is greater than the lion or the jaguar.
5. The tails of cheetahs are more distinctive than any large cat. ➡

6. Cheetahs were only one of the many splendors of our African journey, which was more exciting than any trip I've ever taken.
7. Among other facts, we learned that the area of Sudan is greater than Texas and Alaska combined.
8. The area of the African island of Mahé in the Seychelles, however, is less than New Orleans.
9. All across North Africa lies the awesome Sahara, which is vaster than any desert.
10. Africa is also the home of the mighty Nile, which at four thousand miles is longer than any river in the world.

18.5 Good or Well; Bad or Badly

Always use *good* as an adjective. *Well* may be used as an adverb of manner telling how ably something is done or as an adjective meaning "in good health."

Hiroshi is a **good** violinist. [adjective]

Hiroshi looks **good** in that sweater. [adjective after a linking verb]

Hiroshi plays the violin **well.** [adverb of manner]

Hiroshi is not **well** this week because he has a cold. [adjective meaning "in good health"]

Always use *bad* as an adjective. Therefore, *bad* is used after a linking verb. Use *badly* as an adverb. *Badly* almost always follows an action verb.

The player made a **bad** throw. [adjective]
The skunk smelled **bad.** [adjective following a linking verb]
I felt **bad** about my mistake. [adjective following a linking verb]
Her nose is bleeding **badly.** [adverb following an action verb]

Exercise 6

Choosing the Correct Modifier   On your paper complete the following sentences correctly by filling the blank with *good, well, bad,* or *badly.*

Studying for an Examination
1. A person who studies _____ can be confident of earning good grades on examinations in college.
2. Doing poorly on an examination can make anyone feel _____. ⇒

3. _____ organization is essential to studying effectively.
4. A _____ organized study schedule can cause you to lose a great deal of precious time.
5. A _____ schedule allows enough time for the ideas and the subjects that you find difficult to grasp.
6. Even a student who is doing _____ should give some thought to structuring study time.
7. If you start out _____ in one of your courses, it is especially important to budget additional time for studying that subject.
8. Most people feel _____ when they go into an exam knowing that they have devoted sufficient time to studying.
9. If you do not feel _____ on the day of an examination, your grade might be affected.
10. Some students perform _____ on examinations if they are unduly nervous during the test.

18.6   Double Negatives

In general, do not use a **double negative**, two negative words in the same clause. Use only one negative word to express a negative idea.

INCORRECT	I didn't hear ~~no~~ noise.
CORRECT	I did**n't** hear **any** noise.
INCORRECT	She hasn't had ~~no~~ visitors.
CORRECT	She has**n't** had **any** visitors.
CORRECT	She has had **no** visitors.
INCORRECT	He never reads ~~no~~ magazines.
CORRECT	He **never** reads **any** magazines.
CORRECT	He reads **no** magazines.

Exercise 7

Avoiding Double Negatives   On your paper rewrite the following sentences, eliminating the double negative in each. (Most sentences can be corrected in more than one way.)

The Great Lakes

1. My younger brother hasn't visited none of the Great Lakes.
2. I told him that unlike the other four lakes, Lake Michigan doesn't share no boundary with Canada.
3. Except for the Caspian Sea in Asia, there isn't no lake in ➞

the world larger than Lake Superior.

4. I have never seen no lake as impressive as Lake Superior.
5. My brother could not name none of the four states—Michigan, Wisconsin, Illinois, and Indiana—that border Lake Michigan.
6. There isn't no way to describe how much I loved my camping trip to Lake Huron.
7. Although Lake Ontario is the smallest of the Great Lakes, it isn't no insignificant body of water.
8. Pollution problems in Lake Erie and Lake Michigan are not nowhere as bad as they were two decades ago.
9. If not for the Great Lakes, over two hundred towns and cities in several states would be without no decent water supply.
10. These days my brother and I cannot think of nothing except planning an autumn trip to Lake Superior.

18.7   Misplaced and Dangling Modifiers

Place modifiers as close as possible to the words they modify in order to make the meaning of the sentence clear.

Misplaced modifiers modify the wrong word, or seem to modify more than one word, in a sentence. You can correct a sentence with a misplaced modifier by moving the modifier as close as possible to the word that it modifies.

MISPLACED	**Running at great speed,** the spectators watched the racers. [participial phrase incorrectly modifying *spectators*]
CLEAR	The spectators watched the racers **running at great speed**. [participial phrase correctly modifying *racers*]
MISPLACED	The beaches of Martinique are favored by many tourists **with their beautiful, calm surf.** [prepositional phrase incorrectly modifying *tourists*]
CLEAR	The beaches of Martinique, **with their beautiful, calm surf,** are favored by many tourists. [prepositional phrase correctly modifying *beaches*]

Sometimes a misplaced modifier can be corrected by creating a subordinate clause or by rephrasing the main clause.

MISPLACED	**Blowing from the north,** the pines were tossed by the wind. [participial phrase incorrectly modifying *pines*]
CLEAR	The pines were tossed by the wind, **which blew from the north.** [participial phrase recast as a subordinate clause correctly modifying *wind*]
CLEAR	**Blowing from the north,** the wind tossed the pines. [participial phrase correctly modifying *wind*]

Taken logically, a **dangling modifier** seems to modify no word in the sentence in which it appears. You can correct a sentence with a dangling modifier by supplying a word or phrase the dangling phrase can sensibly modify.

DANGLING	**Using high-powered binoculars,** the lost girl was found. [participial phrase logically modifying no word in the sentence]
CLEAR	**Using high-powered binoculars,** the rescuers found the lost girl. [participial phrase modifying *rescuers*]
CLEAR	The rescuers found the lost girl **because they used high-powered binoculars.** [subordinate clause modifying *found*]
DANGLING	**After searching for hours,** the girl was happily found safe and sound. [prepositional phrase logically modifying no word in the sentence]
CLEAR	**After searching for hours,** the rescuers were happy to find the girl safe and sound. [prepositional phrase modifying *rescuers*]
DANGLING	**Feeling elated,** a celebration with my friends lasted well into the night. [participial phrase logically modifying no word in the sentence]
CLEAR	**Feeling elated,** I celebrated with my friends well into the night. [participial phrase modifying *I*]

Place the adverb *only* immediately before the word or group of words it modifies.

If *only* is positioned incorrectly, the meaning of the sentence may be unclear.

UNCLEAR   Kia **only** has band practice on Tuesday. [Does she have nothing else to do on Tuesday, or is there no band practice on any day but Tuesday? Or is Kia the only person (in a group) who has band practice on Tuesday?]

CLEAR   Kia has **only** band practice on Tuesday. [She does not have any other class or extracurricular activity.]

CLEAR   Kia has band practice **only** on Tuesday. [She does not have band practice on any other day of the week.]

CLEAR   **Only** Kia has band practice on Tuesday. [No one else has band practice on Tuesday.]

Exercise 8

Correcting Misplaced and Dangling Modifiers   On your paper rewrite the following sentences, correcting the misplaced or dangling modifier in each.

Blue Jeans

[1]Created in California during the gold rush, people all over the world now wear blue jeans. [2]Guaranteed not to rip, gold prospectors liked their durability. [3]With a design perfect for rough conditions, only prospectors and laborers wore these denim pants at first. [4]Only jeans gained popularity in the West after cowboys wore them for work and dress. [5]No longer associated with bucking broncos, men and women alike now consider jeans to be high fashion.

Exercise 9

Correcting Misplaced and Dangling Modifiers   On your paper rewrite the following sentences, correcting the misplaced or dangling modifiers in each.

The Aztec Empire

[1]Presenting a lecture on ancient Aztec civilization, we strolled through the museum exhibit and listened to the ➡

curator. [2]After traveling from the Valley of Mexico into central Mexico, the city of Tenochtitlán was founded in 1325. [3]Eventually leading the Aztec Empire in terms of population, we studied an elaborate chart that showed the capital city, Tenochtitlán. [4]Reclaiming swamps and irrigating arid land, agricultural techniques were vital to the Aztecs' survival. [5]Resulting in high productivity, these methods only allowed the area to become rich and populous. [6]Illustrating Aztec domination over millions of people and eighty thousand square miles of the North American continent, our class watched a fascinating film. [7]In a section of central Mexico, another student and I learned that the Aztec language, Nahuatl, is still spoken. [8]In Aztec society I was surprised to learn that there was an elaborate caste system. [9]Ranging from religious and government leaders at the top to serfs at the bottom, the only means of advancement in the caste system was a military career. [10]The arrival of Hernán Cortés and other Spanish explorers only stopped the Aztec Empire from thriving and expanding into the sixteenth century.

Exercise 10: Review

Modifiers   The following contains ten errors in the use of modifiers. Rewrite the paragraph, correcting the errors.

Nikki Giovanni, Poet

[1]Were she to look back over her career, Nikki Giovanni would not have nothing to feel badly about. [2]After spending a happy childhood in Knoxville and Cincinnati, her first books were published when she was in her twenties. [3]It was one of Giovanni's most earliest volumes of poetry, *My House*, that brought her critical acclaim. [4]Many people think Giovanni only writes for adults, but this belief is not the case. [5]Writing books for young adults, readers of all ages can appreciate her poetry. [6]Some of Giovanni's vividest poems convey pride in the poet's racial heritage. [7]More than any book, *The Women and the Men* shows Giovanni exploring questions of personal identity. [8]The most good poems in this book deal with the family. [9]The fact that many Americans know how good Giovanni writes is illustrated by her having been given keys to several cities.

The correct placement of modifiers is essential if a writer wishes to ensure clarity. Dangling and misplaced modifiers confuse the reader and weaken a writer's prose. Notice, for example, the position of the italicized modifiers in the following passage from Julio Cortázar's "Text in a Notebook," translated by Gregory Rabassa:

> *Having reached this conclusion*, I found the rest obvious. *Except at dawn and very late at night*, the Anglo trains are never empty because Buenos Aires people are night owls and there are always a few passengers coming and going before the station gates are closed.

Now think how this passage would read with a dangling participle in the first sentence and a misplaced prepositional phrase in the second sentence.

> *Having reached this conclusion*, the rest was obvious. The Anglo trains are never empty because Buenos Aires people, *except at dawn and very late at night*, are night owls and there are always a few passengers coming and going before the station gates are closed.

Keep these guidelines in mind as you write and revise your own work:

1. Avoid dangling modifiers by making certain to include the word or phrase being modified. In the second example above, "Having reached this conclusion" is a dangling participial phrase. Cortázar's version avoids the problem by including "I," the pronoun that the phrase modifies.

2. Decide whether moving a modifier or other words will make the meaning of your sentence clearer. Often the closer a modifier is to the word it modifies, the clearer the meaning of the sentence will be. Compare the second sentence in each of the two previous examples. Notice how much clearer Cortázar's version is, because he puts the phrase "except at dawn and very late at night" closer to the verb it modifies, "are" in the complete predicate "are never empty."

Apply these guidelines as you revise the following passage on a separate sheet of paper:

> Born during the Depression, poverty haunted Arthur Mitchell's early life. He nevertheless dreamed of becoming a dancer, and he won a scholarship as a teen-ager to study at New York City's High School of Performing Arts. Then, after he graduated from high school, the noted choreographer George Balanchine invited Mitchell to study with the New York City Ballet. Invited to join the ballet troupe in 1955, many of the company productions became Mitchell's star vehicles. He left the New York City Ballet to found the Dance Theater of Harlem and help fulfill the dreams of other aspiring dancers at the height of his career.

Usage Workshop

Using Modifiers Correctly

A Moveable Feast is Ernest Hemingway's memoir of his years in Paris in the 1920s. A poor, struggling writer then, he often had to forgo meals. The following passage has been annotated to show some of the kinds of modifiers covered in this unit.

Literature Model

from A MOVEABLE FEAST
by Ernest Hemingway

Positive form of the adjective *good* —

Superlative form of the adjective *good* —

Comparative forms of the adjectives *clear* and *beautiful* —

Comparative form of the adverb *well* —

Correct placement of the modifier *only* —

You got very hungry when you did not eat enough in Paris because all the bakery shops had such good things in the windows and people ate outside at tables on the sidewalk so that you saw and smelled the food. When you had given up journalism and were writing nothing that anyone in America would buy, explaining at home that you were lunching out with someone, the best place to go was the Luxembourg gardens where you saw and smelled nothing to eat all the way from the Place de l'Observatoire to the rue de Vaugirard. There you could always go into the Luxembourg museum and all the paintings were sharpened and clearer and more beautiful if you were belly-empty, hollow-hungry. I learned to understand Cézanne much better and to see truly how he made landscapes when I was hungry. I used to wonder if he were hungry too when he painted; but I thought possibly it was only that he had forgotten to eat. It was one of those unsound but illuminating thoughts you have when you have been sleepless or hungry. Later I thought Cézanne was probably hungry in a different way.

After you came out of the Luxembourg you could walk down the narrow rue Férou to the Place St.-Sulpice and there were still no restaurants, only the quiet square with its benches and trees. There was a fountain with lions, and pigeons walked on the pavement and perched on the statues of the bishops. There was the church and there ➡

were shops selling religious objects and vestments on the north side of the square.

Correctly placed participial phrase modifying *shops*

From this square you could not go further toward the river without passing shops selling fruits, vegetables, wines, or bakery and pastry shops. But by choosing your way carefully you could work to your right around the gray and white stone church and reach the rue de l'Odéon and turn up to your right toward Sylvia Beach's bookshop and on your way you did not pass too many places where things to eat were sold. The rue de l'Odéon was bare of eating places until you reached the square where there were three restaurants.

By the time you reached 12 rue de l'Odéon your hunger was contained but all of your perceptions were heightened again. The photographs looked different and you saw books that you had never seen before.

"You're too thin, Hemingway," Sylvia would say. "Are you eating enough?"

"Sure."

Usage Workshop Exercise 1

Making Correct Comparisons The following sentences are about some of Ernest Hemingway's friends in Paris in the 1920s. Rewrite each sentence on your paper, substituting the proper comparative or superlative form of the modifier in parentheses for the word or phrase in italics.

SAMPLE   In the 1920s Paris was perhaps the *most beautiful* city in Europe. (lively)

ANSWER   In the 1920s Paris was perhaps the liveliest city in Europe.

1. Of all Hemingway's contemporaries the poet Ezra Pound went *most clearly* in the direction of establishing a new literary style. (far)
2. Few of Hemingway's writer friends in Paris were *more widely* known than F. Scott Fitzgerald. (well)
3. After *The Great Gatsby* was published in 1925, Fitzgerald was often acclaimed as the *finest* American writer. (good)
4. Scott and Zelda Fitzgerald lived a *more glamorous* life than that of many other literary couples. (flamboyant)
5. One of Hemingway's *best* advisers was the innovative writer Gertrude Stein. (helpful)

Usage Workshop Exercise 2

Correcting Incomplete Comparisons   The following sentences are about Paris. Rewrite the sentences, correcting any errors of incomplete comparison. Some of the sentences can be revised in more than one way.

1. To struggling young American artists and writers, Paris in the 1920s was more attractive than any city.
2. Many American artists in the 1920s believed that Paris's cultural life was more diverse and inspiring than New York.
3. The beauty and the variety of the architecture in Paris are not rivaled anywhere.
4. Paris has historical riches that surpass any American city.
5. Few cities can claim a heritage of beauty and culture that matches Paris.

Usage Workshop Exercise 3

Choosing the Correct Modifier   The following sentences are about Sylvia Beach and the bookstore she owned in Paris. For each sentence choose the correct form of the modifier in parentheses, and write it on your paper. Then indicate whether the modifier you have chosen is being used as an *adjective* or an *adverb*.

1. Sylvia Beach, who owned a bookstore in Paris, always treated her customers (good/well).
2. Writers such as Hemingway felt (good/well) about visiting the store, which was called Shakespeare and Company.
3. The store provided a cheerful, warm haven when the weather in Paris turned (bad/badly).
4. Sylvia Beach, confident that Hemingway could write (good/well), lent him many books to encourage his talent.
5. Beach knew how (bad/badly) Hemingway wanted to succeed.

Usage Workshop Exercise 4

Correcting Misplaced Modifiers   The following sentences elaborate on the passage from *A Moveable Feast*. Rewrite the sentences, correcting each misplaced modifier by shifting it or the term it modifies to a position that makes the meaning clearer. If a sentence contains no errors, write *correct*. ➠

SAMPLE	Floating delectably in the air, the streets of Paris were filled with aromas.
ANSWER	The streets of Paris were filled with aromas floating delectably in the air.

1. In the 1920s Hemingway nevertheless enjoyed life having little money in a big city.
2. By choosing his route carefully, Hemingway would only pass a few food shops and cafés.
3. Featuring many of Cézanne's paintings, Hemingway was diverted by the museum at the Luxembourg Gardens.
4. Feeling his perceptions sharpened by hunger, Hemingway thought that he truly understood Cézanne's work.
5. He found a stretch with few cafés along the rue de l'Odéon walking to Sylvia Beach's bookstore.

Usage Workshop Exercise 5

Correcting Dangling Modifiers   The following paragraph is about Gertrude Stein. Read the paragraph. Then rewrite the sentences that follow, correcting each dangling modifier by adding information based on the paragraph. Reword the sentences if necessary. If a sentence contains no errors, write *correct*.

The American writer Gertrude Stein moved to Paris in 1903 after having studied psychology and medicine. A patron of the arts for more than forty years, she warmly supported the avant-garde and often entertained painters and writers. Hemingway visited her salon to discuss books and art. Stein's advocacy of new styles helped to launch the careers of painters such as Matisse and Picasso. She tried to imitate their visual techniques in experimental stories and poems.

SAMPLE	After studying psychology and medicine, literature seemed an unlikely career for Stein.
ANSWER	After studying psychology and medicine, Stein seemed unlikely to pursue a career in literature.

1. Caught up in the creative atmosphere of Paris, patronage of the arts soon occupied Gertrude Stein.
2. Mingling often with other writers and artists, their work received her interest and support.
3. Grateful for her hospitality, Hemingway's attendance at Stein's salon was frequent.
4. Championing new styles, the careers of Matisse and Picasso were launched with Stein's help. ➡

5. Always experimenting with both her prose and her life, Stein was an inspiration to a generation of writers.

Review   Read the following biography of Ernest Hemingway. Then rewrite the sentences below it, correcting any errors in the use of modifiers. If you need additional information for your sentences, consult the biography.

Ernest Hemingway

One of the greatest modern novelists, Ernest Hemingway was born in Oak Park, Illinois, in 1899. After he graduated from high school, he volunteered as an ambulance driver in World War I and was wounded in Italy. In 1920 he went to Paris as a correspondent for the *Toronto Star. A Moveable Feast* recalls his struggle to become a serious writer. His experiences as a journalist during the Spanish civil war inspired *For Whom the Bell Tolls* (1940), which many consider his masterpiece. After World War II Hemingway settled in Cuba. He won the Pulitzer Prize in 1952 for his short novel, *The Old Man and the Sea*, and was awarded the Nobel Prize in 1954. He died in 1961.

1. Of all twentieth-century American novelists, Hemingway may have garnered the greater fame.
2. After graduating from high school, journalism was his first choice as a career.
3. Rejected by the United States Army because of an eye injury, the Red Cross gave Hemingway a job as an ambulance driver in Italy during World War I.
4. He was wounded bad and was decorated by the Italian government.
5. After returning to Michigan to recuperate, a job offer took him to Europe as a foreign correspondent.
6. In Paris Hemingway only decided to write fiction.
7. He soon began to turn out novels and short stories that received more acclaim than his contemporaries.
8. Curiouser than many reporters, Hemingway traveled to Spain in 1937 to cover the civil war there.
9. His novel *For Whom the Bell Tolls* captures better than any work of fiction the tragedy of the Spanish civil war.
10. Several Hollywood movies have been made from Hemingway's novels featuring major stars.

Proofreading The following passage describes the artist Kees van Dongen, whose painting appears below. Rewrite the passage, correcting the errors in spelling, capitalization, punctuation, grammar, and usage. There are ten errors in all.

Kees van Dongen

[1]Born in Rotterdam, Kees van Dongen (1877–1968) studied art in his native Holland, but in 1900 decided to make Paris his permanant home. [2]In France he soon became associated with a group of artists known as the Fauves who were famous—or, in the eyes of conservative critics, infamous for its vibrant colors and fluid brushwork.

[3]While many of the Fauves moved on to other styles Kees van Dongen remained true to his original techniques. [4]He is best known for his witty portraits of actors, writers, and politicians. [5]Regarded at the time as the capitol of modern culture, he also painted many scenes of Paris.

[6]*Avenue du Bois, Paris* is typical of his mature work. [7]The paintings' simplified forms and washes of color clearly show the artist's debt to Fauvism. [8]One can imagine Ernest Hemingway, who was living in Paris at the time, wandering among the crowds depicted in the painting with a notebook.

Kees van Dongen, *Avenue du Bois, Paris,* c. 1925

Unit 18 Review

Using Modifiers Correctly

The Three Degrees of Comparison

[pages 591–592]

Choose the correct modifier.

1. Of the nine planets, Venus is often the **(a)** more visible/**(b)** most visible.
2. Of the two outermost planets Neptune is the **(a)** larger/**(b)** largest.
3. Pluto is the planet **(a)** farrest/**(b)** farthest from the sun.

Double and Incomplete Comparisons

[pages 595–597]

Indicate the correct comparison.

4. The shuttle landed **(a)** sooner/**(b)** more sooner than planned.
5. Astronauts travel farther than **(a)** anyone/**(b)** anyone else.
6. I like astronomy better than **(a)** any/**(b)** any other science.
7. The difference between astronomy and astrology is **(a)** greater/**(b)** more greater than one might think.
8. The gravity of Jupiter is greater than **(a)** Saturn's/**(b)** Saturn.

Using Good or Well, Bad or Badly

[pages 597–598]

Indicate the modifier that is used correctly.

9. It is amazing that astronauts racing through space feel **(a)** good/**(b)** well.
10. I felt **(a)** bad/**(b)** badly about napping.

11. We could see **(a)** good/**(b)** well enough to distinguish craters.
12. Did you do **(a)** bad/**(b)** badly on the quiz?
13. Sally Ride spoke **(a)** good/**(b)** well.

Double Negatives

[pages 598–599]

Indicate the correct usage.

14. I have **(a)** read/**(b)** not read nothing about a space launch.
15. I don't have **(a)** any/**(b)** no doubt that one will occur.
16. No one has been on **(a)** any/**(b)** none of the other planets.

Using Modifiers

[pages 591–603]

Choose the correct sentence.

17. **a.** Visiting Florida, Cape Canaveral is fascinating.
    b. Visiting Florida, tourists find Cape Canaveral fascinating.
18. **a.** Cape Canaveral attracts a huge crowd with its impressive space center.
    b. Cape Canaveral, with its impressive space center, attracts a huge crowd.
19. **a.** Only Munson had witnessed the crime, not committed it.
    b. Munson had only witnessed the crime, not committed it.
20. **a.** Seeing her leap, joy filled the room.
    b. Seeing her leap, I felt joy fill the room.

Writing for Review

Write a paragraph in which you compare one thing with another. Use modifiers.

Unit 19 Usage Glossary

The following glossary describes some particularly troublesome matters of preferred usage. It will help you choose between two words that are often confused. It will also point out certain words and expressions that you should avoid completely in formal speaking and writing.

a, an   Use the article *a* when the word that follows begins with a consonant sound, including a sounded *h: a rocket, a helicopter.* Use *an* when the word that follows begins with a vowel sound or an unsounded *h: an endowment, an heir.* Use *a* before a word that begins with the "yew" sound: *a eucalyptus, a union.*

a lot, alot   You should always write this expression as two words. It means "a large amount." Some authorities suggest avoiding it altogether in formal English.

> **A lot** of people attended the final game of the season.

a while, awhile   *A while* is made up of an article and a noun. *In* or *for* often precedes *a while*, forming a prepositional phrase. *Awhile*, a single word, is used only as an adverb.

> The musicians paused for **a while.**
> The musicians will pause in **a while.**
> The musicians paused **awhile.**

accept, except   *Accept*, a verb, means "to receive" or "to agree to." *Except* may be a preposition or a verb. As a preposition it means "but." As a verb it means "to leave out."

> Please **accept** my apologies.
>
> Everyone **except** Paul can attend the meeting. [preposition]
>
> If you **except** the planet Earth, you can consider the Solar System uninhabited.

adapt, adopt   *Adapt* means "to change something so that it can be used for another purpose" or "to adjust." *Adopt* means "to take something for one's own."

> It was difficult to **adapt** the play for a young audience.
>
> Dinosaurs became extinct because they could not **adapt** to the changing environment.
>
> The general must **adopt** a new strategy to win this battle.

advice, advise   *Advice,* a noun, means "helpful opinion." *Advise,* a verb, means "to give advice or offer counsel."

> Cheryl asked her guidance counselor for **advice** in choosing a college and hoped he would **advise** her well.

affect, effect   *Affect,* a verb, means "to cause a change in, to influence." *Effect* may be a noun or a verb. As a noun it means "result." As a verb it means "to bring about or accomplish."

> This information will certainly **affect** our decision.

> What **effect** will this information have on your decision? [noun meaning "result"]

> What could **effect** such a change in her outlook? [verb meaning "bring about"]

ain't   *Ain't* is unacceptable in formal speaking and writing. Use *ain't* only when quoting somebody's exact words. Otherwise use *I am not; she is not; he is not;* and so on.

all ready, already   *All ready* means "completely ready." *Already,* an adverb, means "before or by this time."

> The boys were **all ready** to take the test, but by the time they arrived, the test had **already** begun.

all right, alright   Always write this expression as two words. Although it is sometimes spelled as one word, *alright,* most authorities prefer that it be spelled *all right.*

> Is it **all right** for the baby to have ice cream?

Exercise 1

Making Usage Choices   For each of the following sentences, choose the correct word or expression from the pair in parentheses.

Ragtime Music

1. Ragtime played (a/an) important role in the development of American music.
2. First popular in the early 1900s, it enjoyed a revival for (a while/awhile) in the 1970s.
3. Americans quickly (adapted/adopted) ragtime as one of their favorite kinds of popular music.
4. Ragtime also (affected/effected) the music of classical composers such as Charles Ives, Igor Stravinsky, and Claude Debussy.
5. The music of the ragtime composer Scott Joplin was ➡

not merely (all right/alright) but quite enjoyable and sometimes even extraordinary.

6. Joplin's "Maple Leaf Rag," (all ready/already) well-known by 1900, helped popularize ragtime throughout the United States.

7. The public quickly (accepted/excepted) a later piece by Joplin, "The Entertainer," which became a famous number and is still heard today.

8. (A lot/Alot) of ragtime pieces were reproduced on piano rolls for player pianos.

9. In his published piano music Joplin offered excellent (advice/advise) on how to play ragtime.

10. Although ragtime compositions (ain't/aren't) easy to play, they remain highly popular with pianists today.

all together, altogether The two words *all together* mean "in a group." The single word *altogether* is an adverb meaning "completely" or "on the whole."

> They decided to leave **all together,** but it was **altogether** impossible for them to fit in one car.

allusion, illusion *Allusion* means "an indirect reference." *Illusion* refers to "a false idea or appearance."

> The candidate made a disparaging **allusion** to his rival's plan for lowering taxes.

> It is an **illusion** that taxes can be lowered this year.

anywheres, everywheres Write these words and others like them without a final *-s: anywhere, everywhere, somewhere.*

bad, badly See Unit 18.

being as, being that Many people use these expressions informally to mean "because" or "since." In formal writing and speech use *because* or *since.*

> **Since** the weather is bad, they have decided to stay at home.
> **Because** the weather is bad, we have decided not to go.

beside, besides *Beside* means "at the side of" or "next to." *Besides* means "moreover" or "in addition to."

> Who is that little girl sitting **beside** Joanne?
> **Besides** Carlos I am inviting James, Lloyd, and Luz.
> Lian is too busy to attend the play; **besides,** she is feeling ill.

between, among　*Between* and *among* are prepositions that are used to state a relationship. Use *between* to refer to two persons or things or to compare one person or thing with another person or thing or with an entire group. Use *between* to refer to more than two persons or things when they are considered equals in a close relationship or are being viewed individually in relation to one another.

> Lucinda sat down **between** Tamara and Geraldo. [*Between* establishes a relationship involving two persons—Tamara and Geraldo.]

> What is the difference **between** this novel and the author's previous books? [*Between* is used to compare one book with an entire group—all of the author's previous books.]

> ANZUS is a treaty **between** Australia, New Zealand, and the United States. [*Between* establishes a relationship in which each country individually has made an agreement with every other country.]

Use *among* to show a relationship in which more than two persons or things are considered as a group.

> The four women talked **among** themselves.
> This soprano is **among** the finest singers in the world.

borrow, lend, loan　*Borrow* and *lend* have opposite meanings. *Borrow* is a verb meaning "to take something with the understanding that it must be returned." *Lend* is a verb meaning "to give something with the understanding that it will be returned." *Loan* is a noun. It may also be used as a verb, but most authorities prefer that *lend* be used instead.

> May I **borrow** your car? [verb]

> Will you **lend** me your car if I return it with a full tank of gas? [verb]

> Florence will ask the bank for an automobile **loan** so she can buy a new car. [noun]

bring, take　Use *bring* to mean "to carry from a distant place to a closer one." Use *take* to mean "to carry from a nearby place to a more distant one."

> Will you **bring** me a pineapple when you come back from Maui?
> Don't forget to **take** your camera when you go to Hawaii.

can, may　Use *can* to indicate the ability to do something. *May* indicates permission to do something or the possibility of doing it.

> Carrie **can** speak several different languages.
> You **may** keep my typewriter till Monday.

Making Usage Choices For each of the following sentences, choose the correct word or expression from the pair in parentheses.

Patchwork Quilts

1. It is certainly an (allusion/illusion) to imagine that patchwork quilts are old-fashioned.
2. Today Americans (everywhere/everywheres) have rediscovered these beautiful and practical coverlets.
3. Patchwork quilts were made by early Americans who needed warm covers (bad/badly).
4. (Being that/Since) these quilts had such beautiful designs, they looked quite extraordinary as bed covers.
5. Some people (can/may) identify the many quaint names of patchwork patterns, such as log cabin, sunburst, nine patch, and Grandma's flower garden.
6. (Beside/Besides) being decorative, some quilt patterns contain symbols that allude to important life-cycle events, such as birth and marriage.
7. (All together/Altogether) there are hundreds of different patchwork patterns.
8. (Among/Between) the two popular patchwork patterns associated with frontier life—the log cabin and the wedding ring—which do you prefer?
9. For my last quilting bee, or quilting party, I needed to (borrow/lend) a tracing wheel and chalk.
10. One guest was asked to (bring/take) to the quilting bee two smooth poles to serve as a frame.

can't hardly, can't scarcely These terms are considered double negatives because *hardly* and *scarcely* by themselves have a negative meaning. Therefore, do not use *hardly* and *scarcely* with *not* or *-n't.*

> That story is so outlandish that I **can hardly** believe it actually happened.

> It is so dark I **can scarcely** see the path.

continual, continuous *Continual* describes action that occurs over and over but with pauses between occurrences. *Continuous* describes an action that continues with no interruption in space or time.

> The **continual** banging of the door and the **continuous** blare from the TV made it difficult to concentrate.

could of, might of, must of, should of, would of   Do not use *of* after *could, might, must, should,* or *would*. Instead, use another verb form, the helping verb *have*.

> I **would have** gone to the meeting if I had known it would be so important and interesting.

different from, different than   In general, the expression *different from* is preferred to *different than*.

> A canoe is **different from** a rowboat.

doesn't, don't   *Doesn't* is the contraction of *does not* and should be used with *he, she, it,* and all singular nouns. *Don't* is the contraction of *do not* and should be used with *I, you, we, they,* and all plural nouns.

> Margie **doesn't** like sweet apples.
> I **don't** like them either.

emigrate, immigrate   Use *emigrate* to mean "to move from one country to another." Use *immigrate* to mean "to enter a country to settle there." Use *from* with *emigrate* and *to* or *into* with *immigrate*.

> Many people **emigrated** from Europe before the turn of the century.

> Thousands of Irish people **immigrated** to the United States during the potato famine of the 1840s.

farther, further   *Farther* should be used to refer to physical distance. *Further* should be used to refer to time or degree.

> My house is five blocks **farther** from the high school than your house is.

> I cannot give you **further** information about the course because the details have not been decided.

fewer, less   Use *fewer* to refer to nouns that can be counted. Use *less* to refer to nouns that cannot be counted. Also use *less* to refer to figures used as a single amount or quantity.

> The store sells **fewer** ice-cream cones during the winter than during the summer.

> People usually eat **less** ice cream during the winter than during the summer.

> The flight from New York to Amsterdam took **less** than seven hours. [*Seven hours* is treated as a single period of time, not as individual hours.]

good, well   See Unit 18.

Making Usage Choices For each of the following sentences, choose the correct word or expression from the pair in parentheses.

United States Immigrants

1. Many people have (emigrated/immigrated) to the United States over the course of the country's two-hundred-year history.

2. Although the flow of immigrants to the United States did slow down at various times, it has been (continuous/continual).

3. During the period between 1890 and 1924 alone, no (fewer/less) than twenty million new immigrants arrived in the United States, hoping to make better lives for themselves and their families.

4. These people (could of/could have) chosen other countries in which to settle, but they recognized the many opportunities open to them in the United States and so decided to come here.

5. Some people (can hardly/can't hardly) believe the contributions in many different fields that immigrants have made to this country.

6. The director Billy Wilder, for example, (emigrated/immigrated) from Austria to the United States, where he found fame directing comedies such as *Some Like It Hot*.

7. My sister (doesn't/don't) realize that the actresses Ingrid Bergman and Marlene Dietrich were not born in the United States.

8. George Balanchine came to the United States from Russia and developed a ballet style very (different from/different than) that of classical ballet.

9. Any physicist knows how (good/well) Chen Ning Yang and Tsung Dao Lee, two Chinese immigrants, did in their field; they won the Nobel Prize for physics in 1957.

10. (Farther/further) evidence that immigrants have contributed to the culture of this country can be found in the work of many foreign-born writers, such as Lucha Corpi, a poet who moved to the United States from Mexico when she was nineteen years old.

had of Do not use *of* between *had* and a past participle.

I wish I **had** seen him before he left for Europe.

hanged, hung Use *hanged* to mean "to put to death by hanging." Use *hung* in all other cases.

> The soldier who had deserted was caught and **hanged.**
> Phil **hung** the picture above his desk.

in, into, in to Use *in* to mean "inside" or "within" and *into* to indicate movement or direction from outside to a point within. *In to* is made up of an adverb (*in*) followed by a preposition (*to*) and should be carefully distinguished from the preposition *into*.

> The president was working **in** his office.

> A secretary walked **into** the office and greeted him.

> Every morning the secretary goes **in to** the president and discusses the day's agenda.

irregardless, regardless Always use *regardless*. The prefix *ir-* and the suffix *-less* both have negative meanings. When used together, they form a double negative.

> Maria maintains an optimistic outlook **regardless** of unfavorable circumstances or events.

this kind, these kinds Because *kind* is singular, it is modified by the singular form *this* or *that*. Similarly, *this* and *that* should be used to modify the nouns *sort* and *type* (*this type, that type, this sort, that sort*). Because *kinds* is plural, it is modified by the plural form *these* or *those*. Similarly, *these* and *those* should be used to modify *sorts* and *types*.

> **This kind** of dog is easy to train.
> **These kinds** of dogs are difficult to train.
> **That sort** of film is entertaining.
> **Those sorts** of films are rare these days.

lay, lie *Lay* means "to put" or "to place," and it takes a direct object. *Lie* means "to recline" or "to be positioned," and it never takes an object.

> Please **lay** the book on the table.
> The cat loves to **lie** in the sun.

To avoid confusion in using the principal parts of these verbs, study the following chart:

BASE FORM	lay	lie
PRESENT PARTICIPLE	laying	lying
PAST FORM	laid	lay
PAST PARTICIPLE	laid	lain

> Daryl **laid** the packages on the chair.
> The cat **lay** next to the fireplace.

learn, teach   *Learn* means "to receive knowledge" or "to acquire skill in." *Teach* means "to impart knowledge or instruction."

> Many young children easily **learn** a second language.
> These instructors **teach** Spanish.

leave, let   *Leave* means "to go away." *Let* means "to allow" or "to permit."

> The plane to Phoenix will **leave** in two hours.
> Please **let** us help with the dishes.

like, as   *Like* is a preposition and introduces a prepositional phrase. *As* and *as if* are subordinating conjunctions and introduce subordinate clauses. Many authorities say that *like* should never be used before a clause.

> He looks **like** a nervous person.
> He felt nervous, **as** he does before every performance.
> He looks **as if** he's nervous.

loose, lose   Use *loose* to mean "free," "not firmly attached," or "not fitting tightly." Use *lose* to mean "to have no longer," "to misplace," or "to fail to win."

> That bracelet is so **loose** that you might **lose** it.

Exercise 4

Making Usage Choices   For each of the following sentences, choose the correct word or expression from the pair in parentheses.

Gary Soto, Author and Teacher

1. The author Gary Soto (teaches/learns) English and Mexican-American studies to students at the University of California at Berkeley.
2. (Regardless/Irregardless) of the kind of class, Soto uses his own life experiences to help relate the subject matter to his students.
3. Years earlier Soto himself (had/had of) acquired a great deal of knowledge by studying with the poet Philip Levine.
4. (This kind/These kinds) of class can inspire young writers to work hard to perfect their craft.
5. Soto himself had to learn to (leave/let) go of his old ideas about poetry in order to develop his own style.
6. During the summer months Soto now goes (in/into/in to) his study, formerly a garage, for three hours each day to work on his writing. ➡

7. Soto says that each time he sits down to write, he feels a tingling sensation around his shoulders, (like/as) he did the very first time he wrote.
8. In one of his books for children, Soto writes about his active cat, who never (lays/lies) around the house like other cats.
9. I liked one of his poems so much that I had it framed and (hanged/hung) it on the wall in my room.
10. Readers of his poetry, short stories, and nonfiction hope Soto never (looses/loses) his desire to write about his world.

passed, past   *Passed* is the past tense and the past participle of the verb *to pass*. *Past* can be an adjective, a preposition, an adverb, or a noun.

> The time **passed** quickly. [verb]
> Kyong has grown during the **past** months. [adjective]
> The truck drove **past** our house this morning. [preposition]
> The truck shifted gears as it went **past**. [adverb]
> All of that happened in the **past**. [noun]

precede, proceed   *Precede* means "to go or come before." *Proceed* means "to continue" or "to move along."

> An elegant dinner **preceded** the concert.
> The speaker **proceeded** to the dais and began her lecture.

raise, rise   *Raise* means "to cause to move upward," and it always takes an object. *Rise* means "to get up"; it is intransitive and therefore never takes an object.

> Many people **raise** their voices when they become angry.
> Antonio **rises** every morning at six and runs two miles.

reason is because   Do not use this expression. Since *because* means "for the reason that," it is repetitious. Use either *reason is that* or *because*.

> The **reason** Jane cannot come to the party **is that** she will be away.

> Jane cannot come to the party **because** she will be away.

respectfully, respectively   *Respectfully* means "with respect." *Respectively* means "in the order named."

> The audience listened **respectfully** to the Nobel laureate.

> Peggy and Michael are, **respectively,** author and editor of the book.

says, said   *Says* is the third-person singular of *say*. *Said* is the past tense of *say*.

> Yesterday he **said** that he would meet us outside the theater before the play began.

> He always **says** he will be on time, but he never is.

sit, set   *Sit* means "to place oneself in a sitting position." It rarely takes an object. *Set* means "to place" or "to put" and usually takes an object. When it is used with *sun* to mean "the sun is going down" or "the sun is sinking out of sight," *set* is intransitive.

> Mother and Father **sit** at opposite ends of the table during the main meal of the day.

> Please **set** this casserole on the table.

> We watched as the sun **set,** leaving the sky streaked with orange and red.

than, then   *Than* is a conjunction that is used to introduce the second element in a comparison; it also shows exception.

> Yesterday was busier **than** today.

> We have had no visitors other **than** Mrs. Peterson, who came early in the morning.

Then is an adverb that means "at that time," "soon afterward," "the time mentioned," "at another time," "for that reason," "in that case," or "besides."

> Ana was in high school **then.**

> The musicians tuned their instruments and **then** played.

> By **then** they had already left town.

> Renee has been to Europe twice; she visited England and Scotland, and **then** she toured France and Italy.

> She found a pleasant hotel and **then** felt contented.

> Sugar is bad for your teeth, but **then** it's bad for your whole body.

this here, that there   Avoid using *here* and *there* after *this* and *that*.

> Debbie visited several stores in the mall and then decided to buy **this** sweater.

> Please hand me **that** pencil on the desk.

who, whom   See Unit 17.

Making Usage Choices   For each of the following sentences, choose the correct word or expression from the pair in parentheses.

The Invention of the Automobile

1. The (passed/past) has taught us that more than one person is usually instrumental in inventing or discovering something.
2. For example, there were many people (who/whom) we could name as having contributed significantly to the invention of the automobile.
3. As early as 1690, Denis Papin, inventor of the pressure cooker, proposed a steam-powered vehicle in which people could (sit/set) and ride.
4. (This/This here) idea of Papin's was not realized until 1769, when Nicolas Cugnot successfully drove his own steam-powered creation down a street in Paris.
5. The reason Cugnot's test ride was not a complete success is (because/that) after reaching a speed of 2.5 miles per hour, his odd-looking contraption crashed into a tree.
6. Today people (raise/rise) few objections when two men, Gottlieb Daimler and Karl Benz, are named as the true fathers of the modern automobile.
7. Never having met each other, both men (preceded/proceeded) to work independently on a gasoline-powered vehicle in 1885.
8. Later, after making successful trial runs with their inventions, each (said/says) that he was the actual inventor of the automobile.
9. Was Daimler's contribution, the internal-combustion engine, more important (then/than) Benz's three-wheeled vehicle?
10. In 1926 Daimler's and Benz's companies, named (respectfully/respectively) Daimler and Benz, joined to form a new company, Daimler, maker of the Mercedes-Benz.

Usage (Part 1)   For each of the following sentences, choose the correct word or expression from the pair in parentheses.

Field Lacrosse

1. Field lacrosse is a sport that has become popular ➡

(between/among) both men and women in the United States.

2. At the beginning of the game, the referee (sets/sits) the ball in the center of the field.

3. The attackers are supposed to get the ball (in/into/in to) the net of the opposing team.

4. As the defenders try to stop them, the attackers (bring/take) the ball toward the defenders' net.

5. Dodging the defending players, the attackers make (continual/continuous) attempts to score.

6. Skill and speed are especially important at (this/this here) point in the game.

7. In their attempts to score, the players on the attacking team must be careful not to (loose/lose) the ball to the defenders who are trying their best to get it.

8. An attacker who is (anywhere/anywheres) near the goal may attempt to score.

9. None of the players (accept/except) the goalies may touch the ball with their hands.

10. (Beside/Besides) needing speed and agility, lacrosse players must be able to judge distance.

11. In lacrosse it is (all right/alright) for players to block one another with their bodies.

12. Players must be careful not to (leave/let) go of the ball too soon.

13. Players who do (good/well) sometimes win scholarships to colleges or universities.

14. It is (a/an) historical fact that the game originated with Native Americans.

15. Lacrosse (might have/might of) never become popular again if college students had not begun to play it.

16. Today lacrosse is (all together/altogether) different from the original game played by the Iroquois and the Huron.

17. It is still fast paced, however, and players (ain't/aren't) allowed to set the ball down on the ground.

18. (Being that/Since) a lacrosse game lasts sixty minutes, players must have endurance.

19. People who know ice hockey will see that that game is not very (different from/different than) lacrosse.

20. Those football players (who/whom) also play lacrosse find that the game enables them to develop their speed and agility.

Usage (Part 2) For each of the following sentences, choose the correct word or expression from the pair in parentheses.

Restored Villages

1. A person who (doesn't/don't) find history interesting might be persuaded to think differently after visiting a restored village.
2. History books describe how people in the (past/passed) probably lived.
3. Restored villages show people actually living (like/as) they did many years ago.
4. Often historians (advice/advise) the people who are carrying out the restorations.
5. The oldest European settlement in North America (can/may) be found in Saint Augustine, Florida.
6. Next to the James River in Virginia (lay/lie) the restored buildings from the Jamestown settlement.
7. At Plimoth Plantation in Massachusetts, restorers (respectfully/respectively) use the original spelling of the town's name.
8. Walking through the streets of restored Williamsburg, Virginia, visitors (can hardly/can't hardly) believe they are in the twentieth century.
9. Artisans at the ancient Cherokee village of Tsa-La-Gi, Oklahoma, are concerned about the (affect/effect) of modern civilization on their heritage.
10. In an effort to preserve their language, (a lot/alot) of these artisans speak only Cherokee.

Usage (Part 3) For each of the following sentences, choose the correct word or expression from the pair in parentheses.

Maria Tallchief, Prima Ballerina

1. For (a while/awhile) Maria Tallchief, a young girl growing up on the Osage Indian Reservation in Oklahoma, studied both piano and ballet.
2. At the age of twelve, she decided she would rather concentrate her efforts on ballet (than/then) on anything else.
3. She knew that she wanted (bad/badly) to be a prima ballerina.
4. (All ready/Already) at the age of fifteen she was dancing ➡

a solo part in a ballet by Nijinska, the sister of the famous dancer Nijinsky.

5. While she was with the Ballet Russe in Ottawa, Canada, she had to (adapt/adopt) to the rigorous discipline and practice, the extremely cold climate, and the resentment of the other dancers.

6. Being with the Ballet Russe (learned/taught) her to confront disappointment since she was continually passed over for leading roles.

7. At one time Tallchief (says/said) that her greatest opportunity came on May 1, 1943, when she was asked to dance a Chopin concerto in place of an ailing ballerina.

8. (Regardless/Irregardless) of the fame her brilliant performance in the concerto brought her, Tallchief was not given other important roles that she was capable of performing, and she again grew discouraged.

9. Tallchief, however, was soon able to go (farther/further) in her career when she started dancing in George Balanchine's productions, specifically *The Song of Norway*, *The Fairy's Kiss*, and *The Firebird*.

10. The reason Maria Tallchief was so successful as a prima ballerina is (because/that) she was able to display not only great emotion but also superb technique in her dancing.

Usage Workshop

Usage Glossary

The following quotations, which have been annotated to show some of the usage items covered in this unit, deal with the paramount importance of freedom to human existence.

Literature Model

QUOTATIONS ABOUT FREEDOM

The articles *a* used before words beginning with consonants and *an* used before a word beginning with a vowel

What woman needs is not as a woman to act or rule, but as a nature to grow, as an intellect to discern, as a soul to live freely and unimpeded, to unfold such powers as were given her when we left our common home.

From Woman in the Nineteenth Century by Margaret Fuller

The conjunction *than* used in a comparison

I would rather sit on a pumpkin and have it all to myself than be crowded on a velvet cushion.

From Walden by Henry David Thoreau

Less used to modify a noun (*cost*) that cannot be counted

The cost of liberty is less than the price of repression.

From John Brown by W. E. B. Du Bois

The relative pronoun *who* in the nominative case because it is the subject of a clause

My first and greatest love affair was with this thing we call freedom, . . . this dangerous and beautiful and sublime being who restores and supplies us all.

From "One Man's Meat" by E. B. White

Usage Workshop Exercise 1

Making Usage Choices The following sentences are about political independence. For each one, choose the correct word or expression in parentheses, and write it on your paper.

SAMPLE	I (can hardly/can't hardly) believe how long it took for some nations to achieve independence.
ANSWER	can hardly →

1. Toussaint L'Ouverture is (a/an) hero in Haiti, where he led the nation to freedom in 1804.
2. (Accept/Except) for French Guiana, an overseas department of France, South America is composed of independent nations.
3. Formerly known as Ceylon, Sri Lanka is one of many countries that have (adapted/adopted) new names since declaring independence.
4. Simón Bolívar, the nineteenth-century freedom fighter, (affected/effected) great change in Latin America.
5. The rest of Central America was (all ready/already) independent when Belize achieved independence in 1981.
6. Although Ireland has (fewer/less) speakers of Gaelic than of English, Gaelic is an official language.
7. Mauritius, an independent island nation, lies (somewheres/somewhere) east of Madagascar.
8. After Algeria achieved independence, many French residents (immigrated/emigrated) from the new nation.
9. Liberia, which (lays/lies) on Africa's west coast, was founded as a haven for freed American slaves.
10. Portugal, the last European nation to (lose/loose) its African colonies, granted independence to Angola and Guinea-Bissau in 1974 and to Mozambique in 1975.

Usage Workshop Exercise 2

Making Usage Choices   For each of the following sentences, choose the correct word or expression in parentheses.

SAMPLE   In the (passed/past) many eloquent people have spoken out for freedom.

ANSWER   past

1. (A lot/Alot) of people have studied the view of Athenian democracy expressed in Pericles' famous funeral oration.
2. As leader of a newly independent Kenya, the skillful orator Jomo Kenyatta told disagreeing factions that (all together/altogether) they could help the nation.
3. The Declaration of Independence makes (allusions/illusions) to some of John Locke's ideas.
4. England's Magna Carta was among the first documents (anywheres/anywhere) that limited the power of kings.
5. America's Declaration of Independence (borrowed/lent/loaned) strength to fighters for independence in many other countries. ➡

6. Thomas Jefferson, (who/whom) we know wrote the Declaration of Independence, saw democracy as a way of life.
7. The American patriot Nathan Hale made a memorable speech before the British (hanged/hung) him.
8. The Fifteenth Amendment gives all citizens the right to vote (irregardless/regardless) of their race.
9. After becoming Senegal's first president, Léopold Sédar Senghor (preceded/proceeded) to make many eloquent speeches concerning the rights of Third World nations.
10. Few speeches are better known (than/then) Martin Luther King's "I Have a Dream" speech.

Usage Workshop Exercise 3

Review For each sentence below choose the correct word or expression in parentheses, and write it on your paper.

SAMPLE   As editor of *The Dial,* Margaret Fuller printed articles that (borrowed/lent/loaned) support to the Transcendentalist movement.

ANSWER   lent

1. The Transcendentalists (excepted/accepted) the young Fuller as an intellectual equal.
2. As did other Transcendentalists, Fuller sometimes sought the (advice/advise) of Ralph Waldo Emerson, an influential proponent of the movement.
3. While Thoreau was associated with Transcendentalism, his views were (different from/different than) Emerson's.
4. Although Thoreau taught (a while/awhile) in a village, he preferred the seclusion of Walden Pond.
5. Thoreau did not join the experimental community of Brook Farm, (like/as) most other Transcendentalists did.
6. W. E. B. Du Bois and Margaret Fuller were the editors of *Crisis* and *The Dial,* (respectfully/respectively).
7. Although Du Bois produced a broad range of literature, he wrote (fewer/less) novels than works of nonfiction.
8. (Being that/Because) Du Bois was interested in African culture, he lived for a time in Ghana.
9. E. B. White, (who/whom) readers admire for his witty essays, was born in Mount Vernon, New York.
10. Many people remember going (in/into/in to) the library and discovering White's classic tale *Charlotte's Web.*

Proofreading The following passage describes the artist George Benjamin Luks, whose painting appears on this page. Rewrite the passage, correcting the errors in spelling, capitalization, punctuation, grammar, and usage. There are ten errors in all.

George Benjamin Luks

[1]George Benjamin Luks (1867–1933) was born in Williamsport, Pennsylvania and attended the Pennsylvania Academy of Fine Arts. [2]It is believed that Luks spent a decade traveling in Europe. [3]Upon his return to the United States in 1894, he excepted a position on the art staff of a Philadelphia newspaper. [4]Later he worked for the *Evening Bulletin* as a war correspondant in Cuba.

[5]After being encouraged by his friends to try painting, Luks preceded to make rapid progress. [6]His subjects were Philadelphia, colorful characters, and social outcasts. [7]These realistic canvasses were painted in a dark aggressive style. [8]As time passed, his works grow more colorful, his style became lighter and more vivacious.

[9]In *Armistice Night* Luks captures the booming festivities that marked the end of World War I. [10]Like the quotations in this workshop, Luk's painting conveys the joyous affect of freedom.

George Benjamin Luks, *Armistice Night*, 1918

Unit 19 Review

Usage Glossary

Preferred Usage

[pages 611–625]

In each sentence indicate the usage that is preferred.

1. Celia could not find him (a) anywhere/
   (b) anywheres.
2. The writer (a) adapted/(b) adopted her
   book for the screen.
3. Edgar Allan Poe's poems frequently make
   (a) allusions/(b) illusions to mythology.
4. After raking the grass (a) a while/
   (b) awhile, my sister decided to take a
   short rest.
5. It seemed that the man walking on stilts
   (a) would of/(b) would have fallen if he
   had taken another step.
6. The columnist Dr. Joyce Brothers gives
   (a) advice/(b) advise to readers.
7. I am (a) all ready/(b) already so full that I
   couldn't eat another bite.
8. Health experts are beginning to discover
   that (a) laying/(b) lying in the sun can be
   dangerous to the skin.
9. I liked the movie made from Kate
   Chopin's novel *The Awakening* better (a)
   than/(b) then any other movie I have seen
   this year.
10. Buffalo, New York, experienced one
    (a) continual/(b) continuous blizzard for
    five days last winter.
11. Many notorious outlaws of the West were
    (a) hanged/(b) hung for their crimes.
12. During the social unrest of the 1840s,
    many people (a) emigrated/(b) immigrated
    from Germany.
13. There are (a) less/(b) fewer seashells on
    the beach today than there were yesterday.
14. New medical discoveries have (a) affected/
    (b) effected the average life expectancy of
    Americans.
15. Some people cannot (a) accept/(b) except
    the facts no matter how clearly they are
    presented.
16. (a) Can/(b) May I borrow the car?
17. If you must know why I can't speak louder,
    the (a) reason is because/(b) reason is that
    I have laryngitis.
18. I (a) can hardly/(b) can't hardly read the
    small print.
19. The basketball finals attracted (a) alot/
    (b) a lot of viewers.
20. After waiting in line for twenty minutes,
    we went (a) into/(b) in the movie theater.

Writing for Review

Demonstrate your knowledge of the
distinction between the terms in each of the
following pairs by writing a sentence using
each term.

all together, altogether

between, among

farther, further

lend, loan

Unit 20 Capitalization

20.1 Capitalization of Sentences and the Pronoun *I*

Capitalize the first word of every sentence, including the first word of a direct quotation that is a complete sentence.

> **D**id you know that Beethoven, who was born in Bonn, Germany, in 1770, was completely deaf by the time he composed his Ninth Symphony?

> **T**he poet Edna St. Vincent Millay responded to a Beethoven symphony by writing, "**S**weet sounds, oh beautiful music, do not cease!"

Capitalize the first word of a sentence in parentheses that stands by itself. Do not capitalize a sentence within parentheses that is contained within another sentence.

> Scott Joplin composed ragtime piano music. (**R**agtime music was originally called rag music.)

> Fiddles and banjos (**t**he piano was used later) were the original instruments in a ragtime band.

Do not capitalize the first word of a quotation unless the entire quotation can stand as a complete sentence.

> The writer Thomas Carlyle said that music is "**t**he speech of angels."

> The American composer Aaron Copland said, "**M**elody is what the piece is about."

Do not capitalize the first word of an indirect quotation. An **indirect quotation,** often introduced by the word *that*, does not repeat a person's exact words.

> Beethoven said that **m**usic should bring tears to the eyes of the listeners.

Always capitalize the pronoun *I* no matter where it appears in the sentence.

> Since **I** already know how to play the drums, **I** do not need to take lessons before **I** join the band.

Capitalizing Sentences and the Pronoun *I* Rewrite correctly any of the following sentences that have one or more errors in capitalization. Write the word *correct* if a sentence has no errors.

What They Said

1. The first line of Margaret Walker's poem "Lineage" is "my grandmothers were strong."
2. The Irish novelist Margaret Wolfe Hungerford's 1878 novel *Molly Bawn* contains the famous line "Beauty is in the eye of the beholder."
3. Less than a week after Britain and France had declared war on Nazi Germany on September 3, 1939 (On September 1 Germany had invaded Poland), the French statesman Paul Reynaud assured radio listeners, "we shall win because we are the stronger."
4. In *Blue Highways* William Least Heat-Moon writes of how he traveled America's back roads "in search of places where change did not mean ruin and where time and men and deeds connected."
5. In her essay "No Name Woman" Maxine Hong Kingston describes how those immigrants in decades past "Who could not reassert brute survival died young and far from home."
6. One of the most practical pieces of advice was given by First Lady Eleanor Roosevelt when she wrote, "no one can make you feel inferior without your consent." (she wrote this in her book *This Is My Story*, published in 1937.)
7. In an interview about her writing techniques, the novelist Toni Morrison declared, "i always know the ending; that's where i start."
8. When asked why the color yellow appeared so frequently in his fiction, Jorge Luis Borges said that Perhaps it was because yellow was the last color he was able to see as he gradually went blind.
9. In a letter the author F. Scott Fitzgerald commented, "all good writing is swimming under water and holding your breath."
10. A week after John F. Kennedy's assassination, President Lyndon Johnson addressed the United States Congress and stated that He regretted having to stand where Kennedy ought to have stood.

20.2   Capitalization of Proper Nouns

Capitalize a proper noun.

Capitalize a common noun only when it is the first word of a sentence.

Capitalize only the important words in proper nouns composed of several words. Do not capitalize articles (*a, an, the*), coordinating conjunctions (*and, but, for, or, nor, yet*), or prepositions of fewer than five letters.

1. Names of individuals

Michael Chang	Buffalo Bill
Ulysses S. Grant	Jackie Joyner-Kersee
Maria Martinez	Catherine the Great

2. Titles of individuals

Capitalize titles used before a proper name and titles used in direct address.

President Bush	Mr. Louis Armstrong
Sir Arthur Conan Doyle	Surgeon General Antonia Novello
Queen Victoria	Rear Admiral Mary F. Hall
Dr. Paul Dudley White	Yes, Senator. [direct address]

In general, do not capitalize titles that follow a proper name or are used alone. Most writers, however, capitalize *president* when referring to the current president of the United States.

In the Oval Office the President met with Corazón Aquino, the president of the Philippines.

Can you tell me who the third president of the United States was?

In general, capitalize a title that describes a family relationship when it is used with or in place of a proper name.

I wrote to Aunt Olga.	*but*	My aunt lives abroad.
We spoke to Father.		Our father is a lawyer.
Did you visit Cousin Arthur?		Our cousin was out.
What did you say, Grandmother?		What did my grandmother say?
Yesterday Grandmother spoke at her garden club.		

3. Names of ethnic groups, national groups, and languages

Mexican Americans	Iroquois
Koreans	Swedish
Indians	Arabic

4. **Names of organizations, institutions, political parties and their members, and firms**

Girl Scouts of America	Democratic party
Salvation Army	a Republican
University of Miami	American Express Company
House of Representatives	Wang Laboratories, Incorporated

Note that the word *party* is not capitalized. Do not capitalize common nouns such as *museum* or *university* unless they are part of a proper noun.

Jesse visited the art museum on his lunch hour.
He visited the Dallas Museum of Fine Arts.

5. **Names of monuments, bridges, buildings, and other structures**

Grant's Tomb	Hoover Dam
Graybar Building	Greater New Orleans Bridge

6. **Trade names**

Toyota	Tide detergent
Bayer aspirin	Ivory soap

7. **Names of documents, awards, and laws**

Magna Carta	Congressional Medal of Honor
Treaty of Paris	Heisman Trophy
Emmy Award	Tax Reform Act of 1986

8. **Geographical terms**

Capitalize the names of continents, countries, states, counties, and cities, as well as the names of specific bodies of water, topographical features, regions, and streets.

North America	Mackinac Island
Greece	Pocono Mountains
Illinois	Red River Valley
West Virginia	Painted Desert
Chester County	Tropic of Capricorn
Richmond	Central America
Indian Ocean	Michigan Avenue

9. **Names of planets and other heavenly bodies**

Mercury	Pleiades
Uranus	Little Dipper
Andromeda galaxy	the constellation Orion

Do not capitalize the words *sun* and *moon*. Capitalize *earth* only when it appears in conjunction with the names of the other planets. It should never be capitalized when it is used with the definite article, *the*.

The **e**arth revolves around the sun.
The planets **M**ars and **E**arth are similar in many respects.

10. Compass points

Capitalize the words *north*, *east*, *south*, and *west* when they refer to a specific area of the country or the world or when they are part of a proper name. Do not capitalize them when they merely indicate direction.

the Far **E**ast	*but*	the **e**ast coast of Australia
South Carolina		Travel **s**outh on Route 9.
the **S**outhwest		a **s**outhwest wind

11. Names of ships, planes, trains, and spacecraft

U.S.S. *Intrepid*	*City of New Orleans*
Concorde	*Apollo 12*

12. Names of most historical events, eras, and calendar items

World **W**ar **I**	**P**leistocene
Great **D**epression	**M**emorial **D**ay

You should not capitalize a historical period that refers to a general span of time.

the **f**ifth century   the **t**hirties

Capitalize the days of the week and the months of the year, but do not capitalize the names of the seasons (*spring, summer, autumn, fall, winter*).

13. Religious terms

Capitalize names of deities, religions and their denominations and adherents, words referring to a supreme deity, and religious books and events.

Allah	**C**hurch of **E**ngland
God	the **A**lmighty
Catholicism	the **B**ible
Islam	the **G**ospels
Shintoism	**G**ood **F**riday
Lutherans	**P**assover

14. Names of school courses

Capitalize only those school courses that are the name of a language or the title of a specific course. Do not capitalize the name of a subject.

French	*but*	**f**oreign **l**anguage
World **H**istory **I**		a course in **w**orld **h**istory
Calculus 303		I am studying **c**alculus.

15. Titles of works

*A **C**onnecticut **Y**ankee in **K**ing **A**rthur's **C**ourt* [book]

"**T**o a **C**hild **R**unning with **O**utstretched **A**rms in **C**anyon de **C**helly" [poem]

the *P**hiladelphia **I**nquirer* [newspaper]

"**H**ome on the **R**ange" [song]

Capitalize articles (*a*, *an*, and *the*) at the beginning of a title only when they are part of the title itself. It is common practice not to capitalize (or italicize) articles preceding the title of a newspaper or a periodical. Do not capitalize (or italicize) the word *magazine* unless it is part of the title of a periodical.

*T**he Invisible Man*	*but*	**a** *Life* **m**agazine photograph
*T**he Red Pony*		**t**he *Chicago Tribune*

Exercise 2

Capitalizing Proper Nouns On your paper rewrite the following sentences correctly, adding or dropping capital letters as necessary.

The Underground Railroad

1. In your History class you may have discussed the Underground railroad—a secret network that helped Slaves escape to freedom in the period before the civil war.
2. In the Decades before the Civil War, the antislavery movement began to flourish in the United States, especially in the north.
3. Pitted against this Movement were those who supported the fugitive slave act—a 1793 law that gave legal support to owners seeking their runaway slaves.
4. The term *underground* in Underground Railroad refers to the secrecy necessary to transport the slaves, most of whom traveled North either at night or in disguise. ➡

5. The operation was called a Railroad because railway terms were used to discuss the slaves' progress from the south to safe locations: routes were called lines; those who helped along the way were conductors; and their charges were known as freight or packages.

6. A wide array of people throughout the country—men and women of all ages, african americans, whites, quakers, presbyterians, congregationalists—worked for the Underground Railroad.

7. Among the most Prominent were two United States representatives, Joshua Giddings and gerrit smith, as well as the reputed leader of the entire operation, Levi Coffin of cincinnati.

8. Using the railroad, many slaves crossed the ohio river to find freedom, and some managed to travel all the way to canada.

9. Harriet Tubman of maryland escaped from slavery in 1849 and became a conductor of hundreds of other slaves along the railroad.

10. The Underground Railroad continues to fascinate people, as we can see by the success of the recent novel *The house of dies drear* by Author Virginia Hamilton.

20.3   Capitalization of Proper Adjectives

Capitalize proper adjectives (adjectives formed from proper nouns).

Below are some of the categories into which most proper adjectives fit:

1. Adjectives formed from names of people

> **G**eorgian architecture
> **M**osaic teachings [the teachings of Moses]
> **C**opernican system
> **J**effersonian agrarianism
> **F**reudian psychology

2. Adjectives formed from place names and names of national, ethnic, and religious groups

> **A**thenian democracy   **I**rish folk music
> **V**irginian soil   **H**ispanic cooking
> **A**frican pottery   **J**ewish holidays

When used as adjectives, many proper nouns do not change form.

Vermont maple syrup	**U**nited **S**tates foreign policy
Eskimo artifacts	**B**eethoven symphonies
Beatles songs	**I**ndia ink

Exercise 3

Capitalizing Proper Adjectives and Proper Nouns
Rewrite the following sentences correctly on your paper. As you write each sentence, add or drop capital letters as necessary.

Columbus's Voyage of Discovery

1. On october 12, 1492, a sailor on the spanish ship *pinta* sighted an island in what are now believed to be the bahamas.
2. The italian captain of the expedition, Christopher Columbus, went ashore with the flag of spain and named the place san salvador.
3. Although Columbus's voyage opened up the americas to the people of europe, this achievement had not been his original goal.
4. Columbus's original goal had been to prove that the important commercial and trading centers of asia—china, japan, and the east indies—could be reached by sailing westward from europe.
5. European demand for chinese, japanese, and indian products was great.
6. Such asian spices as pepper, cinnamon, ginger, and cloves were important products to europeans, who also prized such Asian food as rice, figs, and oranges.
7. On his return to spain, Columbus persuaded queen isabella, who had sponsored his voyage, to give him political control over the lands he had reached.
8. Columbus and his brothers subsequently abused their political power by exploiting and enslaving the Natives of these Lands in the new world.
9. Although he had sailed to a Continent previously unknown to europeans, Columbus still believed that he had reached the east indies.
10. Therefore, Columbus called the new world inhabitants indians.

Summary of Capitalization Rules	
Capitalize	**Do Not Capitalize**
Before making repairs, the mechanic ordered parts for our car. (**O**ur car is a foreign model.)	The mechanic ordered parts for our car (**o**ur car is a foreign model) before making repairs.
Anne Frank said, "**I**n spite of everything, I still believe that people are really good at heart."	Anne Frank said that **i**n spite of all that was happening around her, she believed people are fundamentally good.
Mayor David Dinkins	the **m**ayor
Aunt Carmen	my **a**unt Carmen
Vanderbilt **U**niversity; **S**an **D**iego **Z**oo	the **u**niversity; the **z**oo
a **T**oyota	a **c**ompact **c**ar
the **V**olstead **A**ct	an **a**ct passed by Congress
Mississippi **R**iver; **V**entnor **A**venue	the **r**iver; the **a**venue
Mercury; **P**luto	a **p**lanet; the **s**un; the **m**oon
World **W**ar **II**	Another **w**orld **w**ar began.
the **B**ible; **B**uddhism	a **h**oly **b**ook; a **r**eligion
Geography 101; **C**reative **W**riting	**g**eography; a **c**reative **w**riting class
"**T**he **S**tar-**S**pangled **B**anner"	the **n**ational **a**nthem

Exercise 4: Sentence Writing

Writing a Speech   Imagine that you are going to give a speech about a notable historical event. To prepare for your speech, make notes to help you organize your information. Write down several sentences in which you describe important aspects of the event, such as where and when the activity took place, who was involved in the action, and what impact it had on history.

Capitalization   Write the letter of the one item that is correctly capitalized in each of the following pairs.

1. **a.** After reading the novel *1984*, i shuddered to think of living in an orwellian society.
   b. After reading the novel *1984*, I shuddered to think of living in an Orwellian society.

2. **a.** The author of a recent article published in *Consumer Reports* magazine stated that one kind of Sony videotape was superior to the videotape manufactured by many other companies.
   b. The author of a recent article published in *Consumer Reports* Magazine stated that one kind of Sony Videotape was superior to the videotape manufactured by many other companies.

3. **a.** The National Association for the Advancement of Colored People was established in 1910 to effect racial equality between African Americans and whites throughout the United States.
   b. The national association for the advancement of colored people was established in 1910 to effect racial equality between african americans and whites throughout the United States.

4. **a.** Over a thousand lives were lost when a torpedo from a German submarine struck and sank the British Liner *lusitania* in 1915.
   b. Over a thousand lives were lost when a torpedo from a German submarine struck and sank the British liner *Lusitania* in 1915.

5. **a.** Accepting the Nobel peace prize, Martin Luther King Jr. said that the road from Montgomery, Alabama, to Oslo, norway, would one day "Be widened into a superhighway of justice."
   b. Accepting the Nobel Peace Prize, Martin Luther King Jr. said that the road from Montgomery, Alabama, to Oslo, Norway, would one day "be widened into a superhighway of justice."

6. **a.** Can you ask the librarian to help me find out whether Spanish is widely spoken in Oregon and other parts of the Northwest?
   b. Can you ask the librarian to help me find out whether Spanish is widely spoken in Oregon and other parts of the northwest? ➡

7. **a.** Before boarding *air force one* for his trip to the Middle East, the president said that he was hopeful about the Peace Talks.

   b. Before boarding *Air Force One* for his trip to the Middle East, the President said that he was hopeful about the peace talks.

8. **a.** My cousin Anita met mom and dad at the neighborhood Shopping Mall, and then they all drove in my parents' car to visit Uncle Carlos.

   b. My cousin Anita met Mom and Dad at the neighborhood shopping mall, and then they all drove in my parents' car to visit Uncle Carlos.

9. **a.** Is anyone in history 102 writing a report on life in the urban centers or the rural areas of America in the Nineteenth Century?

   b. Is anyone in History 102 writing a report on life in the urban centers or the rural areas of America in the nineteenth century?

10. **a.** Among the most complex figures in American history is Chief Crazy Horse of the Sioux tribe.

    b. Among the most complex figures in American History is chief Crazy Horse of the Sioux Tribe.

*M*echanics Workshop

Capitalization

The Muses Are Heard is Truman Capote's memoir of a remarkable trip he made to the Soviet Union in 1955 with a troupe of African-American actors who had come to perform George Gershwin's opera, *Porgy and Bess.* In this passage from the book, the Americans are met by their interpreters, a woman named Miss Lydia and three young men, and the delegate from Moscow's Ministry of Culture, Nikolai Savchenko. This excerpt has been annotated to show some of the rules of capitalization covered in this unit.

Literature Model

from THE MUSES ARE HEARD

by Truman Capote

Place name (city) — We reached Brest Litovsk in a luminous twilight. Statues of political heroes, painted cheap-silver like those

Name of a firm — souvenir figures sold at Woolworth's, saluted us along the last mile of track leading to the station. The station was on

Proper adjective formed from a place name — high ground that afforded a partial view of the city, dim and blue and dominated, far-off, by an Orthodox cathedral, whose onion-domes and mosaic towers still projected, despite the failing light, their Oriental colors.

Title used directly before a person's name — It seemed natural that Miss Lydia and the young men should react awkwardly to this, their first encounter with Westerners; understandable that they should hesitate to test

Name of an institution — their English, so tediously learned at Moscow's Institute of Foreign Languages but never before practiced on bona fide foreigners; forgivable that they should, instead, stare as

Name of a national group — though the Americans represented pawns in a chess problem. But Savchenko also gave an impression of being ill at ease, of preferring, in fact, a stretch in Lubyanka [a

Name of a person — prison] to his present chores. . . . He delivered a small speech of welcome in gruff Russian, then had it translated

Name of a language — by Miss Lydia. "We hope each and all have had a pleasant journey. Too bad you see us in the winter. It is not the good

First word of a complete sentence within quotation marks — time of year. But we have the saying, Better now than never. Your visit is a step forward in the march toward ➡

642   *Capitalization*

peace. When the cannons are heard, the muses are silent; when the cannons are silent, the muses are heard."

The muse-cannon metaphor, which was to prove a Savchenko favorite, the starring sentence of all future speeches, was an instant hit with his listeners. ("A beautiful thing." "Just great, Mr. Savchenko." "That's cool cookin', man.") — First word of a sentence that stands by itself in parentheses

We crossed a hundred yards of track, walked down a dirt lane between warehouses, and arrived at what appeared to be a combination of a parking lot and market place. Brightly lighted kiosks circled it like candles burning on a cake. It was puzzling to discover that each of the kiosks sold the same products: cans of Red Star salmon, Red — Trade name Star sardines, dusty bottles of Kremlin perfume, dusty boxes of Kremlin candy.

Mechanics Workshop Exercise 1

Capitalizing Sentences   The following sentences are about the opera *Porgy and Bess*. Rewrite each sentence, correcting any errors in capitalization. If a sentence has no errors, write *correct*.

1. According to the *Oxford Companion to American Theatre*, the play *Porgy* (Written by Dorothy and Dubose Heyward) "Remains one of the greatest of all American folk dramas."
2. The musical *Porgy and Bess* (1935), considered "A folk opera," was based on that play. (the play opened in 1927.)
3. Dubose Heyward and Ira Gershwin wrote the musical's lyrics. (The music was composed by Ira's brother, George.)
4. Experts have said that The distinctly American musical owes much to George Gershwin and his use of jazz rhythms.
5. One review of *Porgy and Bess* asserted, "this opera is one of the great achievements of the American musical theater."

Mechanics Workshop Exercise 2

Capitalizing Proper Nouns and Proper Adjectives   The following sentences are about Saint Petersburg, which was called Leningrad at the time of Capote's visit. Rewrite the sentences, correcting any errors in capitalization. If a sentence has no errors, write *correct*. ➡

1. Saint Petersburg, considered one of the most beautiful cities in Europe, is in the northwestern part of Russia.
2. It has long played an important part in russian history.
3. Built by Peter the Great, it was the capital of the Russian Empire during the Eighteenth and Nineteenth Centuries.
4. Students of Modern History learn of its memorable siege.
5. During world war ii, it was the target of a grueling nine-hundred-day siege by the German and Finnish armies.
6. Saint Petersburg's location produces long, cold nights in the Winter and long, warm days in the Summer.
7. The city is filled with famous Museums, such as the hermitage, and Historic Buildings, such as the marble palace.
8. The City has been known by several names, including Saint petersburg (1703–1914), petrograd (1914–1924), and leningrad (1924–1991).
9. In 1991 the russians restored the name Saint Petersburg.
10. That year the Communists lost power, and former heroes such as Lenin were no longer revered.

Mechanics Workshop Exercise 3

Review   Rewrite the following sentences about Truman Capote [kə pō´ tē]. Correct all the errors in capitalization. If a sentence has no errors, write correct.

Truman Capote

1. truman capote was born truman streckfus persons in 1924.
2. His Mother's second marriage was to Joe Capote.
3. By 1928 Capote had moved to monroeville, alabama.
4. Harper Lee (She later became the Award-winning author of *to Kill A Mockingbird*) was one of his best friends there.
5. at seventeen he was working at the *new yorker* magazine.
6. In 1948 his first novel, *Other voices, other rooms*, became a success. (he was just twenty-four at the time.)
7. Capote trained his powers of recall by memorizing ever longer sections of the Sears, Roebuck catalog.
8. writing about his russian experience helped inspire Capote to pioneer the "nonfiction novel," which uses Novelistic Techniques to report facts.
9. Capote said that He gave his life to the nonfiction novel *In cold blood*, in which he used "Journalism as an art form."
10. Capote won many Prizes, including the edgar award of the Mystery writers of America and an emmy award.

Proofreading   This passage describes Marc Chagall, whose painting appears on this page. Correct the ten errors in spelling, capitalization, punctuation, grammar, and usage.

Marc Chagall

¹Mark Chagall was born in 1887 in Vitebsk a town in Russia near the polish border. ²Although he spends most of his adult life in France, Chagall never forgot the village of his youth. ³His dreamlike paintings are filled with images from the past: Village dances, weddings, harvest festivals, and funerals.

⁴In 1910 Chagall moved to Paris. ⁵Although his work was influenced by the Surrealists he always remained true to his own style. ⁶He returned to Russia after the revolution in October 1917, and served as Commissar of fine arts in Vitebsk. ⁷His irreverent style met with disapproval (A banner he designed to comemorate the revolution showed green cows floating upside down), and he returned to Europe. ⁸In *The Market Place, Vitebsk* Chagall pays tribute to the town where he was born. ⁹Chagall's village is dominated by an Eastern Orthodox cathedral (as is Brest-Litovsk, the town Truman Capote describes).

Marc Chagall, *The Market Place, Vitebsk,* **1917**

Capitalization

Read the following passages, paying attention especially to the underlined text. Then, for each numbered item below, choose the word or group of words that shows the correct capitalization for that underlined item.

Riding the [1]cumbres and toltec Scenic Railroad from Antonio, Colorado [2](the railroad used to run from Denver), to [3]chama, new mexico, is an exciting experience. The train runs in the [4]summer months through october of every year. You can learn more about it from John Albright's article in [5]*the new york times*.

1. **a.** Cumbres and Toltec
   b. cumbres and toltec
2. **a.** (The Railroad
   b. (the Railroad
   c. (the railroad
3. **a.** Chama, New Mexico
   b. chama, new mexico
4. **a.** Summer months through October
   b. Summer months through october
   c. summer months through October
5. **a.** the *New York Times*
   b. the *New York times*

An epigraph in Ernest Hemingway's early novel [6]*the sun also rises* is a quotation attributed to the [7]writer Gertrude Stein. "You," she said in reference to those people who had come into adulthood between [8]world war i and the great depression, [9]"are all a lost generation." According to Stein, she first heard the expression in [10]french from a paris hotel manager.

6. **a.** *the Sun Also Rises*
   b. *the Sun also Rises*
   c. *The Sun Also Rises*
7. **a.** Writer
   b. writer
8. **a.** world war i and the great depression
   b. World War I and the great depression
   c. World War I and the great Depression
   d. World War I and the Great Depression
9. **a.** "are
   b. "Are
10. **a.** French from a paris hotel manager
    b. french from a Paris hotel Manager
    c. French from a Paris hotel manager

Writing for Review

Write a paragraph in which you use several different proper nouns, proper adjectives, titles, and quotations.

Punctuation, Abbreviations, and Numbers

21.1 The Period

Use a period at the end of a declarative sentence and at the end of a polite command.

DECLARATIVE SENTENCE	The banjo is an American folk instrument.
POLITE COMMAND	Think of some other folk instruments besides the banjo.

21.2 The Exclamation Point

Use an exclamation point to show strong feeling and indicate a forceful command.

What a great movie!
How lovely you look!
Don't you dare go without me!

21.3 The Question Mark

Use a question mark to indicate a direct question.

Was Aaron Copland an American composer?
Did Copland write *Appalachian Spring*?

A question mark should not follow a declarative sentence that contains an indirect question.

My friend asked whether Aaron Copland wrote *Appalachian Spring*.

She wondered what folk tune is the central melody in *Appalachian Spring*.

Exercise 1

Using End Punctuation   Read the ten sentences on the following page. Then correct each sentence by adding periods, exclamation points, and question marks wherever they are needed. ➡

Zora Neale Hurston, Author

1. My friend asked me how I enjoyed Zora Neale Hurston's novel *Their Eyes Were Watching God*
2. Wow What a great book that was
3. I wonder why it took me so long to discover this wonderful writer
4. Did you know that Hurston writes tales of African-American folk culture
5. In her autobiography, *Dust Tracks on a Road*, Hurston recounts her early years in Eatonville, Florida; her travels with a theatrical troupe as a teen-ager; and her important work at Columbia University, where she studied anthropology
6. Hurston studied at Columbia with the famous ethnographer of Native American cultures Franz Boas. What a thrill that must have been
7. Are you aware that Hurston traveled widely—to such places as Louisiana, Alabama, Haiti, Jamaica, and the Bahamas—as a scholar and student of African-American folk culture
8. Don't you dare walk away with my only copy of *Mules and Men*
9. After I read *Mules and Men*, I had to ask myself what could be more fascinating than collecting and studying the folk tales, prayers, jokes, and games of an unfamiliar and exotic culture
10. When you finish reading it, please tell me your reactions to *Mule Bone: A Comedy of Negro Life in Three Acts*, the play Zora Neale Hurston wrote with Langston Hughes

21.4   The Colon

Colons to Introduce

1. Lists

Use a colon to introduce a list, especially after a statement that uses such words as *these*, *the following*, or *as follows*.

> The elements of a good detective story are **these:** a crime, interesting characters, and an arrest.

> Listen to a recording of one of **the following** concert vocalists: Justino Diaz, Martina Arroyo, or Jessye Norman.

A teacher often gives **the following** instructions: (1) find books on your topic, (2) take notes, (3) write an outline, and (4) write a first draft.

A colon is not used to introduce a list that immediately follows a verb or a preposition.

Three important American composers **are** Aaron Copland, Scott Joplin, and Arthur Cunningham.

In the 1970s Scott Joplin regained popularity with compositions **like** "The Entertainer" and "Gladiolus Rag."

2. Illustrations or restatements

Use a colon to introduce material that illustrates, explains, or restates the preceding material.

Many African instruments are made of unusual materials: pottery, shells, gourds, and beads are often used to make African percussion instruments.

The cause of the fire was obvious: children were playing with matches.

A complete sentence following a colon is generally lowercased, as in the preceding examples.

Colons Before Quotations

Use a colon to introduce a long or formal quotation. A formal quotation is often preceded by such words as *this, these, the following,* or *as follows.*

Patrick Henry's memorably eloquent speech before the Virginia Convention closed resoundingly with **the following** patriotic exclamation: "I know not what course others may take; but as for me, give me liberty or give me death!"

Quotations of more than one line of poetry and more than a few lines of prose are generally written below the introductory statement (and appear indented on the page).

Walt Whitman celebrated freedom in the following lines:

The earth expanding right hand and left hand,
The picture alive, every part in its best light,
The music falling in where it is wanted, and stopping where it is
    not wanted,
The cheerful voice of the public road, the gay fresh sentiment
    of the road.

Other Uses of Colons

Use a colon between the hour and the minute of the precise time, between the chapter and the verse in biblical references, and after the salutation of a business letter.

6:40 A.M.	Matthew 2:5
9:20 P.M.	Dear Sir or Madam:
Exodus 3:4	Dear Ford Motor Company:

Exercise 2

Using the Colon   Rewrite the following sentences correctly, adding colons where they are needed. For the sentence that does not need a colon, write *correct*. Remember that colons are not needed when a list immediately follows a verb or a preposition.

Memory Skills

1. The information that we need to remember can be classified into the following three categories things we hear, things we see, and things we read.
2. In developing memory skills, you might therefore focus on these three kinds of memory aural memory, visual memory, and memory for written material.
3. Social situations often require you to use aural memory skills at a party, for example, you will want to remember the names of people you meet.
4. Your visual memory will be important if you witness a crime or an accident a police officer may ask you to recall details about a person's appearance or a car's color, make, and license-plate number.
5. Your memory for written material will help you in such subjects as history and social studies, science, spelling, and foreign languages.
6. The following steps will help you to remember information (1) concentrate on the information, (2) repeat the information in your mind, (3) write and rewrite the information, and (4) make up a mnemonic device.
7. A mnemonic device for remembering the colors of the spectrum is the name Roy G. Biv, which stands for the following colors red, orange, yellow, green, blue, indigo, and violet.
8. By using a series of mnemonic devices, Angela memorized portions of the Bible, including Genesis 1 1–31 and Psalms 23 1–6. ➡

9. To remember the locker combination 53-7-15, you could use this mnemonic device "We often have dinner from 5 30 to 7 15."

10. Rhymes and repetition make it easy to memorize the following stanza from "The Raven," a poem by Edgar Allan Poe

> Once upon a midnight dreary, while I pondered, weak and weary,
> Over many a quaint and curious volume of forgotten lore—
> While I nodded, nearly napping, suddenly there came a tapping,
> As of someone gently rapping, rapping at my chamber door—
> " 'Tis some visitor," I muttered, "tapping at my chamber door—
> Only this and nothing more."

21.5   The Semicolon

Semicolons to Separate Main Clauses

Use a semicolon to separate main clauses that are not joined by a coordinating conjunction (*and, but, or, nor, yet,* and *for*).

> George Gershwin wrote music during the Jazz Age; his compositions were influenced by jazz.

Use a semicolon to separate main clauses joined by a conjunctive adverb (such as *however, therefore, nevertheless, moreover, furthermore,* and *consequently*) or by an expression such as *for example* or *that is.*

A comma usually follows a conjunctive adverb or an expression such as *in fact.*

> Much jazz is improvised; however, all the instruments are played in the same key.

Semicolons and Commas

Use a semicolon to separate the items in a series when these items contain commas.

> Three important jazz musicians of the twentieth century were Louis Armstrong, a trumpet player; Duke Ellington, a composer; and Sarah Vaughan, a singer.

Use a semicolon to separate two main clauses joined by a coordinating conjunction when such clauses already contain several commas.

Arthur Mitchell, as a leading dancer with the New York City Ballet, danced in such ballets as *A Midsummer Night's Dream*, *Agon*, and *Western Symphony*; but he is also famous as the founder of the Dance Theater of Harlem, an internationally acclaimed dance company.

Exercise 3

Using the Semicolon   Rewrite the following sentences correctly, adding semicolons where they are needed.

Film Successes

1. "The subjective actress thinks of clothes only as they apply to her the objective actress thinks of them only as they affect others, as a tool for the job."   —Edith Head

2. Film buffs might know that Edith Head, the famous costume designer, won eight Academy Awards for costuming such films as *All About Eve*, *Sabrina*, and *The Sting* but few probably remember that she actually appeared in a movie, *The Oscar*, in which she played herself.

3. The Beatles starred in three movies: *A Hard Day's Night*, made in 1964 *Help!* made in 1965 and *Let It Be*, made in 1970.

4. "I've never sought success in order to get fame and money it's the talent and the passion that count in success."   —Ingrid Bergman

5. Ingrid Bergman was graced with both talent and passion consequently, she made a success of her career.

6. The classic film *Casablanca* was a perfect vehicle for Bergman's talents the film also starred Humphrey Bogart, Peter Lorre, Claude Rains, Sidney Greenstreet, and Dooley Wilson.

7. The story, which unfolds in wartime Morocco, depicts Rick Blaine, the cynical American café owner Ilse Lund, a former flame and Captain Louis Renault, the head of the French police in Morocco.

8. Casablanca has become a refuge for an assortment of characters who have fled the Nazi occupation of France the characters are caught up in the intrigues of the city as they await visas to America.

9. Bogart plays Rick, whose hard-gotten cynicism is ➡

> overcome by memories of his love for Ilse (Bergman) in prewar Paris Rick helps Ilse escape with her husband.
> 10. The famous song of *Casablanca* is "As Time Goes By" the song, like the film itself, has become a favorite among film buffs.

21.6　The Comma

Commas and Compound Sentences

Use commas between the main clauses in a compound sentence.

You should use a comma before a coordinating conjunction (*and, but, or, nor, yet,* or *for*) that joins two main clauses.

> The Marx Brothers were a comedy team, but each of them did work on his own.

> Groucho Marx made wisecracks, and his brother Harpo played music.

The comma may be omitted when two very short main clauses are connected by a coordinating conjunction, unless the comma is needed to avoid confusion.

> Min prepared the meal and Ralph washed the dishes. [clear]

> Min prepared the meal and the dishes needed washing. [confusing]

> Min prepared the meal, and the dishes needed washing. [clear]

Commas in a Series

Use commas to separate three or more words, phrases, or clauses in a series.

> The television show *I Love Lucy* was clever, entertaining, and very funny.

> Langston Hughes wrote poetry, drama, movie screenplays, and popular songs.

> Charles Chaplin wrote, directed, and starred in many film comedies.

> Some movies make audiences laugh, others make them cry, and still others amaze them with dazzling special effects.

Commas are unnecessary when the items are joined by conjunctions.

Langston Hughes's poetry is insightful and expressive and powerful.

Nouns used in pairs (*spaghetti and meatballs, bacon and eggs, pen and ink*) are considered single units and should not be divided by commas. The pairs themselves must be set off from other nouns or groups of nouns in a series.

I like salt and pepper, oil and vinegar, and croutons on my salad.

Commas and Coordinate Adjectives

Place a comma between coordinate adjectives that precede a noun.

Coordinate adjectives modify the same noun to an equal degree. One way to tell whether adjectives in a sentence are coordinate is to reverse their order or put the word *and* between them. The adjectives are coordinate if the sentence still sounds natural.

Julia is a beautiful, happy, intelligent child.

A comma should not be used between adjectives preceding a noun if they sound unnatural with their order reversed or with *and* between them. Adjectives that describe size, age, shape, and material usually do not need a comma between them.

Julia wore a long wool scarf.

Exercise 4

Using the Comma (Part 1) Rewrite the following sentences correctly, adding commas where they are needed. For the one sentence that needs no commas, write *correct*.

The Tomb of Shih Huang-ti

1. Shih Huang-ti was emperor of the Ch'in Dynasty from 221 to 210 B.C. and his accomplishments had long-lasting effects on the history of China.
2. Shih Huang-ti unified the Chinese Empire oversaw construction of the Great Wall and built himself a truly magnificent tomb between 256 and 206 B.C.
3. His very extensive well-equipped funeral compound may be the greatest of his many extraordinary accomplishments.
4. The twenty-square-mile tomb was built two thousand years ago yet it was discovered only in 1974.
5. The compound consists of underground chambers filled with ceramic statues of soldiers bronze chariots and such weapons as spears and swords. ➧

6. The life-size statues number more than six thousand but no two are alike.
7. The ancient ceramic soldiers face east and are poised for battle.
8. The military formation is manned with infantrymen archers and mounted cavalry.
9. Bronze jade and gold artifacts complete the rich treasure buried with Emperor Shih Huang-ti.
10. Shih Huang-ti of Ch'in was the first emperor of the unified nation and his rule gave China its name.

Commas and Nonessential Elements

1. Participles, infinitives, and their phrases

Use commas to set off participles, infinitives, and their phrases if they are not essential to the meaning of the sentence.

> The children, excited, ripped open their presents.
> Mari made her way along the beach, jogging happily.
> I have no idea, to tell you the truth, what this really means.

You should not set off participles, infinitives, and their phrases if they are essential to the meaning of the sentence.

> The most famous documentary film directed by Robert J. Flaherty is *Nanook of the North*. [The participial phrase limits *most famous documentary* to the most famous one that Flaherty directed.]

> Flaherty made the film to show the realities of Eskimo life. [The infinitive phrase tells *why* Flaherty made the film.]

> To film *Nanook of the North* was a difficult undertaking. [The infinitive phrase is used as the subject of the sentence.]

2. Adjective clauses

Use commas to set off a nonessential adjective clause.

A nonessential (nonrestrictive) clause gives additional information about a noun. Because it does not change, but adds to, the meaning of a sentence, it is set off with commas.

> My cousin Ken, who lives in California, works as a film editor.
> [*Who lives in California* is a nonessential clause.]

Avoid using commas in an essential adjective clause. Because an essential (restrictive) clause provides information about a noun, it is needed to convey the precise meaning of the sentence.

The person who actually films a movie is called the camera operator. [*Who actually films a movie* is an essential clause.]

3. Appositives

Use commas to set off an appositive if it is not essential to the meaning of a sentence.

A nonessential (nonrestrictive) appositive can be considered an *extra* appositive and therefore needs commas.

James Wong Howe, a famous camera operator, was born in China.

Howe first worked for Cecil B. De Mille, a director of many Hollywood films.

A nonessential appositive is sometimes positioned before the word to which it refers.

A camera operator for Cecil B. De Mille, James Wong Howe was an important talent in the film industry. [The appositive, *A camera operator for Cecil B. De Mille*, precedes the subject of the sentence, *James Wong Howe*.]

An essential (restrictive) appositive provides necessary information about a noun and is therefore not set off with commas.

James Wong Howe operated the camera for Martin Ritt's film *The Molly Maguires*. [If a comma were placed before the essential appositive, *The Molly Maguires*, the sentence would imply that this was Ritt's only film.]

Commas with Interjections, Parenthetical Expressions, and Conjunctive Adverbs

Use commas to set off interjections (such as *oh* and *well*), parenthetical expressions (such as *on the contrary, on the other hand, in fact, by the way, for example,* and *after all*), and adverbs and conjunctive adverbs (such as *however, moreover,* and *consequently*).

Indeed, director Francis Ford Coppola is also a scriptwriter. He wrote the screenplay for *Patton*, for example.

Coppola is a highly talented director; consequently, he won an Academy Award for directing *The Godfather*.

In fact, Coppola comes from an artistic family.

Talia Shire is Francis Ford Coppola's sister; moreover, she is a talented actress.

Using the Comma (Part 2)   Rewrite the following sentences correctly, adding commas where they are needed. For the one sentence that needs no commas, write *correct*.

Citizen Kane, a Movie Classic

1. Orson Welles's film *Citizen Kane* won only one Academy Award; nevertheless it is now considered one of the finest movies ever made.
2. In fact few American films have been as influential as *Citizen Kane*.
3. The film directed by and starring Orson Welles has a newsreel quality that makes it seem very realistic.
4. The movie which traces the life of a rich and powerful man has had a stormy history to say the least.
5. Some of those criticizing the film thought that Welles had insulted the powerful newspaper publisher William Randolph Hearst.
6. The character Kane played by Orson Welles had many things in common with Hearst.
7. For instance Kane built a great mansion Xanadu just as Hearst built a great mansion San Simeon.
8. Indeed Orson Welles was severely criticized by those people who felt that he had exposed their private lives in order to make his film.
9. On the other hand in 1970 Welles was publicly celebrated as one of the greatest American directors in the history of motion pictures.
10. He also received a special Oscar which was given to him for his outstanding achievements in the film industry.

Commas and Introductory Phrases

1. Prepositional phrases

Use a comma after a short introductory prepositional phrase only if the sentence would be misread without the comma.

> During the winter, snowstorms are common in New England.
> [The comma is needed to prevent misreading.]

> In the distance we saw Mount Washington. [comma not needed]

Use a comma after a long prepositional phrase or after the final phrase in a succession of phrases.

> On the rug by the fireplace, a large dog slept.

A comma is not used if the phrase is immediately followed by a verb.

> On the dresser lay an ivory mirror.

2. Participles and participial phrases

Use commas to set off introductory participles and participial phrases.

> Smiling, I watched Whoopi Goldberg's award-winning performance in the film *Ghost*.

> Beginning as a comic actress, Sally Field graduated to more serious roles.

Commas and Adverb Clauses

Use commas to set off all introductory adverb clauses.

Use commas to set off internal adverb clauses that interrupt the flow of a sentence.

> Although Stanley Kubrick is an American director, he lives and works in Great Britain.

> Denzel Washington, before he became a movie star, appeared in the television series *St. Elsewhere*.

In general, set off an adverb clause at the end of a sentence only if the clause is parenthetical or the sentence would be misread without the comma.

> Ingmar Bergman worked in the theater before he began his career as a film director.

Commas and Antithetical Phrases

Use commas to set off an antithetical phrase.

An **antithetical phrase** uses a word such as *not* or *unlike* to make a contrast.

> Augusta, not Bangor, is the capital of Maine.
> Unlike Kansas, Colorado is very mountainous.

Exercise 6

Using the Comma (Part 3) Read the ten sentences on the following page. Then rewrite the sentences correctly, adding commas where they are needed. If a sentence is correct, write *correct*. ➡

1. Unlike most singers Alberta Hunter turned to a career in music late in life.
2. Retiring from the nursing profession at the age of eighty-two Hunter decided that she would start a new career—as a singer.
3. Hunter had not sung since she was young.
4. With a voice rich in expression Hunter soon became a popular singer.
5. Singing in New York City Hunter was able to fulfill one of her dreams.
6. Hunter because she knew many languages could sing almost anything.
7. She sang French songs when her audience was French.
8. Because she sang the blues so well many audiences requested blues numbers.
9. In each song lyrics and tone blended for a powerful rendition.
10. Although Hunter knew many languages she never learned to read music.

Commas with Titles, Addresses, and Numbers

1. Titles of people

Use commas to set off titles when they follow a person's name.

Henry VIII, king of England, was a songwriter and musician.

2. Addresses, geographical terms, and dates

Use commas to separate the various parts of an address, a geographical term, or a date.

The company is located at 840 Pierce Street, Friendswood, Texas 77546, and has another office in Lansing, Michigan.

Paris, France, is the setting of some of Hemingway's works.

On Friday, October 12, 1492, Christopher Columbus landed on the New World island now called San Salvador.

A comma is not used when only the month and the day or the month and the year are given.

In July 1776 the Declaration of Independence was signed.

The signing of the Declaration of Independence on July 4 is celebrated every year.

3. References

Use commas to set off the parts of a reference that direct the reader to the exact source.

> The theme is expressed in *The Scarlet Letter,* pages 3–4.

> We performed Act I, Scene i, of William Shakespeare's *Julius Caesar.*

Commas and Direct Address

Use commas to set off words or names used in direct address.

> Mona, can you meet me this afternoon?
> You, my dear, are leaving at once.
> Thank you for the book, Mrs. Gomez.

Commas and Tag Questions

Use commas to set off a tag question.

> By using a tag question such as *have you?* or *shouldn't I?* you emphasize an implied answer to the statement that precedes it.

> *Bye Bye Birdie* starred Chita Rivera, didn't it?

> Chita Rivera was not in the film version of *Bye Bye Birdie,* was she?

Commas in Letter Writing

Place a comma after the salutation of an informal letter and after the closing of all letters.

> Dear Mario,
> Dear Cousin Agnes,

> Yours truly,
> Best wishes,

Use the following style for the heading of a letter:

> 23 Silver Lake Road
> Sharon, Connecticut 06069
> February 15, 1992

Misuse of Commas

> Do not use a comma before a conjunction that connects the parts of a compound predicate when there are only two parts.

INCORRECT	Our school never wins the championship, but every year has a spectacular losers' party.
CORRECT	Our school never wins the championship but every year has a spectacular losers' party.

Do not use a comma alone to join two main clauses that are not part of a series. Such a sentence punctuated with a comma alone is called a *run-on sentence* (or a *comma splice* or a *comma fault*). To avoid making this error, use a coordinating conjunction with the comma, or use a semicolon.

INCORRECT	The navigator Juan Rodríguez Cabrillo sighted land in 1542, the history of modern California began.
CORRECT	The navigator Juan Rodríguez Cabrillo sighted land in 1542, **and** the history of modern California began.
CORRECT	The navigator Juan Rodríguez Cabrillo sighted land in 1542; the history of modern California began.

Never use a comma between a subject and its verb or between a verb and its complement.

INCORRECT	What she considered an easy ballet step to master, was quite difficult for me.
CORRECT	What she considered an easy ballet step to master was quite difficult for me.
INCORRECT	Popular tourist attractions in Florida include, Disney World, Palm Beach, and the Everglades.
CORRECT	Popular tourist attractions in Florida include Disney World, Palm Beach, and the Everglades.

Exercise 7

Using the Comma (Part 4)   Rewrite the following letter, adding commas where they are needed or removing them where necessary. (Twenty corrections are needed altogether.)

> 4615 Oak Street
> Kansas City Missouri, 64101
> January 2 1992

Dear Kim

   Happy New Year Kim! We haven't spoken on the phone for some time have we? I am enclosing an article about American colleges that appeared in the Sunday December 30 1991 issue of the *Kansas City Star*. You still haven't decided on a college have you? ➡

I've been looking through the college catalogs at the local library. Mrs. Hom the head librarian was a big help. Colleges I'm thinking of applying to include, Hood College in Frederick Maryland; Kansas State University; and the University of Texas.

The enclosed article contains recent, concise information, and so should prove useful to you. Wouldn't it be nice if we could go to the same college Kim? It's been three years since you moved to Winchester Virginia and left Kansas City. I hope to hear from you soon Kim.

Your friend
Maureen

21.7 The Dash

In typed material a dash is indicated by two hyphens (--). A comma, semicolon, colon, or period should not be placed before or after a dash.

Dashes to Signal Change

Use a dash to indicate an abrupt break or change in thought within a sentence.

"I think the answer is—I've forgotten what I was going to say."

Dashes to Emphasize

Use a dash to set off and emphasize supplemental information or parenthetical comments.

Yellowstone Park's geyser Old Faithful has erupted faithfully—every hour on the hour—for over eighty years.

21.8 Parentheses

Use parentheses to set off supplemental material.

Supplemental material may also be set off by commas and dashes. The difference between the three marks is one of degree. Use commas to set off material that is closely related to the rest of the sentence. Use parentheses to set off material that is not intended to be part of the main statement. Use dashes for emphasis or for material that abruptly interrupts the sentence.

Mary Jane Canary ("Calamity Jane") knew Wild Bill Hickok.

Do not capitalize or add end punctuation to a complete sentence within parentheses if the parenthetical material is contained within another sentence. If a sentence in parentheses stands by itself, both a capital letter and end punctuation are necessary.

> Mary Jane Canary (she was known as Calamity Jane) was a good friend of Wild Bill Hickok's.

> Paul Bunyan is a famous figure in American folklore. (You can learn all about him if you visit the Paul Bunyan Center in Minnesota.)

Parentheses with Other Marks of Punctuation

1. With a comma, semicolon, or colon

Always place a comma, semicolon, or colon *after* the closing parenthesis.

> The writer Bret Harte is associated with the West (his stories include "The Outcasts of Poker Flat" and "The Luck of Roaring Camp"), but this celebrated American author was actually born in Albany, New York.

2. With a period, question mark, or exclamation point

Place a period, a question mark, or an exclamation point *inside* the parentheses if it is part of the parenthetical expression.

> The most famous guide of the Lewis and Clark expedition was Sacajawea. (A novel based on her life was published recently.)

> Owatonna is the name of a Native American princess (a member of the Santee tribe?) who lived hundreds of years ago.

Place a period, a question mark, or an exclamation point *outside* the parentheses if it is part of the entire sentence.

> The code of laws that governed Iroquois society was the Great Binding Law (known as the Iroquois Constitution).

> How surprised I was to learn that the British still call corn *maize* (which comes from the West Indian word for *corn*)!

Exercise 8

Using the Dash and Parentheses   Rewrite the following sentences correctly, adding dashes and parentheses where they are needed. Use the marks of punctuation indicated in parentheses at the end of each sentence. ➡

> ### *American Writers*
>
> 1. Because the novelist Louise Erdrich had supportive parents they encouraged her reading and writing endeavors, she knew at an early age that she wanted to be a writer. (parentheses)
> 2. The gifted writer F. Scott Fitzgerald 1896–1940 wrote the screenplays for several Hollywood films. Did you know that he never liked to publicize this fact? (two sets of parentheses)
> 3. Stephen Crane the author of *The Red Badge of Courage* was once shipwrecked while traveling from the United States to Cuba. What an adventurous life he led! (dashes and parentheses)
> 4. The Chilean poet Gabriela Mistral her real name was Lucila Godoy Alcayaga won the Nobel Prize for literature in 1945. (parentheses)
> 5. I consider the *Narrative of the Life of Frederick Douglass* and I gave this much thought to be one of the most compelling autobiographies I have ever read. (dashes)

21.9 Brackets

Use brackets to enclose information that you insert into a quotation from someones else's work in order to clarify the quotation.

> We cannot be free until they [all Americans] are.
> —James Baldwin

Use brackets to enclose a parenthetical phrase that already appears within parentheses.

> The name Oregon comes from the Algonquian word *wauregan* (which means "beautiful water" [referring to the Columbia River]).

21.10 Ellipsis Points

Use a series of three spaced points, called **ellipsis points,** to indicate the omission of material from a quotation.

Use three spaced points if the omission occurs at the beginning of a sentence. If the omission occurs in the middle or at the end of a sentence, use any necessary punctuation (for example, a comma, a semicolon, or a period) plus the three spaced points. When it is necessary to use a period, do not leave any space between the last word before the omission and the first point, which is the period.

> "I wanted to live deep and suck out all the marrow of life. . . ."
>
> —Henry David Thoreau

21.11   Quotation Marks

Quotation Marks for Direct Quotations

Use quotation marks to enclose a direct quotation.

Place quotation marks around the quoted material *only*, not around introductory or explanatory remarks. Such remarks are generally separated from the actual quotation with a comma.

> "Weave us a garment of brightness," states a Native American song.

> Phil Rizzuto, in an observation famous for its optimism, said, "They still can't steal first base."

When a quotation is interrupted by explanatory words such as *he said* or *she wrote*, use two sets of quotation marks.

Two marks of punctuation, such as two commas or a comma and a period should be used to separate each part of the quotation from the interrupting phrase. If the second part of the quotation is a complete sentence, it should begin with a capital letter.

> "Genius," said the great inventor Thomas A. Edison, "is one percent inspiration and ninety-nine percent perspiration."

> "The Lord prefers common-looking people," Abraham Lincoln once said. "That is the reason he made so many of them."

You should not use quotation marks in an indirect quotation (a quotation that does not repeat a person's exact words).

ORIGINAL QUOTATION	Toni Morrison said, "I wrote my first novel because I wanted to read it."
INDIRECT QUOTATION	Toni Morrison said that she wrote her first novel because she wanted to read it.

Use single quotation marks around a quotation within a quotation.

> In speaking to her students, the teacher said, "Benjamin Franklin once wrote 'Lose no time; be always employed in something useful.'"

In writing dialogue, begin a new paragraph and use a new set of quotation marks every time the speaker changes.

> "Are you going to pass this collection of abalone shells on to your children?" I said.
>
> "No," he said. "I want my children to collect for themselves. I wouldn't give it to them."
>
> "Why?" I said. "When you die?"
>
> Mr. Abe shook his head. "No. Not even when I die," he said. "I couldn't give the children what I see in these shells. The children must go out for themselves and find their own shells."
>
> —Toshio Mori

Quotation Marks with Titles of Short Works

Use quotation marks to enclose titles of short works, such as short stories, short poems, essays, newspaper and magazine articles, book chapters, songs, and single episodes of a television series.

> "Abalone, Abalone, Abalone" [short story]
> "Dream Variations" [poem]
> "A Chicano in China" [essay]
> "The Third Side" [newspaper article]
> "Ahab" [chapter]
> "The Star-Spangled Banner" [song]

Quotation Marks with Unusual Expressions

Use quotation marks to enclose unfamiliar slang and other unusual or original expressions.

> A once-popular expression was "zounds."

Quotation Marks with Definitions

Use quotation marks to enclose a definition that is stated directly.

> *Ukelele* comes from the Hawaiian word for "flea."

Quotation Marks with Other Marks of Punctuation

1. With a comma or a period

Always place a comma or a period *inside* closing quotation marks.

> "Literature is a state of culture," Juan Ramón Jiménez said; "poetry is a state of grace."

2. With a semicolon or a colon

Always place a semicolon or a colon *outside* closing quotation marks.

> Chuck Berry wrote "Johnny B. Goode"; the song was one of the first examples of rock-and-roll music.

> There is only one main character in Ernest Hemingway's short story "Big Two-Hearted River": Nick Adams.

3. With a question mark or an exclamation point

Place the question mark or exclamation point *inside* the closing quotation marks when it is part of the quotation.

> We read Leonard Bernstein's essay "What Makes Music American?"

> Walt Whitman's poem "Beat! Beat! Drums!" is about the Civil War.

Place the question mark or exclamation point outside the closing quotation marks when it is part of the entire sentence.

> Have you read Gwendolyn Brooks's poem "We Real Cool"?
> How I adore old Cole Porter songs like "Anything Goes"!

When the sentence, as well as the quotation at the end of the sentence, needs a question mark (or an exclamation point), use only one question mark (or exclamation point), and place it inside the closing quotation marks.

> What was the name of the French poet who asked, "Where are the snows of yesteryear?"

Exercise 9

Using Quotation Marks Rewrite the following sentences correctly, adding quotation marks where they are needed. For the sentences that need no changes, write *correct*.

General Colin Powell

1. I have been reading about General Colin Powell in preparation for a newspaper article I am writing entitled What Makes a Great Military Mind?
2. My sources tell me that General Powell was born in New York City and graduated from the City College of New York in 1958.
3. My parents, Powell reportedly stated, expected their children to do something with their lives. →

4. Powell has said that he enrolled in the Reserve Officers' Training Corps while he was in college because he felt comfortable with military discipline and had learned to take advantage of any attractive opportunities that came his way.

5. One of Powell's classmates recalled, He displayed rare leadership ability on campus; another said, He motivated many other students to succeed.

6. Over the years Powell completed various tours abroad, won eleven medals for his service in Vietnam, and served as a senior military assistant in Washington, D.C., where one of his associates said of him: He is more of an expediter than a global thinker.

7. Many years later General Powell relinquished command of the Fifth Corps, a seventy-two-thousand-troop force stationed in West Germany, to serve in the White House. I'm a serviceman, a soldier, he explained, and it looked like my service might be of greater use here.

8. As chairman of the National Security Council's policy review group, one of Powell's responsibilities was to turn down what he termed pet rocks, those wild plans that had little chance of approval at higher levels.

9. In 1989, before becoming the first African-American chairman of the Joint Chiefs of Staff, Powell reportedly said, I remember those who suffered and sacrificed to create the conditions and set the stage for me.

10. The word *ideology* means the set of doctrines or opinions of a person or group. A close friend of Powell's once said, He has almost no ideology, unless belief in country and public service qualify as ideology.

21.12   Italics (Underlining)

Italic type is a special type that slants upward and to the right. (*This is printed in italics.*) When typing or writing by hand, indicate italics by underlining. (This is underlined.)

Italics for Titles

Italicize (underline) titles of books, lengthy poems, plays, films and television series, paintings and sculptures, long musical compositions, and court cases. Also italicize the names of newspapers and magazines, ships, trains, airplanes, and spacecraft.

The Invisible Man [novel]
Leaves of Grass [long poem]
A Raisin in the Sun [play]
Casablanca [film]
Nature [television series]
Christina's World [painting]
David [sculpture]
Billy the Kid [ballet]
Brown v. Board of Education of Topeka Kansas [court case]
St. Louis Post-Dispatch [newspaper]
Psychology Today [magazine]
U.S.S. *Intrepid* [ship]*
City of New Orleans [train]
Spruce Goose [airplane]
Apollo 9 [spacecraft]

* Do not italicize abbreviations such as U.S.S. in the name of a ship.

Italicize (underline) and capitalize articles (*a, an, the*) written at the beginning of a title only when they are part of the title itself. It is common practice not to italicize (underline) the article preceding the title of a newspaper or a magazine. Do not italicize the word *magazine* unless it is part of the title of a periodical.

The Color Purple	but	the *Arabian Nights*
A Night at the Opera		a *Business Week* reporter
The Scarlet Letter		the *New Yorker* magazine

Do not italicize the apostrophe and -*s* in the possessive of italicized titles.

*Time***'s** editorial
*Macbeth***'s** plot

Italics with Foreign Words

Italicize (underline) foreign words and expressions that are not used frequently in English.

Such words are not italicized if they are commonly used in English.

James always says **hasta la vista** when he departs.
The health spa offers courses in **judo** and **karate**.

Italics with Words and Other Items Used to Represent Themselves

Italicize (underline) words, letters, and numerals used to represent themselves.

To make your essays read more smoothly, connect ideas with conjunctive adverbs such as **therefore** and **however.**

The **t** and the **v** sometimes stick on this typewriter.

There is no **9** in my phone number.

Should I use the dollar sign (**$**) or spell out the word?

Exercise 10

Using Italics   Rewrite the following sentences correctly, underlining the parts that should be italicized.

Award-Winning Achievers

1. According to books like The World Almanac and magazines like Time and U.S. News & World Report, high achievers in many fields are often recognized by well-known awards.
2. The American composer Samuel Barber twice won Pulitzer Prizes—in 1958 for the opera Vanessa and in 1963 for his piano concerto.
3. In 1984 Haing S. Ngor won an Academy Award for best supporting actor for his role in the film The Killing Fields.
4. A person might use the word impressive to describe Michael Jackson's achievement at the 1983 Grammys, where he won awards for both best record of the year and best album of the year.
5. The actress Ruth Brown won Broadway's Tony Award for best actress for her part in the 1989 hit musical play Black and Blue.
6. Soon after the spacecraft Apollo 11 returned from the moon in l969, Neil Armstrong, Edwin "Buzz" Aldrin, and Michael Collins were awarded the Presidential Medal of Freedom by President Richard M. Nixon.
7. After several of her books were published to great acclaim, Toni Morrison's Beloved won a Pulitzer Prize for fiction in 1987.
8. The award-winning French chef Julia Child ended each of her television broadcasts by looking into the camera and cheerfully saying bon appétit.
9. The poet Juan Ramón Jiménez, winner of the Nobel Prize for literature in 1956, published his most famous volume of prose poems, Platero and I, in 1914.
10. In 1984 Love Medicine, the first novel by Louise Erdrich, won the National Book Critics Circle Award for fiction.

21.13 The Apostrophe

Apostrophes with Possessives

1. Pronouns

Use an apostrophe and -*s* for the possessive of a singular indefinite pronoun.

Do not use an apostrophe with any other possessive pronouns.

no one**'s** business	*but*	**its** engine
each other**'s** books		the car is **hers**

2. Singular Nouns

Use an apostrophe and -*s* to form the possessive of a singular noun, even one that ends in -*s*.

the child**'s** toy	Peru**'s** mountains
the bus**'s** muffler	Ray Charles**'s** music
The duchess**'s** problem	Wallace Stevens**'s** poetry
the lynx**'s** habitat	Mr. Lax**'s** accounts

This rule does have some exceptions, however. For example, to form the possessive of ancient proper nouns that end in -*es* or -*is*, the name *Jesus*, and expressions with words such as *appearance* and *conscience*, add an apostrophe only.

Ulysses**'** journey	Jesus**'** life
Iris**'** apple of discord	for appearance**'** sake

3. Plural nouns ending in -*s*

Use an apostrophe alone to form the possessive of a plural noun that ends in -*s*.

the Girl Scouts**'** badges
the Hugheses**'** vacation
the teachers**'** cafeteria
the tennis rackets**'** strings

4. Plural nouns not ending in -*s*

Use an apostrophe and -*s* to form the possessive of a plural noun that does not end in -*s*.

the children**'s** surprise	his feet**'s** arches
the women**'s** decision	her teeth**'s** crowns

5. Compound nouns

Put only the last word of a compound noun in the possessive form.

> my great-grandfather**'s** watch
> her brother-in-law**'s** family
> the foster child**'s** happiness
> my fellow employees**'** offices

6. Joint possession versus individual possession

If two or more persons (or partners in a company) possess something jointly, use the possessive form for the last person named.

> my father and mother**'s** house
> Lerner and Loewe**'s** musicals
> Lord and Taylor**'s** department store
> Greene, Jones, and Smith**'s** firm

If two or more persons (or companies) possess an item (or items) individually, put each one's name in the possessive form.

> Julio**'s** and Betty**'s** test scores
> the Murphys**'** and the Ramirezes**'** houses
> J. C. Penney**'s** and Kmart**'s** prices

7. Expressions of time and money

Use a possessive form to express amounts of money or time that modify a noun.

You can also express the modifier as a hyphenated adjective. In that case the possessive form is not used.

two hours**'** drive	*but*	a two-hour drive
eighty cents**'** worth		an eighty-cent loaf
five miles**'** walk		a five-mile walk

Apostrophes in Contractions

Use an apostrophe in place of letters omitted in contractions.

A **contraction** is one word that is formed when two words are combined and some letters are omitted. In general, contractions are formed from a pronoun and a verb or a verb and an adverb.

I**'**ve	*formed from*	I have
I**'**d		I had, I would
she**'**ll		she will
he**'**d		he had, he would
can**'**t		cannot

Use an apostrophe in place of the omitted numerals of a particular year.

the **'**92 election results
the summer of **'**62

Apostrophes with Special Plurals

Use an apostrophe and *-s* to form the plural of letters, numerals, symbols, and words used to represent themselves.

Do not italicize the apostrophe or the *-s*. Only the letter, numeral, symbol, or word should be italicized (underlined).

Cross your *t*'**s** and dot your *i*'**s**.
Please be sure to write *and*'**s** instead of *&*'**s**.
I typed *5*'**s** instead of *6*'**s**.

Do not use an apostrophe (or italics) in the plural of dates.

F. Scott Fitzgerald set many of his novels in the 1920s.
The 1990s are proving to be an exciting decade.
The Industrial Revolution began in the 1700s.

Exercise 11

Using the Apostrophe Rewrite the following sentences correctly, adding apostrophes where they are needed. For the one sentence that needs no changes, write *correct.*

Ishi and the Yanas

1. I looked under the *Is* in the encyclopedia to find out about Ishi, the last Stone Age man known to have lived in North America.
2. Ishi was introduced to civilizations wonders by Professor Waterman.
3. Waterman first learned of the mans existence from one of San Franciscos newspapers.
4. The story attracted Waterman because of its human drama.
5. Ishi was a member of the Yanas, a tribe of Native Americans who had lived in California and practiced their ancestors way of life.
6. The Yanas tragedy began in the 1840s, when the white settlers desire for gold overshadowed all else.
7. With Californias gold rush many people moved into the Yanas territory.
8. Theres no need to exaggerate the impact this migration had on the Yanas and other tribes existence. ➡

9. The foreigners desire to take over the land drove away the Yanas.
10. The Yanas culture was practically destroyed in one years time.

21.14   The Hyphen

Hyphens with Prefixes

Usually hyphens are not used to join a prefix to a word. Some exceptions are described below.

Use a hyphen after any prefix joined to a proper noun or a proper adjective. Use a hyphen after the prefixes *all-*, *ex-* (meaning "former"), and *self-* joined to any noun or adjective.

pre-Raphaelite   ex-senator
all-purpose   self-sealing

Use a hyphen after the prefix *anti-* when it joins a word beginning with *i-*. Also use a hyphen after the prefix *vice-*, except in *vice president*.

anti-inflammatory   vice-consul

Use a hyphen to avoid confusion between words beginning with *re-* that look alike but are different in meaning and pronunciation.

re-cover the sofa   *but*   recover a lost watch

Hyphens in Compound Adjectives

Use a hyphen in a compound adjective that precedes a noun.

A compound adjective that follows a noun is generally not hyphenated.

a plum-colored shirt   *but*   The shirt was plum colored.

Compound adjectives beginning with *well*, *ill*, or *little* are usually not hyphenated when they are modified by an adverb.

an ill-tempered man   *but*   a rather ill tempered man

Do not hyphenate an expression when it is made up of an adverb ending in *-ly* and an adjective.

a badly torn blanket   a superbly modeled sculpture

Hyphens in Numbers

1. Compound numbers

Hyphenate any spelled-out cardinal or ordinal compound number up to ninety-nine or ninety-ninth.

twenty-seven	twenty-ninth
fifty-eight	thirty-second

2. Fractions used as adjectives

Hyphenate a fraction used as an adjective (but not one used as a noun).

a one-eighth portion	*but*	one eighth of the pie
a two-thirds majority		two thirds of the population

3. Connected numerals

Hyphenate two numerals to indicate a span.

1899-1968
pages 151-218

When you use the word *from* before a span, use *to* rather than a hyphen. When you use *between* before a span, use *and*.

from 1899 **to** 1968
between 2:45 **and** 3:15 P.M.

Hyphens to Divide Words at the End of a Line

If a word must be divided at the end of a line, divide it between syllables or pronounceable parts. When you are unsure of where to divide a word, check a dictionary.

In general, if a word contains two consonants occurring between two vowels or if it contains a double consonant, divide the word between the two consonants.

con-sonant	pul-ley
per-tinent	scis-sors
com-pete	bar-rel

If a suffix has been added to a complete word that ends in two consonants, divide the word after the two consonants.

dull-est	steward-ship
reck-less	fill-ing
lush-ness	small-ish

Using the Hyphen Rewrite the following sentences, adding hyphens wherever they are needed. If a sentence is correct, write *correct*. Then make a list of all the italicized words, not including the book title, and show where each would be divided if it had to be broken at the end of a line.

Ancient African Civilizations

1. Motivated by antiEgyptian feeling, the people of Kush conquered Egypt around 800 B.C. and emerged as a newly *powerful* African empire.
2. During its seven century reign as a great power, the *Kushite* Empire based its wealth on ironworking.
3. Around A.D. 1000 in the interior sections of Africa, where few nonAfricans dared travel, there existed rising empires, large towns, and *intricate* trading systems.
4. Axum, another ancient African kingdom, was Christianized by fourth century missionaries; this event was the origin of the Coptic *Christian* Church.
5. Axum's farmers *practiced* terracing and irrigation, and its very well trained artisans carved great churches out of solid stone mountains.
6. *According* to an eleventh century Arabic scholar, the kings of the vast empire of Ghana defended their self interests with a vast army.
7. Well trained ironworkers, the Ghanaians *controlled* vast areas of West Africa for almost ten centuries.
8. Mansa Musa, who headed the *kingdom* of Mali for twenty five years, could never be accused of anti intellectualism—he established universities.
9. Fabulously wealthy, this much discussed king *embarked* on a pilgrimage to Mecca in 1324 with sixty thousand followers and more than eighty camels loaded with gold dust.
10. These little known facts, and others about the African empire of Songhay, can be found on pages 75 96 of *Understanding Africa* by E. Jefferson Murphy.

21.15   Abbreviations

Use **abbreviations,** or shortened forms of words, to save space and time and to avoid wordiness. A period follows many abbreviations. Check your dictionary for guidance on how to write a particular abbreviation.

Use only one period if an abbreviation occurs at the end of a sentence that would ordinarily take a period of its own.

If an abbreviation occurs at the end of a sentence that ends with a question mark or an exclamation point, use the period *and* the second mark of punctuation.

> He awoke at 5:00 **A.M.**
> Did he awake at 5:00 **A.M.?**

Capitalization of Abbreviations

Capitalize abbreviations of proper nouns.

Thurs.	**U.S.** Army
U.S.A.	**P.O.** Box 43

Many abbreviations of organizations and government agencies are formed by using the initial letters of the complete name. Most of these abbreviations do not take periods.

UN	RCA
NASA	IRS
ABC	NBA

When abbreviating a person's first and middle names, leave a space after each initial.

> Robert **E.** Lee   **W. H.** Auden

The following abbreviations related to historical dates and times should be capitalized:

A.D. (*anno Domini*), "in the year of the Lord" (since the birth of Christ); place before the date: **A.D.** 67

B.C. (before Christ); place after the date: 500 **B.C.**

B.C.E. (before the common era); place after the date: 1000 **B.C.E.**

C.E. (common era); place after the date: 60 **C.E.**

A.M. (*ante meridiem*), "before noon"

P.M. (*post meridiem*), "after noon"

Abbreviations of Titles of People

Use abbreviations for some personal titles.

Among the titles that are generally abbreviated are *Mrs.*, *Mr.*, and *Jr.* Professional and academic titles, including *Dr.*, *M.D.*, and *Ph.D.*, are almost always abbreviated. When used before a full name, the titles of government and military officials and members of the clergy are also usually abbreviated.

Mr. Ralph Bunche   Lydia Stryk, **Ph.D.**

Mrs. William Buckley   **Dr.** Jonas Salk

Victoria Proudfoot, **M.D.**   Douglas Fairbanks **Jr.**

Michael Marder, **D.D.S.**   Paul Chin, **D.V.M.**

Abbreviations of Units of Measure

Abbreviate units of measure used with numerals in technical or scientific writing but not in ordinary prose.

The abbreviations below stand for plural as well as singular units:

ENGLISH SYSTEM		METRIC SYSTEM	
ft.	foot	**cg**	centigram
gal.	gallon	**cl**	centiliter
in.	inch	**cm**	centimeter
lb.	pound	**g**	gram
mi.	mile	**kg**	kilogram
oz.	ounce	**km**	kilometer
pt.	pint	**l**	liter
qt.	quart	**m**	meter
tbsp.	tablespoon	**mg**	milligram
tsp.	teaspoon	**ml**	milliliter
yd.	yard	**mm**	millimeter

Exercise 13

Using Abbreviations   Write the abbreviations for the italicized words or phrases in the following sentences. Note that in some instances when abbreviations are used, the definite article preceding the name or title is dropped. In this exercise definite articles that are to be dropped appear in italics.

1. Does the Amtrak train to New York leave Cleveland at 2:00 *ante meridiem*?
2. Bernice's car took fifteen *gallons* of gasoline.
3. As the cold war draws to a close, many observers believe that *the North Atlantic Treaty Organization* will have to alter its goals.
4. The poet Sappho was born in the year 612 *before Christ*.
5. *Thomas Stearns* Eliot was the author of "The Love Song of J. Alfred Prufrock."
6. Last week *Doctor* Maria Feliciano announced the engagement of her daughter, Sofia, to *the Reverend* Julio Gomez. ➡

7. In 1965 *the United Nations International Children's Emergency Fund* won the Nobel Peace Prize.
8. Christopher Columbus landed in the New World in *anno Domini* 1492.
9. The *Federal Bureau of Investigation* is part of the United States Department of Justice.
10. Yuki ran ten *kilometers* in record time.

21.16   Numbers and Numerals

In everyday writing, some numbers are spelled out and others are expressed in figures. Numbers expressed in figures are called *numerals*.

Numbers Spelled Out

In general, spell out cardinal and ordinal numbers that can be written in one or two words.

Spell out any number that occurs at the beginning of a sentence.

Two hundred twenty singers performed.

Numerals

In general, use numerals to express numbers that would be written in more than two words.

There were **220** singers in the chorus.

Write large numbers as numerals followed by *million* or *billion*.

The area of Canada is roughly **2.85 million** square miles.

If related numbers appear in the same sentence and some can be written out while others should appear as numerals, use all numerals.

The number of women runners in the local marathon increased from **55** to **429** within a few years.

1. Money, decimals, and percentages

Use numerals to express amounts of money, decimals, and percentages.

She owed me **$2.75**.
The bottle holds **1.5** quarts of liquid.
The bank paid **8** percent interest.

When an amount of money can be expressed in a word or two, it should be spelled out.

forty-four cents   **twenty-two thousand** dollars

2. Dates and time

Use numerals to express the year and day in a date and to express the precise time with the abbreviations A.M. and P.M.

Newfoundland became Canada's tenth province on March **31, 1949.**

The movie was scheduled to begin at **7:05 P.M.**

Spell out expressions of time that do not use the abbreviation A.M. or P.M.

The film starts at **seven** o'clock.

To express a century when the word *century* is used, spell out the number. Likewise, to express a decade when the century is clear from the context, spell out the number.

The **twentieth century** saw the beginnings of rock-and-roll music in the **fifties.**

When a century and a decade are expressed as a single unit, use numerals followed by an -*s*.

The baby boom reached its peak in the **1950s.**

3. Addresses

Use numerals for streets and avenues numbered above ten and for all house, apartment, and room numbers. Spell out numbered streets and avenues with numbers of ten or under.

The office is near **Fifth** Avenue, at **4** West **34th** Street, Room **9.**

Exercise 14

Using Numbers and Numerals   Write out the following sentences, making any necessary changes in the use of numbers and numerals.

American Women Champions

[1]Since the advent of television, America's female athletes have been followed regularly by audiences of as many as fifty million viewers. [2]You can find some interesting statistics on female athletes in *For the Record: Women in Sports*, published in nineteen eighty-five by World Almanac Publications, two hundred Park Avenue, New York, New York. [3]You will learn, ➡

for example, that the ancient Olympics began in Athens, Greece, in the 8th century B.C., whereas the modern Olympics began in Athens in the 1890s; women began competing only in nineteen twelve. [4]The United States record holder in the international figure-skating competition, Carol Heiss, collected 5 world championships and a gold medal; she was runner-up or United States champion for 8 successive years. [5]The 1st African-American gymnast to win a national championship was Dianne Durham of Gary, Indiana (population one hundred forty-three thousand), who accomplished the feat in nineteen eighty-three. [6]Mary Lou Retton, the popular American gymnast, not only achieved 2 perfect scores on 2 successive vaults at the 1984 Olympics in Los Angeles but also won the gold medal for all-around performance. [7].06 of a second behind teammate Evelyn Ashford, sprinter Chandra Cheeseborough finished 6th in the 100-meter dash in the nineteen seventy-six Montreal Olympics. [8]At the Los Angeles games Cheeseborough broke her own previous national record for running 400 meters, coming in at forty-nine and five tenths seconds; yet she was still beaten by her teammate Valerie Brisco-Hooks. [9]At the 1988 Calgary Olympics speed skater Bonnie Blair set a new world's record of thirty-nine and one-tenth seconds for the 500-meter race.

Mechanics Workshop

Punctuation

Best known for her novels, Mary McCarthy was also a fine travel writer, as the following excerpt from *The Stones of Florence* shows. In this passage from the book, which has been annotated to show the kinds of punctuation covered in this unit, McCarthy gives us a deft sketch of one of Italy's most celebrated cities.

Literature Model

from THE STONES OF FLORENCE
by Mary McCarthy

Quotation marks to enclose a direct quotation

Question mark to indicate a direct question

Colon to introduce an explanation of the preceding material

Period at the end of a declarative sentence

Semicolon to separate two main clauses

Parentheses to set off supplemental material

Commas to separate coordinate adjectives

Commas to separate items in a series

"How can you stand it?" This is the first thing the transient visitor to Florence, in summer, wants to know, and the last thing too. . . . He means the noise, the traffic, and the heat, and something else besides, something he hesitates to mention, in view of former raptures: the fact that Florence seems to him dull, drab, provincial. Those who know Florence a little often compare it to Boston. It is full of banks, loan agencies, and insurance companies, of shops selling place mats and doilies and tooled-leather desk sets. The Raphaels and Botticellis in the museums have been copied a thousand times; the architecture and sculpture are associated with the schoolroom. For the contemporary taste, there is too much Renaissance in Florence: too much "David" (copies of Michelangelo's gigantic white nude stand on the Piazza della Signoria and the Piazzale Michelangelo; the original is in the Academy), too much rusticated stone, too much glazed terracotta, too many Madonnas with Bambinos. In the lackluster cafés of the dreary main piazza (which has a parking lot in the middle), stout women in sensible clothing sit drinking tea, and old gentlemen with canes are reading newspapers. Sensible, stout, countrified flowers like zinnias and dahlias are being sold in the Mercato Nuovo, along with straw carryalls, pocketbooks, and marketing baskets. Along the Arno, near Ponte Vecchio, ugly new buildings show where the German bombs fell. . . . ➡

Florence is a manly town, and the cities of art that appeal to the current sensibility are feminine, like Venice and Siena. What irritates the modern tourist about Florence is that it makes no concession to the pleasure principle. It stands four-square and direct, with no air of mystery, no blandishments, no furbelows—almost no Gothic lace or baroque swirls. . . . The general severity is even echoed by the Florentine bird, which is black and white—the swallow, a bachelor, as the Florentines say, wearing a tail coat.

Comma to separate clauses joined by a co-ordinating conjunction

Comma to set off a nonessential adjective clause

Dash to set off and emphasize supplemental material

Mechanics Workshop Exercise 1

Using the Comma   These sentences describe Florence. Rewrite each one, adding or deleting commas as needed.

1. Florence which is known as Firenze in Italian lies 145 miles northwest of Rome the capital of Italy.
2. Often called the Athens of Italy Florence remains a major, world, art center.
3. The magnificent buildings proud bridges and famous statues make the city itself a work of art a treasure to be enjoyed and protected.
4. This great city which is situated on the banks of the River Arno probably dates back to Caesar's Rome.
5. At various times during the Middle Ages walls were built around Florence and parts of a medieval wall still stand.
6. In fact inside the walled section the city takes on a distinctly, medieval flavor that enchants visitors.
7. Making Florence a tourist mecca its churches palaces and artwork attract visitors to the older section of the city.
8. Florence unlike Rome was never sacked but over the years it has suffered from many, damaging floods.
9. On November 4 1966 flood waters rose steeply, and destroyed many glorious irreplaceable works of art.
10. Although the occasional floods can be disastrous, the weather for most of the year is really quite pleasant.

Mechanics Workshop Exercise 2

Review   The following sentences describe Mary McCarthy's life and writings. Rewrite each sentence, correcting all errors in punctuation. ⇒

Mary McCarthy

1. Mary McCarthy was born in Seattle Washington and she grew up in Minneapolis Minnesota.
2. McCarthy did not plan to be a writer: in fact her first ambition was to pursue a career in the theater.
3. Her only brother Kevin McCarthy did pursue that career, and became a noted actor. (He starred in the original version of the film "Invasion of the Body Snatchers".
4. Like the women in her novel "The Group" McCarthy attended Vassar College, and graduated in 1933.
5. Early in her career, McCarthy wrote mostly nonfiction which included literary criticism, and articles, and essays.
6. Although she wrote for the magazines, "the Nation," and "the New Republic" McCarthy is most closely linked to the "Partisan Review."
7. McCarthys' second husband Edmund Wilson—also a famed writer and critic encouraged her to write fiction.
8. McCarthy was thirty years old, when she published her first book of fiction "The Company She Keeps."
9. The book presents a bright, young woman named Margaret Sargent who like McCarthy has a passion for truth.
10. By 1960, McCarthys novels included the following: *The Oasis*, published in 1949, *The Groves of Academe*, published in 1952, and *A Charmed Life*, published in 1955.
11. Need you ask what these novel's popularity did for McCarthy's writing career!
12. Critics of her novels' wondered, why they contained so much autobiographical material?
13. McCarthy answered as follows, What I really do she said is take real plums and put them in an imaginary cake.
14. Some of her books are memoirs, including the following; "Memories of a Catholic Girlhood," and "How I Grew".
15. Her travel writing as you have seen is elegant and she wrote many pieces about Venice as well as Florence.
16. After the publication of her novel, "The Group" in 1962— its my favorite, McCarthy's popularity soared.
17. This book which received mixed reviews tells the story of eight womens' lives, loves and careers.
18. The book was a best seller, moreover it was turned into a movie starring Candice Bergen who went on to star in the television series, "Murphy Brown."
19. Did you read McCarthy's sixth novel "Birds of America."
20. Often called Americas First Lady of Letters, McCarthy is noted for her analytic witty prose style.

Proofreading   The following passage describes the artist Thomas Cole, whose painting appears on this page. Rewrite the passage, correcting the errors in spelling, capitalization, punctuation, grammar, and usage. There are ten errors in all.

Thomas Cole

[1]Born in an industrial town in Lancashire county in England, Thomas Cole (1801–1848) was one of America's great nineteenth-century landscape painters. [2]Before him and his family emigrated to Ohio in 1818, he worked for an engraver and a fabric designer. [3]When he was twenty-two, his family moved to Pittsburgh. [4]There Cole helped out in his father's rug factory and spent his free time: painting portraits and sketching the Pennsylvania countryside.

[5]By the time he was twenty four, Cole had moved to New York City and had began to make a name for himself as a landscape painter. [6]His scenes of the rugged New England Countryside have an epic granduer. [7]Coles' *View of Florence from San Miniato* was inspired by his travels through Italy in the early 1830s. [8]In it are some great monuments of the old city, built in the severe and masculine style that Mary MacCarthy loved.

Thomas Cole, *View of Florence from San Miniato*, 1837

Punctuation, Abbreviations, and Numbers

Read the following passages, paying attention especially to the underlined text. Then, in each numbered item below, choose the word or group of words for which the punctuation, abbreviations, and treatment of numbers are correct as they appear in the passage.

According to [1]W.H. Frey only human beings cry. [2]Animals tears fall if their eyes are [3]irritated however only human beings shed [4]tears when their emotions are touched. [5]Frey a biochemist has made a study of tears. He showed the movie [6]Brians Song [7]1971 to see [8]peoples responses the film is about [9]2 well known football [10]players. One of whom dies young.

When Miguel and Rose made their first trip to [11]Fenway Park they saw the Boston Red Sox play the Texas Rangers.

"I can't wait to see [12]the Green Monster said Rose as they entered the park's gate on Landsdowne Street [13]at 7 00 pm sharp.

"What is [14]that asked [15]Miguel With a skeptical look at his sister, he walked toward the [16]field and she called after [17]him its over [18]thirty feet [19]high Then he saw the [20]monster it was the enormous wall (painted dark green) rising over left field.

1. **a.** W. H. Frey only
   b. W.H. Frey—only
   c. W.H. Frey: only
   d. W. H. Frey, only
2. **a.** Animals **b.** Animal's **c.** Animals'
3. **a.** irritated; however, **b.** irritated, however, **c.** irritated: however,
4. **a.** tears when **b.** tears, when
   c. tears. When
5. **a.** Frey a biochemist, **b.** Frey, a biochemist, **c.** Frey, a biochemist
6. **a.** Brians Song **b.** "Brian's Song"
   c. *Brian's Song*
7. **a.** 1971 **b.** (1971)
   c. (nineteen seventy-one)
8. **a.** peoples' responses. The
   b. people's responses. The
   c. peoples' responses, the
   d. people's responses, the
9. **a.** two well-known **b.** two well known
   c. 2 well-known
10. **a.** players, one **b.** players. One
    c. players: One

11. **a.** Fenway Park they
    b. Fenway Park, they
    c. Fenway Park. They
12. **a.** the 'Green Monster' " said
    b. the "Green Monster"" said
    c. the 'Green Monster,' " said
    d. the "Green Monster,"" said
13. **a.** at 7:00 P.M. sharp.
    b. at 7:00 p.m. sharp.
14. **a.** that," asked **b.** that?" asked
    c. that"? asked
15. **a.** Miguel? **b.** Miguel.
16. **a.** field and **b.** field. And
    c. field, and
17. **a.** him, "it's **b.** him "It's
    c. him; "It's **d.** him, "It's
18. **a.** 30 feet **b.** thirty feet
19. **a.** high"! Then **b.** high!" then
    c. high!" Then
20. **a.** "monster": it
    b. "monster:" It
    c. "monster"; it

Writing for Review

Write a paragraph that includes dialogue.

Part 3

Resources and Skills

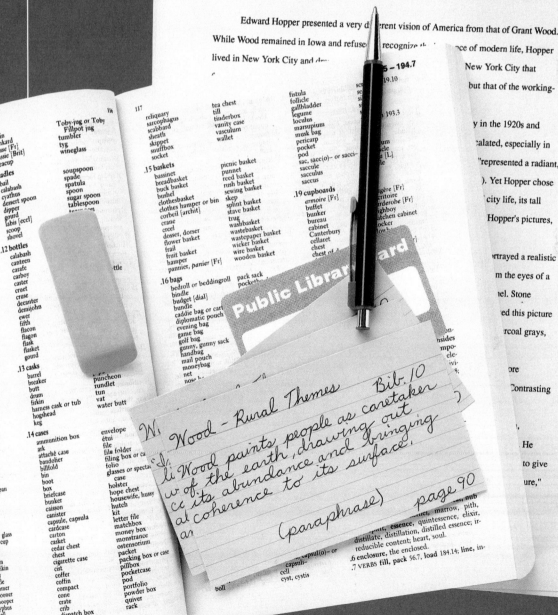

Part 3 Resources and Skills

Unit 22   The English Language

22.1   A Multicultural Linguistic Heritage

When the first English settlers arrived in North America, they spoke a language that had been influenced by centuries of contact with many cultures. This influence was most evident in the settlers' vocabulary.

Words from Many Lands

Throughout its history English has readily borrowed words from other languages. The chart below gives a small sampling of some of these loan words, the languages from which they were borrowed, and the approximate dates they first appeared in English.

Persian illustration, 1554

Early Loan Words in English			
Language	Original Word	English Word	When Borrowed
Latin	crystallum	cristal (crystal)	13th century
	librarius	library	14th century
Greek	kōmōidia	comedy	14th century
	oligarchia	oligarchy	about 1500
Scandinavian languages	vindauga	windowe (window)	13th century
	skule	skoulen (scowl)	14th century
French	atourne	attourney (attorney)	14th century
	magique	magik (magic)	14th century
Portuguese	anchova	anchovy	about 1600
Spanish	sombra	sombrero	about 1600
Italian	madrigale	madrigal	late 16th century
	maccheroni	macaroni	about 1600
Arabic	qutuh	coton (cotton)	14th century
	nāranj	orange	14th century
Persian	kārwān	caravan	late 16th century
	bāzār	bazaar	late 16th century

American English

As the English settlers established communities on the eastern coast of North America, their language and customs were influenced by the many Native American cultures they encountered. As contact with these cultures increased, words from Native American languages soon became part of the settlers' vocabulary. Many of these loan words were place names and names of plants and animals that did not exist in England.

As their numbers increased, the settlers began to push westward, encountering additional Native American cultures. The languages of some of these Native Americans had been heavily influenced by the Spanish language spoken by the *conquistadores,* and thus many Spanish words entered the developing vocabulary of American English.

Early Loan Words in American English		
Original Word	English Word	When Borrowed
Native American languages		
chocolatl (Nahuatl)	chocolate	about 1600
äräkun (Algonquian)	raccoon	early 17th century
mokussin (Narragansett)	moccasin	early 17th century
askoot-asquash (Massachusett)	squash	mid-17th century
pawcohiccora (Algonquian)	hickory	mid-17th century
chitmunk (Algonquian)	chipmunk	early 19th century
Spanish		
mestengo	mustang	early 19th century
patio	patio	early 19th century
estampida	stampede	mid-19th century
cañón	canyon	mid-19th century
bonanza	bonanza	mid-19th century
vigilante	vigilante	mid-19th century
African languages		
banäna (Mandingo)	banana	about 1600
mbanza (Kimbundu)	banjo	mid-18th century
gombo (Bantu)	gumbo	mid-19th century
vodu (Ewe)	voodoo	mid-19th century

Exercise 1

Use a dictionary to discover the language from which each of the following English words originated. If your dictionary provides dates, find out when each word first entered English.

1. circle
2. skirt
3. lieutenant
4. roast
5. trombone
6. hoosegow

Think of at least three more words that originated in another language, and find out when each of them entered English.

Blends and Compounds
The Blend-o-rama

Lewis Carroll, the author of *Alice's Adventures in Wonderland*, loved to experiment with language. In fact, Carroll invented many new words for his stories and poems, such as *chortle, galumph,* and *snark*. What do these words mean, and how did Carroll come to create them?

Chortle, galumph, and *snark* are examples of blends—new words made by combining two existing English words. *Chortle* is a blend of **chuck**le and *snort*; *galumph* is a blend of **gal**lop and *tri-**umph**; *snark* is a blend of **sn**ake and sh**ark**.

As people use English to conduct their daily lives, words that no longer effectively communicate ideas pass gradually out of use, while new, more effective words are born. Thus, in 1598 *twirl* was created out of **tw**ist and wh**irl**. *Dumbfound* was created in 1653, a blend of **dumb** and con**found**. And in 1698 **fl**utter and **hurry** were blended to make *flurry*.

Another way new words are created is by compounding, or joining two words together. Some compounds are closed (one word), such as *greenhouse* and *blackboard*. Others are open (two words), such as *post office* and *ice cream*. Still others are hyphenated: *fire-eater* and *go-between*. Whether a compound is closed, open, or hyphenated is often a seemingly arbitrary matter established by tradition rather than by the application of a set of rules for compounding.

Like blends, compounds have a long history. In Old English, *candel* (candle) and *staef* (stick) were joined to form *candel-staef,* or *candlestick. Full* and *fyllan* were joined to create *fullfyllan* (to fulfill). Despite the long history of compounding, some compounds are short-lived. *Splashdown* was created in the earliest days of the United States space program to describe the return of space capsules that left orbit by parachuting into the ocean. Today's space shuttles glide onto airport runways, relegating *splashdown* to linguistic history.

Blend-o-rama

Try your hand at creating your own blends and compounds. Write three of each, and then use your newly created words in a story, a dialogue, or a poem.

22.2   An African-English Creole

Between 1619 and 1807, slave traders brought 250,000 enslaved Africans to American colonies and Caribbean islands. When the American Revolution started, one in five Americans was of African descent.

Pidgin Speech

The slaves spoke a variety of West African languages. To make communication possible between the colonists and the slaves, who each knew nothing of the other's language, a pidgin slowly evolved. A pidgin is a hybrid language that combines elements of two or more different languages. Pidgins arise out of contact between different cultures through trade, war, colonization, or in this case slavery. Pidgins develop to enable people from different cultures to communicate on a rudimentary level.

The pidgin that enabled slaves and slave owners to communicate was part English and part native Caribbean and African languages. The mixture, which melded different vocabularies, grammars, and pronunciations, flourished in the United States during the eighteenth century and the first half of the nineteenth century. With the end of slavery and the plantation system, this pidgin English slowly died out—except in one area of the United States where it is still spoken today.

A Creole Called Gullah

Many descendants of former slaves still live on the Sea Islands off the coasts of South Carolina and Georgia and on the nearby mainland, where profitable cotton plantations once thrived. These people speak Gullah, sometimes called Geechee, the pidgin English that their ancestors spoke.

Gullah, however, is no longer considered a pidgin by linguists, since from birth its speakers learn it as their primary language. When a pidgin becomes the primary language learned from birth, it is called a creole.

If you heard someone speaking Gullah, you would undoubtedly recognize some of the words. Most words, however, would be completely unfamiliar to you. Read the following Gullah sentence. Which words do you recognize? Can you decipher the meaning of the sentence?

Uma-chil' nyamnyam fufu and t'ree roll roun, but 'e ain't been satify.

Now read the English translation, and compare it with the Gullah original.

The girl ate mush and three biscuits, but she wasn't satisfied.

What is the Gullah verb for *ate*? How is the noun *biscuits* expressed in Gullah? Can you suggest a reason why *uma-chil'* means "girl"?

Gullah exhibits some grammatical patterns derived from English. Notice the auxiliary verbs in the following sentences.

> I be shell 'em. (I am shelling them.)
> I ben shell 'em. (I shelled them.)
> I bina shell 'em. (I have been shelling them.)
> I ben don shell 'em. (I shelled them some time ago.)

Gullah, like any language that started as a pidgin, shows evidence of linguistic inventiveness. *Dawn* in Gullah is an open compound: *day clean*. *Flatter* is a closed compound: *sweetmouth*. Even an intensifier like *very* is expressed inventively. In Gullah, *very ugly* becomes *ugly too much*.

Exercise 2

The people of the Sea Islands have a compelling history. Do some research on their culture and the Gullah language. One source is the article "Sea Change in the Sea Islands," published in *National Geographic*, December 1987. Where did the Gullah-speaking people come from, and how did they come to live on the Sea Islands? Why do you suppose Gullah has thrived on these islands when throughout the rest of the South this language died out with slavery? What is taking place on the Sea Islands today? Do you think the culture of the people will survive?

Illogical Juxtaposition
Include Me Out

> Wagner's music is better than it sounds.

Samuel Goldwyn was a legendary Hollywood studio tycoon, the head of MGM during its golden years. Goldwyn is remembered, however, not just for his movie-making prowess but also for his creativity with the English language. Sam Goldwyn once said of an MGM contract actor, "We're overpaying him, but he's worth it." Another time Goldwyn defended his studio's films by asserting, "Our comedies are not to be laughed at!" And what was a Goldwyn associate to make of the following remark: "I never liked you, and I always will"?

Goldwyn's remarks are illogical juxtapositions. An illogical juxtaposition is a humorous statement that results when two contradictory ideas get tangled up in the same sentence. "Include me out," for example, is an illogical juxtaposition because to *include* means to bring *in,* not to leave *out.* Although illogical juxtapositions are usually unintentional, sometimes they are deliberate, such as Mark Twain's satirical critique, "Wagner's music is better than it sounds."

In addition to Goldwyn and Twain, another well-known practitioner of illogical juxtapositions was New York Yankee catcher Yogi Berra. After Berra turned to managing, reporters wondered whether he would succeed in the dugout after so many years on the field. His answer? "Sometimes you can observe a lot by watching." Berra is also reported to have said of the national pastime, "Ninety-nine percent of this game is half mental."

Illogical juxtapositions remind us that we are, after all, human and that what we say is not always what we mean. Unless, that is, you subscribe to Samuel Goldwyn's oft-quoted philosophy: "I may not always be right, but I'm never wrong!"

Figure It Out

Try translating the following illogical juxtapositions. What did the speaker mean to say?

1. A girl who is seventeen is much more of a woman than a boy who is seventeen.
2. Don't pay any attention to him; don't even ignore him.
3. Her death leaves a void in the community that will be hard to replace.
4. No wonder nobody comes here—it's too crowded.
5. Let's have some new clichés.
6. This book has too much plot and not enough story.

22.3   Immigration and American English

How many languages do you speak? One? Two? You may not realize it, but if you speak English, you are acquainted with quite a few other languages as well: Greek, Latin, Algonquian, Hopi, German, French, Spanish, and Thai, to name just a few. You may not be fluent in any of these languages, but every day you use words from their vocabularies.

In fact, whenever two or more different cultures establish and maintain contact over an extended period of time, the vocabulary of each culture's language reflects word borrowing from each of the other cultures' languages. Throughout its long history, English has borrowed words liberally from other languages to enrich its vocabulary.

In the United States much of this word borrowing has resulted from immigration. From its birth to the present day, the United States has been peopled largely by immigrants. Many immigrants came to this country during two great waves of immigration.

A Cultural Bonanza

The first great wave of immigration to the United States took place from about 1830 to 1850. Millions of people fled poverty and famine in their countries of origin in the hope of improving the quality of their lives in the United States. From western Europe came four million Irish, six million Germans, and two million Scandinavians. In addition, four hundred thousand Chinese arrived from Asia. Each of these groups brought with it a unique culture. The foods, music, literature, history, religious and social traditions, and language of each culture eventually would be woven into the cultural fabric of the developing nation.

Beginning about 1880 and continuing into the 1920s, a second wave of immigration enhanced the cultural vitality of the United States. The new immigrants included five million Italians and Greeks; eight million Poles, Hungarians, and Russians; and smaller numbers of people from other cultures throughout the world. Each of these cultures has expanded the vocabulary of American English.

New Arrivals

The immigration that started with the English colonists continues to this day. Over the past several decades people have immigrated to the United States from Vietnam, Cambodia, Laos, Thailand, Haiti, Central America and South America, Korea, Mexico, Ireland, the Middle East, and the Philippines. Immigrants continue to arrive from Europe, Asia, and Africa. The chart on the next page shows just a few of the words from other languages that have reshaped American English during the past two centuries.

Borrowed Words in American English		
Language	**Word**	**When Borrowed**
French	levee	mid-18th century
	cent	late 18th century
	depot	early 19th century
	jambalaya	late 19th century
Spanish	plaza	mid-19th century
	adobe	mid-19th century
	corral	mid-19th century
	serape	late 19th century
German	pretzel	early 19th century
	kindergarten	mid-19th century
	hamburger	late 19th century
Dutch	cookie	late 18th century
	boss	early 19th century
	bakery	early 19th century
	snoop	early 19th century
Italian	spaghetti	late 19th century
	minestrone	late 19th century
	baloney	early 20th century
Hawaiian	ukulele	early 20th century
Irish	phony	about 1900
Chinese	chop suey	late 19th century
	chow mein	about 1900
	wok	mid-20th century
Japanese	hara-kiri	mid-19th century
	hibachi	mid-19th century

Exercise 3

Use your dictionary to identify the language from which each boldfaced word below was borrowed.

Alberto's mom asked him to go to the **delicatessen** for some **coleslaw**. Alberto replied that he would also pick up some **bagels** while he was there. His sister Marcella reminded him to get some **Parmesan** cheese for the next night's **lasagna**, and their little brother asked Alberto to buy some **tacos**.

Contronyms
Is It a Handicap?

I t's a hot, humid Saturday in July, and your neighbor tells you, "I think it's about time to trim that tree!" What is your neighbor going to do?

It's a cold, snowy Saturday in December, and your neighbor tells you, "I think it's about time to trim that tree!" *Now* what is your neighbor going to do?

It's clear from this example that the word *trim* has two nearly opposite meanings. *Trim* can mean "take away from," as in "**trim** (cut off) some branches," or it can mean "add to," as in "**trim** (hang some ornaments, tinsel, and strings of popcorn on) the tree." *Trim* is a contronym, a word that has two opposite meanings that depend on the context in which the word is used.

English has a number of contronyms. *Left* can mean "departed," as in "Rick and Maria **left** two hours ago." *Left* can also mean "remaining," as in "Only Rick and Maria were **left**."

Wear is another contronym. "That leather **wears** well" means the leather endures. "Rain will **wear** that suede" means the suede will decay.

When you **dust** a table, you remove something. When you **dust** a pan of brownies with powdered sugar, you add something.

How about *cleave?* You can **cleave** to someone (become one together, as in marriage or close friendship), or you can **cleave** a log (split it in two).

It's possible that on some dark night you may find yourself saying, "It's a good thing the moon is **out**, because the lights are **out**!"

Controquizonyms

Test your contronym knowledge. Each of the contronyms below is used to convey a certain meaning in the sentence provided. Think of the opposite meaning for each word, and then write a sentence using that meaning.

1. Clip (to join): I will clip the coupon to the letter.
2. Handicap (advantage): The golfer's handicap allowed competition.
3. Temper (to soften): Temper your anger or it will get you in trouble.
4. Swear (to pledge): The soldier will swear loyalty to her country.
5. Commencement (beginning): At the commencement of the war, the outcome was uncertain.

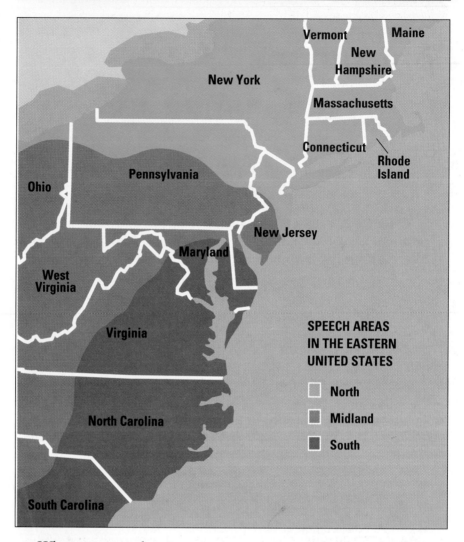

SPEECH AREAS IN THE EASTERN UNITED STATES

- ☐ North
- ☐ Midland
- ☐ South

When you go to the grocery store, are your purchases put in a **bag** or a **sack**? Does the water in your kitchen sink flow from a **tap**, a **faucet**, or a **spigot**? Do you enjoy **cottage cheese, Dutch cheese, smearcase,** or **clabber cheese**? And when you sit down to a summer supper, do you bite into **corn on the cob** or **roasting ears**?

The United States is a land of diversity, and people in different parts of the country speak slightly different forms, or dialects, of English. A dialect is a regional variety of a language that differs from other regional varieties in vocabulary, grammar, and pronunciation. The map above shows the three major dialect regions of the eastern United States: North, Midland, and South. Each dialect can be divided further into many subgroups, some of them distinguished by region and some by socioeconomic factors.

British Influence

Where did these dialects come from? They didn't just spring up in America; their roots go back across the Atlantic to England, where people also speak regional dialects.

When English immigrants began settling in North America, they tended to settle in groups. That is, people who lived in the same area in England often settled together in America as well. One group settled in the southern colonies, while another group settled in the middle colonies. These groups of settlers typically had little contact with each other. Thus, the regional dialects they brought with them from England were preserved in America. Although mass communication has diminished some speech differences, traces of them can still be heard.

One Language, Many Variations

American English dialects differ in vocabulary, grammar, and pronunciation. You have already been introduced to some vocabulary differences. Here's another example: What do you call a sandwich made from cold meats, cheeses, and condiments served on a long slice of French bread? If you're from New York, you probably call it a **hero.** In Florida it's called a **Cuban sandwich.** In New Jersey it's a **hoagie,** and in Iowa, a **Dagwood.** The people of Illinois call it a **sub,** or **submarine,** while in Rhode Island it's a **grinder.** And in New Orleans? Why, it's a **poor boy,** of course!

Grammatical differences in dialects occur as well. A Northerner might say "you might be able to," whereas a Southerner might say "y'all might could." The Northern personal pronouns *ours, yours,* and *his* become *ourn, yourn,* and *hisn* in Midland.

Different dialects also exhibit variations in pronunciation. In some Northern and Southern dialects the *r* in the following words is barely pronounced, if at all: *father, card, far, fort.* In Northern and Midland speech the *s* in *grease* and *greasy* is pronounced like the *ss* in *hiss.* In Southern dialect the *s* has a *z* sound.

Whenever you hear a dialect that is different from yours, remember that "different" English is not incorrect or uneducated English. The Northern, Midland, and Southern dialects, as well as the many socio-economic dialects, are simply different ways to express the same ideas.

Exercise 4

Investigate regional differences in language within your own community. Seek out students and teachers who have moved from other areas of the country. Which expressions that you use are unfamiliar to them? Do they use any expressions that are unfamiliar to you?

Push-Button Words
Button, Button

Think Globally Act Locally

I thought I was wrong once, but I was mistaken

Suppose you want to borrow your sister's car next Saturday. At first she says no, so you have some major persuading to do. Do you remind your sister how *inconsiderate* and *selfish* she can be sometimes, how her *bad attitude* and *unfriendly* manner turn people off, and that lending you her car might make her appear less *self-centered*? Or do you tell her how much you have always *admired* her *openness* and *generosity,* and that you *appreciate* the *trust* she places in you when she lets you use her car?

Assuming you are sincere, the second approach is clearly the better one. Using language that makes people feel good (or bad) is known as "pushing their buttons," because many people react automatically to certain words.

Politicians long ago figured out that certain words evoke either a strong positive or negative response in most people. The power of a push-button word is in its connotations—all the ideas and emotions associated with the word. For example, how many times have you heard *America, freedom,* and *democracy* strung together by politicians? These words are meant to give you a warm emotional glow, stirring up your feelings of pride and patriotism. The politician hopes that these good feelings about your country will inspire good feelings—and votes—for him or her.

Advertisers employ plenty of push-button words as well. Think about the phrase "warm, golden rolls, made just like Grandma baked at home, from all-natural ingredients." Can you identify the push-button words in this pitch? Most people associate pleasant feelings with *warm, golden, Grandma, home,* and *natural.* The advertiser hopes you will feel those same emotions about its dinner rolls, even when the closest anybody's Grandma comes to them is in picking up a package at the grocery store!

Whose Button Is It?

Try this "push-button" activity. For each word in the following list, do some free association. That is, write down whatever words come to you as you think about each word. Try to come up with five to eight words that you associate with each listed word. Then, looking over your responses, note how each word and its associations make you feel. Where might you encounter such words? Compare your words and feelings with those of your classmates. Do you all have the same "buttons"?

- used
- dictator
- antique
- nutritious
- artificial
- wholesome
- improved
- responsibility

SAY NO TO DRUGS

During the 1980s teen-agers of the San Fernando Valley, in Los Angeles, developed a unique manner of speech. It included such colorful expressions as *tubular, to the max, I'm totally sure, gag me with a spoon, grody,* and *narly.* In an earlier era, this way of speaking would have remained localized to southern California and, because it was based largely on slang, eventually would have died out. But something very different happened.

What happened was the intervention of the mass media. Television news shows broadcast stories on the language and culture of "Valley girls" (and boys). Hollywood joined the bandwagon with a popular movie, *Fast Times at Ridgemont High*. Newspapers and magazines ran stories about how young people in the Valley seemed to spend all of their free time at shopping malls. Moon Unit Zappa, daughter of sixties rocker Frank Zappa, had a hit record, *Valley Girl*, that satirized the speech of the Valley teens. Soon, teen-agers all across America and overseas were affecting the language, mannerisms, and even the dress of "the Valley."

Media Presence and Speed

The "Valley" phenomenon is just one example of how the mass media can affect the language we speak. Two critical characteristics of the media enable it to dominate our culture: presence and speed.

First of all, media presence is everywhere. Television, radio, newspapers, magazines, billboards, advertising, movies, records—all spread, influence, and promote popular culture. In 1990 a German automobile manufacturer launched an advertising campaign that used a German word, *fahrvergnügen,* to describe the driving experience its cars offered. The word was plastered across billboards, sung about in television and radio commercials, and featured in magazine ads. Before long, the word was even being joked about on late-night television talk shows. *Fahrvergnügen* will likely never assume a permanent place in the English language, but thanks to the mass media it has certainly made an impact on American consciousness.

The second important characteristic of the media is speed. Throughout history change has come slowly to the English language. Until recently a word from a foreign language might take decades, if not centuries, to become fully integrated into the English language. Today, however, this process has been accelerated. We live in an age in which communication is instantaneous; we can even watch wars fought "live" on network television. This speedy communication makes us aware of language we might otherwise never know.

Before the Persian Gulf War, for example, few Americans knew anything about Scuds, Patriot missiles, Kurds, Shiites, or Sunnis. Yet suddenly, during the weeks of the war, these words became part of the media's vocabulary and, thus, part of our own. When dramatic change was taking place in the Soviet Union, the media introduced us to *glasnost* (openness) and *perestroika* (restructuring). When we talk about the conflicts and personalities in the Middle East, such words as *intifada* (uprising) and *ayatollah* (leader), popularized through the mass media, color our speech.

Future Talk

In the future how will the mass media's ability to create, import, and export language nearly instantaneously influence American English and other languages? Will the constant presence of the mass media in the daily lives of people throughout the world lead one day to a global language that everyone will understand? If it does, will that language resemble any that people now speak?

Already, the world shows signs of moving toward a global language, and many indications suggest that English could become that language. English is standard in international civil aviation, allowing professionals in that field to communicate effectively despite differences in their native languages. In addition, partly because of European colonial expansion during the eighteenth and nineteenth centuries, English is now widely used—and is sometimes even the official language—in countries as varied as India, Jamaica, and Nigeria.

Written communication is more likely to be in English than in any other language. At least 50 percent of books published in the world are in English, and demand for books in English is growing. It has been estimated that at least 70 percent of the world's mail is written in English.

Whether a global language will evolve and what form it will take are questions yet to be answered. But whatever the future holds, one fact about the present has become quite apparent: every day the mass media affects the way we understand and talk about our world.

Exercise 5

Examples of how the mass media affect American English are all around you. Spend some time reading, watching, and listening to advertisements. How many newly invented words or foreign words can you find? Make a list of these words. Which words do you think are likely to endure? Why?

Argot

On the Lam

I f you're a fan of the old gangster movies of the 1930s and 1940s, you've probably already figured out how characters with names like Johnny and Zelda talk. But if phrases like *on the lam* sound completely foreign to you, welcome to the world of argot!

Argot is a special kind of language, the more or less secret lingo of a particular group. Argot is often associated with a shady, underworld culture. Criminals use argot, also called cant, to conceal their plans and to foster a sense of group identity. Some sociologists have suggested that since organized crime is, after all, a profession, it has developed its jargon in the same way other professions develop theirs.

Argot is probably as old as professional crime itself. Argot was described as the special language of crime as early as the sixteenth century. Much later, in 1623 an author identified only as B. E. compiled a dictionary of terms used by what the author called "the canting crew."

Although most argot remains a mystery to the general public, argot has nevertheless enriched American slang with terms such as *hot* (for stolen merchandise), *to take for a ride, to hijack,* and *to muscle in.* And like all living languages, argot continues to evolve and change.

Awright, Wise Guys

Look at the list of argot terms and definitions below. Many terms date from the 1920s, an era famous for its bank robbers and outlaws. Use this list, plus any other argot you may know or can locate in the library, to write a brief scene for a gangster movie. Try to use as many terms as you can, and make the dialogue as realistic as possible. Share your scene with classmates.

- **C-note** (a $100 bill)
- **canary** (one who confesses, or "sings," to the police)
- **cannon** (a pickpocket)
- **cut** (an individual's share of the loot)
- **finger** (to turn in to the law)
- **G-man** (a federal agent)
- **grifter** (a con artist)
- **heater** (a gun)
- **loot** (stolen goods)
- **mark** (a victim)
- **moll** (popularly, a gangster's girlfriend; also, a gun moll, or female pickpocket)
- **on the lam** (running from the law)
- **paperhanger** (one who passes forged checks)
- **rap** (the blame for a crime)
- **slammer** (prison)
- **two-finger** (a pickpocket)
- **up the river** (in or into prison)

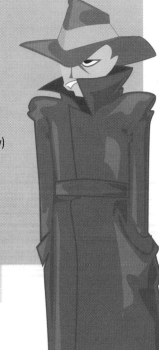

Library Resources

Before 1830 most libraries were private, and only wealthy people and scholars had access to books. Today public libraries appear in almost all communities. Most libraries contain all the basic elements shown below. Ask a reference librarian to help you to familiarize yourself with library resources and their location.

Most Important Parts of a Library

- **Fiction Books** are works of the imagination, such as novels and collections of short stories.

- **Nonfiction Books** are fact-based and are about subjects such as history, science, the arts, and philosophy.

- **Reference Works** include encyclopedias, dictionaries, almanacs, and atlases.

- **Periodicals** include magazines, journals, and newspapers. Periodicals are usually published on a daily, weekly, monthly, or quarterly schedule.

- **Audio-Visual Materials** include films, slides, videos, records, audio cassettes, and compact discs.

- **Catalogs** come either in card form or on a computer. These resources index each book in the library.

23.1   How to Locate Books

For most topics, your search starts at a public library, where you can find books spanning a wide range of topics. Some topics will lead you to specialized libraries, which have more books on particular subject areas such as medical science, law, music, or art. In either kind of library, your search for a book will begin with the catalogs.

Using a Card Catalog

In a card catalog you will find alphabetically arranged cards for each book in the library. The catalog contains two cards for fiction books—one for the author and one for the title. For nonfiction books, the catalog contains an additional card for the subject.

On each card a classification number is printed in the upper left-hand corner. This number, referred to as the call number, corresponds to a number printed on the book's spine. Use this call number to locate the book on the shelf.

Using a Computer Catalog

A computer catalog contains much of the same information as a card catalog, but it stores the information electronically. To use most computer catalogs, you simply follow on-screen directions for looking up a book by subject, title, or author. The screens below show a computerized search.

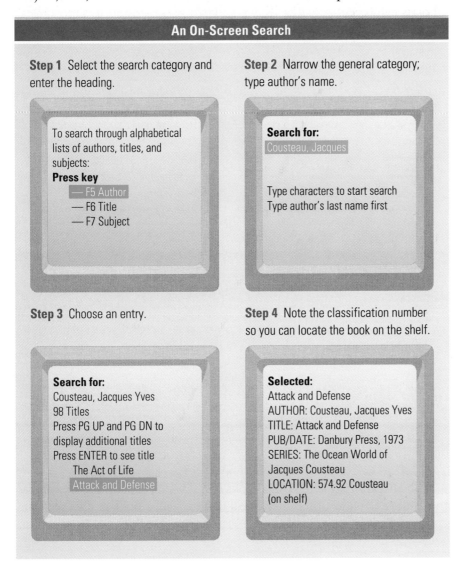

An On-Screen Search

Step 1 Select the search category and enter the heading.

> To search through alphabetical lists of authors, titles, and subjects:
> **Press key**
> — F5 Author
> — F6 Title
> — F7 Subject

Step 2 Narrow the general category; type author's name.

> **Search for:**
> Cousteau, Jacques
>
> Type characters to start search
> Type author's last name first

Step 3 Choose an entry.

> **Search for:**
> Cousteau, Jacques Yves
> 98 Titles
> Press PG UP and PG DN to display additional titles
> Press ENTER to see title
> The Act of Life
> Attack and Defense

Step 4 Note the classification number so you can locate the book on the shelf.

> **Selected:**
> Attack and Defense
> AUTHOR: Cousteau, Jacques Yves
> TITLE: Attack and Defense
> PUB/DATE: Danbury Press, 1973
> SERIES: The Ocean World of Jacques Cousteau
> LOCATION: 574.92 Cousteau (on shelf)

Classification Systems

Libraries use either the Dewey decimal system or the Library of Congress classification system (LC) to organize books. The Dewey decimal system divides nonfiction books into ten numerical categories. Books are shelved by number and then alphabetically by author. You will find fiction works shelved alphabetically by authors' last names and then by title.

The LC uses letters to divide books into twenty general categories, each with subcategories. These letters, along with a combination of numbers, form a book's classification number.

Dewey Decimal System		
Category Numbers	Major Category	Examples of Subcategories
000–099	General works	Encyclopedias, bibliographies
100–199	Philosophy	Ethics, psychology
200–299	Religion	Theology, mythology
300–399	Social sciences	Law, political science, education
400–499	Language	Dictionaries, foreign languages
500–599	Sciences	Chemistry, astronomy, mathematics
600–699	Technology	Medicine, engineering, agriculture
700–799	Arts	Painting, music, theater, sports
800–899	Literature	Poetry, plays, essays
900–999	History and geography	Ancient history, biography, travel

Library of Congress Classification System					
Category Letters	Major Category	Category Letters	Major Category	Category Letters	Major Category
A	General Works	K	Law	S	Agriculture
B	Philosophy and religion	L	Education	T	Technology
		M	Music	U	Military science
C–F	History	N	Fine arts	V	Naval science
G	Geography and anthropology	P	Language and literature	Z	Bibliography and library science
H	Social sciences	Q	Science		
J	Political science	R	Medicine		

The library may keep some books in a separate section. Letters above the catalog classification number will denote such a book and its section.

Exercise 1

Use a card or computer catalog to find a book about some aspect of each of the following subjects. Write the classification number, author, title, and copyright date for each book.

1. American Civil War
2. History of clocks
3. Computer crime
4. Choreography
5. Acid rain
6. Jacques Cousteau
7. Lions
8. Irish poets
9. Nutrition

23.2　How to Locate Periodicals

Periodicals, such as newspapers, magazines, and journals, are the best sources of up-to-date information on current events and on specialized fields of rapid change, such as computer technology. Libraries often keep current issues on the shelves. You may find back issues, however, stored in bound volumes or in microforms, which are small photographs of printed pages that must be magnified to be read. The most common microforms are microfilm (filmstrips) and microfiche (film cards).

To locate periodicals, you may use many different indexes. You will find that some indexes are printed on paper, while others are on microforms or are computerized. Try to use the most current indexes; indexes are updated frequently to accommodate the rapid accumulation of new articles.

Readers' Guide to Periodical Literature

The most popular paper index for magazine articles is the *Readers' Guide to Periodical Literature*. The *Readers' Guide* indexes articles alphabetically, both by author and by subject, that cover a wide range of subjects in more than 175 magazines. Titles for fiction works are sometimes indexed as well. Supplements update the *Readers' Guide* every two weeks. At the end of each year, a hardbound volume indexes all articles published in that year. In the following excerpt from the *Readers' Guide*, notice that entries under subjects are alphabetized by title.

SPEECH
　　See also
　Children—Language
　Deaf children—Language
　Language and languages
　　　Origin
　　See Language and languages—Origin
SPEECH, FREEDOM OF　*See* Freedom of speech
SPEECH PROCESSING SYSTEMS
A computer that recognizes its master's voice? E. Schwartz. il *Business Week* p130–1
　Je 3 '91
Hearing voices [voice recognition module for car audio system] F. Viszard. *Rolling*
　Stone p58 My 2 '91
The human machine [Research at Johns Hopkins Applied Physics Laboratory on chips
　that will enable machines to hear and see; views of Rachel Nowak] *The Wilson*
　Quarterly 15:130 Spr '91
SPEECHES, ADDRESSES, ETC.
　　See also
　Commencement Addresses

> *Cross-references can take two forms: "See also" references refer to related subjects under which additional material may be found. "See" references refer to other forms of subject headings and personal names.*

> *The article by author E. Schwartz appears, illustrated (il), in* Business Week *magazine on pages 130–131 in the June 3, 1991, issue.*

> *"Hearing voices" is the title of an article. Brackets after the title summarize what the article is about: a voice recognition module for a car audio system.*

Other Indexes

Another general magazine index, the *Magazine Index*, covers many fields. Since it's a microfilm index, you'll need to use a special machine that magnifies the text. Ask a librarian for operating instructions if you have never used one before.

If you're doing research in a particular field, you may want to use a specialized periodical index for that field. Every month, for example, the *General Science Index* references 111 science periodicals, and the *Humanities Index* references 347 humanities periodicals. Similarly, the *Business Periodicals Index* references 345 business magazines. You may even find the *Music Index*, which reports articles in the field of music.

You can even expand your library prowess beyond magazine indexes. For newspaper articles, check the *New York Times Index* and the *Wall Street Journal Index*. In addition, the *CBS News Index* offers microform transcripts of its daily television news broadcasts and its other news programs, such as *60 Minutes* and *CBS Reports*.

Computerized Indexes

Some periodical indexes, such as *NEXIS*, are computerized and provide instant access to information from newspapers, news and business magazines, newsletters, wire services, broadcast transcripts, encyclopedias, and other services. Some on-line computer information services, such as ERIC (Educational Resources Information Center), can provide both a bibliographic list of reference sources as well as copies of the sources. Such services are usually available only on a fee-per-use basis. To use any electronic index to its fullest advantage, discuss your research needs with a reference librarian.

Exercise 2

Using the excerpt from the *Readers' Guide* on the previous page, answer the following questions.

1. Which magazine is published quarterly?
2. What is the article "The human machine" about?
3. If you want to get ideas for a speech to deliver at your commencement, under which heading would you look?
4. If you want to read about the origin of speech, which subject heading would provide source articles?
5. Who expresses views about research at Johns Hopkins Applied Physics Laboratory?
6. Under which subject heading would you find articles about how deaf children acquire language?

23.3   Sources of Special Information

General reference works will satisfy many of your research needs, so investigate them first. For some topics, however, you will require very specialized sources to locate information. Some specialized sources include *Arctic Science and Technology Information System Bibliography (ASTIS)*, the *Entertainment Law Reporter* (dealing with legal developments in motion pictures, television, radio, music, sports, and the arts), and the *Jazz Index*.

General Reference Works

You are probably familiar with general reference works such as encyclopedias, dictionaries, and atlases. The information that general works offer should not be underestimated. These sources are easy to find, do not require much time to survey, and provide excellent background information. Take a look at the following chart. It gives examples of some of these resources.

General Reference Works	
Type of Reference	**Examples of Sources**
Dictionaries arrange words alphabetically and include word definitions and pronunciations.	*Random House Webster's College Dictionary, Webster's Ninth New Collegiate Dictionary*
Encyclopedias are multivolume works containing alphabetically arranged articles covering all branches of knowledge.	*World Book Encyclopedia, Encyclopædia Britannica, Random House Encyclopedia, Collier's Encyclopedia, Columbia Encyclopedia*
Biographical Works contain brief histories of living or deceased persons and are usually organized by the particular field in which these persons are best known.	*Contemporary Authors, Current Biography, The International Who's Who, American Authors 1600–1900, European Authors 1000–1900, World Authors, Cyclopedia of World Authors*
Yearbooks and Almanacs contain information and statistics for the past year.	*Information Please Almanac, World Almanac and Book of Facts, Official Associated Press Almanac*
Atlases contain maps, charts, plates, or tables illustrating any subject.	*Hammond Ambassador World Atlas, Cambridge Atlas of Astronomy, Historical Atlas of the United States*
Gazetteers are geographical dictionaries.	*Chambers World Gazetteer, Webster's New Geographical Dictionary*

Specialized Reference Works

Some reference works target specific subject areas (e.g., *Van Nostrand's Scientific Encyclopedia* and the *Encyclopedia of World Art*). Such resources can give you a quick answer to a research question. Other references, such as *Books in Print*, a resource that lists all books currently available from bookstores or publishers, will tell you where to look for an answer. The following chart lists some specialized references that you might use to answer questions about literature.

| Using Literature Reference Works to Answer Questions ||
Questions	Sources for an Answer
1. Who are the main characters in Thomas Hardy's novel *Far from the Madding Crowd*? Where is this novel set?	*Oxford Companion to English Literature, A Literary Gazetteer of England, A Mapbook of English Literature*
2. Who were the most prominent authors in colonial America?	*Oxford Companion to American Literature, American Authors and Books, Cambridge History of American Literature*
3. For which form of poetry is Matsuo Bashō best known?	*Penguin Companion to European Literature, Cassell's Encyclopaedia of World Literature*
4. What are the titles of the epic poems about the Greek hero Odysseus?	*Oxford Companion to Classical Literature; Penguin Companion to Classical, Oriental, and African Literature*
5. Who wrote *Le Misanthrope*? What is it about?	*The New York Public Library Desk Reference, Penguin Companion to European Literature, Oxford Companion to French Literature*

Electronic Sources of Information

As mentioned on page 708, libraries with on-line ERIC services can provide patrons with bibliographies and copies of documents. If you own a computer with a modem, you can access on-line data bases and electronic bulletin boards for yourself.

If you have library privileges at a public or university library, check to see whether or not it is electronically linked to other libraries. Many libraries share a central data base that pools the titles of the books and periodicals in all participating libraries. If a library does not have what you need, one of the other libraries in the network may be able to provide it either electronically or through interlibrary loan. Ask a reference librarian to familiarize you with these services.

Using Parts of a Book

Using all parts of a book, not just the text, can help you to determine whether a book has the information you need. Look for certain kinds of information before the main text; look for other kinds after the text.

Using Parts of a Book

Information Before the Text

Title page This first page contains the full book title and author's name.

Copyright page This page follows the title page and gives the publication date. The copyright date can help you to determine whether the information in the book is too dated for your purposes.

Table of Contents Use this list of the main topics covered as an indication of whether you'll find the kind of information that you need.

Foreword Usually written by someone other than the author, this section often reveals the importance of the book and explains why the book is unique.

Introduction The author's purpose in writing the book or feelings about the subject may be revealed here.

Information After the Text

Afterword or Epilogue This section contains the same kind of information as the foreword, but it is after the text.

Appendix This section (or sections) can contain additional information, such as maps, charts, illustrations, or graphs.

Glossary Special or unfamiliar terms used in the book are alphabetically listed here.

Bibliography This section may list the research sources that the author consulted, or it may list additional sources of information about the subject.

Index This section alphabetically lists all people, places, and significant topics covered in the book. Use it to pinpoint the page numbers of specific information.

Exercise 3

Use the information in this lesson to find three nonfiction books about one topic of your choice. Examine the parts of each book. On your paper, identify the author, title, and copyright date of each book. Then write a paragraph about each book, stating what you learned from examining the parts of the book about its contents and its author's attitudes.

Using Dictionaries

24.1   Varieties of Dictionaries

One of the most famous dictionaries in the English language is the *Oxford English Dictionary*, or *OED*. This multivolume dictionary contains more than 15,000 pages and lists over 80 meanings just for the word *get*.

General Dictionaries

Although people often use the phrase "the dictionary," there are many different kinds of dictionaries, some general and some specialized. General dictionaries are all-purpose dictionaries that contain a broad range of words in common usage.

Types of General Dictionaries   The first dictionary that you used was probably a school dictionary. These dictionaries contain relatively few words and emphasize common words that you are most likely to encounter in your school years.

Later, most people acquire a college dictionary. These dictionaries have more than 150,000 entries with detailed definitions that are sufficient for most college students as well as general users. They also separately list abbreviations, biographical and geographical names, foreign words and phrases, and tables of measures. The *Random House Webster's College Dictionary* and the *American Heritage Dictionary* are well-known college dictionaries.

For the scholar or researcher, unabridged dictionaries provide as many as 500,000 entries that have detailed definitions and extensive word histories. You will find these dictionaries, spanning several volumes, primarily in libraries. Examples of these dictionaries include the *Oxford English Dictionary* and the *Random House Dictionary of the English Language*.

Main Entries   A dictionary entry consists of many elements, such as preferred spellings, plural and capitalized forms, synonyms, and antonyms. Also, the entry may provide American regional expressions (such as "batter-cake" for "pancake"), cross-references, idioms, and other elements. The example on the next page shows many of these elements in a dictionary entry for the word *battle*.

Notice the entry for **battle²**, which indicates it is a homograph, a word that is spelled the same as another word but has a different word history. The label *Archaic* means that particular usage is no longer common. You may encounter archaic terms when you read Shakespeare or classic literature. The label **See BATTLEMENT** is a cross-reference to the entry for the word *battlement*.

bat·tle¹ (bat′l), *n., v.,* **-tled, -tling.** —*n.* **1.** a hostile encounter between opposing military forces. **2.** participation in such an encounter or encounters; *wounds received in battle.* **3.** any fight, conflict, or struggle, as between two persons or teams. **4.** *Archaic.* a battalion. —*v.i.* **5.** to engage in battle. **6.** to struggle; strive. —*v.t.* **7.** to fight (a person, army, cause, etc.). **8.** to force or accomplish by fighting, struggling, etc. **—Idiom.** **9. give** or **do battle,** to engage in conflict; fight. [1250–1300; ME *bataile* < OF < VL *BATTĀLIA, for LL *battuālla* gladiatorial exercises = *battu(ere)* to strike (see **BATE²**) + - *ālia,* neut. pl. of -*ālis* -AL¹] **—bat′tler.** *n.*

bat·tle² (bat′l), *v.t.* **-tled, -tling.** *Archaic.* to furnish with battlements; crenelate [1300–50; ME *batailen* < MF *bataillier.* **See BATTLEMENT**]

Homographs, marked by small raised numbers, are words that are spelled the same but are given separate entries because they have different word histories, called etymologies.

Main entries begin with the syllabicated spelling of the word, its pronunciation, and its part-of-speech label.

Etymologies appear in brackets within entries. The first use of "battle¹" occurred during A.D. 1250 to A.D. 1300.

Using Specialized Dictionaries

Specialized dictionaries provide in-depth information about words in a particular field. For example, a dictionary called *DARE* (*Dictionary of American Regional English*) provides regional definitions of words. Other examples of specialized dictionaries follow.

Specialized Dictionaries	
Questions	**Sources for an Answer**
1. What does a "head gaffer" do on a movie set?	1. *NTC's Mass Media Dictionary*
2. Who is a Middle East mufti?	2. *Political Dictionary of the Arab World*
3. What was Jiang Qing, the last wife of Mao Zedong of China, known for?	3. *Biographical Dictionary and Analysis of China's Party Leadership 1922–1988*
4. Who was the first governor-general of Sierra Leone, Africa?	4. *The Encyclopaedia Africana Dictionary of African Biography, Volume Two: Sierra Leone–Zaire*
5. What was W. C. Handy's full name?	5. *Dictionary of American Negro Biography*
6. When was *Common Sense* first published?	6. *Dictionary of Historic Documents*
7. What does the Biblical name *Canaan* mean?	7. *Dictionary of Bible Place Names*
8. Where was ancient Cahokia, and why is it significant?	8. *The Facts on File Dictionary of Archaeology*
9. Who was nicknamed "Edward Longshanks"?	9. *The Dictionary of Historic Nicknames*
10. What has the German city of Dresden symbolized since World War II?	10. *The Facts on File Dictionary of 20th-Century Allusions*
11. Who was the mythical Loki?	11. *A Dictionary of World Mythology*
12. What was the Gang of Four?	12. *The Facts on File Dictionary of 20th-Century History*
13. Who helped the slave Dred Scott in his lawsuit for freedom?	13. *The Civil War Dictionary, Dictionary of American History*
14. What is the fourth dimension?	14. *The New Age Dictionary*
15. Who said: "Learning without thought is Labor Lost"?	15. *Similes Dictionary*

Decide which of the specialized dictionaries listed in the previous chart might be useful for providing answers to the following questions.

1. What is archaeologist Heinrich Schliemann's greatest find?
2. Where could you learn the identity of the person whom Chief Sitting Bull nicknamed "Little Sure Shot"?
3. Where could you read a summary of the Vietnam War?
4. While studying the Bible as literature, where could you find out whether Mount Sinai is the same as Mount Horeb?
5. Where could you learn whether Abner Doubleday, the founder of baseball, played a role in the Civil War?
6. Where could you learn the political history and significance of the Negev, a tract of land in Palestine/Israel?
7. Where could you find out who said: "Grief sat on his chest like a dragon"?

24.2   Kinds of Thesauruses

Thesauruses list synonyms and are the most commonly used specialized dictionary. Words are arranged by category in a traditional-style thesaurus and alphabetically in a dictionary-style thesaurus.

Traditional Style

The best-known thesaurus is *Roget's Thesaurus*, named for Peter Mark Roget, a British doctor who first developed large categories of words related to a basic concept. Using a traditional *Roget's* involves two steps. First, look up a word in the index, and choose its subentry that is closest to the meaning you have in mind. The subentry is followed by a number. Next, look up that number in the body of the thesaurus to find synonyms for the subentry. Look at the example for *think* that follows. Words similar in meaning are grouped together and set off with semicolons.

If you want a synonym for the verb "think," the index gives you four categories from which to choose. If the meaning that you want is closest to "cogitate," the index directs you to look up 478.8.

478.8 VERBS **think, cogitate,** cerebrate, intellectualize, ideate, conceive, conceptualize, form ideas, entertain ideas; **reason** 482.15; **use one's head,** use *or* exercise the mind, set the brain *or* wits to work, bethink oneself, put on one's thinking *or* considering cap [informal].

Dictionary Style

Thesauruses in dictionary form present words in alphabetical order. Each word is followed by several synonyms and cross-references to any related major category. A major category includes nouns, verbs, and adjectives related to one main idea. See the entry for ELEVATION below.

ELEVATION

Nouns—1, elevation; raising, lifting, erection; sublimation, exaltation; prominence, eminence; advancement, promotion, preferment; uplift, IMPROVEMENT; HEIGHT, hill, mount, mountain.

2, lever, crane, derrick, windlass, capstan, winch, crowbar, jimmy, pulley, crank, jack, dredge, elevator, lift, dumbwaiter, hoist, escalator, moving stairway.

Verbs—1, heighten, elevate, raise, lift, erect, set up, stick up, heave, buoy, weigh.

2, exalt, sublimate, place on a pedestal, promote, advance, improve.

3, take up, fish up; dredge.

4, stand up, spring to one's feet; hold one's head up, rise up, get up, jump up.

Adjectives—1, elevated, raised, lifted up; erect; eminent, lofty; stilted.

2, ennobled, exalted, uplifted

Antonym, **see DEPRESSION.**

Major categories appear in capital letters. ELEVATION is the major category in this example. IMPROVEMENT and HEIGHT are other major categories in which you could find additional synonyms.

Synonyms are listed by part of speech.

For antonyms for "elevation," a cross-reference see DEPRESSION tells you to look under that entry. Not all thesauruses refer you to antonyms.

Exercise 2

Use a thesaurus to find two synonyms for each word below. Then write an original sentence to illustrate the meaning of each synonym. Check the exact meaning of each word in a dictionary before you use it in a sentence.

1. shortness
2. order
3. insanity
4. disclosure
5. converge
6. convex
7. to chance
8. to love
9. to travel
10. authority
11. to broaden
12. to clothe
13. cloudy
14. present (as an adjective)
15. to prepare
16. slowness
17. to prosper
18. test

Vocabulary

25.1 Expanding Your Vocabulary

Most people add new words to their vocabulary through reading and conversation. English as a language acquires new words through contact with other languages; for example, *rodeo, potato,* and *pizza* were once words just in foreign languages.

You can learn the meaning of an unfamiliar word by paying attention to surrounding words and sentences. Sometimes this context provides obvious clues to a word's meaning, but other times you need to verify a word's meaning by looking it up in a dictionary. A dictionary will also provide the pronunciation and the multiple meanings of words.

Specific Context Clues

If you learn to watch and listen for the clues in language, you can often determine the meanings of many new words. In the following paragraph, unfamiliar words are in italic type, and clue words are underscored. Can you guess the meanings of the unfamiliar words?

> The death of Sam Houston's beloved mother served as a *fulcrum,* or a hinge, on which his life turned. Whereas previous personal failures had led him to sink into despair and inactivity, this tragedy *galvanized* Houston's political career. Like his valiant friend, President Andrew Jackson, Houston plunged into public service and became a *stalwart* defender of Jackson's political beliefs.

In the first sentence, the clue word *or* allows you to figure out that a *fulcrum* functions like a hinge. *Or* signals that a restatement or a more familiar explanation follows. Other clue words introducing restatements include *in other words, also known as,* and *also called.*

Contrasts show unfamiliar words as opposites of familiar words. The clue word *Whereas* contrasts "sink into despair and inactivity," and "galvanized Houston's political career"; thus, you know that *galvanized* must mean "stimulated." Other clue words indicating contrasts are *but, although, on the contrary, however, on the other hand,* and *in contrast to.*

Comparisons liken unfamiliar words to familiar ones. The clue word *like* compares the two men, one valiant and the other stalwart. You know that *stalwart* must mean "brave" or "strong of mind." Other clue words introducing comparisons are *also, likewise, similarly, in the same way, similar to, resembling,* and *as.* Try to use the clue words in the paragraph that follows to figure out the meanings of the words in italic type. Jot on scratch paper what you think the words mean before you read the explanation.

> When we visit our cousins in Arizona, we love to dine on their *patio,* <u>which is</u> the little paved courtyard right next to the house. The patio overlooks several Southwestern landforms, <u>such as</u> valley-like canyons and table-<u>like</u> *mesas,* which are always beautiful to gaze upon. I remember how amazed I was the first time I saw an *arroyo* brimming with flood water after a heavy rain, <u>since</u> we had ridden along its dusty bottom only the previous afternoon.

The clue words *which is* in the first sentence signal that a definition for *patio* follows. Other clue words introducing definitions include *which means* and *that is.* Examples illustrate unfamiliar words. You probably deduced that a *mesa* is a table-like landform. Other clue words introducing examples include *for example, for instance, other, these, including,* and *especially.*

An action's unfamiliar cause can be understood by a familiar effect . The context may have been a little more difficult, but the context indicates that an *arroyo* may be a stream bed in a dry region. Other clue words introducing causes and effects include *because, as a result, therefore, when,* and *consequently.*

In addition to clue words, punctuation marks can also supply context clues. For example, many restatements and definitions are set off by commas or dashes. Semicolons are often used before clue words.

General Context Clues

If there are no specific clue words, use general context clues. Begin by determining an unfamiliar word's part of speech. For instance, if you read that "the defendant leaned toward his lawyer, and the two had a brief interlocution," you know that *interlocution* is a noun. You might also guess that an interlocution is a kind of conversation. In the following paragraph, examine the general context of the unfamiliar words in italic type.

> Although Ramone had left for the play in a *jocund* mood, laughing and telling amusing stories to his buddies, he returned home amazingly changed. He described to his parents the *poignant* scene of the play in which Macduff learns that his wife and children have been murdered.

Even if you do not know the meaning of *jocund,* you do know that it is an adjective describing *mood.* You can guess the word's general meaning from supporting details ("laughing and telling amusing stories"), so you may deduce that *jocund* means "merry or cheerful." Using the same process with *poignant,* you might deduce that the scene was sad and touching.

In addition to general context clues the general tone, setting, and situation may provide clues to the meaning of a word, as in the sample paragraph on the next page.

> I don't know how she does it, but my older sister always manages to *cajole* Dad into increasing her allowance. First, she warms him up with excessive flattery. After she flatters him, she reminds him of every little good deed she's done. Then she offers to prepare one of his favorite desserts, and before I know it, she has an allowance that's three times larger than mine. You'd think Dad would recognize a *sycophant* when he sees one.

You know that *cajole* is a verb. It has to do with warming up Dad and flattering him. In fact, *cajole* means "to persuade by pleasant words or to wheedle." The word *sycophant* is a noun and indicates a type of person. You can tell that the writer has a low opinion of her sister's actions, so you may guess that to be called a *sycophant* is not complimentary. In fact, a sycophant is a self-serving flatterer.

Exercise 1

Each of the following sentences contains a word in italic type that may be unfamiliar to you. Try to determine each word's meaning from its context, then write the word and your definition of it on your paper. Check your accuracy with a dictionary.

1. Gold is a very *ductile* metal; it can be hammered quite thin.
2. I would feel like an *ingrate* if I failed to express my gratitude to all those who have so generously assisted me.
3. Schubert's "Ave Maria" is known for how smoothly the notes flow into each other; in contrast, his "Marche Militaire" is known for its dramatic *staccato* notes.
4. We enjoyed the *legerdemain* of the magician and wondered just how she managed to move her hands so quickly.
5. Though usually so graceful, Marcia felt absolutely *maladroit* when she dropped the tray containing tea cups.
6. Some people who have trouble falling asleep have found that drinking a glass of warm milk before going to bed has a *somniferous* effect.
7. The pile of rotting garbage was as *odoriferous* as any skunk.
8. Unlike the *feral* cats in the woods, the domesticated barn cats were friendly and purred as they rubbed against us.
9. Professional mountain climbers almost never suffer from *acrophobia*; on the contrary, the higher the mountain, the happier they are.
10. No one can top Carlos as a *gastronome*; he buys only the finest cheese and the choicest meats, drives to the pier to hand-pick the freshest of fish, and uses only fresh herbs.

25.2   Analyzing Word Parts

Although the English language borrows words from many languages, most English words have their origins in Latin and Greek words and word parts. Knowing some of the Greek and Latin word parts will help you to analyze an unfamiliar word and determine its meaning.

The main part of a word is its root. A root may be a complete word, such as *gram*, or it may be a part of one. Roots such as *jur* and *cand* are unable to stand alone as words and must be combined with other elements in order to form words.

Roots are often combined with a prefix (a word part attached to the beginning of a word), a suffix (a word part attached to the ending of a word), or another root. Many students learn lists of word parts to prepare for the vocabulary portion of college entrance examinations. Look at how you might analyze the word *encryption*.

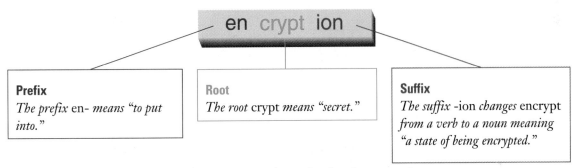

Prefix
The prefix en- *means "to put into."*

Root
The root crypt *means "secret."*

Suffix
The suffix -ion *changes* encrypt *from a verb to a noun meaning "a state of being encrypted."*

The word *encryption* means something that has been put into a secret code or message. Although this word's parts add up to its meaning, sometimes an analysis of a word's parts do not yield its meaning. Use a dictionary to verify a word's meaning.

Word Roots

While prefixes and suffixes can give you hints about a word's meaning, the word's root provides the real clue. In the word *encryption*, the prefix *en-* and the suffix *-ion* have been attached to the root *crypt*. Other words formed from the same root include *cryptic*, meaning mysterious in meaning; *cryptograph*, meaning a message in secret code; and *cryptographer*, meaning a person who specializes in studying the techniques of secret codes. The root *crypt* is also an English word; it is a noun meaning a subterranean chamber that is used as a burial place or as a location for secret meetings.

Look at the list of root words that follows on the next page. Some roots have more than one form. If you have studied a foreign language, you might notice that some root words mean the same thing in another language.

Word Roots		
Roots	**Meanings**	**Examples**
aqua, aqui	water	aquatic, aquifer
astr, astro	star	astral, astronomical
aut, auto	self-acting	autism, autobiography
biblio	book	bibliography, bibliophile
bio	life	biology, biosphere
cand	shine, glow	candle, candescent
chron	time	chronicle, chronological
circ	circle	circular, circus
clin	bend, lean	recline, incline
cogn	know	cognition, incognito
crypt	hidden, secret	cryptic, cryptogram
culp	fault, blame	culprit, exculpate
fac, fec	do, make	factual, infect
fin	end, limit	define, finite
fix	fasten	fixate, fixative
gen	birth, kind	engender, genealogy
geo	earth	geocentric, geode
graph, gram	write, writing	autograph, telegram
hydr, hydra	water	hydroelectric, dehydration
jac, ject	throw, cast, hurl	trajectory, injection
jud	judge	adjudication, prejudge
junct	join	conjunction, juncture
jur, jus	law	jury, justice
log, logy	word, thought, speech	monologue, theology
luc	light	lucid, translucent
meter, metr	measure	thermometer, metric
nym	name	antonym, pseudonym
op, oper	work	operate, operator
omni	all	omnipresent, omnivorous
path, patho	suffering	pathetic, pathology
ped	foot, child	pedicure, pediatrics
port	carry, bear	exportation, portfolio
psych	soul, mind	psychotherapy, psychology
phys	body, nature	physical, physiology
reg, rig	rule, straight	regular, rigid
scop	examine, instrument	periscope, telescope
spect	sight	perspective, spectator
tele	far, distant	telepathy, telephone
terr	earth	terrace, territory
therm	heat	thermal, thermometer
verb	word	verbal, verbose
vid, vis	see	videogame, visual

Word Prefixes

Prefixes are attached to the beginnings of words to change their meanings. Prefixes may show quantity, size, time, direction, or position. Some prefixes reverse the meaning of a root word. Notice that some of the following prefixes have more than one meaning.

Word Prefixes			
	Prefixes	**Meanings**	**Examples**
Prefixes Showing Direction or Position	circum-	around	circumlocution, circumspect
	col-, com-, con-	together	collect, compact, concentrate
	de-	lower	depress, devalue
	en-	in, put into	encapsulate, enlargement
	ex-, exo-	out of	export, exclaim, exotic
	in-, im-	into	insight, immigrant
	inter-	between, among	international, interdependent
	mid-	middle of	midnight, midriff
	peri-	around, about, enclosing	periscope, periphery, peripatetic
	sub-	below, outside of	submarine, subterranean, sublet, subsist
	super-	above, over	supervise, supersede
	trans-	across, over	transmit, transcend
Prefixes Showing Quantity or Size	semi-, hemi-	half	semiannual, hemisphere
	uni-, mon-	one	unicycle, monarchy
	bi-, di-	two	bimonthly, dilemma
	tri-	three	tripod, triangle
	oct-, octa-	eight	octopus, octave
	deca-	ten	decade, decathlon
	cent-	hundred	century, centigrade
	milli-	thousand	milliliter, million
Prefixes Showing Negation	a-, an-	not, without	amoral, aseptic, anemia
	ant-, anti-	against	antacid, antifreeze
	counter-	opposite to	counterclockwise, counterspy
	de-, dis-	do the opposite	defrost, decaffeinate, disarm
	il-, im-, in-, ir-	without, not	illegal, immodest, incomplete, irreligious
	non-, un-		nonconformist, unmoved
	mis-	wrongly, bad	misdeed, misjudge
Prefixes Showing Time	post-	after	postgame, postwar
	pre-, pro-	before	precede, prologue
	re-	again	revisit, rewrite
	syn-	together	synchronized, syncopated

Word Suffixes

Each suffix has its own meaning and is added to the end of a root word to create a new word with a new meaning. Besides having a specific meaning, a suffix may also make a word a different part of speech.

Word Suffixes				
	Suffixes	**Meanings**	**Original Word**	**New Word**
Suffixes That Form Nouns	-ee	receiver of action	train	trainee
	-ance, -ence	state, quality	relevant	relevance
			persist	persistence
	-ant, -eer	agent, doer	contest	contestant
			puppet	puppeteer
	-ist	quality, state	theory	theorist
	-ness	action, state	bright	brightness
	-tion, -ion	the act of	prosecute	prosecution
Suffixes That Form Adjectives	-able	capable of	read	readable
	-al	characterized by	person	personal
	-ful	full of, having	wonder	wonderful
	-ial	relating to	manor	manorial
	-ic	characteristic of	Byron	Byronic
	-ical	related to	geology	geological
	-less	lacking, without	care	careless
	-ly	akin to	queen	queenly
	-ous	full of	joy	joyous
Suffixes That Form Verbs	-ate	become, form	valid	validate
	-en	make, cause to be	length	lengthen
	-ify	cause, make	terror	terrify
	-ize	make, cause to be	eulogy	eulogize

Adding New Words to Your Vocabulary

You can add new words to your spoken and written vocabulary in many ways. For example, you might keep a list of new words as you encounter them and then quiz yourself on your list at regular intervals. If you have a computer, you can use it to create a personal dictionary. Your dictionary may contain the pronunciation, definitions, related words, synonyms, and antonyms for new words. You may even want to create a program to quiz yourself on the words in your dictionary.

The best way of adding new words to your vocabulary is to read a wide variety of material, both fiction and nonfiction. As you read, you will become aware of how words are used in context. Whichever method that you use to learn new words, you will benefit most by consciously using new words as you speak and write every day.

Analyze the following words for their roots, prefixes, and suffixes. (Not every word has all three parts.) Write what you think each word means—but be careful: not every word's meaning will add up to the sum of its parts. Check your accuracy with a dictionary.

antipathy	incandescent
aquaplane	inclination
bicentennial	inoperable
bioengineering	interjection
biped	intermediary
circumscribe	interject
circumspection	millipede
combustible	misdeed
commingle	pedicab
conjunction	preseason
contravene	rehydrate
culpable	seer
deport	spectral
ejection	superstructure
geothermal	trilogy

Use the roots, prefixes, and suffixes that follow, plus words and word parts that you already know, to create a list of fifteen words that you are familiar with or combinations that you think might be words. Use at least one word part in each word. Check your spelling in a dictionary.

Roots	Prefixes	Suffixes
aqua	*anti–*	*–able*
auto	*en–*	*–ance*
clin	*ex–*	*–ee*
fix	*de–*	*–eer*
geo	*in–*	*–en*
gram	*ir–*	*–er*
log	*mid–*	*–ful*
meter	*mis–*	*–ify*
op	*non–*	*–ion*
reg	*sub–*	*–ist*
spect	*trans–*	*–ize*

Spelling

26.1 Mastering the Basics

English spelling is complex; for example, thirteen letter combinations spell just the *sh* sound. If spelling frustrates you at times, you're in good company. Playwright George Bernard Shaw, a frustrated speller, even bequeathed part of his fortune to establish a new system of spelling!

Basic Spelling Rules

Many words follow basic spelling rules; if you learn the rules, you can spell many words correctly. However, not all words follow the rules, so if a word's spelling doesn't look right to you, check a dictionary.

Forming Plurals   Some basic rules can help you form most plurals, but you need to memorize the spellings of plurals that are exceptions to rules. Study the following list to review some of the rules.

Rules for Regular Plurals	Examples
To form the plural of most nouns, including proper nouns, add -*s*. If the noun ends in -*ch*, -*s*, -*sh*, -*x*, or -*z*, add -*es*.	bell + -*s* = bells bunch + -*es* = bunches bus + -*es* = buses
To form the plural of common nouns ending in a consonant + -*y*, change the *y* to *i* and add -*es*.	ally (change the *y* to *i*) + -*es* = allies dairy (change the *y* to *i*) + -*es* = dairies jury (change the *y* to *i*) + -*es* = juries
To form the plural of most nouns ending in -*f*, including all nouns ending in -*ff*, add -*s*. For some nouns ending in -*f*, especially those ending in -*lf*, change the *f* to *v* and add -*es*.	belief + -*s* = beliefs puff + -*s* = puffs loaf (change the *f* to *v*) + -*es* = loaves elf (change the *f* to *v*) + -*es* = elves

Rules for Irregular Plurals	Examples
Some nouns become plural by adding -*en*, -*ren*, or by substituting letters.	child + -*ren* = children woman — women
Some nouns are the same in the singular and the plural.	swine — swine sheep — sheep

Adding Prefixes   You are probably already familiar with some common prefixes, such as *anti-*, *hyper-*, and others mentioned in Unit 25. Look at the rules for spelling words containing prefixes.

Adding Prefixes
When adding a prefix to a word, retain the spelling of the original word. *anti-* + gravity = antigravity   *co-* + authors = coauthors
When adding a prefix to a lowercase word, do not use a hyphen in most cases. When adding a prefix to a capitalized word, use a hyphen. Always use a hyphen with the prefix *ex-* meaning "previous" or "former." *co-* + worker = coworker   *mid-* + ship = midship   *un-* + American = un-American   *ex-* + coach = ex-coach

Many different suffixes can be added to words. Most words that contain suffixes are spelled in a straightforward manner.

Adding Suffix -ly   When adding *-ly* to a word that ends in a single *l*, keep the *l*. When the word ends in a double *l*, drop one *l*. When the word ends in a consonant + *le*, drop the *le*:

equal + *-ly* = equally   dull + *-ly* = dully
comfortable + *-ly* = comfortably.

Adding Suffix -ness   When adding *-ness* to a word that ends in *n*, keep the *n*.

common + *-ness* = commonness   mean + *-ness* = meanness
plain + *-ness* = plainness   brazen+ *-ness* = brazenness

Adding Suffixes to Words Ending in a Silent e   When you are adding a suffix to a word ending in a consonant + silent *e*, pay attention to the first letter of the suffix.

Rules	Examples	Exceptions
Drop the final silent *e* before a suffix that begins with a vowel.	fine + *-est* = finest; value + *-able* = valuable	Drop the final *e* after the letters *u* or *w*: *due, duly; argue, argument; awe, awful.*
Keep the final silent *e* before a suffix that begins with a consonant.	definite + *-ly* = definitely; white + *-ness* = whiteness	

Keep the final *e* in words ending in *-ee* and *-oe*: see, seeing; woe, woeful. Keep the final silent *e* before the suffix *-ing* to avoid ambiguity: singe, singeing; toe, toeing. Keep the final silent *e* in words ending with *-ce* or *-ge* that have suffixes beginning with *a* or *o*: service, serviceable.

Adding Suffixes to Words Ending in a Consonant   The following chart contains rules and examples concerning the doubling of a final consonant when adding a suffix to a word.

IF	THEN
If the original word is a one-syllable word . . .	Double the final consonant: *hop, hopping*
If the original word has its accent on the last syllable and the accent remains there after the suffix is added . . .	Double the final consonant: *begin, beginning*
If the original word is a prefixed word based on a one-syllable word . . .	Double the final consonant: *reset, resetting*

Do *not* double the final consonant . . .
if the accent is not on the last syllable or if the accent shifts when the suffix is added. *saw, sawing*
if the final consonants are *x* or *w*.   *wax, waxing*
when adding a suffix that begins with a consonant to a word that ends in a consonant. *annual, annulment*

Forming Compound Words   When joining a word that ends in a consonant to a word that begins with a consonant, keep both consonants:

air + man = airman

back + ground = background

book + keeper = bookkeeper

row + boat = rowboat

There are many exceptions to this rule. Many compounds are hyphenated: for example, *know-how.* Some compounds remain separate words, such as *cross section*, while related words, such as *crosswalk*, are joined. Use a dictionary to check the spelling of compounds.

ie and ei   Learning this rhyme can save you many misspellings: "Write *i* before *e* except after *c*, or when sounded like *a* as in *neighbor* and *weigh*." There are notable exceptions to the rule, and they include *seize, seizure, leisure, weird, height, either, neither,* and *forfeit.*

-cede, -ceed, and -sede   Because of the relatively few words with *sēd* sounds, these words are worth memorizing.

These words use *-cede:* accede, precede, secede.

One word uses *-sede:* supersede.

Three words use *-ceed:* exceed, proceed, succeed.

Using a Computer Spelling Checker

Although spelling checkers have certain advantages, they are not fool-proof. Use the following tips to learn what spelling checkers can and cannot do for you.

Tips for Using a Spelling Checker

1. When the spelling checker highlights a misspelled word and suggests a replacement, do not rely on the spelling checker's judgment. It searches for words that look similar to the misspelled word, but it does not know the particular word that you need. For example, if you type *mett,* the spelling checker will give you a choice of *met, net, mitt, nit,* and so on.

2. After using the spelling checker, proofread for sense. If you typed *wing* for *ring,* for example, the spelling checker will not pick up the error because both *wing* and *ring* are correctly spelled words. Even grammar checkers that check for grammatical agreement are not very accurate, so don't rely on them. A computer has yet to be invented that has the reasoning ability of a human being.

3. Use the spelling checker to target spelling problems. Keep a list of words that the spelling checker highlights, and quiz yourself on the words until you master them.

Exercise 1

Each of the following sentences contains one, several, or no misspelled words. Write each misspelled word correctly and state whether a rule applies to each case. Check your answers in a dictionary.

1. The ranches hireing cowboys are owned by the Joneses and the Diazes.
2. Midship-men at the Naval Academy are participating in antigravity experiments.
3. I like the plainess of white walls for displaying Southwestern art.
4. My arguement for replacing that aweful wallpaper was finally begining to win her over.
5. Fifteen attorneys representing forty companys are trying to sue the bakery for allowing its chimneys to pollute the air of three valleys.
6. Since the warehouse was empty at mid-day, the railroad delivery service decided to make the delivery at that time.
7. If you precede me on the highway I will probably not excede the speed limit, so let us procede on our journey.
8. You should sieze this opportunity to do a little travelling.

26.2   Spelling Challenges

Not everyone misspells the same words. Each person has an individual set of "problem" words. One strategy for learning these words is to develop a list of words that you frequently misspell in different courses. Keep the list in a notebook, where you can refer to it, and review words until you have mastered their spelling.

Commonly Misspelled Words

Some words fool most spellers at least some of the time because the words contain unusual combinations of letters, do not follow spelling rules, or are not spelled as they sound. A list of such words follows. Try quizzing yourself to see how many of the words you can correctly spell.

Some words have more than one correct spelling; for example, "adviser" is also correctly spelled "advisor."

Commonly Misspelled Words			
abundant	consciousness	inoculate	personnel
accelerator	controlling	intellectual	persuade
accidentally	cruelty	judgment	picnicking
accomplishment	deceitful	larynx	possessed
acknowledge	desirable	license	precede
adequately	devastation	livelihood	prestige
admittance	dilemma	magistrate	prevalent
advantageous	disastrous	maintenance	procedure
adviser	discrimination	manageable	propagate
alliance	dissatisfied	marriageable	questionnaire
apologetically	embarrass	mediocre	rebellion
apparent	emphasize	melodious	recommendation
arrangement	enormous	miniature	referred
ballet	environment	mosquito	remittance
beginning	exhilaration	necessity	reveal
benefited	exuberant	negligence	rhythmical
biscuit	February	negotiable	ridiculous
buffet	feminine	newsstand	salable
burial	fission	nuisance	separation
capitalism	gaiety	occurrence	souvenir
caricature	gauge	omission	sponsor
cataclysm	guidance	opportunity	strategic
calendar	hereditary	outrageous	unscrupulous
changeable	horizontal	pamphlet	vacuum
colleague	ideally	parliament	vaudeville
coming	incidentally	peasant	vengeance
competition	influential	permanent	Wednesday

Easily Confused Words

Some words are frequently confused with other words that have similar pronunciations or spellings. Study the following list of easily confused words. More easily confused words are in Unit 19.

Easily Confused Words		
carat	diamond weight	She wore a two-carat diamond.
caret	proofreader's mark	Use a caret to insert a word.
carrot	vegetable	We like peas and carrots.
complement	to go well with	Tartar sauce complements fish.
compliment	to flatter	Her dress drew compliments.
precedence	priority	What takes precedence over safety?
precedents	previous events	Are there legal precedents?
rap	to knock	Rap on the door.
wrap	to cover	I will wrap the presents.
root	part of a plant	The plant's roots are dry.
rout	to defeat	We will rout our rivals.
route	a traveler's way	Which route should I take?
en route	along the way	We expect trouble en route.
shear	to cut	He should shear the sheep.
sheer	utter, steep	The cliff is a sheer drop.
weather	atmosphere	The weather is sunny and dry.
whether	if	Whether you go is your choice.

Exercise 2

Rewrite the following sentences to correct misspellings.

1. The disasterous buffet included enormus old carots, stale minature biskets, and some rather mediocer fish.
2. When one considers the devestation caused by his unscrupulus enemies, it is no wonder that General Lee exuberantly lead the charge to route them.
3. The wheather analyst's accomplishements were acknoledged by many complements from her colleages.
4. The maintainance personnel sponsered a campaigne for enviromental awareness.
5. Does the calendar show Febuary forth as being a Wensday or a Thursday?

Study Skills

27.1 Boost Your Study Skills

If you want to get better grades, take a tip from the business world: work smarter, not harder. If you study smarter, you will make the most efficient use of the time you spend taking notes, reading, and studying.

Taking Meaningful Notes

Good notes do two things: they condense main ideas and important details, and they show relationships between ideas and details. When you take notes, paraphrase concepts. Double-space your notes, so you can later fill in details and examples that you missed and add information from your reading. Use a question mark to indicate missing information, and then fill in the information after class when the lecture is still fresh in your mind. The following notes are from a biology class.

Identify main ideas by giving them prominence in your notes, and list details underneath them to indicate relationships.

Abbreviate words, such as "2" for "two" and "ident." for "identical," whenever possible to save time.

Taking Notes in Modified Outline Form
Cell Division — 2 Forms
I. Mitosis: cell divides, forms 2 ident. cells
— 4 stages in animals
(1) prophase — chromosomes condense and appear
(2) metaphase —   "   line up midcell
(3) anaphase —   "   move apart
(4) ? —   "   elongate, become invisible
II. Meiosis

Making Study Time Count

The amount of time that you spend studying may not be as important as the quality of your study habits. For example, if you study in front of a blaring television while stretched out on a sofa, you probably will not gain much from your efforts. Similarly, trying to cram a week's studying into a panic-filled two hours is time poorly spent.

Think about when, where, and how you learn best. What works for another student may not work for you, but you might want to experiment with different study habits to discover those that best suit you. Consider some of the suggestions that follow.

1. **Find a quiet place to study.** Distractions will break your concentration and waste time.
2. **Choose a regular time to study.** If studying becomes a routine, it will seem less like a chore.
3. **Set achievable study goals.** Divide long-term assignments into stages, and complete them over a period of time. For nightly homework, prioritize assignments. Do the dreaded assignments first, when you have the most energy.
4. **Before beginning to read or study, skim the material to get a sense of what is before you.** If you preview the material, it will make more sense to you when you read it in depth because you can anticipate how main ideas are connected and will develop.
5. **Study with a pen and paper ready.** Jot down key words and ideas to reinforce them in your mind and to provide yourself with material for review at another study session.
6. **After reviewing the material on your own, ask someone to quiz you to see whether you have mastered the material.** Although you understand the material, you may not know it well enough to rephrase it for a test.
7. **Refresh your attention by taking occasional breaks.**
8. **Don't cram for tests.** Research shows that you will learn more in several short review sessions than in one long one.
9. **If you know the time will be well spent, form a study group.** Quiz each other to prepare for tests.

Reading to Remember

To understand and remember what you read, first spend some time "prereading." Skim chapter headings, key terms, photo captions, and chapter summaries to gain a general sense of the material and an overview of main ideas. The study or review questions at the end of sections or chapters indicate what information the author considers most important.

Next, read in depth. Think as you read, taking notes and finding answers to study or review questions. List any questions of your own that arise. Like reflecting an image with a mirror, your writing will "reflect" the ideas in your mind, reinforcing what you read.

During another study session, review this material. Scan your textbook again for main ideas and supporting details. Reread your notes, the study questions and answers, and the questions and answers you have found for your own questions.

When studying your notes and class handouts, you might use a highlighter pen to emphasize important points. Highlight judiciously: if an entire page is colored in, you will see no differentiation between crucial material and minor details.

Evaluating What You Read

When you read textbooks and library sources, first read to collect information, then read to evaluate it. When you evaluate, you weigh fact against opinion, analyze the completeness of information, and consider the logic of conclusions. Sometimes words in a selection can tip you off to a bias an article has. Other times you may need to rely on your own knowledge or comparisons to other sources to evaluate a source. Look at the following paragraph about pesticides, and try to answer the questions that follow it.

> Many pesticides that are banned in wealthy nations are shipped to Central America, often with disastrous results. Pesticide containers have safety instructions written in a language farmers can't read. Some pesticides are so toxic that anyone applying them should wear a tightly sealed rubber suit and a respirator. Unfortunately, most farmers are too poor to afford any protection; those who can afford the gear don't buy it because rubber suits are impractical in the tropics.
>
> - What are the facts?
> - What additional information do you need to fully understand the situation?
> - Does the writer's selective presentation of the facts affect whether or not you believe the facts?
> - What words are clues to the writer's bias?

In this paragraph the writer presents a one-sided and incomplete picture. Which pesticides are being shipped to Central America? Why have they been banned in wealthier countries? Which pesticides can be used safely if precautions are followed? What evidence is there of "disastrous results"? Why aren't their governments doing something?

Some of the writer's word choices are clues to the writer's bias: *wealthy* countries, *disastrous* results, and *unfortunately*. However, the primary clue to the writer's bias is how the information is slanted. The implication of the paragraph is that greedy manufacturers are either uncaring or are willfully taking advantage of people in developing countries. More facts could justify such an opinion, or they could negate it altogether.

Exercise 1

Find a newspaper news article and an editorial on the same subject. Analyze the news article for fact, opinion, exaggeration, and bias; then do the same for the editorial.

Alternatively, choose a magazine article that you feel contains unsupported opinion or bias, and write a one-page essay stating and defending your views.

27.2   Understanding Graphics

The graphics in your textbooks and other reading materials can clarify complex relationships, untangle complicated descriptions, and summarize key ideas. Interpreting and understanding these visual aids accurately will help you to get the most from your reading. Most graphics are easy to read once you recognize their basic form, usually that of a diagram, table, chart, or graph.

Analyzing Diagrams

Diagrams, such as organizational trees and maps, illustrate the steps in a process or the breakdown of abstract concepts into concrete terms. The diagram below illustrates how a concept can be more easily understood when it is rendered as a diagram.

Abraham Maslow's Psychological Theory of the Hierarchy of Needs		
Stages	**Examples**	**Period of Growth**
Stage 5 Self-actualization	Self-acceptance Self-confidence	Adult
Stage 4 Esteem needs	Respect and acceptance from others	Adolescent
Stage 3 Love needs	Attention from friends and family	Child
Stage 2 Safety needs	Secure environment	Infant
Stage 1 Physiological needs	Air, sustenance, warmth	Developing fetus

Arrows within the diagram provide important information. Why is Stage 1 presented at the bottom of the diagram instead of at the top?

Notice that the overall design of the diagram not only lists the stages of Maslow's theory but also shows that one stage cannot be reached without the previous stage being completed.

Reading Tables, Charts, and Graphs

Suppose you are writing a research paper about trends in home entertainment. How might you use visual aids? You could present information about video sales and rentals in a table, graph, or chart to graphically illustrate a trend: while more people than ever are watching videos, more consumers are renting tapes than are buying them.

Tables　The presentation of several categories of detailed, statistical data is best handled in a table. The following table presents video sales and rentals in millions of dollars over a five-year time span.

Video Sales and Rentals (in millions)		
Year	Video Rentals	Video Sales
1986	$3,308	$ 810
1987	$4,168	$1,004
1988	$5,210	$1,483
1989	$6,096	$2,240
1990	$6,645	$2,800

While the table indicates a trend, you cannot assume that the trend will continue. Other variables, not presented in the table, may affect statistics in the future. For example, the cost of videos may radically decrease and thus increase sales, or a new technology may emerge that makes videos obsolete.

Read tables carefully—numbers are often written in a kind of short-hand in which zeroes are dropped. For example, in the table above, the $3,308 for rentals for the year 1986 means millions of dollars.

Line Graphs　These graphs dramatically show trends, movements, and cycles. Line graphs are often used to show production amounts, sales figures, and temperature or rainfall over a period of time.

The vertical axis, or scale, usually appears on the left side and is used to show the dependent variable, such as dollars or temperature. The horizontal axis usually appears under the graph and increases from left to right; it shows independent variables, such as time. The line graph below presents one column from the table.

If you looked at only the data in the line graph, you might incorrectly assume that video sales have been equally successful. You cannot infer facts beyond those that the graph illustrates. Neither can you infer reasons, such as why people rent videos.

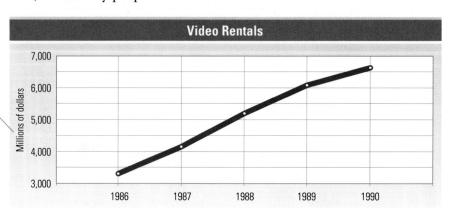

Bar Graphs Bar graphs compare amounts. The bars can be horizontal or vertical. This bar graph uses the same data as the line graph.

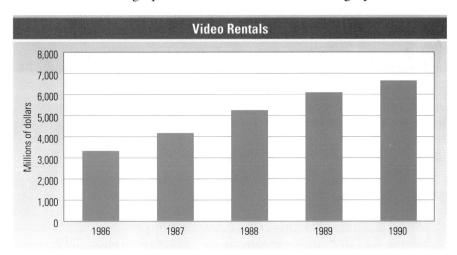

How does your perception of the data change when you see this bar graph versus the same information in the line graph and in the table?

Pie Charts These graphics show a circle representing 100 percent of a whole. Divisions within the circle, "slices" of the pie, represent proportions of the whole and must visually reflect the percentages they represent. To evaluate the accuracy of a pie chart, compare pie slices to divisions on a clock face. In 15 minutes the minute hand travels around 25% of the pie; 30 minutes equals 50%. Use the shapes of these slices to compare to percentages in pie charts.

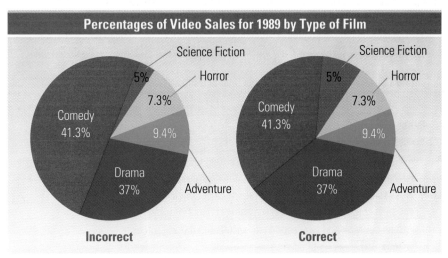

Compare the size of the slice labeled 41.3% on each chart. In the "incorrect" chart, it occupies 50% of the circle.

Exercise 2

Find a table, chart, graph, or diagram. Make a copy of it, and then in writing tell what the visual aid illustrates.

Unit 28 — Test Taking

28.1 Taking Essay Tests

Essay tests require you to use your knowledge of a given topic to produce a well-written essay in a limited amount of time. Thinking on your feet is not the key to writing a successful essay. Prepare thoroughly so you know what you want to write before you walk into class. Then, when you take the test, allocate enough time for each stage of the writing process.

Planning the Essay

Begin planning your answers to essay questions before you see the actual test. As you study, anticipate questions that are likely to appear on the test, and compose answers to them. Set yourself time limits of ten to twenty minutes for each question.

An essay test may consist of one in-depth question or several less complicated ones. When you receive the test, first read it through. If there are several questions, determine how much time to spend on each question. Then, reread the question for words that indicate the thinking processes to employ in your answer: *compare, contrast, analyze, explain, trace, define, summarize,* or *prove.* Look at the following example questions.

Analyzing an Essay Test Question

History Question: Trace the expansion of railroads in the American West.

Analysis: To *trace* is to describe, one stage at a time, how something changes or develops.

What to consider:
- What caused the change to begin?
- What were the stages of change? How long did each last?
- What were the particular elements of each stage? (Consider major political events, people, and obstacles.)
- In each stage, what remained the same? changed? why? (Consider how and why economic, social, and natural forces compelled changes to occur.)
- When and why did the development end?

Similarly, if you are asked to *define* something, such as the system of apartheid, begin with an actual definition. Then, develop and expand the definition. Use examples or illustrations and compare and contrast the system, for example, with other systems.

Analyzing an Essay Test Question

Literature Question: <u>Contrast</u> the poems of Anne Sexton with those of Emily Dickinson.

Analysis: To *contrast* is to describe how items are different.

What to consider:
- Which items (poems) will you contrast?
- Which elements of those items make effective contrasts? (Consider subject matter, tone, images, rhythm, and rhyme.)
- Which details provide the best support? (Consider summarizing poems and paraphrasing lines from poems.)
- How are the poets' lives reflected in their poems?

Writing the Essay

If you must write more than one essay, apportion enough time for each. Begin your answer to a question by brainstorming and prewriting on scratch paper for several minutes. Read the test question again to make sure that you are answering the question. Then, create a rough outline to organize main ideas and key details. Next, jot down your thesis statement. Then begin drafting your answer.

State your thesis in the first paragraph of your draft, so you can refer to it to keep your ideas on track. Use transition words to help one idea move smoothly to the next. Provide complete information, including examples and illustrations, where necessary. Be specific; your teacher will not be impressed if you pad your answer with unnecessary details about the subject.

You won't have time to revise your answer. Instead, spend the remaining minutes that you have proofreading your answer and making corrections neatly.

Exercise 1

Prepare an outline and a thesis statement for each of the following sample essay questions. Spend no more than ten minutes on any one question. Discuss your work in groups.

1. Trace the development of civil rights in the United States.
2. Define "point of view" as it applies to literature, and give examples of the kinds of point of view.
3. Defend or disprove the following statement: "Education is the great emancipator."
4. Contrast the benefits of aerobic exercise and weight lifting.

28.2   Preparing for Standardized Tests

Some Saturday morning you may find yourself in your high school cafeteria or auditorium, taking a morning-long battery of standardized tests. You may be intimidated, knowing that your test results may determine the college to which you go, but preparation can lessen the strain.

The Purpose of Standardized Tests

Standardized tests are given to many people under similar circumstances and are objectively graded to determine an average, or "standard," score. Some standardized tests, such as the California Achievement Tests, evaluate how much you have learned in specific subject areas, such as calculus. Other tests, such as the ACT (American College Testing) and the SAT (Scholastic Aptitude Test), evaluate a broader range of abilities. The ACT measures achievement in English, math, social studies, and natural sciences. The SAT measures verbal and mathematical abilities and is the most frequently administered standardized test.

Colleges use standardized test scores to determine students' admission status and probable success in college courses. Most high school students take the SAT in their junior year and have the option of repeating it in their senior year. If you are not satisfied with your first performance, then repeat the test. In fact, some guidance counselors recommend taking the test for the first time just to demystify the experience.

Preparing to Take Standardized Tests

Because standardized tests of ability, such as the SAT, measure overall scholastic ability, you can't study for them as you would classroom tests. You can, however, almost always ensure a higher score by preparing for them using the methods described in the box that follows.

Before You Take a Standardized Test

- Gather information about the test. Your school counselor's office is a good place to begin your search for information.

- Get a schedule of test dates, and mail in the appropriate forms and any required fees well before the deadline date.

- Take practice exams, such as the PSAT (Preliminary SAT). Practice exams give you an idea of the kinds of questions you can expect and help you to learn how to pace yourself. You can also buy practice books or borrow them from a library.

- Review general principles, but don't cram for the test. Rely on practice exams, books, and study guides. Also ask your counselor about tutors and study groups.

On the morning of the test, be sure that you are well rested and have eaten a sustaining breakfast. Arrive at the testing place early, and have necessary items with you, such as your entrance card, identification, #2 pencils, an eraser, and a watch. The box below provides tips for taking standardized tests.

Tips for Taking Standardized Tests

- If you don't already know, find out whether the test is designed to be completed; some are not. Also find out whether there is a penalty for incorrect answers. If there is a penalty, it is to your advantage not to guess if you don't know an answer. If there is no penalty, do not hesitate to guess.

- Before you begin any section of the test, read the directions carefully. Directions may change from section to section.

- Before beginning each section, check to see how many questions there are so you can pace yourself accordingly.

- If you can't answer a question, don't waste precious minutes dwelling on it. Go on to the next question. If there is time, you can return to the questions you skipped.

- You will probably use a #2 pencil and fill in circles on a computer-readable form. Be sure that your marks are heavy and remain within the answer circle.

- If you skip a question in the test booklet, make sure you skip the corresponding answer circle. Periodically check that the number of the test question matches that of your answer.

Exercise 2

Use a bulletin board in your classroom to create an information center for standardized tests. Your class and other English classes can work together on the project. Use the following suggestions for assigning duties.

1. Visit the counseling center to interview counselors and to gather information, such as sample forms.
2. Make a chart listing application deadlines.
3. See what test-taking resources and practice exams are available in libraries and at bookstores. Prepare a summary of your findings.
4. Write reviews of study guides and practice books. Include prices, quality, and availability.
5. Contact colleges that you and others want to attend. Find out which exams they require, and post your findings.

28.3 Standardized Test Items

Standardized tests such as the SAT test your understanding of word meanings; your level of reading comprehension in various subject areas; and your knowledge of grammar, usage, and mechanics.

Multiple-Choice Vocabulary Questions

Vocabulary test questions are followed by five possible answers. First examine the given words and try to determine the answer before you read the choices. You will be less likely to be confused by a misleading or ambiguous answer choice. Next choose the best answer from those listed.

Antonym Questions   These items require you to choose from a list of words one that is most nearly opposite in meaning from a given capitalized word. Look at the capitalized word below and choose its antonym.

PRELUDE: (A) postpone   (B) preamble   (C) fugue   (D) epilogue   (E) symphony

A *prelude* is "an introductory performance"; in context, it often refers to a piece of music. So you should look for a word that describes the closing of something, such as *epilogue*, choice (D), which is the correct answer even though it refers to the afterword in a novel rather than to a piece of music. You may be distracted by choice (A), *postpone*, which means "to put off," but it's neither a good match nor the same part of speech as *prelude*.

Analogy Questions   These questions test your ability to identify the relationship of a capitalized word pair and then to find a parallel relationship in another word pair from a list of word pairs. Always begin by determining the relationship of the capitalized word pair. Some possible relationships are presented in the chart below.

Analogy Relationships	
Word Pair	**Relationship**
TREPIDATION : PERTURBATION	synonyms
PROCESSIONAL : RECESSIONAL	sequence in time
OEDIPUS REX : DRAMA	an item in a classification
DROUGHT : STARVATION	cause and effect
ASTROLABE : ASTRONOMER	tool and user

To determine an analogy relationship, formulate a sentence that contains and describes the relationship. For ASTROLABE : ASTRONOMER, think, "An astrolabe was used by early astronomers." Determine the relationship of the following capitalized word pair.

PENICILLIN : MEDICINE :: (A) sickness : invalid   (B) aggravation : rash
(C) Ibsen : playwright   (D) noxious : beneficial   (E) punctuation : language

You may decide, "penicillin is a kind of medicine." The relationship of the given pair is *an item in a class*. Now consider the choices, putting each answer choice in your relationship sentence. Thus, "sickness is *not* a kind of invalid"; "aggravation is *not* a kind of rash." (Watch out for answers that would be correct if their order were reversed: a rash is a kind of aggravation.) "Ibsen is *not* a kind of playwright," but he is one author in that class. Neither of the last two choices suits the relationship of object to class. While *punctuation* is related to *language*, "punctuation is *not* a kind of language," nor is it a class of language. Even if your relationship sentence is "penicillin is an example of medicine" or "penicillin is used in the practice of medicine," choice (E) still does not work. Choice (C) is correct.

Sentence-Completion Questions

These questions present sentences in which critical words are missing. You must recognize the relationships among the parts of the sentence in order to choose the word or words that make the sentence correct, both grammatically and logically. Decide which answer choice makes the following sentence correct.

Taking a stand in favor of animal rights, the researcher _____ an end to vivisection and _____ using monkeys in experiments.

(A) applauded . . . extolled   (B) denied . . . continued   (C) condemned . . . supported
(D) cheered . . . threatened   (E) advocated . . . denounced

Before you begin to answer the question, read the sentence through to understand the ideas expressed; then try out each answer choice. Thus, someone in favor of animal rights would certainly *applaud* the end of vivisection but would hardly *extol* the use of monkeys in experiments. To be sure that both words fit the logic and grammar of the sentence, try all the choices in the blanks until you find the best answer. Only answer (E) makes sense in the sentence above.

Reading-Comprehension Questions

This section of the test presents passages of varying length and difficulty from writing in different fields of study. The questions about the passages are designed to test your understanding of what you read. Try the sample questions on the next page. Read the questions first to determine what to look for as you read the passage.

One of the most important archaeological finds in history is the discovery of the tomb of Chinese Emperor Qin Shihuangdi. Qin came to power when he was only 13 years old. As soon as he ascended the throne, he ordered laborers to begin work on his tomb, a project believed to have taken 36 years to complete. An army of life-size terra-cotta figures holding authentic weapons is buried in standing formation with the emperor. Each statue was apparently modeled after a specific soldier—an astounding feat considering the vast number of statues, approximately 6,000 archers, officers, and charioteers with their horses. The tomb was rigged with booby-trapped crossbows intended to protect the emperor's remains against grave robbers.

1. The best title for this passage would be:
   (A) Burial Practices in Ancient China
   (B) Emperor Qin Shihuangdi
   (C) Qin's Army in the Tomb
   (D) Archaeology in China
   (E) A Forgotten Emperor

2. Which of the following conclusions could be made after reading the passage?
   (A) The greatest archaeological finds are in China.
   (B) Qin's society held its emperors in great esteem.
   (C) Qin's soldiers respected him.
   (D) Qin greatly feared his enemies.
   (E) Profiteers are attracted to archaeological sites.

Most questions deal with finding the main idea, drawing inferences, identifying facts, and recognizing tone. The first question above asks for a title, the main idea of the passage. The answer is (C): (A) and (D) are too broad; (B) and (E) focus on the emperor, not the tomb.

The second question asks you to draw an inference. In the passage none of the choices is directly stated. Only answer (D) can be assumed, based on the information provided. When answering a question that asks for facts from a passage, find the choice that answers that question. In evaluating an author's tone, look for words that indicate bias.

English-Composition Questions

These questions test your ability to identify and correct errors in grammar, sentence structure, word usage, and correctness of expression according to standard written American English.

Usage Questions These questions require you to recognize sentence parts that are grammatically incorrect or unclear. Each test question is a sentence that contains several underlined parts labeled (A) through (D), followed by choice (E), "no error." As you read, determine in which part an error exists or, if there is no error, choose (E). Remember that an error can occur only in an underlined section. Try the following question.

> At the Jacobean drama festival honoring Shakespeare's birthday, gaily dressed min-
>   (A)
> strels, playing old ballads and love songs, walked among the crowds; everywhere was
>   (B)   (C)
> music and laughter. no error
>   (D)   (E)

Be sure to read the entire sentence; otherwise, you might overlook an error. In the example sentence, the singular verb "was" in (D) does not agree with the plural subject "music and laughter." Because the sentence structure reverses the order of these elements, the problem may be difficult to recognize.

Sentence-Correction Questions   These questions require you not only to find the error in an underlined part but also to decide on the best revision to correct the error. Your answer, selected from choices that follow the sentence, should reflect the most effective expression and should be free of awkwardness, illogic, and faulty sentence structure. Choice (A) always contains the exact wording of the underlined section and means "no error." As with usage questions, an error can occur only in an underlined portion.

Try to determine the error before reading the answer choices. Read the following sentence and its possible corrections.

> The company president should either resign, or he should learn about responding to employee complaints in a serious way.
>
> (A) he should learn about responding to employee complaints in a serious way.
> (B) he should learn serious responses to employee complaints.
> (C) learn to respond seriously to employee complaints.
> (D) should take the employee complaints with greater seriousness.
> (E) could respond in a serious manner to employee complaints.

Choice (C) contains the most clear and concise wording and corrects the faulty parallelism in the original sentence.

Exercise 3

VOCABULARY QUESTIONS

Antonym Questions   Find the best antonym for each of the words below.

1. RECIDIVISM: (A) advancement (B) deterioration (C) disavow (D) rubbish (E) elitism
2. JOCULAR: (A) irksome (B) angular (C) laughable (D) morose (E) happy ➡

Analogy Questions   For each question, find the pair of words that represents the same relationship expressed in the capitalized word pair.

3. COMPUTER : MICROCHIP : :   (A) program : operate
   (B) injection : rash (C) universe : constellation
   (D) irrigation : flood (E) reporter : news
4. BENEVOLENT : FORGIVES : :   (A) beneficial : helpful
   (B) radiant : obscure (C) proficient : bungles
   (D) musician : concert (E) haughty : boasts

Sentence-Completion Questions   Find the words that best complete each sentence below.

5. When one thinks of _____, Lorraine comes to mind: she always puts the needs of others before her own comfort and convenience.
   (A) goodness (B) affectation (C) altruism
   (D) prestige (E) ennui
6. The dissident writer continued to _____ the current political system in her lectures, even though the government had _____ her books.
   (A) attack . . . banned (B) praise . . . sold
   (C) admonish . . . praised (D) uphold . . . criticized
   (E) laud . . . destroyed

Exercise 4

Reading-Comprehension Questions   Read the passage and answer the questions that follow it.

In ancient times many Arabs who inhabited Asia Minor were Bedouin nomads. They lived in tribes, each made up of related families. Arabs valued family ties because they ensured protection and survival in the harsh desert environment. A sheikh, appointed by the heads of families, led each tribe. A council of elders advised the sheikh, who ruled as long as he had the tribe's consent. Survival in the desert was contingent upon everyone's obeying tribal rules based on such values as honor, loyalty, generosity, and bravery.

7. Which of the following statements is not true?
   (A) A sheikh did not have complete control of the tribe.
   (B) The Bedouin depended upon each other to obey rules.
   (C) Bedouin society was based on familial ties.
   (D) Bedouin lived in villages in the desert. ➥

(E) Bedouin elders advised the sheikh

8. The Bedouin valued family connections because
   (A) they appointed a sheikh as their leader.
   (B) they helped ensure the adherence to values necessary for survival.
   (C) they lived in tribes.
   (D) the sheikh was advised by a council of elders.
   (E) of a system of dowries.

Exercise 5

ENGLISH-COMPOSITION QUESTIONS

Usage Question   Read the sentence below and decide whether any part of it contains an error. Choose (E) if the sentence is grammatically correct.

9. The <u>effect of chlorofluorocarbons</u> on the protective
   (A)
   <u>ozone layer, which surrounds</u> the <u>Earth, will have</u>
   (B)   (C)
   disastrous consequences for plant and animal life unless

   the <u>use of these chemicals is abandoned.</u> <u>no error</u>
   (D)   (E)

Exercise 6

Sentence-Correction Question   Choose the answer that produces the clearest, most effective sentence.

10. As I see it, students who want to pursue a liberal arts education should take classes in history, economics, literature, and philosophy, <u>and they should also take classes in math and science, as well</u>.
    (A) and they should also take classes in math and science, as well.
    (B) as well as in math and science.
    (C) and in math and science, as well.
    (D) and they should, as well, take classes in math and science.
    (E) including classes in math and science.

Unit 29 Listening and Speaking

29.1 Effective Listening

Unlike the written word, the spoken word lasts just an instant. This makes listening a different skill from reading. In this unit you will learn how to understand and remember more of what you hear.

Active Listening

Hearing is perceiving all the sounds and information that make their way into the brain. Listening, on the other hand, only begins with hearing a message. It includes understanding a message, evaluating it, and remembering it. Here are some tips to strengthen your listening skills.

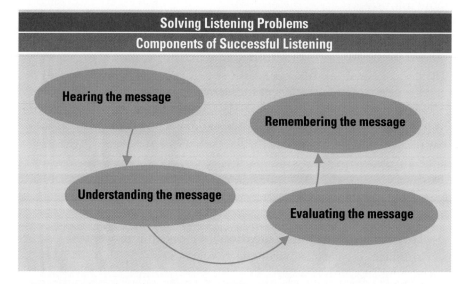

Solving Listening Problems
Components of Successful Listening

- Hearing the message
- Understanding the message
- Evaluating the message
- Remembering the message

How can I keep my mind from wandering when I listen in class?
Take notes and you will become an active listener instead of a passive observer. You will be forced to think about the pattern of what is said and will remain "tuned in."

I think that I understand what I hear in class, but when I take tests, it's obvious that I missed the main points.
If you focus on a lecture's introduction and conclusion and listen carefully for transitional words and important terms, you can take notes in a modified outline form. Your notes will allow you to construct a "mental map" in which main ideas are highlighted. If you mix up "the big picture" and the details, the illogical sequence of information will be obvious. You will need to ask your teacher for clarification.

I can memorize information, but I can't seem to put it all together in a meaningful way.
Make a conscious effort to see what the main ideas are, how they are linked, and why they are significant. Mark your notes to differentiate main ideas and details. Listen for words such as *next, secondly,* and *conversely* that signal linked ideas. To discover the significance of ideas, periodically ask yourself, "Why is this development important?" Find the answer by continued listening, asking your teacher, or reading.

How can I remember what I hear?
No one can remember all that he or she hears. Focus on the main points, and reflect on them. Remembering specific examples will help you to recall the main points.

Critical Listening

Critical listening requires you to do more than understand a message. When you listen critically, you separate fact from opinion, spot errors in logic, and distinguish a speaker's appeal from the message. (See Unit 6 for more information on critical analysis.)

The amount of evaluation that you need to do varies with each listening situation. For example, when your English teacher discusses a work of literature, you hear a mixture of fact and opinion. Your teacher probably expects you to do some analysis to form opinions and conclusions of your own. When you listen to commercials, however, you hear more opinions than facts, and advertisers probably hope that you don't analyze what you hear. When critically examined, many advertising claims are ridiculous: few people find romance by switching to a different toothpaste. Similarly, a celebrity's paid endorsement of a health club or an athletic shoe will not change the intrinsic value of what he or she is selling. Consumers can buy a product or service but not the celebrity's glamour.

Exercise 1

Practice your listening and evaluating skills in one of the following ways.

1. Listen to two radio or television commercials. For each commercial, write a paragraph that rates the ad for its honesty and the amount of factual information that it provides. Use a scale of 1 to 10 in which 10 stands for an extremely honest ad—one containing useful, factual information— and 1 stands for an extremely dishonest or manipulative ad. Defend your rating.
2. Create your own radio commercial. Then have the class evaluate it using the scale mentioned above, and comment on its effectiveness.

29.2　Effective Speaking

A chief surgeon at a leading hospital was asked to give an after-dinner speech at a football banquet. During the dinner a man began choking on something and then collapsed. Thinking quickly, the surgeon rushed to the man's table and opened the choking man's throat with a pen knife. After accompanying the man to a hospital, the surgeon returned to the banquet and gave his speech.

Not all speakers can adapt so appropriately to audience response, but the story illustrates two key rules for good public speaking: be prepared and be responsive to audience needs.

Informal Speeches

People frequently make informal speeches. These speeches can be as brief as an introduction of one friend to another and as casual as telling a group of friends what you did during your family's vacation. You may not realize it, but even informal speeches follow commonly accepted patterns of organization and delivery. Because of their brief, informal nature, however, these speeches rarely require advance preparation.

Making a Formal Speech

Unlike informal speeches, formal speeches are rehearsed and are delivered in more formal settings. In some ways, giving a formal speech is more like writing a research paper because it, too, is more easily managed when divided into stages, such as those that follow.

Consider Your Topic, Purpose, and Audience　Once you have chosen or been assigned a topic, focus on your purpose for making the speech. Do you want to inform your audience, persuade them, or move them to action? Next, evaluate what your audience already knows and believes about your topic. What terms do you need to define? What misconceptions do you need to dispel?

Research Your Topic　Gather facts, examples, and experts' opinions to explain and support your speech. You may gather information through library research, polls, and interviews. The amount of information that you need will depend on the complexity of your topic and the length of time you have been allotted to speak. Include explanations of terms and concepts that will be unfamiliar to your audience.

Organize Your Speech into an Outline　Choose a pattern of organization that effectively presents your information. (See pages 80–81 and 220–232 for methods of organization.) Create a stimulating introduction that grabs your audience's attention. The chart on the next page lists several ideas for beginning your speech.

Use humor
How much string does it take to reach the moon? Just one piece—but it's a very long piece!

Tell a story
When my grandmother came to this country, she expected that the roads would be paved with gold. . . .

Ask a question
If you could spend 60 cents a day to save a child's life, would you do it?

State an amazing fact or statistic
Every minute of every day, 60 acres of rain forest are destroyed.

Create Note Cards   Transfer the main points of your speech to note cards. You will sound more natural and make eye contact with your audience more often if you speak from note cards rather than read from a script. After deciding on the most effective order in which to present your ideas, prepare note cards that contain main ideas, important details, quotations, and statistics. Remember to number your note cards to keep them in order.

Practice Your Speech   If possible, practice before an audience of parents or close friends who will be supportive and honest. Ask them to time your delivery and to offer suggestions. Rehearse several times, but don't rehearse to the point of memorization. If you do memorize your speech, your final delivery will probably sound "canned," or you will be tempted to talk too fast.

Deliver Your Speech   Strive for a natural stance, and use gestures to accentuate your meaning. Make an effort to speak clearly and at a normal pace so that the audience will understand you. If you feel strongly about your topic, let some of that emotion show; it will create empathy in the audience. Be sure to vary your gaze around the room so that everyone in the audience feels included.

Exercise 2

Many local television stations present editorials as a public service. Editorials are short speeches in which the speaker voices an opinion about an issue or expresses pleasure or displeasure with the outcome of a current event. Prepare a three-minute editorial to present to your class. Choose a topic that you feel strongly about and that relates to your school or community.

29.3 Formal Debates

A country lawyer named Abraham Lincoln became so famous for his debating skills that people turned out in droves to hear him. Scholars credit his skill in debating with his winning the presidency of the United States. Indeed, debating skills have many applications.

The Structure of a Debate

A debate is a contest between two people or two teams who argue for or against a given statement or question, known as a proposition. Each side follows rules and time limits set down by a panel of judges. The winner of the debate is the side that presents the most logical and convincing arguments.

When you participate in a school debate, you or your team argues for or against a proposition. Each side has two chances to speak. First, one side presents its case and then the opposition presents its case in what are called constructive speeches. Next, each side refutes the other's arguments in rebuttal speeches. At the end of the debate, a panel of judges selects the winning side. The chart below outlines this process.

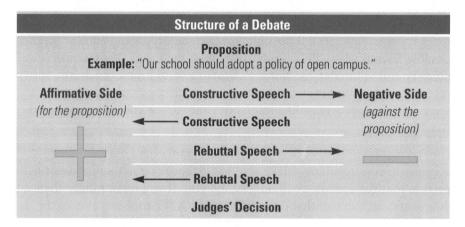

Gathering Information for a Debate

To support your position, use solid evidence to build a case. Your evidence may come from facts, experts' opinions, statistics, and examples of situations similar to the one you are citing. However, gathering information to support your case is not enough. You must also consider the opposing team's case and anticipate its strategy in order to design effective rebuttals. Thus, your goal is twofold: to disprove its case and to prove yours. Sometimes, a school debating team is not told which side of a proposition it will defend until it arrives at the debate, so each team must prepare to defend both sides of the proposition.

Take special care when using statistics to prove your case. You might interpret facts and figures to support your position, but the opposition might use the same facts and figures and interpret them differently. Try also to resist the temptation to flood your case with ambiguous facts in the hope of impressing the judges with a volume of evidence. It's safer to rely on logical reasoning backed up with sound statistics. Consider the following checkpoints as you prepare your case.

Gathering Information for a Debate	
Gathering Information	**Facts** — Accurate? Up-to-date? Relevant? **Examples** — Appropriate? Pertinent? Effective? **Experts** — Qualified in subject area? Best available?
Checking Assumptions	**Interpreting facts** — Can the facts be interpreted in more than one way? **Judges' beliefs** — Are the judges' knowledge and sympathies considered? **Opposition's arguments** — Are the strengths of the opposition's case anticipated?

After you gather information for a debate, put an outline of your speech on note cards. The sample note card below shows an outline for a portion of a debate.

Use large printing so you can read your notes at a glance.

Reasons for Open Campus
1. Cafeteria too crowded
2. Survey of 50 students
   – say cafeteria runs out of best food
   – some lunches too starchy, too greasy
   – often no place to sit
3. Builds responsibility
4. Step toward freedom following high school
5. It works at other high schools

2

Include only key ideas and facts. Write in phrases and abbreviate where possible.

Number your cards to stay organized and as insurance in case you drop your cards during the debate.

Debating Style

A debate is much like a formal speech. In a debate, you or your team will be judged not only on your grasp of the issue, the quality of your research, and your effective reasoning, but also on your oral and physical presentation. How well the judges and audience receive you may depend on your voice quality, body language, eye contact, and enthusiasm.

Support all your claims with facts. While you may wish to show enthusiasm for your position, avoid being overly emotional. You may wish to employ some emotional appeals when appropriate, but be wary of rhetorical pitfalls, such as the bandwagon approach. (See Unit 6.)

To check your effectiveness, videotape yourself or your team in a practice session. Study the tape carefully, and use what you learn about your performance to improve your presentation. The following chart offers some tips on debating style.

Check Your Debating Style	
To Improve . . .	Make Sure That You . . .
Voice	Speak clearly and at a normal pace. Speak loudly enough to be heard by everyone. Omit verbal tics, such as "ummm," "OK," and "you know." Show some enthusiasm in your voice.
Posture	Stand straight but be relaxed; there is a balance between slumping and resembling a museum piece. Do not lean on the lectern; it might topple. Avoid tilting your head to the side.
Gestures	Use hand gestures naturally to emphasize size, a point, a transition, etc. Avoid clutching or drumming on the lectern. Don't shuffle or play with your notes—it distracts the judges and audience.
Eye Contact	Vary your gaze around the room. Include everyone. Avoid staring at your notes or reading from them.
Composure	Stay in control; you're judged for your "cool." Don't become unnerved if someone laughs or leaves; don't assume you are the cause. Smile when appropriate; enjoyment is contagious.

Exercise 3

Work in groups of five or six to practice preparing for a debate. Use the following proposition or one that your teacher assigns: "Our high school should require all athletes to maintain a C average or better in every course." As a team, you may choose to take the positive or the negative side. Discuss ideas that your team could cover in a fifteen-minute constructive argument. Consider the strengths and weaknesses of your case. Present your work in a class discussion.

29.4   Participating in Meetings

Think of the groups in which you participate. Today you're part of a class; after school you may be a member of a team or club; at home, you're one of a family. Later, in college and on the job, participation in groups will remain an element in your life. Therefore, learning participation skills can have lifelong benefits.

Roles in Group Meetings

Some group meetings are as informal and unstructured as a group of friends discussing how to spend a Saturday night. Other group meetings, such as town meetings or student council meetings, are usually more formal and structured.

Formal meetings are often conducted by appointed or elected officers. Most meetings are led by a chairperson who directs the group's activities, maintains order during discussions, and ensures that everyone is heard. A recorder takes notes at meetings to keep a record of the group's activities. The recorder also announces future meetings and manages the group's correspondence. If the group generates money, a treasurer is appointed to serve as accountant for the group's projects.

A large group that must make many complex decisions is further subdivided. For example, members of the United States Senate are divided into various smaller committees with their own chairpersons and recorders. In this way, a large volume of tasks becomes manageable.

Group Meeting Procedures

Formal groups are successful if the members stay focused on their goal, give equal consideration and respect to all participants, and arrive at constructive decisions. Of course, not all participants agree on every point. Often, reaching a decision means ending the discussion and voting. The decision reached by the majority is usually accepted as final.

One way in which formal groups assure that order will prevail during discussions is to follow the rules of parliamentary procedure. Parliamentary procedure is based on the rules set forth in the book *Robert's Rules of Order*. Parliamentary procedure began in the British Parliament and was later adopted by the United States Congress, most large community groups, and student councils.

The basic principles of parliamentary procedure uphold the right of the minority to be heard and the right of the majority to prevail in decisions through voting. To assure order, only one topic may be discussed at a time. Topics are accepted for discussion only after a member makes a motion or a proposal for action. Although everyone has the chance to speak, only one person at a time may air views on the motion.

Personal Interviews

In an interview, it is your job to "sell" your abilities. If you are interviewed by a prospective employer or a college admissions officer, the key to success is to be prepared, to appear responsible and alert, and to use your listening and speaking skills.

Always listen closely to the interviewer, and answer just the question that you are asked. If you don't understand a question, ask for clarification. If you don't know the answer to a question, say so. Some interviewers devise questions that are tests of honesty. Some other suggestions for a successful interview follow.

Build Your Interview Skills

- Nervousness is natural, but try to relax, smile, and appear friendly.

- Look at the person to whom you are speaking.

- If you encounter an objection, such as "I don't think that you have enough experience for this job," evaluate the objection fairly. You may explain why you think you have enough experience, or why you have other qualities (such as your enthusiasm and willingness to learn) that will compensate for your lack of experience.

- Don't assume that an interviewer knows your thoughts. If you disagree with a statement ("You certainly wouldn't want to work in that department"), say so.

- If you need to formulate a complex answer, take time to think before you speak.

- At the conclusion of the interview, thank the interviewer for his or her time, and ask if you have the job or when a decision will be made.

Exercise 4

Practice your interview skills in mock interviews. Divide into groups of three, and take turns interviewing each other for one of the following jobs: clerk at a clothing store, counter person at a fast-food restaurant, or counselor at a summer camp. Before class, each person should prepare to assume each of the following roles: interviewer (What questions will you ask?), interviewee (What questions can you anticipate?), and evaluator. (How will you determine the success of the interview?)

During the mock interviews take turns in the different roles. Allocate your time so that each group member has a chance to be the person interviewed and to take at least one other role. If you have assumed the role of an evaluator, present your evaluations to the class.

Part 4

Strunk and White
The Elements of Style

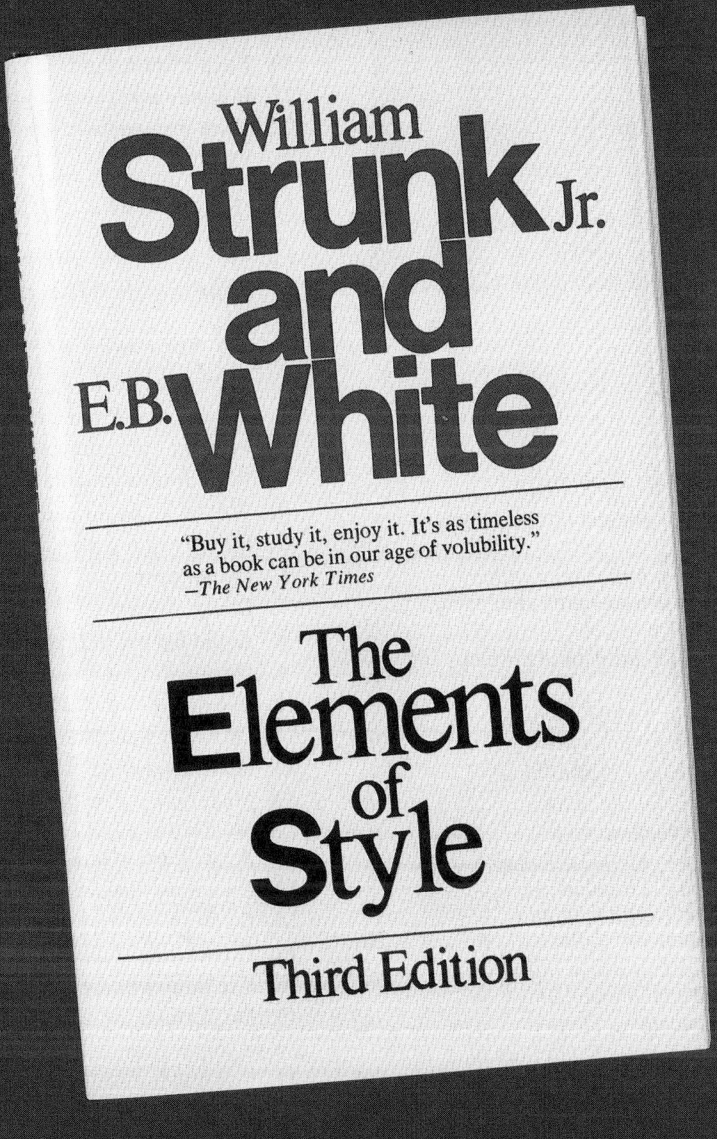

William
Strunk Jr.
and
E.B. White

"Buy it, study it, enjoy it. It's as timeless
as a book can be in our age of volubility."
—The New York Times

The
Elements
of
Style

Third Edition

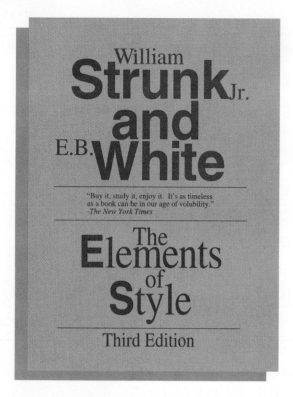

William **Strunk** Jr. **and** E.B. **White**

"Buy it, study it, enjoy it. It's as timeless as a book can be in our age of volubility."
-The New York Times

The **Elements** of **Style**

Third Edition

Contents

I
Elementary Rules of Usage

---

1. *Form the possessive singular of nouns by adding 's.*

Follow this rule whatever the final consonant. Thus write,

> Charles's friend
> Burns's poems
> the witch's malice

Exceptions are the possessives of ancient proper names in *-es* and *-is,* the possessive *Jesus',* and such forms as *for conscience' sake, for righteousness' sake.* But such forms as *Moses' Laws, Isis' temple* are commonly replaced by

> the laws of Moses
> the temple of Isis

The pronominal possessives *hers, its, theirs, yours,* and *ours* have no apostrophe. Indefinite pronouns, however, use the apostrophe to show possession.

> one's rights
> somebody else's umbrella

A common error is to write *it's* for *its,* or vice versa. The first is a contraction, meaning "it is." The second is a possessive.

> It's a wise dog that scratches its own fleas.

---

2. *In a series of three or more terms with a single conjunction, use a comma after each term except the last.*

Thus write,

> red, white, and blue
> gold, silver, or copper
> He opened the letter, read it, and made a note of its contents.

This comma is often referred to as the "serial" comma.

In the names of business firms the last comma is usually omitted. Follow the usage of the individual firm.

> Brown, Shipley and Co.
> Merrill Lynch, Pierce, Fenner & Smith Incorporated

3. *Enclose parenthetic expressions between commas.*

> The best way to see a country, unless you are pressed for time,
> is to travel on foot.

This rule is difficult to apply; it is frequently hard to decide whether a single word, such as *however,* or a brief phrase is or is not parenthetic. If the interruption to the flow of the sentence is but slight, the writer may safely omit the commas. But whether the interruption is slight or considerable, he must never omit one comma and leave the other. There is no defense for such punctuation as

> Marjorie's husband, Colonel Nelson paid us a visit yesterday.

or

> My brother you will be pleased to hear, is now in perfect health.

Dates usually contain parenthetic words or figures. Punctuate as follows:

> February to July, 1972
> April 6, 1956
> Wednesday, November 13, 1929

Note that it is customary to omit the comma in

> 6 April 1958

The last form is an excellent way to write a date; the figures are separated by a word and are, for that reason, quickly grasped.

A name or a title in direct address is parenthetic.

> If, Sir, you refuse, I cannot predict what will happen.
> Well, Susan, this is a fine mess you are in.

The abbreviations *etc., i.e.,* and *e.g.,* the abbreviations for academic degrees, and titles that follow a name are parenthetic and should be punctuated accordingly.

> Letters, packages, etc., should go here.
> Horace Fulsome, Ph.D., presided.
> Rachel Simonds, Attorney
> The Reverend Harry Lang, S.J.

No comma, however, should separate a noun from a restrictive term of identification.

> Billy the Kid
> The novelist John Fowles
> William the Conqueror
> Pliny the Younger

Although *Junior,* with its abbreviation *Jr.,* has commonly been regarded as parenthetic, logic suggests that it is, in fact, restrictive and therefore not in need of a comma.

> James Wright Jr.

Nonrestrictive relative clauses are parenthetic, as are similar clauses introduced by conjunctions indicating time or place. Commas are therefore needed. A nonrestrictive clause is one that does not serve to identify or define the antecedent noun.

> The audience, which had at first been indifferent, became more and more interested.
>
> In 1769, when Napoleon was born, Corsica had but recently been acquired by France.
>
> Nether Stowey, where Coleridge wrote *The Rime of the Ancient Mariner,* is a few miles from Bridgewater.

In these sentences, the clauses introduced by *which, when,* and *where* are nonrestrictive; they do not limit or define, they merely add something. In the first example, the clause introduced by *which* does not serve to tell which of several possible audiences is meant; the reader presumably knows that already. The clause adds, parenthetically, a statement supplementing that in the main clause. Each of the three sentences is a combination of two statements that might have been made independently.

> The audience was at first indifferent. Later it became more and more interested.
>
> Napoleon was born in 1769. At that time Corsica had but recently been acquired by France.
>
> Coleridge wrote *The Rime of the Ancient Mariner* at Nether Stowey. Nether Stowey is a few miles from Bridgewater.

Restrictive clauses, by contrast, are not parenthetic and are not set off by commas. Thus,

> People who live in glass houses shouldn't throw stones.

Here the clause introduced by *who* does serve to tell which people are meant; the sentence, unlike the sentences above, cannot be split into two independent statements. The same principle of comma use applies to participial phrases and to appositives.

> People sitting in the rear couldn't hear. (*restrictive*)
>
> Uncle Bert, being slightly deaf, moved forward. (*nonrestrictive*)
>
> My cousin Bob is a talented harpist. (*restrictive*)
>
> Our oldest daughter, Mary, sings. (*nonrestrictive*)

When the main clause of a sentence is preceded by a phrase or a subordinate clause, use a comma to set off these elements.

> Partly by hard fighting, partly by diplomatic skill, they enlarged their dominions to the east and rose to royal rank with the possession of Sicily.

4. Place a comma before a conjunction introducing an independent clause.

> The early records of the city have disappeared, and the story of its first years can no longer be reconstructed.
>
> The situation is perilous, but there is still one chance of escape.

Two-part sentences of which the second member is introduced by *as* (in the sense of "because"), *for, or, nor,* or *while* (in the sense of "and at the same time") likewise require a comma before the conjunction.

If a dependent clause, or an introductory phrase requiring to be set off by a comma, precedes the second independent clause, no comma is needed after the conjunction.

> The situation is perilous, but if we are prepared to act promptly, there is still one chance of escape.

When the subject is the same for both clauses and is expressed only once, a comma is useful if the connective is *but.* When the connective is *and,* the comma should be omitted if the relation between the two statements is close or immediate.

> I have heard his arguments, but am still unconvinced.
>
> He has had several years' experience and is thoroughly competent.

5. Do not join independent clauses by a comma.

If two or more clauses grammatically complete and not joined by a conjunction are to form a single compound sentence, the proper mark of punctuation is a semicolon.

> Stevenson's romances are entertaining; they are full of exciting adventures.
>
> It is nearly half past five; we cannot reach town before dark.

It is, of course, equally correct to write each of these as two sentences, replacing the semicolons with periods.

> Stevenson's romances are entertaining. They are full of exciting adventures.
>
> It is nearly half past five. We cannot reach town before dark.

If a conjunction is inserted, the proper mark is a comma. (Rule 4.)

> Stevenson's romances are entertaining, for they are full of exciting adventures.
>
> It is nearly half past five, and we cannot reach town before dark.

A comparison of the three forms given above will show clearly the advantage of the first. It is, at least in the examples given, better than the second form because it suggests the close relationship between the two statements in a way that the second does not attempt, and better than the third because it is briefer and therefore more forcible. Indeed, this simple method of indicating relationship between statements is one of the most useful devices of composition. The relationship, as above, is commonly one of cause and consequence.

Note that if the second clause is preceded by an adverb, such as *accordingly, besides, then, therefore,* or *thus,* and not by a conjunction, the semicolon is still required.

> I had never been in the place before; besides, it was dark as a tomb.

An exception to the semicolon rule is worth noting here. A comma is preferable when the clauses are very short and alike in form, or when the tone of the sentence is easy and conversational.

> Man proposes, God disposes.
> The gates swung apart, the bridge fell, the portcullis was drawn up.
> I hardly knew him, he was so changed.
> Here today, gone tomorrow.

6. Do not break sentences in two.

> In other words, do not use periods for commas.

> > I met them on a Cunard liner many years ago. Coming home from Liverpool to New York.

> > He was an interesting talker. A man who had traveled all over the world and lived in half a dozen countries.

In both these examples, the first period should be replaced by a comma and the following word begun with a small letter.

It is permissible to make an emphatic word or expression serve the purpose of a sentence and to punctuate it accordingly:

> > Again and again he called out. No reply.

The writer must, however, be certain that the emphasis is warranted, lest his clipped sentence seem merely a blunder in syntax or in punctuation. Generally speaking, the place for broken sentences is in dialogue, when a character happens to speak in a clipped or fragmentary way.

Rules 3, 4, 5, and 6 cover the most important principles that govern punctuation. They should be so thoroughly mastered that their application becomes second nature.

7. Use a colon after an independent clause to introduce a list of particulars, an appositive, an amplification, or an illustrative quotation.

A colon tells the reader that what follows is closely related to the preceding clause. The colon has more effect than the comma, less power to separate than the semicolon, and more formality than the dash. It usually follows an independent clause and should not separate a verb from its complement or a preposition from its object. The examples in the left-hand column, below, are wrong; they should be rewritten as in the right-hand column.

Your dedicated whittler requires: a knife, a piece of wood, and a back porch.	Your dedicated whittler requires three props: a knife, a piece of wood, and a back porch.
Understanding is that penetrating quality of knowledge that grows from: theory, practice, conviction, assertion, error, and humiliation.	Understanding is that penetrating quality of knowledge that grows from theory, practice, conviction, assertion, error, and humiliation.

Join two independent clauses with a colon if the second interprets or amplifies the first.

> But even so, there was a directness and dispatch about animal burial: there was no stopover in the undertaker's foul parlor, no wreath or spray.

A colon may introduce a quotation that supports or contributes to the preceding clause.

> The squalor of the streets reminded him of a line from Oscar Wilde: "We are all in the gutter, but some of us are looking at the stars."

The colon also has certain functions of form: to follow the salutation of a formal letter, to separate hour from minute in a notation of time, and to separate the title of a work from its subtitle or a Bible chapter from a verse.

> Dear Mr. Montague:
>
> *Practical Calligraphy: An Introduction to Italic Script*
>
> departs at 10:48 P.M.
>
> Nehemiah 11:7

8. *Use a dash to set off an abrupt break or interruption, and to announce a long appositive or summary.*

A dash is a mark of separation stronger than a comma, less formal than a colon, and more relaxed than parentheses.

> His first thought on getting out of bed—if he had any thought at all—was to get back in again.
>
> The rear axle began to make a noise—a grinding, chattering, teeth-gritting rasp.
>
> The increasing reluctance of the sun to rise, the extra nip in the breeze, the patter of shed leaves dropping— all the evidences of fall drifting into winter were clearer each day.

Use a dash only when a more common mark of punctuation seems inadequate.

Her father's suspicions proved well-founded—it was not Edward she cared for—it was San Francisco.	Her father's suspicions proved well-founded. It was not Edward she cared for, it was San Francisco.
Violence—the kind you see on television—is not honestly violent—there lies its harm.	Violence, the kind you see on television, is not honestly violent. There lies its harm.

9. *The number of the subject determines the number of the verb.*

Words that intervene between subject and verb do not affect the number of the verb.

The bittersweet flavor of youth—its trials, its joys, its adventures, its challenges—are not soon forgotten.

The bittersweet flavor of youth—its trials, its joys, its adventures, its challenges—is not soon forgotten.

A common blunder is the use of a singular verb form in a relative clause following "one of . . ." or a similar expression when the relative is the subject.

One of the ablest men who has attacked this problem

One of the ablest men who have attacked this problem

One of those people who is never ready on time

One of those people who are never ready on time

Use a singular verb form after *each, either, everyone, everybody, neither, nobody, someone*.

Everybody thinks he has a sense of humor.
Although both clocks strike cheerfully, neither keeps good time.

With *none,* use the singular verb when the word means "no one" or "not one."

None of us are perfect.   None of us is perfect.

A plural verb is commonly used when *none* suggests more than one thing or person.

None are so fallible as those who are sure they're right.

A compound subject formed of two or more nouns joined by *and* almost always requires a plural verb.

The walrus and the carpenter were walking close at hand.

But certain compounds, often clichés, are so inseparable they are considered a unit and so take a singular verb, as do compound subjects qualified by *each* or *every.*

The long and the short of it is . . .
Bread and butter was all she served.
Give and take is essential to a happy household.
Every window, picture, and mirror was smashed.

A singular subject remains singular even if other nouns are connected to it by *with, as well as, in addition to, except, together with,* and *no less than.*

His speech as well as his manner is objectionable.

A linking verb agrees with the number of its subject.

What is wanted is a few more pairs of hands.
The trouble with truth is its many varieties.

Some nouns that appear to be plural are usually construed as singular and given a singular verb.

> Politics is an art, not a science.

> The Republican Headquarters is on this side of the tracks.

But

> The general's quarters are over the river.

In these cases the writer must simply learn the idioms. The contents of a book is singular. The contents of a jar may be either singular or plural, depending on what's in the jar—jam or marbles.

10. Use the proper case of pronoun.

The personal pronouns, as well as the pronoun *who,* change form as they function as subject or object.

> Will Jane or he be hired, do you think?
>
> The culprit, it turned out, was he.
>
> We heavy eaters would rather walk than ride.
>
> Who knocks?
>
> Give this work to whoever looks idle.

In the last example, *whoever* is the subject of *looks idle;* the object of the preposition *to* is the entire clause *whoever looks idle.* When *who* introduces a subordinate clause, its case depends on its function in that clause.

> Virgil Soames is the candidate whom we think will win.

> Virgil Soames is the candidate who we think will win.

> Virgil Soames is the candidate who we hope to elect.

> Virgil Soames is the candidate whom we hope to elect.

A pronoun in a comparison is nominative if it is the subject of a stated or understood verb.

> Sandy writes better than I. (Than I write.)

In general, avoid "understood" verbs by supplying them.

> I think Horace admires Jessica more than I.

> I think Horace admires Jessica more than I do.

> Polly loves cake more than me.

> Polly loves cake more than she loves me.

The objective case is correct in the following examples.

> The ranger offered Shirley and him some advice on campsites.
>
> They came to meet the Baldwins and us.
>
> Let's talk it over between us, then, you and me.
>
> Whom should I ask?
>
> A group of us taxpayers protested.

Us in the last example is in apposition to taxpayers, the object of the preposition *of.* The wording, although grammatically defensible, is rarely apt. "A group of us protested as taxpayers" is better, if not exactly equivalent.

Use the simple personal pronoun as a subject.

Blake and myself stayed home.	Blake and I stayed home.
Howard and yourself brought the lunch, I thought.	Howard and you brought the lunch, I thought.

The possessive case of pronouns is used to show ownership. It has two forms: the adjectival modifier, *your* hat, and the noun form, a hat of *yours.*

> The dog has buried one of your gloves and one of mine in the flower bed.

Gerunds usually require the possessive case.

> Mother objected to our driving on the icy roads.

A present participle as a verbal, on the other hand, takes the objective case.

> They heard him singing in the shower.

The difference between a verbal participle and a gerund is not always obvious, but note what is really said in each of the following.

> Do you mind me asking a question?
> Do you mind my asking a question?

In the first sentence, the queried objection is to *me,* as opposed to other members of the group, putting one of the questions. In the second example, the issue is whether a question may be asked at all.

11. A participial phrase at the beginning of a sentence must refer to the grammatical subject.

> Walking slowly down the road, he saw a woman accompanied by two children.

The word *walking* refers to the subject of the sentence, not to the woman. If the writer wishes to make it refer to the woman, he must recast the sentence.

> He saw a woman, accompanied by two children, walking slowly down the road.

Participial phrases preceded by a conjunction or by a preposition, nouns in apposition, adjectives, and adjective phrases come under the same rule if they begin the sentence.

On arriving in Chicago, his friends met him at the station.	On arriving in Chicago, he was met at the station by his friends.
A soldier of proved valor, they entrusted him with the defense of the city.	A soldier of proved valor, he was entrusted with the defense of the city.

| Young and inexperienced, the task seemed easy to me. | Young and inexperienced, I thought the task easy. |
| Without a friend to counsel him, the temptation proved irresistible. | Without a friend to counsel him, he found the temptation irresistible. |

Sentences violating Rule 11 are often ludicrous:

Being in a dilapidated condition, I was able to buy the house very cheap.

Wondering irresolutely what to do next, the clock struck twelve.

As a mother of five, with another on the way, my ironing board is always up.

II
Elementary Principles of Composition

---

12. *Choose a suitable design and hold to it.*

A basic structural design underlies every kind of writing. The writer will in part follow this design, in part deviate from it, according to his skill, his needs, and the unexpected events that accompany the act of composition. Writing, to be effective, must follow closely the thoughts of the writer, but not necessarily in the order in which those thoughts occur. This calls for a scheme of procedure. In some cases the best design is no design, as with a love letter, which is simply an outpouring, or with a casual essay, which is a ramble. But in most cases planning must be a deliberate prelude to writing. The first principle of composition, therefore, is to foresee or determine the shape of what is to come and pursue that shape.

A sonnet is built on a fourteen-line frame, each line containing five feet. Hence, the sonneteer knows exactly where he is headed, although he may not know how to get there. Most forms of composition are less clearly defined, more flexible, but all have skeletons to which the writer will bring the flesh and the blood. The more clearly he perceives the shape, the better are his chances of success.

---

13. *Make the paragraph the unit of composition.*

The paragraph is a convenient unit; it serves all forms of literary work. As long as it holds together, a paragraph may be of any length—a single, short sentence or a passage of great duration.

If the subject on which you are writing is of slight extent, or if you intend to treat it briefly, there may be no need to divide it into topics. Thus, a brief description, a brief book review, a brief account of a single incident, a narrative merely outlining an action, the setting forth of a single idea—any one of these is best written in a single paragraph. After the paragraph has been written, examine it to see whether division will improve it.

Ordinarily, however, a subject requires division into topics, each of which should be dealt with in a paragraph. The object of treating each topic in a paragraph by itself is, of course, to aid the reader. The beginning of each paragraph is a signal to him that a new step in the development of the subject has been reached.

As a rule, single sentences should not be written or printed as paragraphs. An exception may be made of sentences of transition, indicating the relation between the parts of an exposition or argument.

In dialogue, each speech, even if only a single word, is usually a paragraph by itself; that is, a new paragraph begins with each change of speaker. The application of this rule when dialogue and narrative are combined is best learned from examples in well-edited works of fiction. Sometimes a writer, seeking to create an effect of rapid talk or for some other reason, will elect not to set off each speech in a separate paragraph and instead will run speeches together. The common practice, however, and the one that serves best in most instances, is to give each speech a paragraph of its own.

As a rule, begin each paragraph either with a sentence that suggests the topic or with a sentence that helps the transition. If a paragraph forms part of a larger composition, its relation to what precedes, or its function as a part of the whole, may need to be expressed. This can sometimes be done by a mere word or phrase (*again; therefore; for the same reason*) in the first sentence. Sometimes, however, it is expedient to get into the topic slowly, by way of a sentence or two of introduction or transition.

In narration and description, the paragraph sometimes begins with a concise, comprehensive statement serving to hold together the details that follow.

> The breeze served us admirably.
> The campaign opened with a series of reverses.
> The next ten or twelve pages were filled with a curious set of entries.

But when this device, or any device, is too often used, it becomes a mannerism. More commonly the opening sentence simply indicates by its subject the direction the paragraph is to take.

> At length I thought I might return toward the stockade.
> He picked up the heavy lamp from the table and began to explore.
> Another flight of steps, and they emerged on the roof.

In animated narrative, the paragraphs are likely to be short and without any semblance of a topic sentence, the writer rushing headlong, event following event in rapid succession. The break between such paragraphs merely serves the purpose of a rhetorical pause, throwing into prominence some detail of the action.

In general, remember that paragraphing calls for a good eye as well as a logical mind. Enormous blocks of print look formidable to a reader. He has a certain reluctance to tackle them; he can lose his way in them. Therefore, breaking long paragraphs in two, even if it is not necessary to do so for sense, meaning, or logical development, is often a visual help. But remember, too, that firing off many short paragraphs in quick succession can be distracting. Paragraph breaks used only for show read like the writing of commerce or of display advertising. Moderation and a sense of order should be the main considerations in paragraphing.

14. Use the active voice.

The active voice is usually more direct and vigorous than the passive:

> I shall always remember my first visit to Boston.

This is much better than

> My first visit to Boston will always be remembered by me.

The latter sentence is less direct, less bold, and less concise. If the writer tries to make it more concise by omitting "by me,"

> My first visit to Boston will always be remembered,

it becomes indefinite: is it the writer or some person undisclosed or the world at large that will always remember this visit?

This rule does not, of course, mean that the writer should entirely discard the passive voice, which is frequently convenient and sometimes necessary.

> The dramatists of the Restoration are little esteemed today.
> Modern readers have little esteem for the dramatists of the Restoration.

The first would be the preferred form in a paragraph on the dramatists of the Restoration, the second in a paragraph on the tastes of modern readers. The need of making a particular word the subject of the sentence will often, as in these examples, determine which voice is to be used.

The habitual use of the active voice, however, makes for forcible writing. This is true not only in narrative concerned principally with action but in writing of any kind. Many a tame sentence of description or exposition can be made lively and emphatic by substituting a transitive in the active voice for some such perfunctory expression as *there is* or *could be heard*.

There were a great number of dead leaves lying on the ground.	Dead leaves covered the ground.
At dawn the crowing of a rooster could be heard.	The cock's crow came with dawn.
The reason he left college was that his health became impaired.	Failing health compelled him to leave college.
It was not long before he was very sorry that he had said what he had.	He soon repented his words.

Note, in the examples above, that when a sentence is made stronger, it usually becomes shorter. Thus, brevity is a by-product of vigor.

---

15. Put statements in positive form.

Make definite assertions. Avoid tame, colorless, hesitating, noncommittal language. Use the word *not* as a means of denial or in antithesis, never as a means of evasion.

He was not very often on time.	He usually came late.
He did not think that studying Latin was a sensible way to use one's time.	He thought the study of Latin a waste of time.
The Taming of the Shrew is rather weak in spots. Shakespeare does not portray Katharine as a very admirable character, nor does Bianca remain long in memory as an important character in Shakespeare's works.	The women in *The Taming of the Shrew* are unattractive. Katharine is disagreeable, Bianca insignificant.

The last example, before correction, is indefinite as well as negative. The corrected version, consequently, is simply a guess at the writer's intention.

All three examples show the weakness inherent in the word *not*. Consciously or unconsciously, the reader is dissatisfied with being told only what is not; he wishes to be told what is. Hence, as a rule, it is better to express even a negative in positive form.

not honest	dishonest
not important	trifling
did not remember	forgot
did not pay any attention to	ignored
did not have much confidence in	distrusted

Placing negative and positive in opposition makes for a stronger structure.

> Not charity, but simple justice.
> Not that I loved Caesar less, but that I loved Rome more.
> Ask not what your country can do for you—ask what you can do for your country.

Negative words other than *not* are usually strong.

> Her loveliness I never knew/Until she smiled on me.

Statements qualified with unnecessary auxiliaries or conditionals sound irresolute.

If you would let us know the time of your arrival, we would be happy to arrange your transportation from the airport.	If you will let us know the time of your arrival, we shall be happy to arrange your transportation from the airport.
The applicant can make a good impression by being neat and punctual.	The applicant will make a good impression if he is neat and punctual.
Keats may be ranked among those romantic poets who died young.	Keats was one of those romantic poets who died young.

If your every sentence admits a doubt, your writing will lack authority. Save the auxiliaries *would, should, could, may, might,* and *can* for situations involving real uncertainty.

16. Use definite, specific, concrete language.

Prefer the specific to the general, the definite to the vague, the concrete to the abstract.

A period of unfavorable weather set in.	It rained every day for a week.
He showed satisfaction as he took possession of his well-earned reward.	He grinned as he pocketed the coin.

If those who have studied the art of writing are in accord on any one point, it is on this: the surest way to arouse and hold the attention of the reader is by being specific, definite, and concrete. The greatest writers—Homer, Dante, Shake-speare—are effective largely because they deal in particulars and report the details that matter. Their words call up pictures.

Jean Stafford, to cite a modern author, demonstrates in her short story "In the Zoo" how prose is made vivid by the use of words that evoke images and sensations:

> . . . Daisy and I in time found asylum in a small menagerie down by the railroad tracks. It belonged to a gentle alcoholic ne'er-do-well, who did nothing all day long but drink bathtub gin in rickeys and play solitaire and smile to himself and talk to his animals. He had a little, stunted red vixen and a deodorized skunk, a parrot from Tahiti that spoke Parisian French, a woebegone coyote, and two capuchin monkeys, so serious and human-ized, so small and sad and sweet, and so religious-looking with their ton-sured heads that it was impossible not to think their gibberish was really an ordered language with a grammar that someday some philologist would understand.
>
> Gran knew about our visits to Mr. Murphy and she did not object, for it gave her keen pleasure to excoriate him when we came home. His vice was not a matter of guesswork; it was an established fact that he was half-seas over from dawn till midnight. "With the black Irish," said Gran, "the taste for drink is taken in with the mother's milk and is never mastered. Oh, I know all about those promises to join the temperance movement and not to touch another drop. The way to Hell is paved with good intentions."
>
> We were still little girls when we discovered Mr. Murphy, before the shattering disease of adolescence was to make our bones and brains ache even more painfully than before, and we loved him and we hoped to marry him when we grew up. We loved him, and we loved his monkeys to exactly the same degree and in exactly the same way; they were husbands and fathers and brothers, these little, ugly, dark, secret men who minded their own business and let us mind ours. If we stuck our fingers through the bars of the cage, the monkeys would sometimes take them in their tight, tiny hands and look into our faces with a tentative, somehow absent-minded sorrow, as if they terribly regretted that they could not place us but were glad to see us all the same. Mr. Murphy, playing a solitaire game of cards called "once in a blue moon" on a kitchen table in his back yard beside the pens, would occasionally look up and blink his beautiful blue eyes and say, "You're peaches to make over my wee friends. I love you for it." There was nothing demanding in his voice, and nothing sticky; on his lips the word "love" was jocose and forthright, it had no strings attached. We would sit on either side of him and watch him regiment his ranks of cards and stop to drink as deeply as if he were dying of thirst and wave to his animals and say to them, "Yes, lads, you're dandies."*

If the experiences of Walter Mitty, of Dick Diver, of Rabbit Angstrom have seemed for the moment real to countless readers, if in reading Faulkner we have almost the sense of inhabiting Yoknapatawpha County during the decline of the South, it is because the details used are definite, the terms concrete. It is not that every detail is given—that would be impossible, as well as to no purpose—but that all the significant details are given, and with such accuracy and vigor that the reader, in imagination, can project himself into the scene.

---

* A selection from "In the Zoo" from *Bad Characters* by Jean Stafford. Copyright © 1953, 1964 by Jean Stafford. This selection appeared originally in *The New Yorker.* Reprinted with the permission of Farrar, Straus & Giroux, Inc.

In exposition and in argument, the writer must likewise never lose his hold upon the concrete; and even when he is dealing with general principles, he must furnish particular instances of their application.

In his *Philosophy of Style*, Herbert Spencer gives two sentences to illustrate how the vague and general can be turned into the vivid and particular:

In proportion as the manners, customs, and amusements of a nation are cruel and barbarous, the regulations of its penal code will be severe.	In proportion as men delight in battles, bullfights, and combats of gladiators, will they punish by hanging, burning, and the rack.

To show what happens when strong writing is deprived of its vigor, George Orwell once took a passage from the Bible and drained it of its blood. On the left, below, is Orwell's translation; on the right, the verse from Ecclesiastes (King James Version).

Objective consideration of contemporary phenomena compels the conclusion that success or failure in competitive activities exhibits no tendency to be commensurate with innate capacity, but that a considerable element of the unpredictable must inevitably be taken into account.	I returned, and saw under the sun, that the race is not to the swift, nor the battle to the strong, neither yet bread to the wise, nor yet riches to men of understanding, nor yet favor to men of skill; but time and chance happeneth to them all.

17. *Omit needless words.*

Vigorous writing is concise. A sentence should contain no unnecessary words, a paragraph no unnecessary sentences, for the same reason that a drawing should have no unnecessary lines and a machine no unnecessary parts. This requires not that the writer make all his sentences short, or that he avoid all detail and treat his subjects only in outline, but that every word tell.

Many expressions in common use violate this principle.

the question as to whether	whether (the question whether)
there is no doubt but that	no doubt (doubtless)
used for fuel purposes	used for fuel
he is a man who	he
in a hasty manner	hastily
this is a subject that	this subject
His story is a strange one.	His story is strange.
the reason why is that	because

An expression that is especially debilitating is *the fact that*. It should be revised out of every sentence in which it occurs.

owing to the fact that	since (because)
in spite of the fact that	though (although)
call your attention to the fact that	remind you (notify you)
I was unaware of the fact that	I was unaware that (did not know)
the fact that he had not succeeded	his failure
the fact that I had arrived	my arrival

See also the words *case, character, nature* in Chapter IV.
Who is, which was, and the like are often superfluous.

His brother, who is a member of the same firm	His brother, a member of the same firm
Trafalgar, which was Nelson's last battle	Trafalgar, Nelson's last battle

As a positive statement is more concise than a negative one, and the active voice more concise than the passive, many of the examples given under Rules 14 and 15 illustrate this rule as well.

A common way to fall into wordiness is to present a single complex idea, step by step, in a series of sentences that might to advantage be combined into one.

Macbeth was very ambitious. This led him to wish to become king of Scotland. The witches told him that this wish of his would come true. The king of Scotland at this time was Duncan. Encouraged by his wife, Macbeth murdered Duncan. He was thus enabled to succeed Duncan as king. (51 words)	Encouraged by his wife, Macbeth achieved his ambition and realized the prediction of the witches by murdering Duncan and becoming king of Scotland in his place. (26 words)

18. Avoid a succession of loose sentences.

This rule refers especially to loose sentences of a particular type: those consisting of two clauses, the second introduced by a conjunction or relative. A writer may err by making his sentences too compact and periodic. An occasional loose sentence prevents the style from becoming too formal and gives the reader a certain relief. Consequently, loose sentences are common in easy, unstudied writing. The danger is that there may be too many of them.

An unskilled writer will sometimes construct a whole paragraph of sentences of this kind, using as connectives *and, but,* and, less frequently, *who, which, when, where,* and *while,* these last in nonrestrictive senses. (See Rule 3.)

> The third concert of the subscription series was given last evening, and a large audience was in attendance. Mr. Edward Appleton was the soloist, and the Boston Symphony Orchestra furnished the instrumental music. The former showed himself to be an artist of the first rank, while the latter proved itself fully deserving of its high reputation. The interest aroused by the series has been very gratifying to the Committee, and it is planned to give a similar series annually hereafter. The fourth concert will be given on Tuesday, May l0, when an equally attractive program will be presented.

Apart from its triteness and emptiness, the paragraph above is bad because of the structure of its sentences, with their mechanical symmetry and singsong. Compare these sentences from the chapter "What I Believe" in E. M. Forster's *Two Cheers for Democracy:*

> I believe in aristocracy, though—if that is the right word, and if a democrat may use it. Not an aristocracy of power, based upon rank and influence, but an aristocracy of the sensitive, the considerate and the plucky. Its members are to be found in all nations and classes, and all through the ages, and there is a secret understanding between them when they meet. They represent the true human tradition, the one permanent victory of our queer race over cruelty and chaos. Thousands of them perish in obscurity, a few are great names. They are sensitive for others as well as for themselves, they are considerate without being fussy, their pluck is not swankiness but the power to endure, and they can take a joke.*

If the writer finds that he has written a series of loose sentences, he should recast enough of them to remove the monotony, replacing them by simple sentences, by sentences of two clauses joined by a semicolon, by periodic sentences of two clauses, by sentences (loose or periodic) of three clauses—whichever best represent the real relations of the thought.

19. Express coordinate ideas in similar form.

This principle, that of parallel construction, requires that expressions similar in content and function be outwardly similar. The likeness of form enables the reader to recognize more readily the likeness of content and function. The familiar Beatitudes exemplify the virtue of parallel construction.

> Blessed are the poor in spirit: for theirs is the kingdom of heaven.
> Blessed are they that mourn: for they shall be comforted.
> Blessed are the meek: for they shall inherit the earth.
> Blessed are they which do hunger and thirst after righteousness: for they shall be filled.

The unskillful writer often violates this principle, from a mistaken belief that he should constantly vary the form of his expressions. When repeating a statement to emphasize it, the writer may need to vary its form. But apart from this he should follow the principle of parallel construction.

| Formerly, science was taught by the textbook method, while now the laboratory method is employed. | Formerly, science was taught by the textbook method; now it is taught by the laboratory method. |

The left-hand version gives the impression that the writer is undecided or timid; he seems unable or afraid to choose one form of expression and hold to it. The right-hand version shows that the writer has at least made his choice and abided by it.

* From *Two Cheers for Democracy,* copyright, 1951, by E. M. Forster. Published by Harcourt, Brace and Company, Inc.

By this principle, an article or a preposition applying to all the members of a series must either be used only before the first term or else be repeated before each term.

the French, the Italians, Spanish, and Portuguese	the French, the Italians, the Spanish, and the Portuguese
in spring, summer, or in winter	in spring, summer, or winter (in spring, in summer, or in winter)

Some words require a particular preposition in certain idiomatic uses. When such words are joined in a compound construction, all the appropriate prepositions must be included, unless they are the same.

His speech was marked by disagreement and scorn for his opponent's position.	His speech was marked by disagreement with and scorn for his opponent's position.

Correlative expressions (*both, and; not, but; not only, but also; either, or; first, second, third;* and the like) should be followed by the same grammatical construction. Many violations of this rule can be corrected by rearranging the sentence.

It was both a long ceremony and very tedious.	The ceremony was both long and tedious.
A time not for words but action.	A time not for words but for action.
Either you must grant his request or incur his ill will.	You must either grant his request or incur his ill will.
My objections are, first, the injustice of the measure; second, that it is unconstitutional.	My objections are, first, that the measure is unjust; second, that it is unconstitutional.

It may be asked, what if a writer needs to express a rather large number of similar ideas—say, twenty? Must he write twenty consecutive sentences of the same pattern? On closer examination he will probably find that the difficulty is imaginary—that his twenty ideas can be classified in groups, and that he need apply the principle only within each group. Otherwise he had best avoid the difficulty by putting his statements in the form of a table.

20. Keep related words together.

The position of the words in a sentence is the principal means of showing their relationship. Confusion and ambiguity result when words are badly placed. The writer must, therefore, bring together the words and groups of words that are related in thought and keep apart those that are not so related.

He noticed a large stain in the rug that was right in the center.	He noticed a large stain right in the center of the rug.
You can call your mother in London and tell her all about George's taking you out to dinner for just sixty cents.	For just sixty cents you can call your mother in London and tell her all about George's taking you out to dinner.

New York's first commercial human-sperm bank opened Friday with semen samples from 18 men frozen in a stainless steel tank.	New York's first commercial human-sperm bank opened Friday when semen samples were taken from 18 men. The samples were then frozen and stored in a stainless steel tank.

In the left-hand version of the first example, the reader has no way of knowing whether the stain was in the center of the rug or the rug was in the center of the room. In the left-hand version of the second example, the reader may well wonder which cost sixty cents—the phone call or the dinner. In the left-hand version of the third example, the reader's heart goes out to those eighteen poor fellows frozen in a steel tank.

The subject of a sentence and the principal verb should not, as a rule, be separated by a phrase or clause that can be transferred to the beginning.

Wordsworth, in the fifth book of *The Excursion,* gives a minute description of this church.	In the fifth book of *The Excursion,* Wordsworth gives a minute description of this church.
A dog, if you fail to discipline him, becomes a household pest.	Unless disciplined, a dog becomes a household pest.

Interposing a phrase or a clause, as in the left-hand examples above, interrupts the flow of the main clause. This interruption, however, is not usually bothersome when the flow is checked only by a relative clause or by an expression in apposition. Sometimes, in periodic sentences, the interruption is a deliberate device for creating suspense. (See examples under Rule 22.)

The relative pronoun should come, in most instances, immediately after its antecedent.

There was a stir in the audience that suggested disapproval.	A stir that suggested disapproval swept the audience.
He wrote three articles about his adventures in Spain, which were published in *Harper's Magazine*	He published three articles in *Harper's Magazine* about his adventures in Spain.
This is a portrait of Benjamin Harrison, grandson of William Henry Harrison, who became President in 1889.	This is a portrait of Benjamin Harrison, who became President in 1889. He was the grandson of William Henry Harrison.

If the antecedent consists of a group of words, the relative comes at the end of the group, unless this would cause ambiguity.

> The Superintendent of the Chicago Division, who

No ambiguity results from the above.   But

> A proposal to amend the Sherman Act, which has been variously judged

leaves the reader wondering whether it is the proposal or the Act that has been variously judged. The relative clause must be moved forward, to read, "A proposal, which has been variously judged, to amend the Sherman Act. . . ."

Similarly

The grandson of William Henry Harrison, who	William Henry Harrison's grandson, Benjamin Harrison, who

A noun in apposition may come between antecedent and relative, because in such a combination no real ambiguity can arise.

> The Duke of York, his brother, who was regarded with hostility by the Whigs

Modifiers should come, if possible, next to the word they modify. If several expressions modify the same word, they should be so arranged that no wrong relation is suggested.

All the members were not present.	Not all the members were present.
He only found two mistakes.	He found only two mistakes.
The chairman said he hoped all members would give generously to the Fund at a meeting of the committee yesterday.	At a meeting of the committee yesterday, the chairman said he hoped all members would give generously to the Fund.
Major R. E. Joyce will give a lecture on Tuesday evening in Bailey Hall, to which the public is invited on "My Experiences in Mesopotamia" at eight P.M.	On Tuesday evening at eight, Major R. E. Joyce will give a lecture in Bailey Hall on his experiences in Mesopotamia. The public is invited.

Note, in the last left-hand example, how swiftly meaning departs when words are wrongly juxtaposed.

---

21. In summaries, keep to one tense.

In summarizing the action of a drama, the writer should use the present tense. In summarizing a poem, story, or novel, he should also use the present, though he may use the past if it seems more natural to do so. If the summary is in the present tense, antecedent action should be expressed by the perfect; if in the past, by the past perfect.

> Chance prevents Friar John from delivering Friar Lawrence's letter to Romeo. Meanwhile, owing to her father's arbitrary change of the day set for her wedding, Juliet has been compelled to drink the potion on Tuesday night, with the result that Balthasar informs Romeo of her supposed death before Friar Lawrence learns of the nondelivery of the letter.

But whichever tense is used in the summary, a past tense in indirect discourse or in indirect question remains unchanged.

> The Friar confesses that it was he who married them.

Apart from the exceptions noted, whichever tense the writer chooses he should use throughout. Shifting from one tense to another gives the appearance of uncertainty and irresolution.

In presenting the statements or the thought of someone else, as in summarizing an essay or reporting a speech, the writer should not overwork such expressions as "he said," "he stated," "the speaker added," "the speaker then went on to say," "the author also thinks." He should indicate clearly at the outset, once for all, that what follows is summary, and then waste no words in repeating the notification.

In notebooks, in newspapers, in handbooks of literature, summaries of one kind or another may be indispensable, and for children in primary schools retelling a story in their own words is a useful exercise. But in the criticism or interpretation of literature the writer should be careful to avoid dropping into summary. He may find it necessary to devote one or two sentences to indicating the subject, or the opening situation, of the work he is discussing; he may cite numerous details to illustrate its qualities. But he should aim at writing an orderly discussion supported by evidence, not a summary with occasional comment. Similarly, if the scope of his discussion includes a number of works, he will as a rule do better not to take them up singly in chronological order but to aim from the beginning at establishing general conclusions.

22. *Place the emphatic words of a sentence at the end.*

The proper place in the sentence for the word or group of words that the writer desires to make most prominent is usually the end.

Humanity has hardly advanced in fortitude since that time, though it has advanced in many other ways.	Since that time, humanity has advanced in many ways, but it has hardly advanced in fortitude.
This steel is principally used for making razors, because of its hardness.	Because of its hardness, this steel is used principally for making razors.

The word or group of words entitled to this position of prominence is usually the logical predicate—that is, the *new* element in the sentence, as it is in the second example.

The effectiveness of the periodic sentence arises from the prominence it gives to the main statement.

> Four centuries ago, Christopher Columbus, one of the Italian mariners whom the decline of their own republics had put at the service of the world and of adventure, seeking for Spain a westward passage to the Indies to offset the achievement of Portuguese discoverers, lighted on America.

> With these hopes and in this belief I would urge you, laying aside all hindrance, thrusting away all private aims, to devote yourself unswervingly and unflinchingly to the vigorous and successful prosecution of this war.

The other prominent position in the sentence is the beginning. Any element in the sentence other than the subject becomes emphatic when placed first.

> Deceit or treachery he could never forgive.

Vast and rude, fretted by the action of nearly three thousand years, the fragments of this architecture may often seem, at first sight, like works of nature.

Home is the sailor.

A subject coming first in its sentence may be emphatic, but hardly by its position alone. In the sentence

Great kings worshiped at his shrine

the emphasis upon *kings* arises largely from its meaning and from the context. To receive special emphasis, the subject of a sentence must take the position of the predicate.

Through the middle of the valley flowed a winding stream.

The principle that the proper place for what is to be made most prominent is the end applies equally to the words of a sentence, to the sentences of a paragraph, and to the paragraphs of a composition.

III
A Few Matters of Form

Colloquialisms.

If you use a colloquialism or a slang word or phrase, simply use it; do not draw attention to it by enclosing it in quotation marks. To do so is to put on airs, as though you were inviting the reader to join you in a select society of those who know better.

Exclamations.

Do not attempt to emphasize simple statements by using a mark of exclamation.

It was a wonderful show!   It was a wonderful show.

The exclamation mark is to be reserved for use after true exclamations or commands.

What a wonderful show!
Halt!

Headings.

If a manuscript is to be submitted for publication, leave plenty of space at the top of page 1. The editor will need this space for his penciled directions to the compositor. Place the heading, or title, at least a fourth of the way down the page. Leave a blank line, or its equivalent in space, after the heading. On succeeding pages, begin near the top, but not so near as to give a crowded appearance. Omit the period after a title or heading. A question mark or an exclamation point may be used if the heading calls for it.

Hyphen.

When two or more words are combined to form a compound adjective, a hyphen is usually required. "He belonged to the leisure class and enjoyed leisure-class pursuits." "He entered his boat in the round-the-island race."

Do not use a hyphen between words that can better be written as one word: *water-fowl, waterfowl.* Your common sense will aid you in the decision, but a dictionary is more reliable. The steady evolution of the language seems to favor union: two words eventually become one, usually after a period of hyphenation.

bed chamber	bed-chamber	bedchamber
wild life	wild-life	wildlife
bell boy	bell-boy	bellboy

The hyphen can play tricks on the unwary, as it did in Chattanooga when two newspapers merged—the *News* and the *Free Press*. Someone introduced a hyphen into the merger, and the paper became *The Chattanooga News-Free Press*, which sounds as though the paper were news-free, or devoid of news. Obviously, we ask too much of a hyphen when we ask it to cast its spell over words it does not adjoin.

Margins.

Keep right-hand and left-hand margins roughly the same width. Exception: If a great deal of annotating or editing is anticipated, the left-hand margin should be roomy enough to accommodate this work.

Numerals.

Do not spell out dates or other serial numbers. Write them in figures or in Roman notation, as may be appropriate.

August 9, 1968	Chapter XII
Rule 3	352d Infantry

Exception: When they occur in dialogue, most dates and numbers are best spelled out.

"I arrived home on August ninth."
"In the year 1970, I turned twenty-one."
"I shall read Chapter Twelve."

Parentheses.

A sentence containing an expression in parentheses is punctuated outside the marks of parenthesis exactly as if the parenthetical expression were absent. The expression within the marks is punctuated as if it stood by itself, except that the final stop is omitted unless it is a question mark or an exclamation point.

I went to his house yesterday (my third attempt to see him), but he had left town.
He declares (and why should we doubt his good faith?) that he is now certain of success.

(When a wholly detached expression or sentence is parenthesized, the final stop comes before the last mark of parenthesis.)

Quotations.

Formal quotations cited as documentary evidence are introduced by a colon and enclosed in quotation marks.

> The United States Coast Pilot has this to say of the place: "Bracy Cove, 0.5 mile eastward of Bear Island, is exposed to southeast winds, has a rocky and uneven bottom, and is unfit for anchorage."

A quotation grammatically in apposition or the direct object of a verb is preceded by a comma and enclosed in quotation marks.

> I am reminded of the advice of my neighbor, "Never worry about your heart till it stops beating."
>
> Mark Twain says, "A classic is something that everybody wants to have read and nobody wants to read."

When a quotation is followed by an attributive phrase, the comma is enclosed within the quotation marks.

> "I can't attend," she said.

Typographical usage dictates that the comma be inside the marks, though logically it often seems not to belong there.

> "The Clerks," "Luke Havergal," and "Richard Cory" are in Robinson's *Children of the Night.*

When quotations of an entire line, or more, of either verse or prose are to be distinguished typographically from text matter, as are the quotations in this book, begin on a fresh line and indent. Quotation marks should not be used unless they appear in the original, as in dialogue.

> Wordsworth's enthusiasm for the French Revolution was at first unbounded:
>
> > Bliss was it in that dawn to be alive,
> > But to be young was very heaven!

Quotations introduced by *that* are indirect discourse and not enclosed in quotation marks.

> Keats declares that beauty is truth, truth beauty.

Proverbial expressions and familiar phrases of literary origin require no quotation marks.

> These are the times that try men's souls.
> He lives far from the madding crowd.

References.

In scholarly work requiring exact references, abbreviate titles that occur frequently, giving the full forms in an alphabetical list at the end. As a general practice, give the references in parentheses or in footnotes, not in the body of the

sentence. Omit the words *act, scene, line, book, volume, page,* except when referring by only one of them. Punctuate as indicated below.

in the second scene of the third act   in III.ii (Still better, simply insert
                                                III.ii in parentheses at the proper place
                                                in the sentence.)

After the killing of Polonius, Hamlet is placed under guard (IV.ii. 14) .

2 Samuel i:17–27

Othello II.iii. 264–267, III.iii. 155–161

Syllabication.

When a word must be divided at the end of a line, consult a dictionary to learn
the syllables between which division should be made. The student will do well to
examine the syllable division in a number of pages of any carefully printed book.

Titles.

For the titles of literary works, scholarly usage prefers italics with capitalized
initials. The usage of editors and publishers varies, some using italics with capitalized initials, others using Roman with capitalized initials and with or without
quotation marks. Use italics (indicated in manuscript by underscoring) except in
writing for a periodical that follows a different practice. Omit initial *A* or *The*
from titles when you place the possessive before them.

A Tale of Two Cities; Dickens's *Tale of Two Cities.*

Many of the words and expressions here listed are not so much bad English as bad style, the commonplaces of careless writing. As is illustrated under *Feature,* the proper correction is likely to be not the replacement of one word or set of words by another but the replacement of vague generality by definite statement.

The shape of our language is not rigid; in questions of usage we have no lawgiver whose word is final. Students whose curiosity is aroused by the interpretations that follow, or whose doubts are raised, will wish to pursue their investigations further. Books useful in such pursuits are *Webster's New Collegiate Dictionary,* Revised Edition; *The Random House College Dictionary; The American Heritage Dictionary of the English Language; Webster's New International Dictionary of the English Language,* Second Edition; H. W. Fowler's *Dictionary of Modern English Usage,* Second Edition; *Watch Your Language,* by Theodore M. Bernstein; and Roy H. Copperud's *American Usage: The Consensus.*

Aggravate. Irritate.

The first means "to add to" an already troublesome or vexing matter or condition. The second means "to vex" or "to annoy" or "to chafe."

All right.

Idiomatic in familiar speech as a detached phrase in the sense "Agreed," or "Go ahead," or "O.K." Properly written as two words—*all right.*

Allude.

Do not confuse with *elude.* You *allude* to a book; you *elude* a pursuer. Note, too, that *allude* is not synonymous with *refer.* An allusion is an indirect mention, a reference is a specific one.

Allusion.

Easily confused with *illusion.* The first means "an indirect reference"; the second means "an unreal image" or "a false impression."

Alternate. Alternative.

The words are not always interchangeable as nouns or adjectives. The first means every other one in a series; the second, one of two possibilities. As the other one of a series of two, an *alternate* may stand for "a substitute," but an *alternative*, although used in a similar sense, connotes a matter of choice that is never present with *alternate*.

> As the flooded road left them no alternative, they took the alternate route.

Among. Between.

When more than two things or persons are involved, *among* is usually called for: "The money was divided among the four players." When, however, more than two are involved but each is considered individually, *between* is preferred: "an agreement between the six heirs."

And/or.

A device, or shortcut, that damages a sentence and often leads to confusion or ambiguity.

> First of all, would an honor system successfully cut down on the amount of stealing and/or cheating?

> First of all, would an honor system reduce the incidence of stealing or cheating or both?

Anticipate.

Use *expect* in the sense of simple expectation.

> I anticipated that she would look older.

> I expected that she would look older.

> My brother anticipated the upturn in the market.

> My brother expected the upturn in the market.

In the second example, the word *anticipated* is ambiguous. It could mean simply that the brother believed the upturn would occur, or it could mean that he acted in advance of the expected upturn—by buying stock, perhaps.

Anybody.

In the sense of "any person" not to be written as two words. *Any body* means "any corpse," or "any human form," or "any group." The rule holds equally for *everybody, nobody,* and *somebody*.

Anyone.

In the sense of "anybody," written as one word. *Any one* means "any single person" or "any single thing."

As good or better than.

Expressions of this type should be corrected by rearranging the sentences.

My opinion is as good or better than his.

My opinion is as good as his, or better (if not better) .

As to whether.

Whether is sufficient.

As yet.

Yet nearly always is as good, if not better.

No agreement has been reached as yet.

No agreement has yet been reached.

The chief exception is at the beginning of a sentence, where *yet* means something different.

Yet (*or* despite everything) he has not succeeded.

As yet (*or* so far) he has not succeeded.

Being.

Not appropriate after *regard . . . as.*

He is regarded as being the best dancer in the club.

He is regarded as the best dancer in the club.

But.

Unnecessary after *doubt* and *help.*

I have no doubt but that
He could not help but see that

I have no doubt that
He could not help seeing that

The too-frequent use of *but* as a conjunction leads to the fault discussed under Rule 18. A loose sentence formed with *but* can usually be converted into a periodic sentence formed with *although,* as illustrated under Rule 4.

Particularly awkward is one *but* closely following another, thus making a contrast to a contrast, or a reservation to a reservation. This is easily corrected by rearrangement.

America had vast resources, but she seemed almost wholly unprepared for war. But within a year she had created an army of four million men.

America seemed almost wholly unprepared for war, but she had vast resources. Within a year she had created an army of four million men.

Can.

Means "am (is, are) able." Not to be used as a substitute for *may.*

Case.

Often unnecessary.

In many cases, the rooms were poorly ventilated.	Many of the rooms were poorly ventilated.
It has rarely been the case that any mistake has been made.	Few mistakes have been made.

Certainly.

Used indiscriminately by some speakers, much as others use *very,* in an attempt to intensify any and every statement. A mannerism of this kind, bad in speech, is even worse in writing.

Character.

Often simply redundant, used from a mere habit of wordiness.

acts of a hostile character	hostile acts

Claim (verb).

With object-noun, means "lay claim to." May be used with a dependent clause if this sense is clearly intended: "He claimed that he was the sole heir." (But even here *claimed to be* would be better.) Not to be used as a substitute for *declare, maintain,* or *charge*.

He claimed he knew how.	He declared he knew how.

Clever.

Note that the word means one thing when applied to men, another when applied to horses. A clever horse is a good-natured one, not an ingenious one.

Compare.

To *compare to* is to point out or imply resemblances between objects regarded as essentially of a different order; to *compare with* is mainly to point out differences between objects regarded as essentially of the same order. Thus, life has been *compared to* a pilgrimage, *to* a drama, *to* a battle; Congress may be compared with the British Parliament. Paris has been *compared to* ancient Athens; it may be *compared with* modern London.

Comprise.

Literally, "embrace": A zoo comprises mammals, reptiles, and birds (because it "embraces," or "includes," them). But animals do not comprise ("embrace") a zoo—they constitute a zoo.

Consider.

Not followed by *as* when it means "believe to be."

I consider him as competent.   I consider him competent.

When *considered* means "examined" or "discussed," it is followed by *as:*

The lecturer considered Eisenhower first as soldier and second as administrator.

Contact.

As a transitive verb, the word is vague and self-important. Do not *contact* anybody; get in touch with him, or look him up, or phone him, or find him, or meet him.

Cope.

An intransitive verb used with *with*. In formal writing, one doesn't "cope," one "copes with" something or somebody.

I knew she'd cope. (jocular)   I knew she would cope with the situation.

Currently.

In the sense of *now* with a verb in the present tense, *currently* is usually redundant; emphasis is better achieved through a more precise reference to time.

We are currently reviewing your application.   We are at this moment reviewing your application.

Data.

Like *strata, phenomena,* and *media, data* is a plural and is best used with a plural verb. The word, however, is slowly gaining acceptance as a singular.

The data is misleading.   These data are misleading.

Different than.

Here logic supports established usage: one thing differs *from* another, hence, *different from.* Or, *other than, unlike.*

Disinterested.

Means "impartial." Do not confuse it with *uninterested*, which means "not interested in."

> Let a disinterested person judge our dispute. (an impartial person)

> This man is obviously uninterested in our dispute. (couldn't care less)

Divided into.

Not to be misused for *composed of.* The line is sometimes difficult to draw; doubtless plays are divided into acts, but poems are composed of stanzas. An apple, halved, is divided into sections, but an apple is composed of seeds, flesh, and skin.

Due to.

Loosely used for *through, because of,* or *owing to,* in adverbial phrases.

He lost the first game due to carelessness.	He lost the first game because of carelessness.

In correct use synonymous with *attributable to:* "The accident was due to bad weather"; "losses due to preventable fires."

Each and every one.

Pitchman's jargon. Avoid, except in dialogue.

It should be a lesson to each and every one of us.	It should be a lesson to every one of us (to us all).

Effect.

As a noun, means "result"; as a verb, means "to bring about," "to accomplish" (not to be confused with *affect,* which means "to influence").

As a noun, often loosely used in perfunctory writing about fashions, music, painting, and other arts: "an Oriental effect"; "effects in pale green"; "very delicate effects"; "subtle effects"; "a charming effect was produced." The writer who has a definite meaning to express will not take refuge in such vagueness.

Enormity.

Use only in the sense "monstrous wickedness." Misleading, if not wrong, when used to express bigness.

Enthuse.

An annoying verb growing out of the noun *enthusiasm.* Not recommended.

She was enthused about her new car.	She was enthusiastic about her new car.
She enthused about her new car. (expressed enthusiasm)	She talked enthusiastically about her new car.

Etc.

Literally, "and other things"; sometimes loosely used to mean "and other persons." The phrase is equivalent to *and the rest, and so forth,* and hence is not to be used if one of these would be insufficient—that is, if the reader would be left in doubt as to any important particulars. Least open to objection when it represents the last terms of a list already given almost in full, or immaterial words at the end of a quotation.

At the end of a list introduced by *such as, for example,* or any similar expression, *etc.* is incorrect. In formal writing, *etc.* is a misfit. An item important enough to call for *etc.* is probably important enough to be named.

Fact.

Use this word only of matter capable of direct verification, not of matters of judgment. That a particular event happened on a given date, that lead melts at a certain temperature are facts. But such conclusions as that Napoleon was the greatest of modern generals or that the climate of California is delightful, however defensible they may be, are not properly called facts.

Facility.

Why must jails, hospitals, schools suddenly become "facilities"?

Parents complained bitterly about the fire hazard in the wooden facility.	Parents complained bitterly about the fire hazard in the wooden schoolhouse.
He has been appointed warden of the new facility.	He has been appointed warden of the new prison.

Factor.

A hackneyed word; the expressions of which it forms part can usually be replaced by something more direct and idiomatic.

His superior training was the great factor in his winning the match.	He won the match by being better trained.
Air power is becoming an increasingly important factor in deciding battles.	Air power is playing a larger and larger part in deciding battles.

Farther. Further.

The two words are commonly interchanged, but there is a distinction worth observing: *farther* serves best as a distance word, *further* as a time or quantity word. You chase a ball *farther* than the other fellow; you pursue a subject *further*.

Feature.

Another hackneyed word; like *factor*, it usually adds nothing to the sentence in which it occurs.

A feature of the entertainment especially worthy of mention was the singing of Miss A.	(Better use the same number of words to tell what Miss A. sang and how she sang it.)

As a verb, in the sense of "offer as a special attraction," to be avoided.

Finalize.

A pompous, ambiguous verb. (See Chapter V, Reminder 21.)

Fix.

Colloquial in America for *arrange, prepare, mend.* The usage is well established. But bear in mind that this verb is from *figere:* "to make firm," "to place definitely." These are the preferred meanings of the word.

Flammable.

An oddity, chiefly useful in saving lives. The common word meaning "combustible" is *inflammable*. But some people are thrown off by the *in-* and think *inflammable* means "not combustible." For this reason, trucks carrying gasoline or explosives are now marked FLAMMABLE. Unless you are operating such a truck and hence are concerned with the safety of children and illiterates, use *inflammable*.

Folk.

A collective noun, equivalent to *people*. Use the singular form only. *Folks,* in the sense of "parents," "family," "those present," is colloquial and too folksy for formal writing.

Her folks arrived by the afternoon train.	Her father and mother arrived by the afternoon train.

Fortuitous.

Limited to what happens by chance. Not to be used for *fortunate* or *lucky.*

Get.

The colloquial *have got* for *have* should not be used in writing. The preferable form of the participle is *got,* not *gotten.*

He has not got any sense.	He has no sense.
They returned without having gotten any.	They returned without having got any.

Gratuitous.

Means "unearned," or "unwarranted."

The insult seemed gratuitous. (undeserved)

He is a man who.

A common type of redundant expression; see Rule 17.

He is a man who is very ambitious.	He is very ambitious.
Vermont is a state that attracts visitors because of its winter sports.	Vermont attracts visitors because of its winter sports.

Hopefully.

This once-useful adverb meaning "with hope" has been distorted and is now widely used to mean "I hope" or "it is to be hoped." Such use is not merely wrong, it is silly. To say, "Hopefully I'll leave on the noon plane" is to talk nonsense. Do you mean you'll leave on the noon plane in a hopeful frame of mind? Or do you mean you hope you'll leave on the noon plane? Whichever you mean, you haven't said it clearly. Although the word in its new, free-floating capacity may be pleasurable and even useful to many, it offends the ear of many others, who do not like to see words dulled or eroded, particularly when the erosion leads to ambiguity, softness, or nonsense.

However.

Avoid starting a sentence with *however* when the meaning is "nevertheless." The word usually serves better when not in first position.

> The roads were almost impassable. However, we at last succeeded in reaching camp.

> The roads were almost impassable. At last, however, we succeeded in reaching camp.

When *however* comes first, it means "in whatever way" or "to whatever extent."

> However you advise him, he will probably do as he thinks best.
> However discouraging the prospect, he never lost heart.

Illusion.

See *allusion*.

Imply. Infer.

Not interchangeable. Something implied is something suggested or indicated, though not expressed. Something inferred is something deduced from evidence at hand.

> Farming implies early rising.
> Since he was a farmer, we inferred that he got up early.

Importantly.

Avoid by rephrasing.

> More importantly, he paid for the damages.

> What's more, he paid for the damages.

> With the breeze freshening, he altered course to pass inside the island. More importantly, as things turned out, he tucked in a reef.

> With the breeze freshening, he altered course to pass inside the island. More important, as things turned out, he tucked in a reef.

In regard to.

Often wrongly written *in regards to*. But *as regards* is correct, and means the same thing.

In the last analysis.

A bankrupt expression.

Inside of. Inside.

The *of* following *inside* is correct in the adverbial meaning "in less than." In other meanings *of* is unnecessary.

> Inside of five minutes I'll be inside the bank.

Insightful.

The word is a suspicious overstatement for "perceptive." If it is to be used at all, it should be used for instances of remarkably penetrating vision. Usually, it crops up merely to inflate the commonplace.

That was an insightful remark you made.	That was a perceptive remark you made.

In terms of

A piece of padding usually best omitted.

The job was unattractive in terms of salary.	The salary made the job unattractive.

Interesting.

An unconvincing word; avoid it as a means of introduction. Instead of announcing that what you are about to tell is interesting, make it so.

An interesting story is told of	(Tell the story without preamble.)
In connection with the forthcoming visit of Mr. B. to America, it is interesting to recall that he	Mr. B., who will soon visit America

Also to be avoided in introduction is the word *funny*. Nothing becomes funny by being labeled so.

Irregardless.

Should be *regardless*. The error results from failure to see the negative in *-less* and from a desire to get it in as a prefix, suggested by such words as *irregular, irresponsible,* and, perhaps especially, *irrespective*.

-ize.

Do not coin verbs by adding this tempting suffix. Many good and useful verbs do end in *-ize: summarize, temporize, fraternize, harmonize, fertilize.* But there is a growing list of abominations: *containerize, customize, prioritize, finalize,* to name four. Be suspicious of *-ize;* let your ear and your eye guide you. Never tack *-ize* onto a noun to create a verb. Usually you will discover that a useful verb already exists. Why say "moisturize" when there is the simple, unpretentious word *moisten*?

Kind of.

Except in familiar style, not to be used as a substitute for *rather* or *something like*. Restrict it to its literal sense: "Amber is a kind of fossil resin"; "I dislike that kind of publicity." The same holds true of *sort of*.

Lay.

A transitive verb. Except in slang ("Let it lay"), do not misuse it for the intransitive verb *lie*. The hen, or the play, *lays* an egg; the llama *lies* down. The playwright went home and *lay* down.

> lie; lay; lain; lying
> lay; laid; laid; laying

Leave.

Not to be misused for *let*.

Leave it stand the way it is.	Let it stand the way it is.
Leave go of that rope!	Let go of that rope!

Less.

Should not be misused for *fewer*.

He had less men than in the previous campaign.	He had fewer men than in the previous campaign.

Less refers to quantity, *fewer* to number. "His troubles are less than mine" means "His troubles are not so great as mine." "His troubles are fewer than mine" means "His troubles are not so numerous as mine."

Like.

Not to be used for the conjunction *as*. *Like* governs nouns and pronouns; before phrases and clauses the equivalent word is *as*.

We spent the evening like in the old days.	We spent the evening as in the old days.
Chloë smells good, like a pretty girl should.	Chloë smells good, as a pretty girl should.

The use of *like* for *as* has its defenders; they argue that any usage that achieves currency becomes valid automatically. This, they say, is the way the language is

The Elements of Style

formed. It is and it isn't. An expression sometimes merely enjoys a vogue, much as an article of apparel does. *Like* has long been widely misused by the illiterate; lately it has been taken up by the knowing and the well-informed, who find it catchy, or liberating, and who use it as though they were slumming. If every word or device that achieved currency were immediately authenticated, simply on the ground of popularity, the language would be as chaotic as a ball game with no foul lines. For the student, perhaps the most useful thing to know about *like* is that most carefully edited publications regard its use before phrases and clauses as simple error.

Line. Along these lines.

Line in the sense of "course of procedure, conduct, thought" is allowable, but has been so overworked, particularly in the phrase *along these lines,* that a writer who aims at freshness or originality had better discard it entirely.

Mr. B. also spoke along the same lines.	Mr. B. also spoke to the same effect.
He is studying along the line of French literature.	He is studying French literature.

Literal. Literally.

Often incorrectly used in support of exaggeration or violent metaphor.

a literal flood of abuse	a flood of abuse
literally dead with fatigue	almost dead with fatigue (dead tired)

Loan.

A noun. As a verb, prefer *lend.*

Lend me your ears.
the loan of your ears

Meaningful.

A bankrupt adjective. Choose another, or rephrase.

His was a meaningful contribution.	His contribution counted heavily.
We are instituting many meaningful changes in the curriculum.	We are improving the curriculum in many ways.

Memento.

Often incorrectly written *momento.*

Most.

Not to be used for *almost* in formal composition.

most everybody	almost everybody
most all the time	almost all the time

Nature.

Often simply redundant, used like *character.*

acts of a hostile nature	hostile acts

Nature should be avoided in such vague expressions as "a lover of nature," "poems about nature." Unless more specific statements follow, the reader cannot tell whether the poems have to do with natural scenery, rural life, the sunset, the untracked wilderness, or the habits of squirrels.

Nauseous. Nauseated.

The first means "sickening to contemplate"; the second means "sick at the stomach." Do not, therefore, say "I feel nauseous," unless you are sure you have that effect on others.

Nice.

A shaggy, all-purpose word, to be used sparingly in formal composition. "I had a nice time." "It was nice weather." "She was so nice to her mother." The meanings are indistinct. *Nice* is most useful in the sense of "precise" or "delicate": "a nice distinction."

Nor.

Often used wrongly for *or* after negative expressions.

He cannot eat nor sleep.	He cannot eat or sleep.
	He can neither eat nor sleep.
	He cannot eat nor can he sleep.

Noun used as verb.

Many nouns have lately been pressed into service as verbs. Not all are bad, but all are suspect.

Be prepared for kisses when you gift your girl with this merry scent.	Be prepared for kisses when you give your girl this merry scent.

The candidate hosted a dinner for fifty of his workers.	The candidate gave a dinner for fifty of his workers.
The meeting was chaired by Mr. Oglethorp.	Mr. Oglethorp was chairman of the meeting.
He headquarters in Newark.	He has headquarters in Newark.
She debuted last fall.	She made her debut last fall.

Offputting. Ongoing.

Newfound adjectives, to be avoided because they are inexact and clumsy. *Ongoing* is a mix of "continuing" and "active" and is usually superfluous.

She devoted all her spare time to the ongoing program for aid to the elderly.	She devoted all her spare time to the program for aid to the elderly.

Offputting might mean "objectionable," "disconcerting," "distasteful." Select instead a word whose meaning is clear. As a simple test, transform the participles to verbs. It is possible to *upset* something. But to *offput?* To *ongo?*

One.

In the sense of "a person," not to be followed by *his.*

One must watch his step.	One must watch one's step. (You must watch your step.)

One of the most.

Avoid this feeble formula. "One of the most exciting developments of modern science is . . ."; "Switzerland is one of the most beautiful countries of Europe." There is nothing wrong with the grammar; the formula is simply threadbare.

-oriented.

A clumsy, pretentious device, much in vogue. Find a better way of indicating orientation or alignment or direction.

His was a manufacturing-oriented company.	His was a company chiefly concerned with manufacturing.
Many of the skits are situation-oriented.	Many of the skits rely on situation.

Partially.

Not always interchangeable with *partly.* Best used in the sense of "to a certain degree," when speaking of a condition or state: "I'm partially resigned to it."

Partly carries the idea of a part as distinct from the whole—usually a physical object.

The log was partially submerged.	The log was partly submerged.
He was partially in and partially out.	He was partly in and partly out.
	He was part in, part out.

Participle for verbal noun.

There was little prospect of the Senate accepting even this compromise.	There was little prospect of the Senate's accepting even this compromise.

In the left-hand column, *accepting* is a present participle; in the right-hand column, it is a verbal noun (gerund). The construction shown in the left-hand column is occasionally found, and has its defenders. Yet it is easy to see that the second sentence has to do not with a prospect of the Senate but with a prospect of accepting.

Any sentence in which the use of the possessive is awkward or impossible should of course be recast.

In the event of a reconsideration of the whole matter's becoming necessary	If it should become necessary to reconsider the whole matter
There was great dissatisfaction with the decision of the arbitrators being favorable to the company.	There was great dissatisfaction with the arbitrators' decision in favor of the company.

People.

A word with many meanings. (*The American Heritage Dictionary* gives ten.) *The people* is a political term, not to be confused with *the public*. From the people comes political support or opposition; from the public comes artistic appreciation or commercial patronage.

The word *people* is best not used with words of number, in place of *persons*. If of "six people" five went away, how many people would be left? Answer: one people.

Personalize.

A pretentious word, often carrying bad advice. Do not *personalize* your prose; simply make it good and keep it clean. See Chapter V, Reminder 1.

a highly personalized affair	a highly personal affair
Personalize your stationery.	Get up a letterhead.

Personally.

Often unnecessary.

Personally, I thought it was a good book.	I thought it a good book.

Possess.

Often used because to the writer it sounds more impressive than *have* or *own*. Such usage is not incorrect but is to be guarded against.

He possessed great courage.	He had great courage (was very brave).
He was the fortunate possessor of	He was lucky enough to own

Presently.

Has two meanings: "in a short while" and "currently." Because of this ambiguity it is best restricted to the first meaning: "He'll be here presently" ("soon," or "in a short time").

Prestigious.

Often an adjective of last resort. It's in the dictionary, but that doesn't mean you have to use it.

Refer.

See *allude*.

Regretful.

Sometimes carelessly used for *regrettable:* "The mixup was due to a regretful breakdown in communications."

Relate.

Not to be used intransitively to suggest rapport.

I relate well to Janet.	Janet and I see things the same way.
	Janet and I have a lot in common.

Respective. Respectively.

These words may usually be omitted with advantage.

Works of fiction are listed under the names of their respective authors.	Works of fiction are listed under the names of their authors.
The mile run and the two-mile run were won by Jones and Cummings respectively.	The mile run was won by Jones, the two-mile run by Cummings.

Secondly, thirdly, etc.

Unless you are prepared to begin with *firstly* and defend it (which will be difficult), do not prettify numbers with *-ly*. Modern usage prefers *second, third,* and so on.

Shall. Will.

In formal writing, the future tense requires *shall* for the first person, *will* for the second and third. The formula to express the speaker's belief regarding his future action or state is *I shall; I will* expresses his determination or his consent. A swimmer in distress cries, "I shall drown; no one will save me!" A suicide puts it the other way: "I will drown; no one shall save me!" In relaxed speech, however, the words *shall* and *will* are seldom used precisely; our ear guides us or fails to guide us, as the case may be, and we are quite likely to drown when we want to survive and survive when we want to drown.

So.

Avoid, in writing, the use of *so* as an intensifier: "so good"; "so warm"; "so delightful."

Sort of.

See *kind of*.

Split infinitive.

There is precedent from the fourteenth century down for interposing an adverb between *to* and the infinitive it governs, but the construction should be avoided unless the writer wishes to place unusual stress on the adverb.

to diligently inquire	to inquire diligently

For another side to the split infinitive, see Chapter V, Reminder 14.

State.

Not to be used as a mere substitute for *say, remark*. Restrict it to the sense of "express fully or clearly": "He refused to state his objections."

Student body.

Nine times out of ten a needless and awkward expression, meaning no more than the simple word *students*.

a member of the student body	a student
popular with the student body	liked by the students

Than.

Any sentence with *than* (to express comparison) should be examined to make sure no essential words are missing.

I'm probably closer to my mother than my father. (Ambiguous.)	I'm probably closer to my mother than to my father.
	I'm probably closer to my mother than my father is.
It looked more like a cormorant than a heron.	It looked more like a cormorant than like a heron.

Thanking you in advance.

This sounds as if the writer meant, "It will not be worth my while to write to you again." In making your request, write, "Will you please," or "I shall be obliged." Then, later, if you feel moved to do so, or if the circumstances call for it, write a letter of acknowledgment.

That. Which.

That is the defining, or restrictive pronoun, *which* the nondefining, or nonrestrictive. See Rule 3.

> The lawn mower that is broken is in the garage. (Tells which one)
>
> The lawn mower, which is broken, is in the garage. (Adds a fact about the only mower in question)

The use of *which* for *that* is common in written and spoken language ("Let us now go even unto Bethlehem, and see this thing which is come to pass.") Occasionally *which* seems preferable to *that,* as in the sentence from the Bible. But it would be a convenience to all if these two pronouns were used with precision. The careful writer, watchful for small conveniences, goes *which*-hunting, removes the defining *whiches,* and by so doing improves his work.

The foreseeable future.

A cliché, and a fuzzy one. How much of the future is foreseeable? Ten minutes? Ten years? Any of it? By whom is it foreseeable? Seers? Experts? Everybody?

The truth is. . . . The fact is. . . .

A bad beginning for a sentence. If you feel you are possessed of the truth, or of the fact, simply state it. Do not give it advance billing.

They.

Not to be used when the antecedent is a distributive expression such as *each, each one, everybody, every one, many a man.* Use the singular pronoun.

Every one of us knows they are fallible.	Every one of us knows he is fallible.
Everyone in the community, whether they are a member of the Association or not, is invited to attend.	Everyone in the community, whether he is a member of the Association or not, is invited to attend.

A similar fault is the use of the plural pronoun with the antecedent *anybody, anyone, somebody, someone,* the intention being either to avoid the awkward "he or she" or to avoid committing oneself to one or the other. Some bashful speakers even say, "A friend of mine told me that they. . . ."

The use of *he* as pronoun for nouns embracing both genders is a simple, practical convention rooted in the beginnings of the English language. *He* has lost all suggestion of maleness in these circumstances. The word was unquestionably biased to begin with (the dominant male), but after hundreds of years it has become seemingly indispensable. It has no pejorative connotation; it is never incorrect. Substituting *he or she* in its place is the logical thing to do if it works. But it often doesn't work, if only because repetition makes it sound boring or silly. Consider the following unexceptional sentences from *The Summing Up,* by W. Somerset Maugham:

> Another cause of obscurity is that the writer is himself not quite sure of his meaning. He has a vague impression of what he wants to say, but has not, either from lack of mental power or from laziness, exactly formulated it in his mind, and it is natural enough that he should not find a precise expression for a confused idea.

Rewritten to affirm equality of the sexes, the same statement verges on nonsense:

> Another cause of obscurity is that the writer is herself or himself not quite sure of her or his meaning. He or she has a vague impression of what he or she wants to say, but has not, either from lack of mental power or from laziness, exactly formulated it in her or his mind, and it is natural enough that he or she should not find a precise expression for a confused idea.

No one need fear to use *he* if common sense supports it. The furor recently raised about *he* would be more impressive if there were a handy substitute for the word. Unfortunately, there isn't—or, at least, no one has come up with one yet. If you think *she* is a handy substitute for *he,* try it and see what happens. Alternatively, put all controversial nouns in the plural and avoid the choice of sex altogether, and you may find your prose sounding general and diffuse as a result.

This.

The pronoun *this*, referring to the complete sense of a preceding sentence or clause, can't always carry the load and so may produce an imprecise statement.

Visiting dignitaries watched yesterday as ground was broken for the new high-energy physics laboratory with a blowout safety wall. This is the first visible evidence of the university's plans for modernization and expansion.	Visiting dignitaries watched yesterday as ground was broken for the new high-energy physics laboratory with a blowout safety wall. The ceremony afforded the first visible evidence of the university's plans for modernization and expansion.

In the left-hand example above, *this* does not immediately make clear what the first visible evidence is.

Thrust.

This showy noun, suggestive of power, hinting of sex, is the darling of executives, politicos, and speech-writers. Use it sparingly. Save it for specific application.

Our reorganization plan has a tremendous thrust.	The piston has a five-inch thrust.
The thrust of his letter was that he was working more hours than he'd bargained for.	The point he made in his letter was that he was working more hours than he'd bargained for.

Tortuous. Torturous.

A winding road is *tortuous,* a painful ordeal is *torturous*. Both words carry the idea of "twist," the twist having been a form of torture.

Transpire.

Not to be used in the sense of "happen," "come to pass." Many writers so use it (usually when groping toward imagined elegance), but their usage finds little support in the Latin "breathe across or through." It is correct, however, in the sense of "become known." "Eventually, the grim account of his villainy transpired" (literally, "leaked through or out").

The
Elements
of
Style

Try.

Takes the infinitive: "try to mend it," not "try *and* mend it." Students of the language will argue that *try and* has won through and become idiom. Indeed it has, and it is relaxed and acceptable. But *try to* is precise, and when you are writing formal prose, try and write *try to*.

Type.

Not a synonym for *kind of*. The examples below are common vulgarisms.

that type employee	that kind of employee
I dislike that type publicity.	I dislike that kind of publicity.
small, home-type hotels	small, homelike hotels
a new type plane	a plane of a new design (new kind)

Unique.

Means "without like or equal." Hence, there can be no degrees of uniqueness.

It was the most unique egg beater on the market.	It was a unique egg beater.
The balancing act was very unique.	The balancing act was unique.
Of all the spiders, the one that lives in a bubble under water is the most unique.	Among spiders, the one that lives in a bubble under water is unique.

Utilize.

Prefer *use*.

I utilized the facilities.	I used the toilet.
She utilized the dishwasher.	She used the dishwasher.

Verbal.

Sometimes means "word for word" and in this sense may refer to something expressed in writing. *Oral* (from Latin *ōs,* "mouth") limits the meaning to what is transmitted by speech. *Oral agreement* is more precise than *verbal agreement*.

Very.

Use this word sparingly. Where emphasis is necessary, use words strong in themselves.

While.

Avoid the indiscriminate use of this word for *and, but,* and *although.* Many writers use it frequently as a substitute for *and* or *but,* either from a mere desire to vary the connective or from doubt about which of the two connectives is the more appropriate. In this use it is best replaced by a semicolon.

The office and salesrooms are on the ground foor, while the rest of the building is used for manufacturing.	The office and salesrooms are on the ground floor; the rest of the building is used for manufacturing.

Its use as a virtual equivalent of *although* is allowable in sentences where this leads to no ambiguity or absurdity.

> While I admire his energy, I wish it were employed in a better cause.

This is entirely correct, as is shown by the paraphrase

> I admire his energy; at the same time, I wish it were employed in a better cause.

Compare:

> While the temperature reaches 90 or 95 degrees in the daytime, the nights are often chilly.

The paraphrase shows why the use of *while* is incorrect:

> The temperature reaches 90 or 95 degrees in the daytime; at the same time the nights are often chilly.

In general, the writer will do well to use *while* only with strict literalness, in the sense of "during the time that."

-wise.

Not to be used indiscriminately as a pseudosuffix: *taxwise, pricewise, marriagewise, prosewise, saltwater taffywise.* Chiefly useful when it means "in the manner of": *clockwise.* There is not a noun in the language to which *-wise* cannot be added if the spirit moves one to add it. The sober writer will abstain from the use of this wild additive.

Worth while.

Overworked as a term of vague approval and (with *not*) of disapproval. Strictly applicable only to actions: "Is it worth while to telegraph?"

His books are not worth while.	His books are not worth reading (are not worth one's while to read; do not repay reading).

The adjective *worthwhile* (one word) is acceptable but emaciated. Use a stronger word.

<table>
<tr><td>a worthwhile project</td><td>a promising (useful, valuable, exciting) project</td></tr>
</table>

Would.

Commonly used to express habitual or repeated action. ("He would get up early and prepare his own breakfast before he went to work.") But when the idea of habit or repetition is expressed, in such phrases as *once a year, every day, each Sunday,* the past tense, without *would*, is usually sufficient, and, from its brevity, more emphatic.

<table>
<tr><td>Once a year, he would visit the old mansion.</td><td>Once a year he visited the old mansion.</td></tr>
</table>

In narrative writing, always indicate the transition from the general to the particular—that is, from sentences that merely state a general habit to those that express the action of a specific day or period. Failure to indicate the change will cause confusion.

> Townsend would get up early and prepare his own breakfast. If the day was cold, he filled the stove and had a warm fire burning before he left the house. On his way out to the garage, he noticed that there were footprints in the new-fallen snow on the porch.

The reader is lost, having received no signal that Townsend has changed from a mere man of habit to a man who has seen a particular thing on a particular day.

> Townsend would get up early and prepare his own breakfast. If the day was cold, he filled the stove and had a warm fire burning before he left the house. One morning in January on his way out to the garage, he noticed footprints in the new-fallen snow on the porch.

V
An Approach to Style
(With a List of Reminders)

Up to this point, the book has been concerned with what is correct, or acceptable, in the use of English. In this final chapter, we approach style in its broader meaning: style in the sense of what is distinguished and distinguishing. Here we leave solid ground. Who can confidently say what ignites a certain combination of words, causing them to explode in the mind? Who knows why certain notes in music are capable of stirring the listener deeply, though the same notes slightly rearranged are impotent? These are high mysteries, and this chapter is a mystery story, thinly disguised. There is no satisfactory explanation of style, no infallible guide to good writing, no assurance that a person who thinks clearly will be able to write clearly, no key that unlocks the door, no inflexible rule by which the young writer may shape his course. He will often find himself steering by stars that are disturbingly in motion.

The preceding chapters contain instructions drawn from established English usage; this one contains advice drawn from a writer's experience of writing. Since the book is a rule book, these cautionary remarks, these subtly dangerous hints, are presented in the form of rules, but they are, in essence, mere gentle reminders: they state what most of us know and at times forget.

Style is an increment in writing. When we speak of Fitzgerald's style, we don't mean his command of the relative pronoun, we mean the sound his words make on paper. Every writer, by the way he uses the language, reveals something of his spirit, his habits, his capacities, his bias. This is inevitable as well as enjoyable. All writing is communication; creative writing is communication through revelation—it is the Self escaping into the open. No writer long remains incognito.

If the student doubts that style is something of a mystery, let him try rewriting a familiar sentence and see what happens. Any much-quoted sentence will do. Suppose we take "These are the times that try men's souls." Here we have eight short, easy words, forming a simple declarative sentence. The sentence contains no flashy ingredient such as "Damn the torpedoes!" and the words, as you see, are ordinary. Yet in that arrangement they have shown great durability; the sentence is almost into its third century. Now compare a few variations:

> Times like these try men's souls.
> How trying it is to live in these times!
> These are trying times for men's souls.
> Soulwise, these are trying times.

It seems unlikely that Thomas Paine could have made his sentiment stick if he had couched it in any of these forms. But why not? No fault of grammar can be detected in them, and in every case the meaning is clear. Each version is correct, and each, for some reason that we can't readily put our finger on, is marked for oblivion. We could, of course, talk about "rhythm" and "cadence," but the talk would be vague and unconvincing. We could declare *soulwise* to be a silly word, inappropriate to the occasion; but even that won't do—it does not answer the main question. Are we even sure *soulwise* is silly? If *otherwise* is a serviceable word, what's the matter with *soulwise*?

Here is another sentence, this one by a later Tom. It is not a famous sentence, although its author (Thomas Wolfe) is well known. "Quick are the mouths of earth, and quick the teeth that fed upon this loveliness." The sentence would not take a prize for clarity, and rhetorically it is at the opposite pole from "These are the times." Try it in a different form, without the inversions:

> The mouths of earth are quick, and the teeth that fed upon this loveli-
> ness are quick, too.

The author's meaning is still intact, but not his overpowering emotion. What was poetical and sensuous has become prosy and wooden; instead of the secret sounds of beauty, we are left with the simple crunch of mastication. (Whether Mr. Wolfe was guilty of overwriting is, of course, another question—one that is not pertinent here.)

With some writers, style not only reveals the spirit of the man but reveals his identity, as surely as would his fingerprints. Here, following, are two brief passages from the works of two American novelists. The subject in each case is languor. In both, the words used are ordinary, and there is nothing eccentric about the construction.

> He did not still feel weak, he was merely luxuriating in that supremely
> gutful lassitude of convalescence in which time, hurry, doing, did not
> exist, the accumulating seconds and minutes and hours to which in its well
> state the body is slave both waking and sleeping, now reversed and time
> now the lip-server and mendicant to the body's pleasure instead of the
> body thrall to time's headlong course.

> Manuel drank his brandy. He felt sleepy himself. It was too hot to go
> out into the town. Besides there was nothing to do. He wanted to see
> Zurito. He would go to sleep while he waited.

Anyone acquainted with Faulkner and Hemingway will have recognized them in these passages and perceived which was which. How different are their languors!

Or take two American poets, stopping at evening. One stops by woods, the other by laughing flesh.

> My little horse must think it queer
> To stop without a farmhouse near
> Between the woods and frozen lake
> The darkest evening of the year.*

> I have perceived that to be with those I like is enough,
> To stop in company with the rest at evening is enough,
> To be surrounded by beautiful, curious, breathing,
>   laughing flesh is enough . . .

*From "Stopping by Woods on a Snowy Evening" from *The Poetry of Robert Frost*, edited by Edward Connery Latham. Copyright 1923, © 1969 by Holt, Rinehart, and Winston, Inc. Copyright 1951 by Robert Frost. Reprinted by permission of Holt, Rinehart, and Winston, Inc., and Jonathan Cape Ltd.

Strunk Jr. **and** E.B. **White**

Because of the characteristic styles, there is little question about identity here, and if the situations were reversed, with Whitman stopping by woods and Frost by laughing flesh (not one of his regularly scheduled stops), the reader would still know who was who.

Young writers often suppose that style is a garnish for the meat of prose, a sauce by which a dull dish is made palatable. Style has no such separate entity; it is nondetachable, unfilterable. The beginner should approach style warily, realizing that it is himself he is approaching, no other; and he should begin by turning resolutely away from all devices that are popularly believed to indicate style—all mannerisms, tricks, adornments. The approach to style is by way of plainness, simplicity, orderliness, sincerity.

Writing is, for most, laborious and slow. The mind travels faster than the pen; consequently, writing becomes a question of learning to make occasional wing shots, bringing down the bird of thought as it flashes by. A writer is a gunner, sometimes waiting in his blind for something to come in, sometimes roaming the countryside hoping to scare something up. Like other gunners, he must cultivate patience; he may have to work many covers to bring down one partridge. Here, following, are some suggestions and cautionary hints that may help the beginner find his way to a satisfactory style.

1. Place yourself in the background.

Write in a way that draws the reader's attention to the sense and substance of the writing, rather than to the mood and temper of the author. If the writing is solid and good, the mood and temper of the writer will eventually be revealed, and not at the expense of the work. Therefore, the first piece of advice is this: to achieve style, begin by affecting none—that is, place yourself in the background. A careful and honest writer does not need to worry about style. As he becomes proficient in the use of the language, his style will emerge, because he himself will emerge, and when this happens he will find it increasingly easy to break through the barriers that separate him from other minds, other hearts—which is, of course, the purpose of writing, as well as its principal reward. Fortunately, the act of composition, or creation, disciplines the mind; writing is one way to go about thinking, and the practice and habit of writing not only drain the mind but supply it, too.

2. Write in a way that comes naturally.

Write in a way that comes easily and naturally to you, using words and phrases that come readily to hand. But do not assume that because you have acted naturally your product is without flaw.

The use of language begins with imitation. The infant imitates the sounds made by its parents; the child imitates first the spoken language, then the stuff of books. The imitative life continues long after the writer is on his own in the language, for it is almost impossible to avoid imitating what one admires. Never imitate consciously, but do not worry about being an imitator; take pains instead to admire what is good. Then when you write in a way that comes naturally, you will echo the halloos that bear repeating.

3. *Work from a suitable design.*

Before beginning to compose something, gauge the nature and extent of the enterprise and work from a suitable design. (See Chapter II, Rule 12.) Design informs even the simplest structure, whether of brick and steel or of prose. You raise a pup tent from one sort of vision, a cathedral from another. This does not mean that you must sit with a blueprint always in front of you, merely that you had best anticipate what you are getting into. To compose a laundry list, a writer can work directly from the pile of soiled garments, ticking them off one by one. But to write a biography the writer will need at least a rough scheme; he cannot plunge in blindly and start ticking off fact after fact about his man, lest he miss the forest for the trees and there be no end to his labors.

Sometimes, of course, impulse and emotion are more compelling than design. A deeply troubled person, composing a letter appealing for mercy or for love, had best not attempt to organize his emotions; his prose will have a better chance if he leaves his emotions in disarray—which he'll probably have to do anyway, since one's feelings do not usually lend themselves to rearrangement. But even the kind of writing that is essentially adventurous and impetuous will on examination be found to have a secret plan: Columbus didn't just sail, he sailed west, and the New World took shape from this simple and, we now think, sensible design.

4. *Write with nouns and verbs.*

Write with nouns and verbs, not with adjectives and adverbs. The adjective hasn't been built that can pull a weak or inaccurate noun out of a tight place. This is not to disparage adjectives and adverbs; they are indispensable parts of speech. Occasionally they surprise us with their power, as in

> Up the airy mountain,
>   Down the rushy glen,
> We daren't go a-hunting
>   For fear of little men . . .

The nouns *mountain* and *glen* are accurate enough, but had the mountain not become airy, the glen rushy, William Allingham might never have got off the ground with his poem. In general, however, it is nouns and verbs, not their assistants, that give to good writing its toughness and color.

5. *Revise and rewrite.*

Revising is part of writing. Few writers are so expert that they can produce what they are after on the first try. Quite often the writer will discover, on examining the completed work, that there are serious flaws in the arrangement of the material, calling for transpositions. When this is the case, he can save himself much labor and time by using scissors on his manuscript, cutting it to pieces and fitting the pieces together in a better order. If the work merely needs shortening, a pencil is the most useful tool; but if it needs rearranging, or stirring up, scissors should be brought into play. Do not be afraid to seize whatever you have written and cut it to ribbons; it can always be restored to its original condition in the morning, if that course seems best. Remember, it is no sign of weakness or defeat that your manuscript ends up in need of major surgery. This is a common occurrence in all writing, and among the best writers.

6. Do not overwrite.

Rich, ornate prose is hard to digest, generally unwholesome, and sometimes nauseating. If the sickly-sweet word, the overblown phrase are a writer's natural form of expression, as is sometimes the case, he will have to compensate for it by a show of vigor, and by writing something as meritorious as the Song of Songs, which is Solomon's.

7. Do not overstate.

When you overstate, the reader will be instantly on guard, and everything that has preceded your overstatement as well as everything that follows it will be suspect in his mind because he has lost confidence in your judgment or your poise. Overstatement is one of the common faults. A single overstatement, wherever or however it occurs, diminishes the whole, and a single carefree superlative has the power to destroy, for the reader, the object of the writer's enthusiasm.

8. Avoid the use of qualifiers.

Rather, very, little, pretty—these are the leeches that infest the pond of prose, sucking the blood of words. The constant use of the adjective *little* (except to indicate size) is particularly debilitating; we should all try to do a little better, we should all be very watchful of this rule, for it is a rather important one and we are pretty sure to violate it now and then.

9. Do not affect a breezy manner.

The volume of writing is enormous, these days, and much of it has a sort of windiness about it, almost as though the author were in a state of euphoria. "Spontaneous me," sang Whitman, and, in his innocence, let loose the hordes of uninspired scribblers who would one day confuse spontaneity with genius.

The breezy style is often the work of an egocentric, the person who imagines that everything that pops into his head is of general interest and that uninhibited prose creates high spirits and carries the day. Open any alumni magazine, turn to the class notes, and you are quite likely to encounter old Spontaneous Me at work —an aging collegian who writes something like this:

> Well, chums, here I am again with my bagful of dirt about your disorderly classmates, after spending a helluva weekend in N'Yawk trying to view the Columbia game from behind two bumbershoots and a glazed cornea. And speaking of news, howzabout tossing a few chirce nuggets my way?

This is an extreme example, but the same wind blows, at lesser velocities, across vast expanses of journalistic prose. The author in this case has managed in two sentences to commit most of the unpardonable sins: he obviously has nothing to say, he is showing off and directing the attention of the reader to himself, he is using slang with neither provocation nor ingenuity, he adopts a patronizing air by throwing in the word *chirce,* he is tasteless, humorless (though full of fun), dull, and empty. He has not done his work. Compare his opening remarks with the following—a plunge directly into the news:

> Clyde Crawford, who stroked the varsity shell in 1928, is swinging an oar again after a lapse of forty years. Clyde resigned last spring as executive sales manager of the Indiana Flotex Company and is now a gondolier in Venice.

This, although conventional, is compact, informative, unpretentious. The writer has dug up an item of news and presented it in a straightforward manner. What the first writer tried to accomplish by cutting rhetorical capers and by breeziness, the second writer managed to achieve by good reporting, by keeping a tight rein on his material, and by staying out of the act.

10. Use orthodox spelling.

In ordinary composition, use orthodox spelling. Do not write *nite* for *night, thru* for *through, pleez* for *please,* unless you plan to introduce a complete system of simplified spelling and are prepared to take the consequences.

In the original edition of *The Elements of Style,* there was a chapter on spelling. In it, the author had this to say:

> The spelling of English words is not fixed and invariable, nor does it depend on any other authority than general agreement. At the present day there is practically unanimous agreement as to the spelling of most words. . . . At any given moment, however, a relatively small number of words may be spelled in more than one way. Gradually, as a rule, one of these forms comes to be generally preferred, and the less customary form comes to look obsolete and is discarded. From time to time new forms, mostly simplifications, are introduced by innovators, and either win their place or die of neglect.
>
> The practical objection to unaccepted and oversimplified spellings is the disfavor with which they are received by the reader. They distract his attention and exhaust his patience. He reads the form *though* automatically, without thought of its needless complexity; he reads the

abbreviation *tho* and mentally supplies the missing letters, at the cost of a fraction of his attention. The writer has defeated his own purpose.

The language manages somehow to keep pace with events. A word that has taken hold in our century is *thruway;* it was born of necessity and is apparently here to stay. In combination with *way, thru* is more serviceable than *through;* it is a high-speed word for readers who are going sixty. *Throughway* would be too long to fit on a road sign, too slow to serve the speeding eye. It is conceivable that because of our thruways, *through* will eventually become *thru*—after many more thousands of miles of travel.

11. *Do not explain too much.*

It is seldom advisable to tell all. Be sparing, for instance, in the use of adverbs after "he said," "she replied," and the like: "he said consolingly"; "she replied grumblingly." Let the conversation itself disclose the speaker's manner or condition. Dialogue heavily weighted with adverbs after the attributive verb is cluttery and annoying. Inexperienced writers not only overwork their adverbs but load their attributives with explanatory verbs: "he consoled," "she congratulated." They do this, apparently, in the belief that the word *said* is always in need of support, or because they have been told to do it by experts in the art of bad writing.

12. *Do not construct awkward adverbs.*

Adverbs are easy to build. Take an adjective or a participle, add *-ly,* and behold! you have an adverb. But you'd probably be better off without it. Do not write *tangledly.* The word itself is a tangle. Do not even write *tiredly.* Nobody says *tangledly* and not many people say *tiredly.* Words that are not used orally are seldom the ones to put on paper.

He climbed tiredly to bed.	He climbed wearily to bed.
The lamp cord lay tangledly beneath his chair.	The lamp cord lay in tangles beneath his chair.

Do not dress words up by adding *ly* to them, as though putting a hat on a horse.

overly	over
muchly	much
thusly	thus

13. *Make sure the reader knows who is speaking.*

Dialogue is a total loss unless you indicate who the speaker is. In long dialogue passages containing no attributives, the reader may become lost and be compelled to go back and reread in order to puzzle the thing out. Obscurity is an imposition on the reader, to say nothing of its damage to the work.

In dialogue, make sure that your attributives do not awkwardly interrupt a spoken sentence. Place them where the break would come naturally in speech—

that is, where the speaker would pause for emphasis, or take a breath. The best test for locating an attributive is to speak the sentence aloud.

"Now, my boy, we shall see," he said, "how well you have learned your lesson."

"Now, my boy," he said, "we shall see how well you have learned your lesson."

"What's more, they would never," he added, "consent to the plan."

"What's more," he added, "they would never consent to the plan."

14. Avoid fancy words.

Avoid the elaborate, the pretentious, the coy, and the cute. Do not be tempted by a twenty-dollar word when there is a ten-center handy, ready and able. Anglo-Saxon is a livelier tongue than Latin, so use Anglo-Saxon words. In this, as in so many matters pertaining to style, one's ear must be one's guide: *gut* is a lustier noun than *intestine*, but the two words are not interchangeable, because *gut* is often inappropriate, being too coarse for the context. Never call a stomach a tummy without good reason.

If you admire fancy words, if every sky is *beauteous,* every blonde *curvaceous,* if you are tickled by *discombobulate,* you will have a bad time with Reminder 14. What is wrong, you ask, with *beauteous*? No one knows, for sure. There is nothing wrong, really, with any word—all are good, but some are better than others. A matter of ear, a matter of reading the books that sharpen the ear.

The line between the fancy and the plain, between the atrocious and the felicitous, is sometimes alarmingly fine. The opening phrase of the Gettysburg address is close to the line, at least by our standards today, and Mr. Lincoln, knowingly or unknowingly, was flirting with disaster when he wrote "Four score and seven years ago." The President could have got into his sentence with plain "Eighty-seven"—a saving of two words and less of a strain on the listeners' powers of multiplication. But Lincoln's ear must have told him to go ahead with four score and seven. By doing so, he achieved cadence while skirting the edge of fanciness. Suppose he had blundered over the line and written, "In the year of our Lord seventeen hundred and seventy-six." His speech would have sustained a heavy blow. Or suppose he had settled for "Eighty-seven." In that case he would have got into his introductory sentence too quickly; the timing would have been bad.

The question of ear is vital. Only the writer whose ear is reliable is in a position to use bad grammar deliberately; only he knows for sure when a colloquialism is better than formal phrasing; only he is able to sustain his work at the level of good taste. So cock your ear. Years ago, students were warned not to end a sentence with a preposition; time, of course, has softened that rigid decree. Not only is the preposition acceptable at the end, sometimes it is more effective in that spot than anywhere else. "A claw hammer, not an ax, was the tool he murdered her with." This is preferable to "A claw hammer, not an ax, was the tool with which he murdered her." Why? Because it sounds more violent, more like murder. A matter of ear.

And would you write "The worst tennis player around here is I" or "The worst tennis player around here is me"? The first is good grammar, the second is good judgment—although the *me* might not do in all contexts.

The split infinitive is another trick of rhetoric in which the ear must be quicker than the handbook. Some infinitives seem to improve on being split, just as a stick of round stovewood does. "I cannot bring myself to really like the fellow." The sentence is relaxed, the meaning is clear, the violation is harmless and scarcely perceptible. Put the other way, the sentence becomes stiff, needlessly formal. A matter of ear.

There are times when the ear not only guides us through difficult situations but also saves us from minor or major embarrassments of prose. The ear, for example must decide when to omit *that* from a sentence, when to retain it. "He knew he could do it" is preferable to "He knew that he could do it"—simpler and just as clear. But in many cases the *that* is needed. "He felt that his big nose, which was sunburned, made him look ridiculous." Omit the *that* and you have "He felt his big nose. . . ."

15. Do not use dialect unless your ear is good.

Do not attempt to use dialect unless you are a devoted student of the tongue you hope to reproduce. If you use dialect, be consistent. The reader will become impatient or confused if he finds two or more versions of the same word or expression. In dialect it is necessary to spell phonetically, or at least ingeniously, to capture unusual inflections. Take, for example, the word *once.* It often appears in dialect writing as *oncet,* but *oncet* looks as though it should be pronounced "onset." A better spelling would be *wunst.* But if you write it *oncet* once, write it that way throughout. The best dialect writers, by and large, are economical of their talents, they use the minimum, not the maximum, of deviation from the norm, thus sparing the reader as well as convincing him.

16. Be clear.

Clarity is not the prize in writing, nor is it always the principal mark of a good style. There are occasions when obscurity serves a literary yearning, if not a literary purpose, and there are writers whose mien is more overcast than clear. But since writing is communication, clarity can only be a virtue. And although there is no substitute for merit in writing, clarity comes closest to being one. Even to a writer who is being intentionally obscure or wild of tongue we can say, "Be obscure clearly! Be wild of tongue in a way we can understand!" Even to writers of market letters, telling us (but not telling us) which securities are promising, we can say, "Be cagey plainly! Be elliptical in a straightforward fashion!"

Clarity, clarity, clarity. When you become hopelessly mired in a sentence, it is best to start fresh; do not try to fight your way through against the terrible odds of syntax. Usually what is wrong is that the construction has become too involved at some point; the sentence needs to be broken apart and replaced by two or more shorter sentences.

Muddiness is not merely a disturber of prose, it is also a destroyer of life, of hope: death on the highway caused by a badly worded road sign, heartbreak among lovers caused by a misplaced phrase in a well-intentioned letter, anguish of a traveler expecting to be met at a railroad station and not being met because of a slipshod telegram. Usually we think only of the ludicrous aspect of ambiguity; we enjoy it when the *Times* tells us that Nelson Rockefeller is "chairman of the Museum of Modern Art, which he entered in a fireman's raincoat during a recent fire, and founded the Museum of Primitive Art." This we all love. But think of the tragedies that are rooted in ambiguity; think of that side, and be clear! When you say something, make sure you have said it. The chances of your having said it are only fair.

17. Do not inject opinion.

Unless there is a good reason for its being there, do not inject opinion into a piece of writing. We all have opinions about almost everything, and the temptation to toss them in is great. To air one's views gratuitously, however, is to imply that the demand for them is brisk, which may not be the case, and which, in any event, may not be relevant to the discussion. Opinions scattered indiscriminately about leave the mark of egotism on a work. Similarly, to air one's views at an improper time may be in bad taste. If you have received a letter inviting you to speak at the dedication of a new cat hospital, and you hate cats, your reply, declining the invitation, does not necessarily have to cover the full range of your emotions. You must make it clear that you will not attend, but you do not have to let fly at cats. The writer of the letter asked a civil question; attack cats, then, only if you can do so with good humor, good taste, and in such a way that your answer will be courteous as well as responsive. Since you are out of sympathy with cats, you may quite properly give this as a reason for not appearing at the dedicatory ceremonies of a cat hospital. But bear in mind that your opinion of cats was not sought, only your services as a speaker. Try to keep things straight.

18. Use figures of speech sparingly.

The simile is a common device and a useful one, but similes coming in rapid fire, one right on top of another, are more distracting than illuminating. The reader needs time to catch his breath; he can't be expected to compare everything with something else, and no relief in sight.

When you use metaphor, do not mix it up. That is, don't start by calling something a swordfish and end by calling it an hourglass.

19. Do not take shortcuts at the cost of clarity.

Do not use initials for the names of organizations or movements unless you are certain the initials will be readily understood. Write things out. Not everyone knows that SALT means Strategic Arms Limitation Talks, and even if everyone did, there are babies being born every minute who will someday encounter the name for the first time. They deserve to see the words, not simply the initials. A good rule is to start your article by writing out names in full, and then, later, when the reader has got his bearings, to shorten them.

Many shortcuts are self-defeating; they waste the reader's time instead of conserving it. There are all sorts of rhetorical stratagems and devices that attract writers who hope to be pithy, but most of them are simply bothersome. The longest way round is usually the shortest way home, and the one truly reliable shortcut in writing is to choose words that are strong and sure-footed to carry the reader on his way.

20. Avoid foreign languages.

The writer will occasionally find it convenient or necessary to borrow from other languages. Some writers, however, from sheer exuberance or a desire to show off, sprinkle their work liberally with foreign expressions, with no regard for the reader's comfort. It is a bad habit. Write in English.

21. Prefer the standard to the offbeat.

The young writer will be drawn at every turn toward eccentricities in language. He will hear the beat of new vocabularies, the exciting rhythms of special segments of his society, each speaking a language of its own. All of us come under the spell of these unsettling drums; the problem for the beginner is to listen to them, learn the words, feel the vibrations, and not be carried away.

Youth invariably speaks to youth in a tongue of his own devising: he renovates the language with a wild vigor, as he would a basement apartment. By the time this paragraph sees print, *uptight, ripoff, rap, dude, vibes, copout,* and *funky* will be the words of yesteryear, and we will be fielding more recent ones that have come bouncing into our speech—some of them into our dictionary as well. A new word is always up for survival. Many do survive. Others grow stale and disappear. Most are, at least in their infancy, more appropriate to conversation than to composition.

Today, the language of advertising enjoys an enormous circulation. With its deliberate infractions of grammatical rules and its crossbreeding of the parts of speech, it profoundly influences the tongues and pens of children and adults. Your new kitchen range is so revolutionary it *obsoletes* all other ranges. Your counter top is beautiful because it is *accessorized* with gold-plated faucets. Your cigarette tastes good *like* a cigarette should. And, *like the man says,* you will want to try one. You will also, in all probability, want to try writing that way, using that language. You do so at your peril, for it is the language of mutilation.

Advertisers are quite understandably interested in what they call "attention getting." The man photographed must have lost an eye or grown a pink beard, or he must have three arms or be sitting wrong-end-to on a horse. This technique is proper in its place, which is the world of selling, but the young writer had best not adopt the device of mutilation in ordinary composition, whose purpose is to engage, not paralyze, the reader's senses. Buy the gold-plated faucets if you will, but do not accessorize your prose. To use the language well, do not begin by hacking it to bits; accept the whole body of it, cherish its classic form, its variety, and its richness.

Another segment of society that has constructed a language of its own is business. The businessman says that ink erasers are in *short supply,* that he has *updated* the next shipment of these erasers, and that he will *finalize* his recommendations at the next meeting of the board. He is speaking a language that is familiar to him and dear to him. Its portentous nouns and verbs invest ordinary events with high adventure; the executive walks among ink erasers, caparisoned like a knight. We should tolerate him—every man of spirit wants to ride a white horse. The only question is whether his vocabulary is helpful to ordinary prose. Usually, the same ideas can be expressed less formidably, if one makes the effort. A good many of the special words of business seem designed more to express the user's dreams than to express his precise meaning. Not all such words, of course, can be dismissed summarily; indeed, no word in the language can be dismissed offhand by anyone who has a healthy curiosity. *Update* isn't a bad word; in the right setting it is useful. In the wrong setting, though, it is destructive, and the trouble with adopting coinages too quickly is that they will bedevil one by insinuating themselves where they do not belong. This may sound like rhetorical snobbery, or plain stuffiness; but the writer will discover, in the course of his work, that the setting of a word is just as restrictive as the setting of a jewel. The general rule here is to prefer the standard. *Finalize,* for instance, is not standard; it is special, and it is a peculiarly fuzzy and silly word. Does it mean "terminate," or does it mean "put into final form"? One can't be sure, really, what it means, and one gets the impression that the person using it doesn't know, either, and doesn't want to know.

The special vocabularies of the law, of the military, of government are familiar to most of us. Even the world of criticism has a modest pouch of private words (*luminous, taut),* whose only virtue is that they are exceptionally nimble and can escape from the garden of meaning over the wall. Of these Critical words, Wolcott Gibbs once wrote, ". . . they are detached from the language and inflated like little balloons." The young writer should learn to spot them—words that at first glance seem freighted with delicious meaning but that soon burst in air, leaving nothing but a memory of bright sound.

The language is perpetually in flux: it is a living stream, shifting, changing, receiving new strength from a thousand tributaries, losing old forms in the backwaters of time. To suggest that a young writer not swim in the main stream of this turbulence would be foolish indeed, and such is not the intent of these cautionary remarks. The intent is to suggest that in choosing between the formal and the informal, the regular and the offbeat, the general and the special, the orthodox and the heretical, the beginner err on the side of conservatism, on the side of established usage. No idiom is taboo, no accent forbidden; there is simply a better chance of doing well if the writer holds a steady course, enters the stream of English quietly, and does not thrash about.

"But," the student may ask, "what if it comes natural to me to experiment rather than conform? What if I am a pioneer, or even a genius?" Answer: then be one. But do not forget that what may seem like pioneering may be merely evasion, or laziness—the disinclination to submit to discipline. Writing good standard English is no cinch, and before you have managed it you will have encountered enough rough country to satisfy even the most adventurous spirit.

Style takes its final shape more from attitudes of mind than from principles of composition, for, as an elderly practitioner once remarked, "Writing is an act of faith, not a trick of grammar." This moral observation would have no place in a rule book were it not that style *is* the writer, and therefore what a man is, rather than what he knows, will at last determine his style. If one is to write, one must believe—in the truth and worth of the scrawl, in the ability of the reader to receive and decode the message. No one can write decently who is distrustful of the reader's intelligence, or whose attitude is patronizing.

Many references have been made in this book to "the reader"—he has been much in the news. It is now necessary to warn the writer that his concern for the reader must be pure: he must sympathize with the reader's plight (most readers are in trouble about half the time) but never seek to know his wants. The whole duty of a writer is to please and satisfy himself, and the true writer always plays to an audience of one. Let him start sniffing the air, or glancing at the Trend Machine, and he is as good as dead, although he may make a nice living.

Full of his beliefs, sustained and elevated by the power of his purpose, armed with the rules of grammar, the writer is ready for exposure. At this point, he may well pattern himself on the fully exposed cow of Robert Louis Stevenson's rhyme. This friendly and commendable animal, you may recall, was "blown by all the winds that pass/And wet with all the showers." And so must the young writer be. In our modern idiom, we would say that he must get wet all over. Mr. Stevenson, working in a plainer style, said it with felicity, and suddenly one cow, out of so many, received the gift of immortality. Like the steadfast writer, she is at home in the wind and the rain; and, thanks to one moment of felicity, she will live on and on and on.

Index

Boldfaced numerals refer to pages in the reprinted Strunk and White, *Elements of Style*.

A

A, an, 416, 611, 636
Abbott, Bud, 64
Abbreviations, 676–677
  capitalization of, 677
  initials as, **817–818**
  periods in, 677
  for titles of people, 677–678, **758**
  for units of measure, 678
Absolute phrases, 471, 473
  diagraming, 515
Abstract nouns, 397
Academic degrees
  abbreviations of, 677–678
  punctuating, **758**
Accept, except, 611
Action verbs, 409, 533–534
Active listening, 746–747
Active voice of verbs, 533–534, 537, **768–769**
Adams, Douglas, 224
Adapt, adopt, 611
Addresses
  commas in, 659
  numerals in, 680
Adjective clauses, 489–490
  commas to set off nonessential, 655–656
  diagraming, 517
  subject-verb agreement with, 554–555
Adjectives
  articles as, 416, 611, 636
  comparative form of, 415, 591–592
  comparison of, 240, 415, 591–592
  compound, 674, **780**
  coordinate, 654
  definition of, 415
  diagraming, 511
  fractions used as, 675
  hyphens in compound, 674
  infinitive used as, 469

as object complements, 450
  participial phrase as, 467
  positive form of, 591–592
  predicate, 451
  prepositional phrases as, 463
  proper, 416, 637–638
  superlative form of, 591–592
  using specific, 418
Adopt, adapt, 611
Adverb clauses, 490–491
  commas to set off introductory, 658
  diagraming, 517–518
  elliptical, 492
Adverbs
  avoiding awkward, **814**
  for clarity, 422
  comparative form of, 419, 591–592
  comparison of, 240, 419, 591–592
  conjunctive, 429
  definition of, 419
  diagraming, 511
  in dialogue, **814–815**
  for emphasis, 422
  infinitive used as, 469
  negative words as, 419, 422
  positive form of, 419, 591–592
  prepositional phrases as, 463
  superlative form of, 419, 591–592
Advice, advise, 612
Affect, effect, 612, **789**
Afterword, 711
Aggravate, irritate, **784**
Agreement. *See* Pronoun-antecedent agreement; Subject-verb agreement
Ain't, 612
Alcott, Louisa May, 15
Algebra, writing topics in, 211
All ready, already, 612
All right, alright, 612, **784**
All together, altogether, 613
Allude, elude, **784**
Allusion, illusion, 613, **784**
Almost, most, **797**
Along these lines, line, **796**
Alternate, alternative, **784–785**
Ambiguous reference, correcting, 87, 580

American Childhood, An (Dillard), 104–108
American history, writing topics in, 133, 137, 211, 233, 299
American literature, writing topics in, 13, 29, 145, 229, 241
Among, between, 614, **785**
Analogies, 156, 273
And, as conjunction, **760**
And/or, **785**
Anecdotes
  in narrative writing, 6–7, 178
  in personal writing, 9
  in persuasive speech, 298
  in problem-solving essays, 227
Angelou, Maya, 136, 242
Antecedents. *See also* Pronoun-antecedent agreement
  definition of, 573
  position in sentence, **776**
Anthony, Susan B., 279
Anticipate, **785**
Antithetical phrases, commas to set off, 658
Anybody, **785**
Anyone, **785**
Apostrophes
  in contractions, 672–673
  correcting missing or misplaced, 392-393
  with possessives, 397, 671–672, **757**
  with special plurals, 673
Appendix, 711
Appositive phrases, 465, 473
  diagraming, 514
Appositives, 465–466
  commas to set off, 395, 656
  diagraming, 514
  gerunds used as, 468
  pronouns with and as, 567–568
"Arab World, The" (Hall), 236
Archaeology writing, case study in, 116–121
Arctic Science and Technology Information System Bibliography (ASTIS), 709
"Are You My Mother?" (Taylor), 30
Argot, 703
Art, list of works herein. *See* xvii
Art, writing topics in, 17, 25, 59,

Art, writing topics in *(continued)* 67, 71, 85, 89, 99, 141, 183, 215, 267, 275, 287, 295, 339
Articles (*a, an, the*)
  as adjectives, 416, 611
  capitalizing, in titles, 636
  in series, **775**
As, pronouns after, 569
As, like, 619, **795–796**
As good, better than, **786**
As to whether, **786**
As yet, **786**
Audience. *See also* Guided Assignment
  in expository writing, 209, 214
  in personal writing, 23
  in persuasive writing, 266
  in prewriting, 68–71
Audio-visual materials, 704
Auditory learner, 20
Aunt Erma's Cope Book (Bombeck), 70
Auxiliary verbs, 411–412, **770**
Awards, capitalizing names of, 634
A while, awhile, 611

B

Bad, badly, 597, 613
Baker, Russell, 166
Bandwagon reasoning, 283
Bar graphs, 735
Begley, Sharon, 208
Being, **786**
Being as, being that, 613
Bennett, Joan Frances, 14
Berra, Yogi, 694
Beside, besides, 613
Better than, as good, **786**
Between, among, 614, **785**
Biblical references, colon in, 650, **762**
Bibliography, 711
  in a book, 711
  developing, for research paper, 331–335
Bibliography cards, for research paper, 318–319
Biographical sketch, 172–175
  editing, 174
  keeping and discarding details, 174
  literature model for, 172, 174

narrowing subject in, 173
  prewriting, 173
Black Ice (Cary), 38–42
Blends, 691
Bombeck, Erma, 70
Book, parts of, 711
Borrow, lend, loan, 614, **796**
Borrowed words, 689, 690, 696
Boudreau, Cléo, 4–8
Brackets, 664
Bradstreet, Anne, 242
Brainstorming, 9, 13, 25, 67, 79, 81, 89, 103, 135, 145, 155, 211, 227, 252, 253, 267, 311
Brandon, Barbara, 50–55
Bridges, capitalizing names of, 634
Bring, take, 614
Bryan, C. D. B., 168
Buildings, capitalizing names of, 634
"Burning, The" (Trambley), 66
Business education, writing in, 179
Business letters, colon after salutation in, 650
Business Periodicals Index, 708
But, as conjunction, 425, **760, 786**
Butler, Samuel, 94

C

Calendar items, capitalizing names of, 635
Can, may, 614, **787**
Canemaker, John, 216
Can't hardly, can't scarcely, 615
Capitalization
  of abbreviations, 677
  of articles in titles of works, 636, **783**
  of first word in sentence, 631
  Mechanics Workshop for, 642–644
  of pronoun *I,* 631
  of proper adjectives, 416, 637–638
  of proper nouns, 398, 633–636
Capital letters, in outlines, 323
Capote, Truman, 642
Card catalog, 704
Cary, Lorene, 38
Case, **787**
Case of Harry Houdini, The, (Epstein), 188–194

Case Study feature
  in descriptive writing, 116–121
  in expository writing, 202–207
  in narrative writing, 160–165
  in personal writing, 4–9
  in persuasive writing, 258–263
  in writing process, 50–55
Causal chain, 217
Cause-and-effect fallacy, 284
Cause-and-effect organization, 209
Cause-and-effect writing, 208–209, 216–219. *See also* Expository Writing
  details for, 209
  in essay, 218
  literature model in, 218
  transitions for, 210
CBS News Index, 708
Certainly, **787**
Character, **787**
Character descriptions, 166–171
  adding dialogue to, 169
  editing, 169
  portraying real-life, 167
  prewriting, 167
  using vivid descriptions in, 168
Characters
  analysis of, in play, 100–103
  in descriptive writing, 155
  in determining theme, 181
  in narratives, 171
  rounding out your, 170
  strategies for revealing, 167, 168
Character sketch
  adding clues to, 136
  editing, 135
  prewriting, 134
Charts, in prewriting, 11, 32, 228, 253
Chemistry, writing topics in, 89, 129, 233
"Chief Joseph of the Nez Percé" (Warren), 184, 185
Chronological order, 45, 80, 178, 322
Circular reasoning, 282–283
Claim (verb), **787**
Clarity, importance of, **816–817**
Clauses
  adjective, 489–490, 517, 554–555, 655–656
  adverb, 490–491, 492, 517–518, 658

Computers. *See* Computer Option

Conclusion
  in building hypothesis, 236
  drafting, 83, 112, 329

Concrete nouns, 397

"Confessions of a Tape–Deck Owner" (Goodman), 84

Conjunctions
  and/or as, **785**
  but as, **786**
  coordinating, 425, 485, 498
  correlative, 426
  definition of, 425
  guidelines for using, 432
  subordinating, 427–428, 483–484, 489, 492

Conjunctive adverbs, 429

Connected numerals, 675

Consider, **788**

Contact, **788**

Context clues
  general, 717–718
  specific, 716–717

Contexts for writing. *See* Guided Assignment; Writing Process in Action lessons

Continual, continuous, 615

Contractions, apostrophes in, 672–673

Contronyms, 697

Cooperative Learning, 9, 29, 33, 37, 55, 75, 79, 93, 121, 129, 133, 137, 145, 165, 171, 175, 179, 187, 207, 219, 225, 237, 245, 263, 271, 291, 299

Coordinate adjectives, commas with, 654

Coordinate ideas, use of parallel construction for, **774–775**

Coordinating conjunctions, 425, 485, 498

Cope, **788**

Copyright page, 711

Correlative conjunctions, 426, **775**

Costello, Lou, 64

Could of, might of, must of, should of, would of, 616

Country of the Pointed Firs, The (Jewett), 558–559

Crane, Stephen, 474–475

Creole, 692

Criteria, 47, 113, 157, 199, 255, 313

Critical analysis

of character in play, 100–102
  comparing and contrasting two authors in, 238–241
  comparing and contrasting two poems in, 242–245
  of mood in play, 142–145
  of nonfiction article, 30–33
  of persuasive speech, 296–299
  responding to narrative poetry in, 184–187
  responding to poetry in, 34–37

Critical listening, 747

Critical thinking. *See* Thinking Skills

Cross-curricular writing topics. *See* Writing Across the Curriculum

Currently, **788**

D

Dangling modifiers, 391, 600–601, 603

Dashes, **762**
  to emphasize, 662
  to signal change, 662

Data, **788**

Dates
  abbreviations for, 677
  commas in, 659, **758**
  forming plurals of, 673
  methods for writing, **758**
  numerals for, 680

Debates
  gathering information for, 750–751
  structure of, 750
  style in, 751–752

Decimals, numerals to express, 679

Declarative sentences, 496

Deductive reasoning, 278–281
  pitfalls of, 280

Definite articles, 416

Definitions, quotation marks with, 666

De la Rosa, Denise M., 214

Demonstrative pronouns, 404

Dependent clauses. *See* Subordinate clauses

Descriptive writing
  case study in, 116–121
  character sketch in, 134–137
  choosing vantage point for,

138–139
  creating mood in, 130–133
  creating vivid description in, 122–125
  describing event in, 138–141
  drafting in, 139, 141, 156
  editing in, 157
  literature model for, 122, 126, 132, 136, 138
  organization in, 123–124
  paragraphing in, **768**
  presenting in, 157
  prewriting in, 127, 154–155
  revising in, 123, 128, 141, 156–157
  sensory details in, 126–129
  sentence combining in, 352–355

Details
  in biographical sketch, 174
  in descriptive writing, 122–125
  in personal narrative, 44–45
  in personal writing, 25
  in prewriting, 72–75
  reading for, in editing, 94–95
  sensory, in descriptive writing, 126–129
  supporting theme with, 182

Dewey decimal system, 705–706

Diagraming sentences, 511–520

Diagrams, using, 77, 173, 217, 311, 733

Dialect, 698, 699, **816**

Dialogue, **814–815**
  adverbs in, **814**
  in character description, 169
  dialect in, **816**
  paragraph in, **767–768**
  in personal narrative, 45–46
  quotation marks in writing, 666
  writing, 33, 112–113

Dictionaries
  general, 712
  specialized, 713

Different from, different than, 616, **789**

Dillard, Annie, 10, 104

Direct objects, 448
  diagraming, 512, 518
  noun clauses as, 493, 518

Direct quotations
  in note taking, 319, 320
  quotation marks for, 665

Disinterested, **789**

Divided into, **789**

names of, 635
Historical writing, present tense in, 525
Home economics, writing topics in, 63
Hopefully, **792**
Houston Post, review in (Morris), 298
However, **793**
punctuating, **758**
How-to writing. *See* Process explanation
Hughes, Langston, 291, 584
Humanities Index, 708
Hung, hanged, 618
Hurst, Fannie, 24
Hurston, Zora Neale, 24
Hyperbole, 284–285
HyperCard, 175
Hyphens
in compound adjectives, 674, **780**
in compound words, 691, 726, **780–781**
to divide words at end of lines, 675
in numbers, 675
with prefixes, 674
Hypothesis building, 209, 234–237
prewriting, 235

I

I, capitalization of, 631
Idiomatic expressions, **775**
I Know Why the Caged Bird Sings (Angelou), 136
Illogical juxtaposition, 694
Illusion, allusion, 613, **784**
Illustrations, colon to introduce, 649, **761**
Imperative mood, 535
Imperative sentences, 496
Imply, infer, **793**
Importance, order of, 80, 123, 124, 129, 156, 265, 322
Importantly, **793**
Impression, order of, 123, 124, 129, 156, 253, 322
In, into, 618
Incomplete comparisons, 596
Indefinite articles, 416, 611

Indefinite pronouns, 406–407
as antecedents, 383
and pronoun-antecedent agreement, 578
and subject-verb agreement, 381, 553–554
Independent clauses, punctuating, **760–761**
Index, of a book, 711
Indicative mood, 535
Indirect objects, 449
diagraming, 512
Indirect quotations, 665, **782**
Individuals, capitalizing names of, 633
Inductive reasoning, 276–277
pitfalls in, 278
Infer, imply, **793**
Infinitive clauses, 470
Infinitive phrases, 470, 473
diagraming, 515
Infinitives, 469–470
commas to set off nonessential, 394, 655
diagraming, 514–515
split, **801, 816**
Informal speeches, 748
Information sources, 317–319
documenting, for research paper, 330–331
electronic, 710
evaluating, for research paper, 335
formatting citations for, 331–334
Infotrak, 33
Initials, **817–818**
In regard to, **793**
"In Retrospect" (Angelou), 242
Inside, inside of, **794**
Insightful, **794**
Institutions, capitalizing names of, 634
Integrating the language arts. *See* Grammar Workshop, Journal Activity; Listening; Literature Selections; Mechanics Workshop; Portfolio & Reflection; Sentence Combining; Sentence Writing exercises; Usage Workshop; Writing about literature; Writer's Choice activities; Writing Process in Action lessons

Intensive pronouns, 404, 570
Interesting, **794**
Interjections, 433
commas with, 395
In terms of, **794**
Interrogative pronouns, 405
Interrogative sentences, 496, 501
who/whom in, 571, 583
Intervening expressions, and subject-verb agreement, 378, 381, 551
Interview of John McPhee on National Public Radio's "Fresh Air," 56
In the last analysis, **793**
Intransitive verbs, 409
Introduction, 711
drafting effective, 328
"Inventing the Truth: The Art and Craft of Memoir" (Zinsser), 47
Invention. *See* Prewriting
Inverted sentences, and subject-verb agreement, 547–548, 557
Irregardless, regardless, 618, **794**
Irregular verbs, 388, 522–523
Irritate, aggravate, **784**
Italics
with foreign words, 669
for titles of works, 636, 668–669, **783**
with words representing themselves, 669–670
It's, its, 393, 566, 583, **757**
I Wonder As I Wander (Hughes), 584–585
–ize, **794–795**

J

Jackson, Andrew, 268
Jargon, **818–819**
Jewett, Sarah Orne, 558
Johnson, Malvin Gray, 10
Jordan, Barbara, 297
Journal Activity, 11, 15, 17, 19, 23, 27, 31, 33, 35, 57, 61, 63, 65, 69, 77, 81, 83, 87, 91, 95, 97, 101, 123, 127, 131, 139, 143, 167, 169, 173, 177, 181, 185, 209, 213, 217, 221, 227, 235, 239, 243, 265, 269, 273, 277,

M

N

Punctuation. *See also* specific
  marks
  Mechanics Workshop for,
    682–685
Purpose
  determining, in prewriting,
    68–71
  in personal writing, 23
Push-button words, 700

742–743
multiple-choice vocabulary
questions, 740–741
preparing to take, 738–739
purpose of, 738
reading-comprehension questions, 741–742
sentence-completion questions,
741
State, **802**
Stein, Gertrude, 16
Stones of Florence, The (McCarthy),
682–683
Student body, **802**
Student models, 15, 18, 22, 26,
36, 60, 76, 83, 87, 102, 140,
144, 169, 170, 182, 212,
220–221, 228, 290, 342–347
Study skills. *See also* Library; Tests
evaluating what you read, 732
for exam, 21
making study time count,
730–731
note taking in, 730
reading to remember, 731
Subject
adding to sentence fragment,
374, 375
complete, 443
compound, 380–381, 444–445,
550–551
noun clause as, 493
position in sentence, 446, **776**
simple, 443
Subject approach, in
compare-and-
contrast essay, 223
Subject complements, 451
diagraming, 512
predicate adjectives, 451
predicate nominatives, 378, 451
Subject-verb agreement
in adjective clauses, 554–555
with collective nouns, 379, 549,
763
with compound subjects,
550–551, **763**
correcting problems in,
378–381
with indefinite pronouns as
subjects, 553–554
with intervening expressions,
545, 551, **763**
in inverted sentences, 547–548
with linking verbs, 546

with nouns of amount, 549
with special nouns, 549
with titles, 550
Usage Workshop for, 558–563
Subjunctive mood, 535
Subordinate clauses, 406,
483–484
correcting as sentence fragments, 375
who, whom in, 571, 583
Subordinating conjunctions,
427–428, 483
to introduce subordinate
clauses, 483–484, 489, 492,
759
Suffixes, 722, 725–726
–ize as, **794–795**
–wise as, **806**
Summaries, verb tense in,
777–778
Summarizing, in note taking, 319,
320
Superlative form
of adjectives, 415, 591–592
of adverbs, 419, 591–592
Syllabication, 675, **783**
Symbols, apostrophe to form
plural of, 673
Synonyms. *See* Thesauruses

T

Table of contents, 711
Tables, 734
Tag questions, commas to set off,
660
Take, bring, 614
Teach, learn, 619
Tests. *See also* Study skills
English-composition questions,
742–743
essay, 736–737
multiple-choice vocabulary
questions, 740–741
reading-comprehension questions, 741–742
sentence-completion questions,
741
standardized, 738–743
studying for, 21
Than, **802**
pronouns after, 569
Than, then, 621

Thanking you in advance, **802**
That, which, 489–490, **802**
That there, this here, 621
Theater arts, writing in, 33, 125
Theme
characters in determining, 181
definition of, 180
identifying, in narrative writing,
180–183
plot in determining, 181
point of view in determining,
181
setting in determining, 181
supporting, with details, 182
Then, than, 621
Thesauruses
dictionary style, 715
electronic, 245
traditional style, 714
These kinds, this kind, 618
Thesis statement
in compare-and-contrast
essays, 221
creating, 324–325
in expository writing, 253, 254
in narrative writing, 198
in persuasive writing, 265, 311
revising, 324–325
They, **803–804**
indefinite use of, 385, 580–581
Thinking Skills, 23, 27, 31, 57,
83, 91, 95, 101, 123, 131, 135,
139, 167, 173, 181, 209, 213,
217, 221, 231, 243, 265, 273,
283, 285, 289, 293
Thirdly, **801**
This, **804**
This here, that there, 621
This kind, these kinds, 618
Thompson, Dorothy, 285
Thoreau, Henry David, 16
Thrust, **804**
Time
abbreviations for, 678
colons in expressions of, 650,
762
numerals in, 680
forming possessive of, in
expressions, 672
transitions for, 210
Time lines, 177, 179, 230, 233
Title page, 711
Titles of persons
abbreviations of, 677–678, **758**
capitalizing, 633

Titles of persons (continued)
commas with, 659
Titles of works, **783**
capitalizing, 636
italics for, 668–669, **783**
selecting for writing, 98
subject-verb agreement with, 550
quotation marks for short, 666
"To My Dear and Loving Husband" (Bradstreet), 242
Tone, in personal narrative, 45–46
Topic
finding, in prewriting, 60–63
investigating and limiting for research paper, 317
for personal narrative, 44
selecting, in expository , 209
Topic sentence. *See* Thesis statement
Tortuous, torturous, **804**
Trade names, capitalizing, 634
Trains, capitalizing names of, 635
Trambley, Estela Portillo, 66
Transitional words
in achieving coherence, 224
in building hypothesis, 236
in expository writing, 210, 254
in organizing writing, 210
in personal narrative, 45
Transitive verbs, 409
Transpire, **804**
Tree diagram, 61, 62, 63, 253, 324
Troubleshooter, 373–396
Truth is, **803**
Try, **805**
Twain, Mark, 694
Type, **805**

U

Underlining. *See* Italics
Understanding, Maintaining and Riding the Ten-Speed Bicycle (de la Rosa and Kolin), 214
"Under the Auchincloss Shell" (Bryan), 168
Unique, **805**
Unit reviews, 442, 462, 482, 510, 520, 544, 564, 590, 610, 630, 646, 686
See also Portfolio & Reflection

Unity, achieving in drafting, 76–79
Usage
glossary of, 611–630
subject-verb agreement, 545–564
using modifiers correctly, 591–610
using pronouns correctly, 565–590
verb tenses, voice, and mood, 521–544
Usage Workshop. *See also* Grammar Workshop; Mechanics Workshop
for modifiers, 604–609
for pronouns, 584–589
for subject-verb agreement, 558–563
for usage glossary, 626–629
for verb tenses, voice, and mood, 538–543
Utilize, 805

V

Vague references, correcting, 579–580
Vantage point, choosing, for descriptive writing, 138–139
Venn diagram, 222, 225, 241
Verbal nouns, **799**
Verbal phrases, 466
Verbals, **805**
gerunds, 468–469
infinitives, 469–470
participles, 466, **799**
Verb phrases, 411–412
Verbs. *See also* Verb tense
action, 409, 533–534
active voice for, 533–534, **768–769**
adding complete, to sentence fragments, 374, 375
auxiliary, 411–412, **770**
avoiding "understood," **764**
conditional, **770**
confusion between past form and past participle, 388–389
definition of, 408
helping, 411–412
intransitive, 409
irregular, 388, 522–523

linking, 410
mood of, 535
nouns used as, **797–798**
passive, 533–534
position in sentence, **776**
principal parts of, 521
regular, 521–523
transitive, 409
Usage Workshop on tenses, voice, and mood, 538–543
using vivid, 414, **770**, **811**
voice of, 533–534
Verb tense, 218, 408
compatibility of, 532
correcting problems in, 387–389
emphatic forms, 530
future, 526
future perfect, 529
past, 525
past perfect, 528
present perfect, 524–525, 528
progressive forms, 530
in summaries, **777–778**
Very, **805**
Viewpoint. *See* Point of View
Visual learning. *Writer's Choice* contains numerous instructional visuals. 11, 57, 61, 69, 77, 80, 81, 101, 173, 177, 181, 209, 213, 217, 222, 223, 228, 230–233, 235, 240, 244, 265, 277, 279, 280, 282, 284, 290, 316, 698, 705
Vocabulary. *See also* Words
adding new words in, 722
analyzing word parts, 719–723
context clues in, 716–718
Voice
active, 533–534, 537, **768–769**
passive, 533–534, 537
in personal narrative, 45

W

Wall Street Journal Index, 708
Warren, Robert Penn, 184, 185
Way Things Work, The (Macaulay), 214
Way to Rainy Mountain, The (Momaday), 132
"Wealth" (Emerson), 238
Weizenbaum, Joseph, 222

Acknowledgments *(continued from page iv)*

Text

10 From *The Writing Life* by Annie Dillard. Copyright © 1989 by Annie Dillard. Published by Harper & Row, Publishers, Inc. **14** From *Members of the Class Will Keep Daily Journals: The Barnard College Journals of Tobi Gillian Sanders and Joan Frances Bennett, Spring 1968* (New York: Winter House, 1970). Copyright © 1970 by Tobi Gillian Sanders and Joan Frances Bennett. Reprinted by permission of Joan Frances Bennett.(t); From *The Lost Notebooks of Loren Eiseley* by Loren Eiseley. Copyright © 1987 by the estate of Mabel L. Eiseley. Published by Little, Brown and Company (b). **15** From *Revelations: Diaries of Women* edited by Mary Jane Moffat and Charlotte Painter. Copyright 1974 by Mary Jane Moffat and Charlotte Painter. Published by Random House. **16** From *A Writer's Diary* by Virginia Woolf. Copyright © 1953, 1954 by Leonard Woolf. Published by Vintage Books. **24** Zora Neale Hurston, courtesy of the Harry Ransom Humanities Research Center, The University of Texas at Austin (t); Fannie Hurst, courtesy of the Harry Ransom Humanities Research Center, The University of Texas at Austin (b). **28** From *100 Successful College Applications*, edited by Christopher J. Georges and Gigi E. Georges with members of the staff of the *Harvard Independent*. Copyright © 1988 by Harvard Independent. Published by Penguin U.S.A. **30** "Are You My Mother" by Elizabeth Taylor. Copyright © 1989 by Time Magazine. Reprinted by permission. **32** From "Step-Siblings" by Ann Patchet from *Seventeen Magazine*. Copyright © June 1991 by News America Publications Inc. **34** "On Remembering The Beara Landscape" by Christopher Nolan from *Dam-Burst of Dreams* by Christopher Nolan. Copyright © 1981 by Christopher Nolan. Published by the Ohio University Press. **38-42** From *Black Ice* by Lorene Cary. Copyright © 1991 by Lorene Cary. Published by Alfred A. Knopf, Inc. **56** John McPhee spoke with Terry Gross on *Fresh Air*, which is distributed by National Public Radio and produced at WHYY-FM. Copyright © 1990. **62** "Knoxville, Tennessee" by Nikki Giovanni from *Black Sister: Poetry By Black American Women, 1746–1980.* Copyright © 1981 by Erlene Stetson. Published by Indiana University Press. **64** From "Who's On First?" by Abbott & Costello from *Lou's on First* by Chris Costello with Raymond Strait. Copyright © 1981 by Chris Costello and Raymond Strait. Published by St. Martin's Press. **66** "The Burning" by Estela Portillo Trambley from *The Third Woman: Minority Women Writers of the United States.* Copyright © 1975 by Estella Portillo Trambley. Published by Houghton Mifflin. **70** From *Laurel's Kitchen: A Handbook for Vegetarian Cookery & Nutrition* by Laurel Robertson, Carol Flinders and Bronwen Godfrey. Copyright © 1976 by Nilgiri Press. Published by Bantam Books, Inc. (t); From "Aunt Erma's Cope Book" by Erma Bombeck from *Four of a Kind: A Treasury of Favorite Works by America's Best-Loved Humorists* by Erma Bombeck. Copyright © 1985 by Erma Bombeck. Published by McGraw-Hill (b). **73** "Royal Beatings" by Alice Munro from *We Are the Stories We Tell: The Best Short Stories of North American Women Since 1945.* Copyright © 1990 by Wendy Martin. Published by Pantheon Books. **84** From "Confessions of a Tape-Deck Owner" by Ellen Goodman from *Keeping In Touch* by Ellen Goodman. Copyright © by The Washington Post Company. Published by Ballantine Books. **88** From *The River Why* by David James Duncan. Copyright © 1983 by David James Duncan. Published by The Sierra Club. **94** From *The Note-books of Samuel Butler* by Samuel Butler from *Telling Writing* by Ken Macrorie. Copyright © 1980 by Hayden Book Company. Published by Hayden Book Company. **100** From *The Glass Menagerie* by Tennessee Williams. Copyright © 1945 by Tennessee Williams. Published by New Directions Publishing Corporation. **104-08** From *An American Childhood* by Annie Dillard. Copyright © 1987 by Annie Dillard. Published by Harper & Row Publishers, Inc. **122** From *Listening Woman* by Tony Hillerman. Copyright © 1978 by Anthony G. Hillerman. Published by Harper Collins. **126** From "Mysteries of the Ancient World" by Judith E. Rinard. Copyright © 1979 by National Geographic Society. Published by the National Geographic Society. **132** From "The Way to Rainy Mountain" by N. Scott Momaday

from *The Dolphin Reader.* Copyright © 1969 by The University of New Mexico Press. First published in *The Reporter*, January 26, 1967. Reprinted by The University of New Mexico Press. **136** From *I Know Why the Caged Bird Sings* by Maya Angelou. Copyright © 1969 by Maya Angelou. Published by Random House, Inc. **138** From *G is for Gumshoe* by Sue Grafton. Copyright © 1990 by Sue Grafton. Published by Henry Holt and Company, Inc. **142-43** From *Sherlock Holmes* by Arthur Conan Doyle and William Gillette, from *Plays of the Year* edited by J.C. Trewin. Copyright © 1975 by Plays of the Year Company and Paul Elek Books Ltd. Published by Paul Elek Books Limited. **146** From "The Signature" by Elizabeth Enright. Reprinted by permission of Russell & Volkening as agents for the estate of Elizabeth Enright. Copyright © 1951 by Elizabeth Enright, renewed in 1979 by Elizabeth Enright. **166** From *The Good Times* by Russell Baker. Copyright © 1989 by Russell Baker. Published by William Morrow and Company. **168** From "Under the Auchincloss Shell" by C. D. B. Bryan from *Developing Writing Skills; Fourth Edition.* Copyright © 1979 by C. D. B. Bryan. Published by Brandt & Brandt Literary Agents, Inc. **172** From *Elizabeth Regina: The Age of Triumph 1588–1603* by Alison Plowden. Copyright © 1980 by Alison Plowden. Published by Times Books Company. **174** From *Richard Milhous Nixon* by Roger Morris. Copyright © 1990 by Roger Morris. Published by Henry Holt and Company, Inc. **176** From *Sojourner Truth: A Self-Made Woman* by Victoria Ortiz. Copyright © 1974 by Victoria Ortiz. Published by J.B. Lippincott Company. **178** From "Obāchan" by Gail Y. Miyasaki from *The Third Woman: Minority Women Writers of the United States*. Copyright © 1971 by *Asian Women's Journal.* Published by *Asian Women's Journal.* **184, 185** From *Chief Joseph of the Nez Perce* by Robert Penn Warren. Copyright © 1983 by Robert Penn Warren. Published by Random House. **188-94** "The Case of Harry Houdini," from *Star of Wonder* by Daniel Mark Epstein. Copyright © 1986 by Daniel Mark Epstein. Published by the Overlook Press, Lewis Hollow Road, Woodstock, NY 12498. **208** "Wilder Places for Wild Things" by Sharon Begley. Copyright © 1989 by Newsweek. Published by Newsweek. **212-13** From *Encounters with the Archdruid* by John McPhee. Copyright © 1971 by John McPhee. Published by Farrar, Straus, and Giroux. **214** From *The Way Things Work* by David Macaulay. Copyright © 1988 by David Macaulay and Neil Ardley. Published by Houghton Mifflin Company (t); From *Understanding, Maintaining, and Riding the Ten-Speed Bicycle* by Denise M. de la Rosa and Michael Kolin. Copyright © 1979 by Denise M. de la Rosa and Michael Kolin. Published by Rodale Press (b). **216** From "Once Again, 'Toons' Are Tops" by John Canemaker from *World Book Year Book.* Copyright 1991 by *World Book Year Book.* Published by World Book, Inc. **218** From "Skyscrapers: Above the Crowd" by William S. Ellis from National Geographic. Copyright © 1989 by National Geographic Society. Published by National Geographic Society. **222** From "Science and the Compulsive Programmer" by Joseph Weizenbaum from Partisan Review. Copyright © 1975 by Partisan Review. Published by Partisan Review. **224** From *Last Chance to See* by Douglas Adams. Copyright © 1990 by Serious Productions Ltd. and Mark Carwardine. Published by Harmony Books. **226** From "Gridlock!" by Stephen Koepp. Copyright © 1988 by Time Warner Inc. Reprinted by permission. **234** From "Arsenic and Old Zach" as appeared in the Newsweek article July 1, 1991. Copyright © 1991. Published by Newsweek. **236** From "The Arab World" by Edward T. Hall from *The Hidden Dimension* by Edward T. Hall. Copyright © 1966 by Edward T. Hall. Published by Doubleday & Co. **238** From "Wealth" by Ralph Waldo Emerson from *English Traits* by Ralph Waldo Emerson. Copyright © 1876 by Ralph Waldo Emerson. Published by Houghton Mifflin Company. **242** "To My Dear and Loving Husband" by Anne Bradstreet. Copyright © 1967 by the President and Fellows of Harvard College. Published by Harvard University Press (t); "In Retrospect" by Maya Angelou from *And Still I Rise* by Maya Angelou. Copyright © 1978 by Maya Angelou. Published by Random House (b). **246-50** From *The Soul Of A New Machine* by Tracy Kidder. Copyright © 1981 by John Tracy Kidder. Published Little, Brown and Company. **264** From *The Writings of Benjamin Franklin* by Albert Henry Smyth. Copyright © 1906 by The Macmillan Company. Published by The Macmillan Company. **266** From "Fourth of July Oration" by Frederick Douglass from *Rhetoric of Black Revolution* by Arthur Smith.

Copyright © 1969 by Allyn and Bacon, Inc. Published by Allyn and Bacon, Inc. **268** From *Trail of Tears: The Rise and Fall of the Cherokee Nation* by John Ehle. Copyright © 1988 by John Ehle. Published by Doubleday Publishing, Inc. (t); From *Cherokee Sunset: A Nation Betrayed* by Samuel Carter. Copyright © 1976 by Samuel Carter. Published by Doubleday & Company, Inc. (b). **271** From "What's Wrong with Animal Rights," by Vicki Hearne, in *Harper's*, Sept. 1991. **272-73** From "Irving Harris' address to City Club of Cleveland" in *Vital Speeches of the Day*. Copyright © 1989 by *Vital Speeches of the Day*. **274** From *The World's Greatest Speeches* edited by Lewis Copeland and Lawrence W. Lamm. Copyright © 1973 by Copeland and Lamm, Inc. Published by Dover Publications, Inc. **275** From *Forbes*, September 17, 1990. Copyright © September 17, 1990 by Forbes Inc. **276** From "Extinctions" by Rick Gore, in *National Geographic*, June 1989. **279** From *The World's Greatest Speeches* edited by Lewis Copeland and Lawrence W. Lamm. Copyright © 1973 by Copeland and Lamm, Inc. Published by Dover Publications, Inc. **285** From *The World's Greatest Speeches* edited by Lewis Copeland and Lawrence W. Lamm. Copyright © 1973 by Copeland and Lamm, Inc. Published by Dover Publications, Inc. **288** From *Speechwriting: The Master Touch* by Joseph J. Kelley. Copyright © 1980 by Joseph J. Kelley. Published by Don Mills. **291** From "A Red Light for Scofflaws," by Frank Trippet, from *Time*, (l); "Harlem" by Langston Hughes from *The Panther and the Lash* by Langston Hughes. Copyright © 1951 by Langston Hughes. Published by Alfred A. Knopf (r). **297** From *From the Ghetto to the Capitol* by Ira B. Bryant. Copyright © 1977 by Ira B. Bryant. Published by D. Armstrong Co., Inc. **298** From "Jordan Steals Show in NYC" by Donald Morris. Copyright © 1976 by Houston Post. Published by the Houston Post. **300-08** From "Of Accidental Judgements and Casual Slaughter" by Kai Erikson from *The Best American Essays 1986*. Copyright © 1985 by Kai Erikson. First published by *The Nation*. **342-47** From *The Concord Review*, Spring 1990, Volume Two, Number Three. Copyright © 1990 by *The Concord Review*, P. O. Box 661, Concord, MA 01742. Reprinted with permission. **414** Excerpt from "A Summer Tragedy," by Arna Bontemps. Reprinted by permission of the author. **415** Excerpt from *I Know the Way to Rainy Mountain* by N. Scott Momaday. Reprinted by permission of N. Scott Momaday. **418** Excerpt from *Blue Highways: A Journey into America* by William Least Heat Moon. Copyright © 1982 by William Least Heat Moon. Used by permission of Little, Brown & Co. **434** Excerpts from *Love in the Time of Cholera* by Gabriel García Márquez. Copyright © 1988 by Gabriel García Márquez. Reprinted by permission of Alfred A. Knopf, Inc. **454** Excerpt from *Main Street* by Sinclair Lewis. Copyright 1920 by Harcourt Brace Jovanovich, Inc. Copyright 1948 by Sinclair Lewis. Reprinted by permission of Harcourt Brace Jovanovich, Inc. **473** Excerpt from *The Women of Brewster Place* by Gloria Naylor. Reprinted by permission of Penguin USA. **501** Excerpt from "The Signature" from *The Riddle of the Fly and Other Stories* by Elizabeth Enright. Copyright 1951 by Elizabeth Enright, renewed in 1979 by Elizabeth Enright. Reprinted by permission of Russell & Volkening as agents for the author. **502** Excerpt from *The Great Gatsby* by F. Scott Fitzgerald. Copyright 1925 by Charles Scribner's Sons; renewal copyright 1953 by Francis Scott Fitzgerald Lanahan. Reprinted with permission of Charles Scribner's Sons, an imprint of Macmillan Publishing Company. **537** Excerpt from "The First Seven Years" from *The Magic Barrel* by Bernard Malamud. Copyright © 1950 and renewal copyright © 1977 by Bernard Malamud. Reprinted by permission of Farrar, Straus & Giroux. **538** Excerpt from *Roots* by Alex Haley. Copyright © 1976 by Alex Haley. Used by permission of Dell, a division of Bantam Doubleday Dell Publishing Group, Inc. **584** Excerpt from *I Wonder As I Wander* by Langston Hughes. Copyright © 1956 by Langston Hughes. Reprinted by permission of Hill and Wang, a division of Farrar, Straus & Giroux. **604** Excerpt from *A Moveable Feast* by Ernest Hemingway. Copyright © 1964 by Mary Hemingway. Reprinted with permission of Charles Scribner's Sons, an imprint of Macmillan Publishing Company. **642** Excerpts from *The Muses Are Heard* by Truman Capote. Copyright © 1956 by Truman Capote. Reprinted by permission of Random House, Inc. **666** Excerpt from "Abalone, Abalone, Abalone" from *The Chauvinist and Other Stories* by Toshio Mori. Reprinted by permission of Steven Mori for the Estate of Toshio Mori and the Asian American Studies Center. **682** Excerpt from *The Stones of Florence* by Mary McCarthy. Copyright by Mary McCarthy. Reprinted by permission of Harcourt Brace Jovanovich, Inc. **707** From *Readers' Guide to Periodical Literature*, July 1991, Volume 91, Number Seven. Copyright © 1991 by The H.W. Wilson Company. **713** From *Webster's College Dictionary*. Copyright © 1991 by Random House, Inc. **714** From *Roget's International Thesaurus*, revised by Robert L. Chapman. Copyright © 1977 by Harper & Row, Publishers, Inc. **715** From *The New American Roget's Thesaurus*, revised by Philip D. Morehead. Copyright © 1958, 1962 by Albert H. Morehead; copyright © 1978 by Andrew T. Morehead and Philip D. Morehead. **757–819** *Elements of Style* (Third Edition), by William Strunk Jr. and E. B. White, copyright © 1979, Macmillan Publishing Co., Inc. Earlier editions © 1959 and © copyright 1972 by Macmillan Publishing Co., Inc. Reprinted by permission of Macmillan Publishing Co.

Photos

AR=Art Resource, New York; EF=Eric Futran; RJB=Ralph J. Brunke; SB=Stock Boston, Inc.; SK=Stephen Kennedy; TIB=The Image Bank, Chicago, Schlowsky=Schlowsky Photography.

Front Cover Fernand Léger, Follow the Arrow, 1919, oil on canvas, 54.1-by-65.7 cm, Joseph Winterbotham Collection, © 1991 The Art Institute of Chicago, photo by RJB. **Back Cover** Herman Zapf and his design philosophy. © 1987, by Herman Zapf. American Center for Design. **ii** Frank Siteman (tl); Chris Denney (cl); DeScoise Productions (tc); Mark Tuschman (c); Eric Roth (cr); Don Herbert (tr); EF (bottom half of the page). **1** Fernand Léger, Follow the Arrow, 1919, oil on canvas, 54.1-by-65.7 cm, Joseph Winterbotham Collection, © 1991 The Art Institute of Chicago, photo by RJB. **3** The Detroit Institute of Arts, Bequest of Robert H. Tannahill. **4** Don Hebert. **5** Don Hebert. **6** Don Hebert (both). **7** Jane Burton/Bruce Coleman, Inc. (cr); The St. Thomas Courier/ photo by Schlowsky (b). **9** Schlowsky. **10** National Museum of American Art, Washington, D.C./AR, NY 1967.57.30 (detail). **12** Mike and Carol Werner/COMSTOCK, Inc. (cl); Jeffry W. Myers/FPG International (cr); Jeffry W. Myers/FPG International (tl). **14** Ms. Joan Bennett. **15** Schlowsky. **17** Musee d'Orsay, ©photo by R.M.N. **18** Schlowsky. **20** John Elk, III/ Bruce Coleman, Inc. **22** Schlowsky. **24** Culver Pictures, Inc. (c); UPI/ Bettmann (b). **25** Marc Riboud/Magnum Photos, Inc. **26** Michael Quackenbush/TIB. **28** © (1987) Universal Press Syndicate. Reprinted with permission. All rights reserved. **30** Judith Aronson/Ligature, Inc. **34** Bernd Kappelmeyer/FPG International. **37** Musees Royaux Des Beaux-Arts De Belgique, Brussels/Bridgeman Art Library. **39** Collection of the artist. **41** Zurich, Private Collection/AR, NY. **43** EF (both). **49** Picasso, Pablo. *Three Musicians. Fountainebleau,* summer 1921. Collection, The Museum of Modern Art, NY. Mrs. Simon Guggenheim Fund. **50** Chris Denney. **51** Illustration by Barbara Brandon/Schlowsky (t); Brumsic Brandon, Jr./Los Angeles Times (b). **52** Chris Denney. **53** Courtesy of Barbara Brandon/photo by Schlowsky. **54** Courtesy of Barbara Brandon (both). **55** Courtesy of Jaime Farrow and Nathan Boyer (both). **59** Collection Haags Gemeentemusem-The Hague. **62** COMSTOCK, Inc. **64** ©1945, Universal Pictures, Inc./Superstock, Kobal Collection. **67** National Gallery of Art, Washington D.C.; John Hay Whitney Collection. **68** © 1985 Universal Press Syndicate. Reprinted with permission. All rights reserved. **71** Pablo Picasso *Carafe, Jug, and Fruit Bowl.* 1909 (summer); Solomon R. Guggenheim Museum, NY. Gift, Solomon R. Guggenheim, 1937; Photograph by David Heald; "Photograph © The Solomon R. Guggenheim Foundation." **72** National Gallery of Art, Washington. Collection of Mr. and Mrs. Paul Mellon (detail). **73** Robert Houser/COMSTOCK, Inc. **76** Michael Rothwell/FPG International. **80** Tate Gallery, London/AR, NY. **85** Private Collection/AR, NY. **86** Culver Pictures, Inc. **89** Giraudon/AR, NY. **94** Ken Sherman/Bruce Coleman, Inc. **99** Courtesy Sidney Janis Gallery, NY. **107** Collection of Douglas and Beverly Feurring, Courtesy of Tibor de Nagy Gallery, NY. **109** EF (both). **115** Rene Magritte, Belgian, 1898–1967, *Time Transfixed*, oil on canvas, 1938, 147-by-98.7 cm, Joseph Winterbotham Collection, 1970.426 © The Art Institute of Chicago, all rights reserved. **116** Eric Roth. **117** David Henderson/Eric Roth Studio (t); Eric Roth (br). **118** Eric Roth (both). **119** Eric Roth (all). **120** Eric Roth.

121 Schlowsky. 122 © Charles Cambell/Westlight. 124 Roger Farrington/ The Wang Center, Boston. 125 The Metropolitan Museum of Art, Wolfe Fund, 1906. Catherine Lorillard Wolfe Collection. (06.1234). 126 Schlowsky. 129 The Metropolitan Museum of Art, George A. Hearn Fund, 1943. (43.159.1). 130 Harold Lambert/Superstock. 134 Drawing by David Levine. Reprinted with permission from The New York Review of Books. © 1966. 135 Scott Darrow/Superstock. 136 Schlowsky. 138 David Henderson/Eric Roth Studio. 141 '29-134-16: Philadelphia Museum of Art: Given by Mrs. Thomas Eakins and Miss Mary Adeline Williams. 144 © 1972 by Edward Gorey from "The Listing Attic" in Amphigorey. Published by G.P. Putnam & Sons. 148 AR, NY. 151 Milano, Coll. Jesi/ AR, NY. 153 EF (both). 159 National Gallery of Art, Washington, D.C. Paul Mellon Collection. 160 Mark Tuschman. 161 Schlowsky. 162 Mark Tuschman. 163 Mark Tuschman (both). 164 © Meckler Publishing Corporation/photo by Schlowsky. 165 Schlowsky. 166 UPI/Bettmann. 171 Muskegon Museum of Art. 172 Nicholas Hilliard by Courtesy of the Board of Trustees of the Victoria and Albert Museum/Bridgeman Art Library (l); Methuen Collection, Corsham Court, England (r). 177 Sopia Smith Collection, Smith College. 183 The Metropolitan Museum of Art, Purchase Alfred N. Punnett Endowment Fund and George D. Pratt Gift, 1934. 184 Russ Kinney/COMSTOCK, Inc. 186 Smithsonian Institution, photo no. 43201B. 191 Brown Brothers. 193 Posters Please, Inc. 195 EF (both). 201 City Number Eleven, A Watercolor by Richard French, F.W.S. 202 Frank Siteman. 203 Titanic Historical Society. 204 Woods Hole Oceanographic Institution (cl); © McGraw-Hill Publishing Co./photo by Schlowsky (tl). 205 Woods Hole Oceanographic Institution. 206 Schlowsky (b); Woods Hole Oceanographic Institution (t). 207 Schlowsky. 208 Jen and Des Barltlett/ Bruce Coleman, Inc. 212 Jack Elness/ COMSTOCK, Inc. 215 Giraudon/AR, NY. 216 ©Warner Brothers, Inc. 219 Culver Pictures, Inc. 220 Drawing by Jonik © 1991 The New Yorker Magazine, Inc. 225 Alan Berner. 234 Schlowsky (tl); White House Historical Assoc. (cl). 237 Edward Hopper. Gas. 1940. Oil on canvas, 26.1/4-by-40.1/4 inches. Collection, The Museum of Modern Art, NY. Mrs. Simon Guggenheim Fund. 238 Yale University Art Gallery, The Mabel Brady Garvan Collection. 242 Abby Aldrich Rockefeller Folk Art Center. 243 Maria Taglienti/TIB. 249 David Em "Transjovian Pipeline" 1979 © David Em/Represented by Speickerman Associates, SF. 251 EF (both). 257 Private Collection (detail). 258–259 DeSciose Productions. 260 Wheeler Pictures/Bruce Coleman, Inc. 261 Linda J. Echo-Hawk. 262 DeSciose Productions (both). 263 Schlowsky. 267 Collection of

Pembroke Herbert. 268 Smithsonian Institution, Washington D.C. 270 Phil Cantor/Superstock. 272 Cadge Productions/TIB. 275 Collection of The Montclair Art Museum, Museum purchase, Friends of Agnes White Everett. 278 Grant V. Faint/TIB. 283 Ralph Morse/Life Magazine ©1958 Time Inc. 287 Laget Collection, photo courtesy of Sally Fox. 288 photo. no. KN-C29248 in the John F. Kennedy Library. 295 Ant Farm © 1974. 296 ©Curtis Publishing Company. 297 Uniphoto Picture Agency/ Consolidated Press. 305 Francine Seders Gallery, Seattle, photo by Chris Eden. 309 EF (both). 315 Des Moines Art Center, purchased with funds from the Edmundson Art Foundation, Inc. 1958.2. 316 W. King/FPG International. 319 Edward Hopper by Lloyd Goodrich ©1978 Harry N. Abrams, Edward Hopper "Light Years" © 1988 Hirschl and Adler Galleries/ photo by Schlowsky. 322 Edward Hopper. (Drawing for painting Cape Cod Evening). 1939. conte on paper. 8 1/2-by-11 inches. Collection of the Whitney Museum of American Art, NY, Josephine N. Hopper Bequest. 70.183a. 326 Schlowsky. 330 Schlowsky (tl); Group III/Bruce Coleman, Inc. (c). 336 Grant Wood, American, 1892-1942, American Gothic, oil on beaver board, 1930, 76-by-63.3 cm, Friends of American Art Collection, 1930.934 © 1990 The Art Institute of Chicago, All Rights Reserved. 340 The Joslyn Art Museum, Omaha, Nebraska. 349 ATS, NY/photo courtesy of Leo Castelli, Leo Castelli Gallery. 371 RJB. 441 Patricia Gonzalez "Sleep" 1985, oil on paper, 36.25-by-36.5 inches. 461 Courtesy Journal Communications. 481 The Metropolitan Museum of Art, Gift of Mrs. Frank B. Porter, 1992 (22.207). 509 The Metropolitan Museum of Art, Gift of Chester Dale, 1963. 543 University Museum, University of Pennsylvania, neg. no T4-9c2. 563 National Museum of American Art/AR, NY. 589 Courtesy Mary-Anne Martin/Fine Art. 609 The Metropolitan Museum of Art, Robert Lehman Collection, 1975 (1975.1.227). 629 George Luks. Armistice Night. 1918. Oil on Canvas. 37-by-68 3/4 inches. Collection of Whitney Museum of American Art. Gift of an anonymous donor. 54.58. 645 The Metropolitan Museum of Art, Bequest of Scofield Thayer, 1982. (1984.443.6). 685 The Cleveland Museum of Art, Mr. and Mrs. William H. Marlatt Fund, 61.39. 687 RJB. 689 Giraudon/AR, NY. 693 Southern Historical Collection, Wilson Library, University of North Carolina at Chapel Hill. 694 Drawing by David Levine. Reprinted with permission for The New York Review of Books. ©1966. 755 © Macmillan Publishing Co., photo by RJB.

Picture Research by Ligature, Inc., and Picture Research Consultants, Inc.